The Harbrace Anthology of Short Fiction

FIFTH EDITION

D0760091

The Harbrace Anthology of Short Fiction

FIFTH EDITION

EDITORS

Jon C. Stott, Emeritus
University of Alberta

Raymond E. Jones, Emeritus
University of Alberta

NELSON / EDUCATION

NELSON / EDUCATION

The Harbrace Anthology of Short Fiction, Fifth Edition
by Jon C. Stott and Raymond E. Jones

Vice President, Editorial Director:
Evelyn Veitch

Editor-in-Chief, Higher Education:
Anne Williams

Executive Editor:
Laura Macleod

Senior Marketing Manager:
Amanda Henry

Developmental Editor:
Jacquelyn Busby

Permissions Coordinator:
Natalie Russell

Content Production Manager:
Claire Horsnell

Production Service:
Integra

Copy Editor:
Carrie MacGregor

Proofreader:
Nancy Ahr

Indexer:
Edwin Durbin

Senior Production Coordinator:
Ferial Suleman

Design Director:
Ken Phipps

Managing Designer:
Franca Amore

Interior Design:
Katherine Strain

Cover Design:
Sharon Lucas

Cover Image:
Helen Vaughn/Getty Images

Compositor:
Integra

Printer:
RR Donnelley

Library and Archives Canada Cataloguing in Publication Data

Main entry under title:

The Harbrace anthology of short fiction / senior editors, Jon C. Stott, Raymond E. Jones.—5th ed.

Includes bibliographical references and index.
ISBN 978-0-17-650276-8

1. Short stories, English. 2. Short stories, Canadian (English). 3. Short stories, American. 4. College readers. I. Stott, Jon C., 1939– II. Jones, Raymond E

PN6120.2.H37 2010
823'.0108
C2010-903918-1

ISBN-13: 978-0-17-650276-8
ISBN-10: 0-17-650276-9

CONTENTS

PREFACE

"We imagine ourselves, we create ourselves, we touch ourselves into being with words, words that are important to us," writes Native North American author Gerald Vizenor. One means by which we imagine or create ourselves is through the reading of literature.

The Harbrace Anthology of Short Fiction uses three approaches to encourage its readers in this activity. First, it presents significant and representative works from the increasingly widening canon of literature in English. Second, it provides strategies to assist readers in their appreciation of works of literature. Third, by introducing readers to the language of literature, both simple and complex, and by suggesting methods for articulating responses, it provides opportunities to explore literature and to respond to language in its rich and varied forms.

Although no anthology can include all of its readers' favourite works, the editors have attempted to make their selections as varied and diverse as possible. Thus, *The Harbrace Anthology of Short Fiction* offers many contemporary short stories, by men and women alike, from a variety of cultures and backgrounds, in addition to many of those works that have always formed an integral part of the accepted canon of literature in English. It also includes a large sampling of English-Canadian literature in the belief that Canadian students should have the opportunity to experience the works of their literary tradition both on their own terms and within the larger context of literature written in English.

Individual works in *The Harbrace Anthology of Short Fiction* mirror the diversity of backgrounds and interests of Canadian students as well as reflecting an expanded canon. The short stories reveal many of the characteristic themes and artistic techniques of their authors; they also reflect the cultural and social contexts in which they were written. In particular, they embody, as the eighteenth-century poet Alexander Pope observed, "what oft was thought but ne'er so well expressed." Most readers of this anthology will find its works speaking directly to them and addressing their most deeply felt concerns.

The Harbrace Anthology of Short Fiction is organized by author. Selections are chronological, according to the birth dates of their authors. Following a selection, its date of publication is printed in parentheses on the right; when it differs significantly and is known, the date of composition appears in parentheses on the left. Such an organizational pattern, based on chronology rather than on pedagogical or theoretical concerns, invites a broad range of responses to a work, unencumbered by artificial or purely technical groupings based on content or theme. It does, of course, implicitly suggest a historical continuity in literature: that works from a specific period often have technical and thematic similarities; and that earlier works and authors can influence later ones.

The General Introduction considers the reading of literature both as a personal, necessary, lifelong activity and as a discipline. It explores how reading poems and short stories allows individuals to understand their own lives and responses to literature in relation to those of other people. It also demonstrates how readers can engage more deeply with a text, experiencing it more fully and relating it more completely to their own lives.

The introduction to each genre focuses directly on the characteristics and conventions of the genre, using examples from the literature presented in *The Harbrace Anthology of Short Fiction*. Discussions of individual characteristics are intended not to offer explanations or explications, but to indicate ways in which authors have used the various elements of the genre. For the reader, an awareness of these characteristics may assist in engagement with the text and lead to a broader range of responses.

Each work in the anthology is prefaced by a brief headnote establishing a biographical and literary context. The headnote may also touch on technique or theme. Explanatory footnotes identify historical, fictional, and mythological personages; literary and artistic works; real and fictional places; and terms not usually found in standard dictionaries. This material provides resources to assist readers in the personal creation of meaning—not to impose a critical viewpoint or to force interpretation in a specific, narrow direction.

For this short fiction anthology, the Glossary has been tailored to offer definitions of key terms, providing for readers both an awareness of essential concepts and a standard vocabulary for use in discussing short fiction.

A Note from the Publisher

Thank you for selecting *The Harbrace Anthology of Literature*, Fifth Edition, edited by Jon C. Stott and Raymond E. Jones. The editors and publisher have devoted considerable time and care to the development of this book. We appreciate your recognition of this effort and accomplishment.

A Note on the Harbrace Anthologies of Poetry and Short Fiction

The publisher has made available individual anthologies representing two of the genres previously included in *The Harbrace Anthology of Literature*. These are *The Harbrace Anthology of Poetry* and *The Harbrace Anthology of Short Fiction*. These one-genre anthologies offer greater choice to instructors teaching courses in these areas. Each of the one-genre anthologies includes the following elements:

- the general introduction to literature
- the introduction to the specific genre
- a glossary, tailored to the specific genre

GENERAL INTRODUCTION

One of the favourite folktales of the Ashanti people of Ghana recounts how Anansi the Spiderman acquires stories for the people. The Sky-God, who possesses all the stories, agrees to give them to him only if he succeeds in completing four impossible tasks. Ridiculing him as small and insignificant, the Sky-God reminds him that other, apparently more capable, individuals had previously failed to complete the tasks and therefore had not earned the right to the stories. Anansi is not deterred. Armed with only a few very simple props and the talent of knowing how to use words and also when not to use them, he captures a leopard, a python, a swarm of hornets, and a dancing fairy. When he returns with his captives, the Sky-God praises him and gives him stories, which Anansi takes home and shares with others. For the first time, therefore, people have stories. Anansi succeeds because he is a storyteller: he deceives his victims with simple narratives. Skilled with words himself, he receives the gift of words formed into stories.

The popularity of this story among the Ashanti, as well as the popularity of similar tales among many other peoples, indicates how important stories—and, by extension, literature in general—have been for preliterate cultures. In addition to myths, legends, and folktales about such topics as the creation of the world, the seasonal cycles, and the characteristics of the physical world, these cultures created narratives that explained the origins of what some people have called a basic need: literature. Canadian literary critic Northrop Frye, for instance, emphasized the importance of literature, observing that "whenever a society is reduced to the barest primary requirements of food, sex, and shelter, the arts, including poetry, stand out sharply in relief as ranking with those primary requirements."

While some literature may simply entertain or allow escape from everyday lives, the works that ultimately stay with their readers are those that challenge, engage, or make demands. Well-crafted literature invites its readers to laugh, to cry, to wonder, to analyze, to explore, to understand.

Throughout our lives, we seek to understand ourselves, our emotions, our experiences, and our relationships with others. We also attempt to define our connections to larger social and cultural institutions. One way that we can do so is through literature, for works of literature are the records of individual response to the world in which we live.

Because of our own experiences, we are able to understand the self-doubts and uncertainties expressed in T. S. Eliot's "The Love Song of J. Alfred Prufrock," the anguish of Phyllis Webb's "Treblinka Gas Chamber," and the wife's sense of betrayal in "Bliss." The specific experiences may be different from our own, but we recognize similarities in the thoughts and emotions of the characters; examination and reflection may lead to clearer insights into our own lives.

Because works of literature are often demanding, they offer great rewards. Readers come to fuller awareness of themselves and others. They discover both the uniqueness and the universality of human experience; they explore both their own world and worlds they may never otherwise see. Through critical response to literature, readers question a work, examine their relationship to the author, consider the author's role, and develop an appreciation of the work, both on its own terms and as an expression of the author's vision of life. Readers may also explore a work in the context of its times, whether social, historical, or ideological.

Until fairly recently, much of the literature studied in English courses was chosen from a list of works deemed important by a majority of critics and scholars, a list referred to as the canon of English literature. Like most of these critics and scholars, most of the writers were white, male, and British or of British descent. The list usually began with the anonymous creator of the Anglo-Saxon epic "Beowulf" and ended with such early-twentieth-century writers as T. S. Eliot, W. H. Auden, and Dylan Thomas. Because it included very few works by women, members of ethnic minorities, or writers from the British colonies, however, it could not be said to reflect the diversity of writing in English.

The past 50 years have seen a remarkable change in our society as a whole: the recognition of the equal place of all people in it, regardless of gender or ethnic origin. As a consequence, many literary scholars and critics have vigorously sought to expand the canon so that it speaks to everyone. They have demanded the inclusion of the many voices whose stories and poems are worthy of study, both on their own merits and because of the insights they offer into a very large segment of the population of the English-speaking world. Such critics have argued that literature should certainly present universal human concerns but should also help readers understand how gender, cultural background, and social position influence responses to life. The works in this anthology reflect this expanded canon.

Reading and reflecting on works of literature reveal human similarities as well as differences. The poetry of Oodgeroo Noonuccal (Kath Walker) reveals a modern Australian aboriginal woman examining her people's past and its troubled relationships with both government and newcomers. Thomas King's "Borders" captures the sense of alienation many aboriginal Canadians feel in their own land.

Readers who come actively to such works with an open, questioning mind will be able to join with their authors in making explicit the implicit. They will appreciate that an author has used language connotatively, choosing words that, in addition to their dictionary meanings, suggest a range of emotions, ideas, or associations. They will recognize the symbolic nature of actions, characters, and objects. As the German literary critic Wolfgang Iser has commented, literary texts are incomplete; they contain gaps that readers fill in or bridge to create meaning. Readers anticipate, make inferences, draw conclusions; in short, they actively work with the language of a piece of literature to arrive at meaning.

Reading for meaning is a very personal act. It is not simply a matter of paraphrasing or summarizing a story of transforming poetry into prose, or of examining literary technique or metaphorical language. Each reader is unique and will, therefore, respond differently—perhaps slightly, perhaps dramatically—to a work. A Dubliner will no doubt react differently to James Joyce's "Araby" than will a Winnipegger; a woman will react differently to Margaret Atwood's "The Resplendent Quetzal" than will a man. People who have read many works of each of these authors or who have a well-developed knowledge of literature would likely have a different and broader interpretation of these works than someone who seldom reads. Readers draw on personal experience, knowledge, and awareness of both specific literature and literary techniques to appreciate and interpret a literary work.

One way readers can increase their understanding and appreciation of the works with which they engage is to make use of some of the critical and theoretical approaches that specialists have developed for the study of literature. These approaches are many and varied, and they frequently overlap each other. In discussing them, we shall, for convenience, categorize them as either textual (approaches that focus on elements found entirely within the texts, the works of literature themselves) or contextual (approaches that relate the works to elements outside of the texts).

Formalism, the first of three textual approaches that we will briefly consider, holds that a work of literature has a unity that is created through the interrelationship of the parts. Formalist critics, therefore, examine a work analytically, reading a text closely and finding relationships among the elements in it in order to discover its form or pattern. New Criticism, a critical school within formalism, applies this approach to a detailed analysis of such elements as imagery, symbolism, paradox, and irony, particularly in shorter poems, but also in passages of longer poems and works of prose. Structuralism also maintains that literature forms patterns; it maintains, however, that the patterns of significance are not the unique ones found in single works, but the general forms of which specific works are individual embodiments. Structural critics therefore conduct a systematic analysis of many works, seeking the conventions, patterns, and systems that they believe exist in literature.

Whereas formalist and structuralist critics attempt to discover and define objectively recognizable fixed patterns within individual works or within literature in general, deconstructionist critics deny that any patterns found in literature are stable or fixed. That is because language, they argue, is unstable and cannot create fixed, definite meaning. These critics thus look closely at works of literature to show how the meanings they appear to communicate break down. Because meanings do deconstruct, works can have alternate, conflicting, and ambiguous meanings.

Several of the contextual approaches can be termed historical because they consider biographical factors and influences of literary, political, and cultural history on authors and their writings. Biographical criticism studies works in relation to authors' lives. By examining facts about, among other things, authors' education and reading, places of residence and travels, friends and relatives, and recreation and employment, readers may acquire factual information that casts light on details in pieces of literature and that helps them to understand better the work as a whole. They can also discover the process of creation that has led to the completion of a work and can see to what extent the content is autobiographical and, if it is, how the facts of the author's life have been altered.

Historical critics examine a work within the various contexts of its time. Knowledge of social, political, and cultural beliefs and events can increase understanding of both specific details and overall themes of a work. They also discuss how a work reflects and comments on its physical and intellectual context. They thus consider not only physical conditions, but also fashions in literature and in the arts, political trends and events, scientific discoveries, and various ideologies. As well, they study the forces that influence the creation, production, and sale of works of literature, seeking to answer a variety of complex questions: In what ways does popular taste influence or affect writers? Why do publishers decide to print certain books? Why are some books better received by reviewers and more popular with buyers? Why do readers re-discover books that have been virtually unknown for decades or even centuries? Historical scholars also examine attitudes toward various cultural and social groups, including women and minorities, in particular time periods and how these attitudes influence the writing and publishing of books and the way these people are portrayed.

Psychological critics use the tenets of such well-known psychiatrists as Sigmund Freud, Carl Jung, and Jacques Lacan to cast light on authors and their works. Freud advanced the theory that dreams were symbolic manifestations of repressed, unconscious drives and that the interpretation of dreams provided a means for understanding the problems experienced by the dreamers. Similarly, he stated that works of art, although more fixed, were manifestations of the unconscious of their creators. Many critics have applied these principles to the study of literature, using their analysis to better understand the authors. Other critics, following Freud's lead, also use the ideas of psychoanalysis to study the motivations and conflicts of characters in literature, suggesting that, even if the authors didn't know Freud's work, they intuitively understood the psychological elements that he articulated. Students of Jung and Lacan have similarly applied psychological principles to both authors and works.

Gender criticism is closely related to psychological criticism insofar as it examines the nature of males and females. Some critics argue that, by nature, men and women perceive, feel, and think differently from each other and, therefore, that they read and write differently. These critics enumerate the differences that they find in works written by men and women. Such an approach has also been applied to gay and lesbian writers.

Other critics disagree with this kind of approach toward gender, arguing that cultural attitudes and beliefs about gender have much greater influence on how people behave. Accordingly, they study the attitudes toward gender that have prevailed in different times and different cultures in order to understand not only how these have influenced the portrayals of men and women in literature, but also how they have, in part, influenced which works were published and which were well received.

In addition to exploring the way mainstream literature has sought to impose on culture ideas about how women should behave and even how they should feel about themselves, feminist criticism also studies the history of women's writing and the economic and social conditions under which women wrote and published. As a result, these critics have re-discovered many works that had been little read or had been unread for many years and have introduced them to new and generally receptive audiences. Some of them have also suggested feminist reconsiderations of traditional "male" literature.

The above approaches focus on contexts influencing the creation and publication of texts and the texts themselves. Reader response criticism focuses on the way texts are received. Critics taking this contextual approach insist that a work does not possess a fixed meaning; it can have as many meanings as it has readers. Reader response critics argue that people give the words meaning as they read them and as they reflect on them after reading. According to these critics, the process of reading involves readers in developing a series of expectations about a work, modifying these in the process of moving through the text, and coming up with some kind of meaning on completing it. Subsequent readings may result in readers creating new or modified meanings. The contexts readers bring to their encounters with a text influence the meanings they create. Their own personalities and experiences, their factual knowledge, the cultural environment in which they live, and their previous literary experiences, including earlier encounters with the work at hand, influence the nature of their encounters. By being aware of the various elements that they bring to their encounter with a specific work, readers can further enrich their literary experiences.

What are the rewards of becoming active readers and interpreters? An answer can be found by returning to this introduction's opening discussion of essential human needs. Poems and short stories are artistic and articulate responses to life that offer emotional, intellectual, and imaginative nourishment to their readers. Anthologies such as this provide exposure to literature that enhances the readers' knowledge of themselves and the world outside of themselves. Such experiences can lead to self-discovery and a lifelong love of reading.

SHORT FICTION

INTRODUCTION

In her Introduction to *Favorite Folktales from Around the World*, editor Jane Yolen wrote: "Stories distinguish us from animals more than any opposable thumb." She was emphasizing what, to her, was the unique characteristic of human beings. However, until we pause to consider it, most of us do not realize what an important place stories occupy in our lives and how much of our time is occupied with them. In fact, our daily lives are full of stories, sometimes written down, but, more often, not. People imagine, develop plans for a successful day, relate accounts (sometimes true, sometimes embroidered) about what they have done, or gossip about other people. They personalize, modify, and extend stories they have heard or read; retell and sometimes add variations to jokes and anecdotes; read newspaper stories; look at comic strips; listen to country and western ballads; and watch movies, television programs, and commercials (which are often minidramas).

Stories play an important role in relating people to their social and cultural groups. Novelist Leslie Silko wrote: "It's stories that make us into a community. There have to be stories. That's how you know; that's how you belong; that's how you know you belong." People receive some of their religious and political messages in the form of stories included in sermons and election speeches. More important, the great myths and epics, along with folktales, are stories in which cultures express and perpetuate the beliefs and values that bind their members together.

The processes of creating, transmitting, and receiving stories are among the most basic human activities. "One wants to tell a story, like Scheherazade," novelist Carlos Fuentes wrote, "in order not to die. It's one of the oldest urges of mankind. It's a way of stalling death." Like eating, sleeping, and breathing, it is a necessary human activity, and like breathing, so natural that we are often unaware that it is occurring. In *Tellers and Listeners: The Narrative Imagination*, the noted British critic Barbara Hardy has written:

> Nature, not art, makes us all story-tellers. Daily and nightly we devise fictions and chronicles, calling some of them daydreams or dreams, some of them nightmares, some of them truths, records, reports, and plans. Some of them we call, or refuse to call lies. Narrative imagination is a common human possession, differentiating us . . . from the animals.

The creation of all stories involves the selection and structuring of details that assist the storytellers in achieving their intended purposes. While in the types of stories described by Hardy these activities may be casual and haphazard, in those written as short stories and novels they are usually very deliberate and precise. Authors include only those characters, events, objects, and details that they consider to be necessary for their stories, and they arrange them in artistically satisfying and meaningful patterns. As an example, we know that in their day-to-day lives people spend much time on routine activities such as obtaining, preparing, and eating food. Although some people have transformed them into highly entertaining events, authors describe these only when they are important to their stories in some way: to development of plot and conflict, perhaps, or to portray character.

Some stories make few demands on their readers, offering light entertainment. Others require attentive readers, not only because their characters and themes are more complex and involved, but also because their authors frequently imply, rather than explain, elements of character and theme. Authors may, for example, leave the significance of actions, dialogue, and objects for readers to discover. They may create narrators who are not reliable reporters or interpreters. Moreover, they may present events in other than chronological order or may not supply clear links or bridges between sections of a story.

Readers easily recognize the basic elements of most stories—characters, actions, and settings—and the basic organizing pattern, which is the introduction, development, and resolution of one or more conflicts. An understanding of the varied and complex ways in which both these elements and the pattern of conflict are used by authors, along with an awareness of the significance of such techniques as narrative point of view, symbolism, and irony, will bring to readers fuller, richer comprehension of the stories they encounter. Careful attention to these elements is especially important in the reading of short stories, in which authors must achieve their purposes within a limited space, generally a few thousand words. Like lyric poets, to whom they have been frequently compared, they cannot waste words and must make each word contribute to their stories' total effect and meaning.

PLOT AND CONFLICT

Key to many stories are the incidents they contain; readers want to know what happens next and how a story ends. Authors select and organize events and then add details that contribute to the **plot** and lead toward a satisfying conclusion. The plot of a story provides more than factual information about who did what and when; it helps readers understand why these events occurred.

In most short stories, the plot begins with an **exposition** and then is organized around the introduction, development, and **resolution** of one or more **conflicts**. The exposition provides necessary background about characters, settings, and events. Those stories told or narrated in the same order in which the events occurred, that is, chronological order, usually introduce the conflict near the beginning. The events that follow form the **rising action**, or sequence of actions, leading to the **climax** or turning point, which is the most significant moment in the story. The **dénouement**, or final outcome or consequence of events, and the resolution of the conflict usually follow quickly. "Bliss" presents events in chronological order, helping to reveal both the relationships between actions and the nature of the characters' responses to them.

Many writers use **flashbacks**, interrupting the chronological presentation of events to introduce earlier actions that clarify the immediate present of the narrative. For example, during a Christmas vacation in Mexico, Sarah and Edward, the childless couple in "The Resplendent Quetzal," think about their courtship and unhappy married life in Toronto. By presenting these thoughts, which neither communicates to the other, the author clarifies the significance of their actions during an excursion to some Aztec ruins. After she has become a widow, the title character in "Hazel" has brief memories of confronting her deceased husband about his affairs with her friends. These memories help her to better prepare for her new life and give readers a fuller sense of what her married life was like. Other writers use **foreshadowing**, providing clues that hint at significant events that occur later in the story. In "A Rose for Emily," the reasons for the title character's purchase of arsenic are not explained. Only at the conclusion are her motivations and the ironic significance of the notation on the package, "For rats," made clear.

Most readers demand more than an exciting plot to stimulate their imaginations or develop their understanding of themselves and the world around them. This is particularly the case in many modern short stories, where the plot is minimal, there are few, if any, physical actions, and the events may initially appear to be almost trivial. Interest in the motivations of characters and their responses frequently leads to a re-reading of such stories. Do they develop during the course of a plot? Do they gain clearer understandings of themselves and their situations? What are the causes of the changes or insights, or the failure to achieve them?

When they change, the central characters, or **protagonists**, often do so as a result of conflicts with one or more of three kinds of opposing characters or forces, often referred to as **antagonists**. First, individuals may be in conflict with themselves. In "Bartleby, the Scrivener," the narrator must face his own conscience as he deals with his employee. Some of the self-justifications he makes may be his attempts to resolve satisfactorily for himself the inner conflicts he feels about his actions. In contrast, the narrator's mother in "Borders" is in conflict with the immigration officials who demand that she declare herself either a Canadian or an American citizen. Her struggle symbolizes that between Native peoples and colonial powers that will not allow subjects to define themselves in their own terms.

Second, characters find themselves in conflict with those around them—quite often brothers and sisters, parents and children, husbands and wives. Because family conflicts are among the most intense and intimate that most people experience, the frequency with which these occur in stories is not surprising. Often, in quarrelling with those closest to them, individuals are trying to define themselves and to define their positions in the relationships. "Out on Main Street" reveals the tensions the narrator feels between herself and her companion, other groups of Indian immigrants to Canada, and white Canadians. The reclusive heroine of "A Rose for Emily," the last member of a once-proud and wealthy Southern family, asserts her own status by defying the townspeople, refusing to pay taxes, and flaunting her Northern lover before them. In both "Squatter" and "The Motor Car," young immigrants to Canada find themselves in conflict with the cultures of their new country.

Third, conflict may place the central characters in opposition to natural or supernatural forces. In "An Outpost of Progress," two colonial administrators, deprived of the structure and familiarity of European life, cannot cope with living at the edge of an uncharted jungle. In "The Fall of the House of Usher," the decaying mansion seems to possess supernatural forces that drive Roderick Usher mad.

Most stories present conflicts of more than one type and usually examine the interrelationships between them. The narrator of "Bartleby, the Scrivener," while attempting to understand the motives behind Bartleby's behaviour, is also wrestling with his own opposing attitudes and with the dehumanizing effect of life in New York.

Not all stories conclude with conflicts resolved. In some, the characters confront forces or realities they cannot alter, as is the case in "A Clean, Well-Lighted Place." In others, their own inner flaws do not permit resolution. The narrator of "Why I Live at the P.O." believes she has triumphed over her family by leaving home. Although she does not appear to realize it, it is she who has created many of the situations that have made conditions intolerable at the house, and, in her account of events, she unconsciously reveals that her anger and hostility, the sources of much of the conflict, remain.

CHARACTER AND CHARACTERIZATION

Short stories generally focus on one or two major **characters**. These are almost always **rounded**; that is, they possess the complexities, contradictions, and depths of personality associated with actual human beings. They are distinguished from **flat characters**, whose personalities are presented briefly and in little depth. They may also be **dynamic**, changing during the course of a story. The change may be positive, as it is for the main character in "Hazel." Recently widowed and, at age fifty, entering the work force for the first time, she discovers talents and inner strengths of which she has been unaware and succeeds in a business controlled by men younger than she is. Character change can also be negative, as in the case of "Young Goodman Brown." At first the main character is foolish and naively overconfident of his ability successfully to survive his perilous journey. However, his inability to deal with what he believes he saw in the forest transforms him into "a stern, a darkly meditative, a distrustful, if not a desperate man."

In some modern short stories, characters are **static**, undergoing no development. Lack of change may be a result of the brevity of a story; there simply may not be the space to portray development. It may also be a reflection of the characters' inability to grow or to develop, or it may represent a thematic and philosophical position that views people as subject to outside forces that they can neither understand nor control.

In "A Clean, Well-Lighted Place," for example, the older waiter, who is sympathetic to the old man who frequents the café, does not change as a result of his knowledge of the meaninglessness of life, a condition he cannot change. He merely accepts what is.

At the conclusion of many short stories, one or more of the major characters may experience what James Joyce called an **"epiphany,"** a moment of revelation that brings understanding of a character's situation in life. In "Araby," the boy, while standing in the darkness, perceives the truth of his motivations for coming to the bazaar and the nature of his feelings for his friend's older sister. The young wife in "Bliss" perceives the nature of the relationship between her husband and a woman she has befriended.

In presenting characters confronting the conflicts in their lives, authors seldom engage in direct character analysis. Instead, they employ a variety of devices, especially **dialogue** and **action**, that reveal character implicitly. The conversation of the two waiters in "A Clean, Well-Lighted Place" consists of short, often abrupt phrases and sentences that seem very similar in style; however, the younger man asks a number of questions that reveal his lack of understanding of either his fellow worker or their customer. His partner gives simple answers without elaboration; these are the facts he accepts without questioning or resistance.

In these stories, the contrasting actions of people in the same situations reveal character. "Bartleby, the Scrivener" and "The Boat" also use this method, and there are many other examples. In the former story, the work patterns of Turkey and Nippers, two copyists for a New York lawyer, represent contrasts that the cautious narrator is able to keep in balance. While each exhibits some extreme behaviours, the fact that their personalities complement each other allows the lawyer to maintain the calmness of his daily routine. However, the arrival of the title character upsets both his routine and his peace of mind. The lives of the mother and father in "The Boat" have been tied to the sea since their youth, but each views the attachment and their children's attitude to the sea differently. The father seems to have sacrificed his love of literature to the necessity of fishing; the mother, who has never read a book since high school, sees making a living on the water the natural and honourable thing to do. Not surprisingly, the father is more sympathetic to his daughters' desires to leave; the mother sees their departures as almost a desertion.

Characters' thoughts and statements about themselves and other people also cast light on their own personalities. Their analyses and judgements should not necessarily be taken at face value. Rather, the reasons for them should be analyzed to discover what there is about particular characters that makes them view themselves and other people the way they do. For example, the narrator of "Why I Live at the P.O.," in expressing her negative opinion of her sister, reveals her own insecurity and resentment. In "Bartleby, the Scrivener," the narrator's satisfaction with his occupation and his position in New York legal circles may help to explain why he reacts to Bartleby as he does.

Physical objects, such as possessions or clothing, can reveal character. The items belonging to the dead priest in "Araby" reveal a great deal about both him and the young narrator. By wearing her best silk dress to travel into the United States to visit her daughter, the mother of the narrator in "Borders" is indicating elements of her character that will become more evident in her confrontation with the officials. In "Rope," the husband's purchase of a length of rope and his wife's reaction reveal the tensions in their marriage.

Finally, authors' descriptions of the physical appearance of individuals assist in the delineation of character. Melville carefully describes not only the clothing, but also the faces of the three scriveners in "Bartleby." While Turkey and Nippers are obvious, simple contrasts in looks and behaviour, Bartleby, considered in relation to them, is far more ambiguous. In the opening paragraph of "A Whisper in the Dark," the narrator describes her uncle in a way that reveals both his potential danger to her and her attraction toward him. Handsome and yet threatening, his face reveals personality traits that will seriously affect her life.

SETTING

Settings of stories, the locations and times in which the actions occur, can be specific social or cultural contexts, such as a character's home, neighbourhood, or place of work; larger, more generalized geographical regions; specific times of the day or of the year; and historical periods. Even weather conditions may be an important part of setting. In addition to assisting readers in visualizing events, settings provide contexts for the actions and contribute to the delineation of character, the creation of mood, and the development of theme. Settings are frequently symbolic, representing internal emotional states of characters. Readers who interpret settings rather than simply read them literally, who question why authors have selected particular times and places for their stories, will gain fuller understanding of the works they encounter. In "Young Goodman Brown," the dark forest, into which shafts of moonlight briefly penetrate, is a reflection of the dark confusion the young man experiences as he progresses further on his journey.

A major setting in many stories is the home of the central character, a place that should represent security, stability, and nurturance. Frequently, characters leave homes that do not possess these qualities. In "The Motor Car," Calvin departs from Barbados because his life there seems unfulfilling compared with the lives of the Canadian tourists who visit the island. He believes that Toronto will be everything for him that his home is not. The decaying condition of the House of Usher, which is described in detail by Poe's narrator, parallels the psychological state of the man for whom it is home. Introverted and melancholy, his withdrawal from the larger world leads to his destruction, just as the instability of the house leads to its collapsing in on itself.

Even though the characters in many stories have dwellings to which they can return, these places do not always offer them security. In "The

Resplendent Quetzal," the fact that Sarah and Edward spend Christmas, a time associated with home and family, on vacation in Mexico implies much about their lives back in Canada. Unlike his younger colleague, the older waiter in "A Clean, Well-Lighted Place" is not anxious to return to his lodgings, preferring to stay until dawn in a bar where he can better endure his life.

POINT OF VIEW

The narrator of a story, the person reporting on the characters, actions, and settings of a story, is as important as these elements themselves. While authors write their stories, they do not tell them directly; they create **narrators**, through whose voices the stories are related. By the choice of narrative **point of view**, the perspective from which a story is told, an author influences its interpretation. Third-person narrators are not characters in the stories they tell. They may be objective, reporting only the observable facts of the story without direct comment; omniscient, delving into the minds of several or all of the characters; or limited, delving only into the mind of the central character. First-person narrators are present in the stories they tell, either as observers or minor participants, or as major characters. It is interesting, after reading a story, to speculate how its meaning might have been altered had the author selected a different point of view or narrator.

Each type of narrator provides specific advantages to an author. Immediately observable in objective third-person narrators is their detachment from the scenes they recount. During most of Hemingway's "A Clean, Well-Lighted Place," the narrator describes, without comment, the bar and café, the actions of the old man, and the conversations between the two waiters. Only at the conclusion of the story does the narrator present the thoughts of the older waiter. This shift from objective to limited third-person narration casts light on the "facts" of the earlier part of the narration. Knowing the attitude of the waiter, readers can perceive that the apparently objective reporting earlier in the story consisted of elements carefully selected to reveal the characters' attitudes toward life.

Choosing a third-person omniscient narrator who reports on the emotions and thoughts of several characters allows an author to develop comparisons between individuals and to portray more fully the nature of the relationships between them. Atwood's "The Resplendent Quetzal" consists of five sections. In the first four, the narrator reports alternately on the thoughts of Sarah and her husband, Edward, each of whom is in a different part of the Aztec ruins they are touring. Even in the concluding section, when Edward returns to his wife, the narrator presents the thoughts first of one and then the other. The abruptly shifting point of view indicates the nature of the couple's relationship.

Although able to enter into the mind of only one character, a limited third-person narrator is able to explore that character fully, often exposing the character's failure to perceive the nature of the situations in which she finds herself, as is the case in "Bliss," or presenting aspects of the character not understood by those around her, as in "The Story of an Hour." In the latter story, other people attribute the heroine's death to her shock of joy on discovering that her husband, presumed dead, is still alive. The narrator, in presenting the woman's thoughts as she sits alone after receiving the news of her husband's supposed death, provides readers with information that explains the true cause of her death.

Because they are characters in the stories they report on, first-person narrators usually have access to less information than do third-person narrators. The words of first-person narrators raise such questions as: "How reliably does the narrator interpret events, his or her own character, and the characters of other people?" The observer narrator, a representative of the townspeople in "A Rose for Emily," recounts incidents he has heard of or seen from a distance. Using such phrases as "we believed," "we said," and "we were sure," he also presents hypotheses about the recluse. Only after her death, when he, along with other townsmen, has entered her bedroom, does he make a discovery that provides an explanation of the elderly woman's life and casts light on the accuracy of her neighbours' suppositions about it. Through the use of this type of narrator, Faulkner creates a story that is as much about the townspeople who interpret and judge Emily Grierson as it is about her life itself.

First-person narrators who are the main characters in a story are also limited by the extent of the knowledge they possess. Moreover, qualities of their personalities may cause them to ignore, overlook, or misinterpret the significance of the actions in which they are involved and the characters with whom they interact, as is the case in "Why I Live at the P.O." Other narrators may be more aware of themselves, and their narratives may present their consciousness of character change, as in "Bartleby, the Scrivener," in which the narrator seems to be as interested in explaining how the young man influenced him as he is in analyzing Bartleby himself. For the mature narrator of "The Boat," the remembrance of his boyhood relationship with his father provides him with fuller understanding of important aspects of his childhood and adolescence.

SYMBOLISM

Through an author's careful employment of **symbols**—objects, characters, or actions that stand for something beyond themselves—specific elements of many stories assume greater significance. Universal symbols, often called **archetypes**, are interpreted in much the same way in many different cultures. The use of the cycles of day and night and of the seasons to present the phases of human life is a familiar example. Cultural symbols hold special meanings for a specific group. For example, the cross embodies a number of complex spiritual beliefs for Christians. **Contextual symbols** are given or take on meaning only within the stories that contain them.

When employing universal or cultural symbols, authors usually assume their readers' general knowledge of the relationship between the literal objects, events, and characters and their symbolic meanings. Readers use this knowledge to interpret the symbols and hence to understand the stories they read more fully. In "An Outpost of Progress," the manner of death of Kayerts resembles Christ's crucifixion. Readers are invited to consider whether the man's death could be considered sacrificial, and, if it was, to what extent.

In "The Resplendent Quetzal," a cultural symbol takes on contextual meanings unique to the story. A sacred bird, whose feathers symbolize the souls of unborn babies to the Aztecs, is the only bird Sarah decides she wishes to see. Edward, who "felt he was allowed to see birds only when they wanted him to," does not think there are any in the area they are visiting. He is correct: neither one sees a quetzal. An understanding of what the bird symbolizes for each of them illuminates aspects of their characters. Atwood also draws on the fact that male quetzals play an important role in the hatching and raising of offspring, staying close to and assisting their mates during the entire process.

In "Borders" and "The Loons," the titles introduce the major contextual symbols, which acquire additional meanings each time they appear. In the former story, the international boundary between Canada and the United States, the "border," comes to represent divisions, not only between countries, but also between cultures and even between members of a family. In "The Loons," the calls of the shy, elusive birds were "plaintive, and yet with a quality of chilling mockery . . . [and] belonged to a world separated by aeons from our neat world of summer cottages and the lighted lamps of home." To the teenage narrator of the story, they stand for Piquette, a young, lonely Métis woman whom she had tried unsuccessfully to befriend.

IRONY

Irony, one of the most frequently used techniques in stories, is of three types. Verbal irony is created when there is a difference between the apparent and actual meanings of a speaker's words. In "An Outpost of Progress," the company director "made a speech to Kayerts and Carlier, pointing out to them the promising aspect of their situation." After he has left them, however, he reveals his actual assessment of their situation: " 'I always thought the station on this river useless, and they just fit the situation.' " In the case of dramatic irony, readers have clearer perceptions of situations than do the characters involved in them. The narrator in "Araby" is so involved in his emotions about Mangan's sister that he does not see how his thoughts and actions are indications of infatuation and sexual arousal, emotions that Joyce makes clear to the reader. In "Why I Live at the P.O.," the narrator, who reports throughout the story what she considers to be the failings of her family members, does not realize that her statements also reveal a great deal about her own failings and character flaws.

In some stories, the situational irony is of cosmic dimensions, as characters struggle against natural or supernatural forces that frequently defeat them. In "The Boat," the sea is the source of the family's livelihood. However, it is also a place of great danger, where fishermen die. In "An Outpost of Progress," Kayerts and Carlier are victims not only of their own character deficiencies, but also of the vast, natural, uncivilized world that surrounds them, an environment against which their European training has not given them adequate defenses.

Katherine Mansfield's "Bliss" contains all three types of irony. Harry practises verbal irony when speaking of Miss Fulton, a dinner guest, in terms that conceal his true attitude about her. The situational irony is introduced in the title, "Bliss," which refers to the emotion Bertha experiences for the first time. Because of it, she is "waiting for something . . . divine to happen . . . that she knew must happen . . . infallibly." However, the events of the evening result in her feeling far from blissful. Bertha perceives the blossoming pear tree as a visual embodiment of her emotion and believes that Miss Fulton does as well. She is correct, but does not realize the cause of the other woman's feelings. On first reading, an attentive reader may notice in "Bliss" several instances of dramatic irony that subtly foreshadow the story's conclusion. These hints provide an undercurrent that contrasts Bertha's perceptions and anticipations with the realities of her situation.

INTERPRETATION AND PERSONAL RESPONSE

Because of differences in gender, age, cultural background, and personal experience, readers respond individually to short stories. Their interpretations begin with the words of the works themselves, for as creations of other individuals, these are influenced by their authors' gender, age, cultural and literary background, and personal experience. Full, informed response to a work requires that readers initially relinquish freedom of response, giving consideration to the contexts out of which a story emerged and the technical aspects of language used in writing it. Careful, analytical attention to a story will lead to speculation on an author's purpose in writing. Based on such inquiry, readers can engage in more informed evaluation of a work, considering how clearly and artistically the author has communicated and judging the validity of the work's theme. Then, having responded to it on its own terms, they can respond to it personally, relating it to their own lives, identifying with or reacting against the characters, accepting or rejecting the author's attitudes toward or interpretation of life, or modifying their own views in the light of those presented. In making informed personal responses, readers achieve a new freedom, one that helps them to enjoy stories more fully and to make the creating, telling, and reading of stories an integral part of their lives.

Nathaniel Hawthorne (1804–1864)

A native of Salem, Massachusetts, where an ancestor was a judge at the witch trials of 1692, Nathaniel Hawthorne set many of his short stories and *The Scarlet Letter,* his best-known novel, in colonial New England. He was more than a creator of historical fiction, however, describing himself as a writer who delved into "our common human nature." The events in "Young Goodman Brown," set on All Hallows Eve, at which time the devil was supposed to initiate new converts at a ceremony deep in the forest, take place before the famous witch trials and makes reference to three women, Sarah Cloyse, Martha Corey, and Martha Carrier, who were accused of witchcraft. Carrier was convicted and executed. Using the widely used symbol of the dark forest as a place of moral and psychological confusion and evil, Hawthorne carefully portrays events from the point of view of the young man, but casts doubt on the actuality of what Brown thinks he sees. This ambiguity invites the reader to ask, "If these events happened, what is the meaning of Brown's reactions? If they did not happen and are a creation of Brown's mind, what does this reflect about him?"

YOUNG GOODMAN BROWN

Young Goodman Brown came forth, at sunset, into the street of Salem village, but put his head back, after crossing the threshold, to exchange a parting kiss with his young wife. And Faith, as the wife was aptly named, thrust her own pretty head into the street, letting the wind play with the pink ribbons of her cap, while she called to Goodman Brown.

"Dearest heart," whispered she, softly and rather sadly, when her lips were close to his ear, "pr'y thee, put off your journey until sunrise, and sleep in your own bed to-night. A lone woman is troubled with such dreams and such thoughts, that she's afeard of herself, sometimes. Pray, tarry with me this night, dear husband, of all nights in the year!"

"My love and my Faith," replied young Goodman Brown, "of all nights in the year, this one night must I tarry away from thee. My journey, as thou callest it, forth and back again, must needs be done 'twixt now and sunrise. What, my sweet, pretty wife, dost thou doubt me already, and we but three months married!"

"Then, God bless you!" said Faith, with the pink ribbons, "and may you find all well, when you come back."

5   "Amen!" cried Goodman Brown. "Say thy prayers, dear Faith, and go to bed at dusk, and no harm will come to thee."

So they parted; and the young man pursued his way, until, being about to turn the corner by the meeting-house, he looked back, and saw the head of Faith still peeping after him, with a melancholy air, in spite of her pink ribbons.

"Poor little Faith!" thought he, for his heart smote him. "What a wretch am I, to leave her on such an errand! She talks of dreams, too. Methought, as she spoke, there was trouble in her face, as if a dream had warned her what work is to be done to-night. But no, no! 'twould kill her to think it. Well; she's a blessed angel on earth; and after this one night, I'll cling to her skirts and follow her to Heaven."

With this excellent resolve for the future, Goodman Brown felt himself justified in making more haste on his present evil purpose. He had taken a dreary road, darkened by all the gloomiest trees of the forest, which barely stood aside to let the narrow path creep through, and closed immediately behind. It was all as lonely as could be; and there is this peculiarity in such a solitude, that the traveller knows not who may be concealed by the innumerable trunks and the thick boughs overhead; so that, with lonely footsteps, he may yet be passing through an unseen multitude.

"There may be a devilish Indian behind every tree," said Goodman Brown, to himself; and he glanced fearfully behind him, as he added, "What if the devil himself should be at my very elbow!"

His head being turned back, he passed a crook of the road, and looking forward again, beheld the figure of a man, in grave and decent attire, seated at the foot of an old tree. He arose, at Goodman Brown's approach, and walked onward, side by side with him.

"You are late, Goodman Brown," said he. "The clock of the Old South[1] was striking as I came through Boston; and that is full fifteen minutes agone."

"Faith kept me back awhile," replied the young man, with a tremor in his voice, caused by the sudden appearance of his companion, though not wholly unexpected.

It was now deep dusk in the forest, and deepest in that part of it where these two were journeying. As nearly as could be discerned, the second traveller was about fifty years old, apparently in the same rank of life as Goodman Brown, and bearing a considerable resemblance to him, though perhaps more in expression than features. Still, they might have been taken for father and son. And yet, though the elder person was as simply clad as the younger, and as simple in manner too, he had an indescribable air of one who knew the world, and would not have felt abashed at the governor's dinner-table, or in King William's[2] court, were it possible that his affairs should call him thither. But the only thing about him, that could be fixed upon as remarkable, was his staff, which bore the likeness of a great black snake, so curiously wrought, that it might almost be seen to twist and wriggle itself, like a living serpent. This, of course, must have been an ocular deception, assisted by the uncertain light.

"Come, Goodman Brown!" cried his fellow-traveller, "this is a dull pace for the beginning of a journey. Take my staff, if you are so soon weary."

"Friend," said the other, exchanging his slow pace for a full stop, "having kept covenant by meeting thee here, it is my purpose now to return whence I came. I have scruples, touching the matter thou wot'st of."

"Sayest thou so?" replied he of the serpent, smiling apart. "Let us walk on, nevertheless, reasoning as we go, and if I convince thee not, thou shalt turn back. We are but a little way in the forest, yet."

---

[1]the Old South Church was located in Boston, 25 km southwest of Salem. [2]King William III ruled England from 1689 to 1702.

"Too far, too far!" exclaimed the goodman, unconsciously resuming his walk. "My father never went into the woods on such an errand, nor his father before him. We have been a race of honest men and good Christians, since the days of the martyrs. And shall I be the first of the name of Brown, that ever took this path, and kept—"

"Such company, thou wouldst say," observed the elder person, interpreting his pause. "Well said, Goodman Brown! I have been as well acquainted with your family as with ever a one among the Puritans; and that's no trifle to say. I helped your grandfather, the constable, when he lashed the Quaker woman so smartly through the streets of Salem. And it was I that brought your father a pitch-pine knot, kindled at my own hearth, to set fire to an Indian village, in King Philip's war.[3] They were my good friends, both; and many a pleasant walk have we had along this path, and returned merrily after midnight. I would fain be friends with you, for their sake."

"If it be as thou sayest," replied Goodman Brown, "I marvel they never spoke of these matters. Or, verily, I marvel not, seeing that the least rumor of the sort would have driven them from New-England. We are a people of prayer, and good works to boot, and abide no such wickedness."

20   "Wickedness or not," said the traveller with the twisted staff, "I have a very general acquaintance here in New-England. The deacons of many a church have drunk the communion wine with me; the selectmen, of divers towns, make me their chairman; and a majority of the Great and General Court are firm supporters of my interest. The governor and I, too—but these are state-secrets."

"Can this be so!" cried Goodman Brown, with a stare of amazement at his undisturbed companion. "Howbeit, I have nothing to do with the governor and council; they have their own ways, and are no rule for a simple husbandman, like me. But, were I to go on with thee, how should I meet the eye of that good old man, our minister, at Salem village? Oh, his voice would make me tremble, both Sabbath-day and lecture-day!"

Thus far, the elder traveller had listened with due gravity, but now burst into a fit of irrepressible mirth, shaking himself so violently, that his snake-like staff actually seemed to wriggle in sympathy.

"Ha! ha! ha!" shouted he, again and again; then composing himself, "Well, go on, Goodman Brown, go on; but pr'y thee, don't kill me with laughing!"

"Well, then, to end the matter at once," said Goodman Brown, considerably nettled, "there is my wife, Faith. It would break her dear little heart; and I'd rather break my own!"

25   "Nay, if that be the case," answered the other, "e'en go thy ways, Goodman Brown. I would not, for twenty old women like the one hobbling before us, that Faith should come to any harm."

As he spoke, he pointed his staff at a female figure on the path, in whom Goodman Brown recognized a very pious and exemplary dame, who had

---

[3] in 1676, Chief Metacomet (King Philip) led an Indian uprising against Massachusetts colonists.

taught him his catechism, in youth, and was still his moral and spiritual adviser, jointly with the minister and Deacon Gookin.

"A marvel, truly, that Goody Cloyse should be so far in the wilderness, at night-fall! said he. "But, with your leave, friend, I shall take a cut through the woods, until we have left this Christian woman behind. Being a stranger to you, she might ask whom I was consorting with, and whither I was going."

"Be it so," said his fellow-traveller. "Betake you to the woods, and let me keep the path."

Accordingly, the young man turned aside, but took care to watch his companion, who advanced softly along the road, until he had come within a staff's length of the old dame. She, meanwhile, was making the best of her way, with singular speed for so aged a woman, and mumbling some indistinct words, a prayer, doubtless, as she went. The traveller put forth his staff, and touched her withered neck with what seemed the serpent's tail.

"The devil!" screamed the pious old lady.

"Then Goody Cloyse knows her old friend?" observed the traveller, confronting her, and leaning on his writhing stick.

"Ah, forsooth, and is it your worship, indeed?" cried the good dame. "Yea, truly is it, and in the very image of my old gossip, Goodman Brown, the grandfather of the silly fellow that now is. But—would your worship believe it?—my broomstick hath strangely disappeared, stolen, as I suspect, by that unhanged witch, Goody Cory, and that, too, when I was all anointed with the juice of smallage and cinque-foil and wolf's bane—"[4]

"Mingled with fine wheat and the fat of a new-born babe," said the shape of old Goodman Brown.

"Ah, your worship knows the receipt," cried the old lady, cackling aloud. "So, as I was saying, being all ready for the meeting, and no horse to ride on, I made up my mind to foot it; for they tell me, there is a nice young man to be taken into communion to-night. But now your good worship will lend me your arm, and we shall be there in a twinkling."

"That can hardly be," answered her friend. "I may not spare you my arm, Goody Cloyse, but here is my staff, if you will."

So saying, he threw it down at her feet, where, perhaps, it assumed life, being one of the rods which its owner had formerly lent to the Egyptian Magi.[5] Of this fact, however, Goodman Brown could not take cognizance. He had cast up his eyes in astonishment, and looking down again, beheld neither Goody Cloyse nor the serpentine staff, but his fellow-traveller alone, who waited for him as calmly as if nothing had happened.

"That old woman taught me my catechism!" said the young man; and there was a world of meaning in this simple comment.

They continued to walk onward, while the elder traveller exhorted his companion to make good speed and persevere in the path, discoursing so aptly, that his arguments seemed rather to spring up in the bosom of his auditor, than to be suggested by himself. As they went, he plucked a branch

[4]plants supposedly possessing magical qualities reported to be used by witches. [5]Moses commanded his brother Aaron to throw down a rod before the Egyptian pharaoh. When he did so, it turned into a serpent. Exodus 7:9–10.

of maple, to serve for a walking-stick, and began to strip it of the twigs and little boughs, which were wet with evening dew. The moment his fingers touched them, they became strangely withered and dried up, as with a week's sunshine. Thus the pair proceeded, at a good free pace, until suddenly, in a gloomy hollow of the road, Goodman Brown sat himself down on the stump of a tree, and refused to go any farther.

"Friend," said he, stubbornly, "my mind is made up. Not another step will I budge on this errand. What if a wretched old woman do choose to go to the devil, when I thought she was going to Heaven! Is that any reason why I should quit my dear Faith, and go after her?"

40   "You will think better of this, by-and-by," said his acquaintance, composedly. "Sit here and rest yourself awhile; and when you feel like moving again, there is my staff to help you along."

Without more words, he threw his companion the maple stick, and was as speedily out of sight, as if he had vanished into the deepening gloom. The young man sat a few moments, by the road-side, applauding himself greatly, and thinking with how clear a conscience he should meet the minister, in his morning-walk, nor shrink from the eye of good old Deacon Gookin. And what calm sleep would be his, that very night, which was to have been spent so wickedly, but purely and sweetly now, in the arms of Faith! Amidst these pleasant and praiseworthy meditations, Goodman Brown heard the tramp of horses along the road, and deemed it advisable to conceal himself within the verge of the forest, conscious of the guilty purpose that had brought him thither, though now so happily turned from it.

On came the hoof-tramps and the voices of the riders, two grave old voices, conversing soberly as they drew near. These mingled sounds appeared to pass along the road, within a few yards of the young man's hiding-place; but owing, doubtless, to the depth of the gloom, at that particular spot, neither the travellers nor their steeds were visible. Though their figures brushed the small boughs by the way-side, it could not be seen that they intercepted, even for a moment, the faint gleam from the strip of bright sky, athwart which they must have passed. Goodman Brown alternately crouched and stood on tip-toe, pulling aside the branches, and thrusting forth his head as far as he durst, without discerning so much as a shadow. It vexed him the more, because he could have sworn, were such a thing possible, that he recognized the voices of the minister and Deacon Gookin, jogging along quietly, as they were wont to do, when bound to some ordination or ecclesiastical council. While yet within hearing, one of the riders stopped to pluck a switch.

"Of the two, reverend Sir," said the voice like the deacon's, "I had rather miss an ordination-dinner than to-night's meeting. They tell me that some of our community are to be here from Falmouth and beyond, and others from Connecticut and Rhode-Island; besides several of the Indian powows, who, after their fashion, know almost as much deviltry as the best of us. Moreover, there is a goodly young woman to be taken into communion."

"Mighty well, Deacon Gookin!" replied the solemn old tones of the minister. "Spur up, or we shall be late. Nothing can be done, you know, until I get on the ground."

45 The hoofs clattered again, and the voices, talking so strangely in the empty air, passed on through the forest, where no church had ever been gathered, nor solitary Christian prayed. Whither, then, could these holy men be journeying, so deep into the heathen wilderness? Young Goodman Brown caught hold of a tree, for support, being ready to sink down on the ground, faint and overburthened with the heavy sickness of his heart. He looked up to the sky, doubting whether there really was a Heaven above him. Yet, there was the blue arch, and the stars brightening in it.

"With Heaven above, and Faith below, I will yet stand firm against the devil!" cried Goodman Brown.

While he still gazed upward, into the deep arch of the firmament, and had lifted his hands to pray, a cloud, though no wind was stirring, hurried across the zenith, and hid the brightening stars. The blue sky was still visible, except directly overhead, where this black mass of cloud was sweeping swiftly northward. Aloft in the air, as if from the depths of the cloud, came a confused and doubtful sound of voices. Once, the listener fancied that he could distinguish the accents of town's-people of his own, men and women, both pious and ungodly, many of whom he had met at the communion-table, and had seen others rioting at the tavern. The next moment, so indistinct were the sounds, he doubted whether he had heard aught but the murmur of the old forest, whispering without a wind. Then came a stronger swell of those familiar tones, heard daily in the sunshine, at Salem village, but never, until now, from a cloud of night. There was one voice, of a young woman, uttering lamentations, yet with an uncertain sorrow, and entreating for some favor, which, perhaps, it would grieve her to obtain. And all the unseen multitude, both saints and sinners, seemed to encourage her onward.

"Faith!" shouted Goodman Brown, in a voice of agony and desperation; and the echoes of the forest mocked him, crying—"Faith! Faith!" as if bewildered wretches were seeking her, all through the wilderness.

The cry of grief, rage, and terror, was yet piercing the night, when the unhappy husband held his breath for a response. There was a scream, drowned immediately in a louder murmur of voices, fading into far-off laughter, as the dark cloud swept away, leaving the clear and silent sky above Goodman Brown. But something fluttered lightly down through the air, and caught on the branch of a tree. The young man seized it, and beheld a pink ribbon.

50 "My Faith is gone!" cried he, after one stupefied moment. "There is no good on earth; and sin is but a name. Come, devil! for to thee is this world given."

And maddened with despair, so that he laughed loud and long, did Goodman Brown grasp his staff and set forth again, at such a rate, that he seemed to fly along the forest-path, rather than to walk or run. The road grew wilder and drearier, and more faintly traced, and vanished at length, leaving him in the heart of the dark wilderness, still rushing onward, with the instinct that guides mortal man to evil. The whole forest was peopled with frightful sounds; the creaking of the trees, the howling of wild beasts, and the yell of Indians; while, sometimes, the wind tolled like a distant church-bell, and sometimes gave a broad roar around the traveller, as if all

Nature were laughing him to scorn. But he was himself the chief horror of the scene, and shrank not from its other horrors.

"Ha! ha! ha!" roared Goodman Brown, when the wind laughed at him. "Let us hear which will laugh loudest! Think not to frighten me with your deviltry! Come witch, come wizard, come Indian powow, come devil himself! and here comes Goodman Brown. You may as well fear him as he fear you!"

In truth, all through the haunted forest, there could be nothing more frightful than the figure of Goodman Brown. On he flew, among the black pines, brandishing his staff with frenzied gestures, now giving vent to an inspiration of horrid blasphemy, and now shouting forth such laughter, as set all the echoes of the forest laughing like demons around him. The fiend in his own shape is less hideous, than when he rages in the breast of man. Thus sped the demoniac on his course, until, quivering among the trees, he saw a red light before him, as when the felled trunks and branches of a clearing have been set on fire, and throw up their lurid blaze against the sky, at the hour of midnight. He paused, in a lull of the tempest that had driven him onward, and heard the swell of what seemed a hymn, rolling solemnly from a distance, with the weight of many voices. He knew the tune; it was a familiar one in the choir of the village meeting-house. The verse died heavily away, and was lengthened by a chorus, not of human voices, but of all the sounds of the benighted wilderness, pealing in awful harmony together. Goodman Brown cried out; and his cry was lost to his own ear, by its unison with the cry of the desert.

In the interval of silence, he stole forward, until the light glared full upon his eyes. At one extremity of an open space, hemmed in by the dark wall of the forest, arose a rock, bearing some rude, natural resemblance either to an altar or a pulpit, and surrounded by four blazing pines, their tops aflame, their stems untouched, like candles at an evening meeting. The mass of foliage, that had overgrown the summit of the rock, was all on fire, blazing high into the night, and fitfully illuminating the whole field. Each pendent twig and leafy festoon was in a blaze. As the red light arose and fell, a numerous congregation alternately shone forth, then disappeared in shadow, and again grew, as it were, out of the darkness, peopling the heart of the solitary woods at once.

55   "A grave and dark-clad company!" quoth Goodman Brown.

In truth, they were such. Among them, quivering to-and-fro, between gloom and splendor, appeared faces that would be seen, next day, at the council-board of the province, and others which, Sabbath after Sabbath, looked devoutly heavenward, and benignantly over the crowded pews, from the holiest pulpits in the land. Some affirm, that the lady of the governor was there. At least, there were high dames well known to her, and wives of honored husbands, and widows, a great multitude, and ancient maidens, all of excellent repute, and fair young girls, who trembled, lest their mothers should espy them. Either the sudden gleams of light, flashing over the obscure field, bedazzled Goodman Brown, or he recognized a score of the church-members of Salem village, famous for their especial sanctity. Good old Deacon Gookin had arrived, and waited at the skirts of that venerable saint, his revered pastor. But, irreverently consorting with these grave, reputable, and pious people, these elders of the church, these chaste dames and dewy virgins, there were men of dissolute lives and women of spotted fame, wretches given over to all mean and filthy vice, and suspected even of horrid crimes. It was strange to see, that the good shrank not from the wicked, nor were the sinners abashed by the saints. Scattered, also, among their pale-faced enemies, were the Indian priests, or powows, who had often scared their native forest with more hideous incantations than any known to English witchcraft.

"But, where is Faith?" thought Goodman Brown; and, as hope came into his heart, he trembled.

Another verse of the hymn arose, a slow and mournful strain, such as the pious love, but joined to words which expressed all that our nature can conceive of sin, and darkly hinted at far more. Unfathomable to mere mortals is the lore of fiends. Verse after verse was sung, and still the chorus of the desert swelled between, like the deepest tone of a mighty organ. And, with the final peal of that dreadful anthem, there came a sound, as if the roaring wind, the rushing streams, the howling beasts, and every other voice of the unconverted wilderness, were mingling and according with the voice of guilty man, in homage to the prince of all. The four blazing pines threw up a loftier flame, and obscurely discovered shapes and visages of horror on the smoke-wreaths, above the impious assembly. At the same moment, the fire on the rock shot redly forth, and formed a glowing arch above its base, where now appeared a figure. With reverence be it spoken, the figure bore no slight similitude, both in garb and manner, to some grave divine of the New-England churches.

"Bring forth the converts!" cried a voice, that echoed through the field and rolled into the forest.

60 At the word, Goodman Brown stept forth from the shadow of the trees, and approached the congregation, with whom he felt a loathful brotherhood, by the sympathy of all that was wicked in his heart. He could have well nigh sworn, that the shape of his own dead father beckoned him to advance, looking downward from a smoke-wreath, while a woman, with dim features of despair, threw out her hand to warn him back. Was it his mother? But he had no power to retreat one step, nor to resist, even in thought, when the minister and good old Deacon Gookin seized his arms, and led him to the blazing rock. Thither came also the slender form of a veiled female, led between Goody Cloyse, that pious teacher of the catechism, and Martha Carrier, who had received the devil's promise to be queen of hell. A rampant hag was she! And there stood the proselytes, beneath the canopy of fire.

"Welcome, my children," said the dark figure, "to the communion of your race! Ye have found, thus young, your nature and your destiny. My children, look behind you!"

They turned; and flashing forth, as it were, in a sheet of flame, the fiend-worshippers were seen; the smile of welcome gleamed darkly on every visage.

"There," resumed the sable form, "are all whom ye have reverenced from youth. Ye deemed them holier than yourselves, and shrank from your own sin, contrasting it with their lives of righteousness, and prayerful aspirations heavenward. Yet, here are they all, in my worshipping assembly! This night it shall be granted you to know their secret deeds; how hoary-bearded elders of the church have whispered wanton words to the young maids of their households; how many a woman, eager for widow's weeds, has given her husband a drink at bed-time, and let him sleep his last sleep in her bosom; how beardless youths have made haste to inherit their fathers' wealth; and how fair damsels—blush not, sweet ones!—have dug little graves in the garden, and bidden me, the sole guest, to an infant's funeral. By the sympathy of your human hearts for sin, ye shall scent out all the places—whether in church, bed-chamber, street, field, or forest—where crime has been committed, and shall exult to behold the whole earth one stain of guilt, one mighty blood-spot. Far more than this! It shall be yours to penetrate, in every bosom, the deep mystery of sin, the fountain of all wicked arts, and which inexhaustibly supplies more evil impulses than human power—than my power, at its utmost!—can make manifest in deeds. And now, my children, look upon each other."

They did so; and, by the blaze of the hell-kindled torches, the wretched man beheld his Faith, and the wife her husband, trembling before that unhallowed altar.

65   "Lo! there ye stand, my children," said the figure, in a deep and solemn tone, almost sad, with its despairing awfulness, as if his once angelic nature could yet mourn for our miserable race. "Depending upon one another's hearts, ye had still hoped, that virtue were not all a dream. Now are ye undeceived! Evil is the nature of mankind. Evil must be your only happiness. Welcome, again, my children, to the communion of your race!"

"Welcome!" repeated the fiend-worshippers, in one cry of despair and triumph.

And there they stood, the only pair, as it seemed, who were yet hesitating on the verge of wickedness, in this dark world. A basin was hollowed, naturally, in the rock. Did it contain water, reddened by the lurid light? or was it blood? or, perchance, a liquid flame? Herein did the Shape of Evil dip his hand, and prepare to lay the mark of baptism upon their foreheads, that they might be partakers of the mystery of sin, more conscious of the secret guilt of others, both in deed and thought, than they could now be of their own. The husband cast one look at his pale wife, and Faith at him. What polluted wretches would the next glance shew them to each other, shuddering alike at what they disclosed and what they saw!

"Faith! Faith!" cried the husband. "Look up to Heaven, and resist the Wicked One!"

Whether Faith obeyed, he knew not. Hardly had he spoken, when he found himself amid calm night and solitude, listening to a roar of the wind, which died heavily away through the forest. He staggered against the rock and felt it chill and damp, while a hanging twig, that had been all on fire, besprinkled his cheek with the coldest dew.

70   The next morning, young Goodman Brown came slowly into the street of Salem village, staring around him like a bewildered man. The good old minister was taking a walk along the grave-yard, to get an appetite for breakfast and meditate his sermon, and bestowed a blessing, as he passed, on Goodman Brown. He shrank from the venerable saint, as if to avoid an

anathema. Old Deacon Gookin was at domestic worship, and the holy words of his prayer were heard through the open window. "What God doth the wizard pray to?" quoth Goodman Brown. Goody Cloyse, that excellent old Christian, stood in the early sunshine, at her own lattice, catechising a little girl, who had brought her a pint of morning's milk. Goodman Brown snatched away the child, as from the grasp of the fiend himself. Turning the corner by the meeting-house, he spied the head of Faith, with the pink ribbons, gazing anxiously forth, and bursting into such joy at sight of him, that she skipt along the street, and almost kissed her husband before the whole village. But, Goodman Brown looked sternly and sadly into her face, and passed on without a greeting.

Had Goodman Brown fallen asleep in the forest, and only dreamed a wild dream of a witch-meeting?

Be it so, if you will. But, alas! it was a dream of evil omen for young Goodman Brown. A stern, a sad, a darkly meditative, a distrustful, if not a desperate man, did he become, from the night of that fearful dream. On the Sabbath-day, when the congregation were singing a holy psalm, he could not listen, because an anthem of sin rushed loudly upon his ear, and drowned all the blessed strain. When the minister spoke from the pulpit, with power and fervid eloquence, and, with his hand on the open Bible, of the sacred truths of our religion, and of saint-like lives and triumphant deaths, and of future bliss or misery unutterable, then did Goodman Brown turn pale, dreading, lest the roof should thunder down upon the gray blasphemer and his hearers. Often, awaking suddenly at midnight, he shrank from the bosom of Faith, and at morning or eventide, when the family knelt down at prayer, he scowled, and muttered to himself, and gazed sternly at his wife, and turned away. And when he had lived long, and was borne to his grave, a hoary corpse, followed by Faith, an aged woman, and children and grand-children, a goodly procession, besides neighbors, not a few, they carved no hopeful verse upon his tomb-stone; for his dying hour was gloom.

(1835)

Edgar Allan Poe   (1809–1849)

Born in Boston and raised by foster parents in Richmond, Virginia, Edgar Allan Poe struggled all his adult life to earn a living as a professional author, serving as a magazine editor and writing poetry, short stories, and reviews. A controversial figure before and after his death, he is remembered as a poet whose works influenced late-nineteenth- and early-twentieth-century French, British, and American poets, and as one of the first major writers of the short story. He developed a theory of the short story as a brief prose piece, capable of being read in no more than an hour, in which all details are selected and arranged to create a unified effect. Poe applied this theory skillfully in his story "The Fall of the House of Usher." The narrator's response to the setting, the Usher twins, and the events communicates a sense of increasing horror.

THE FALL OF THE HOUSE OF USHER

Son coeur est un luth suspendu;
Sitôt qu'on le touche il résonne.
                            —De Béranger[1]

During the whole of a dull, dark, and soundless day in the autumn of the year, when the clouds hung oppressively low in the heavens, I had been passing alone, on horseback, through a singularly dreary tract of country; and at length found myself, as the shades of the evening drew on, within view of the melancholy House of Usher. I know not how it was—but, with the first glimpse of the building, a sense of insufferable gloom pervaded my spirit. I say insufferable; for the feeling was unrelieved by any of that half-pleasurable, because poetic, sentiment, with which the mind usually receives even the sternest natural images of the desolate or terrible. I looked upon the scene before me—upon the mere house, and the simple landscape features of the domain—upon the bleak walls—upon the vacant eye-like windows—upon a few rank sedges—and upon a few white trunks of decayed trees—with an utter depression of soul which I can compare to no earthly sensation more properly than to the after-dream of the reveller upon opium—the bitter lapse into everyday life—the hideous dropping off of the veil. There was an iciness, a sinking, a sickening of the heart—an unredeemed dreariness of thought which no goading of the imagination could torture into aught of the sublime. What was it—I paused to think—what was it that so unnerved me in the contemplation of the House of Usher? It was a mystery all insoluble; nor could I grapple with the shadowy fancies that crowded upon me as I pondered. I was forced to fall back upon the unsatisfactory conclusion, that while, beyond doubt, there are combinations

---

[1]"His heart is a tightly stringed lute; as soon as one touches it, it resonates"—based on eighteenth-century French poet Pierre-Jean de Béranger's "Le Rufus."

of very simple natural objects which have the power of thus affecting us, still the analysis of this power lies among considerations beyond our depth. It was possible, I reflected, that a mere different arrangement of the particulars of the scene, of the details of the picture, would be sufficient to modify, or perhaps to annihilate its capacity for sorrowful impression; and, acting upon this idea, I reined my horse to the precipitous brink of a black and lurid tarn that lay in unruffled lustre by the dwelling, and gazed down—but with a shudder even more thrilling than before—upon the remodelled and inverted images of the gray sedge, and the ghastly tree-stems, and the vacant and eye-like windows.

Nevertheless, in this mansion of gloom I now proposed to myself a sojourn of some weeks. Its proprietor, Roderick Usher, had been one of my boon companions in boyhood; but many years had elapsed since our last meeting. A letter, however, had lately reached me in a distant part of the country—a letter from him—which, in its wildly importunate nature, had admitted of no other than a personal reply. The MS. gave evidence of nervous agitation. The writer spoke of acute bodily illness—of a mental disorder which oppressed him—and of an earnest desire to see me, as his best, and indeed his only personal friend, with a view of attempting, by the cheerfulness of my society, some alleviation of his malady. It was the manner in which all this, and much more, was said—it was the apparent *heart* that went with his request—which allowed me no room for hesitation; and I accordingly obeyed forthwith what I still considered a very singular summons.

Although, as boys, we had been even intimate associates, yet I really knew little of my friend. His reserve had been always excessive and habitual. I was aware, however, that his very ancient family had been noted, time out of mind, for a peculiar sensibility of temperament, displaying itself, through long ages, in many works of exalted art, and manifested, of late, in repeated deeds of munificent yet unobtrusive charity, as well as in a passionate devotion to the intricacies, perhaps even more than to the orthodox and easily recognisable beauties, of musical science. I had learned, too, the very remarkable fact, that the stem of the Usher race, all time-honoured as it was, had put forth, at no period, any enduring branch; in other words, that the entire family lay in the direct line of descent, and had always, with very trifling and very temporary variation, so lain. It was this deficiency, I considered, while running over in thought the perfect keeping of the character of the premises with the accredited character of the people, and while speculating upon the possible influence which the one, in the long lapse of centuries, might have exercised upon the other—it was this deficiency, perhaps, of collateral issue, and the consequent undeviating transmission, from sire to son, of the patrimony with the name, which had, at length, so identified the two as to merge the original title of the estate in the quaint and equivocal appellation of the "House of Usher"—an appellation which seemed to include, in the minds of the peasantry who used it, both the family and the family mansion.

I have said that the sole effect of my somewhat childish experiment—that of looking down within the tarn—had been to deepen the first singular impression. There can be no doubt that the consciousness of the rapid increase of my superstition—for why should I not so term it?—served mainly to accelerate the increase itself. Such, I have long known, is the paradoxical law of all sentiments having terror as a basis. And it might have been for this reason only, that, when I again uplifted my eyes to the house itself, from its image in the pool, there grew in my mind a strange fancy—a fancy so ridiculous, indeed, that I but mention it to show the vivid force of the sensations which oppressed me. I had so worked upon my imagination as really to believe that about the whole mansion and domain there hung an atmosphere peculiar to themselves and their immediate vicinity—an atmosphere which had no affinity with the air of heaven, but which had reeked up from the decayed trees, and the gray wall, and the silent tarn—a pestilent and mystic vapour, dull, sluggish, faintly discernible, and leaden-hued.

5   Shaking off from my spirit what *must* have been a dream, I scanned more narrowly the real aspect of the building. Its principal feature seemed to be that of an excessive antiquity. The discoloration of ages had been great. Minute fungi overspread the whole exterior, hanging in a fine tangled webwork from the eaves. Yet all this was apart from any extraordinary dilapidation. No portion of the masonry had fallen; and there appeared to be a wild inconsistency between its still perfect adaptation of parts, and the crumbling condition of the individual stones. In this there was much that reminded me of the specious totality of old wood-work which has rotted for long years in some neglected vault, with no disturbance from the breath of the external air. Beyond this indication of extensive decay, however, the fabric gave little token of instability. Perhaps the eye of a scrutinizing observer might have discovered a barely perceptible fissure, which, extending from the roof of the building in front, made its way down the wall in a zigzag direction, until it became lost in the sullen waters of the tarn.

Noticing these things, I rode over a short causeway to the house. A servant in waiting took my horse, and I entered the Gothic archway of the hall. A valet, of stealthy step, thence conducted me, in silence, through many dark and intricate passages in my progress to the *studio* of his master. Much that I encountered on the way contributed, I know not how, to heighten the vague sentiments of which I have already spoken. While the objects around me—while the carvings of the ceilings, the sombre tapestries of the walls, the ebon blackness of the floors, and the phantasmagoric armorial trophies which rattled as I strode, were but matters to which, or to such as which, I had been accustomed from my infancy—while I hesitated not to acknowledge how familiar was all this—I still wondered to find how unfamiliar were the fancies which ordinary images were stirring up. On one of the staircases, I met the physician of the family. His countenance, I thought, wore a mingled expression of low cunning and perplexity. He accosted me with trepidation and passed on. The valet now threw open a door and ushered me into the presence of his master.

The room in which I found myself was very large and lofty. The windows were long, narrow, and pointed, and at so vast a distance from the black oaken floor as to be altogether inaccessible from within. Feeble gleams of encrimsoned light made their way through the trellised panes, and served to render sufficiently distinct the more prominent objects around; the eye, however, struggled in vain to reach the remoter angles of the chamber, or the recesses of the vaulted and fretted ceiling. Dark draperies hung upon the walls. The general furniture was profuse, comfortless, antique, and tattered. Many books and musical instruments lay scattered about, but failed to give any vitality to the scene. I felt that I breathed an atmosphere of sorrow. An air of stern, deep, and irredeemable gloom hung over and pervaded all.

Upon my entrance, Usher arose from a sofa on which he had been lying at full length, and greeted me with a vivacious warmth which had much in it, I at first thought, of an overdone cordiality—of the constrained effort of the *ennuyé* man of the world. A glance, however, at his countenance, convinced me of his perfect sincerity. We sat down; and for some moments, while he spoke not, I gazed upon him with a feeling half of pity, half of awe. Surely, man had never before so terribly altered, in so brief a period, as had Roderick Usher! It was with difficulty that I could bring myself to admit the identity of the wan being before me with the companion of my early boyhood. Yet the character of his face had been at all times remarkable. A cadaverousness of complexion; an eye large, liquid, and luminous beyond comparison; lips somewhat thin and very pallid, but of a surpassingly beautiful curve; a nose of a delicate Hebrew model, but with a breadth of nostril unusual in similar formations; a finely moulded chin, speaking, in its want of prominence, of a want of moral energy; hair of a more than web-like softness and tenuity; these features, with an inordinate expansion above the regions of the temple, made up altogether a countenance not easily to be forgotten. And now in the mere exaggeration of the prevailing character of these features, and of the expression they were wont to convey, lay so much of change that I doubted to whom I spoke. The now ghastly pallor of the skin, and the now miraculous lustre of the eye, above all things startled and even awed me. The silken hair, too, had been suffered to grow all unheeded, and as, in its wild gossamer texture, it floated rather than fell about the fact, I could not, even with effort, connect its Arabesque expression with any idea of simple humanity.

In the manner of my friend I was at once struck with an incoherence—an inconsistency; and I soon found this to arise from a series of feeble and futile struggles to overcome an habitual trepidancy—an excessive nervous agitation. For something of this nature I had indeed been prepared, no less by his letter, than by reminiscences of certain boyish traits, and by conclusions deduced from his peculiar physical conformation and temperament. His action was alternately vivacious and sullen. His voice varied rapidly from a tremulous indecision (when the animal spirits seemed utterly in abeyance) to that species of energetic concision—that abrupt, weighty, unhurried, and hollow-sounding enunciation—that leaden, self-balanced and perfectly modulated guttural utterance, which may be observed in the lost drunkard, or the irreclaimable eater of opium, during the periods of his most intense excitement.

It was thus that he spoke of the object of my visit, of his earnest desire to see me, and of the solace he expected me to afford him. He entered, at some length, into what he conceived to be the nature of

10

his malady. It was, he said, a constitutional and a family evil, and one for which he despaired to find a remedy—a mere nervous affection, he immediately added, which would undoubtedly soon pass off. It displayed itself in a host of unnatural sensations. Some of these, as he detailed them, interested and bewildered me; although, perhaps, the terms, and the general manner of the narration had their weight. He suffered much from a morbid acuteness of the senses; the most insipid food was alone endurable; he could wear only garments of certain texture; the odours of all flowers were oppressive; his eyes were tortured by even a faint light; and there were but peculiar sounds, and these from stringed instruments, which did not inspire him with horror.

To an anomalous species of terror I found him a bounden slave. "I shall perish," said he, "I *must* perish in this deplorable folly. Thus, thus, and not otherwise, shall I be lost. I dread the events of the future, not in themselves, but in their results. I shudder at the thought of any, even the most trivial, incident, which may operate upon this intolerable agitation of soul. I have, indeed, no abhorrence of danger, except in its absolute effect—in terror. In this unnerved—in this pitiable condition—I feel that the period will sooner or later arrive when I must abandon life and reason together, in some struggle with the grim phantasm, Fear."

I learned, moreover, at intervals, and through broken and equivocal hints, another singular feature of his mental condition. He was enchained by certain superstitious impressions in regard to the dwelling which he tenanted, and whence, for many years, he had never ventured forth—in regard to an influence whose supposititious force was conveyed in terms too shadowy here to be re-stated—an influence which some peculiarities in the mere form and substance of his family mansion, had, by dint of long sufferance, he said, obtained over his spirit—an effect which the *physique* of the gray walls and turrets, and of the dim tarn into which they all looked down, had, at length, brought about upon the *morale* of his existence.

He admitted, however, although with hesitation, that much of the peculiar gloom which thus afflicted him could be traced to a more natural and far more palpable origin—to the severe and long-continued illness—indeed to the evidently approaching dissolution—of a tenderly beloved sister—his sole companion for long years—his last and only relative on earth. "Her decease," he said, with a bitterness which I can never forget, "would leave him (him the hopeless and the frail) the last of the ancient race of the Ushers." While he spoke, the lady Madeline (for so was she called) passed slowly through a remote portion of the apartment, and, without having noticed my presence, disappeared. I regarded her with an utter astonishment not unmingled with dread—and yet I found it impossible to account for such feelings. A sensation of stupor oppressed me, as my eyes followed her retreating steps. When a door, at length, closed upon her, my glance sought instinctively and eagerly the countenance of the brother—but he had buried his face in his hands, and I could only perceive that a far more than ordinary wanness had overspread the emaciated fingers through which trickled many passionate tears.

The disease of the lady Madeline had long baffled the skill of her physicians. A settled apathy, a gradual wasting away of the person, and frequent although transient affections of a partially cataleptical character, were the unusual diagnosis. Hitherto she had steadily borne up against the pressure of her malady, and had not betaken herself finally to bed; but, on the closing in of the evening of my arrival at the house, she succumbed (as her brother told me at night with inexpressible agitation) to the prostrating power of the destroyer; and I learned that the glimpse I had obtained of her person would thus probably be the last I should obtain—that the lady, at least while living, would be seen by me no more.

For several days ensuing, her name was unmentioned by either Usher or myself: and during this period I was busied in earnest endeavours to alleviate the melancholy of my friend. We painted and read together; or I listened, as if in a dream, to the wild improvisations of his speaking guitar. And thus, as a closer and still closer intimacy admitted me more unreservedly into the recesses of his spirit, the more bitterly did I perceive the futility of all attempt at cheering a mind from which darkness, as if an inherent positive quality, poured forth upon all objects of the moral and physical universe, in one unceasing radiation of gloom.

I shall ever bear about me a memory of the many solemn hours I thus spent alone with the master of the House of Usher. Yet I should fail in any attempt to convey an idea of the exact character of the studies, or of the occupations, in which he involved me, or led me the way. An excited and highly distempered ideality threw a sulphureous lustre over all. His long improvised dirges will ring forever in my ears. Among other things, I hold painfully in mind a certain singular perversion and amplification of the wild air of the last waltz of Von Weber.[2] From the paintings over which his elaborate fancy brooded, and which grew, touch by touch, into vaguenesses at which I shuddered the more thrillingly, because I shuddered knowing not why;—from these paintings (vivid as their images now are before me) I would in vain endeavour to educe more than a small portion which should lie within the compass of merely written words. By the utter simplicity, by the nakedness of his designs, he arrested and overawed attention. If ever mortal painted an idea, that mortal was Roderick Usher. For me at least— in the circumstances then surrounding me—there arose out of the pure abstractions which the hypochondriac contrived to throw upon his canvas, an intensity of intolerable awe, no shadow of which felt I ever yet in the contemplation of the certainly glowing yet too concrete reveries of Fuseli.[3]

One of the phantasmagoric conceptions of my friend, partaking not so rigidly of the spirit of abstraction, may be shadowed forth, although feebly, in words. A small picture presented the interior of an immensely long and rectangular vault or tunnel, with low walls, smooth, white, and without interruption or device. Certain accessory points of the design served well to

15

---

[2]Composed by Karl Gottlieb Reissiger in honour of Karl Maria von Weber, nineteenth-century German composer of operas. [3]late-eighteenth- early-nineteenth century Swiss painter interested in psychological horror and the supernatural.

convey the idea that this excavation lay at an exceeding depth below the surface of the earth. No outlet was observed in any portion of its vast extent, and no torch, or other artificial source of light was discernible; yet a flood of intense rays rolled throughout, and bathed the whole in a ghastly and inappropriate splendour.

I have just spoken of that morbid condition of the auditory nerve which rendered all music intolerable to the sufferer, with the exception of certain effects of stringed instruments. It was, perhaps, the narrow limits to which he thus confined himself upon the guitar, which gave birth, in great measure, to the fantastic character of his performances. But the fervid *facility* of his *impromptus* could not be so accounted for. They must have been, and were, in the notes, as well as in the words of his wild fantasias (for he not unfrequently accompanied himself with rhymed verbal improvisations), the result of that intense mental collectedness and concentration to which I have previously alluded as observable only in particular moments of the highest artificial excitement. The words of one of these rhapsodies I have easily remembered. I was, perhaps, the more forcibly impressed with it, as he gave it, because, in the under or mystic current of its meaning, I fancied that I perceived, and for the first time, a full consciousness on the part of Usher, of the tottering of his lofty reason upon her throne. The verses, which were entitled "The Haunted Palace," ran very nearly, if not accurately, thus:

I.

In the greenest of our valleys,
    By good angels tenanted,
Once a fair and stately palace—
    Radiant palace—reared its head.
In the monarch Thought's dominion—
    It stood there!
Never seraph spread a pinion
    Over fabric half so fair.

II.

Banners yellow, glorious, golden,
    On its roof did float and flow;
(This—all this—was in the olden
    Time long ago)
And every gentle air that dallied,
    In that sweet day,
Along the ramparts plumed and pallid,
    A winged odour went away.

III.

Wanderers in that happy valley
    Through two luminous windows saw
Spirits moving musically
    To a lute's well-tuned law,

Round about a throne, where sitting
  (Porphyrogene!)[4]
In state his glory well befitting,
  The ruler of the realm was seen.

IV.

And all with pearl and ruby glowing
  Was the fair palace door,
Through which came flowing, flowing, flowing
  And sparkling evermore,
A troop of Echoes whose sweet duty
  Was but to sing,
In voices of surpassing beauty,
  The wit and wisdom of their king.

V.

But evil things, in robes of sorrow,
  Assailed the monarch's high estate;
(Ah, let us mourn, for never morrow
  Shall dawn upon him, desolate!)
And, round about his home, the glory
  That blushed and bloomed
Is but a dim-remembered story
  Of the old time entombed.

VI.

And travellers now within that valley,
  Through the red-litten windows, see
Vast forms that move fantastically
  To a discordant melody;
While, like a rapid ghastly river,
  Through the pale door,
A hideous throng rush out forever,
  And laugh—but smile no more.

25   I well remember that suggestions arising from this ballad, led us into a train of thought wherein there became manifest an opinion of Usher's which I mention not so much on account of its novelty, (for other men have thought thus,) as on account of the pertinacity with which he maintained it. This opinion, in its general form, was that of the sentience of all vegetable things. But, in his disordered fancy, the idea had assumed a more daring character, and trespassed, under certain conditions, upon the kingdom of inorganization. I lack words to express the full extent, or the earnest *abandon* of his persuasion. The belief, however, was connected (as I have previously hinted) with the gray stones of the home of his forefathers. The conditions

[4]of royal birth.

of the sentience had been here, he imagined, fulfilled in the method of col-location of these stones—in the order of their arrangement, as well as in that of the many *fungi* which overspread them, and of the decayed trees which stood around—above all, in the long undisturbed endurance of this arrange-ment, and in its reduplication in the still waters of the tarn. Its evidence—the evidence of the sentience—was to be seen, he said (and I here started as he spoke,) in the gradual yet certain condensation of an atmosphere of their own about the waters and the walls. The result was discoverable, he added, in that silent, yet importunate and terrible influence which for centuries had moulded the destinies of his family, and which made *him* what I now saw him—what he was. Such opinions need no comment, and I will make none.

Our books[5]—the books which, for years, had formed no small portion of the mental existence of the invalid—were, as might be supposed, in strict keeping with this character of phantasm. We pored together over such works as the Ververt et Chartreuse of Gresset; the Belphegor of Machiavelli; the Heaven and Hell of Swedenborg; the Subterranean Voyage of Nicholas Klimm by Holberg; the Chiromancy of Robert Flud, of Jean D'Indaginé, and of De la Chambre; the Journey into the Blue Distance of Tieck; and the City of the Sun of Campanella. One favourite volume was a small octavo edition of the *Directorium Inquisitorum*, by the Dominican Eymeric de Gironne; and there were passages in Pomponius Mela, about the old African Satyrs and Ægipans, over which Usher would sit dreaming for hours. His chief delight, however, was found in the perusal of an exceedingly rare and curious book in quarto Gothic—the manual of a forgotten church—the *Vigiliae Mortuorum Secundum Chorum Ecclesiae Maguntinæ*.

I could not help thinking of the wild ritual of this work, and of its prob-able influence upon the hypochondriac, when, one evening, having informed me abruptly that the lady Madeline was no more, he stated his intention of preserving her corpse for a fortnight, (previously to its final interment,) in one of the numerous vaults within the main walls of the building. The worldly reason, however, assigned for this singular proceeding, was one which I did not feel at liberty to dispute. The brother had been led to his resolution (so he told me) by consideration of the unusual character of the malady of the deceased, of certain obtrusive and eager inquiries on the part of her medical men, and of the remote and exposed situation of the burial-ground of the family. I will not deny that when I called to mind the sinister countenance of the person whom I met upon the staircase, on the day of my arrival at the house, I had no desire to oppose what I regarded as at best but a harmless, and by no means an unnatural, precaution.

At the request of Usher, I personally aided him in the arrangements for the temporary entombment. The body having been encoffined, we two alone bore it to its rest. The vault in which we placed it (and which had been so long unopened that our torches, half smothered in its oppressive atmosphere, gave us little opportunity for investigation) was small, damp, and entirely without means of admission for light; lying, at great depth, immediately beneath that portion of the building in which was my own

[5]these obscure books deal with supernatural occurrences, death, and damnation.

sleeping apartment. It had been used, apparently, in remote feudal times, for the worst purposes of a donjon-keep, and, in later days, as a place of deposit for powder, or some other highly combustible substance, as a portion of its floor, and the whole interior of a long archway through which we reached it, were carefully sheathed with copper. The door, of massive iron, had been, also, similarly protected. Its immense weight caused an unusually sharp grating sound, as it moved upon its hinges.

Having deposited our mournful burden upon tressels within this region of horror, we partially turned aside the yet unscrewed lid of the coffin, and looked upon the face of the tenant. A striking similitude between the brother and sister now first arrested my attention; and Usher, divining, perhaps, my thoughts, murmured out some few words from which I learned that the deceased and himself had been twins, and that sympathies of a scarcely intelligible nature had always existed between them. Our glances, however, rested not long upon the dead—for we could not regard her unawed. The disease which had thus entombed the lady in the maturity of youth, had left, as usual in all maladies of a strictly cataleptical character, the mockery of a faint blush upon the bosom and the face, and that suspiciously lingering smile upon the lip which is so terrible in death. We replaced and screwed down the lid, and, having secured the door of iron, made our way, with toil, into the scarcely less gloomy apartments of the upper portion of the house.

30 And now, some days of bitter grief having elapsed, an observable change came over the features of the mental disorder of my friend. His ordinary manner had vanished. His ordinary occupations were neglected or forgotten. He roamed from chamber to chamber with hurried, unequal, and objectless step. The pallor of his countenance had assumed, if possible, a more ghastly hue—but the luminousness of his eye had utterly gone out. The once occasional huskiness of his tone was heard no more; and a tremulous quaver, as if of extreme terror, habitually characterized his utterance. There were times, indeed, when I thought his unceasingly agitated mind was labouring with some oppressive secret, to divulge which he struggled for the necessary courage. At times, again, I was obliged to resolve all into the mere inexplicable vagaries of madness, for I beheld him gazing upon vacancy for long hours, in an attitude of the profoundest attention, as if listening to some imaginary sound. It was no wonder that his condition terrified—that it infected me. I felt creeping upon me, by slow yet certain degrees, the wild influences of his own fantastic yet impressive superstitions.

It was, especially, upon retiring to bed late in the night of the seventh or eighth day after the placing of the lady Madeline within the donjon, that I experienced the full power of such feelings. Sleep came not near my couch—while the hours waned and waned away. I struggled to reason off the nervousness which had dominion over me. I endeavoured to believe that much, if not all of what I felt, was due to the bewildering influence of the gloomy furniture of the room—of the dark and tattered draperies, which, tortured into motion by the breath of a rising tempest, swayed fitfully to and fro upon the walls, and rustled uneasily about the decorations of the bed. But my efforts were fruitless. An irrepressible tremour gradually pervaded my frame; and, at length, there sat upon my very heart an incubus of utterly causeless alarm. Shaking this off with a gasp and a struggle, I uplifted myself upon the pillows, and, peering earnestly within the intense darkness of the chamber, hearkened—I know not why, except that an instinctive spirit prompted me—to certain low and indefinite sounds which came, through the pauses of the storm, at long intervals, I knew not whence. Overpowered by an intense sentiment of horror, unaccountable yet unendurable, I threw on my clothes with haste (for I felt that I should sleep no more during the night), and endeavoured to arouse myself from the pitiable condition into which I had fallen, by pacing rapidly to and fro through the apartment.

I had taken but few turns in this manner, when a light step on an adjoining staircase arrested my attention. I presently recognised it as that of Usher. In an instant afterward he rapped, with a gentle touch, at my door, and entered, bearing a lamp. His countenance was, as usual, cadaverously wan—but, moreover, there was a species of mad hilarity in his eyes—an evidently restrained *hysteria* in his whole demeanour. His air appalled me—but anything was preferable to the solitude which I had so long endured, and I even welcomed his presence as a relief.

"And you have not seen it?" he said abruptly, after having stared about him for some moments in silence—"you have not then seen it?—but, stay! you shall." Thus speaking, and having carefully shaded his lamp, he hurried to one of the casements, and threw it freely open to the storm.

The impetuous fury of the entering gust nearly lifted us from our feet. It was, indeed, a tempestuous yet sternly beautiful night, and one wildly singular in its terror and its beauty. A whirlwind had apparently collected its force in our vicinity; for there were frequent and violent alterations in the direction of the wind; and the exceeding density of the clouds (which hung so low as to press upon the turrets of the house) did not prevent our perceiving the life-like velocity with which they flew careering from all points against each other, without passing away into the distance. I say that even their exceeding density did not prevent our perceiving this—yet we had no glimpse of the moon or stars—nor was there any flashing forth of the lightning. But the under surfaces of the huge masses of agitated vapour, as well as all terrestrial objects immediately around us, were glowing in the unnatural light of a faintly luminous and distinctly visible gaseous exhalation which hung about and enshrouded the mansion.

35   "You must not—you shall not behold this!" said I, shudderingly, to Usher, as I led him, with a gentle violence, from the window to a seat. "These appearances, which bewilder you, are merely electrical phenomena not uncommon—or it may be that they have their ghastly origin in the rank miasma of the tarn. Let us close this casement;—the air is chilling and dangerous to your frame. Here is one of your favourite romances. I will read, and you shall listen;—and so we will pass away this terrible night together."

The antique volume which I had taken up was the "Mad Trist" of Sir Launcelot Canning;[6] but I had called it a favourite of Usher's more in sad jest than in earnest; for, in trust, there is little in its uncouth and unimaginative prolixity which could have had interest for the lofty and spiritual

[6]the author and book are imaginary; Poe wrote the descriptions to fit this story.

ideality of my friend. It was, however, the only book immediately at hand; and I indulged a vague hope that the excitement which now agitated the hypochondriac, might find relief (for the history of mental disorder is full of similar anomalies) even in the extremeness of the folly which I should read. Could I have judged, indeed, by the wild overstrained air of vivacity with which he hearkened, or apparently hearkened, to the words of the tale, I might well have congratulated myself upon the success of my design.

I had arrived at that well-known portion of the story where Ethelred, the hero of the Trist, having sought in vain for peaceable admission into the dwelling of the hermit, proceeds to make good an entrance by force. Here, it will be remembered, the words of the narrative runs thus:

"And Ethelred, who was by nature of a doughty heart, and who was now mighty withal, on account of the powerfulness of the wine which he had drunken, waited no longer to hold parley with the hermit, who, in sooth, was of an obstinate and maliceful turn, but, feeling the rain upon his shoulders, and fearing the rising of the tempest, uplifted his mace outright, and, with blows, made quickly room in the plankings of the door for his gauntleted hand; and now pulling therewith sturdily, he so cracked, and ripped, and tore all asunder, that the noise of the dry and hollow-sounding wood alarmed and reverberated throughout the forest."

At the termination of this sentence I started, and for a moment, paused; for it appeared to me (although I at once concluded that my excited fancy had deceived me)—it appeared to me that, from some very remote portion of the mansion, there came, indistinctly, to my ears, what might have been, in its exact similarity of character, the echo (but a stifled and full one certainly) of the very cracking and ripping sound which Sir Launcelot had so particularly described. It was, beyond doubt, the coincidence alone which had arrested my attention; for, amid the rattling of the sashes of the casements, and the ordinary commingled noises of the still increasing storm, the sound, in itself, had nothing, surely, which should have interested or disturbed me. I continued the story:

40

"But the good champion Ethelred, now entering within the door, was sore enraged and amazed to perceive no signal of the maliceful hermit; but, in the stead thereof, a dragon of a scaly and prodigious demeanour, and of a fiery tongue, which sate in guard before a palace of gold, with a floor of silver; and upon the wall there hung a shield of shining brass with this legend enwritten—

Who entereth herein, a conqueror hath bin;
Who slayeth the dragon, the shield he shall win;

And Ethelred uplifted his mace, and struck upon the head of the dragon, which fell before him, and gave up his pesty breath, with a shriek so horrid and harsh, and withal so piercing, that Ethelred had fain to close his ears with his hands against the dreadful noise of it, the like whereof was never before heard."

Here again I paused abruptly, and now with a feeling of wild amazement—for there could be no doubt whatever that, in this instance, I did actually hear (although from what direction it proceeded I found it impossible to say) a low and apparently distant, but harsh, protracted, and most unusual screaming or grating sound—the exact counterpart of what my fancy had already conjured up for the dragon's unnatural shriek as described by the romancer.

Oppressed, as I certainly was, upon the occurrence of the second and most extraordinary coincidence, by a thousand conflicting sensations, in which wonder and extreme terror were predominant, I still retained sufficient presence of mind to avoid exciting, by any observation, the sensitive nervousness of my companion. I was by no means certain that he had noticed the sounds in question; although, assuredly, a strange alteration had, during the last few minutes, taken place in his demeanour. From a position fronting my own, he had gradually brought round his chair, so as to sit with his face to the door of the chamber; and thus I could but partially perceive his features, although I saw that his lips trembled as if he were murmuring inaudibly. His head had dropped upon his breast—yet I knew that he was not asleep, from the wide and rigid opening of the eye as I caught a glance of it in profile. The motion of his body, too, was at variance with this idea—for he rocked from side to side with a gentle yet constant and uniform sway. Having rapidly taken notice of all this, I resumed the narrative of Sir Launcelot, which thus proceeded:

"And now, the champion, having escaped from the terrible fury of the dragon, bethinking himself of the brazen shield, and of the breaking up of the enchantment which was upon it, removed the carcass from out of the way before him, and approached valorously over the silver pavement of the castle to where the shield was upon the wall; which in sooth tarried not for his full coming, but fell down at his feet upon the silver floor, with a mighty great and terrible ringing sound."

No sooner had these syllables passed my lips, than—as if a shield of brass had indeed, at the moment, fallen heavily upon a floor of silver—I became aware of a distinct, hollow, metallic, and clangorous, yet apparently muffled reverberation. Completely unnerved, I leaped to my feet; but the measured rocking movement of Usher was undisturbed. I rushed to the chair in which he sat. His eyes were bent fixedly before him, and throughout his whole countenance there reigned a stony rigidity. But, as I placed my hand upon his shoulder, there came a strong shudder over his whole person; a sickly smile quivered about his lips; and I saw that he spoke in a low, hurried, and gibbering murmur, as if unconscious of my presence. Bending closely over him, I at length drank in the hideous import of his words.

45 "Not hear it?—yes, I hear it, and *have* heard it. Long—long—long—many minutes, many hours, many days, have I heard it—yet I dared not—oh, pity me, miserable wretch that I am!—I dared not—I *dared* not speak! *We have put her living in the tomb!* Said I not that my senses were acute? I *now* tell you that I heard her first feeble movements in the hollow coffin. I heard them, many, many days ago—yet I dared not—*I dared not speak!* And now—to-night—Ethelred—ha! ha!—the breaking of the hermit's door, and the death-cry of the dragon, and the clangour of the shield!—say, rather, the rending of her coffin, and the grating of the iron hinges of her prison, and

her struggles within the coppered archway of the vault! Oh whither shall I fly? Will she not be here anon? Is she not hurrying to upbraid me for my haste? Have I not heard her footstep on the stair? Do I not distinguish that heavy and horrible beating of her heart? MADMAN!" Here he sprang furiously to his feet, and shrieked out his syllables, as if in the effort he were giving up his soul—"MADMAN! I TELL YOU THAT SHE NOW STANDS WITHOUT THE DOOR!"

As if in the superhuman energy of his utterance there had been found the potency of a spell—the huge antique panels to which the speaker pointed, threw slowly back, upon the instant, their ponderous and ebony jaws. It was the work of the rushing gust—but then without those doors there DID stand the lofty and enshrouded figure of the lady Madeline of Usher. There was blood upon her white robes, and the evidence of some bitter struggle upon every portion of her emaciated frame. For a moment she remained trembling and reeling to and fro upon the threshold, then, with a low moaning cry, fell heavily inward upon the person of her brother, and in her violent and now final death-agonies, bore him to the floor a corpse, and a victim to the terrors he had anticipated.

From that chamber, and from that mansion, I fled aghast. The storm was still abroad in all its wrath as I found myself crossing the old causeway. Suddenly there shot along the path a wild light, and I turned to see whence a gleam so unusual could have issued; for the vast house and its shadows were alone behind me. The radiance was that of the full, setting, and blood-red moon which now shone vividly through that once barely discernible fissure of which I have before spoken as extending from the roof of the building, in a zigzag direction, to the base. While I gazed, this fissure rapidly widened—there came a fierce breath of the whirlwind—the entire orb of the satellite burst at once upon my sight—my brain reeled as I saw the mighty walls rushing asunder—there was a long tumultuous shouting sound like the voice of a thousand waters—and the deep and dank tarn at my feet closed sullenly and silently over the fragments of the "HOUSE OF USHER."

(1839)

Herman Melville (1819–1891)

Born in New York City, Herman Melville spent many years as a sailor, including a cruise on a whaling ship, before becoming a writer. His most famous book, *Moby-Dick,* combined factual details about whaling with a symbolic examination about the nature of reality, particularly the conflict between good and evil. It is narrated by Ishmael, a quiet, thoughtful crew member, and presents the monomaniacal quest of Captain Ahab to slay a great white whale. Although "Bartleby, the Scrivener," written shortly after the novel, is much shorter and is set in a large city, it bears many similarities to *Moby-Dick.* The unnamed narrator is fascinated by a character who is much different from him, as Ishmael was fascinated by Ahab. The realistic and mundane details of a law office are given symbolic meanings, particularly the blank wall at which Bartleby stares. The story may be as much a revelation of the narrator's character, as revealed by his responses to his employees, as it is an examination of Bartleby.

BARTLEBY, THE SCRIVENER

A Story of Wall-Street

I am a rather elderly man. The nature of my avocations for the last thirty years has brought me into more than ordinary contact with what would seem an interesting and somewhat singular set of men, of whom as yet nothing that I know of has ever been written:—I mean the law-copyists or scriveners. I have known very many of them, professionally and privately, and if I pleased, could relate divers histories, at which good-natured gentlemen might smile, and sentimental souls might weep. But I waive the biographies of all other scriveners for a few passages in the life of Bartleby, who was a scrivener the strangest I ever saw or heard of. While of other law-copyists I might write the complete life, of Bartleby nothing of that sort can be done. I believe that no materials exist for a full and satisfactory biography of this man. It is an irreparable loss to literature. Bartleby was one of those beings of whom nothing is ascertainable, except from the original sources, and in his case those are very small. What my own astonished eyes saw of Bartleby, *that* is all I know of him, except, indeed, one vague report which will appear in the sequel.

Ere introducing the scrivener, as he first appeared to me, it is fit I make some mention of myself, my *employés,* my business, my chambers, and general surroundings; because some such description is indispensable to an adequate understanding of the chief character about to be presented.

Imprimis: I am a man who, from his youth upwards, has been filled with a profound conviction that the easiest way of life is the best. Hence, though I belong to a profession proverbially energetic and nervous, even to turbulence, at times, yet nothing of that sort have I ever suffered to invade my peace. I am one of those unambitious lawyers who never addresses a jury, or in any way draws down public applause; but in the cool tranquillity of a snug retreat, do a snug business among rich men's bonds and mortgages and title-deeds. All who know me, consider me an eminently *safe* man. The late John Jacob Astor,[1] a personage little given to poetic enthusiasm, had no hesitation in pronouncing my first grand point to be prudence; my next, method. I do not speak it in vanity, but simply record the fact, that I was not unemployed in my profession by the late John Jacob Astor; a name which, I admit, I love to repeat, for it hath a rounded and orbicular sound to it, and rings like unto bullion. I will freely add, that I was not insensible to the late John Jacob Astor's good opinion.

Some time prior to the period at which this little history begins, my avocations had been largely increased. The good old office, now extinct in the State of New-York, of a Master in Chancery,[2] had been conferred upon me. It was not a very arduous office, but very pleasantly remunerative. I seldom lose my temper; much more seldom indulge in dangerous indignation at wrongs and outrages; but I must be permitted to be rash here and declare, that I consider the sudden and violent abrogation of the office of Master in Chancery, by the new Constitution, as a—premature act; inasmuch as I had counted upon a life-lease of the profits, whereas I only received those of a few short years. But this is by the way.

5   My chambers were up stairs at No. — Wall-street.[3] At one end they looked upon the white wall of the interior of a spacious sky-light shaft, penetrating the building from top to bottom. This view might have been considered rather tame than otherwise, deficient in what landscape painters call "life." But if so, the view from the other end of my chambers offered, at least, a contrast, if nothing more. In that direction my windows commanded an unobstructed view of a lofty brick wall, black by age and everlasting shade; which wall required no spy-glass to bring out its lurking beauties, but for the benefit of all near-sighted spectators, was pushed up to within ten feet of my window panes. Owing to the great height of the surrounding buildings, and my chambers being on the second floor, the interval between this wall and mine not a little resembled a huge square cistern.

At the period just preceding the advent of Bartleby, I had two persons as copyists in my employment, and a promising lad as an office-boy. First, Turkey; second, Nippers; third, Ginger Nut. These may seem names, the like of which are not usually found in the Directory. In truth they were nicknames, mutually conferred upon each other by my three clerks, and were deemed expressive of their respective persons or characters. Turkey was a short, pursy Englishman of about my own age, that is, somewhere not far from sixty. In the morning, one might say, his face was of a fine florid hue, but after twelve o'clock, meridian—his dinner hour—it blazed like a grate full of Christmas coals; and continued blazing—but, as it were, with a gradual wane—till 6 o'clock, P.M. or thereabouts, after which I saw no more of the proprietor of the face, which gaining its meridian with the sun, seemed to set with it, to rise, culminate, and decline the following day, with the like

---

[1] at the time of his death in 1848, Astor was the richest man in the United States. [2] officer of the court whose duties included taking testimonies, administering oaths, and acknowledging deeds. [3] located in New York City, the financial centre of the United States.

regularity and undiminished glory. There are many singular coincidences I have known in the course of my life, not the least among which was the fact, that exactly when Turkey displayed his fullest beams from his red and radiant countenance, just then, too, at that critical moment, began the daily period when I considered his business capacities as seriously disturbed for the remainder of the twenty-four hours. Not that he was absolutely idle, or averse to business then; far from it. The difficulty was, he was apt to be altogether too energetic. There was a strange, inflamed, flurried, flighty recklessness of activity about him. He would be incautious in dipping his pen into his inkstand. All his blots upon my documents, were dropped there after twelve o'clock, meridian. Indeed, not only would he be reckless and sadly given to making blots in the afternoon, but some days he went further, and was rather noisy. At such times, too, his face flamed with augmented blazonry, as if cannel coal had been heaped on anthracite. He made an unpleasant racket with his chair; spilled his sandbox; in mending his pens, impatiently split them all to pieces, and threw them on the floor in a sudden passion; stood up and leaned over his table, boxing his papers about in a most indecorous manner, very sad to behold in an elderly man like him. Nevertheless, as he was in many ways a most valuable person to me, and all the time before twelve o'clock, meridian, was the quickest, steadiest creature too, accomplishing a great deal of work in a style not easy to be matched—for these reasons, I was willing to overlook his eccentricities, though indeed, occasionally, I remonstrated with him. I did this very gently, however, because, though the civilest, nay, the blandest and most reverential of men in the morning, yet in the afternoon he was disposed, upon provocation, to be slightly rash with his tongue, in fact, insolent. Now, valuing his morning services as I did, and resolved not to lose them; yet, at the same time made uncomfortable by his inflamed ways after twelve o'clock; and being a man of peace, unwilling by my admonitions to call forth unseemly retorts from him; I took upon me, one Saturday noon (he was always worse on Saturdays), to hint to him, very kindly, that perhaps now that he was growing old, it might be well to abridge his labors; in short, he need not come to my chambers after twelve o'clock, but, dinner over, had best go home to his lodgings and rest himself till teatime. But no; he insisted upon his afternoon devotions. His countenance became intolerably fervid, as he oratorically assured me—gesticulating with a long ruler at the other end of the room—that if his services in the morning were useful, how indispensable, then, in the afternoon?

"With submission, sir," said Turkey on this occasion, "I consider myself your right-hand man. In the morning I but marshal and deploy my columns; but in the afternoon I put myself at their head, and gallantly charge the foe, thus!"—and he made a violent thrust with the ruler.

"But the blots, Turkey," intimated I.

"True,—but, with submission, sir, behold these hairs! I am getting old. Surely, sir, a blot or two of a warm afternoon is not to be severely urged against gray hairs. Old age—even if it blot the page—is honorable. With submission, sir, we *both* are getting old."

This appeal to my fellow-feeling was hardly to be resisted. At all events, I saw that go he would not. So I made up my mind to let him

10

stay, resolving, nevertheless, to see to it, that during the afternoon he had to do with my less important papers.

Nippers, the second on my list, was a whiskered, sallow, and, upon the whole, rather piratical-looking young man of about five and twenty. I always deemed him the victim of two evil powers—ambition and indigestion. The ambition was evinced by a certain impatience of the duties of a mere copyist, an unwarrantable usurpation of strictly professional affairs, such as the original drawing up of legal documents. The indigestion seemed betokened in an occasional nervous testiness and grinning irritability, causing the teeth to audibly grind together over mistakes committed in copying; unnecessary maledictions, hissed, rather than spoken, in the heat of business; and especially by a continual discontent with the height of the table where he worked. Though of a very ingenious mechanical turn, Nippers could never get this table to suit him. He put chips under it, blocks of various sorts, bits of pasteboard, and at last went so far as to attempt an exquisite adjustment by final pieces of folded blotting-paper. But no invention would answer. If, for the sake of easing his back, he brought the table lid at a sharp angle well up towards his chin, and wrote there like a man using the steep roof of a Dutch house for his desk:—then he declared that it stopped the circulation in his arms. If now he lowered the table to his waistbands, and stooped over it in writing, then there was a sore aching in his back. In short, the truth of the matter was, Nippers knew not what he wanted. Or, if he wanted any thing, it was to be rid of a scrivener's table altogether. Among the manifestations of his diseased ambition was a fondness he had for receiving visits from certain ambiguous-looking fellows in seedy coats, whom he called his clients. Indeed I was aware that not only was he, at times, considerable of a ward-politician,[4] but he occasionally did a little business at the Justices' courts, and was not unknown on the steps of the Tombs.[5] I have good reason to believe, however, that one individual who called upon him at my chambers, and who, with a grand air, he insisted was his client, was no other than a dun, and the alleged title-deed, a bill. But with all his failings, and the annoyances he caused me, Nippers, like his compatriot Turkey, was a very useful man to me; wrote a neat, swift hand; and, when he chose, was not deficient in a gentlemanly sort of deportment. Added to this, he always dressed in a gentlemanly sort of way; and so, incidentally, reflected credit upon my chambers. Whereas with respect to Turkey, I had much ado to keep him from being a reproach to me. His clothes were apt to look oily and smell of eating-houses. He wore his pantaloons very loose and baggy in summer. His coats were execrable; his hat not to be handled. But while the hat was a thing of indifference to me, inasmuch as his natural civility and deference, as a dependent Englishman, always led him to doff it the moment he entered the room, yet his coat was another matter. Concerning his coats, I reasoned with him; but with no effect. The truth was, I suppose, that a man with so small an income, could not afford to sport such a lustrous face and a lustrous coat at one and the same time. As Nippers once observed, Turkey's

[4]similar to an alderman or town-councillor. [5]New York City prison.

money went chiefly for red ink. One winter day I presented Turkey with a highly-respectable looking coat of my own, a padded gray coat, of a most comfortable warmth, and which buttoned straight up from the knee to the neck. I thought Turkey would appreciate the favor, and abate his rashness and obstreperousness of afternoons. But no. I verily believe that buttoning himself up in so downy and blanket-like a coat had a pernicious effect upon him; upon the same principle that too much oats are bad for horses. In fact, precisely as a rash, restive horse is said to feel his oats, so Turkey felt his coat. It made him insolent. He was a man whom prosperity harmed.

Though concerning the self-indulgent habits of Turkey I had my own private surmises, yet touching Nippers I was well persuaded that whatever might be his faults in other respects, he was, at least, a temperate young man. But indeed, nature herself seemed to have been his vintner, and at his birth charged him so thoroughly with an irritable, brandy-like disposition, that all subsequent potations were needless. When I consider how, amid the stillness of my chambers, Nippers would sometimes impatiently rise from his seat, and stooping over his table, spread his arms wide apart, seize the whole desk, and move it, and jerk it, with a grim, grinding motion on the floor, as if the table were a perverse voluntary agent, intent on thwarting and vexing him; I plainly perceive that for Nippers, brandy and water were altogether superfluous.

It was fortunate for me that, owing to its peculiar cause—indigestion—the irritability and consequent nervousness of Nippers, were mainly observable in the morning, while in the afternoon he was comparatively mild. So that Turkey's paroxysms only coming on about twelve o'clock, I never had to do with their eccentricities at one time. Their fits relieved each other like guards. When Nippers' was on, Turkey's was off; and *vice versa*. This was a good natural arrangement under the circumstances.

Ginger Nut, the third on my list, was a lad some twelve years old. His father was a carman,[6] ambitious of seeing his son on the bench instead of a cart, before he died. So he sent him to my office as student at law, errand boy, and cleaner and sweeper, at the rate of one dollar a week. He had a little desk to himself, but he did not use it much. Upon inspection, the drawer exhibited a great array of the shells of various sorts of nuts. Indeed, to this quick-witted youth the whole noble science of the law was contained in a nut-shell. Not the least among the employments of Ginger Nut, as well as one which he discharged with the most alacrity, was his duty as cake and apple purveyor for Turkey and Nippers. Copying law papers being proverbially a dry, husky sort of business, my two scriveners were fain to moisten their mouths very often with Spitzenbergs[7] to be had at the numerous stalls nigh the Custom House and Post Office. Also, they sent Ginger Nut very frequently for that peculiar cake—small, flat, round, and very spicy—after which he had been named by them. Of a cold morning when business was but dull, Turkey would gobble up scores of these cakes, as if they were mere wafers—indeed they sell them at the rate of six or eight for a penny—the scrape of his pen blending with the crunching of the crisp particles in his mouth. Of all the fiery

[6]driver of a cart. [7]variety of apple.

afternoon blunders and flurried rashnesses of Turkey, was his once moistening a ginger-cake between his lips, and clapping it on to a mortgage for a seal. I came within an ace of dismissing him then. But he mollified me by making an oriental bow, and saying—"With submission, sir, it was generous of me to find you in stationery on my own account."

15 Now my original business—that of a conveyancer[8] and title hunter, and drawer-up of recondite documents of all sorts—was considerably increased by receiving the master's office. There was now great work for scriveners. Not only must I push the clerks already with me, but I must have additional help. In answer to my advertisement, a motionless young man one morning, stood upon my office threshold, the door being open, for it was summer. I can see that figure now—pallidly neat, pitiably respectable, incurably forlorn! It was Bartleby.

After a few words touching his qualifications, I engaged him, glad to have among my corps of copyists a man of so singularly sedate an aspect, which I thought might operate beneficially upon the flighty temper of Turkey, and the fiery one of Nippers.

I should have stated before that ground glass folding-doors divided my premises into two parts, one of which was occupied by my scriveners, the other by myself. According to my humor I threw open these doors, or closed them. I resolved to assign Bartleby a corner by the folding-doors, but on my side of them, so as to have this quiet man within easy call, in case any trifling thing was to be done. I placed his desk close up to a small side-window in that part of the room, a window which originally had afforded a lateral view of certain grimy back-yards and bricks, but which, owing to subsequent erections, commanded at present no view at all, though it gave some light. Within three feet of the panes was a wall, and the light came down from far above, between two lofty buildings, as from a very small opening in a dome. Still further to a satisfactory arrangement, I procured a high green folding screen, which might entirely isolate Bartleby from my sight, though not remove him from my voice. And thus, in a manner, privacy and society were conjoined.

At first Bartleby did an extraordinary quantity of writing. As if long famishing for something to copy, he seemed to gorge himself on my documents. There was no pause for digestion. He ran a day and night line, copying by sun-light and by candle-light. I should have been quite delighted with his application, had he been cheerfully industrious. But he wrote on silently, palely, mechanically.

It is, of course, an indispensable part of a scrivener's business to verify the accuracy of his copy, word by word. Where there are two or more scriveners in an office, they assist each other in this examination, one reading from the copy, the other holding the original. It is a very dull, wearisome, and lethargic affair. I can readily imagine that to some sanguine temperaments it would be altogether intolerable. For example, I cannot credit that the mettlesome poet Byron[9] would have contentedly sat down with

[8]person who prepares documents for property transfers. [9]an English poet of the early nineteenth century, Byron was known for his flamboyant temperament.

Bartleby to examine a law document of, say five hundred pages, closely written in a crimpy hand.

Now and then, in the haste of business, it had been my habit to assist in comparing some brief document myself, calling Turkey or Nippers for this purpose. One object I had in placing Bartleby so handy to me behind the screen, was to avail myself of his services on such trivial occasions. It was on the third day, I think, of his being with me, and before any necessity had arisen for having his own writing examined, that, being much hurried to complete a small affair I had in hand, I abruptly called to Bartleby. In my haste and natural expectancy of instant compliance, I sat with my head bent over the original on my desk, and my right hand sideways, and somewhat nervously extended with the copy, so that immediately upon emerging from his retreat, Bartleby might snatch it and proceed to business without the least delay.

In this very attitude did I sit when I called to him, rapidly stating what it was I wanted him to do—namely, to examine a small paper with me. Imagine my surprise, nay, my consternation, when without moving from his privacy, Bartleby in a singularly mild, firm voice, replied, "I would prefer not to."

I sat awhile in perfect silence, rallying my stunned faculties. Immediately it occurred to me that my ears had deceived me, or Bartleby had entirely misunderstood my meaning. I repeated my request in the clearest tone I could assume. But in quite as clear a one came the previous reply, "I would prefer not to."

"Prefer not to," echoed I, rising in high excitement, and crossing the room with a stride. "What do you mean? Are you moon-struck? I want you to help me compare this sheet here—take it," and I thrust it towards him.

"I would prefer not to," said he.

I looked at him steadfastly. His face was leanly composed; his gray eye dimly calm. Not a wrinkle of agitation rippled him. Had there been the least uneasiness, anger, impatience or impertinence in his manner; in other words, had there been any thing ordinarily human about him, doubtless I should have violently dismissed him from the premises. But as it was, I should have as soon thought of turning my pale plaster-of-paris bust of Cicero out of doors. I stood gazing at him awhile, as he went on with his own writing, and then reseated myself at my desk. This is very strange, thought I. What had one best do? But my business hurried me. I concluded to forget the matter for the present, reserving it for my future leisure. So calling Nippers from the other room, the paper was speedily examined.

A few days after this, Bartleby concluded four lengthy documents, being quadruplicates of a week's testimony taken before me in my High Court of Chancery. It became necessary to examine them. It was an important suit, and great accuracy was imperative. Having all things arranged I called Turkey, Nippers and Ginger Nut from the next room, meaning to place the four copies in the hands of my four clerks, while I should read from the original.

Accordingly Turkey, Nippers and Ginger Nut had taken their seats in a row, each with his document in hand, when I called to Bartleby to join this interesting group.

"Bartleby! quick, I am waiting."

I heard a slow scrape of his chair legs on the uncarpeted floor, and soon he appeared standing at the entrance of his hermitage.

30   "What is wanted?" said he mildly.

"The copies, the copies," said I hurriedly. "We are going to examine them. There"—and I held towards him the fourth quadruplicate.

"I would prefer not to," he said, and gently disappeared behind the screen.

For a few moments I was turned into a pillar of salt,[10] standing at the head of my seated column of clerks. Recovering myself, I advanced towards the screen, and demanded the reason for such extraordinary conduct.

"*Why* do you refuse?"

35   "I would prefer not to."

With any other man I should have flown outright into a dreadful passion, scorned all further words, and thrust him ignominiously from my presence. But there was something about Bartleby that not only strangely disarmed me, but in a wonderful manner touched and disconcerted me. I began to reason with him.

"These are your own copies we are about to examine. It is labor saving to you, because one examination will answer for your four papers. It is common usage. Every copyist is bound to help examine his copy. Is it not so? Will you not speak? Answer!"

"I prefer not to," he replied in a flute-like tone. It seemed to me that while I had been addressing him, he carefully revolved every statement that I made; fully comprehended the meaning; could not gainsay the irresistible conclusion; but, at the same time, some paramount consideration prevailed with him to reply as he did.

"You are decided, then, not to comply with my request—a request made according to common usage and common sense?"

40   He briefly gave me to understand that on that point my judgment was sound. Yes: his decision was irreversible.

It is not seldom the case that when a man is browbeaten in some unprecedented and violently unreasonable way, he begins to stagger in his own plainest faith. He begins, as it were, vaguely to surmise that, wonderful as it may be, all the justice and all the reason is on the other side. Accordingly, if any distinterested persons are present, he turns to them for some reinforcement for his own faltering mind.

"Turkey," said I, "what do you think of this? Am I not right?"

"With submission, sir," said Turkey, with his blandest tone, "I think that you are."

"Nippers," said I, "what do *you* think of it?"

45   "I think I should kick him out of the office."

(The reader of nice perceptions will here perceive that, it being morning, Turkey's answer is couched in polite and tranquil terms, but Nippers replies in ill-tempered ones. Or, to repeat a previous sentence, Nippers's ugly mood was on duty, and Turkey's off.)

---

[10]in Genesis 19, Lot's wife is turned into a pillar of salt for disobeying God's orders not to look at the evil city of Sodom, which God was destroying.

"Ginger Nut," said I, willing to enlist the smallest suffrage in my behalf, "what do *you* think of it?"

"I think, sir, he's a little *luny*," replied Ginger Nut, with a grin.

"You hear what they say," said I, turning towards the screen, "come forth and do your duty."

But he vouchsafed no reply. I pondered a moment in sore perplexity. But once more business hurried me. I determined again to postpone the consideration of this dilemma to my future leisure. With a little trouble we made out to examine the papers without Bartleby, though at every page or two, Turkey deferentially dropped his opinion that this proceeding was quite out of the common; while Nippers, twitching in his chair with a dyspeptic nervousness, ground out between his set teeth occasional hissing maledictions against the stubborn oaf behind the screen. And for his (Nippers's) part, this was the first and the last time he would do another man's business without pay.

Meanwhile Bartleby sat in his hermitage, oblivious to every thing but his own peculiar business there.

Some days passed, the scrivener being employed upon another lengthy work. His late remarkable conduct led me to regard his ways narrowly. I observed that he never went to dinner; indeed that he never went any where. As yet I had never of my personal knowledge known him to be outside of my office. He was a perpetual sentry in the corner. At about eleven o'clock though, in the morning, I noticed that Ginger Nut would advance toward the opening in Bartleby's screen, as if silently beckoned thither by a gesture invisible to me where I sat. The boy would then leave the office jingling a few pence, and reappear with a handful of ginger-nuts which he delivered in the hermitage, receiving two of the cakes for his trouble.

He lives, then, on ginger-nuts, thought I; never eats a dinner, properly speaking; he must be a vegetarian then; but no; he never eats even vegetables, he eats nothing but ginger-nuts. My mind then ran on in reveries concerning the probable effects upon the human constitution of living entirely on ginger-nuts. Ginger-nuts are so called because they contain ginger as one of their peculiar constituents, and the final flavoring one. Now what was ginger? A hot, spicy thing. Was Bartleby hot and spicy? Not at all. Ginger, then, had no effect upon Bartleby. Probably he preferred it should have none.

Nothing so aggravates an earnest person as a passive resistance. If the individual so resisted be of a not inhumane temper, and the resisting one perfectly harmless in his passivity; then, in the better moods of the former, he will endeavor charitably to construe to his imagination what proves impossible to be solved by his judgment. Even so, for the most part, I regarded Bartleby and his ways. Poor fellow! thought I, he means no mischief; it is plain he intends no insolence; his aspect sufficiently evinces that his eccentricities are involuntary. He is useful to me. I can get along with him. If I turn him away, the chances are he will fall in with some less indulgent employer, and then he will be rudely treated, and perhaps driven forth miserably to starve. Yes. Here I can cheaply purchase a delicious self-approval. To befriend Bartleby; to humor him in his strange wilfulness, will cost me little or nothing, while I lay up in my soul what will eventually prove a sweet morsel for my conscience. But this mood was not invariable with me. The passiveness of Bartleby sometimes irritated me. I felt strangely goaded on to encounter him in new opposition, to elicit some angry spark from him answerable to my own. But indeed I might as well have essayed to strike fire with my knuckles against a bit of Windsor soap.[11] But one afternoon the evil impulse in me mastered me, and the following little scene ensued:

55   "Bartleby," said I, "when those papers are all copied, I will compare them with you."

"I would prefer not to."

"How? Surely you do not mean to persist in that mulish vagary?"

No answer.

I threw open the folding-doors near by, and turning upon Turkey and Nippers, exclaimed:

60   "Bartleby a second time says, he won't examine his papers. What do you think of it, Turkey?"

It was afternoon, be it remembered. Turkey sat glowing like a brass boiler, his bald head steaming, his hands reeling among his blotted papers.

"Think of it?" roared Turkey; "I think I'll just step behind his screen, and black his eyes for him!"

So saying, Turkey rose to his feet and threw his arms into a pugilistic position. He was hurrying away to make good his promise, when I detained him, alarmed at the effect of incautiously rousing Turkey's combativeness after dinner.

"Sit down, Turkey," said I, "and hear what Nippers has to say. What do you think of it, Nippers? Would I not be justified in immediately dismissing Bartleby?"

65   "Excuse me, that is for you to decide, sir. I think his conduct quite unusual, and indeed unjust, as regards Turkey and myself. But it may only be a passing whim."

"Ah," exclaimed I, "you have strangely changed your mind then—you speak very gently of him now."

"All beer," cried Turkey; "gentleness is effects of beer—Nippers and I dined together to-day. You see how gentle *I* am, sir. Shall I go and black his eyes?"

"You refer to Bartleby, I suppose. No, not to-day, Turkey," I replied; "pray, put up your fists."

I closed the doors, and again advanced towards Bartleby. I felt additional incentives tempting me to my fate. I burned to be rebelled against again. I remembered that Bartleby never left the office.

70   "Bartleby," said I, "Ginger Nut is away; just step round to the Post Office, won't you? (it was but a three minutes walk,) and see if there is any thing for me."

"I would prefer not to."

"You *will* not?"

"I *prefer* not."

I staggered to my desk, and sat there in a deep study. My blind inveteracy returned. Was there any other thing in which I could procure myself to be

[11]brown-coloured, scented soap.

ignominiously repulsed by this lean, penniless wight?—my hired clerk? What added thing is there, perfectly reasonable, that he will be sure to refuse to do?

75   "Bartleby!"

No answer.

"Bartleby," in a louder tone.

No answer.

"Bartleby," I roared.

80   Like a very ghost, agreeably to the laws of magical invocation, at the third summons, he appeared at the entrance of his hermitage.

"Go to the next room, and tell Nippers to come to me."

"I prefer not to," he respectfully and slowly said, and mildly disappeared.

"Very good, Bartleby," said I, in a quiet sort of serenely severe self-possessed tone, intimating the unalterable purpose of some terrible retribution very close at hand. At the moment I half intended something of the kind. But upon the whole, as it was drawing towards my dinner-hour, I thought it best to put on my hat and walk home for the day, suffering much from perplexity and distress of mind.

Shall I acknowledge it? The conclusion of this whole business was, that it soon became a fixed fact of my chambers, that a pale young scrivener, by the name of Bartleby, had a desk there; that he copied for me at the usual rate of four cents a folio (one hundred words); but he was permanently exempt from examining the work done by him, that duty being transferred to Turkey and Nippers, out of compliment doubtless to their superior acuteness; moreover, said Bartleby was never on any account to be dispatched on the most trivial errand of any sort; and that even if entreated to take upon him such a matter, it was generally understood that he would prefer not to—in other words, that he would refuse point-blank.

85   As days passed on, I became considerably reconciled to Bartleby. His steadiness, his freedom from all dissipation, his incessant industry (except when he chose to throw himself into a standing revery behind his screen), his great stillness, his unalterableness of demeanor under all circumstances, made him a valuable acquisition. One prime thing was this,—*he was always there*;—first in the morning, continually through the day, and the last at night. I had a singular confidence in his honesty. I felt my most precious papers perfectly safe in his hands. Sometimes to be sure I could not, for the very soul of me, avoid falling into sudden spasmodic passions with him. For it was exceeding difficult to bear in mind all the time those strange peculiarities, privileges, and unheard of exemptions, forming the tacit stipulations on Bartleby's part under which he remained in my office. Now and then, in the eagerness of dispatching pressing business, I would inadvertently summon Bartleby, in a short, rapid tone, to put his finger, say, on the incipient tie of a bit of red tape with which I was about compressing some papers. Of course, from behind the screen the usual answer, "I prefer not to," was sure to come; and then, how could a human creature with the common infirmities of our nature, refrain from bitterly exclaiming upon such perverseness—such unreasonableness. However, every added repulse of this sort which I received only tended to lessen the probability of my repeating the inadvertence.

Here it must be said, that according to the custom of most legal gentlemen occupying chambers in densely populated law buildings, there were
several keys to my door. One was kept by a woman residing in the attic,
which person weekly scrubbed and daily swept and dusted my apartments.
Another was kept by Turkey for convenience sake. The third I sometimes
carried in my own pocket. The fourth I knew not who had.

Now, one Sunday morning I happened to go to Trinity Church, to hear
a celebrated preacher, and finding myself rather early on the ground,
I thought I would walk round to my chambers for a while. Luckily I had
my key with me; but upon applying it to the lock, I found it resisted by
something inserted from the inside. Quite surprised, I called out; when to my
consternation a key was turned from within; and thrusting his lean visage at
me, and holding the door ajar, the apparition of Bartleby appeared, in his
shirt sleeves, and otherwise in a strangely tattered dishabille, saying quietly
that he was sorry, but he was deeply engaged just then, and—preferred not
admitting me at present. In a brief word or two, he moreover added, that
perhaps I had better walk round the block two or three times, and by that
time he would probably have concluded his affairs.

Now, the utterly unsurmised appearance of Bartleby, tenanting my law-
chambers of a Sunday morning, with his cadaverously gentlemanly *noncha-
lance*, yet withal firm and self-possessed, had such a strange effect upon me,
that incontinently I slunk away from my own door, and did as desired. But
not without sundry twinges of impotent rebellion against the mild effrontery
of this unaccountable scrivener. Indeed, it was his wonderful mildness
chiefly, which not only disarmed me, but unmanned me, as it were. For
I consider that one, for the time, is sort of unmanned when he tranquilly
permits his hired clerk to dictate to him, and order him away from his own
premises. Furthermore, I was full of uneasiness as to what Bartleby could
possibly be doing in my office in his shirt sleeves, and in an otherwise
dismantled condition of a Sunday morning. Was any thing amiss going on?
Nay, that was out of the question. It was not to be thought of for a moment
that Bartleby was an immoral person. But what could he be doing there?—
copying? Nay again, whatever might be his eccentricities, Bartleby was an
eminently decorous person. He would be the last man to sit down to his desk
in any state approaching to nudity. Besides, it was Sunday; and there was
something about Bartleby that forbade the supposition that he would by any
secular occupation violate the proprieties of the day.

Nevertheless, my mind was not pacified; and full of a restless curiosity,
at last I returned to the door. Without hindrance I inserted my key, opened
it, and entered. Bartleby was not to be seen. I looked round anxiously,
peeped behind his screen; but it was very plain that he was gone. Upon more
closely examining the place, I surmised that for an indefinite period Bartleby
must have ate, dressed, and slept in my office, and that too without plate,
mirror, or bed. The cushioned seat of a ricketty old sofa in one corner
bore the faint impress of a lean, reclining form. Rolled away under his desk,
I found a blanket; under the empty grate, a blacking box and brush; on a
chair, a tin basin, with soap and a ragged towel; in a newspaper a few crumbs
of ginger-nuts and a morsel of cheese. Yes, thought I, it is evident enough

that Bartleby has been making his home here, keeping bachelor's hall all by himself. Immediately then the thought came sweeping across me, What miserable friendlessness and loneliness are here revealed! His poverty is great; but his solitude, how horrible! Think of it. Of a Sunday, Wall-street is deserted as Petra;[12] and every night of every day it is an emptiness. This building too, which of week-days hums with industry and life, at nightfall echoes with sheer vacancy, and all through Sunday is forlorn. And here Bartleby makes his home; sole spectator of a solitude which he has seen all populous—a sort of innocent and transformed Marius[13] brooding among the ruins of Carthage![14]

90   For the first time in my life a feeling of overpowering stinging melancholy seized me. Before, I had never experienced aught but a not-unpleasing sadness. The bond of a common humanity now drew me irresistibly to gloom. A fraternal melancholy! For both I and Bartleby were sons of Adam. I remembered the bright silks and sparkling faces I had seen that day, in gala trim, swan-like sailing down the Mississippi of Broadway; and I contrasted them with the pallid copyist, and thought to myself, Ah, happiness courts the light, so we deem the world is gay; but misery hides aloof, so we deem that misery there is none. These sad fancyings—chimeras, doubtless, of a sick and silly brain—led on to other and more special thoughts, concerning the eccentricities of Bartleby. Presentiments of strange discoveries hovered round me. The scrivener's pale form appeared to me laid out, among uncaring strangers, in its shivering winding sheet.

Suddenly I was attracted by Bartleby's closed desk, the key in open sight left in the lock.

I mean no mischief, seek the gratification of no heartless curiosity, thought I; besides, the desk is mine, and its contents too, so I will make bold to look within. Every thing was methodically arranged, the papers smoothly placed. The pigeon holes were deep, and removing the files of documents, I groped into their recesses. Presently I felt something there, and dragged it out. It was an old bandanna handkerchief, heavy and knotted. I opened it, and saw it was a savings' bank.

I now recalled all the quiet mysteries which I had noted in the man. I remembered that he never spoke but to answer; that though at intervals he had considerable time to himself, yet I had never seen him reading—no, not even a newspaper; that for long periods he would stand looking out, at his pale window behind the screen, upon the dead brick wall; I was quite sure he never visited any refectory or eating house; while his pale face clearly indicated that he never drank beer like Turkey, or tea and coffee even, like other men; that he never went any where in particular that I could learn; never went out for a walk, unless indeed that was the case at present; that he had declined telling who he was, or whence he came, or whether he had any relatives in the world; that though so thin and pale, he never complained of ill health. And more than all, I remembered a certain unconscious air of

[12]destroyed and abandoned city in north Africa. [13]Roman military commander who fled to Africa in the first century B.C. [14]north African city destroyed by the Romans in the second century B.C.

pallid—how shall I call it?—of pallid haughtiness, say, or rather an austere reserve about him, which had positively awed me into my tame compliance with his eccentricities, when I had feared to ask him to do the slightest incidental thing for me, even though I might know, from his long-continued motionlessness, that behind his screen he must be standing in one of those dead-wall reveries of his.

Revolving all these things, and coupling them with the recently discovered fact that he made my office his constant abiding place and home, and not forgetful of his morbid moodiness; revolving all these things, a prudential feeling began to steal over me. My first emotions had been those of pure melancholy and sincerest pity; but just in proportion as the forlornness of Bartleby grew and grew to my imagination, did that same melancholy merge into fear, that pity into repulsion. So true it is, and so terrible too, that up to a certain point the thought or sight of misery enlists our best affections; but, in certain special cases, beyond that point it does not. They err who would assert that invariably this is owing to the inherent selfishness of the human heart. It rather proceeds from a certain hopelessness of remedying excessive and organic ill. To a sensitive being, pity is not seldom pain. And when at last it is perceived that such pity cannot lead to effectual succor, common sense bids the soul be rid of it. What I saw that morning persuaded me that the scrivener was the victim of innate and incurable disorder. I might give alms to his body; but his body did not pain him; it was his soul that suffered, and his soul I could not reach.

95   I did not accomplish the purpose of going to Trinity Church that morning. Somehow, the things I had seen disqualified me for the time from church-going. I walked homeward, thinking what I would do with Bartleby. Finally, I resolved upon this;—I would put certain calm questions to him the next morning, touching his history, &c., and if he declined to answer them openly and unreservedly (and I supposed he would prefer not), then to give him a twenty dollar bill over and above whatever I might owe him, and tell him his services were no longer required; but that if in any other way I could assist him, I would be happy to do so, especially if he desired to return to his native place, wherever that might be, I would willingly help to defray the expenses. Moreover, if, after reaching home, he found himself at any time in want of aid, a letter from him would be sure of a reply.

The next morning came.

"Bartleby," said I, gently calling to him behind his screen.

No reply.

"Bartleby," said I, in a still gentler tone, "come here; I am not going to ask you to do any thing you would prefer not to do—I simply wish to speak to you."

100   Upon this he noiselessly slid into view.

"Will you tell me, Bartleby, where you were born?"

"I would prefer not to."

"Will you tell me *any thing* about yourself?"

"I would prefer not to."

105   "But what reasonable objection can you have to speak to me? I feel friendly towards you."

He did not look at me while I spoke, but kept his glance fixed upon my bust of Cicero,[15] which as I then sat, was directly behind me, some six inches above my head.

"What is your answer, Bartleby?" said I, after waiting a considerable time for a reply, during which his countenance remained immovable, only there was the faintest conceivable tremor of the white attenuated mouth.

"At present I prefer to give no answer," he said, and retired into his hermitage.

It was rather weak in me I confess, but his manner on this occasion nettled me. Not only did there seem to lurk in it a certain calm disdain, but his perverseness seemed ungrateful, considering the undeniable good usage and indulgence he had received from me.

110   Again I sat ruminating what I should do. Mortified as I was at his behavior, and resolved as I had been to dismiss him when I entered my office, nevertheless I strangely felt something superstitious knocking at my heart, and forbidding me to carry out my purpose, and denouncing me for a villain if I dared to breathe one bitter word against this forlornest of mankind. At last, familiarly drawing my chair behind his screen, I sat down and said: "Bartleby, never mind then about revealing your history; but let me entreat you as a friend, to comply as far as may be with the usages of this office. Say now you will help to examine papers to-morrow or next day: in short, say now that in a day or two you will begin to be a little reasonable:—say so, Bartleby."

"At present I would prefer not to be a little reasonable," was his mildly cadaverous reply.

Just then the folding-doors opened, and Nippers approached. He seemed suffering from an unusually bad night's rest, induced by severer indigestion than common. He overheard those final words of Bartleby.

"*Prefer not*, eh?" gritted Nippers—"I'd *prefer* him, if I were you, sir," addressing me—"I'd *prefer* him; I'd give him preferences, the stubborn mule! What is it, sir, pray, that he *prefers* not to do now?"

Bartleby moved not a limb.

115   "Mr. Nippers," said I, "I'd prefer that you would withdraw for the present."

Somehow, of late I had got into the way of involuntarily using this word "prefer" upon all sorts of not exactly suitable occasions. And I trembled to think that my contact with the scrivener had already and seriously affected me in a mental way. And what further and deeper aberration might it not yet produce? This apprehension had not been without efficacy in determining me to summary measures.

As Nippers, looking very sour and sulky, was departing, Turkey blandly and deferentially approached.

"With submission, sir," said he, "yesterday I was thinking about Bartleby here, and I think that if he would but prefer to take a quart of good ale every day, it would do much towards mending him, and enabling him to assist in examining his papers."

---

[15]renowned Roman orator of the first century B.C.

"So you have got the word too," said I, slightly excited.

"With submission, what word, sir," asked Turkey, respectfully crowding himself into the contracted space behind the screen, and by so doing, making me jostle the scrivener. "What word, sir?"

"I would prefer to be left alone here," said Bartleby, as if offended at being mobbed in his privacy.

"*That's* the word, Turkey," said I—"*that's* it."

"Oh, *prefer?* oh yes—queer word. I never use it myself. But, sir, as I was saying, if he would but prefer—"

"Turkey," interrupted I, "you will please withdraw."

"Oh certainly, sir, if you prefer that I should."

As he opened the folding-doors to retire, Nippers at his desk caught a glimpse of me, and asked whether I would prefer to have a certain paper copied on blue paper or white. He did not in the least roguishly accent the word prefer. It was plain that it involuntarily rolled from his tongue. I thought to myself, surely I must get rid of a demented man, who already has in some degree turned the tongues, if not the heads of myself and clerks. But I thought it prudent not to break the dismission at once.

The next day I noticed that Bartleby did nothing but stand at his window in his dead-wall revery. Upon asking him why he did not write, he said that he had decided upon doing no more writing.

"Why, how now? what next?" exclaimed I, "do no more writing?"

"No more."

"And what is the reason?"

"Do you not see the reason for yourself," he indifferently replied.

I looked steadfastly at him, and perceived that his eyes looked dull and glazed. Instantly it occurred to me, that his unexampled diligence in copying by his dim window for the first few weeks of his stay with me might have temporarily impaired his vision.

I was touched. I said something in condolence with him. I hinted that of course he did wisely in abstaining from writing for a while; and urged him to embrace that opportunity of taking wholesome exercise in the open air. This, however, he did not do. A few days after this, my other clerks being absent, and being in a great hurry to dispatch certain letters by the mail, I thought that, having nothing else earthly to do, Bartleby would surely be less inflexible than usual, and carry these letters to the post-office. But he blankly declined. So, much to my inconvenience, I went myself.

Still added days went by. Whether Bartleby's eyes improved or not, I could not say. To all appearance, I thought they did. But when I asked him if they did, he vouchsafed no answer. At all events, he would do no copying. At last, in reply to my urgings, he informed me that he had permanently given up copying.

"What!" exclaimed I; "suppose your eyes should get entirely well— better than ever before—would you not copy then?"

"I have given up copying," he answered, and slid aside.

He remained as ever, a fixture in my chamber. Nay—if that were possible—he became still more of a fixture than before. What was to be done? He would do nothing in the office: why should he stay there? In plain fact, he had now become a millstone to me, not only useless as a necklace, but afflictive to bear. Yet I was sorry for him. I speak less than truth when I say that, on his own account, he occasioned me uneasiness. If he would but have named a single relative or friend, I would instantly have written, and urged their taking the poor fellow away to some convenient retreat. But he seemed alone, absolutely alone in the universe. A bit of wreck in the mid Atlantic. At length, necessities connected with my business tyrannized over all other considerations. Decently as I could, I told Bartleby that in six days' time he must unconditionally leave the office. I warned him to take measures, in the interval, for procuring some other abode. I offered to assist him in this endeavor, if he himself would but take the first step towards a removal. "And when you finally quit me, Bartleby," added I, "I shall see that you go not away entirely unprovided. Six days from this hour, remember."

At the expiration of that period, I peeped behind the screen, and lo! Bartleby was there.

I buttoned up my coat, balanced myself; advanced slowly towards him, touched his shoulder, and said, "The time has come; you must quit this place; I am sorry for you; here is money, but you must go."

140 "I would prefer not," he replied, with his back still towards me.

"You *must*."

He remained silent.

Now I had an unbounded confidence in this man's common honesty. He had frequently restored to me sixpences and shillings carelessly dropped upon the floor, for I am apt to be very reckless in such shirt-button affairs. The proceeding then which followed will not be deemed extraordinary.

"Bartleby," said I, "I owe you twelve dollars on account; here are thirty-two; the odd twenty are yours.—Will you take it?" and I handed the bills towards him.

145 But he made no motion.

"I will leave them here then," putting them under a weight on the table. Then taking my hat and cane and going to the door I tranquilly turned and added—"After you have removed your things from these offices, Bartleby, you will of course lock the door—since every one is now gone for the day but you—and if you please, slip your key underneath the mat, so that I may have it in the morning. I shall not see you again; so good-bye to you. If hereafter in your new place of abode I can be of any service to you, do not fail to advise me by letter. Good-bye, Bartleby, and fare you well."

But he answered not a word; like the last column of some ruined temple, he remained standing mute and solitary in the middle of the otherwise deserted room.

As I walked home in a pensive mood, my vanity got the better of my pity. I could not but highly plume myself on my masterly management in getting rid of Bartleby. Masterly I call it, and such it must appear to any dispassionate thinker. The beauty of my procedure seemed to consist in its perfect quietness. There was no vulgar bullying, no bravado of any sort, no choleric hectoring, and striding to and fro across the apartment, jerking out vehement commands for Bartleby to bundle himself off with his beggarly traps. Nothing of the kind. Without loudly bidding Bartleby depart—as an inferior genius might have done—I *assumed* the ground that depart he must; and upon that assumption built all I had to say. The more I thought over my procedure, the more I was charmed with it. Nevertheless, next morning, upon awakening, I had my doubts,—I had somehow slept off the fumes of vanity. One of the coolest and wisest hours a man has, is just after he wakes in the morning. My procedure seemed as sagacious as ever,—but only in theory. How it would prove in practice—there was the rub. It was truly a beautiful thought to have assumed Bartleby's departure; but, after all, that assumption was simply my own, and none of Bartleby's. The great point was, not whether I had assumed that he would quit me, but whether he would prefer so to do. He was more a man of preferences than assumptions.

After breakfast, I walked down town, arguing the probabilities *pro* and *con*. One moment I thought it would prove a miserable failure, and Bartleby would be found all alive at my office as usual; the next moment it seemed certain that I should find his chair empty. And so I kept veering about. At the corner of Broadway and Canal-street, I saw quite an excited group of people standing in earnest conversation.

150 "I'll take odds he doesn't," said a voice as I passed.

"Doesn't go?—done!" said I, "put up your money."

I was instinctively putting my hand in my pocket to produce my own, when I remembered that this was an election day. The words I had over-heard bore no reference to Bartleby, but to the success or non-success of some candidate for the mayoralty. In my intent frame of mind, I had, as it were, imagined that all Broadway shared in my excitement, and were debating the same question with me. I passed on, very thankful that the uproar of the street screened my momentary absent-mindedness.

As I had intended, I was earlier than usual at my office door. I stood listening for a moment. All was still. He must be gone. I tried the knob. The door was locked. Yes, my procedure had worked to a charm; he indeed must be vanished. Yet a certain melancholy mixed with this: I was almost sorry for my brilliant success. I was fumbling under the door mat for the key, which Bartleby was to have left there for me, when accidentally my knee knocked against a panel, producing a summoning sound, and in response a voice came to me from within—"Not yet; I am occupied."

155 It was Bartleby.

I was thunderstruck. For an instant I stood like the man who, pipe in mouth, was killed one cloudless afternoon long ago in Virginia, by summer lightning; at his own warm open window he was killed, and remained leaning out there upon the dreamy afternoon, till some one touched him, when he fell.

"Not gone!" I murmured at last. But again obeying that wondrous ascendancy which the inscrutable scrivener had over me, and from which ascendancy, for all my chafing, I could not completely escape, I slowly went down stairs and out into the street, and while walking round the block, con-sidered what I should next do in this unheard-of perplexity. Turn the man out by an actual thrusting I could not; to drive him away by calling him hard names would not do; calling in the police was an unpleasant idea; and yet, permit him to enjoy his cadaverous triumph over me,—this too I could not think of. What was to be done? or, if nothing could be done, was there any thing further that I could *assume* in the matter? Yes, as before I had prospectively assumed that Bartleby would depart, so now I might retrospectively assume that departed he was. In the legitimate carrying out of this assumption, I might enter my office in a great hurry, and pretending not to see Bartleby at all, walk straight against him as if he were air. Such a proceeding would in a singular degree have the appearance of a home-thrust. It was hardly possible that Bartleby could withstand such an application of the doctrine of assumptions. But upon second thoughts the success of the plan seemed rather dubious. I resolved to argue the matter over with him again.

"Bartleby," said I, entering the office, with a quietly severe expression, "I am seriously displeased. I am pained, Bartleby. I had thought better of you. I had imagined you of such a gentlemanly organization, that in any delicate dilemma a slight hint would suffice—in short, an assumption. But it appears I am deceived. Why," I added, unaffectedly starting, "you have not even touched that money yet," pointing to it, just where I had left it the evening previous.

He answered nothing.

160   "Will you, or will you not, quit me?" I now demanded in a sudden passion, advancing close to him.

"I would prefer *not* to quit you," he replied, gently emphasizing the *not*.

"What earthly right have you to stay here? Do you pay any rent? Do you pay my taxes? Or is this property yours?"

He answered nothing.

"Are you ready to go on and write now? Are your eyes recovered? Could you copy a small paper for me this morning? or help examine a few lines? or step round to the post-office? In a word, will you do any thing at all, to give a coloring to your refusal to depart the premises?"

165   He silently retired into his hermitage.

I was now in such a state of nervous resentment that I thought it but prudent to check myself at present from further demonstrations. Bartleby and I were alone. I remembered the tragedy of the unfortunate Adams and the still more unfortunate Colt[16] in the solitary office of the latter; and how poor Colt, being dreadfully incensed by Adams, and imprudently permitting himself to get wildly excited, was at unawares hurried into his fatal act—an act which certainly no man could possibly deplore more than the actor himself. Often it had occurred to me in my ponderings upon the subject, that had that altercation taken place in the public street, or at a private residence, it would not have terminated as it did. It was the circumstance of being alone in a solitary office, up stairs, of a building entirely unhallowed by humanizing domestic associations—an uncarpeted office, doubtless, of a dusty, haggard sort of appearance;—this it must have been, which greatly helped to enhance the irritable desperation of the hapless Colt.

But when this old Adam[17] of resentment rose in me and tempted me concerning Bartleby, I grappled him and threw him. How? Why, simply by

---

[16]Samuel Adams was killed in 1841 in a fight with John Colt, a brother of the manufacturer of guns. [17]reference to the biblical first man, whose temperament was believed to have been passed on to all the human race.

recalling the divine injunction: "A new commandment give I unto you, that ye love one another." Yes, this it was that saved me. Aside from higher considerations, charity often operates as a vastly wise and prudent principle—a great safeguard to its possessor. Men have committed murder for jealousy's sake, and anger's sake, and hatred's sake, and selfishness' sake, and spiritual pride's sake; but no man that ever I heard of, ever committed a diabolical murder for sweet charity's sake. Mere self-interest, then, if no better motive can be enlisted, should, especially with high-tempered men, prompt all beings to charity and philanthropy. At any rate, upon the occasion in question, I strove to drown my exasperated feelings towards the scrivener by benevolently construing his conduct. Poor fellow, poor fellow! thought I, he don't mean any thing; and besides, he has seen hard times, and ought to be indulged.

I endeavored also immediately to occupy myself, and at the same time to comfort my despondency. I tried to fancy that in the course of the morning, at such time as might prove agreeable to him, Bartleby, of his own free accord, would emerge from his hermitage, and take up some decided line of march in the direction of the door. But no. Half-past twelve o'clock came; Turkey began to glow in the face, overturn his inkstand, and become generally obstreperous; Nippers abated down into quietude and courtesy; Ginger Nut munched his noon apple; and Bartleby remained standing at his window in one of his profoundest dead-wall reveries. Will it be credited? Ought I to acknowledge it? That afternoon I left the office without saying one further word to him.

Some days now passed, during which, at leisure intervals I looked a little into "Edwards on the Will,"[18] and "Priestley on Necessity."[19] Under the circumstances, those books induced a salutary feeling. Gradually I slid into the persuasion that these troubles of mine touching the scrivener, had been all predestinated from eternity, and Bartleby was billeted upon me for some mysterious purpose of an all-wise Providence, which it was not for a mere mortal like me to fathom. Yes, Bartleby, stay there behind your screen, thought I; I shall persecute you no more; you are harmless and noiseless as any of these old chairs; in short, I never feel so private as when I know you are here. At last I see it, I feel it; I penetrate to the predestinated purpose of my life. I am content. Others may have loftier parts to enact; but my mission in this world, Bartleby, is to furnish you with office-room for such period as you may see fit to remain.

170   I believe that this wise and blessed frame of mind would have continued with me, had it not been for the unsolicited and uncharitable remarks obtruded upon me by my professional friends who visited the rooms. But thus it often is, that the constant friction of illiberal minds wears out at last the best resolves of the more generous. Though to be sure, when I reflected upon it, it was not strange that people entering my office should be struck by the peculiar aspect of the unaccountable Bartleby, and so be tempted to throw out

[18]eighteenth-century American philosopher who believed that human beings' will was controlled by God. [19]eighteenth-century English philosopher who believed that, to prevent revolution, rulers should act in the interests of those they govern.

some sinister observations concerning him. Sometimes an attorney having business with me, and calling at my office, and finding no one but the scrivener there, would undertake to obtain some sort of precise information from him touching my whereabouts; but without heeding his idle talk, Bartleby would remain standing immovable in the middle of the room. So after contemplating him in that position for a time, the attorney would depart, no wiser than he came.

Also, when a Reference[20] was going on, and the room full of lawyers and witnesses and business was driving fast; some deeply occupied legal gentleman present, seeing Bartleby wholly unemployed, would request him to run round to his (the legal gentleman's) office and fetch some papers for him. Thereupon, Bartleby would tranquilly decline, and yet remain idle as before. Then the lawyer would give a great stare, and turn to me. And what could I say? At last I was made aware that all through the circle of my professional acquaintance, a whisper of wonder was running round, having reference to the strange creature I kept at my office. This worried me very much. And as the idea came upon me of his possibly turning out a longlived man, and keep occupying my chambers, and denying my authority; and perplexing my visitors; and scandalizing my professional reputation; and casting a general gloom over the premises; keeping soul and body together to the last upon his savings (for doubtless he spent but half a dime a day), and in the end perhaps outlive me, and claim possession of my office by right of his perpetual occupancy: as all these dark anticipations crowded upon me more and more, and my friends continually intruded their relentless remarks upon the apparition in my room; a great change was wrought in me. I resolved to gather all my faculties together, and for ever rid me of this intolerable incubus.

Ere revolving any complicated project, however, adapted to this end, I first simply suggested to Bartleby the propriety of his permanent departure. In a calm and serious tone, I commended the idea to his careful and mature consideration. But having taken three days to meditate upon it, he apprised me that his original determination remained the same; in short, that he still preferred to abide with me.

What shall I do? I now said to myself, buttoning up my coat to the last button. What shall I do? what ought I to do? what does conscience say I *should* do with this man, or rather ghost? Rid myself of him, I must; go, he shall. But how? You will not thrust him, the poor, pale, passive mortal,—you will not thrust such a helpless creature out of your door? you will not dishonor yourself by such cruelty? No, I will not, I cannot do that. Rather would I let him live and die here, and then mason up his remains in the wall. What then will you do? For all your coaxing, he will not budge. Bribes he leaves under your own paper-weight on your table; in short, it is quite plain that he prefers to cling to you.

Then something severe, something unusual must be done. What! surely you will not have him collared by a constable, and commit his innocent pallor to the common jail? And upon what ground could you procure such a thing to be done?—a vagrant, is he? What! he a vagrant, a wanderer, who refuses to

[20]legal hearing in which two parties submit their differences to an arbitrator.

budge? It is because he will *not* be a vagrant, then, that you seek to count him *as* a vagrant. That is too absurd. No visible means of support: there I have him. Wrong again: for undubitably he *does* support himself, and that is the only unanswerable proof that any man can show of his possessing the means so to do. No more then. Since he will not quit me, I must quit him. I will change my offices; I will move elsewhere; and give him fair notice, that if I find him on my new premises I will then proceed against him as a common trespasser.

175   Acting accordingly, next day I thus addressed him: "I find these chambers too far from the City Hall; the air is unwholesome. In a word, I propose to remove my offices next week, and shall no longer require your services. I tell you this now, in order that you may seek another place."

He made no reply, and nothing more was said.

On the appointed day I engaged carts and men, proceeded to my chambers, and having but little furniture, every thing was removed in a few hours. Throughout, the scrivener remained standing behind the screen, which I directed to be removed the last thing. It was withdrawn; and being folded up like a huge folio, left him the motionless occupant of a naked room. I stood in the entry watching him a moment, while something from within me upbraided me.

I re-entered, with my hand in my pocket—and—and my heart in my mouth.

"Good-bye, Bartleby; I am going—good-bye, and God some way bless you; and take that," slipping something in his hand. But it dropped upon the floor, and then,—strange to say—I tore myself from him whom I had so longed to be rid of.

180   Established in my new quarters, for a day or two I kept the door locked, and started at every footfall in the passages. When I returned to my rooms after any little absence, I would pause at the threshold for an instant, and attentively listen, ere applying my key. But these fears were needless. Bartleby never came nigh me.

I thought all was going well, when a perturbed looking stranger visited me, inquiring whether I was the person who had recently occupied rooms at No. — Wall-street.

Full of forebodings, I replied that I was.

"Then sir," said the stranger, who proved a lawyer, "you are responsible for the man you left there. He refuses to do any copying; he refuses to do any thing; he says he prefers not to; and he refuses to quit the premises."

"I am very sorry, sir" said I, with assumed tranquillity, but an inward tremor, "but, really, the man you allude to is nothing to me—he is no relation or apprentice of mine, that you should hold me responsible for him."

185   "In mercy's name, who is he?"

"I certainly cannot inform you. I know nothing about him. Formerly I employed him as a copyist; but he has done nothing for me now for some time past."

"I shall settle him then,—good morning, sir."

Several days passed, and I heard nothing more; and though I often felt a charitable prompting to call at the place and see poor Bartleby, yet a certain squeamishness of I know not what withheld me.

All is over with him, by this time, thought I at last, when through another week no further intelligence reached me. But coming to my room the day after, I found several persons waiting at my door in a high state of nervous excitement.

190 "That's the man—here he comes," cried the foremost one, whom I recognized as the lawyer who had previously called upon me alone.

"You must take him away, sir, at once," cried a portly person among them, advancing upon me, and whom I knew to be the landlord of No. — Wall-street. "These gentlemen, my tenants, cannot stand it any longer; Mr. B——" pointing to the lawyer, "has turned him out of his room, and he now persists in haunting the building generally, sitting upon the banisters of the stairs by day, and sleeping in the entry by night. Every body is concerned; clients are leaving the offices; some fears are entertained of a mob; something you must do, and that without delay."

Aghast at this torrent, I fell back before it, and would fain have locked myself in my new quarters. In vain I persisted that Bartleby was nothing to me—no more than to any one else. In vain:—I was the last person known to have any thing to do with him, and they held me to the terrible account. Fearful then of being exposed in the papers (as one person present obscurely threatened) I considered the matter, and at length said, that if the lawyer would give me a confidential interview with the scrivener, in his (the lawyer's) own room, I would that afternoon strive my best to rid them of the nuisance they complained of.

Going up stairs to my old haunt, there was Bartleby silently sitting upon the banister at the landing.

"What are you doing here, Bartleby?" said I.

195 "Sitting upon the banister," he mildly replied.

I motioned him into the lawyer's room, who then left us.

"Bartleby," said I, "are you aware that you are the cause of great tribulation to me, by persisting in occupying the entry after being dismissed from the office?"

No answer.

"Now one of two things must take place. Either you must do something, or something must be done to you. Now what sort of business would you like to engage in? Would you like to re-engage in copying for some one?"

200 "No; I would prefer not to make any change."

"Would you like a clerkship in a dry-goods store?"

"There is too much confinement about that. No, I would not like a clerkship; but I am not particular."

"Too much confinement," I cried, "why you keep yourself confined all the time!"

205 "I would prefer not to take a clerkship," he rejoined, as if to settle that little item at once.

"How would a bar-tender's business suit you? There is no trying of the eyesight in that."

"I would not like it at all; though, as I said before, I am not particular."

His unwonted wordiness inspirited me. I returned to the charge.

"Well then, would you like to travel through the country collecting bills for the merchants? That would improve your health."

210   "No, I would prefer to be something else."

"How then would going as a companion to Europe, to entertain some young gentleman with your conversation,—how would that suit you?"

"Not at all. It does not strike me that there is any thing definite about that. I like to be stationary. But I am not particular."

"Stationary you shall be then," I cried, now losing all patience, and for the first time in all my exasperating connection with him fairly flying into a passion. "If you do not go away from these premises before night, I shall feel bound—indeed I *am* bound—to—to—to quit the premises myself!" I rather absurdly concluded, knowing not with what possible threat to try to frighten his immobility into compliance. Despairing of all further efforts, I was precipitately leaving him, when a final thought occurred to me—one which had not been wholly unindulged before.

215   "Bartleby," said I, in the kindest tone I could assume under such exciting circumstances, "will you go home with me now—not to my office, but my dwelling—and remain there till we can conclude upon some convenient arrangement for you at our leisure? Come, let us start now, right away."

"No: at present I would prefer not to make any change at all."

I answered nothing; but effectually dodging every one by the suddenness and rapidity of my flight, rushed from the building, ran up Wall-street towards Broadway, and jumping into the first omnibus was soon removed from pursuit. As soon as tranquillity returned I distinctly perceived that I had now done all that I possibly could, both in respect to the demands of the landlord and his tenants, and with regard to my own desire and sense of duty, to benefit Bartleby, and shield him from rude persecution. I now strove to be entirely care-free and quiescent; and my conscience justified me in the attempt; though indeed it was not so successful as I could have wished. So fearful was I of being again hunted out by the incensed landlord and his exasperated tenants, that, surrendering my business to Nippers, for a few days I drove about the upper part of the town and through the suburbs, in my rockaway;[21] crossed over to Jersey City and Hoboken, and paid fugitive visits to Manhattanville and Astoria. In fact I almost lived in my rockaway for the time.

When again I entered my office, lo, a note from the landlord lay upon the desk. I opened it with trembling hands. It informed me that the writer had sent to the police, and had Bartleby removed to the Tombs as a vagrant. Moreover, since I knew more about him than any one else, he wished me to appear at that place, and make a suitable statement of the facts. These tidings had a conflicting effect upon me. At first I was indignant; but at last almost approved. The landlord's energetic, summary disposition, had led him to adopt a procedure which I do not think I would have decided upon myself; and yet as a last resort, under such peculiar circumstances, it seemed the only plan.

[21]luxury carriage.

As I afterwards learned, the poor scrivener, when told that he must be conducted to the Tombs, offered not the slightest obstacle, but in his pale unmoving way, silently acquiesced.

220 Some of the compassionate and curious bystanders joined the party; and headed by one of the constables arm in arm with Bartleby, the silent procession filed its way through all the noise, and heat, and joy of the roaring thoroughfares at noon.

The same day I received the note I went to the Tombs, or to speak more properly, the Halls of Justice. Seeking the right officer, I stated the purpose of my call, and was informed that the individual I described was indeed within. I then assured the functionary that Bartleby was a perfectly honest man, and greatly to be compassionated, however unaccountably eccentric. I narrated all I knew, and closed by suggesting the idea of letting him remain in as indulgent confinement as possible till something less harsh might be done—though indeed I hardly knew what. At all events, if nothing else could be decided upon, the alms-house must receive him. I then begged to have an interview.

Being under no disgraceful charge, and quite serene and harmless in all his ways, they had permitted him freely to wander about the prison, and especially in the inclosed grass-platted yards thereof. And so I found him there, standing all alone in the quietest of the yards, his face towards a high wall, while all around, from the narrow slits of the jail windows, I thought I saw peering out upon him the eyes of murderers and thieves.

"Bartleby!"

"I know you," he said, without looking round,—"and I want nothing to say to you."

225 "It was not I that brought you here, Bartleby," said I, keenly pained at his implied suspicion. "And to you, this should not be so vile a place. Nothing reproachful attaches to you by being here. And see, it is not so sad a place as one might think. Look, there is the sky, and here is the grass."

"I know where I am," he replied, but would say nothing more, and so I left him.

As I entered the corridor again, a broad meat-like man, in an apron, accosted me, and jerking his thumb over his shoulder said—"Is that your friend?"

"Yes."

230 "Does he want to starve? If he does, let him live on the prison fare, that's all."

"Who are you?" asked I, not knowing what to make of such an unofficially speaking person in such a place.

"I am the grub-man. Such gentlemen as have friends here, hire me to provide them with something good to eat."

"Is this so?" said I, turning to the turnkey.

235 He said it was.

"Well then," said I, slipping some silver into the grub-man's hands (for so they called him). "I want you to give particular attention to my friend there; let him have the best dinner you can get. And you must be as polite to him as possible."

"Introduce me, will you?" said the grub-man, looking at me with an expression which seemed to say he was all impatience for an opportunity to give a specimen of his breeding.

Thinking it would prove of benefit to the scrivener, I acquiesced; and asking the grub-man his name, went up with him to Bartleby.

"Bartleby, this is Mr. Cutlets; you will find him very useful to you."

240 "Your sarvant, sir, your sarvant," said the grub-man, making a low salutation behind his apron. "Hope you find it pleasant here, sir; nice grounds— cool apartments, sir—hope you'll stay with us some time—try to make it agreeable. May Mrs. Cutlets and I have the pleasure of your company to dinner, sir, in Mrs. Cutlet's private room?"

"I prefer not to dine to-day," said Bartleby, turning away. "It would disagree with me; I am unused to dinners." So saying he slowly moved to the other side of the inclosure, and took up a position fronting the dead-wall.

"How's this?" said the grub-man, addressing me with a stare of astonishment. "He's odd, aint he?"

"I think he is a little deranged," said I, sadly.

"Deranged? deranged is it? Well now, upon my word, I thought that friend of yourn was a gentleman forger; they are always pale and genteel-like, them forgers. I can't help pity 'em—can't help it, sir. Did you know Monroe Edwards?" he added touchingly, and paused. Then, laying his hand pityingly on my shoulder, sighed, "he died of consumption at Sing-Sing.[22] So you weren't acquainted with Monroe?"

245 "No, I was never socially acquainted with any forgers. But I cannot stop longer. Look to my friend yonder. You will not lose by it. I will see you again."

Some few days after this, I again obtained admission to the Tombs, and went through the corridors in quest of Bartleby; but without finding him.

"I saw him coming from his cell not long ago," said a turnkey, "may be he's gone to loiter in the yards."

So I went in that direction.

250 "Are you looking for the silent man?" said another turnkey passing me. "Yonder he lies—sleeping in the yard there. 'Tis not twenty minutes since I saw him lie down."

The yard was entirely quiet. It was not accessible to the common prisoners. The surrounding walls, of amazing thickness, kept off all sounds behind them. The Egyptian character of the masonry weighed upon me with its gloom. But a soft imprisoned turf grew under foot. The heart of the eternal pyramids, it seemed, wherein, by some strange magic, through the clefts, grass-seed, dropped by birds, had sprung.

Strangely huddled at the base of the wall, his knees drawn up, and lying on his side, his head touching the cold stones, I saw the wasted Bartleby. But nothing stirred. I paused; then went close up to him; stooped over, and saw that his dim eyes were open; otherwise he seemed profoundly sleeping. Something prompted me to touch him. I felt his hand, when a tingling shiver ran up my arm and down my spine to my feet.

[22]state prison north of New York City.

The round face of the grub-man peered upon me now. "His dinner is ready. Won't he dine to-day, either? Or does he live without dining?"

"Lives without dining," said I, and closed the eyes.

255 "Eh!—He's asleep, aint he?"

"With kings and counsellors,"[23] murmured I.

*****

There would seem little need for proceeding further in this history. Imagination will readily supply the meagre recital of poor Bartleby's interment. But ere parting with the reader, let me say, that if this little narrative has sufficiently interested him, to awaken curiosity as to who Bartleby was, and what manner of life he led prior to the present narrator's making his acquaintance, I can only reply, that in such curiosity I fully share, but am wholly unable to gratify it. Yet here I hardly know whether I should divulge one little item of rumor, which came to my ear a few months after the scrivener's decease. Upon what basis it rested, I could never ascertain; and hence, how true it is I cannot now tell. But inasmuch as this vague report has not been without a certain strange suggestive interest to me, however sad, it may prove the same with some others; and so I will briefly mention it. The report was this: that Bartleby had been a subordinate clerk in the Dead Letter Office at Washington, from which he had been suddenly removed by a change in the administration. When I think over this rumor, hardly can I express the emotions which seize me. Dead letters! does it not sound like dead men? Conceive a man by nature and misfortune prone to a pallid hopelessness, can any business seem more fitted to heighten it than that of continually handling these dead letters, and assorting them for the flames? For by the cart-load they are annually burned. Sometimes from out the folded paper the pale clerk takes a ring:—the finger it was meant for, perhaps, moulders in the grave; a bank-note sent in swiftest charity: he whom it would relieve, nor eats nor hungers any more; pardon for those who died despairing; hope for those who died unhoping; good tidings for those who died stifled by unrelieved calamities. On errands of life, these letters speed to death.

Ah Bartleby! Ah humanity!

(1853)

---

[23]see Job 3:14. A reference to death as a condition of tranquillity.

Louisa May Alcott   (1832–1888)

The daughter of Bronson Alcott, a mid-nineteenth-century radical philosopher-educator, Louisa May Alcott grew up around Concord, Massachusetts, and knew such celebrated authors as Nathaniel Hawthorne, Ralph Waldo Emerson, and Henry David Thoreau. Her most famous work is the children's classic *Little Women*. However, she also published adult short stories and novels, many of them anonymously. Although the stories were written in the style of the popular romances and melodramas of the time, they have, during the later decades of the twentieth century, received praise for their portrayal of women in Alcott's time and for their examination of intense psychological conflicts. "A Whisper in the Dark" is a good example of these types of short stories. The narrative is filled with exciting plots and vivid characters. On a thematic level, it presents a detailed study of a number of power struggles—between older and younger people, males and females, fathers and sons. The portrayal of the changing mental state of women imprisoned because of suspected madness is found in many nineteenth-century works, including Charlotte Perkins Gilman's "The Yellow Wallpaper."

A WHISPER IN THE DARK

As we rolled along, I scanned my companion covertly, and saw much to interest a girl of seventeen. My uncle was a handsome man, with all the polish of foreign life fresh upon him; yet it was neither comeliness nor graceful ease which most attracted me; for even my inexperienced eye caught glimpses of something stern and somber below these external charms, and my long scrutiny showed me the keenest eye, the hardest mouth, the subtlest smile I ever saw—a face which in repose wore the look that comes to those who have led lives of pleasure and learned their emptiness. He seemed intent on some thought that absorbed him, and for a time rendered him forgetful of my presence, as he sat with folded arms, fixed eyes, and restless lips. While I looked, my own mind was full of deeper thought than it had ever been before; for I was recalling, word for word, a paragraph in that half-read letter:

> At eighteen Sybil[1] is to marry her cousin, the compact having been made between my brother and myself in their childhood. My son is with me now, and I wish them to be together during the next few months, therefore my niece must leave you sooner than I at first intended. Oblige me by preparing her for an immediate and final separation, but leave all disclosures to me, as I prefer the girl to remain ignorant of the matter for the present.

That displeased me. Why was I to remain ignorant of so important an affair? Then I smiled to myself, remembering that I did know, thanks to the willful curiosity that prompted me to steal a peep into the letter that

---

[1]in ancient Greece, a sybil was a prophetess or oracle.

Mme. Bernard had pored over with such an anxious face. I saw only a single paragraph, for my own name arrested my eye; and, though wild to read all, I had scarcely time to whisk the paper back into the reticule the forgetful old soul had left hanging on the arm of her chair. It was enough, however, to set my girlish brain in a ferment, and keep me gazing wistfully at my uncle, conscious that my future now lay in his hands; for I was an orphan and he my guardian, though I had seen him but seldom since I was confided to Madame a six years' child.

Presently my uncle became cognizant of my steady stare, and returned it with one as steady for a moment, then said, in a low, smooth tone, that ill accorded with the satirical smile that touched his lips, "I am a dull companion for my little niece. How shall I provide her with pleasanter amusement than counting my wrinkles or guessing my thoughts?"

5   I was a frank, fearless creature, quick to feel, speak, and act, so I answered readily, "Tell me about my cousin Guy. Is he as handsome, brave, and clever as Madame says his father was when a boy?"

My uncle laughed a short laugh, touched with scorn, whether for Madame, himself, or me I could not tell, for his countenance was hard to read.

"A girl's question and artfully put; nevertheless I shall not answer it, but let you judge for yourself."

"But, sir, it will amuse me and beguile the way. I feel a little strange and forlorn at leaving Madame, and talking of my new home and friends will help me to know and love them sooner. Please tell me, for I've had my own way all my life, and can't bear to be crossed."

My petulance seemed to amuse him, and I became aware that he was observing me with a scrutiny as keen as my own had been; but I smilingly sustained it, for my vanity was pleased by the approbation his eye betrayed. The evident interest he now took in all I said and did was sufficient flattery for a young thing, who felt her charms and longed to try their power.

10   "I, too, have had my own way all my life; and as the life is double the length, the will is double the strength of yours, and again I say no. What next, mademoiselle?"

He was blander than ever as he spoke, but I was piqued, and resolved to try coaxing, eager to gain my point, lest a too early submission now should mar my freedom in the future.

"But that is ungallant, Uncle, and I still have hopes of a kinder answer, both because you are too generous to refuse so small a favor to your 'little niece,' and because she can be charmingly wheedlesome when she likes. Won't you say yes now, Uncle?" And pleased with the daring of the thing, I put my arm about his neck, kissed him daintily, and perched myself upon his knee with most audacious ease.

He regarded me mutely for an instant, then, holding me fast, deliberately returned my salute on lips, cheeks, and forehead, with such warmth that I turned scarlet and struggled to free myself, while he laughed that mirthless laugh of his till my shame turned to anger, and I imperiously commanded him to let me go.

"Not yet, young lady. You came here for your own pleasure, but shall stay for mine, till I tame you as I see you must be tamed. It is a short process with me, and I possess experience in the work; for Guy, though by nature as wild as a hawk, has learned to come at my call as meekly as a dove. Chut! What a little fury it is!"

15   I was just then; for exasperated at his coolness, and quite beside myself, I had suddenly stooped and bitten the shapely white hand that held both my own. I had better have submitted; for slight as the foolish action was, it had an influence on my afterlife as many another such has had. My uncle stopped laughing, his hand tightened its grasp, for a moment his cold eye glittered and a grim look settled round the mouth, giving to his whole face a ruthless expression that entirely altered it. I felt perfectly powerless. All my little arts had failed, and for the first time I was mastered. Yet only physically; my spirit was rebellious still. He saw it in the glance that met his own, as I sat erect and pale, with something more than childish anger. I think it pleased him, for swiftly as it had come the dark look passed, and quietly, as if we were the best of friends, he began to relate certain exciting adventures he had known abroad, lending to the picturesque narration the charm of that peculiarly melodious voice, which soothed and won me in spite of myself, holding me intent till I forgot the past; and when he paused I found that I was leaning confidentially on his shoulder, asking for more, yet conscious of an instinctive distrust of this man whom I had so soon learned to fear yet fancy.

As I was recalled to myself, I endeavored to leave him; but he still detained me, and, with a curious expression, produced a case so quaintly fashioned that I cried out in admiration, while he selected two cigarettes, mildly aromatic with the herbs they were composed of, lit them, offered me one, dropped the window, and leaning back surveyed me with an air of extreme enjoyment, as I sat meekly puffing and wondering what prank I should play a part in next. Slowly the narcotic influence of the herbs diffused itself like a pleasant haze over all my senses; sleep, the most grateful, fell upon my eyelids, and the last thing I remember was my uncle's face dreamily regarding me through a cloud of fragrant smoke. Twilight wrapped us in its shadows when I woke, with the night wind blowing on my forehead, the muffled roll of wheels sounding in my ear, and my cheek pillowed upon my uncle's arm. He was humming a French *chanson* about "love and wine, and the Seine tomorrow!" I listened till I caught the air, and presently joined him, mingling my girlish treble with his flutelike tenor. He stopped at once and, in the coolly courteous tone I had always heard in our few interviews, asked if I was ready for lights and home.

"Are we there?" I cried; and looking out saw that we were ascending an avenue which swept up to a pile of buildings that rose tall and dark against the sky, with here and there a gleam along its gray front.

"Home at last, thank heaven!" And springing out with the agility of a young man, my uncle led me over a terrace into a long hall, light and warm, and odorous with the breath of flowers blossoming here and there in graceful groups. A civil, middle-aged maid received and took me to my room, a bijou[2] of a place, which increased my wonder when told that my uncle had

[2]jewel.

chosen all its decorations and superintended their arrangement. "He understands women," I thought, handling the toilet ornaments, trying luxurious chair and lounge, and ending by slipping my feet into the scarlet-and-white Turkish slippers, coquettishly turning up their toes before the fire. A few moments I gave to examination, and, having expressed my satisfaction, was asked by my maid if I would be pleased to dress, as "the master" never allowed dinner to wait for anyone. This recalled to me the fact that I was doubtless to meet my future husband at that meal, and in a moment every faculty was intent upon achieving a grand toilette for this first interview. The maid possessed skill and taste, and I a wardrobe lately embellished with Parisian gifts from my uncle which I was eager to display in his honor.

When ready, I surveyed myself in the long mirror as I had never done before, and saw there a little figure, slender, yet stately, in a dress of foreign fashion, ornamented with lace and carnation ribbons which enhanced the fairness of neck and arms, while blond hair, wavy and golden, was gathered into an antique knot of curls behind, with a carnation fillet, and below a blooming dark-eyed face, just then radiant with girlish vanity and eagerness and hope.

"I'm glad I'm pretty!"

"So am I, Sybil."

I had unconsciously spoken aloud, and the echo came from the doorway where stood my uncle, carefully dressed, looking comelier and cooler than ever. The disagreeable smile flitted over his lips as he spoke, and I started, then stood abashed, till beckoning, he added in his most courtly manner, "You were so absorbed in the contemplation of your charming self that Janet answered my tap and took herself away unheard. You are mistress of my table now. It waits; will you come down?"

With a last touch to that unruly hair of mine, a last, comprehensive glance and shake, I took the offered arm and rustled down the wide staircase, feeling that the romance of my life was about to begin. Three covers were laid, three chairs set, but only two were occupied, for no Guy appeared. I asked no questions, showed no surprise, but tried to devour my chagrin with my dinner, and exerted myself to charm my uncle into the belief that I had forgotten my cousin. It was a failure, however, for that empty seat had an irresistible fascination for me, and more than once, as my eye returned from its furtive scrutiny of napkin, plate, and trio of colored glasses, it met my uncle's and fell before his penetrative glance. When I gladly rose to leave him to his wine—for he did not ask me to remain—he also rose, and, as he held the door for me, he said, "You asked me to describe your cousin. You have seen one trait of his character tonight; does it please you?"

I knew he was as much vexed as I at Guy's absence, so quoting his own words, I answered saucily, "Yes, for I'd rather see the hawk free than coming tamely at your call, Uncle."

He frowned slightly, as if unused to such liberty of speech, yet bowed when I swept him a stately little curtsy and sailed away to the drawing room, wondering if my uncle was as angry with me as I was with my cousin. In solitary grandeur I amused myself by strolling through the suite of handsome rooms henceforth to be my realm, looked at myself in the long mirrors, as every woman is apt to do when alone and in costume, danced over the mossy carpets, touched the grand piano, smelled the flowers, fingered the orna-ments on étagère and table, and was just giving my handkerchief a second drench of some refreshing perfume from a filigree flask that had captivated me when the hall door was flung wide, a quick step went running upstairs, boots tramped overhead, drawers seemed hastily opened and shut, and a bold, blithe voice broke out into a hunting song in a tone so like my uncle's that I involuntarily flew to the door, crying, "Guy is come!"

Fortunately for my dignity, no one heard me, and hurrying back I stood ready to skim into a chair and assume propriety at a minute's notice, con-scious, meanwhile, of the new influence which seemed suddenly to gift the silent house with vitality, and add the one charm it needed—that of cheerful companionship. "How will he meet me? And how shall I meet him?" I thought, looking up at the bright-faced boy, whose portrait looked back at me with a mirthful light in the painted eyes and a trace of his father's disdainful smile in the curves of the firm-set lips. Presently the quick steps came flying down again, past the door, straight to the dining room opposite, and, as I stood listening with a strange flutter at my heart, I heard an impe-rious young voice say rapidly, "Beg pardon, sir, unavoidably detained. Has she come? Is she bearable?"

"I find her so. Dinner is over, and I can offer you nothing but a glass of wine."

My uncle's voice was frostily polite, making a curious contrast to the other, so impetuous and frank, as if used to command or win all but one.

"Never mind the dinner! I'm glad to be rid of it; so I'll drink your health, Father, and then inspect our new ornament."

"Impertinent boy!" I muttered, yet at the same moment resolved to deserve his appellation, and immediately grouped myself as effectively as possible, laughing at my folly as I did so. I possessed a pretty foot, therefore one little slipper appeared quite naturally below the last flounce of my dress; a bracelet glittered on my arm as it emerged from among the lace and carnation knots; that arm supported my head. My profile was well cut, my eyelashes long, therefore I read with face half averted from the door. The light showered down, turning my hair to gold; so I smoothed my curls, retied my snood, and, after a satisfied survey, composed myself with an absorbed aspect and a quickened pulse to await the arrival of the gentlemen.

Soon they came. I knew they paused on the threshold, but never stirred till an irrepressible "You are right, sir!" escaped the younger.

Then I rose prepared to give him the coldest greeting, yet I did not. I had almost expected to meet the boyish face and figure of the picture; I saw instead a man comely and tall. A dark moustache half hid the proud mouth; the vivacious eyes were far kinder, though quite as keen as his father's; and the freshness of unspoiled youth lent a charm which the older man had lost forever. Guy's glance of pleased surprise was flatteringly frank, his smile so cordial, his "Welcome, cousin!" such a hearty sound that my coldness melted in a breath, my dignity was all forgotten, and before I could restrain myself I had offered both hands with the impulsive exclamation "Cousin Guy, I know I shall be very happy here! Are you glad I have come?"

"Glad as I am to see the sun after a November fog."

And bending his tall head, he kissed my hand in the graceful foreign fashion he had learned abroad. It pleased me mightily, for it was both affectionate and respectful. Involuntarily I contrasted it with my uncle's manner, and flashed a significant glance at him as I did so. He understood it, but only nodded with the satirical look I hated, shook out his paper, and began to read. I sat down again, careless of myself now; and Guy stood on the rug, surveying me with an expression of surprise that rather nettled my pride.

35 "He is only a boy, after all; so I need not be daunted by his inches or his airs. I wonder if he knows I am to be his wife, and likes it."

The thought sent the color to my forehead, my eyes fell, and despite my valiant resolution I sat like any bashful child before my handsome cousin. Guy laughed a boyish laugh as he sat down on his father's footstool, saying, while he warmed his slender brown hands, "I beg your pardon, Sybil. (We won't be formal, will we?) But I haven't seen a lady for a month, so I stare like a boor at sight of a silk gown and highbred face. Are those people coming, sir?"

"If Sybil likes, ask her."

"Shall we have a flock of people here to make it gay for you, Cousin, or do you prefer our quiet style better; just riding, driving, lounging, and enjoying life, each in his own way? Henceforth it is to be as you command in such matters."

"Let things go on as they have done then. I don't care for society, and strangers wouldn't make it gay to me, for I like freedom; so do you, I think."

40 "Ah, don't I!"

A cloud flitted over his smiling face, and he punched the fire, as if some vent were necessary for the sudden gust of petulance that knit his black brows into a frown, and caused his father to tap him on the shoulder with the bland request, as he rose to leave the room, "Bring the portfolios and entertain your cousin; I have letters to write, and Sybil is too tired to care for music tonight."

Guy obeyed with a shrug of the shoulder his father touched, but lingered in the recess till my uncle, having made his apologies to me, had left the room; then my cousin rejoined me, wearing the same cordial aspect I first beheld. Some restraint was evidently removed, and his natural self appeared. A very winsome self it was, courteous, gay, and frank, with an undertone of deeper feeling than I thought to find. I watched him covertly, and soon owned to myself that he was all I most admired in the ideal hero every girl creates in her romantic fancy; for I no longer looked upon this young man as my cousin, but my lover, and through all our future intercourse this thought was always uppermost, full of a charm that never lost its power.

Before the evening ended Guy was kneeling on the rug beside me, our two heads close together, while he turned the contents of the great portfolio spread before us, looking each other freely in the face, as I listened and he described, both breaking into frequent peals of laughter at some odd adventure or comical mishap in his own travels, suggested by the pictured scenes before us. Guy was very charming, I my blithest, sweetest self, and when we parted late, my cousin watched me up the stairs with still another "Good night, Sybil," as if both sight and sound were pleasant to him.

"Is that your horse Sultan?" I called from my window next morning, as I looked down upon my cousin, who was coming up the drive from an early gallop on the moors.

"Yes, bonny Sybil; come and admire him," he called back, hat in hand, and a quick smile rippling over his face.

I went, and standing on the terrace, caressed the handsome creature, while Guy said, glancing up at his father's undrawn curtains, "If your saddle had come, we would take a turn before 'my lord' is ready for breakfast. This autumn air is the wine you women need."

I yearned to go, and when I willed the way soon appeared; so careless of bonnetless head and cambric gown, I stretched my hands to him, saying boldly, "Play young Lochinvar,[3] Guy; I am little and light; take me up before you and show me the sea."

He liked the daring feat, held out his hand, I stepped on his boot toe, sprang up, and away we went over the wide moor, where the sun shone in a cloudless heaven, the lark soared singing from the green grass at our feet, and the September wind blew freshly from the sea. As we paused on the upland slope, that gave us a free view of the country for miles, Guy dismounted, and standing with his arm about the saddle to steady me in my precarious seat, began to talk.

"Do you like your new home, Cousin?"

"More than I can tell you!"

"And my father, Sybil?"

"Both yes and no to that question, Guy; I hardly know him yet."

"True, but you must not expect to find him as indulgent and fond as many guardians would be to such as you. It's not his nature. Yet you can win his heart by obedience, and soon grow quite at ease with him."

"Bless you! I'm that already, for I fear no one. Why, I sat on his knee yesterday and smoked a cigarette of his own offering, though Madame would have fainted if she had seen me; then I slept on his arm an hour, and he was fatherly kind, though I teased him like a gnat."

"The deuce he was!"

With which energetic expression Guy frowned at the landscape and harshly checked Sultan's attempt to browse, while I wondered what was amiss between father and son, and resolved to discover; but finding the conversation at an end, started it afresh by asking, "Is any of my property in this part of the country, Guy? Do you know I am as ignorant as a baby about my own affairs; for, as long as every whim was gratified and my purse full, I left the rest to Madame and Uncle, though the first hadn't a bit of judgment, and the last I scarcely knew. I never cared to ask questions before, but now I am intensely curious to know how matters stand."

"All you see is yours, Sybil" was the brief answer.

"What, that great house, the lovely gardens, these moors, and the forest stretching to the sea? I'm glad! I'm glad! But where, then, is your home, Guy?"

[3] in "Lochinvar," a poem by Scottish writer Sir Walter Scott (1771–1832), the title hero, a knight, rescues his beloved just before she is about to wed a person she does not love.

"Nowhere."

60   At this I looked so amazed that his gloom vanished in a laugh, as he explained, but briefly, as if this subject were no pleasanter than the first, "By your father's will you were desired to take possession of the old place at eighteen. You will be that soon; therefore, as your guardian, my father has prepared things for you, and is to share your home until you marry."

"When will that be, I wonder?" And I stole a glance from under my lashes, wild to discover if Guy knew of the compact and was a willing party to it.

His face was half averted, but over his dark cheek I saw a deep flush rise, as he answered, stooping to pull a bit of heather, "Soon, I hope, or the gentleman sleeping there below will be tempted to remain a fixture with you on his knee as 'Madame my wife.' He is not your own uncle, you know."

I smiled at the idea, but Guy did not see it; and seized with a whim to try my skill with the hawk that seemed inclined to peck at its master, I said demurely, "Well, why not? I might be very happy if I learned to love him, as I should, if he were always in that kindest mood of his. Would you like me for a little mamma, Guy?"

"No!" short and sharp as a pistol shot.

65   "Then you must marry and have a home of your own, my son."

"Don't, Sybil! I'd rather you didn't see me in a rage, for I'm not a pleasant sight, I assure you; and I'm afraid I shall be in one if you go on. I early lost my mother, but I love her tenderly, because my father is not much to me, and I know if she had lived I should not be what I am."

Bitter was his voice, moody his mien, and all the sunshine gone at once. I looked down and touched his black hair with a shy caress, feeling both penitent and pitiful.

"Dear Guy, forgive me if I pained you. I'm a thoughtless creature, but I'm not malicious, and a word will restrain me if kindly spoken. My home is always yours, and when my fortune is mine you shall never want, if you are not too proud to accept help from your own kin. You are a little proud, aren't you?"

"As Lucifer,[4] to most people. I think I should not be to you, for you understand me, Sybil, and with you I hope to grow a better man."

70   He turned then, and through the lineaments his father had bequeathed him I saw a look that must have been his mother's, for it was womanly, sweet, and soft, and lent new beauty to the dark eyes, always kind, and just then very tender. He had checked his words suddenly, like one who has gone too far, and with that hasty look into my face had bent his own upon the ground, as if to hide the unwonted feeling that had mastered him. It lasted but a moment, then his old manner returned, as he said gaily, "There drops your slipper. I've been wondering what kept it on. Pretty thing! They say it is a foot like this that oftenest tramples on men's hearts. Are you cruel to your lovers, Sybil?"

"I never had one, for Madame guarded me like a dragon, and I led the life of a nun; but when I do find one I shall try his mettle well before I give up my liberty."

[4]a name for Satan.

"Poets say it is sweet to give up liberty for love, and they ought to know," answered Guy, with a sidelong glance.

I liked that little speech, and recollecting the wistful look he had given me, the significant words that had escaped him, and the variations of tone and manner constantly succeeding one another, I felt assured that my cousin was cognizant of the family league, and accepted it, yet with the shyness of a young lover, knew not how to woo. This pleased me, and quite satisfied with my morning's work, I mentally resolved to charm my cousin slowly, and enjoy the romance of a genuine wooing, without which no woman's life seems complete—in her own eyes at least. He had gathered me a knot of purple heather, and as he gave it I smiled my sweetest on him, saying, "I commission you to supply me with nosegays, for you have taste, and I love wild flowers. I shall wear this at dinner in honor of its giver. Now take me home; for my moors, though beautiful, are chilly, and I have no wrapper but this microscopic handkerchief."

Off went his riding jacket, and I was half smothered in it. The hat followed next, and as he sprang up behind I took the reins, and felt a thrill of delight in sweeping down the slope with that mettlesome creature tugging at the bit, that strong arm around me, and the happy hope that the heart I leaned on might yet learn to love me.

75   The day so began passed pleasantly, spent in roving over house and grounds with my cousin, setting my possessions in order, and writing to dear old Madame. Twilight found me in my bravest attire, with Guy's heather in my hair, listening for his step, and longing to run and meet him when he came. Punctual to the instant he appeared, and this dinner was a far different one from that of yesterday, for both father and son seemed in their gayest and most gallant mood, and I enjoyed the hour heartily. The world seemed all in tune now, and when I went to the drawing room I was moved to play my most stirring marches, sing my blithest songs, hoping to bring one at least of the gentlemen to join me. It brought both, and my first glance showed me a curious change in each. My uncle looked harassed and yet amused; Guy looked sullen and eyed his father with covert glances.

The morning's chat flashed into my mind, and I asked myself, "Is Guy jealous so soon?" It looked a little like it, for he threw himself upon a couch and lay there silent and morose; while my uncle paced to and fro, thinking deeply, while apparently listening to the song he bade me finish. I did so, then followed the whim that now possessed me, for I wanted to try my power over them both, to see if I could restore that gentler mood of my uncle's, and assure myself that Guy cared whether I was friendliest with him or not.

"Uncle, come and sing with me; I like that voice of yours."

"Tut, I am too old for that; take this indolent lad instead. His voice is fresh and young, and will chord well with yours."

"Do you know that pretty *chanson* about 'love and wine, and the Seine tomorrow,' cousin Guy?" I asked, stealing a sly glance at my uncle.

80   "Who taught you that?" And Guy eyed me over the top of the couch with an astonished expression which greatly amused me.

"No one; Uncle sang a bit of it in the carriage yesterday. I like the air, so come and teach me the rest."

"It is no song for you, Sybil. You choose strange entertainment for a lady, sir."

A look of unmistakable contempt was in the son's eye, of momentary annoyance in the father's, yet his voice betrayed none as he answered, still pacing placidly along the room, "I thought she was asleep, and unconsciously began it to beguile a silent drive. Sing on, Sybil; that Bacchanalian snatch[5] will do you no harm."

But I was tired of music now they had come, so I went to him, and passing my arm through his, walked beside him, saying with my most persuasive aspect, "Tell me about Paris, Uncle; I intend to go there as soon as I'm of age, if you will let me. Does your guardianship extend beyond that time?"

85 "Only till you marry."

"I shall be in no haste, then, for I begin to feel quite homelike and happy here with you, and shall be content without other society; only you'll soon tire of me, and leave me to some dismal governess, while you and Guy go pleasuring."

"No fear of that, Sybil; I shall hold you fast till some younger guardian comes to rob me of my merry ward."

As he spoke, he took the hand that lay upon his arm into a grasp so firm, and turned on me a look so keen, that I involuntarily dropped my eyes lest he should read my secret there. Eager to turn the conversation, I asked, pointing to a little miniature hanging underneath the portrait of his son, before which he had paused, "Was that Guy's mother, sir?"

"No, your own."

90 I looked again, and saw a face delicate yet spirited, with dark eyes, a passionate mouth, and a head crowned with hair as plenteous and golden as my own; but the whole seemed dimmed by age, the ivory was stained, the glass cracked, and a faded ribbon fastened it. My eyes filled as I looked, and a strong desire seized me to know what had defaced this little picture of the mother whom I never knew.

"Tell me about her, Uncle; I know so little, and often long for her so much. Am I like her, sir?"

Why did my uncle avert his eyes as he answered, "You are a youthful image of her, Sybil"?

"Go on, please, tell me more; tell me why this is so stained and worn; you know all, and surely I am old enough now to hear any history of pain and loss."

Something caused my uncle to knit his brows, but his bland voice never varied a tone as he placed the picture in my hand and gave me this brief explanation:

95 "Just before your birth your father was obliged to cross the Channel, to receive the last wishes of a dying friend. There was an accident; the vessel foundered, and many lives were lost. He escaped, but by some mistake his name appeared in the list of missing passengers; your mother saw it, the shock destroyed her, and when your father returned he found only a motherless little daughter to welcome him. This miniature, which he always

[5]a few bars of a rowdy drinking song.

carried with him, was saved with his papers at the last moment; but though the seawater ruined it he would never have it copied or retouched, and gave it to me when he died in memory of the woman I had loved for his sake. It is yours now, my child; keep it, and never feel that you are fatherless or motherless while I remain."

Kind as was both act and speech, neither touched me, for something seemed wanting. I felt yet could not define it, for then I believed in the sincerity of all I met.

"Where was she buried, Uncle? It may be foolish, but I should like to see my mother's grave."

"You shall someday, Sybil," and a curious change came over my uncle's face as he averted it.

"I have made him melancholy, talking of Guy's mother and my own; now I'll make him gay again if possible, and pique that negligent boy," I thought, and drew my uncle to a lounging chair, established myself on the arm thereof, and kept him laughing with my merriest gossip, both of us apparently unconscious of the long dark figure stretched just opposite, feigning sleep, but watching us through half-closed lids, and never stirring except to bow silently to my careless "Good night."

100   As I reached the stairhead, I remembered that my letter to Madame, full of the frankest criticisms upon people and things, was lying unsealed on the table in the little room my uncle had set apart for my boudoir; fearing servants' eyes and tongues, I slipped down again to get it. The room adjoined the parlors, and just then was lit only by a ray from the hall lamp.

I had secured the letter, and was turning to retreat, when I heard Guy say petulantly, as if thwarted yet submissive, "I *am* civil when you leave me alone; I *do* agree to marry her, but I won't be hurried or go a-wooing except in my own way. You know I never liked the bargain, for it's nothing else; yet I can reconcile myself to being sold, if it relieves you and gives us both a home. But, Father, mind this, if you tie me to that girl's sash too tightly I shall break away entirely, and then where are we?"

"I should be in prison and you a houseless vagabond. Trust me, my boy, and take the good fortune which I secured for you in your cradle. Look in pretty Sybil's face, and resignation will grow easy; but remember time presses, that this is our forlorn hope, and for God's sake be cautious, for she is a headstrong creature, and may refuse to fulfill her part if she learns that the contract is not binding against her will."

"I think she'll not refuse, sir; she likes me already. I see it in her eyes; she has never had a lover, she says, and according to your account a girl's first sweetheart is apt to fare the best. Besides, she likes the place, for I told her it was hers, as you bade me, and she said she could be very happy here, if my father was always kind."

"She said that, did she? Little hypocrite! For your father, read yourself, and tell me what else she babbled about in that early *tête-à-tête* of yours."

105   "You are as curious as a woman, sir, and always make me tell you all I do and say, yet never tell me anything in return, except this business, which I hate, because my liberty is the price, and my poor little cousin is kept in the dark. I'll tell her all, before I marry her, Father."

"As you please, hothead. I am waiting for an account of the first love passage, so leave blushing to Sybil and begin."

I knew what was coming and stayed no longer, but caught one glimpse of the pair. Guy in his favorite place, erect upon the rug, half laughing, half frowning as he delayed to speak, my uncle serenely smoking on the couch; then I sped away to my own room, thinking, as I sat down in a towering passion, "So he does know of the baby betrothal and hates it, yet submits to please his father, who covets my fortune—mercenary creatures! I can annul the contract, can I? I'm glad to know that, for it makes me mistress of them both. I like you already, do I, and you see it in my eyes? Coxcomb! I'll be the thornier for that. Yet I do like him; I do wish he cared for me, I'm so lonely in the world, and he can be so kind."

So I cried a little, brushed my hair a good deal, and went to bed, resolving to learn all I could when, where, and how I pleased, to render myself as charming and valuable as possible, to make Guy love me in spite of himself, and then say yes or no, as my heart prompted me.

That day was a sample of those that followed, for my cousin was by turns attracted or repelled by the capricious moods that ruled me. Though conscious of a secret distrust of my uncle, I could not resist the fascination of his manner when he chose to exert its influence over me; this made my little plot easier of execution, for jealousy seemed the most effectual means to bring my wayward cousin to subjection. Full of this fancy, I seemed to tire of his society, grew thorny as a brier rose to him, affectionate as a daughter to my uncle, who surveyed us both with that inscrutable glance of his, and slowly yielded to my dominion as if he had divined my purpose and desired to aid it. Guy turned cold and gloomy, yet still lingered near me as if ready for a relenting look or word. I liked that, and took a wanton pleasure in prolonging the humiliation of the warm heart I had learned to love, yet not to value as I ought, until it was too late.

110

One dull November evening as I went wandering up and down the hall, pretending to enjoy the flowers, yet in reality waiting for Guy, who had left me alone all day, my uncle came from his room, where he had sat for many hours with the harassed and anxious look he always wore when certain foreign letters came.

"Sybil, I have something to show and tell you," he said, as I garnished his buttonhole with a spray of heliotrope, meant for the laggard, who would understand its significance, I hoped. Leading me to the drawing room, my uncle put a paper into my hands, with the request "This is a copy of your father's will; oblige me by reading it."

He stood watching my face as I read, no doubt wondering at my composure while I waded through the dry details of the will, curbing my impatience to reach the one important passage. There it was, but no word concerning my power to dissolve the engagement if I pleased; and, as I realized the fact, a sudden bewilderment and sense of helplessness came over me, for the strange law terms seemed to make inexorable the paternal decree which I had not seen before. I forgot my studied calmness, and asked several questions eagerly.

"Uncle, did my father really command that I should marry Guy, whether we loved each other or not?"

"You see what he there set down as his desire; and I have taken measures that you *should* love one another, knowing that few cousins, young, comely, and congenial, could live three months together without finding themselves ready to mate for their own sakes, if not for the sake of the dead and living fathers to whom they owe obedience."

115   "You said I need not, if I didn't choose; why is it not here?"

"I said that? Never, Sybil!" and I met a look of such entire surprise and incredulity it staggered my belief in my own senses, yet also roused my spirit, and, careless of consequences, I spoke out at once.

"I heard you say it myself the night after I came, when you told Guy to be cautious, because I could refuse to fulfill the engagement, if I knew that it was not binding against my will."

This discovery evidently destroyed some plan, and for a moment threw him off his guard; for, crumpling the paper in his hand, he sternly demanded, "You turned eavesdropper early; how often since?"

"Never, Uncle; I did not mean it then, but going for a letter in the dark, I heard your voices, and listened for an instant. It was dishonorable, but irresistible; and if you force Guy's confidence, why should not I steal yours? All is fair in war, sir, and I forgive as I hope to be forgiven."

120   "You have a quick wit and a reticence I did not expect to find under that frank manner. So you have known your future destiny all these months then, and have a purpose in your treatment of your cousin and myself?"

"Yes, Uncle."

"May I ask what?"

I was ashamed to tell; and in the little pause before my answer came, my pique at Guy's desertion was augmented by anger at my uncle's denial of his own words the ungenerous hopes he cherished, and a strong desire to perplex and thwart him took possession of me, for I saw his anxiety concerning the success of this interview, though he endeavored to repress and conceal it. Assuming my coldest mien, I said, "No, sir, I think not; only I can assure you that my little plot has succeeded better than your own."

"But you intend to obey your father's wish, I hope, and fulfill your part of the compact, Sybil?"

125   "Why should I? It is not binding, you know, and I'm too young to lose my liberty just yet; besides, such compacts are unjust, unwise. What right had my father to mate me in my cradle? How did he know what I should become, or Guy? How could he tell that I should not love someone else better? No! I'll not be bargained away like a piece of merchandise, but love and marry when I please!"

At this declaration of independence my uncle's face darkened ominously, some new suspicion lurked in his eye, some new anxiety beset him; but his manner was calm, his voice blander than ever as he asked, "Is there then someone whom you love? Confide in me, my girl."

"And if there were, what then?"

"All would be changed at once, Sybil. But who is it? Some young lover left behind at Madame's?"

"No, sir."

130 "Who, then? You have led a recluse life here. Guy has no friends who visit him, and mine are all old, yet you say you love."

"With all my heart, Uncle."

"Is this affection returned, Sybil?"

"I think so."

"And it is not Guy?"

135 I was wicked enough to enjoy the bitter disappointment he could not conceal at my decided words, for I thought he deserved that momentary pang; but I could not as decidedly answer that last question, for I would not lie, neither would I confess just yet; so, with a little gesture of impatience, I silently turned away, lest he should see the telltale color in my cheeks. My uncle stood an instant in deep thought, a slow smile crept to his lips, content returned to his mien, and something like a flash of triumph glittered for a moment in his eye, then vanished, leaving his countenance earnestly expectant. Much as this change surprised me, his words did more, for, taking both my hands in his, he gravely said, "Do you know that I am your uncle by adoption and not blood, Sybil?"

"Yes, sir; I heard so, but forgot about it," and I looked up at him, my anger quite lost in astonishment.

"Let me tell you then. Your grandfather was childless for many years, my mother was an early friend, and when her death left me an orphan, he took me for his son and heir. But two years from that time your father was born. I was too young to realize the entire change this might make in my life. The old man was too just and generous to let me feel it, and the two lads grew up together like brothers. Both married young, and when you were born a few years later than my son, your father said to me, 'Your boy shall have my girl, and the fortune I have innocently robbed you of shall make us happy in our children.' Then the family league was made, renewed at his death, and now destroyed by his daughter, unless—Sybil, I am forty-five, you not eighteen, yet you once said you could be very happy with me, if I were always kind to you. I can promise that I will be, for I love you. My darling, you reject the son, will you accept the father?"

If he had struck me, it would scarcely have dismayed me more. I started up, and snatching away my hands, hid my face in them, for after the first tingle of surprise an almost irresistible desire to laugh came over me, but I dared not, and gravely, gently he went on.

"I am a bold man to say this, yet I mean it most sincerely. I never meant to betray the affection I believed you never could return, and would only laugh at as a weakness; but your past acts, your present words, give me courage to confess that I desire to keep my ward mine forever. Shall it be so?"

140 He evidently mistook my surprise for maidenly emotion, and the suddenness of this unforeseen catastrophe seemed to deprive me of words. All thought of merriment or ridicule was forgotten in a sense of guilt, for if he feigned the love he offered it was well done, and I believed it then. I saw at once the natural impression conveyed by my conduct; my half confession and the folly of it all oppressed me with a regret and shame I could not master. My mind was in dire confusion, yet a decided "No" was rapidly emerging from the chaos, but was not uttered; for just at this crisis, as I stood

with my uncle's arm about me, my hand again in his, and his head bent down to catch my answer, Guy swung himself gaily into the room.

A glance seemed to explain all, and in an instant his face assumed that expression of pale wrath so much more terrible to witness than the fiercest outbreak; his eye grew fiery, his voice bitterly sarcastic, as he said, "Ah, I see; the play goes on, but the actors change parts. I congratulate you, sir, on your success, and Sybil on her choice. Henceforth I am *de trop*, but before I go allow me to offer my wedding gift. You have taken the bride, let me supply the ring."

He threw a jewel box upon the table, adding, in that unnaturally calm tone that made my heart stand still:

"A little candor would have spared me much pain, Sybil; yet I hope you will enjoy your bonds as heartily as I shall my escape from them. A little confidence would have made me your ally, not your rival, Father. I have not your address; therefore I lose, you win. Let it be so. I had rather be the vagabond this makes me than sell myself, that you may gamble away that girl's fortune as you have your own and mine. You need not ask me to the wedding, I will not come. Oh, Sybil, I so loved, so trusted you!"

And with that broken exclamation he was gone.

145 The stormy scene had passed so rapidly, been so strange and sudden, Guy's anger so scornful and abrupt, I could not understand it, and felt like a puppet in the grasp of some power I could not resist; but as my lover left the room I broke out of the bewilderment that held me, imploring him to stay and hear me.

It was too late, he was gone, and Sultan's tramp was already tearing down the avenue. I listened till the sound died, then my hot temper rose past control, and womanlike asserted itself in vehement and voluble speech. I was angry with my uncle, my cousin, and myself, and for several minutes poured forth a torrent of explanations, reproaches, and regrets, such as only a passionate girl could utter.

My uncle stood where I had left him when I flew to the door with my vain cry; he now looked baffled, yet sternly resolved, and as I paused for breath his only answer was "Sybil, you ask me to bring back that headstrong boy; I cannot; he will never come. This marriage was distasteful to him, yet he submitted for my sake, because I have been unfortunate, and we are poor. Let him go, forget the past, and be to me what I desire, for I loved your father and will be a faithful guardian to his daughter all my life. Child, it must be— come, I implore, I command you.

He beckoned imperiously as if to awe me, and held up the glittering betrothal ring as if to tempt me. The tone, the act, the look put me quite beside myself. I did go to him, did take the ring, but said as resolutely as himself, "Guy rejects me, and I have done with love. Uncle, you would have deceived me, used me as a means to your own selfish ends. I will accept neither yourself nor your gifts, for now I despise both you and your commands." And as the most energetic emphasis I could give to my defiance, I flung the ring, case and all, across the room; it struck the great mirror, shivered it just in the middle, and sent several loosened fragments crashing to the floor.

"Great heavens! Is the young lady mad?" exclaimed a voice behind us. Both turned and saw Dr. Karnac, a stealthy, sallow-faced Spaniard, for whom I had an invincible aversion. He was my uncle's physician, had been visiting a sick servant in the upper regions, and my adverse fate sent him to the door just at that moment with that unfortunate exclamation on his lips.

150

"What do you say?"

My uncle wheeled about and eyed the newcomer intently as he repeated his words. I have no doubt I looked like one demented, for I was desperately angry, pale and trembling with excitement, and as they fronted me with a curious expression of alarm on their faces, a sudden sense of the absurdity of the spectacle came over me; I laughed hysterically a moment, then broke into a passion of regretful tears, remembering that Guy was gone. As I sobbed behind my hands, I knew the gentlemen were whispering together and of me, but I never heeded them, for as I wept myself calmer a comforting thought occurred to me. Guy could not have gone far, for Sultan had been out all day, and though reckless of himself he was not of his horse, which he loved like a human being; therefore he was doubtless at the house of a humble friend nearby. If I could slip away unseen, I might undo my miserable work, or at least see him again before he went away into the world, perhaps never to return. This hope gave me courage for anything, and dashing away my tears, I took a covert survey. Dr. Karnac and my uncle still stood before the fire, deep in their low-toned conversation; their backs were toward me; and hushing the rustle of my dress, I stole away with noiseless steps into the hall, seized Guy's plaid,[6] and, opening the great door unseen, darted down the avenue.

Not far, however; the wind buffeted me to and fro, the rain blinded me, the mud clogged my feet and soon robbed me of a slipper; groping for it in despair, I saw a light flash into the outer darkness; heard voices calling, and soon the swift tramp of steps behind me. Feeling like a hunted doe, I ran on, but before I had gained a dozen yards my shoeless foot struck a sharp stone, and I fell half stunned upon the wet grass of the wayside bank. Dr. Karnac reached me first, took me up as if I were a naughty child, and carried me back through a group of staring servants to the drawing room, my uncle following with breathless entreaties that I would be calm, and a most uncharacteristic display of bustle.

I was horribly ashamed; my head ached with the shock of the fall, my foot bled, my heart fluttered, and when the doctor put me down the crisis came, for as my uncle bent over me with the strange question "My poor girl, do you know me?" an irresistible impulse impelled me to push him from me, crying passionately, "Yes, I know and hate you; let me go! Let me go, or it will be too late!" Then, quite spent with the varying emotions of the last hour, for the first time in my life I swooned away.

Coming to myself, I found I was in my own room, with my uncle, the doctor, Janet, and Mrs. Best, the housekeeper, gathered about me, the latter saying, as she bathed my temples, "She's a sad sight, poor thing, so young, so bonny, and so unfortunate. Did you ever see her so before, Janet?"

[6] a cloak.

155 "Bless you, no, ma'am; there was no signs of such a tantrum when I dressed her for dinner."

"What do they mean? Did they never see anyone angry before?" I dimly wondered, and presently, through the fast disappearing stupor that had held me, Dr. Karnac's deep voice came distinctly, saying, "If it continues, you are perfectly justified in doing so."

"Doing what?" I demanded sharply, for the sound both roused and irritated me, I disliked the man so intensely.

"Nothing, my dear, nothing," purred Mrs. Best, supporting me as I sat up, feeling weak and dazed, yet resolved to know what was going on. I was "a sad sight" indeed: my drenched hair hung about my shoulders, my dress was streaked with mud, one shoeless foot was red with blood, the other splashed and stained, and a white, wild-eyed face completed the ruinous image the opposite mirror showed me. Everything looked blurred and strange, and a feverish unrest possessed me, for I was not one to subside easily after such a mental storm. Leaning on my arm, I scanned the room and its occupants with all the composure I could collect. The two women eyed me curiously yet pitifully; Dr. Karnac stood glancing at me furtively as he listened to my uncle, who spoke rapidly in Spanish as he showed the little scar upon his hand.

That sight did more to restore me than the cordial just administered, and I rose erect, saying abruptly, "Please, everybody, go away; my head aches, and I want to be alone."

160 "Let Janet stay and help you, dear; you are not fit," began Mrs. Best; but I peremptorily stopped her.

"No, go yourself, and take her with you; I'm tired of so much stir about such foolish things as a broken glass and a girl in a pet."

"You will be good enough to take this quieting draft before I go, Miss Sybil."

"I shall do nothing of the sort, for I need only solitude and sleep to be perfectly well," and I emptied the glass the doctor offered into the fire.

He shrugged his shoulders with a disagreeable smile, and quietly began to prepare another draft, saying, "You are mistaken, my dear young lady; you need much care, and should obey, that your uncle may be spared further apprehension and anxiety."

165 My patience gave out at this assumption of authority; and I determined to carry matters with a high hand, for they all stood watching me in a way which seemed the height of impertinent curiosity.

"He is not my uncle! Never has been, and deserves neither respect nor obedience from me! I am the best judge of my own health, and you are not bettering it by contradiction and unnecessary fuss. This is my house, and you will oblige me by leaving it, Dr. Karnac; this is my room, and I insist on being left in peace immediately."

I pointed to the door as I spoke; the women hurried out with scared faces; the doctor bowed and followed, but paused on the threshold, while my uncle approached me, asking in a tone inaudible to those still hovering round the door, "Do you still persist in your refusal, Sybil?"

"How dare you ask me that again? I tell you I had rather die than marry you!"

"The Lord be merciful to us! Just hear how she's going on now about marrying Master. Ain't it awful, Jane?" ejaculated Mrs. Best, bobbing her head in for a last look.

170 "Hold your tongue, you impertinent creature!" I called out; and the fat old soul bundled away in such comical haste I laughed, in spite of languor and vexation.

My uncle left me, and I heard him say as he passed the doctor, "You see how it is."

"Nothing uncommon; but that virulence is a bad symptom," answered the Spaniard, and closing the door locked it, having dexterously removed the key from within.

I had never been subjected to restraint of any kind; it made me reckless at once, for this last indignity was not to be endured.

"Open this instantly!" I commanded, shaking the door. No one answered, and after a few ineffectual attempts to break the lock I left it, threw up the window and looked out; the ground was too far off for a leap, but the trellis where summer vines had clung was strong and high, a step would place me on it, a moment's agility bring me to the terrace below. I was now in just the state to attempt any rash exploit, for the cordial had both strengthened and excited me; my foot was bandaged, my clothes still wet; I could suffer no new damage, and have my own way at small cost. Out I crept, climbed safely down, and made my way to the lodge as I had at first intended. But Guy was not there; and returning, I boldly went in at the great door, straight to the room where my uncle and the doctor were still talking.

175 "I wish the key of my room" was my brief command.

Both started as if I had been a ghost, and my uncle exclaimed, "You here! How in heaven's name came you out?"

"By the window. I am no child to be confined for a fit of anger. I will not submit to it; tomorrow I shall go to Madame; till then I will be mistress in my own house. Give me the key, sir."

"Shall I?" asked the doctor of my uncle, who nodded with a whispered "Yes, yes; don't excite her again."

It was restored, and without another word I went loftily up to my room, locked myself in, and spent a restless, miserable night. When morning came, I breakfasted abovestairs, and then busied myself packing trunks, burning papers, and collecting every trifle Guy had ever given me. No one annoyed me, and I saw only Janet, who had evidently received some order that kept her silent and respectful, though her face still betrayed the same curiosity and pitiful interest as the night before. Lunch was brought up, but I could not eat, and began to feel that the exposure, the fall, and excitement of the evening had left me weak and nervous, so I gave up the idea of going to Madame till the morrow; and as the afternoon waned, tried to sleep, yet could not, for I had sent a note to several of Guy's haunts, imploring him to see me; but my messenger brought word that he was not to be found, and my heart was too heavy to rest.

180 When summoned to dinner, I still refused to go down; for I heard Dr. Karnac's voice, and would not meet him, so I sent word that I wished the carriage early the following morning, and to be left alone till then. In a few

minutes, back came Janet, with a glass of wine set forth on a silver salver, and a card with these words: "Forgive, forget, for your father's sake, and drink with me, 'Oblivion to the past.'"

It touched and softened me. I knew my uncle's pride, and saw in this an entire relinquishment of the hopes I had so thoughtlessly fostered in his mind. I was passionate, but not vindictive. He had been kind, I very willful. His mistake was natural, my resentment ungenerous. Though my resolution to go remained unchanged, I was sorry for my part in the affair; and remembering that through me his son was lost to him, I accepted his apology, drank his toast, and sent him back a dutiful "Good night."

I was unused to wine. The draft I had taken was powerful with age, and, though warm and racy to the palate, proved too potent for me. Still sitting before my fire, I slowly fell into a restless drowse, haunted by a dim dream that I was seeking Guy in a ship, whose motion gradually lulled me into perfect unconsciousness.

Waking at length, I was surprised to find myself in bed, with a shimmer of daylight peeping through the curtains. Recollecting that I was to leave early, I sprang up, took one step, and remained transfixed with dismay, for the room was not my own! Utterly unfamiliar was every object on which my eyes fell. The place was small, plainly furnished, and close, as if long unused. My trunks stood against the wall, my clothes lay on a chair, and on the bed I had left trailed a fur-lined cloak I had often seen on my uncle's shoulders. A moment I stared about me bewildered, then hurried to the window. It was grated!

A lawn, sere and sodden, lay without, and a line of somber firs hid the landscape beyond the high wall which encompassed the dreary plot. More and more alarmed, I flew to the door and found it locked. No bell was visible, no sound audible, no human presence near me, and an ominous foreboding thrilled cold through nerves and blood, as, for the first time, I felt the paralyzing touch of fear. Not long, however. My native courage soon returned, indignation took the place of terror, and excitement gave me strength. My temples throbbed with a dull pain, my eyes were heavy, my limbs weighed down by an unwonted lassitude, and my memory seemed strangely confused; but one thing was clear to me: I must see somebody, ask questions, demand explanations, and get away to Madame without delay.

185

With trembling hands I dressed, stopping suddenly with a cry; for lifting my hands to my head, I discovered that my hair, my beautiful, abundant hair, was gone! There was no mirror in the room, but I could feel that it had been shorn away close about face and neck. This outrage was more than I could bear, and the first tears I shed fell for my lost charm. It was weak, perhaps, but I felt better for it, clearer in mind and readier to confront whatever lay before me. I knocked and called. Then, losing patience, shook and screamed; but no one came or answered me; and wearied out at last, I sat down and cried again in impotent despair.

An hour passed, then a step approached, the key turned, and a hard-faced woman entered with a tray in her hand. I had resolved to be patient, if possible, and controlled myself to ask quietly, though my eyes kindled, and my voice trembled with resentment, "Where am I, and why am I here against my will?"

"This is your breakfast, miss; you must be sadly hungry" was the only reply I got.

"I will never eat till you tell me what I ask."

"Will you be quiet, and mind me if I do, miss?"

190   "You have no right to exact obedience from me, but I'll try."

"That's right. Now all I know is that you are twenty miles from the Moors, and came because you are ill. Do you like sugar in your coffee?"

"When did I come? I don't remember it."

"Early this morning; you don't remember because you were put to sleep before being fetched, to save trouble."

"Ah, that wine! Who brought me here?"

195   "Dr. Karnac, miss."

"Alone?"

"Yes, miss; you were easier to manage asleep than awake, he said."

I shook with anger, yet still restrained myself, hoping to fathom the mystery of this nocturnal journey.

"What is your name, please?" I meekly asked.

200   "You can call me Hannah."

"Well, Hannah, there is a strange mistake somewhere. I am not ill—you see I am not—and I wish to go away at once to the friend I was to meet today. Get me a carriage and have my baggage taken out."

"It can't be done, miss. We are a mile from town, and have no carriages here; besides, you couldn't go if I had a dozen. I have my orders, and shall obey 'em."

"But Dr. Karnac has no right to bring or keep me here."

"Your uncle sent you. The doctor has the care of you, and that is all I know about it. Now I have kept my promise, do you keep yours, miss, and eat your breakfast, else I can't trust you again."

205   "But what is the matter with me? How can I be ill and not know or feel it?" I demanded, more and more bewildered.

"You look it, and that's enough for them as is wise in such matters. You'd have had a fever, if it hadn't been seen to in time."

"Who cut my hair off?"

"I did; the doctor ordered it."

"How dared he? I hate that man, and never will obey him."

210   "Hush, miss, don't clench your hands and look in that way, for I shall have to report everything you say and do to him, and it won't be pleasant to tell that sort of thing."

The woman was civil, but grim and cool. Her eye was unsympathetic, her manner businesslike, her tone such as one uses to a refractory child, half soothing, half commanding. I conceived a dislike to her at once, and resolved to escape at all hazards, for my uncle's inexplicable movements filled me with alarm. Hannah had left my door open, a quick glance showed me another door also ajar at the end of a wide hall, a glimpse of green, and a gate. My plan was desperately simple, and I executed it without delay. Affecting to eat, I presently asked the woman for my handkerchief from the bed. She crossed the room to get it. I darted out, down the passage, along the walk, and tugged vigorously at the great bolt of the gate, but it was also locked. In despair I flew into the garden, but a high wall enclosed it on every side; and as I ran round and round, vainly looking for some outlet, I saw Hannah, accompanied by a man as gray and grim as herself, coming leisurely toward me, with no appearance of excitement or displeasure. Back I would not go; and inspired with a sudden hope, swung myself into one of the firs that grew close against the wall. The branches snapped under me, the slender tree swayed perilously, but up I struggled, till the wide coping of the wall was gained. There I paused and looked back. The woman was hurrying through the gate to intercept my descent on the other side, and close behind me the man, sternly calling me to stop. I looked down; a stony ditch was below, but I would rather risk my life than tamely lose my liberty, and with a flying leap tried to reach the bank; failed, fell heavily among the stones, felt an awful crash, and then came an utter blank.

For many weeks I lay burning in a fever, fitfully conscious of Dr. Karnac and the woman's presence; once I fancied I saw my uncle, but was never sure, and rose at last a shadow of my former self, feeling pitifully broken, both mentally and physically. I was in a better room now, wintry winds howled without, but a generous fire glowed behind the high closed fender, and books lay on my table.

I saw no one but Hannah, yet could wring no intelligence from her beyond what she had already told, and no sign of interest reached me from the outer world. I seemed utterly deserted and forlorn, my spirit was crushed, my strength gone, my freedom lost, and for a time I succumbed to despair, letting one day follow another without energy or hope. It is hard to live with no object to give zest to life, especially for those still blessed with youth, and even in my prison house I soon found one quite in keeping with the mystery that surrounded me.

As I sat reading by day or lay awake at night, I became aware that the room above my own was occupied by some inmate whom I never saw. A peculiar person it seemed to be; for I heard steps going to and fro, hour after hour, in a tireless march that wore upon my nerves, as many a harsher sound would not have done. I could neither tease nor surprise Hannah into any explanation of the thing, and day after day I listened to it, till I longed to cover up my ears and implore the unknown walker to stop, for heaven's sake. Other sounds I heard and fretted over: a low monotonous murmur, as of someone singing a lullaby; a fitful tapping, like a cradle rocked on a carpet-less floor; and at rare intervals cries of suffering, sharp but brief, as if forcibly suppressed. These sounds, combined with the solitude, the confinement, and the books I read, a collection of ghostly tales and weird fancies, soon wrought my nerves to a state of terrible irritability, and wore upon my health so visibly that I was allowed at last to leave my room.

215   The house was so well guarded that I soon relinquished all hope of escape, and listlessly amused myself by roaming through the unfurnished rooms and echoing halls, seldom venturing into Hannah's domain; for there her husband sat, surrounded by chemical apparatus, poring over crucibles and retorts. He never spoke to me, and I dreaded the glance of his cold eye, for it looked unsoftened by a ray of pity at the little figure that

sometimes paused a moment on his threshold, wan and wasted as the ghost of departed hope.

The chief interest of these dreary walks centered in the door of the room above my own, for a great hound lay before it, eyeing me savagely as he rejected all advances, and uttering his deep bay if I approached too near. To me this room possessed an irresistible fascination. I could not keep away from it by day, I dreamed of it by night, it haunted me continually, and soon became a sort of monomania, which I condemned, yet could not control, till at length I found myself pacing to and fro as those invisible feet paced over-head. Hannah came and stopped me, and a few hours later Dr. Karnac appeared. I was so changed that I feared him with a deadly fear. He seemed to enjoy it; for in the pride of youth and beauty I had shown him contempt and defiance at my uncle's, and he took an ungenerous satisfaction in annoying me by a display of power. He never answered my questions or entreaties, regarded me as being without sense or will, insisted on my trying various mixtures and experiments in diet, gave me strange hooks to read, and weekly received Hannah's report of all that passed. That day he came, looked at me, said, "Let her walk," and went away, smiling that hateful smile of his.

Soon after this I took to walking in my sleep, and more than once woke to find myself roving lampless through that haunted house in the dead of night. I concealed these unconscious wanderings for a time, but an ominous event broke them up at last and betrayed them to Hannah.

I had followed the steps one day for several hours, walking below as they walked above; had peopled that mysterious room with every mournful shape my disordered fancy could conjure up; had woven tragical romances about it, and brooded over the one subject of interest my unnatural life possessed with the intensity of a mind upon which its uncanny influence was telling with perilous rapidity. At midnight I woke to find myself standing in a streak of moonlight, opposite the door whose threshold I had never crossed. The April night was warm, a single pane of glass high up in that closed door was drawn aside, as if for air; and as I stood dreamily collecting my sleep-drunken senses, I saw a ghostly hand emerge and beckon, as if to me. It startled me broad awake, with a faint exclamation and a shudder from head to foot. A cloud swept over the moon, and when it passed the hand was gone, but shrill through the keyhole came a whisper that chilled me to the marrow of my bones, so terribly distinct and imploring was it.

"Find it! For God's sake find it before it is too late!"

220   The hound sprang up with an angry growl; I heard Hannah leave her bed nearby; and with an inspiration strange as the moment, I paced slowly on with open eyes and lips apart, as I had seen Amina[7] in the happy days when kind old Madame took me to the theater, whose mimic horrors I had never thought to equal with such veritable ones. Hannah appeared at her door with a light, but on I went in a trance of fear; for I was only kept from dropping in a swoon by the blind longing to fly from that spectral voice and

[7]in Vincenzo Bellini's popular opera La Sonnambula (1831), the heroine, Amina, is a sleep-walker.

hand. Past Hannah I went, she following; and as I slowly laid myself in bed, I heard her say to her husband, who just then came up, "Sleepwalking, John; it's getting worse and worse, as the doctor foretold; she'll settle down like the other presently, but she must be locked up at night, else the dog will do her a mischief."

The man yawned and grumbled; then they went, leaving me to spend hours of unspeakable suffering, which aged me more than years. What was I to find? Where was I to look? And when would it be too late? These questions tormented me; for I could find no answers to them, divine no meaning, see no course to pursue. Why was I here? What motive induced my uncle to commit such an act? And when should I be liberated? were equally unanswerable, equally tormenting, and they haunted me like ghosts I had no power to exorcise or forget. After that I walked no more, because I slept no more; sleep seemed scared away, and waking dreams harassed me with their terrors. Night after night I paced my room in utter darkness—for I was allowed no lamp—night after night I wept bitter tears wrung from me by anguish, for which I had no name; and night after night the steps kept time to mine, and the faint lullaby came down to me as if to soothe and comfort my distress. I felt that my health was going, my mind growing confused and weak; my thoughts wandered vaguely, memory began to fail, and idiocy or madness seemed my inevitable fate; but through it all my heart clung to Guy, yearning for him with a hunger that would not be appeased.

At rare intervals I was allowed to walk in the neglected garden, where no flowers bloomed, no birds sang, no companion came to me but surly John, who followed with his book or pipe, stopping when I stopped, walking when I walked, keeping a vigilant eye upon me, yet seldom speaking except to decline answering my questions. These walks did me no good, for the air was damp and heavy with vapors from the marsh; for the house stood near a half-dried lake, and hills shut it in on every side. No fresh winds from upland moor or distant ocean ever blew across the narrow valley; no human creature visited the place, and nothing but a vague hope that my birthday might bring some change, some help, sustained me. It did bring help, but of such an unexpected sort that its effects remained through all my afterlife. My birthday came, and with it my uncle. I was in my room, walking restlessly— for the habit was a confirmed one now—when the door opened, and Hannah, Dr. Karnac, my uncle, and a gentleman whom I knew to be his lawyer entered, and surveyed me as if I were a spectacle. I saw my uncle start and turn pale; I had never seen myself since I came, but if I had not suspected that I was a melancholy wreck of my former self, I should have known it then, such sudden pain and pity softened his ruthless countenance for a single instant. Dr. Karnac's eye had a magnetic power over me; I had always felt it, but in my present feeble state I dreaded, yet submitted to it with a helpless fear that should have touched his heart—it was on me then, I could not resist it, and paused fixed and fascinated by that repellent yet potent glance.

Hannah pointed to the carpet worn to shreds by my weary march, to the walls which I had covered with weird, grotesque, or tragic figures to while away the heavy hours, lastly to myself, mute, motionless, and scared, saying, as if in confirmation of some previous assertion, "You see, gentlemen, she is, as I said, quiet, but quite hopeless."

I thought she was interceding for me; and breaking from the bewilderment and fear that held me, I stretched my hands to them, crying with an imploring cry, "Yes, I *am* quiet! I *am* hopeless! Oh, have pity on me before this dreadful life kills me or drives me mad!"

225   Dr. Karnac came to me at once with a black frown, which I alone could see; I evaded him, and clung to Hannah, still crying frantically—for this seemed my last hope—"Uncle, let me go! I will give you all I have, will never ask for Guy, will be obedient and meek if I may only go to Madame and never hear the feet again, or see the sights that terrify me in this dreadful room. Take me out! For God's sake take me out!"

My uncle did not answer me, but covered up his face with a despairing gesture, and hurried from the room; the lawyer followed, muttering pitifully, "Poor thing! Poor thing!" and Dr. Karnac laughed the first laugh I had ever heard him utter as he wrenched Hannah from my grasp and locked me in alone. My one hope died then, and I resolved to kill myself rather than endure this life another month; for now it grew clear to me that they believed me mad, and death of the body was far more preferable than that of the mind. I think I *was* a little mad just then, but remember well the sense of peace that came to me as I tore strips from my clothing, braided them into a cord, hid it beneath my mattress, and serenely waited for the night. Sitting in the last twilight I thought to see in this unhappy world, I recollected that I had not heard the feet all day, and fell to pondering over the unusual omission. But if the steps had been silent in that room, voices had not, for I heard a continuous murmur at one time: the tones of one voice were abrupt and broken, the other low, yet resonant, and that, I felt assured, belonged to my uncle. Who was he speaking to? What were they saying? Should I ever know? And even then, with death before me, the intense desire to possess the secret filled me with its old unrest.

Night came at last; I heard the clock strike one, and listening to discover if John still lingered up, I heard through the deep hush a soft grating in the room above, a stealthy sound that would have escaped ears less preternaturally alert than mine. Like a flash came the thought, "Someone is filing bars or picking locks: will the unknown remember me and let me share her flight?" The fatal noose hung ready, but I no longer cared to use it, for hope had come to nerve me with the strength and courage I had lost. Breathlessly I listened; the sound went on, stopped; a dead silence reigned; then something brushed against my door, and with a suddenness that made me tingle from head to foot like an electric shock, through the keyhole came again that whisper, urgent, imploring, and mysterious, "Find it! For God's sake find it before it is too late!" Then fainter, as if breath failed, came the broken words, "The dog—a lock of hair—there is yet time."

Eagerness rendered me forgetful of the secrecy I should preserve, and I cried aloud, "What shall I find? Where shall I look?" My voice, sharpened by fear, rang shrilly through the house; Hannah's quick tread rushed down the hall; something fell; then loud and long rose a cry that made my heart stand still, so helpless, so hopeless was its wild lament. I had betrayed and

I could not save or comfort the kind soul who had lost liberty through me. I was frantic to get out, and beat upon my door in a paroxysm of impatience, but no one came; and all night long those awful cries went on above, cries of mortal anguish, as if soul and body were being torn asunder. Till dawn I listened, pent in that room which now possessed an added terror; till dawn I called, wept, and prayed, with mingled pity, fear, and penitence; and till dawn the agony of that unknown sufferer continued unabated. I heard John hurry to and fro, heard Hannah issue orders with an accent of human sympathy in her hard voice; heard Dr. Karnac pass and repass my door; and all the sounds of confusion and alarm in that once quiet house. With daylight all was still, a stillness more terrible than the stir; for it fell so suddenly, remained so utterly unbroken, that there seemed no explanation of it but the dread word death.

At noon Hannah, a shade paler but grim as ever, brought me some food, saying she forgot my breakfast, and when I refused to eat, yet asked no questions, she bade me go into the garden and not fret myself over last night's flurry. I went, and passing down the corridor, glanced furtively at the door I never saw without a thrill; but I experienced a new sensation then, for the hound was gone, the door was open, and with an impulse past control, I crept in and looked about me. It was a room like mine, the carpet worn like mine, the windows barred like mine; there the resemblance ended, for an empty cradle stood beside the bed, and on that bed, below a sweeping cover, stark and still a lifeless body lay. I was inured to fear now, and an unwholesome craving for new terrors seemed to have grown by what it fed on: an irresistible desire led me close, nerved me to lift the cover and look below— a single glance—then with a cry as panic-stricken as that which rent the silence of the night, I fled away, for the face I saw was a pale image of my own. Sharpened by suffering, pallid with death, the features were familiar as those I used to see; the hair, beautiful and blond as mine had been, streamed long over the pulseless breast, and on the hand, still clenched in that last struggle, shone the likeness of a ring I wore, a ring bequeathed me by my father. An awesome fancy that it was myself assailed me; I had plotted death, and with the waywardness of a shattered mind, I recalled legends of spirits returning to behold the bodies they had left.

Glad now to seek the garden, I hurried down, but on the threshold of the great hall door was arrested by the sharp crack of a pistol; and as a little cloud of smoke dispersed, I saw John drop the weapon and approach the hound, who lay writhing on the bloody grass. Moved by compassion for the faithful brute whose long vigilance was so cruelly repaid, I went to him, and kneeling there, caressed the great head that never yielded to my touch before. John assumed his watch at once, and leaning against a tree, cleaned the pistol, content that I should amuse myself with the dying creature, who looked into my face with eyes of almost human pathos and reproach. The brass collar seemed to choke him as he gasped for breath, and leaning nearer to undo it, I saw, half hidden in his own black hair, a golden lock wound tightly round the collar, and so near its color as to be unobservable, except upon a close inspection. No accident could have placed it there; no head but mine in that house wore hair of that sunny hue—yes, one other, and my

230

heart gave a sudden leap as I remembered the shining locks just seen on that still bosom.

"Find it—the dog—the lock of hair," rang in my ears, and swift as light came the conviction that the unknown help was found at last. The little band was woven close. I had no knife, delay was fatal. I bent my head as if lamenting over the poor beast and bit the knot apart, drew out a folded paper, hid it in my hand, and rising, strolled leisurely back to my own room, saying I did not care to walk till it was warmer. With eager eyes I examined my strange treasure trove. It consisted of two strips of thinnest paper, without address or signature, one almost illegible, worn at the edges and stained with the green rust of the collar; the other fresher, yet more feebly written, both abrupt and disjointed, but terribly significant to me. This was the first:

> I have never seen you, never heard your name, yet I know that you are young, that you are suffering, and I try to help you in my poor way. I think you are not crazed yet, as I often am; for your voice is sane, your plaintive singing not like mine, your walking only caught from me, I hope. I sing to lull the baby whom I never saw; I walk to lessen the long journey that will bring me to the husband I have lost—stop! I must not think of those things or I shall forget. If you are not already mad, you will be; I suspect you were sent here to be made so; for the air is poison, the solitude is fatal, and Karnac remorseless in his mania for prying into the mysteries of human minds. What devil sent you I may never know, but I long to warn you. I can devise no way but this; the dog comes into my room sometimes, you sometimes pause at my door and talk to him; you may find the paper I shall hide about his collar. Read, destroy, but obey it. I implore you to leave this house before it is too late.

The other paper was as follows:

> I have watched you, tried to tell you where to look, for you have not found my warning yet, though I often tie it there and hope. You fear the dog, perhaps, and my plot fails; yet I know by your altered step and voice that you are fast reaching my unhappy state; for I am fitfully mad, and shall be till I die. Today I have seen a familiar face; it seems to have calmed and strengthened me, and though he would not help you, I shall make one desperate attempt. I may not find you, so leave my warning to the hound, yet hope to breathe a word into your sleepless ear that shall send you back into the world the happy thing you should be. Child! Woman! Whatever you are, leave this accursed house while you have power to do it.

235   That was all. I did not destroy the papers, but I obeyed them, and for a week watched and waited till the propitious instant came. I saw my uncle, the doctor, and two others follow the poor body to its grave beside the lake, saw all depart but Dr. Karnac, and felt redoubled hatred and contempt for the men who could repay my girlish slights with such a horrible revenge. On the seventh day, as I went down for my daily walk, I saw John and Dr. Karnac so deep in some uncanny experiment that I passed out unguarded. Hoping to profit by this unexpected chance, I sprang down the steps, but the next moment dropped half stunned upon the grass; for behind me rose a crash, a shriek, a sudden blaze that flashed up and spread, sending a noisome vapor rolling out with clouds of smoke and flame.

Aghast, I was just gathering myself up when Hannah fled out of the house, dragging her husband senseless and bleeding, while her own face was ashy with affright. She dropped her burden beside me, saying, with white lips and a vain look for help where help was not, "Something they were at has burst, killed the doctor, and fired the house! Watch John till I get help, and leave him at your peril." Then flinging open the gate she sped away.

"Now is my time," I thought, and only waiting till she vanished, I boldly followed her example, running rapidly along the road in an opposite direction, careless of bonnetless head and trembling limbs, intent only upon leaving that prison house far behind me. For several hours, I hurried along that solitary road; the spring sun shone, birds sang in the blooming hedges, green nooks invited me to pause and rest; but I heeded none of them, steadily continuing my flight, till spent and footsore I was forced to stop a moment by a wayside spring. As I stooped to drink, I saw my face for the first time in many months, and started to see how like that dead one it had grown, in all but the eternal peace which made that beautiful in spite of suffering and age. Standing thus and wondering if Guy would know me, should we ever meet, the sound of wheels disturbed me. Believing them to be coming from the place I had left, I ran desperately down the hill, turned a sharp corner, and before I could check myself passed a carriage slowly ascending. A face sprang to the window, a voice cried "Stop!" but on I flew, hoping the traveler would let me go unpursued. Not so, however; soon I heard fleet steps following, gaining rapidly, then a hand seized me, a voice rang in my ears, and with a vain struggle I lay panting in my captor's hold, fearing to look up and meet a brutal glance. But the hand that had seized me tenderly drew me close, the voice that had alarmed cried joyfully, "Sybil, it is Guy: Lie still, poor child, you are safe at last."

Then I knew that my surest refuge was gained, and too weak for words, clung to him in an agony of happiness, which brought to his kind eyes the tears I could not shed.

The carriage returned; Guy took me in, and for a time cared only to soothe and sustain my worn soul and body with the cordial of his presence, as we rolled homeward through a blooming world, whose beauty I had never truly felt before. When the first tumult of emotion had subsided, I told the story of my captivity and my escape, ending with a passionate entreaty not to be returned to my uncle's keeping, for henceforth there could be neither affection nor respect between us.

240

"Fear nothing, Sybil; Madame is waiting for you at the Moors, and my father's unfaithful guardianship has ended with his life."

Then with averted face and broken voice Guy went on to tell his father's purposes, and what had caused this unexpected meeting. The facts were briefly these: The knowledge that my father had come between him and a princely fortune had always rankled in my uncle's heart, chilling the ambitious hopes he cherished even in his boyhood, and making life an eager search for pleasure in which to drown his vain regrets. This secret was suspected by my father, and the household league was formed as some atonement for the innocent offense. It seemed to soothe my uncle's resentful nature, and as years went on he lived freely, assured that ample means would be his through his son. Luxurious, self-indulgent, fond of all excitements, and reckless in their pursuit, he took no thought for the morrow till a few months before his return. A gay winter in Paris reduced him to those straits of which women know so little; creditors were oppressive, summer friends failed him, gambling debts harassed him, his son reproached him, and but one resource remained—Guy's speedy marriage with the half-forgotten heiress. The boy had been educated to regard this fate as a fixed fact, and submitted, believing the time to be far distant; but the sudden summons came, and he rebelled against it, preferring liberty to love. My uncle pacified the claimants by promises to be fulfilled at my expense, and hurried home to press on the marriage, which now seemed imperative. I was taken to my future home, approved by my uncle, beloved by my cousin, and, but for my own folly, might have been a happy wife on that May morning when I listened to the unveiling of the past. My mother had been melancholy mad since that unhappy rumor of my father's death; this affliction had been well concealed from me, lest the knowledge should prey upon my excitable nature and perhaps induce a like misfortune. I believed her dead, yet I had seen her, knew where her solitary grave was made, and still carried in my bosom the warning she had sent me, prompted by the unerring instinct of a mother's heart. In my father's will a clause was added just below the one confirming my betrothal, a clause decreeing that, if it should appear that I inherited my mother's malady, the fortune should revert to my cousin, with myself a mournful legacy, to be cherished by him whether his wife or not. This passage, and that relating to my freedom of choice, had been omitted in the copy shown me on the night when my seeming refusal of Guy had induced his father to believe that I loved him, to make a last attempt to keep the prize by offering himself, and, when that failed, to harbor a design that changed my little comedy into the tragical experience I have told.

Dr. Karnac's exclamation had caused the recollection of that clause respecting my insanity to flash into my uncle's mind—a mind as quick to conceive as fearless to execute. I unconsciously abetted the stratagem, and Dr. Karnac was an unscrupulous ally, for love of gain was as strong as love of science; both were amply gratified, and I, poor victim, was given up to be experimented upon, till by subtle means I was driven to the insanity which would give my uncle full control of my fortune and my fate. How the black plot prospered has been told; but retribution speedily overtook them both, for Dr. Karnac paid his penalty by the sudden death that left his ashes among the blackened ruins of that house of horrors, and my uncle had preceded him. For before the change of heirs could be effected my mother died, and the hours spent in that unhealthful spot insinuated the subtle poison of the marsh into his blood; years of pleasure left little vigor to withstand the fever, and a week of suffering ended a life of generous impulses perverted, fine endowments wasted, and opportunities forever lost. When death drew near, he sent for Guy (who, through the hard discipline of poverty and honest labor, was becoming a manlier man), confessed all, and implored him to save me before it was too late. He did, and when all was told, when each saw the other by the light of this strange and sad experience—Guy poor again, I free, the old bond still existing, the barrier of misunderstanding gone—it was easy to see our way, easy to submit, to forgive, forget, and begin anew the life these clouds had darkened for a time.

Home received me, kind Madame welcomed me, Guy married me, and I was happy; but over all these years, serenely prosperous, still hangs for me the shadow of the past, still rises that dead image of my mother, still echoes that spectral whisper in the dark.

(1863)

Kate Chopin   (1851–1904)

Kate Chopin, who received a traditional Catholic upbringing and moved in the society circles of her native city, St. Louis, Missouri, began a career as an author after the death of her husband. She stated that she strove to present "human existence in its subtle, complex, true meaning, stripped of the veil with which ethical and conventional standards have draped it." Her novel *The Awakening* (1899), now considered a classic, is the story of a young mother's escape from her socially imposed roles; it was condemned as immoral and was mostly ignored until the 1960s, as were such stories as "A Shameful Affair" and "The Storm." "The Story of an Hour," which is praised for its conciseness and its presentation of "daring" themes, focuses on the surface and the secret life of the central character. Chopin's use of the limited third-person narrator and the surprise ending enables readers to understand the conventional attitudes of the other characters and Mrs. Mallard's own, unspoken views.

THE STORY OF AN HOUR

Knowing that Mrs. Mallard was afflicted with a heart trouble, great care was taken to break to her as gently as possible the news of her husband's death.

It was her sister Josephine who told her, in broken sentences; veiled hints that revealed in half concealing. Her husband's friend Richards was there, too, near her. It was he who had been in the newspaper office when intelligence of the railroad disaster was received, with Brently Mallard's name leading the list of "killed." He had only taken the time to assure himself of its truth by a second telegram, and had hastened to forestall any less careful, less tender friend in bearing the sad message.

She did not hear the story as many women have heard the same, with a paralyzed inability to accept its significance. She wept at once, with sudden, wild abandonment, in her sister's arms. When the storm of grief had spent itself she went away to her room alone. She would have no one follow her.

There stood, facing the open window, a comfortable, roomy armchair. Into this she sank, pressed down by a physical exhaustion that haunted her body and seemed to reach into her soul.

5 She could see in the open square before her house the tops of trees that were all aquiver with the new spring life. The delicious breath of rain was in the air. In the street below a peddler was crying his wares. The notes of a distant song which some one was singing reached her faintly, and countless sparrows were twittering in the eaves.

There were patches of blue sky showing here and there through the clouds that had met and piled one above the other in the west facing her window.

She sat with her head thrown back upon the cushion of the chair, quite motionless, except when a sob came up into her throat and shook her, as a child who has cried itself to sleep continues to sob in its dreams.

She was young, with a fair, calm face, whose lines bespoke repression and even a certain strength. But now there was a dull stare in her eyes, whose gaze was fixed away off yonder on one of those patches of blue sky. It was not a glance of reflection, but rather indicated a suspension of intelligent thought.

There was something coming to her and she was waiting for it, fearfully. What was it? She did not know; it was too subtle and elusive to name. But she felt it, creeping out of the sky, reaching toward her through the sounds, the scents, the color that filled the air.

10   Now her bosom rose and fell tumultuously. She was beginning to recognize this thing that was approaching to possess her, and she was striving to beat it back with her will—as powerless as her two white slender hands would have been.

When she abandoned herself a little whispered word escaped her slightly parted lips. She said it over and over under her breath: "free, free, free!" The vacant stare and the look of terror that had followed it went from her eyes. They stayed keen and bright. Her pulses beat fast, and the coursing blood warmed and relaxed every inch of her body.

She did not stop to ask if it were or were not a monstrous joy that held her. A clear and exalted perception enabled her to dismiss the suggestion as trivial.

She knew that she would weep again when she saw the kind, tender hands folded in death; the face that had never looked save with love upon her, fixed and gray and dead. But she saw beyond that bitter moment a long procession of years to come that would belong to her absolutely. And she opened and spread her arms out to them in welcome.

There would be no one to live for her during those coming years; she would live for herself. There would be no powerful will bending hers in that blind persistence with which men and women believe they have a right to impose a private will upon a fellow-creature. A kind intention or a cruel intention made the act seem no less a crime as she looked upon it in that brief moment of illumination.

15   And yet she had loved him—sometimes. Often she had not. What did it matter! What could love, the unsolved mystery, count for in face of this possession of self-assertion which she suddenly recognized as the strongest impulse of her being!

"Free! Body and soul free!" she kept whispering.

Josephine was kneeling before the closed door with her lips to the keyhole, imploring for admission. "Louise, open the door! I beg; open the door—you will make yourself ill. What are you doing, Louise? For heaven's sake open the door."

"Go away. I am not making myself ill." No; she was drinking in a very elixir of life through that open window.

Her fancy was running riot along those days ahead of her. Spring days, and summer days, and all sorts of days that would be her own. She breathed a quick prayer that life might be long. It was only yesterday she had thought with a shudder that life might be long.

20   She arose at length and opened the door to her sister's importunities. There was a feverish triumph in her eyes, and she carried herself unwittingly like a goddess of Victory. She clasped her sister's waist, and together they descended the stairs. Richards stood waiting for them at the bottom.

Some one was opening the front door with a latchkey. It was Brently Mallard who entered, a little travel-stained, composedly carrying his grip-sack and umbrella. He had been far from the scene of accident, and did not even know there had been one. He stood amazed at Josephine's piercing cry; at Richards' quick motion to screen him from the view of his wife.

But Richards was too late.

When the doctors came they said she had died of heart disease—of joy that kills.

(1894)

Joseph Conrad   (1857–1924)

Born in the Ukraine of Polish parents, Joseph Conrad worked at sea for twenty years before settling in England. There he began writing novels and short stories, all in his third language, English, which he did not learn until he was an adult. His novels, such as *Lord Jim* and *Nostromo,* are dominated by a concern with the complexities of character and motivation, and focus on the degeneration and corruption of the human spirit. Like *Heart of Darkness* (1902), his best-known short novel, the story "An Outpost of Progress" is an analysis of the impact of the European traders on the African continent and its influence on them.

AN OUTPOST OF PROGRESS

I

There were two white men in charge of the trading station. Kayerts, the chief, was short and fat; Carlier, the assistant, was tall, with a large head and a very broad trunk perched upon a long pair of thin legs. The third man on the staff was a Sierra Leone nigger, who maintained that his name was Henry Price. However, for some reason or other, the natives down the river had given him the name of Makola, and it stuck to him through all his wanderings about the country. He spoke English and French with a warbling accent, wrote a beautiful hand, understood bookkeeping, and cherished in his innermost heart the worship of evil spirits. His wife was a negress from Loanda, very large and very noisy. Three children rolled about in sunshine before the door of his low, shed-like dwelling. Makola, taciturn and impenetrable, despised the two white men. He had charge of a small clay storehouse with a dried-grass roof, and pretended to keep a correct account of beads, cotton cloth, red kerchiefs, brass wire, and other trade goods it contained. Besides the storehouse and Makola's hut, there was only one large building in the cleared ground of the station. It was built neatly of reeds, with a verandah on all the four sides. There were three rooms in it. The one in the middle was the living-room, and had two rough tables and a few stools in it. The other two were the bedrooms for the white men. Each had a bedstead and a mosquito net for all furniture. The plank floor was littered with the belongings of the white men; open half-empty boxes, town wearing apparel, old boots; all the things dirty, and all the things broken, that accumulate mysteriously round untidy men. There was also another dwelling-place some distance away from the buildings. In it, under a tall cross much out of the perpendicular, slept the man who had seen the beginning of all this; who had planned and had watched the construction of this outpost of progress. He had been, at home, an unsuccessful painter who, weary of pursuing fame on an empty stomach, had gone out there through high protections. He had been the first chief of that station. Makola had watched the energetic artist die of fever in the just finished house with his usual kind of "I told you so" indifference. Then, for a time, he dwelt alone with his family, his account

books, and the Evil Spirit that rules the lands under the equator. He got on
very well with his god. Perhaps he had propitiated him by a promise of more
white men to play with, by and by. At any rate the director of the Great
Trading Company, coming up in a steamer that resembled an enormous
sardine box with a flat-roofed shed erected on it, found the station in good
order, and Makola as usual quietly diligent. The director had the cross put up
over the first agent's grave, and appointed Kayerts to the post. Carlier was
told off as second in charge. The director was a man ruthless and efficient,
who at times, but very imperceptibly, indulged in grim humour. He made a
speech to Kayerts and Carlier, pointing out to them the promising aspect of
their station. The nearest trading-post was about three hundred miles away.
It was an exceptional opportunity for them to distinguish themselves and to
earn percentages on the trade. This appointment was a favour done to
beginners. Kayerts was moved almost to tears by his director's kindness. He
would, he said, by doing his best, try to justify the flattering confidence, &c., &c.
Kayerts had been in the Administration of the Telegraphs, and knew how to
express himself correctly. Carlier, an ex-non-commissioned officer of cavalry
in an army guaranteed from harm by several European Powers, was less
impressed. If there were commissions to get, so much the better; and, trailing
a sulky glance over the river, the forests, the impenetrable bush that seemed
to cut off the station from the rest of the world, he muttered between his
teeth, "We shall see, very soon."

Next day, some bales of cotton goods and a few cases of provisions
having been thrown on shore, the sardine-box steamer went off, not to
return for another six months. On the deck the director touched his cap to
the two agents, who stood on the bank waving their hats, and turning to an
old servant of the Company on his passage to headquarters, said, "Look at
those two imbeciles. They must be mad at home to send me such specimens.
I told those fellows to plant a vegetable garden, build new storehouses and
fences, and construct a landing-stage. I bet nothing will be done! They
won't know how to begin. I always thought the station on this river useless,
and they just fit the station!

"They will form themselves there," said the old stager with a quiet smile.

"At any rate, I am rid of them for six months," retorted the director.

The two men watched the steamer round the bend, then, ascending arm
in arm the slope of the bank, returned to the station. They had been in this
vast and dark country only a very short time, and as yet always in the midst
of other white men, under the eye and guidance of their superiors. And now,
dull as they were to the subtle influences of surroundings, they felt
themselves very much alone, when suddenly left unassisted to face the
wilderness; a wilderness rendered more strange, more incomprehensible by
the mysterious glimpses of the vigorous life it contained. They were two
perfectly insignificant and incapable individuals, whose existence is only
rendered possible through the high organization of civilized crowds. Few
men realize that their life, the very essence of their character, their
capabilities and their audacities, are only the expression of their belief in the
safety of their surroundings. The courage, the composure, the confidence;
the emotions and principles; every great and every insignificant thought

belongs not to the individual but to the crowd: to the crowd that believes blindly in the irresistible force of its institutions and of its morals, in the power of its police and of its opinion. But the contact with pure unmitigated savagery, with primitive nature and primitive man, brings sudden and profound trouble into the heart. To the sentiment of being alone of one's kind, to the clear perception of the loneliness of one's thoughts, of one's sensations—to the negation of the habitual, which is safe, there is added the affirmation of the unusual, which is dangerous; a suggestion of things vague, uncontrollable, and repulsive, whose discomposing intrusion excites the imagination and tries the civilized nerves of the foolish and the wise alike.

Kayerts and Carlier walked arm in arm, drawing close to one another as children do in the dark; and they had the same, not altogether unpleasant, sense of danger which one half suspects to be imaginary. They chatted persistently in familiar tones. "Our station is prettily situated," said one. The other assented with enthusiasm, enlarging volubly on the beauties of the situation. Then they passed near the grave. "Poor devil!" said Kayerts. "He died of fever, didn't he?" muttered Carlier, stopping short. "Why," retorted Kayerts, with indignation, "I've been told that the fellow exposed himself recklessly to the sun. The climate here, everybody says, is not at all worse than at home, as long as you keep out of the sun. Do you hear that, Carlier? I am chief here, and my orders are that you should not expose yourself to the sun!" He assumed his superiority jocularly, but his meaning was serious. The idea that he would, perhaps, have to bury Carlier and remain alone, gave him an inward shiver. He felt suddenly that this Carlier was more precious to him here, in the centre of Africa, than a brother could be anywhere else. Carlier, entering into the spirit of the thing, made a military salute and answered in a brisk tone, "Your orders shall be attended to, chief!" Then he burst out laughing, slapped Kayerts on the back and shouted, "We shall let life run easily here! Just sit still and gather in the ivory those savages will bring. This country has its good points, after all!" They both laughed loudly while Carlier thought: That poor Kayerts; he is so fat and unhealthy. It would be awful if I had to bury him here. He is a man I respect . . . . Before they reached the verandah of their house they called one another "my dear fellow."

The first day they were very active, pottering about with hammers and nails and red calico, to put up curtains, make their house habitable and pretty; resolved to settle down comfortably to their new life. For them an impossible task. To grapple effectually with even purely material problems requires more serenity of mind and more lofty courage than people generally imagine. No two beings could have been more unfitted for such a struggle. Society, not from any tenderness, but because of its strange needs, had taken care of those two men, forbidding them all independent thought, all initiative, all departure from routine; and forbidding it under pain of death. They could only live on condition of being machines. And now, released from the fostering care of men with pens behind the ears, or of men with gold lace on the sleeves, they were like those lifelong prisoners who, liberated after many years, do not know what use to make of their freedom. They did not know what use to make of their faculties, being both, through want of practice, incapable of independent thought.

At the end of two months Kayerts often would say, "If it was not for my Melie, you wouldn't catch me here." Melie was his daughter. He had thrown up his post in the Administration of the Telegraphs, though he had been for seventeen years perfectly happy there, to earn a dowry for his girl. His wife was dead, and the child was being brought up by his sisters. He regretted the streets, the pavements, the cafés, his friends of many years; all the things he used to see, day after day; all the thoughts suggested by familiar things—the thoughts effortless, monotonous, and soothing of a Government clerk; he regretted all the gossip, the small enmities, the mild venom, and the little jokes of Government offices. "If I had had a decent brother-in-law," Carlier would remark, "a fellow with a heart, I would not be here." He had left the army and had made himself so obnoxious to his family by his laziness and impudence, that an exasperated brother-in-law had made superhuman efforts to procure him an appointment in the Company as a second-class agent. Having not a penny in the world he was compelled to accept this means of livelihood as soon as it became quite clear to him that there was nothing more to squeeze out of his relations. He, like Kayerts, regretted his old life. He regretted the clink of sabre and spurs on a fine afternoon, the barrack-room witticisms, the girls of garrison towns; but, besides, he had also a sense of grievance. He was evidently a much ill-used man. This made him moody, at times. But the two men got on well together in the fellowship of their stupidity and laziness. Together they did nothing, absolutely nothing, and enjoyed the sense of idleness for which they were paid. And in time they came to feel something resembling affection for one another.

They lived like blind men in a large room, aware only of what came in contact with them (and of that only imperfectly), but unable to see the general aspect of things. The river, the forest, all the great land throbbing with life, were like a great emptiness. Even the brilliant sunshine disclosed nothing intelligible. Things appeared and disappeared before their eyes in an unconnected and aimless kind of way. The river seemed to come from nowhere and flow nowhither. It flowed through a void. Out of that void, at times, came canoes, and men with spears in their hands would suddenly crowd the yard of the station. They were naked, glossy black, ornamented with snowy shells and glistening brass wire, perfect of limb. They made an uncouth babbling noise when they spoke, moved in a stately manner, and sent quick, wild glances out of their startled, never-resting eyes. Those warriors would squat in long rows, four or more deep, before the verandah, while their chiefs bargained for hours with Makola over an elephant tusk. Kayerts sat on his chair and looked down on the proceedings, understanding nothing. He stared at them with his round blue eyes, called out to Carlier, "Here, look! look at that fellow there—and that other one, to the left. Did you ever see such a face? Oh, the funny brute!"

10   Carlier, smoking native tobacco in a short wooden pipe, would swagger up twirling his moustaches, and surveying the warriors with haughty indulgence, would say—

"Fine animals. Brought any bone? Yes? It's not any too soon. Look at the muscles of that fellow—third from the end. I wouldn't care to get a punch on the nose from him. Fine arms, but legs no good below the knee. Couldn't make cavalry men of them." And after glancing down complacently at his own shanks, he always concluded: "Pah! Don't they stink! You, Makola! Take that herd over to the fetish" (the storehouse was in every station called the fetish, perhaps because of the spirit of civilization it contained) "and give them up some of the rubbish you keep there. I'd rather see it full of bone than full of rags."

Kayerts approved.

"Yes, yes! Go and finish that palaver over there, Mr. Makola. I will come round when you are ready, to weigh the tusk. We must be careful." Then turning to his companion: "This is the tribe that lives down the river; they are rather aromatic. I remember, they had been once before here. D'ye hear that row? What a fellow has got to put up with in this dog of a country! My head is split."

Such profitable visits were rare. For days the two pioneers of trade and progress would look on their empty courtyard in the vibrating brilliance of vertical sunshine. Below the high bank, the silent river flowed on glittering and steady. On the sands in the middle of the stream, hippos and alligators sunned themselves side by side. And stretching away in all directions, surrounding the insignificant cleared spot of the trading post, immense forests, hiding fateful complications of fantastic life, lay in the eloquent silence of mute greatness. The two men understood nothing, cared for nothing but for the passage of days that separated them from the steamer's return. Their predecessor had left some torn books. They took up these wrecks of novels, and, as they had never read anything of the kind before, they were surprised and amused. Then during long days there were interminable and silly discussions about plots and personages. In the centre of Africa they made acquaintance of Richelieu and of d'Artagnan, of Hawk's Eye and of Father Goriot, and of many other people.[1] All these imaginary personages became subjects for gossip as if they had been living friends. They discounted their virtues, suspected their motives, decried their successes; were scandalized at their duplicity or were doubtful about their courage. The accounts of crimes filled them with indignation, while tender or pathetic passages moved them deeply. Carlier cleared his throat and said in a soldierly voice, "What nonsense!" Kayerts, his round eyes suffused with tears, his fat cheeks quivering, rubbed his bald head, and declared, "This is a splendid book. I had no idea there were such clever fellows in the world." They also found some old copies of a home paper. That print discussed what it was pleased to call "Our Colonial Expansion" in high-flown language. It spoke much of the rights and duties of civilization, of the sacredness of the civilizing work, and extolled the merits of those who went about bringing light, and faith and commerce to the dark places of the earth. Carlier and Kayerts read, wondered, and began to think better of themselves. Carlier said one evening, waving his hand about, "In a hundred years, there will be perhaps a town here. Quays, and warehouses, and barracks, and—and— billiard-rooms. Civilization, my boy, and virtue—and all. And then, chaps

---

[1]heroes in popular adventure novels by Alexandre Dumas, James Fenimore Cooper, and Honoré de Balzac, respectively.

will read that two good fellows, Kayerts and Carlier, were the first civilized men to live in this very spot!" Kayerts nodded, "Yes, it is a consolation to think of that." They seemed to forget their dead predecessor; but, early one day, Carlier went out and replanted the cross firmly. "It used to make me squint whenever I walked that way," he explained to Kayerts over the morning coffee. "It made me squint, leaning over so much. So I just planted it upright. And solid, I promise you! I suspended myself with both hands to the cross-piece. Not a move. Oh, I did that properly."

15   At times Gobila came to see them. Gobila was the chief of the neighbouring villages. He was a gray-headed savage, thin and black, with a white cloth round his loins and a mangy panther skin hanging over his back. He came up with long strides of his skeleton legs, swinging a staff as tall as himself, and, entering the common room of the station, would squat on his heels to the left of the door. There he sat, watching Kayerts, and now and then making a speech which the other did not understand. Kayerts, without interrupting his occupation, would from time to time say in a friendly manner: "How goes it, you old image?" and they would smile at one another. The two whites had a liking for that old and incomprehensible creature, and called him Father Gobila. Gobila's manner was paternal, and he seemed really to love all white men. They all appeared to him very young, indistinguishably alike (except for stature), and he knew that they were all brothers, and also immortal. The death of the artist, who was the first white man whom he knew intimately, did not disturb this belief, because he was firmly convinced that the white stranger had pretended to die and got himself buried for some mysterious purpose of his own, into which it was useless to inquire. Perhaps it was his way of going home to his own country? At any rate, these were his brothers, and he transferred his absurd affection to them. They returned it in a way. Carlier slapped him on the back, and recklessly struck off matches for his amusement. Kayerts was always ready to let him have a sniff at the ammonia bottle. In short, they behaved just like that other white creature that had hidden itself in a hole in the ground. Gobila considered them attentively. Perhaps they were the same being with the other—or one of them was. He couldn't decide—clear up that mystery; but he remained always very friendly. In consequence of that friendship the women of Gobila's village walked in single file through the reedy grass, bringing every morning to the station, fowls, and sweet potatoes, and palm wine, and sometimes a goat. The Company never provisions the stations fully, and the agents required those local supplies to live. They had them through the good-will of Gobila, and lived well. Now and then one of them had a bout of fever, and the other nursed him with gentle devotion. They did not think much of it. It left them weaker, and their appearance changed for the worse. Carlier was hollow-eyed and irritable. Kayerts showed a drawn, flabby face above the rotundity of his stomach, which gave him a weird aspect. But being constantly together, they did not notice the change that took place gradually in their appearance, and also in their dispositions.

Five months passed in that way.

Then, one morning, as Kayerts and Carlier, lounging in their chairs under the verandah, talked about the approaching visit of the steamer, a knot of armed men came out of the forest and advanced towards the station.

They were strangers to that part of the country. They were tall, slight, draped classically from neck to heel in blue fringed cloths, and carried percussion muskets over their bare right shoulders. Makola showed signs of excitement, and ran out of the storehouse (where he spent all his days) to meet these visitors. They came into the courtyard and looked about them with steady, scornful glances. Their leader, a powerful and determined-looking negro with bloodshot eyes, stood in front of the verandah and made a long speech. He gesticulated much, and ceased very suddenly.

There was something in his intonation, in the sounds of the long sentences he used, that startled the two whites. It was like a reminiscence of something not exactly familiar, and yet resembling the speech of civilized men. It sounded like one of those impossible languages which sometimes we hear in our dreams.

"What lingo is that?" said the amazed Carlier. "In the first moment I fancied the fellow was going to speak French. Anyway, it is a different kind of gibberish to what we ever heard."

"Yes," replied Kayerts. "Hey, Makola, what does he say? Where do they come from? Who are they?

But Makola, who seemed to be standing on hot bricks, answered hurriedly, "I don't know. They come from very far. Perhaps Mrs. Price will understand. They are perhaps bad men."

The leader, after waiting for a while, said something sharply to Makola, who shook his head. Then the man, after looking round, noticed Makola's hut and walked over there. The next moment Mrs. Makola was heard speaking with great volubility. The other strangers—they were six in all—strolled about with an air of ease, put their heads through the door of the storeroom, congregated round the grave, pointed understandingly at the cross, and generally made themselves at home.

"I don't like those chaps—and, I say, Kayerts, they must be from the coast; they've got firearms," observed the sagacious Carlier.

Kayerts also did not like those chaps. They both, for the first time, became aware that they lived in conditions where the unusual may be dangerous, and that there was no power on earth outside of themselves to stand between them and the unusual. They became uneasy, went in and loaded their revolvers. Kayerts said, "We must order Makola to tell them to go away before dark."

The strangers left in the afternoon, after eating a meal prepared for them by Mrs. Makola. The immense woman was excited, and talked much with the visitors. She rattled away shrilly, pointing here and there at the forests and at the river. Makola sat apart and watched. At times he got up and whispered to his wife. He accompanied the strangers across the ravine at the back of the station-ground, and returned slowly looking very thoughtful. When questioned by the white men he was very strange, seemed not to understand, seemed to have forgotten French—seemed to have forgotten how to speak altogether. Kayerts and Carlier agreed that the nigger had had too much palm wine.

There was some talk about keeping a watch in turn, but in the evening everything seemed so quiet and peaceful that they retired as usual. All night they were disturbed by a lot of drumming in the villages. A deep, rapid roll near by would be followed by another far off—then all ceased. Soon short appeals would rattle out here and there, then all mingle together, increase, become vigorous and sustained, would spread out over the forest, roll through the night, unbroken and ceaseless, near and far, as if the whole land had been one immense drum booming out steadily an appeal to heaven. And through the deep and tremendous noise sudden yells that resembled snatches of songs from a madhouse darted shrill and high in discordant jets of sound which seemed to rush far above the earth and drive all peace from under the stars.

Carlier and Kayerts slept badly. They both thought they had heard shots fired during the night—but they could not agree as to the direction. In the morning Makola was gone somewhere. He returned about noon with one of yesterday's strangers, and eluded all Kayerts' attempts to close with him: had become deaf apparently. Kayerts wondered. Carlier, who had been fishing off the bank, came back and remarked while he showed his catch, "The niggers seem to be in a deuce of a stir; I wonder what's up. I saw about fifteen canoes cross the river during the two hours I was there fishing." Kayerts, worried, said, "Isn't this Makola very queer to-day?" Carlier advised, "Keep all our men together in case of some trouble."

II

There were ten station men who had been left by the Director. Those fellows, having engaged themselves to the Company for six months (without having any idea of a month in particular and only a very faint notion of time in general), had been serving the cause of progress for upwards of two years. Belonging to a tribe from a very distant part of the land of darkness and sorrow, they did not run away, naturally supposing that as wandering strangers they would be killed by the inhabitants of the country; in which they were right. They lived in straw huts on the slope of a ravine overgrown with reedy grass, just behind the station buildings. They were not happy, regretting the festive incantations, the sorceries, the human sacrifices of their own land; where they also had parents, brothers, sisters, admired chiefs, respected magicians, loved friends, and other ties supposed generally to be human. Besides, the rice rations served out by the Company did not agree with them, being a food unknown to their land, and to which they could not get used. Consequently they were unhealthy and miserable. Had they been of any other tribe they would have made up their minds to die—for nothing is easier to certain savages than suicide—and so have escaped from the puzzling difficulties of existence. But belonging, as they did, to a warlike tribe with filed teeth, they had more grit, and went on stupidly living through disease and sorrow. They did very little work, and had lost their splendid physique. Carlier and Kayerts doctored them assiduously without being able to bring them back into condition again. They were mustered every morning and told off to different tasks—grass-cutting, fence-building, tree-felling, &c, &c., which no power on earth could induce them to execute efficiently. The two whites had practically very little control over them.

In the afternoon Makola came over to the big house and found Kayerts watching three heavy columns of smoke rising above the forests. "What is that?" asked Kayerts. "Some villages burn," answered Makola, who seemed to have regained his wits. Then he said abruptly: "We have got very little ivory; bad six months' trading. Do you like get a little more ivory?"

"Yes," said Kayerts, eagerly. He thought of percentages which were low.

"Those men who came yesterday are traders from Loanda who have got more ivory than they can carry home. Shall I buy? I know their camp."

"Certainly," said Kayerts. "What are those traders?"

"Bad fellows," said Makola, indifferently. "They fight with people, and catch women and children. They are bad men, and got guns. There is a great disturbance in the country. Do you want ivory?"

"Yes," said Kayerts. Makola said nothing for a while. Then: "Those workmen of ours are no good at all," he muttered, looking round. "Station in very bad order, sir. Director will growl. Better get a fine lot of ivory, then he say nothing."

"I can't help it; the men won't work," said Kayerts. "When will you get that ivory?"

"Very soon," said Makola. "Perhaps to-night. You leave it to me, and keep indoors, sir. I think you had better give some palm wine to our men to make a dance this evening. Enjoy themselves. Work better to-morrow. There's plenty palm wine—gone a little sour."

Kayerts said yes, and Makola, with his own hands, carried big calabashes to the door of his hut. They stood there till the evening, and Mrs. Makola looked into every one. The men got them at sunset. When Kayerts and Carlier retired, a big bonfire was flaring before the men's huts. They could hear their shouts and drumming. Some men from Gobila's village had joined the station hands, and the entertainment was a great success.

In the middle of the night, Carlier waking suddenly, heard a man shout loudly; then a shot was fired. Only one. Carlier ran out and met Kayerts on the verandah. They were both startled. As they went across the yard to call Makola, they saw shadows moving in the night. One of them cried, "Don't shoot! It's me, Price." Then Makola appeared close to them. "Go back, go back, please," he urged, "you spoil all." "There are strange men about," said Carlier. "Never mind; I know," said Makola. Then he whispered, "All right. Bring ivory. Say nothing! I know my business." The two white men reluctantly went back to the house, but did not sleep. They heard footsteps, whispers, some groans. It seemed as if a lot of men came in, dumped heavy things on the ground, squabbled a long time, then went away. They lay on their hard beds and thought: "This Makola is invaluable." In the morning Carlier came out, very sleepy, and pulled at the cord of the big bell. The station hands mustered every morning to the sound of the bell. That morning nobody came. Kayerts turned out also, yawning. Across the yard they saw Makola come out of his hut, a tin basin of soapy water in his hand. Makola, a civilized nigger, was very neat in his person. He threw the soapsuds skilfully over a wretched little yellow cur he had, then turning his face to the agent's house, he shouted from the distance, "All the men gone last night!"

They heard him plainly, but in their surprise they both yelled out together: "What!" Then they stared at one another. "We are in a proper fix now," growled Carlier. "It's incredible!" muttered Kayerts. "I will go to the huts and see," said Carlier, striding off. Makola coming up found Kayerts standing alone.

40 "I can hardly believe it," said Kayerts, tearfully. "We took care of them as if they had been our children."

"They went with the coast people," said Makola after a moment of hesitation.

"What do I care with whom they went—the ungrateful brutes!" exclaimed the other. Then with sudden suspicion, and looking hard at Makola, he added: "What do you know about it?"

Makola moved his shoulders, looking down on the ground. "What do I know? I think only. Will you come and look at the ivory I've got there? It is a fine lot. You never saw such."

He moved towards the store. Kayerts followed him mechanically, thinking about the incredible desertion of the men. On the ground before the door of the fetish lay six splendid tusks.

45 "What did you give for it?" asked Kayerts, after surveying the lot with satisfaction.

"No regular trade," said Makola. "They brought the ivory and gave it to me. I told them to take what they most wanted in the station. It is a beautiful lot. No station can show such tusks. Those traders wanted carriers badly, and our men were no good here. No trade, no entry in books; all correct."

Kayerts nearly burst with indignation. "Why!" he shouted, "I believe you have sold our men for these tusks!" Makola stood impassive and silent. "I—I—will—I," stuttered Kayerts. "You fiend!" he yelled out.

"I did the best for you and the Company," said Makola, imperturbably. "Why you shout so much? Look at this tusk."

"I dismiss you! I will report you—I won't look at the tusk. I forbid you to touch them. I order you to throw them into the river. You—you!"

50 "You very red, Mr. Kayerts. If you are so irritable in the sun, you will get fever and die—like the first chief!" pronounced Makola impressively.

They stood still, contemplating one another with intense eyes, as if they had been looking with effort across immense distances. Kayerts shivered. Makola had meant no more than he said, but his words seemed to Kayerts full of ominous menace! He turned sharply and went away to the house. Makola retired into the bosom of his family; and the tusks, left lying before the store, looked very large and valuable in the sunshine.

Carlier came back on the verandah. "They're all gone, hey?" asked Kayerts from the far end of the common room in a muffled voice. "You did not find anybody?"

"Oh, yes," said Carlier, "I found one of Gobila's people lying dead before the huts—shot through the body. We heard that shot last night."

Kayerts came out quickly. He found his companion staring grimly over the yard at the tusks, away by the store. They both sat in silence for a while. Then Kayerts related his conversation with Makola. Carlier said nothing.

At the midday meal they ate very little. They hardly exchanged a word that day. A great silence seemed to lie heavily over the station and press on their lips. Makola did not open the store; he spent the day playing with his children. He lay full-length on a mat outside his door, and the youngsters sat on his chest and clambered all over him. It was a touching picture. Mrs. Makola was busy cooking all day as usual. The white men made a somewhat better meal in the evening. Afterwards, Carlier smoking his pipe strolled over to the store; he stood for a long time over the tusks, touched one or two with his foot, even tried to lift the largest one by its small end. He came back to his chief, who had not stirred from the verandah, threw himself in the chair and said—

55   "I can see it! They were pounced upon while they slept heavily after drinking all that palm wine you've allowed Makola to give them. A put-up job! See? The worst is, some of Gobila's people went there, and got carried off too, no doubt. The least drunk woke up, and got shot for his sobriety. This is a funny country. What will you do now?"

"We can't touch it, of course," said Kayerts.

"Of course not," assented Carlier.

"Slavery is an awful thing," stammered out Kayerts in an unsteady voice.

"Frightful—the sufferings," grunted Carlier with conviction.

60   They believed their words. Everybody shows a respectful deference to certain sounds that he and his fellows can make. But about feelings people really know nothing. We talk with indignation or enthusiasm; we talk about oppression, cruelty, crime, devotion, self-sacrifice, virtue, and we know nothing real beyond the words. Nobody knows what suffering or sacrifice mean—except, perhaps the victims of the mysterious purpose of these illusions.

Next morning they saw Makola very busy setting up in the yard the big scales used for weighing ivory. By and by Carlier said: "What's that filthy scoundrel up to?" and lounged out into the yard. Kayerts followed. They stood watching. Makola took no notice. When the balance was swung true, he tried to lift a tusk into the scale. It was too heavy. He looked up helplessly without a word, and for a minute they stood round that balance as mute and still as three statues. Suddenly Carlier said: "Catch hold of the other end, Makola—you beast!" and together they swung the tusk up. Kayerts trembled in every limb. He muttered, "I say! O! I say!" and putting his hand in his pocket found there a dirty bit of paper and the stump of a pencil. He turned his back on the others, as if about to do something tricky, and noted stealthily the weights which Carlier shouted out to him with unnecessary loudness. When all was over Makola whispered to himself: "The sun's very strong here for the tusks." Carlier said to Kayerts in a careless tone: "I say, chief, I might just as well give him a lift with this lot into the store."

As they were going back to the house Kayerts observed with a sigh: "It had to be done." And Carlier said: "It's deplorable, but, the men being Company's men the ivory is Company's ivory. We must look after it." "I will report to the Director, of course," said Kayerts. "Of course; let him decide," approved Carlier.

At midday they made a hearty meal. Kayerts sighed from time to time. Whenever they mentioned Makola's name they always added to it an opprobrious epithet. It eased their conscience. Makola gave himself a half-holiday, and bathed his children in the river. No one from Gobila's villages came near the station that day. No one came the next day, and the next, nor for a whole week. Gobila's people might have been dead and buried for any sign of life they gave. But they were only mourning for those they had lost by the witchcraft of white men, who had brought wicked people into their country. The wicked people were gone, but fear remained. Fear always remains. A man may destroy everything within himself, love and hate and belief, and even doubt; but as long as he clings to life he cannot destroy fear: the fear, subtle, indestructible, and terrible, that pervades his being; that tinges his thoughts; that lurks in his heart; that watches on his lips the struggle of his last breath. In his fear, the mild old Gobila offered extra human sacrifices to all the Evil Spirits that had taken possession of his white friends. His heart was heavy. Some warriors spoke about burning and killing, but the cautious old savage dissuaded them. Who could foresee the woe those mysterious creatures, if irritated, might bring.? They should be left alone. Perhaps in time they would disappear into the earth as the first one had disappeared. His people must keep away from them, and hope for the best.

Kayerts and Carlier did not disappear, but remained above on this earth, that, somehow, they fancied had become bigger and very empty. It was not the absolute and dumb solitude of the post that impressed them so much as an inarticulate feeling that something from within them was gone, something that worked for their safety, and had kept the wilderness from interfering with their hearts. The images of home; the memory of people like them, of men that thought and felt as they used to think and feel, receded into distances made indistinct by the glare of unclouded sunshine. And out of the great silence of the surrounding wilderness, its very hopelessness and savagery seemed to approach them nearer, to draw them gently, to look upon them, to envelop them with a solicitude irresistible, familiar, and disgusting.

65

Days lengthened into weeks, then into months. Gobila's people drummed and yelled to every new moon, as of yore, but kept away from the station. Makola and Carlier tried once in a canoe to open communications, but were received with a shower of arrows, and had to fly back to the station for dear life. That attempt set the country up and down the river into an uproar that could be very distinctly heard for days. The steamer was late. At first they spoke of delay jauntily, then anxiously, then gloomily. The matter was becoming serious. Stores were running short. Carlier cast his lines off the bank, but the river was low, and the fish kept out in the stream. They dared not stroll far away from the station to shoot. Moreover, there was no game in the impenetrable forest. Once Carlier shot a hippo in the river. They had no boat to secure it, and it sank. When it floated up it drifted away, and Gobila's people secured the carcase. It was the occasion for a national holiday, but Carlier had a fit of rage over it and talked about the necessity of exterminating all the niggers before the country could be made habitable. Kayerts mooned about silently; spent hours looking at the portrait of his Melie. It represented a little girl with long bleached tresses and a rather sour face. His legs were much swollen, and he could hardly walk. Carlier, undermined by fever, could not swagger any more, but kept tottering about, still with a devil-may-care air, as became a man who remembered his crack regiment. He had become hoarse, sarcastic, and inclined to say unpleasant things. He called it "being frank with you." They had long ago reckoned their percentages on trade, including in them that last deal of "this infamous Makola." They had also concluded not to say anything about it. Kayerts hesitated at first—was afraid of the Director.

"He has seen worse things done on the quiet," maintained Carlier, with a hoarse laugh. "Trust him! He won't thank you if you blab. He is no better than you or me. Who will talk if we hold our tongues? There is nobody here."

That was the root of the trouble! There was nobody there; and being left there alone with their weakness, they became daily more like a pair of accomplices than like a couple of devoted friends. They had heard nothing from home for eight months. Every evening they said, "To-morrow we shall see the steamer." But one of the Company's steamers had been wrecked, and the Director was busy with the other, relieving very distant and important stations on the main river. He thought that the useless station, and the useless men, could wait. Meantime Kayerts and Carlier lived on rice boiled without salt, and cursed the Company, all Africa, and the day they were born. One must have lived on such diet to discover what ghastly trouble the necessity of swallowing one's food may become. There was literally nothing else in the station but rice and coffee; they drank the coffee without sugar. The last fifteen lumps Kayerts had solemnly locked away in his box, together with a half-bottle of Cognâc, "in case of sickness," he explained. Carlier approved. "When one is sick," he said, "any little extra like that is cheering."

They waited. Rank grass began to sprout over the courtyard. The bell never rang now. Days passed, silent, exasperating, and slow. When the two men spoke, they snarled; and their silences were bitter, as if tinged by the bitterness of their thoughts.

One day after a lunch of boiled rice, Carlier put down his cup untasted, and said: "Hang it all! Let's have a decent cup of coffee for once. Bring out that sugar, Kayerts!"

70   "For the sick," muttered Kayerts, without looking up.

"For the sick," mocked Carlier. "Bosh! . . . Well! I am sick."

"You are no more sick than I am, and I go without," said Kayerts in a peaceful tone.

"Come! out with that sugar, you stingy old slave-dealer."

Kayerts looked up quickly. Carlier was smiling with marked insolence. And suddenly it seemed to Kayerts that he had never seen that man before. Who was he? He knew nothing about him. What was he capable of? There was a surprising flash of violent emotion within him, as if in the presence of something undreamt-of, dangerous, and final. But he managed to pronounce with composure—

75   "That joke is in very bad taste. Don't repeat it."

"Joke!" said Carlier, hitching himself forward on his seat. "I am hungry—I am sick—I don't joke! I hate hypocrites. You are a hypocrite. You are a slave-dealer. I am a slave-dealer. There's nothing but slave-dealers in this cursed country. I mean to have sugar in my coffee to-day, anyhow!"

"I forbid you to speak to me in that way," said Kayerts with a fair show of resolution.

"You!—What?" shouted Carlier, jumping up.

Kayerts stood up also. "I am your chief," he began, trying to master the shakiness of his voice.

80   "What?" yelled the other. "Who's chief? There's no chief here. There's nothing here: there's nothing but you and I. Fetch the sugar—you potbellied ass."

"Hold your tongue. Go out of this room," screamed Kayerts. "I dismiss you—you scoundrel!"

Carlier swung a stool. All at once he looked dangerously in earnest. "You flabby, good-for-nothing civilian—take that!" he howled.

Kayerts dropped under the table, and the stool struck the grass inner wall of the room. Then, as Carlier was trying to upset the table, Kayerts in desperation made a blind rush, head low, like a cornered pig would do, and over-turning his friend, bolted along the verandah, and into his room. He locked the door, snatched his revolver, and stood panting. In less than a minute, Carlier was kicking at the door furiously, howling, "If you don't bring out that sugar, I will shoot you at sight, like a dog. Now then—one—two—three. You won't? I will show you who's the master."

Kayerts thought the door would fall in, and scrambled through the square hole that served for a window in his room. There was then the whole breadth of the house between them. But the other was apparently not strong enough to break in the door, and Kayerts heard him running round. Then he also began to run laboriously on his swollen legs. He ran as quickly as he could, grasping the revolver, and unable yet to understand what was happening to him. He saw in succession Makola's house, the store, the river, the ravine, and the low bushes; and he saw all those things again as he ran for the second time round the house. Then again they flashed past him. That morning he could not have walked a yard without a groan.

85   And now he ran. He ran fast enough to keep out of sight of the other man.

Then as, weak and desperate, he thought, "Before I finish the next round I shall die," he heard the other man stumble heavily, then stop. He stopped also. He had the back and Carlier the front of the house, as before. He heard him drop into a chair cursing, and suddenly his own legs gave way, and he slid down into a sitting posture with his back to the wall. His mouth was as dry as a cinder, and his face was wet with perspiration—and tears. What was it all about? He thought it must be a horrible illusion; he thought he was dreaming; he thought he was going mad! After a while he collected his senses. What did they quarrel about? That sugar! How absurd! He would give it to him—didn't want it himself. And he began scrambling to his feet with a sudden feeling of security. But before he had fairly stood upright, a common-sense reflection occurred to him and drove him back into despair. He thought: If I give way now to that brute of a soldier, he will begin this horror again to-morrow—and the day after—every day—raise other pretensions, trample on me, torture me, make me his slave—and I will be lost! Lost! The steamer may not come for days—may never come. He shook so that he had to sit down on the floor again. He shivered forlornly. He felt he could not, would not move any more. He was completely distracted by the sudden perception that the position was without issue—that death and life had in a moment become equally difficult and terrible.

All at once he heard the other push his chair back; and he leaped to his feet with extreme facility. He listened and got confused. Must run again! Right or left? He heard footsteps. He darted to the left, grasping his revolver, and at the very same instant, as it seemed to him, they came into violent collision. Both shouted with surprise. A loud explosion took place between them; a roar of red fire, thick smoke; and Kayerts, deafened and blinded, rushed back thinking: I am hit—it's all over. He expected the other to come round—to gloat over his agony. He caught hold of an upright of the roof—"All over!" Then he heard a crashing fall on the other side of the house, as if somebody had tumbled headlong over a chair—then silence. Nothing more happened. He did not die. Only his shoulder felt as if it had been badly wrenched, and he had lost his revolver. He was disarmed and helpless! He waited for his fate. The other man made no sound. It was a stratagem. He was stalking him now! Along what side? Perhaps he was taking aim this very minute!

After a few moments of an agony frightful and absurd, he decided to go and meet his doom. He was prepared for every surrender. He turned the corner, steadying himself with one hand on the wall; made a few paces, and nearly swooned. He had seen on the floor, protruding past the other corner, a pair of turned-up feet. A pair of white naked feet in red slippers. He felt deadly sick, and stood for a time in profound darkness. Then Makola appeared before him, saying quietly: "Come along, Mr. Kayerts. He is dead." He burst into tears of gratitude; a loud, sobbing fit of crying. After a time he found himself sitting in a chair and looking at Carlier, who lay stretched on his back. Makola was kneeling over the body.

"Is this your revolver?" asked Makola, getting up.

90 "Yes," said Kayerts; then he added very quickly, "He ran after me to shoot me—you saw!"

"Yes, I saw," said Makola. "There is only one revolver; where's his?"

"Don't know," whispered Kayerts in a voice that had become suddenly very faint.

"I will go and look for it," said the other, gently. He made the round along the verandah, while Kayerts sat still and looked at the corpse. Makola came back empty-handed, stood in deep thought, then stepped quietly into the dead man's room, and came out directly with a revolver, which he held up before Kayerts. Kayerts shut his eyes. Everything was going round. He found life more terrible and difficult than death. He had shot an unarmed man.

After meditating for a while, Makola said softly, pointing at the dead man who lay there with his right eye blown out—

95 "He died of fever." Kayerts looked at him with a stony stare. "Yes," repeated Makola, thoughtfully, stepping over the corpse, "I think he died of fever. Bury him to-morrow."

And he went away slowly to his expectant wife, leaving the two white men alone on the verandah.

Night came, and Kayerts sat unmoving on his chair. He sat quiet as if he had taken a dose of opium. The violence of the emotions he had passed through produced a feeling of exhausted serenity. He had plumbed in one short afternoon the depths of horror and despair, and now found repose in the conviction that life had no more secrets for him: neither had death! He sat by the corpse thinking; thinking very actively, thinking very new thoughts. He seemed to have broken loose from himself altogether. His old thoughts, convictions, likes and dislikes, things he respected and things he abhorred, appeared in their true light at last! Appeared contemptible and childish, false and ridiculous. He revelled in his new wisdom while he sat by the man he had killed. He argued with himself about all things under heaven with that kind of wrong-headed lucidity which may be observed in some lunatics. Incidentally he reflected that the fellow dead there had been a noxious beast anyway; that men died every day in thousands; perhaps in hundreds of thousands—who could tell?—and that in the number, that one death could not possibly make any difference; couldn't have any importance, at least to a thinking creature. He, Kayerts, was a thinking creature. He had been all his life, till that moment, a believer in a lot of nonsense like the rest of mankind—who are fools; but now he thought! He knew! He was at peace; he was familiar with the highest wisdom! Then he tried to imagine himself dead, and Carlier sitting in his chair watching him; and his attempt met with such unexpected success, that in a very few moments he became not at all sure who was dead and who was alive. This extraordinary achievement of his fancy startled him, however, and by a clever and timely effort of mind he saved himself just in time from becoming Carlier. His heart thumped, and he felt hot all over at the thought of that danger. Carlier! What a beastly thing! To compose his now disturbed nerves—and no wonder!—he tried to whistle a little. Then, suddenly, he fell asleep, or thought he had slept; but at any rate there was a fog, and somebody had whistled in the fog.

He stood up. The day had come, and a heavy mist had descended upon the land: the mist penetrating, enveloping, and silent; the morning mist of tropical lands; the mist that clings and kills; the mist white and deadly, immaculate and poisonous. He stood up, saw the body, and threw his arms above his head with a cry like that of a man who, waking from a trance, finds himself immured forever in a tomb. "*Help! . . . My God!*"

A shriek inhuman, vibrating and sudden, pierced like a sharp dart the white shroud of that land of sorrow. Three short, impatient screeches followed, and then, for a time, the fog-wreaths rolled on, undisturbed, through a formidable silence. Then many more shrieks, rapid and piercing, like the yells of some exasperated and ruthless creature, rent the air. Progress was calling to Kayerts from the river. Progress and civilization and all the virtues. Society was calling to its accomplished child to come, to be taken care of, to be instructed, to be judged, to be condemned; it called him to return to that rubbish heap from which he had wandered away, so that justice could be done.

Kayerts heard and understood. He stumbled out of the verandah, leaving the other man quite alone for the first time since they had been thrown there together. He groped his way through the fog, calling in his

100

ignorance upon the invisible heaven to undo its work. Makola flitted by in the mist, shouting as he ran—

"Steamer! Steamer! They can't see. They whistle for the station. I go ring the bell. Go down to the landing, sir. I ring."

He disappeared. Kayerts stood still. He looked upwards; the fog rolled low over his head. He looked round like a man who has lost his way; and he saw a dark smudge, a cross-shaped stain, upon the shifting purity of the mist. As he began to stumble towards it, the station bell rang in a tumultuous peal its answer to the impatient clamour of the steamer.

The Managing Director of the Great Civilizing Company (since we know that civilization follows trade) landed first, and incontinently lost sight of the steamer. The fog down by the river was exceedingly dense; above, at the station, the bell rang unceasing and brazen.

The Director shouted loudly to the steamer:

105 "There is nobody down to meet us; there may be something wrong, though they are ringing. You had better come, too!"

And he began to toil up the steep bank. The captain and the engine-driver of the boat followed behind. As they scrambled up the fog thinned, and they could see their Director a good way ahead. Suddenly they saw him start forward, calling to them over his shoulder:—"Run! Run to the house! I've found one of them. Run, look for the other!"

He had found one of them! And even he, the man of varied and startling experience, was somewhat discomposed by the manner of this finding. He stood and fumbled in his pockets (for a knife) while he faced Kayerts, who was hanging by a leather strap from the cross. He had evidently climbed the grave, which was high and narrow, and after tying the end of the strap to the arm, had swung himself off. His toes were only a couple of inches above the ground; his arms hung stiffly down; he seemed to be standing rigidly at attention, but with one purple cheek playfully posed on the shoulder. And, irreverently, he was putting out a swollen tongue at his Managing Director.

(1897)

Charlotte Perkins Gilman   (1860–1935)

Although "The Yellow Wallpaper" has recently been praised as a major feminist short story, it was virtually unknown until the early 1960s, and its author, a native of Hartford, Connecticut, was remembered chiefly as an important theorist in the women's movement during the early decades of this century. In such book-length tracts as *Women and Economics* (1898) and short stories as "If I Were a Man" and "The Widow's Might," she studied the nature of women's lives and their relationships with men. "The Yellow Wallpaper," one of her first short stories, was based on the extreme mental depression she suffered in part as the result of psychiatric treatments prescribed after the birth of her daughter. It was written, she later stated, "not . . . to drive people crazy, but to save people from being driven crazy. . . ."

THE YELLOW WALLPAPER

It is very seldom that mere ordinary people like John and myself secure ancestral halls for the summer.

A colonial mansion, a hereditary estate, I would say a haunted house and reach the height of romantic felicity—but that would be asking too much of fate!

Still I will proudly declare that there is something queer about it.

Else, why should it be let so cheaply? And why have stood so long untenanted?

5 John laughs at me, of course, but one expects that.

John is practical in the extreme. He has no patience with faith, an intense horror of superstition, and he scoffs openly at any talk of things not to be felt and seen and put down in figures.

John is a physician, and *perhaps*—(I would not say it to a living soul, of course, but this is dead paper and a great relief to my mind)—*perhaps* that is one reason I do not get well faster.

You see, he does not believe I am sick! And what can one do?

If a physician of high standing, and one's own husband, assures friends and relatives that there is really nothing the matter with one but temporary nervous depression—a slight hysterical tendency—what is one to do?

10 My brother is also a physician, and also of high standing, and he says the same thing.

So I take phosphates or phosphites—whichever it is—and tonics, and air and exercise, and journeys, and am absolutely forbidden to "work" until I am well again.

Personally, I disagree with their ideas.

Personally, I believe that congenial work, with excitement and change, would do me good.

But what is one to do?

15 I did write for a while in spite of them; but it *does* exhaust me a good deal—having to be so sly about it, or else meet with heavy opposition.

I sometimes fancy that in my condition, if I had less opposition and more society and stimulus—but John says the very worst thing I can do is to think about my condition, and I confess it always makes me feel bad.

So I will let it alone and talk about the house.

The most beautiful place! It is quite alone, standing well back from the road, quite three miles from the village. It makes me think of English places that you read about, for there are hedges and walls and gates that lock, and lots of separate little houses for the gardeners and people.

There is a *delicious* garden! I never saw such a garden—large and shady, full of box-bordered paths, and lined with long grape-covered arbors with seats under them.

There were greenhouses, but they are all broken now.

There was some legal trouble, I believe, something about the heirs and co-heirs; anyhow, the place has been empty for years.

That spoils my ghostliness, I am afraid, but I don't care—there is something strange about the house—I can feel it.

I even said so to John one moonlight evening, but he said what I felt was a draught, and shut the window.

I get unreasonably angry with John sometimes. I'm sure I never used to be so sensitive. I think it is due to this nervous condition.

But John says if I feel so I shall neglect proper self-control; so I take pains to control myself—before him, at least, and that makes me very tired.

I don't like our room a bit. I wanted one downstairs that opened onto the piazza and had roses all over the window, and such pretty old-fashioned chintz hangings! But John would not hear of it.

He said there was only one window and not room for two beds, and no near room for him if he took another.

He is very careful and loving, and hardly lets me stir without special direction.

I have a schedule prescription for each hour in the day; he takes all care from me, and so I feel basely ungrateful not to value it more.

He said he came here solely on my account, that I was to have perfect rest and all the air I could get. "Your exercise depends on your strength, my dear," said he, "and your food somewhat on your appetite; but air you can absorb all the time." So we took the nursery at the top of the house.

It is a big, airy room, the whole floor nearly, with windows that look all ways, and air and sunshine galore. It was nursery first, and then playroom and gymnasium, I should judge, for the windows are barred for little children, and there are rings and things in the walls.

The paint and paper look as if a boys' school had used it. It is stripped off—the paper—in great patches all around the head of my bed, about as far as I can reach, and in a great place on the other side of the room low down. I never saw a worse paper in my life. One of those sprawling, flamboyant patterns committing every artistic sin.

It is dull enough to confuse the eye in following, pronounced enough constantly to irritate and provoke study, and when you follow the lame uncertain curves for a little distance they suddenly commit suicide—plunge off at outrageous angles, destroy themselves in unheard-of contradictions.

The color is repellent, almost revolting: a smouldering unclean yellow, strangely faded by the slow-turning sunlight. It is a dull yet lurid orange in some places, a sickly sulphur tint in others.

No wonder the children hated it! I should hate it myself if I had to live in this room long.

There comes John, and I must put this away—he hates to have me write a word.

We have been here two weeks, and I haven't felt like writing before, since that first day.

I am sitting by the window now, up in this atrocious nursery, and there is nothing to hinder my writing as much as I please, save lack of strength.

John is away all day, and even some nights when his cases are serious.

I am glad my case is not serious!

But these nervous troubles are dreadfully depressing.

John does not know how much I really suffer. He knows there is no reason to suffer, and that satisfies him.

Of course it is only nervousness. It does weigh on me so not to do my duty in any way!

I meant to be such a help to John, such a real rest and comfort, and here I am a comparative burden already!

Nobody would believe what an effort it is to do what little I am able—to dress and entertain, and order things.

It is fortunate Mary is so good with the baby. Such a dear baby!

And yet I *cannot* be with him, it makes me so nervous.

I suppose John never was nervous in his life. He laughs at me so about this wallpaper!

At first he meant to repaper the room, but afterward he said that I was letting it get the better of me, and that nothing was worse for a nervous patient than to give way to such fancies.

He said that after the wallpaper was changed it would be the heavy bedstead, and then the barred windows, and then that gate at the head of the stairs, and so on.

"You know the place is doing you good," he said, "and really, dear, I don't care to renovate the house just for a three months' rental."

"Then do let us go downstairs," I said. "There are such pretty rooms there."

Then he took me in his arms and called me a blessed little goose, and said he would go down cellar, if I wished, and have it whitewashed into the bargain.

But he is right enough about the beds and windows and things.

It is as airy and comfortable a room as anyone need wish, and, of course, I would not be so silly as to make him uncomfortable just for a whim.

I'm really getting quite fond of the big room, all but that horrid paper.

Out of one window I can see the garden—those mysterious deep-shaded arbors, the riotous old-fashioned flowers, and bushes and gnarly trees.

Out of another I get a lovely view of the bay and a little private wharf belonging to the estate. There is a beautiful shaded lane that runs down there from the house. I always fancy I see people walking in these numerous paths and arbors, but John has cautioned me not to give way to fancy in the least. He says that with my imaginative power and habit of story-making, a nervous weakness like mine is sure to lead to all manner of excited fancies, and that I ought to use my will and good sense to check the tendency. So I try.

I think sometimes that if I were only well enough to write a little it would relieve the press of ideas and rest me.

But I find I get pretty tired when I try.

It is so discouraging not to have any advice and companionship about my work. When I get really well, John says we will ask Cousin Henry and Julia down for a long visit; but he says he would as soon put fireworks in my pillow-case as to let me have those stimulating people about now.

I wish I could get well faster.

But I must not think about that. This paper looks to me as if it *knew* what a vicious influence it had!

There is a recurrent spot where the pattern lolls like a broken neck and two bulbous eyes stare at you upside down.

I get positively angry with the impertinence of it and the everlasting-ness. Up and down and sideways they crawl, and those absurd unblinking eyes are everywhere. There is one place where two breadths didn't match, and the eyes go all up and down the line, one a little higher than the other.

I never saw so much expression in an inanimate thing before, and we all know how much expression they have! I used to lie awake as a child and get more entertainment and terror out of blank walls and plain furniture than most children could find in a toy-store.

I remember what a kindly wink the knobs of our big old bureau used to have, and there was one chair that always seemed like a strong friend.

I used to feel that if any of the other things looked too fierce I could always hop into that chair and be safe.

The furniture in this room is no worse than inharmonious, however, for we had to bring it all from downstairs. I suppose when this was used as a playroom they had to take the nursery things out, and no wonder! I never saw such ravages as the children have made here.

The wallpaper, as I said before, is torn off in spots, and it sticketh closer than a brother—they must have had perseverance as well as hatred.

Then the floor is scratched and gouged and splintered, the plaster itself is dug out here and there, and this great heavy bed, which is all we found in the room, looks as if it had been through the wars.

But I don't mind it a bit—only the paper.

There comes John's sister. Such a dear girl as she is, and so careful of me! I must not let her find me writing.

She is a perfect and enthusiastic housekeeper, and hopes for no better profession. I verily believe she thinks it is the writing which made me sick!

But I can write when she is out, and see her a long way off from these windows.

There is one that commands the road, a lovely shaded winding road, and one that just looks off over the country. A lovely country, too, full of great elms and velvet meadows.

This wallpaper has a kind of sub-pattern in a different shade, a particularly irritating one, for you can only see it in certain lights, and not clearly then.

But in the places where it isn't faded and where the sun is just so—I can see a strange, provoking, formless sort of figure that seems to skulk about behind that silly and conspicuous front design.

There's sister on the stairs!

80   Well, the Fourth of July[1] is over! The people are all gone, and I am tired out. John thought it might do me good to see a little company, so we just had Mother and Nellie and the children down for a week.

Of course I didn't do a thing. Jennie sees to everything now.

But it tired me all the same.

John says if I don't pick up faster he shall send me to Weir Mitchell[2] in the fall.

But I don't want to go there at all. I had a friend who was in his hands once, and she says he is just like John and my brother, only more so!

85   Besides, it is such an undertaking to go so far.

I don't feel as if it was worthwhile to turn my hand over for anything, and I'm getting dreadfully fretful and querulous.

I cry at nothing, and cry most of the time.

Of course I don't when John is here, or anybody else, but when I am alone.

And I am alone a good deal just now. John is kept in town very often by serious cases, and Jennie is good and lets me alone when I want her to.

90   So I walk a little in the garden or down that lovely lane, sit on the porch under the roses, and lie down up here a good deal.

I'm getting really fond of the room in spite of the wallpaper. Perhaps *because* of the wallpaper.

It dwells in my mind so!

I lie here on this great immovable bed—it is nailed down, I believe—and follow that pattern about by the hour. It is as good as gymnastics, I assure you. I start, we'll say, at the bottom, down in the corner over there where it has not been touched, and I determine for the thousandth time that I *will* follow that pointless pattern to some sort of a conclusion.

I know a little of the principle of design, and I know this thing was not arranged on any laws of radiation, or alternation, or repetition, or symmetry, or anything else that I ever heard of.

95   It is repeated, of course, by the breadths, but not otherwise.

Looked at in one way, each breadth stands alone; the bloated curves and flourishes—a kind of "debased Romanesque"[3] with delirium tremens—go waddling up and down in isolated columns of fatuity.

---

[1]American Independence Day. [2]Gilman's own physician, Silas Weir Mitchell, popularized the "rest cure" for people suffering from nervous disorders. [3]style of architecture prevalent from the ninth to the twelfth century in Europe, when the Gothic style began to replace it. It is characterized by thick walls and plain, rounded arches supported by columns.

But, on the other hand, they connect diagonally, and the sprawling outlines run off in great slanting waves of optic horror, like a lot of wallowing sea-weeds in full chase.

The whole thing goes horizontally, too, at least it seems so, and I exhaust myself trying to distinguish the order of its going in that direction.

They have used a horizontal breadth for a frieze, and that adds wonderfully to the confusion.

100 There is one end of the room where it is almost intact, and there, when the crosslights fade and the low sun shines directly upon it, I can almost fancy radiation after all—the interminable grotesque seems to form around a common center and rush off in headlong plunges of equal distraction.

It makes me tired to follow it. I will take a nap, I guess.

I don't know why I should write this.

I don't want to.

I don't feel able.

105 And I know John would think it absurd. But I *must* say what I feel and think in some way—it is such a relief!

But the effort is getting to be greater than the relief.

Half the time now I am awfully lazy, and lie down ever so much. John says I mustn't lose my strength, and has me take cod liver oil and lots of tonics and things, to say nothing of ale and wine and rare meat.

Dear John! He loves me very dearly, and hates to have me sick. I tried to have a real earnest reasonable talk with him the other day, and tell him how I wish he would let me go and make a visit to Cousin Henry and Julia.

But he said I wasn't able to go, nor able to stand it after I got there; and I did not make out a very good case for myself, for I was crying before I had finished.

110 It is getting to be a great effort for me to think straight. Just this nervous weakness, I suppose.

And dear John gathered me up in his arms, and just carried me upstairs and laid me on the bed, and sat by me and read to me till it tired my head.

He said I was his darling and his comfort and all he had, and that I must take care of myself for his sake, and keep well.

He says no one but myself can help me out of it, that I must use my will and self-control and not let any silly fancies run away with me.

There's one comfort—the baby is well and happy, and does not have to occupy this nursery with the horrid wallpaper.

115 If we had not used it, that blessed child would have! What a fortunate escape! Why, I wouldn't have a child of mine, an impressionable little thing, live in such a room for worlds.

I never thought of it before, but it is lucky that John kept me here after all; I can stand it so much easier than a baby, you see.

Of course I never mention it to them any more—I am too wise—but I keep watch for it all the same.

There are things in that wallpaper that nobody knows about but me, or ever will.

Behind that outside pattern the dim shapes get clearer every day.

It is always the same shape, only very numerous.

And it is like a woman stooping down and creeping about behind that pattern. I don't like it a bit. I wonder—I begin to think—I wish John would take me away from here!

It is so hard to talk with John about my case, because he is so wise, and because he loves me so.

But I tried it last night.

It was moonlight. The moon shines in all around just as the sun does.

I hate to see it sometimes, it creeps so slowly, and always comes in by one window or another.

John was asleep and I hated to waken him, so I kept still and watched the moonlight on that undulating wallpaper till I felt creepy.

The faint figure behind seemed to shake the pattern, just as if she wanted to get out.

I got up softly and went to feel and see if the paper *did* move, and when I came back John was awake.

"What is it, little girl?" he said. "Don't go walking about like that— you'll get cold."

I thought it was a good time to talk, so I told him that I really was not gaining here, and that I wished he would take me away.

"Why, darling!" said he. "Our lease will be up in three weeks, and I can't see how to leave before.

"The repairs are not done at home, and I cannot possibly leave town just now. Of course, if you were in any danger, I could and would, but you really are better, dear, whether you can see it or not. I am a doctor, dear, and I know. You are gaining flesh and color, your appetite is better, I feel really much easier about you."

"I don't weigh a bit more," said I, "nor as much; and my appetite may be better in the evening when you are here but it is worse in the morning when you are away!"

"Bless her little heart!" said he with a big hug. "She shall be as sick as she pleases! But now let's improve the shining hours by going to sleep, and talk about it in the morning!"

"And you won't go away?" I asked gloomily.

"Why, how can I, dear? It is only three weeks more and then we will take a nice little trip of a few days while Jennie is getting the house ready. Really, dear, you are better!"

"Better in body perhaps—" I began, and stopped short, for he sat up straight and looked at me with such a stern, reproachful look that I could not say another word.

"My darling," said he, "I beg of you, for my sake and for our child's sake, as well as for your own, that you will never for one instant let that idea enter your mind! There is nothing so dangerous, so fascinating, to a temperament like yours. It is a false and foolish fancy. Can you not trust me as a physician when I tell you so?"

So of course I said no more on that score, and we went to sleep before long. He thought I was asleep first, but I wasn't, and lay there for hours trying to decide whether that front pattern and the back pattern really did move together or separately.

On a pattern like this, by daylight, there is a lack of sequence, a defiance of law, that is a constant irritant to a normal mind.

The color is hideous enough, and unreliable enough, and infuriating enough, but the pattern is torturing.

You think you have mastered it, but just as you get well under way in following, it turns a back-somersault and there you are. It slaps you in the face, knocks you down, and tramples upon you. It is like a bad dream.

The outside pattern is a florid arabesque,[4] reminding one of a fungus. If you can imagine a toadstool in joints, an interminable string of toadstools, budding and sprouting in endless convolutions—why, that is something like it.

That is, sometimes!

There is one marked peculiarity about this paper, a thing nobody seems to notice but myself, and that is that it changes as the light changes.

When the sun shoots in through the east window—I always watch for that first long, straight ray—it changes so quickly that I never can quite believe it.

That is why I watch it always.

By moonlight—the moon shines in all night when there is a moon—I wouldn't know it was the same paper.

At night in any kind of light, in twilight, candlelight, lamplight, and worst of all by moonlight, it becomes bars! The outside pattern, I mean, and the woman behind it is as plain as can be.

I didn't realize for a long time what the thing was that showed behind, that dim sub-pattern, but now I am quite sure it is a woman.

By daylight she is subdued, quiet. I fancy it is the pattern that keeps her so still. It is so puzzling. It keeps me quiet by the hour.

I lie down ever so much now. John says it is good for me, and to sleep all I can.

Indeed he started the habit by making me lie down for an hour after each meal.

It is a very bad habit, I am convinced, for you see, I don't sleep.

And that cultivates deceit, for I don't tell them I'm awake—oh, no!

The fact is I am getting a little afraid of John.

He seems very queer sometimes, and even Jennie has an inexplicable look.

It strikes me occasionally, just as a scientific hypothesis, that perhaps it is the paper!

I have watched John when he did not know I was looking, and come into the room suddenly on the most innocent excuses, and I've caught him several times *looking at the paper*! And Jennie too. I caught Jennie with her hand on it once.

She didn't know I was in the room, and when I asked her in a quiet, a very quiet voice, with the most restrained manner possible, what she was doing with the paper, she turned around as if she had been caught stealing, and looked quite angry—asked me why I should frighten her so!

[4]interwoven pattern of flowers and designs.

Then she said that the paper stained everything it touched, that she had found yellow smooches on all my clothes and John's and she wished we would be more careful!

Did not that sound innocent? But I know she was studying that pattern, and I am determined that nobody shall find it out but myself!

Life is very much more exciting now than it used to be. You see, I have something more to expect, to look forward to, to watch. I really do eat better, and am more quiet than I was.

John is so pleased to see me improve! He laughed a little the other day, and said I seemed to be flourishing in spite of my wallpaper.

165   I turned it off with a laugh. I had no intention of telling him it was *because* of the wallpaper—he would make fun of me. He might even want to take me away.

I don't want to leave now until I have found it out. There is a week more, and I think that will be enough.

I'm feeling so much better!

I don't sleep much at night, for it is so interesting to watch developments; but I sleep a good deal during the daytime.

In the daytime it is tiresome and perplexing.

170   There are always new shoots on the fungus, and new shades of yellow all over it. I cannot keep count of them, though I have tried conscientiously.

It is the strangest yellow, that wallpaper! It makes me think of all the yellow things I ever saw—not beautiful ones like buttercups, but old, foul, bad yellow things.

But there is something else about that paper—the smell! I noticed it the moment we came into the room, but with so much air and sun it was not bad. Now we have had a week of fog and rain, and whether the windows are open or not, the smell is here.

It creeps all over the house.

I find it hovering in the dining-room, skulking in the parlor, hiding in the hall, lying in wait for me on the stairs.

175   It gets into my hair.

Even when I go to ride, if I turn my head suddenly and surprise it—there is that smell!

Such a peculiar odor, too! I have spent hours in trying to analyze it, to find what it smelled like.

It is not bad—at first—and very gentle, but quite the subtlest, most enduring odor I ever met.

In this damp weather it is awful. I wake up in the night and find it hanging over me.

180   It used to disturb me at first. I thought seriously of burning the house— to reach the smell.

But now I am used to it. The only thing I can think of that it is like is the *color* of the paper! A yellow smell.

There is a very funny mark on this wall, low down, near the mopboard. A streak that runs round the room. It goes behind every piece of furniture, except the bed, a long, straight, even *smooch*, as if it had been rubbed over and over.

I wonder how it was done and who did it, and what they did it for. Round and round and round—round and round and round—it makes me dizzy!

I really have discovered something at last.

Through watching so much at night, when it changes so, I have finally found out.

The front pattern *does* move—and no wonder! The woman behind shakes it!

Sometimes I think there are a great many women behind, and sometimes only one, and she crawls around fast, and her crawling shakes it all over.

Then in the very bright spots she keeps still, and in the very shady spots she just takes hold of the bars and shakes them hard.

And she is all the time trying to climb through. But nobody could climb through that pattern—it strangles so; I think that is why it has so many heads.

They get through, and then the pattern strangles them off and turns them upside down, and makes their eyes white!

If those heads were covered or taken off it would not be half so bad.

I think that woman gets out in the daytime!

And I'll tell you why—privately—I've seen her!

I can see her out of every one of my windows!

It is the same woman, I know, for she is always creeping, and most women do not creep by daylight.

I see her in that long shaded lane, creeping up and down. I see her in those dark grape arbors, creeping all around the garden.

I see her on that long road under the trees, creeping along, and when a carriage comes she hides under the blackberry vines.

I don't blame her a bit. It must be very humiliating to be caught creeping by daylight!

I always lock the door when I creep by daylight. I can't do it at night, for I know John would suspect something at once.

And John is so queer now that I don't want to irritate him. I wish he would take another room! Besides, I don't want anybody to get that woman out at night but myself.

I often wonder if I could see her out of all the windows at once.

But, turn as fast as I can, I can only see out of one at one time.

And though I always see her, she *may* be able to creep faster than I can turn! I have watched her sometimes away off in the open country, creeping as fast as a cloud shadow in a wind.

If only that top pattern could be gotten off from the under one! I mean to try it, little by little.

I have found out another funny thing, but I shan't tell it this time! It does not do to trust people too much.

There are only two more days to get this paper off, and I believe John is beginning to notice. I don't like the look in his eyes.

And I heard him ask Jennie a lot of professional questions about me. She had a very good report to give.

She said I slept a good deal in the daytime.

John knows I don't sleep very well at night, for all I'm so quiet!

210   He asked me all sorts of questions, too, and pretended to be very loving and kind.

As if I couldn't see through him!

Still, I don't wonder he acts so, sleeping under this paper for three months.

It only interests me, but I feel sure John and Jennie are affected by it.

Hurrah! This is the last day, but it is enough. John is to stay in town over night, and won't be out until this evening.

215   Jennie wanted to sleep with me—the sly thing; but I told her I should undoubtedly rest better for a night all alone.

That was clever, for really I wasn't alone a bit! As soon as it was moonlight and that poor thing began to crawl and shake the pattern, I got up and ran to help her.

I pulled and she shook. I shook and she pulled, and before morning we had peeled off yards of that paper.

A strip about as high as my head and half around the room.

And then when the sun came and that awful pattern began to laugh at me, I declared I would finish it today!

220   We go away tomorrow, and they are moving all my furniture down again to leave things as they were before.

Jennie looked at the wall in amazement, but I told her merrily that I did it out of pure spite at the vicious thing.

She laughed and said she wouldn't mind doing it herself, but I must not get tired.

How she betrayed herself that time!

But I am here, and no person touches this paper but Me—not *alive!*

225   She tried to get me out of the room—it was too patent! But I said it was so quiet and empty and clean now that I believed I would lie down again and sleep all I could, and not to wake me even for dinner—I would call when I woke.

So now she is gone, and the servants are gone, and the things are gone, and there is nothing left but that great bedstead nailed down, with the canvas mattress we found on it.

We shall sleep downstairs tonight, and take the boat home tomorrow.

I quite enjoy the room, now it is bare again.

How those children did tear about here!

230   This bedstead is fairly gnawed!

But I must get to work.

I have locked the door and thrown the key down into the front path.

I don't want to go out, and I don't want to have anybody come in, till John comes.

I want to astonish him.

235   I've got a rope up here that even Jennie did not find. If that woman does get out, and tries to get away, I can tie her!

But I forgot I could not reach far without anything to stand on!

This bed will *not* move!

I tried to lift and push it until I was lame, and then I got so angry I bit off a little piece at one corner—but it hurt my teeth.

Then I peeled off all the paper I could reach standing on the floor. It sticks horribly and the pattern just enjoys it! All those strangled heads and bulbous eyes and waddling fungus growths just shriek with derision!

I am getting angry enough to do something desperate. To jump out of the window would be admirable exercise, but the bars are too strong even to try.

Besides I wouldn't do it. Of course not. I know well enough that a step like that is improper and might be misconstrued.

I don't like to *look* out of the windows even—there are so many of those creeping women, and they creep so fast.

I wonder if they all come out of that wallpaper as I did?

But I am securely fastened now by my well-hidden rope—you don't get *me* out in the road there!

I suppose I shall have to get back behind the pattern when it comes night, and that is hard!

It is so pleasant to be out in this great room and creep around as I please!

I don't want to go outside. I won't, even if Jennie asks me to.

For outside you have to creep on the ground, and everything is green instead of yellow.

But here I can creep smoothly on the floor, and my shoulder just fits in that long smooch around the wall, so I cannot lose my way.

Why, there's John at the door!

It is no use, young man, you can't open it!

How he does call and pound!

Now he's crying to Jennie for an axe.

It would be a shame to break down that beautiful door!

"John, dear!" said I in the gentlest voice. "The key is down by the front steps, under a plantain leaf!"

That silenced him for a few moments.

Then he said, very quietly indeed, "Open the door, my darling!"

"I can't," said I. "The key is down by the front door under a plantain leaf!" And then I said it again, several times, very gently and slowly, and said it so often that he had to go and see, and he got it of course, and came in. He stopped short by the door.

"What is the matter?" he cried. "For God's sake, what are you doing!"

I kept on creeping just the same, but I looked at him over my shoulder.

"I've got out at last," said I, "in spite of you and Jane. And I've pulled off most of the paper, so you can't put me back!"

Now why should that man have fainted? But he did, and right across my path by the wall, so that I had to creep over him every time!

(1892)

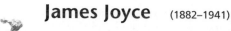

James Joyce (1882–1941)

Although Dublin-born, James Joyce lived most of his adult life in Europe, including twenty years in Paris, where he wrote most of his books about Dublin and its people: *Dubliners,* a collection of short stories; and three novels, *A Portrait of the Artist as a Young Man, Ulysses,* and *Finnegans Wake.* The first three of these were filled with minutely depicted presentations of scenes and characters of Dublin. In *Dubliners,* from which "Araby" is taken, the details are given symbolic meanings that transform specific aspects of late-nineteenth-century Irish life into the universal. Many of the characters experience what Joyce called an "epiphany," a moment of insight in which they understand the nature of their lives. From the opening sentence's reference to a "blind" street to the concluding one's references to the darkness of the bazaar, Joyce carefully selects and arranges details to emphasize the boy's changing attitudes toward himself and his world.

ARABY[1]

North Richmond Street, being blind,[2] was a quiet street except at the hour when the Christian Brothers' School set the boys free. An uninhabited house of two storeys stood at the blind end, detached from its neighbours in a square ground. The other houses of the street, conscious of decent lives within them, gazed at one another with brown imperturbable faces.

The former tenant of our house, a priest, had died in the back drawing-room. Air, musty from having been long enclosed, hung in all the rooms, and the waste room behind the kitchen was littered with old useless papers. Among these I found a few paper-covered books, the pages of which were curled and damp: *The Abbot,*[3] by Walter Scott, *The Devout Communicant*[4] and *The Memoirs of Vidocq.*[5] I liked the last best because its leaves were yellow. The wild garden behind the house contained a central apple-tree and a few straggling bushes under one of which I found the late tenant's rusty bicycle-pump. He had been a very charitable priest; in his will he had left all his money to institutions and the furniture of his house to his sister.

When the short days of winter came dusk fell before we had well eaten our dinners. When we met in the street the houses had grown sombre. The space of sky above us was the colour of ever-changing violet and towards it the lamps of the street lifted their feeble lanterns. The cold air stung us and we played till our bodies glowed. Our shouts echoed in the silent street. The career of our play brought us through the dark muddy lanes behind the houses where we ran the gantlet of the rough tribes from the cottages, to

---

[1]Dublin charity bazaar with a name evoking the romance and mystery of Arabia.
[2]dead-end street. [3]in Sir Walter Scott's 1820 novel set in the sixteenth century, a young man loyally serves Mary Queen of Scots. [4]nineteenth-century religious tract. [5]François Vidocq was an early-nineteenth-century French thief turned detective.

the back doors of the dark dripping gardens where odours arose from the ash-pits, to the dark odorous stables where a coachman smoothed and combed the horse or shook music from the buckled harness. When we returned to the street light from the kitchen windows had filled the areas. If my uncle was seen turning the corner we hid in the shadow until we had seen him safely housed. Or if Mangan's sister came out on the doorstep to call her brother in to his tea we watched her from our shadow peer up and down the street. We waited to see whether she would remain or go in and, if she remained, we left our shadow and walked up to Mangan's steps resignedly. She was waiting for us, her figure defined by the light from the half-opened door. Her brother always teased her before he obeyed and I stood by the railings looking at her. Her dress swung as she moved her body and the soft rope of her hair tossed from side to side.

Every morning I lay on the floor in the front parlour watching her door. The blind was pulled down to within an inch of the sash so that I could not be seen. When she came out on the doorstep my heart leaped. I ran to the hall, seized my books and followed her. I kept her brown figure always in my eye and, when we came near the point at which our ways diverged, I quickened my pace and passed her. This happened morning after morning. I had never spoken to her, except for a few casual words, and yet her name was like a summons to all my foolish blood.

Her image accompanied me even in places the most hostile to romance. On Saturday evenings when my aunt went marketing I had to go to carry some of the parcels. We walked through the flaring streets, jostled by drunken men and bargaining women, amid the curses of labourers, the shrill litanies of shop-boys who stood on guard by the barrels of pigs' cheeks, the nasal chanting of street-singers, who sang a *come-all-you* about O'Donovan Rossa,[6] or a ballad about the troubles in our native land. These noises converged in a single sensation of life for me: I imagined that I bore my chalice safely through a throng of foes. Her name sprang to my lips at moments in strange prayers and praises which I myself did not understand. My eyes were often full of tears (I could not tell why) and at times a flood from my heart seemed to pour itself out into my bosom. I thought little of the future. I did not know whether I would ever speak to her or not or, if I spoke to her, how I could tell her of my confused adoration. But my body was like a harp and her words and gestures were like fingers running upon the wires.

One evening I went into the back drawing-room in which the priest had died. It was a dark rainy evening and there was no sound in the house. Through one of the broken panes I heard the rain impinge upon the earth, the fine incessant needles of water playing in the sodden beds. Some distant lamp or lighted window gleamed below me. I was thankful that I could see so little. All my senses seemed to desire to veil themselves and, feeling that I was about to slip from them, I pressed the palms of my hands together until they trembled, murmuring: *O love! O love!* many times.

At last she spoke to me. When she addressed the first words to me I was so confused that I did not know what to answer. She asked me was I going

[6]popular street ballad about a nineteenth-century Irish revolutionary

to *Araby*. I forget whether I answered yes or no. It would be a splendid bazaar, she said; she would love to go.

—And why can't you? I asked.

While she spoke she turned a silver bracelet round and round her wrist. She could not go, she said, because there would be a retreat that week in her convent. Her brother and two other boys were fighting for their caps and I was alone at the railings. She held one of the spikes, bowing her head towards me. The light from the lamp opposite our door caught the white curve of her neck, lit up her hair that rested there and, falling, lit up the hand upon the railing. It fell over one side of her dress and caught the white border of a petticoat, just visible as she stood at ease.

10 —It's well for you, she said.

—If I go, I said, I will bring you something.

What innumerable follies laid waste my waking and sleeping thoughts after that evening! I wished to annihilate the tedious intervening days. I chafed against the work of school. At night in my bedroom and by day in the classroom her image came between me and the page I strove to read. The syllables of the word *Araby* were called to me through the silence in which my soul luxuriated and cast an Eastern enchantment over me. I asked for leave to go to the bazaar on Saturday night. My aunt was surprised and hoped it was not some Freemason[7] affair. I answered few questions in class. I watched my master's face pass from amiability to sternness; he hoped I was not beginning to idle. I could not call my wandering thoughts together. I had hardly any patience with the serious work of life which, now that it stood between me and my desire, seemed to me child's play, ugly monotonous child's play.

On Saturday morning I reminded my uncle that I wished to go to the bazaar in the evening. He was fussing at the hallstand, looking for the hat-brush, and answered me curtly:

—Yes, boy, I know.

15 As he was in the hall I could not go into the front parlour and lie at the window. I left the house in bad humour and walked slowly towards the school. The air was pitilessly raw and already my heart misgave me.

When I came home to dinner my uncle had not yet been home. Still it was early. I sat staring at the clock for some time and, when its ticking began to irritate me, I left the room. I mounted the staircase and gained the upper part of the house. The high cold empty gloomy rooms liberated me and I went from room to room singing. From the front window I saw my companions playing below in the street. Their cries reached me weakened and indistinct and, leaning my forehead against the cool glass, I looked over at the dark house where she lived. I may have stood there for an hour, seeing nothing but the brown-clad figure cast by my imagination, touched discreetly by the lamplight at the curved neck, at the hand upon the railings and at the border below the dress.

When I came downstairs again I found Mrs Mercer sitting at the fire. She was an old garrulous woman, a pawnbroker's widow, who collected used

[7]the Protestant Masons were considered enemies of Irish Roman Catholics.

stamps for some pious purpose. I had to endure the gossip of the tea-table. The meal was prolonged beyond an hour and still my uncle did not come. Mrs Mercer stood up to go: she was sorry she couldn't wait any longer, but it was after eight o'clock and she did not like to be out late, as the night air was bad for her. When she had gone I began to walk up and down the room, clenching my fists. My aunt said:

—I'm afraid you may put off your bazaar for this night of Our Lord.

At nine o'clock I heard my uncle's latchkey in the halldoor. I heard him talking to himself and heard the hallstand rocking when it had received the weight of his overcoat. I could interpret these signs. When he was midway through his dinner I asked him to give me the money to go to the bazaar. He had forgotten.

20   —The people are in bed and after their first sleep now, he said.

I did not smile. My aunt said to him energetically:

—Can't you give him the money and let him go? You've kept him late enough as it is.

My uncle said he was very sorry he had forgotten. He said he believed in the old saying: *All work and no play makes Jack a dull boy.* He asked where I was going and, when I had told him a second time he asked me did I know *The Arab's Farewell to his Steed.*[8] When I left the kitchen he was about to recite the opening lines of the piece to my aunt.

I held a florin[9] tightly in my hand as I strode down Buckingham Street towards the station. The sight of the streets thronged with buyers and glaring with gas recalled to me the purpose of my journey. I took my seat in a third-class carriage of a deserted train. After an intolerable delay the train moved out of the station slowly. It crept onward among ruinous houses and over the twinkling river. At Westland Row Station a crowd of people pressed to the carriage doors; but the porters moved them back, saying that it was a special train for the bazaar. I remained alone in the bare carriage. In a few minutes the train drew up beside an improvised wooden platform. I passed out on to the road and saw by the lighted dial of a clock that it was ten minutes to ten. In front of me was a large building which displayed the magical name.

25   I could not find any sixpenny entrance and, fearing that the bazaar would be closed, I passed in quickly through a turnstile, handing a shilling to a weary-looking man. I found myself in a big hall girdled at half its height by a gallery. Nearly all the stalls were closed and the greater part of the hall was in darkness. I recognized a silence like that which pervades a church after a service. I walked into the centre of the bazaar timidly. A few people were gathered about the stalls which were still open. Before a curtain, over which the words *Café Chantant* were written in coloured lamps, two men were counting money on a salver. I listened to the fall of the coins.

Remembering with difficulty why I had come I went over to one of the stalls and examined porcelain vases and flowered tea-sets. At the door of the

---

[8] sentimental nineteenth-century poem about a man who, disconsolate at selling his horse, reclaims it. [9] two-shilling coin worth about 50 cents at that time.

stall a young lady was talking and laughing with two young gentlemen. I remarked their English accents and listened vaguely to their conversation.

—Oh, I never said such a thing!

—O, but you did!

—O, but I didn't!

30   —Didn't she say that?

—Yes. I heard her.

—O, there's a . . . fib!

Observing me the young lady came over and asked me did I wish to buy anything. The tone of her voice was not encouraging; she seemed to have spoken to me out of a sense of duty. I looked humbly at the great jars that stood like eastern guards at either side of the dark entrance to the stall and murmured:

—No, thank you.

35   The young lady changed the position of one of the vases and went back to the two young men. They began to talk of the same subject. Once or twice the young lady glanced at me over her shoulder.

I lingered before her stall, though I knew my stay was useless, to make my interest in her wares seem the more real. Then I turned away slowly and walked down the middle of the bazaar. I allowed the two pennies to fall against the sixpence in my pocket. I heard a voice call from one end of the gallery that the light was out. The upper part of the hall was now completely dark.

Gazing up into the darkness I saw myself as a creature driven and derided by vanity; and my eyes burned with anguish and anger.

(1914)

Katherine Mansfield (1888–1923)

Born in Wellington, New Zealand, Katherine Mansfield (the pseudonym of Kathleen Beauchamp) moved to London when she was twenty and shortly after began her career as a writer. Critics have compared her works to those of Russian author Anton Chekhov, whose ironic view of life and whose technical innovations, particularly the use of small details to reveal character, she greatly admired. In her collections of short stories, three of which—*In a German Pension, Bliss,* and *The Garden Party*—were published during her life, she examined the nature of childhood and the troubled relationships between men and women. The description of the heroine's activities in the early pages of "Bliss" reveals the happiness Bertha feels as she prepares for a dinner party, while later details indicate her changing emotions.

BLISS

Although Bertha Young was thirty she still had moments like this when she wanted to run instead of walk, to take dancing steps on and off the pavement, to bowl a hoop, to throw something up in the air and catch it again, or to stand still and laugh at—nothing—at nothing, simply.

What can you do if you are thirty and, turning the corner of your own street, you are overcome, suddenly, by a feeling of bliss—absolute bliss!—as though you'd suddenly swallowed a bright piece of that late afternoon sun and it burned in your bosom, sending out a little shower of sparks into every particle, into every finger and toe? . . .

Oh, is there no way you can express it without being "drunk and disorderly"? How idiotic civilization is! Why be given a body if you have to keep it shut up in a case like a rare, rare fiddle?

"No, that about the fiddle is not quite what I mean," she thought, running up the steps and feeling in her bag for the key—she's forgotten it, as usual—and rattling the letter-box. "It's not what I mean, because—Thank you, Mary"—she went into the hall. "Is nurse back?"

5   "Yes, M'm."

"And has the fruit come?"

"Yes, M'm. Everything's come."

"Bring the fruit up to the dining-room, will you? I'll arrange it before I go upstairs."

It was dusky in the dining-room and quite chilly. But all the same Bertha threw off her coat; she could not bear the tight clasp of it another moment, and the cold air fell on her arms.

10   But in her bosom there was still that bright glowing place—that shower of little sparks coming from it. It was almost unbearable. She hardly dared to breathe for fear of fanning it higher, and yet she breathed deeply, deeply. She hardly dared to look into the cold mirror—but she did look, and it gave her back a woman, radiant, with smiling, trembling lips, with big, dark eyes and an air of listening, waiting for something . . . divine to happen . . . that she knew must happen . . . infallibly.

Mary brought in the fruit on a tray and with it a glass bowl, and a blue dish, very lovely, with a strange sheen on it as though it had been dipped in milk.

"Shall I turn on the light, M'm?"

"No, thank you. I can see quite well."

There were tangerines and apples stained with strawberry pink. Some yellow pears, smooth as silk, some white grapes covered with a silver bloom and a big cluster of purple ones. These last she had bought to tone in with the new dining-room carpet. Yes, that did sound rather far-fetched and absurd, but it was really why she had bought them. She had thought in the shop: "I must have some purple ones to bring the carpet up to the table." And it had seemed quite sense at the time.

15   When she had finished with them and had made two pyramids of these bright round shapes, she stood away from the table to get the effect—and it really was most curious. For the dark table seemed to melt into the dusky light and the glass dish and the blue bowl to float in the air. This, of course in her present mood, was so incredibly beautiful . . . . She began to laugh.

"No, no. I'm getting hysterical." And she seized her bag and coat and ran upstairs to the nursery.

Nurse sat at a low table giving Little B her supper after her bath. The baby had on a white flannel gown and a blue woollen jacket, and her dark, fine hair was brushed up into a funny little peak. She looked up when she saw her mother and began to jump.

"Now, my lovey, eat it up like a good girl," said Nurse, setting her lips in a way that Bertha knew, and that meant she had come into the nursery at another wrong moment.

"Has she been good, Nanny?"

20   "She's been a little sweet all the afternoon," whispered Nanny. "We went to the park and I sat down on a chair and took her out of the pram and a big dog came along and put his head on my knee and she clutched its ear, tugged it. Oh, you should have seen her."

Bertha wanted to ask if it wasn't rather dangerous to let her clutch at a strange dog's ear. But she did not dare to. She stood watching them, her hands by her side, like the poor little girl in front of the rich little girl with the doll.

The baby looked up at her again, stared, and then smiled so charmingly that Bertha couldn't help crying:

"Oh, Nanny, do let me finish giving her her supper while you put the bath things away."

"Well, M'm, she oughtn't to be changed hands while she's eating," said Nanny, still whispering. "It unsettles her; it's very likely to upset her."

25   How absurd it was. Why have a baby if it has to be kept—not in a case like a rare, rare fiddle—but in another woman's arms?

"Oh, I must!" said she.

Very offended, Nanny handed her over.

"Now, don't excite her after her supper. You know you do, M'm. And I have such a time with her after!"

Thank heaven! Nanny went out of the room with the bath towels.

30   "Now I've got you to myself, my little precious," said Bertha, as the baby leaned against her.

She ate delightfully, holding up her lips for the spoon and then waving her hands. Sometimes she wouldn't let the spoon go; and sometimes, just as Bertha had filled it, she waved it away to the four winds.

When the soup was finished Bertha turned round to the fire.

"You're nice—you're very nice!" said she, kissing her warm baby. "I'm fond of you. I like you."

And, indeed, she loved Little B so much—her neck as she bent forward, her exquisite toes as they shone transparent in the firelight—that all her feeling of bliss came back again, and again she didn't know how to express it—what to do with it.

35 "You're wanted on the telephone," said Nanny, coming back in triumph and seizing *her* Little B.

Down she flew. It was Harry.

"Oh, is that you, Ber? Look here. I'll be late. I'll take a taxi and come along as quickly as I can, but get dinner put back ten minutes—will you? All right?"

"Yes, perfectly. Oh, Harry!"

"Yes?"

40 What had she to say? She'd nothing to say. She only wanted to get in touch with him for a moment. She couldn't absurdly cry: "Hasn't it been a divine day!"

"What is it?" rapped out the little voice.

"Nothing. *Entendu*,"[1] said Bertha, and hung up the receiver, thinking how more than idiotic civilization was.

They had people coming to dinner. The Norman Knights—a very sound couple—he was about to start a theatre, and she was awfully keen on interior decoration, a young man, Eddie Warren, who had just published a little book of poems and whom everybody was asking to dine, and a "find" of Bertha's called Pearl Fulton. What Miss Fulton did, Bertha didn't know. They had met at the club and Bertha had fallen in love with her, as she always did fall in love with beautiful women who had something strange about them.

The provoking thing was that, though they had been about together and met a number of times and really talked, Bertha couldn't yet make her out. Up to a certain point Miss Fulton was rarely, wonderfully frank, but the certain point was there, and beyond that she would not go.

45 Was there anything beyond it? Harry said "No." Voted her dullish, and "cold like all blond women, with a touch, perhaps, of anaemia of the brain." But Bertha wouldn't agree with him; not yet, at any rate.

"No, the way she has of sitting with her head a little on one side, and smiling, has something behind it, Harry, and I must find out what that something is."

"Most likely it's a good stomach," answered Harry.

He made a point of catching Bertha's heels with replies of that kind . . . "liver frozen, my dear girl," or "pure flatulence," or "kidney disease," . . . and

[1]understood, agreed.

so on. For some strange reason Bertha liked this, and almost admired it in him very much.

She went into the drawing-room and lighted the fire; then, picking up the cushions, one by one, that Mary had disposed so carefully, she threw them back on to the chairs and the couches. That made all the difference; the room came alive at once. As she was about to throw the last one she surprised herself by suddenly hugging it to her, passionately, passionately. But it did not put out the fire in her bosom. Oh, on the contrary!

50 The windows of the drawing-room opened on to a balcony overlooking the garden. At the far end, against the wall, there was a tall, slender pear tree in fullest, richest bloom; it stood perfect, as though becalmed against the jade-green sky. Bertha couldn't help feeling, even from this distance, that it had not a single bud or a faded petal. Down below, in the garden beds, the red and yellow tulips, heavy with flowers, seemed to lean upon the dusk. A grey cat, dragging its belly, crept across the lawn, and a black one, its shadow, trailed after. The sight of them, so intent and so quick, gave Bertha a curious shiver.

"What creepy things cats are!" she stammered, and she turned away from the window and began walking up and down. . . .

How strong the jonquils smelled in the warm room. Too strong? Oh, no. And yet, as though overcome, she flung down on a couch and pressed her hands to her eyes.

"I'm too happy—too happy!" she murmured.

And she seemed to see on her eyelids the lovely pear tree with its wide open blossoms as a symbol of her own life.

55 Really—really—she had everything. She was young. Harry and she were as much in love as ever, and they got on together splendidly and were really good pals. She had an adorable baby. They didn't have to worry about money. They had this absolutely satisfactory house and garden. And friends—modern, thrilling friends, writers and painters and poets or people keen on social questions—just the kind of friends they wanted. And then there were books, and there was music, and she had found a wonderful little dressmaker, and they were going abroad in the summer, and their new cook made the most superb omelettes. . . .

"I'm absurd! Absurd!" She sat up; but she felt quite dizzy, quite drunk. It must have been the spring.

Yes, it was the spring. Now she was so tired she could not drag herself upstairs to dress.

A white dress, a string of jade beads, green shoes and stockings. It wasn't intentional. She had thought of this scheme hours before she stood at the drawing-room window.

Her petals rustled softly into the hall, and she kissed Mrs. Norman Knight, who was taking off the most amusing orange coat with a procession of black monkeys round the hem and up the fronts.

60 ". . . Why! Why! Why is the middle-class so stodgy—so utterly without a sense of humour! My dear, it's only by a fluke that I am here at all—Norman being the protective fluke. For my darling monkeys so upset the train that it rose to a man and simply ate me with its eyes. Didn't

laugh—wasn't amused—that I should have loved. No, just stared—and bored me through and through."

"But the cream of it was," said Norman, pressing a large tortoise-shell-rimmed monocle into his eye, "you don't mind me telling this, Face, do you?" (In their home and among their friends they called each other Face and Mug.) "The cream of it was when she, being full fed, turned to the woman beside her and said: 'Haven't you ever seen a monkey before?'"

"Oh, yes!" Mrs. Norman Knight joined in the laughter. "Wasn't that too absolutely creamy?"

And a funnier thing still was that now her coat was off she did look like a very intelligent monkey—who had even made that yellow silk dress out of scraped banana skins. And her amber ear-rings; they were like little dangling nuts.

"This is a sad, sad fall!" said Mug, pausing in front of Little B's perambulator. "When the perambulator comes into the hall—" and he waved the rest of the quotation away.

65   The bell rang. It was lean, pale Eddie Warren (as usual) in a state of acute distress.

"It *is* the right house, *isn't it?*" he pleaded.

"Oh, I think so—I hope so," said Bertha brightly.

"I have had such a *dreadful* experience with a taxi-man; he was *most* sinister. I couldn't get him to *stop*. The *more* I knocked and called the *faster* he went. And *in* the moonlight this *bizarre* figure with the *flattened* head *crouching* over the *lit-tle* wheel. . . ."

He shuddered, taking off an immense white silk scarf. Bertha noticed that his socks were white, too—most charming.

70   "But how dreadful!" she cried.

"Yes, it really was," said Eddie, following her into the drawing-room. "I saw myself *driving* through Eternity in a *timeless* taxi."

He knew the Norman Knights. In fact, he was going to write a play for N.K. when the theatre scheme came off.

"Well, Warren, how's the play?" said Norman Knight, dropping his monocle and giving his eye a moment in which to rise to the surface before it was screwed down again.

And Mrs. Norman Knight: "Oh, Mr. Warren, what happy socks?"

75   "I *am* so glad you like them," said he, staring at his feet. "They seem to have got so *much* whiter since the moon rose." And he turned his lean sorrowful young face to Bertha. "There *is* a moon, you know."

She wanted to cry: "I am sure there is—often—often!"

He really was a most attractive person. But so was Face, crouched before the fire in her banana skins, and so was Mug, smoking a cigarette and saying as he flicked the ash: "Why doth the bridegroom tarry?"

"There he is, now."

Bang went the front door open and shut. Harry shouted: "Hullo, you people. Down in five minutes." And they heard him swarm up the stairs. Bertha couldn't help smiling; she knew how he loved doing things at high pressure. What, after all, did an extra five minutes matter? But he would pretend to himself that they mattered beyond measure. And then he would make a great point of coming into the drawing-room, extravagantly cool and collected.

Harry had such a zest for life. Oh, how she appreciated it in him. And his passion for fighting—for seeking in everything that came up against him another test of his power and of his courage—that, too, she understood. Even when it made him just occasionally, to other people, who didn't know him well, a little ridiculous perhaps. . . . For there were moments when he rushed into battle where no battle was. . . . She talked and laughed and positively forgot until he had come in (just as she had imagined) that Pearl Fulton had not turned up.

"I wonder if Miss Fulton has forgotten?"

"I expect so," said Harry. "Is she on the 'phone?"

"Ah! There's a taxi, now." And Bertha smiled with that little air of proprietorship that she always assumed while her women finds were new and mysterious. "She lives in taxis."

"She'll run to fat if she does," said Harry coolly, ringing the bell for dinner. "Frightful danger for blond women."

"Harry—don't," warned Bertha, laughing up at him.

Came another tiny moment, while they waited, laughing and talking, just a trifle too much at their ease, a trifle too unaware. And then Miss Fulton, all in silver, with a silver fillet binding her pale blond hair, came in smiling, her head a little on one side.

"Am I late?"

"No, not at all," said Bertha. "Come along." And she took her arm and they moved into the dining-room.

What was there in the touch of that cool arm that could fan—fan—start blazing—blazing—the fire of bliss that Bertha did not know what to do with?

Miss Fulton did not look at her; but then she seldom did look at people directly. Her heavy eyelids lay upon her eyes and the strange half smile came and went upon her lips as though she lived by listening rather than seeing. But Bertha knew, suddenly, as if the longest, most intimate look had passed between them—as if they had said to each other: "You, too?"—that Pearl Fulton, stirring the beautiful red soup in the grey plate, was feeling just what she was feeling.

And the others? Face and Mug, Eddie and Harry, their spoons rising and falling—dabbing their lips with their napkins, crumbling bread, fiddling with the forks and glasses and talking.

"I met her at the Alpha shore—the weirdest little person. She'd not only cut off her hair, but she seemed to have taken a dreadfully good snip off her legs and arms and her neck and her poor little nose as well."

"Isn't she very *liée*[2] with Michael Oat?"

"The man who wrote *Love in False Teeth?*"

"He wants to write a play for me. One act. One man. Decides to commit suicide. Gives all the reasons why he should and why he shouldn't. And just as he has made up his mind either to do it or not to do it—curtain. Not half a bad idea."

___

[2]attached (involved).

"What's he going to call it—'Stomach Trouble'?"

"I *think* I've come across the *same* idea in a lit-tle French review, *quite* unknown in England."

No, they didn't share it. They were dears—dears—and she loved having them there, at her table, and giving them delicious food and wine. In fact, she longed to tell them how delightful they were, and what a decorative group they made, how they seemed to set one another off and how they reminded her of a play by Tchekof![3]

Harry was enjoying his dinner. It was part of his—well, not his nature, exactly, and certainly not his pose—his—something or other—to talk about food and to glory in his "shameless passion for the white flesh of the lobster" and "the green of pistachio ices—green and cold like the eyelids of Egyptian dancers."

100   When he looked up at her and said: "Bertha, this is a very admirable *soufflée!*" she almost could have wept with child-like pleasure.

Oh, why did she feel so tender towards the whole world tonight? Everything was good—was right. All that happened seemed to fill again her brimming cup of bliss.

And still, in the back of her mind, there was the pear tree. It would be silver now, in the light of poor dear Eddie's moon, silver as Miss Fulton, who sat there turning a tangerine in her slender fingers that were so pale a light seemed to come from them.

What she simply couldn't make out—what was miraculous—was how she should have guessed Miss Fulton's mood so exactly and so instantly. For she never doubted for a moment that she was right, and yet what had she to go on? Less than nothing.

"I believe this does happen very, very rarely between women. Never between men," thought Bertha. "But while I am making the coffee in the drawing-room perhaps she will 'give a sign.'"

105   What she meant by that she did not know, and what would happen after that she could not imagine.

While she thought like this she saw herself talking and laughing. She had to talk because of her desire to laugh.

"I must laugh or die."

But when she noticed Face's funny little habit of tucking something down the front of her bodice—as if she kept a tiny, secret hoard of nuts there, too—Bertha had to dig her nails into her hands—so as not to laugh too much.

It was over at last. And: "Come and see my new coffee machine," said Bertha.

110   "We only have a new coffee machine once a fortnight," said Harry. Face took her arm this time; Miss Fulton bent her head and followed after.

The fire had died down in the drawing-room to a red, flickering "nest of baby phoenixes," said Face.

"Don't turn up the light for a moment. It is so lovely." And down she crouched by the fire again. She was always cold . . . "without her little red flannel jacket, of course," thought Bertha.

[3]Anton Chekhov, nineteenth-century Russian writer of ironic dramas and short stories.

At that moment Miss Fulton "gave the sign."

"Have you a garden?" said the cool, sleepy voice.

115   This was so exquisite on her part that all Bertha could do was to obey. She crossed the room, pulled the curtains apart, and opened those long windows.

"There!" she breathed.

And the two women stood side by side looking at the slender, flowering tree. Although it was so still it seemed, like the flame of a candle, to stretch up, to point, to quiver in the bright air, to grow taller and taller as they gazed—almost to touch the rim of the round, silver moon.

How long did they stand there? Both, as it were, caught in that circle of unearthly light, understanding each other perfectly, creatures of another world, and wondering what they were to do in this one with all this blissful treasure that burned in their bosoms and dropped, in silver flowers, from their hair and hands?

For ever—for a moment? And did Miss Fulton murmur: "Yes. Just *that*." Or did Bertha dream it?

120   Then the light was snapped on and Face made the coffee and Harry said: "My dear Mrs. Knight, don't ask me about my baby. I never see her. I shan't feel the slightest interest in her until she has a lover," and Mug took his eye out of the conservatory for a moment and then put it under glass again and Eddie Warren drank his coffee and set down the cup with a face of anguish as though he had drunk and seen the spider.

"What I want to do is to give the young men a show. I believe London is simply teeming with first-chop, unwritten plays. What I want to say to 'em is: 'Here's the theatre. Fire ahead.'"

"You know, my dear, I am going to decorate a room for the Jacob Nathans. Oh, I am so tempted to do a fried fish scheme, with the backs of the chairs shaped like frying pans and lovely chip potatoes embroidered all over the curtains."

"The trouble with our young writing men is that they are still too romantic. You can't put out to sea without being seasick and wanting a basin. Well, why won't they have the courage of those basins?"

"A *dreadful* poem about a *girl* who was *violated* by a beggar *without* a nose in a lit-tle wood. . . ."

125   Miss Fulton sank into the lowest, deepest chair and Harry handed round the cigarettes.

From the way he stood in front of her shaking the silver box and saying abruptly: "Egyptian? Turkish? Virginian? They're all mixed up," Bertha realized that she not only bored him; he really disliked her. And she decided from the way Miss Fulton said: "No, thank you, I won't smoke," that she felt it, too, and was hurt.

"Oh, Harry, don't dislike her. You are quite wrong about her. She's wonderful, wonderful. And, besides, how can you feel so differently about some one who means so much to me. I shall try to tell you when we are in bed tonight what has been happening. What she and I have shared."

At those last words something strange and almost terrifying darted into Bertha's mind. And this something blind and smiling whispered to her: "Soon these people will go. The house will be quiet—quiet. The lights will be out. And you and he will be alone together in the dark room—the warm bed. . . ."

She jumped up from her chair and ran over to the piano.

130 "What a pity some one does not play!" she cried. "What a pity somebody does not play."

For the first time in her life Bertha Young desired her husband.

Oh, she'd loved him—she'd been in love with him, of course, in every other way, but just not in that way. And, equally, of course, she'd understood that he was different. They'd discussed it so often. It had worried her dreadfully at first to find that she was so cold, but after a time it had not seemed to matter. They were so frank with each other—such good pals. That was the best of being modern.

But now—ardently! ardently! The word ached in her ardent body! Was this what that feeling of bliss had been leading up to? But then—then—

"My dear," said Mrs. Norman Knight, "you know our shame. We are the victims of time and train. We live in Hampstead. It's been so nice."

135 "I'll come with you into the hall," said Bertha. "I love having you. But you must not miss the last train. That's so awful, isn't it?"

"Have a whisky, Knight, before you go?" called Harry.

"No, thanks, old chap."

Bertha squeezed his hand for that as she shook it.

"Good night, good-bye," she cried from the top step, feeling that this self of hers was taking leave of them for ever.

140 When she got back into the drawing-room the others were on the move.

" . . . Then you can come part of the way in my taxi."

"I shall be *so* thankful *not* to have to face *another* drive *alone* after my *dreadful* experience."

"You can get a taxi at the rank just at the end of the street. You won't have to walk more than a few yards."

"That's comfort. I'll go and put on my coat."

145 Miss Fulton moved towards the hall and Bertha was following when Harry almost pushed past.

"Let me help you."

Bertha knew that he was repenting his rudeness—she let him go. What a boy he was in some ways—so impulsive—so—simple.

And Eddie and she were left by the fire.

"I *wonder* if you have seen Bilks' *new* poem called *Table d'Hôte*," said Eddie softly. "It's *so* wonderful. In the last Anthology. Have you got a copy? I'd *so* like to *show* it to you. It begins with an *incredibly* beautiful line: 'Why Must it Always be Tomato Soup?' "

150 "Yes," said Bertha. And she moved noiselessly to a table opposite the drawing-room door and Eddie glided noiselessly after her. She picked up the little book and gave it to him; they had not made a sound.

While he looked it up she turned her head towards the hall. And she saw . . . Harry with Miss Fulton's coat in his arms and Miss Fulton with her back turned to him and her head bent. He tossed the coat away, put his hands on her shoulders and turned her violently to him. His lips said:

"I adore you," and Miss Fulton laid her moonbeam fingers on his cheeks and smiled her sleepy smile. Harry's nostrils quivered; his lips curled back in a hideous grin while he whispered: "Tomorrow," and with her eyelids Miss Fulton said "Yes."

"Here it is," said Eddie. " 'Why Must it Always be Tomato Soup?' It's so *deeply* true, don't you feel? Tomato soup is so *dreadfully* eternal."

"If you prefer," said Harry's voice, very loud, from the hall, "I can 'phone you a cab to come to the door."

"Oh, no. It's not necessary," said Miss Fulton, and she came up to Bertha and gave her the slender fingers to hold.

155 "Good-bye. Thank you so much."

"Good-bye," said Bertha.

Miss Fulton held her hand a moment longer.

"Your lovely pear tree!" she murmured.

And then she was gone, with Eddie following, like the black cat following the grey cat.

160 "I'll shut up shop," said Harry, extravagantly cool and collected.

"Your lovely pear tree—pear tree—pear tree!"

Bertha simply ran over to the long windows.

"Oh, what is going to happen now?" she cried.

But the pear tree was as lovely as ever and as full of flower and as still.

(1918)

Katherine Anne Porter   (1890–1980)

Born in Indian Creek, Texas, Katherine Anne Porter lived and worked in Fort Worth, Chicago, Denver, New York, Mexico, and Germany, all places that she used as settings for her short stories, which she referred to as outgrowths of her "constant exercise of memory." Her works, many of which are set in the rural South, are noted for their compression, intensity of emotion, and precise use of small details to portray the complexities of the characters and their strained relationships. "Rope," which relates in part to the breakup of her second marriage, is set in an unspecified country location, whose isolation seems to intensify the animosity the husband and wife feel toward each other. Their reactions to the length of rope bought by the husband reveal the complexity of the conflicts they face.

ROPE

On the third day after they moved to the country he came walking back from the village carrying a basket of groceries and a twenty-four-yard coil of rope. She came out to meet him, wiping her hands on her green smock. Her hair was tumbled, her nose was scarlet with sunburn; he told her that already she looked like a born country woman. His gray flannel shirt stuck to him, his heavy shoes were dusty. She assured him he looked like a rural character in a play.

Had he brought the coffee? She had been waiting all day long for coffee. They had forgot it when they ordered at the store the first day.

Gosh, no, he hadn't. Lord, now he'd have to go back. Yes, he would if it killed him. He thought, though, he had everything else. She reminded him it was only because he didn't drink coffee himself. If he did he would remember it quick enough. Suppose they ran out of cigarettes? Then she saw the rope. What was that for? Well, he thought it might do to hang clothes on, or something. Naturally she asked him if he though they were going to run a laundry? They already had a fifty-foot line hanging right before his eyes? Why, hadn't he noticed it, really? It was a blot on the landscape to her.

He thought there were a lot of things a rope might come in handy for. She wanted to know what, for instance. He thought a few seconds, but nothing occurred. They could wait and see, couldn't they? You need all sorts of strange odds and ends around a place in the country. She said, yes, that was so; but she thought just at that time when every penny counted, it seemed funny to buy more rope. That was all. She hadn't meant anything else. She hadn't just seen, not at first, why he felt it was necessary.

5   Well, thunder, he had bought it because he wanted to, and that was all there was to it. She thought that was reason enough, and couldn't understand why he hadn't said so, at first. Undoubtedly it would be useful, twenty-four yards of rope, there were hundreds of things, she couldn't think of any at the moment, but it would come in. Of course. As he had said, things always did in the country.

But she was a little disappointed about the coffee, and oh, look, look, look at the eggs! Oh, my, they're all running! What had he put on top of them? Hadn't he known eggs mustn't be squeezed? Squeezed, who had squeezed them, he wanted to know. What a silly thing to say. He had simply brought them along in the basket with the other things. If they got broke it was the grocer's fault. He should know better than to put heavy things on top of eggs.

She believed it was the rope. That was the heaviest thing in the pack, she saw him plainly when he came in from the road, the rope was a big package on top of everything. He desired the whole wide world to witness that this was not a fact. He had carried the rope in one hand and the basket in the other, and what was the use of her having eyes if that was the best they could do for her?

Well, anyhow, she could see one thing plain: no eggs for breakfast. They'd have to scramble them now, for supper. It was too damned bad. She had planned to have steak for supper. No ice, meat wouldn't keep. He wanted to know why she couldn't finish breaking the eggs in a bowl and set them in a cool place.

Cool place! If he could find one for her, she'd be glad to set them there. Well, then, it seemed to him they might very well cook the meat at the same time they cooked the eggs and then warm up the meat for tomorrow. The idea simply choked her. Warmed-over meat, when they might as well have had it fresh. Second best and scraps and makeshifts, even to the meat! He rubbed her shoulder a little. It doesn't really matter so much, does it darling? Sometimes when they were playful, he would rub her shoulder and she would arch and purr. This time she hissed and almost clawed. He was getting ready to say that they could surely manage somehow when she turned on him and said, if he told they could manage somehow she would certainly slap his face.

10 He swallowed the words red hot, his face burned. He picked up the rope and started to put it on the top shelf. She would not have it on the top shelf, the jars and tins belonged there; positively she would not have the top shelf cluttered up with a lot of rope. She had borne all the clutter she meant to bear in the flat in town, there was space here at least and she meant to keep things in order.

Well, in that case, he wanted to know what the hammer and nails were doing up there? And why had she put them there when she knew very well he needed that hammer and those nails upstairs to fix the window sashes? She simply slowed down everything and made double work on the place with her insane habit of changing things around and hiding them.

She was sure she begged his pardon, and if she had had any reason to believe he was going to fix the sashes this summer she would have left the hammer and nails right where he put them; in the middle of the bedroom floor where they could step on them in the dark. And now if he didn't clear the whole mess out of there she would throw them down the well.

Oh, all right, all right—could he put them in the closet? Naturally not, there were brooms and mops and dustpans in the closet, and why couldn't he find a place for his rope outside her kitchen? Had he stopped to consider there were seven God-forsaken rooms in the house, and only one kitchen?

He wanted to know what of it? And did she realize she was making a complete fool of herself? And what did she take him for, a three-year-old idiot? The whole trouble with her was she needed something weaker than she was to heckle and tyrannize over. He wished to God now they had a couple of children she could take it out on. Maybe he'd get some rest.

Her face changed at this, she reminded him he had forgot the coffee and had bought a worthless piece of rope. And when she thought of all the things they actually needed to make the place even decently fit to live in, well, she could cry, that was all. She looked so forlorn, so lost and despairing he couldn't believe it was only a piece of rope that was causing all the racket. What *was* the matter, for God's sake?

Oh, would he please hush and go away, and *stay* away, if he could, for five minutes? By all means, yes, he would. He'd stay away indefinitely if she wished. Lord, yes, there was nothing he'd like better than to clear out and never come back. She couldn't for the life of her see what was holding him, then. It was a swell time. Here she was, stuck, miles from a railroad, with a half-empty house on her hands, and not a penny in her pocket, and everything on earth to do; it seemed the God-sent moment for him to get out from under. She was surprised he hadn't stayed in town as it was until she had come out and done the work and got things straightened out. It was his usual trick.

It appeared to him that this was going a little far. Just a touch out of bounds, if she didn't mind his saying so. Why the hell had he stayed in town the summer before? To do a half-dozen extra jobs to get the money he had sent her. That was it. She knew perfectly well they couldn't have done it otherwise. She had agreed with him at the time. And that was the only time so help him he had ever left her to do anything by herself.

Oh, he could tell that to his great-grandmother. She had her notion of what had kept him in town. Considerably more than a notion, if he wanted to know. So, she was going to bring all that up again, was she? Well, she could just think what she pleased. He was tired of explaining. It may have looked funny but he had simply got hooked in, and what could he do? It was impossible to believe that she was going to take it seriously. Yes, yes, she knew how it was with a man: if he was left by himself a minute, some woman was certain to kidnap him. And naturally he couldn't hurt her feelings by refusing!

Well, what was she raving about? Did she forget she had told him those two weeks alone in the country were the happiest she had known for four years? And how long had they been married when she said that? All right, shut up! If she thought that hadn't stuck in his craw.

She hadn't meant she was happy because she was away from him. She meant she was happy getting the devilish house nice and ready for him. That was what she had meant, and now look! Bringing up something she had said a year ago simply to justify himself for forgetting her coffee and breaking the eggs and buying a wretched piece of rope they couldn't afford. She really thought it was time to drop the subject, and now she wanted only two things in the world. She wanted him to get that rope from underfoot, and go back to the village and get her coffee, and if he could remember it, he might bring a metal mitt for the skillets and two more curtain rods, and if there were any rubber gloves in the village, her hands were simply raw, and a bottle of milk of magnesia from the drugstore.

He looked out at the dark blue afternoon sweltering on the slopes, and mopped his forehead and sighed heavily and said, if only she could wait a minute for *anything,* he was going back. He had said so, hadn't he, the very instant they found he had overlooked it?

Oh, yes, well . . . run along. She was going to wash windows. The country was so beautiful! She doubted they'd have a moment to enjoy it. He meant to go, but he could not until he had said that if she wasn't such a hopeless melancholiac she might see that this was only for a few days. Couldn't she remember anything pleasant about the other summers? Hadn't they ever had any fun? She hadn't time to talk about it, and now would he please not leave that rope lying around for her to trip on? He picked it up, somehow it had toppled off the table, and walked out with it under his arm.

Was he going this minute? He certainly was. She thought so. Sometimes it seemed to her he had second sight about the precisely perfect moment to leave her ditched. She had meant to put the mattresses out to sun, if they put them out this minute they would get at least three hours, he must have heard her say that morning she meant to put them out. So of course he would walk off and leave her to it. She supposed he thought the exercise would do her good.

Well, he was merely going to get her coffee. A four-mile walk for two pounds of coffee was ridiculous, but he was perfectly willing to do it. The habit was making a wreck of her, but if she wanted to wreck herself there was nothing he could do about it. If he thought it was coffee that was making a wreck of her, she congratulated him: he must have a damned easy conscience.

25   Conscience or no conscience, he didn't see why the mattresses couldn't very well wait until tomorrow. And anyhow, for God's sake, were they living *in* the house, or were they going to let the house ride them to death? She paled at this, her face grew livid about the mouth, she looked quite dangerous, and reminded him that housekeeping was no more her work than it was his: she had other work to do as well, and when did he think she was going to find time to do it at this rate!

Was she going to start on that again? She knew as well as he did that his work brought in the regular money, hers was only occasional, if they depended on what *she* made—and she might as well get straight on this question once for all!

That was positively not the point. The question was, when both of them were working on their own time, was there going to be a division of the housework, or wasn't there? She merely wanted to know, she had to make her plans. Why, he thought that was all arranged. It was understood that he was to help. Hadn't he always, in summers?

Hadn't he, though? Oh, just hadn't he? And when, and where, and doing what? Lord, what an uproarious joke!

It was such a very uproarious joke that her face turned slightly purple, and she screamed with laughter. She laughed so hard she had to sit down, and finally a rush of tears spurted from her eyes and poured down into the lifted corners of her mouth. He dashed towards her and dragged her up to her feet and tried to pour water on her head. The dipper hung by a string on a nail and he broke it loose. Then he tried to pump water with one hand while she struggled in the other. So he gave it up and shook her instead.

30 She wrenched away, crying out for him to take his rope and go to hell, she had simply given him up: and ran. He heard her high-heeled bedroom slippers clattering and stumbling on the stairs.

He went out around the house and into the lane; he suddenly realized he had a blister on his heel and his shirt felt as if it were on fire. Things broke so suddenly you didn't know where you were. She could work herself into a fury about simply nothing. She was terrible, damn it: not an ounce of reason. You might as well talk to a sieve as that woman when she got going. Damned if he'd spend his life humoring her! Well, what to do now? He would take back the rope and exchange it for something else. Things accumulated, things were mountainous, you couldn't move them or sort them out or get rid of them. They just lay and rotted around. He'd take it back. Hell, why should he? He wanted it. What was it anyhow? A piece of rope. Imagine anybody caring more about a piece of rope than about a man's feelings. What earthly right had she to say a word about it? He remembered all the useless, meaningless things she bought for herself: Why? because I wanted it, that's why! He stopped and selected a large stone by the road. He would put the rope behind it. He would put it in the tool-box when he got back. He's heard enough about it last him a life-time.

When he came back she was leaning against the post box beside the road waiting. It was pretty late, the smell of broiled steak floated nose high in the cooling air. Her face was young and smooth and fresh-looking. Her unmanageable funny black hair was all on end. She waved to him from a distance, and he speeded up. She called out that supper was ready and waiting, was he starved?

You bet he was starved. Here was the coffee. He waved it at her. She looked at his other hand. What was that he had there?

Well, it was the rope again. He stopped short. He had meant to exchange it but forgot. She wanted to know why he should exchange it, if it was some-thing he really wanted. Wasn't the air sweet now, and wasn't it fine to be here?

35 She walked beside him with one hand hooked into his leather belt. She pulled and jostled him a little as he walked, and leaned against him. He put his arm clear around her and patted her stomach. They exchanged wary smiles. Coffee, coffee for the Ootsum-Wootsums! He felt as if he were bringing her a beautiful present.

He was a love, she firmly believed, and if she had had her coffee in the morning, she wouldn't have behaved so funny . . . There was a whippoorwill still coming back, imagine, clear out of season, sitting in the crab-apple tree calling all by himself. Maybe his girl stood him up. Maybe she did. She hoped to hear him once more, she loved whippoorwills . . . He knew how she was, didn't he?

Sure, he knew how she was.

(1928)

William Faulkner   (1897–1962)

In his 1950 acceptance speech for the Nobel Prize for literature, William Faulkner defined his subject matter as "the human heart in conflict with itself, which alone can make good writing because only that is worth writing about." Universal in their themes, most of his novels and short stories are set in Yoknapatawpha County, a fictionalized version of West Lafayette County, Mississippi, where he was born and lived most of his life. A major focus in many of his works is the central characters' awareness of the degeneration of their families from a once glorious past and their sense of imprisonment in memories of that past. In such novels as *Absalom, Absalom!* and *The Reivers,* Faulkner is as interested in attempts by the characters to understand the past as he is in that past itself. "A Rose for Emily," which begins after the death of the title character, presents an unnamed townsman's account and interpretation of details of Emily Grierson's life and death.

A ROSE FOR EMILY

I

When Miss Emily Grierson died, our whole town went to her funeral: the men through a sort of respectful affection for a fallen monument, the women mostly out of curiosity to see the inside of her house, which no one save an old man-servant—a combined gardener and cook—had seen in at least ten years.

It was a big, squarish frame house that had once been white, decorated with cupolas and spires and scrolled balconies in the heavily lightsome style of the seventies, set on what had once been our most select street. But garages and cotton gins had encroached and obliterated even the august names of that neighborhood; only Miss Emily's house was left, lifting its stubborn and coquettish decay above the cotton wagons and the gasoline pumps—an eyesore among eyesores. And now Miss Emily had gone to join the representatives of those august names where they lay in the cedar-bemused cemetery among the ranked and anonymous graves of Union and Confederate soldiers[1] who fell at the battle of Jefferson.[2]

Alive, Miss Emily had been a tradition, a duty, and a care; a sort of hereditary obligation upon the town, dating from that day in 1894 when Colonel Sartoris, the mayor—he who fathered the edict that no Negro woman should appear on the streets without an apron—remitted her taxes, the dispensation dating from the death of her father on into perpetuity. Not that Miss Emily would have accepted charity. Colonel Sartoris invented an involved tale to the effect that Miss Emily's father had loaned money to the town, which the town, as a matter of business, preferred this way of repaying.

[1] soldiers who fought for the North and South, respectively, during the American Civil War.
[2] Civil War battle fought in Mississippi; Jefferson is Faulkner's fictional name for Oxford, Mississippi.

Only a man of Colonel Sartoris' generation and thought could have invented it, and only a woman could have believed it.

When the next generation, with its more modern ideas, became mayors and aldermen, this arrangement created some little dissatisfaction. On the first of the year they mailed her a tax notice. February came, and there was no reply. They wrote her a formal letter, asking her to call at the sheriff's office at her convenience. A week later the mayor wrote her himself, offering to call or to send his car for her, and received in reply a note on paper of an archaic shape, in a thin, flowing calligraphy in faded ink, to the effect that she no longer went out at all. The tax notice was also enclosed, without comment.

5   They called a special meeting of the Board of Aldermen. A deputation waited upon her, knocked at the door through which no visitor had passed since she ceased giving china-painting lessons eight or ten years earlier. They were admitted by the old Negro into a dim hall from which a stairway mounted into still more shadow. It smelled of dust and disuse—a close, dank smell. The Negro led them into the parlor. It was furnished in heavy, leather-covered furniture. When the Negro opened the blinds of one window, they could see that the leather was cracked; and when they sat down, a faint dust rose sluggishly about their thighs, spinning with slow motes in the single sun-ray. On a tarnished gilt easel before the fireplace stood a crayon portrait of Miss Emily's father.

They rose when she entered—a small, fat woman in black, with a thin gold chain descending to her waist and vanishing into her belt, leaning on an ebony cane with a tarnished gold head. Her skeleton was small and spare; perhaps that was why what would have been merely plumpness in another was obesity in her. She looked bloated, like a body long submerged in motionless water, and of that pallid hue. Her eyes, lost in the fatty ridges of her face, looked like two small pieces of coal pressed into a lump of dough as they moved from one face to another while the visitors stated their errand.

She did not ask them to sit. She just stood in the door and listened quietly until the spokesman came to a stumbling halt. Then they could hear the invisible watch ticking at the end of the gold chain.

Her voice was dry and cold. "I have no taxes in Jefferson. Colonel Sartoris explained it to me. Perhaps one of you can gain access to the city records and satisfy yourselves."

"But we have. We are the city authorities, Miss Emily. Didn't you get a notice from the sheriff, signed by him?"

10   "I received a paper, yes," Miss Emily said. "Perhaps he considers himself the sheriff . . . I have no taxes in Jefferson."

"But there is nothing on the books to show that, you see. We must go by the—"

"See Colonel Sartoris. I have no taxes in Jefferson."

"But, Miss Emily—"

"See Colonel Sartoris." (Colonel Sartoris had been dead almost ten years.) "I have no taxes in Jefferson. Tobe!" The Negro appeared. "Show these gentlemen out."

II

15   So she vanquished them, horse and foot, just as she had vanquished their fathers thirty years before about the smell. That was two years after her father's death and a short time after her sweetheart—the one we believed would marry her—had deserted her. After her father's death she went out very little; after her sweetheart went away, people hardly saw her at all. A few of the ladies had the temerity to call, but were not received, and the only sign of life about the place was the Negro man—a young man then—going in and out with a market basket.

"Just as if a man—any man—could keep a kitchen properly," the ladies said; so they were not surprised when the smell developed. It was another link between the gross, teeming world and the high and mighty Griersons.

A neighbor, a woman, complained to the mayor, Judge Stevens, eighty years old.

"But what will you have me do about it, madam?" he said.

"Why, send her word to stop it," the woman said. "Isn't there a law?"

20   "I'm sure that won't be necessary," Judge Stevens said. "It's probably just a snake or a rat that nigger of hers killed in the yard. I'll speak to him about it."

The next day he received two more complaints, one from a man who came in diffident deprecation. "We really must do something about it, Judge. I'd be the last one in the world to bother Miss Emily, but we've got to do something." That night the Board of Aldermen met—three graybeards and one younger man, a member of the rising generation.

"It's simple enough," he said. "Send her word to have her place cleaned up. Give her a certain time to do it in, and if she don't . . ."

"Dammit, sir," Judge Stevens said, "will you accuse a lady to her face of smelling bad?"

So the next night, after midnight, four men crossed Miss Emily's lawn and slunk about the house like burglars, sniffing along the base of the brickwork and at the cellar openings while one of them performed a regular sowing motion with his hand out of a sack slung from his shoulder. They broke open the cellar door and sprinkled lime there, and in all the outbuildings. As they recrossed the lawn, a window that had been dark was lighted and Miss Emily sat in it, the light behind her, and her upright torso motionless as that of an idol. They crept quietly across the lawn and into the shadow of the locusts that lined the street. After a week or two the smell went away.

25   That was when people had begun to feel really sorry for her. People in our town, remembering how old lady Wyatt, her great-aunt, had gone completely crazy at last, believed that the Griersons held themselves a little too high for what they really were. None of the young men were quite good enough for Miss Emily and such. We had long thought of them as a tableau, Miss Emily a slender figure in white in the background, her father a spraddled silhouette in the foreground, his back to her and clutching a horsewhip, the two of them framed by the back-flung front door. So when she got to be thirty and was still single, we were not pleased exactly, but vindicated; even with insanity in the family she wouldn't have turned down all of her chances if they had really materialized.

When her father died, it got about that the house was all that was left to her; and in a way, people were glad. At last they could pity Miss Emily. Being left alone, and a pauper, she had become humanized. Now she too would know the old thrill and the old despair of a penny more or less.

The day after his death all the ladies prepared to call at the house and offer condolence and aid, as is our custom. Miss Emily met them at the door, dressed as usual and with no trace of grief on her face. She told them that her father was not dead. She did that for three days, with the ministers calling on her, and the doctors, trying to persuade her to let them dispose of the body. Just as they were about to resort to law and force, she broke down, and they buried her father quickly.

We did not say she was crazy then. We believed she had to do that. We remembered all the young men her father had driven away, and we knew that with nothing left, she would have to cling to that which had robbed her, as people will.

III

She was sick for a long time. When we saw her again, her hair was cut short, making her look like a girl, with a vague resemblance to those angels in colored church windows—sort of tragic and serene.

30　　The town had just let the contracts for paving the sidewalks, and in the summer after her father's death they began the work. The construction company came with niggers and mules and machinery, and a foreman named Homer Barron, a Yankee—a big, dark, ready man, with a big voice and eyes lighter than his face. The little boys would follow in groups to hear him cuss the niggers, and the niggers singing in time to the rise and fall of picks. Pretty soon he knew everybody in town. Whenever you heard a lot of laughing anywhere about the square, Homer Barron would be in the center of the group. Presently we began to see him and Miss Emily on Sunday afternoons driving in the yellow-wheeled buggy and the matched team of bays from the livery stable.

At first we were glad that Miss Emily would have an interest, because the ladies all said, "Of course a Grierson would not think seriously of a Northerner, a day laborer." But there were still others, older people, who said that even grief could not cause a real lady to forget *noblesse oblige*[3]— without calling it *noblesse oblige*. They just said, "Poor Emily. Her kinsfolk should come to her." She had some kin in Alabama; but years ago her father had fallen out with them over the estate of old lady Wyatt, the crazy woman, and there was no communication between the two families. They had not even been represented at the funeral.

And as soon as the old people said, "Poor Emily," the whispering began. "Do you suppose it's really so?" they said to one another. "Of course it is. What else could . . ." This behind their hands; rustling of craned silk and satin behind jalousies closed upon the sun of Sunday afternoon as the thin, swift clop-clop-clop of the matched team passed: "Poor Emily."

[3]the responsibility of privileged, high-born people to be honourable.

She carried her head high enough—even when we believed that she was fallen. It was as if she demanded more than ever the recognition of her dignity as the last Grierson; as if it had wanted that touch of earthiness to reaffirm her imperviousness. Like when she bought the rat poison, the arsenic. That was over a year after they had begun to say "Poor Emily," and while the two female cousins were visiting her.

"I want some poison," she said to the druggist. She was over thirty then, still a slight woman, though thinner than usual, with cold, haughty black eyes in a face the flesh of which was strained across the temples and about the eye-sockets as you imagine a lighthouse-keeper's face ought to look. "I want some poison," she said.

35   "Yes, Miss Emily. What kind? For rats and such? I'd recom—"

"I want the best you have. I don't care what kind."

The druggist named several. "They'll kill anything up to an elephant. But what you want is—"

"Arsenic," Miss Emily said. "Is that a good one?"

"Is . . . arsenic? Yes, ma'am. But what you want—"

40   "I want arsenic."

The druggist looked down at her. She looked back at him, erect, her face like a strained flag. "Why, of course," the druggist said. "If that's what you want. But the law requires you to tell what you are going to use it for."

Miss Emily just stared at him, her head tilted back in order to look him eye for eye, until he looked away and went and got the arsenic and wrapped it up. The Negro delivery boy brought her the package; the druggist didn't come back. When she opened the package at home there was written on the box, under the skull and bones: "For rats."

IV

So the next day we all said, "She will kill herself"; and we said it would be the best thing. When she had first begun to be seen with Homer Barron, we had said, "She will marry him." Then we said, "She will persuade him yet," because Homer himself had remarked—he liked men, and it was known that he drank with the younger men in the Elks' Club—that he was not a marrying man. Later we said, "Poor Emily" behind the jalousies as they passed on Sunday afternoon in the glittering buggy, Miss Emily with her head high and Homer Barron with his hat cocked and a cigar in his teeth, reins and whip in a yellow glove.

Then some of the ladies began to say that it was a disgrace to the town and a bad example to the young people. The men did not want to interfere, but at last the ladies forced the Baptist minister—Miss Emily's people were Episcopal[4]—to call upon her. He would never divulge what happened during that interview, but he refused to go back again. The next Sunday they again drove about the streets, and the following day the minister's wife wrote to Miss Emily's relations in Alabama.

[4]the Anglican Church in the United States.

45   So she had blood-kin under her roof again and we sat back to watch developments. At first nothing happened. Then we were sure that they were to be married. We learned that Miss Emily had been to the jeweler's and ordered a man's toilet set in silver, with the letters H.B. on each piece. Two days later we learned that she had bought a complete outfit of men's clothing, including a nightshirt, and we said, "They are married." We were really glad. We were glad because the two female cousins were even more Grierson than Miss Emily had ever been.

So we were not surprised when Homer Barron—the streets had been finished some time since—was gone. We were a little disappointed that there was not a public blowing-off, but we believed that he had gone on to prepare for Miss Emily's coming, or to give her a chance to get rid of the cousins. (By that time it was a cabal, and we were all Miss Emily's allies to help circumvent the cousins.) Sure enough, after another week they departed. And, as we had expected all along, within three days Homer Barron was back in town. A neighbor saw the Negro man admit him at the kitchen door at dusk one evening.

And that was the last we saw of Homer Barron. And of Miss Emily for some time. The Negro man went in and out with the market basket, but the front door remained closed. Now and then we would see her at a window for a moment, as the men did that night when they sprinkled the lime, but for almost six months she did not appear on the streets. Then we knew that this was to be expected too; as if that quality of her father which had thwarted her woman's life so many times had been too virulent and too furious to die.

When we next saw Miss Emily, she had grown fat and her hair was turning gray. During the next few years it grew grayer and grayer until it attained an even pepper-and-salt iron-gray, when it ceased turning. Up to the day of her death at seventy-four it was still that vigorous iron-gray, like the hair of an active man.

From that time on her front door remained closed, save for a period of six or seven years, when she was about forty, during which she gave lessons in china-painting. She fitted up a studio in one of the downstairs rooms, where the daughters and granddaughters of Colonel Sartoris' contemporaries were sent to her with the same regularity and in the same spirit that they were sent to church on Sundays with a twenty-five-cent piece for the collection plate. Meanwhile her taxes had been remitted.

50   Then the newer generation became the backbone and the spirit of the town, and the painting pupils grew up and fell away and did not send their children to her with boxes of color and tedious brushes and pictures cut from the ladies' magazines. The front door closed upon the last one and remained closed for good. When the town got free postal delivery, Miss Emily alone refused to let them fasten the metal numbers above her door and attach a mailbox to it. She would not listen to them.

Daily, monthly, yearly we watched the Negro grow grayer and more stooped, going in and out with the market basket. Each December we sent her a tax notice, which would be returned by the post office a week later, unclaimed. Now and then we would see her in one of the downstairs windows—she had evidently shut up the top floor of the house—like the carven torso of an idol in a niche, looking or not looking at us, we could never tell which. Thus she passed from generation to generation—dear, inescapable, impervious, tranquil, and perverse.

And so she died. Fell ill in the house filled with dust and shadows, with only a doddering Negro man to wait on her. We did not even know she was sick; we had long since given up trying to get any information from the Negro. He talked to no one, probably not even to her, for his voice had grown harsh and rusty, as if from disuse.

She died in one of the downstairs rooms, in a heavy walnut bed with a curtain, her gray head propped on a pillow yellow and moldy with age and lack of sunlight.

The Negro met the first of the ladies at the front door and let them in, with their hushed, sibilant voices and their quick, curious glances, and then he disappeared. He walked right through the house and out the back and was not seen again.

The two female cousins came at once. They held the funeral on the second day, with the town coming to look at Miss Emily beneath a mass of bought flowers, with the crayon face of her father musing profoundly above the bier and the ladies sibilant and macabre, and the very old men—some in their brushed Confederate uniforms—on the porch and the lawn, talking of Miss Emily as if she had been a contemporary of theirs, believing that they had danced with her and courted her perhaps, confusing time with its mathematical progression, as the old do, to whom all the past is not a diminishing road but, instead, a huge meadow which no winter ever quite touches, divided from them now by the narrow bottle-neck of the most recent decade of years.

Already we knew that there was one room in that region above stairs which no one had seen in forty years, and which would have to be forced. They waited until Miss Emily was decently in the ground before they opened it.

The violence of breaking down the door seemed to fill this room with pervading dust. A thin, acrid pall as of the tomb seemed to lie everywhere upon this room decked and furnished as for a bridal: upon the valance curtains of faded rose color, upon the rose-shaded lights, upon the dressing table, upon the delicate array of crystal and the man's toilet things backed with tarnished silver, silver so tarnished that the monogram was obscured. Among them lay a collar and tie, as if they had just been removed, which, lifted, left upon the surface a pale crescent in the dust. Upon a chair hung the suit, carefully folded; beneath it the two mute shoes and the discarded socks.

The man himself lay in the bed.

For a long while we just stood there, looking down at the profound and fleshless grin. The body had apparently once lain in the attitude of an embrace, but now the long sleep that outlasts love, that conquers even the grimace of love, had cuckolded him. What was left of him, rotted beneath what was left of the nightshirt, had become inextricable from the bed in which he lay; and upon him and upon the pillow beside him lay that even coating of the patient and biding dust.

60   Then we noticed that in the second pillow was the indentation of a head. One of us lifted something from it, and leaning forward, that faint and invisible dust dry and acrid in the nostrils, we saw a long strand of iron-gray hair.

(1930)

Ernest Hemingway   (1899–1961)

A native of Oak Park, Illinois, Ernest Hemingway began his writing career as a newspaper correspondent. The short sentences, crisp description of settings and actions, and relative lack of authorial comment that are distinguishing features of his mature style no doubt reflect his background in journalism. Hemingway's experiences in Italy during World War I, where he was injured while serving as an ambulance driver, and in Paris during the 1920s, where he was a member of the so-called Lost Generation (individuals who no longer believed in absolute moral or religious values), contributed to the development of his major theme: the need of the individual to live with control and dignity in a world devoid of spiritual meaning. Most fully developed in *The Sun Also Rises* (1926) and *A Farewell to Arms* (1929), two of his finest novels, these ideas are also expressed in "A Clean, Well-Lighted Place." The prose, which at first appears simply reportorial, implicitly develops the themes and symbols of the story.

A CLEAN, WELL-LIGHTED PLACE

It was late and every one had left the café except an old man who sat in the shadow the leaves of the tree made against the electric light. In the day time the street was dusty, but at night the dew settled the dust and the old man liked to sit late because he was deaf and now at night it was quiet and he felt the difference. The two waiters inside the café knew that the old man was a little drunk, and while he was a good client they knew that if he became too drunk he would leave without paying, so they kept watch on him.

"Last week he tried to commit suicide," one waiter said.

"Why?"

"He was in despair."

"What about?"

"Nothing."

"How do you know it was nothing?"

"He has plenty of money."

They sat together at a table that was close against the wall near the door of the café and looked at the terrace where the tables were all empty except where the old man sat in the shadow of the leaves of the tree that moved slightly in the wind. A girl and a soldier went by in the street. The street light shone on the brass number on his collar. The girl wore no head covering and hurried beside him.

"The guard will pick him up," one waiter said.

"What does it matter if he gets what he's after?"

"He had better get off the street now. The guard will get him. They went by five minutes ago."

The old man sitting in the shadow rapped on his saucer with his glass. The younger waiter went over to him.

"What do you want?"

15 The old man looked at him. "Another brandy," he said.

"You'll be drunk," the waiter said. The old man looked at him. The waiter went away.

"He'll stay all night," he said to his colleague. "I'm sleepy now. I never get into bed before three o'clock. He should have killed himself last week."

The waiter took the brandy bottle and another saucer from the counter inside the café and marched out to the old man's table. He put down the saucer and poured the glass full of brandy.

"You should have killed yourself last week," he said to the deaf man. The old man motioned with his finger. "A little more," he said. The waiter poured on into the glass so that the brandy slopped over and ran down the stem into the top saucer of the pile. "Thank you," the old man said. The waiter took the bottle back inside the café. He sat down at the table with his colleague again.

20 "He's drunk now," he said.

"He's drunk every night."

"What did he want to kill himself for?"

"How should I know."

"How did he do it?"

25 "He hung himself with a rope."

"Who cut him down?"

"His niece."

"Why did she do it?"

"Fear for his soul."

30 "How much money has he got?"

"He's got plenty."

"He must be eighty years old."

"Anyway I should say he was eighty."

"I wish he would go home. I never get to bed before three o'clock. What kind of hour is that to go to bed?"

35 "He stays up because he likes it."

"He's lonely. I'm not lonely. I have a wife waiting in bed for me."

"He had a wife once too."

"A wife would be no good to him now."

"You can't tell. He might be better with a wife."

40 "His niece looks after him. You said she cut him down."

"I know."

"I wouldn't want to be that old. An old man is a nasty thing."

"Not always. This old man is clean. He drinks without spilling. Even now, drunk. Look at him."

"I don't want to look at him. I wish he would go home. He has no regard for those who must work."

45 The old man looked from his glass across the square, then over at the waiters.

"Another brandy," he said, pointing to his glass. The waiter who was in a hurry came over.

"Finished," he said, speaking with that omission of syntax stupid people employ when talking to drunken people or foreigners. "No more tonight. Close now."

"Another," said the old man.

"No. Finished." The waiter wiped the edge of the table with a towel and shook his head.

50   The old man stood up, slowly counted the saucers, took a leather coin purse from his pocket and paid for the drinks, leaving half a peseta tip.

The waiter watched him go down the street, a very old man walking unsteadily but with dignity.

"Why didn't you let him stay and drink?" the unhurried waiter asked. They were putting up the shutters. "It is not half-past two."

"I want to go home to bed."

"What is an hour?"

55   "More to me than to him."

"An hour is the same."

"You talk like an old man yourself. He can buy a bottle and drink at home."

"It's not the same."

"No, it is not," agreed the waiter with a wife. He did not wish to be unjust. He was only in a hurry.

60   "And you? You have no fear of going home before your usual hour?"

"Are you trying to insult me?"

"No, hombre, only to make a joke."

"No," the waiter who was in a hurry said, rising from pulling down the metal shutters. "I have confidence. I am all confidence."

"You have youth, confidence, and a job," the older waiter said. "You have everything."

65   "And what do you lack?"

"Everything but work."

"You have everything I have."

"No. I have never had confidence and I am not young."

"Come on. Stop talking nonsense and lock up."

70   "I am with those who like to stay late at the café," the older waiter said. "With all those who do not want to go to bed. With all those who need a light for the night."

"I want to go home and into bed."

"We are of two different kinds," the older waiter said. He was now dressed to go home. "It is not only a question of youth and confidence although those things are very beautiful. Each night I am reluctant to close up because there may be some one who needs the café."

"Hombre, there are bodegas open all night long."

"You do not understand. This is a clean and pleasant café. It is well lighted. The light is very good and also, now, there are shadows of the leaves."

75   "Good night," said the younger waiter.

"Good night," the other said. Turning off the electric light he continued the conversation with himself. It is the light of course but it is necessary that the place be clean and pleasant. You do not want music. Certainly you do not want music. Nor can you stand before a bar with dignity although that is all that is provided for these hours. What did he fear? It was not fear or dread. It was a nothing that he knew too well. It was all a nothing and a man was nothing too. It was only that and light was all it needed and a certain cleanness and order. Some lived in it and never felt it but he knew it all was nada y pues nada y nada y pues nada.[1] Our nada who art in nada, nada be thy name thy kingdom nada thy will be nada in nada as it is in nada. Give us this nada our daily nada and nada us our nada as we nada our nadas and nada us not into nada but deliver us from nada; pues nada. Hail nothing full of nothing, nothing is with thee. He smiled and stood before a bar with a shining steam pressure coffee machine.

"What's yours?" asked the barman.

"Nada."

"Otro loco mas,"[2] said the barman and turned away.

80   "A little cup," said the waiter.

The barman poured it for him.

"The light is very bright and pleasant but the bar is unpolished," the waiter said.

The barman looked at him but did not answer. It was too late at night for conversation.

"You want another copita?"[3]

85   "No, thank you," said the waiter and went out. He disliked bars and bodegas. A clean, well-lighted café was a very different thing. Now, without thinking further, he would go home to his room. He would lie in the bed and finally, with daylight, he would go to sleep. After all, he said to himself, it is probably only insomnia. Many must have it.

(1933)

---

[1]nothing, and therefore nothing. [2]another crazy one. [3]small cup.

Eudora Welty   (1909–2001)

Like fellow Mississippian William Faulkner, whose works she admired, Eudora Welty set most of her short stories in and around the city where she was born and lived most of her life: Jackson. Family and a sense of place are most important for her characters, for a place of one's own provides "a base of reference," and enables "individuals to put out roots." "Why I Live at the P.O.," which takes place on July 4, American Independence Day, traditionally a time of family reunions, focuses on the developing hostility the narrator feels toward her family and her own declaration of independence from them. Ironically, in its portrayal of the disintegrating interrelationships, the story provides a negative example of Welty's belief that "communication and hope of it are conditions of life itself."

WHY I LIVE AT THE P.O.

I was getting along fine with Mama, Papa-Daddy and Uncle Rondo until my sister Stella-Rondo just separated from her husband and came back home again. Mr. Whitaker! Of course I went with Mr. Whitaker first, when he first appeared here in China Grove,[1] taking "Pose Yourself" photos, and Stella-Rondo broke us up. Told him I was one-sided. Bigger on one side than the other, which is a deliberate, calculated falsehood: I'm the same. Stella-Rondo is exactly twelve months to the day younger than I am and for that reason she's spoiled.

She's always had anything in the world she wanted and then she'd throw it away. Papa-Daddy gave her this gorgeous Add-a-Pearl necklace when she was eight years old and she threw it away playing baseball when she was nine, with only two pearls.

So as soon as she got married and moved away from home the first thing she did was separate! From Mr. Whitaker! This photographer with the popeyes she said she trusted. Came home from one of those towns up in Illinois and to our complete surprise brought this child of two.

Mama said she like to made her drop dead for a second. "Here you had this marvelous blonde child and never so much as wrote your mother a word about it," says Mama. "I'm thoroughly ashamed of you." But of course she wasn't.

5   Stella-Rondo just calmly takes off this *hat*, I wish you could see it. She says, "Why, Mama, Shirley-T.'s adopted, I can prove it."

"How?" says Mama, but all I says was, "H'm!" There I was over the hot stove, trying to stretch two chickens over five people and a completely unexpected child into the bargain, without one moment's notice.

"What do you mean—'H'm!'?" says Stella-Rondo, and Mama says, "I heard that, Sister."

I said that oh, I didn't mean a thing, only that whoever Shirley-T. was, she was the spit-image of Papa-Daddy if he'd cut off his beard, which of course he'd never do in the world. Papa-Daddy's Mama's papa and sulks.

[1]town in central Mississippi.

Stella-Rondo got furious! She said, "Sister, I don't need to tell you you got a lot of nerve and always did have and I'll thank you to make no future reference to my adopted child whatsoever."

"Very well," I said. "Very well, very well. Of course I noticed at once she looks like Mr. Whitaker's side too. That frown. She looks like a cross between Mr. Whitaker and Papa-Daddy."

"Well, all I can say is she isn't."

"She looks exactly like Shirley Temple[2] to me," says Mama, but Shirley-T. just ran away from her.

So the first thing Stella-Rondo did at the table was turn Papa-Daddy against me.

"Papa-Daddy," she says. He was trying to cut up his meat. "Papa-Daddy!" I was taken completely by surprise. Papa-Daddy is about a million years old and's got this long-long beard. "Papa-Daddy, Sister says she fails to understand why you don't cut off your beard."

So Papa-Daddy l-a-y-s down his knife and fork! He's real rich. Mama says he is, he says he isn't. So he says, "Have I heard correctly? You don't understand why I don't cut off my beard?"

"Why," I says, "Papa-Daddy, of course I understand, I did not say any such of a thing, the idea!"

He says, "Hussy!"

I says, "Papa-Daddy, you know I wouldn't any more want you to cut off your beard than the man in the moon. It was the farthest thing from my mind! Stella-Rondo sat there and made that up while she was eating breast of chicken."

But he says, "So the postmistress fails to understand why I don't cut off my beard. Which job I got you through my influence with the government. 'Bird's nest'—is that what you call it?"

Not that it isn't the next to smallest P.O. in the entire state of Mississippi.

I says, "Oh, Papa-Daddy," I says, "I didn't say any such of a thing, I never dreamed it was a bird's nest, I have always been grateful though this is the next to smallest P.O. in the state of Mississippi, and I do not enjoy being referred to as a hussy by my own grandfather."

But Stella-Rondo says, "Yes, you did say it too. Anybody in the world could of heard you, that had ears."

"Stop right there," says Mama, looking at *me*.

So I pulled my napkin straight back through the napkin ring and left the table.

As soon as I was out of the room Mama says, "Call her back, or she'll starve to death," but Papa-Daddy says, "This is the beard I started growing on the Coast when I was fifteen years old." He would of gone on till nightfall if Shirley-T. hadn't lost the Milky Way she ate in Cairo.[3]

So Papa-Daddy says, "I am going out and lie in the hammock, and you can all sit here and remember my words: I'll never cut off my beard as long

---

[2]American child movie star of the 1930s. [3]town in southern Illinois.

as I live, even one inch, and I don't appreciate it in you at all." Passed right by me in the hall and went straight out and got in the hammock.

It would be a holiday. It wasn't five minutes before Uncle Rondo suddenly appeared in the hall in one of Stella-Rondo's flesh-colored kimonos, all cut on the bias, like something Mr. Whitaker probably thought was gorgeous.

"Uncle Rondo!" I says. "I didn't know who that was! Where are you going?"

"Sister," he says, "get out of my way, I'm poisoned."

30   "If you're poisoned stay away from Papa-Daddy," I says. "Keep out of the hammock. Papa-Daddy will certainly beat you on the head if you come within forty miles of him. He thinks I deliberately said he ought to cut off his beard after he got me the P.O., and I've told him and told him and told him, and he acts like he just don't hear me. Papa-Daddy must of gone stone deaf."

"He picked a fine day to do it then," says Uncle Rondo, and before you could say "Jack Robinson" flew out in the yard.

What he'd really done, he'd drunk another bottle of that prescription. He does it every single Fourth of July as sure as shooting, and it's horribly expensive. Then he falls over in the hammock and snores. So he insisted on zigzagging right on out to the hammock, looking like a half-wit.

Papa-Daddy woke up with this horrible yell and right there without moving an inch he tried to turn Uncle Rondo against me. I heard every word he said. Oh, he told Uncle Rondo I didn't learn to read till I was eight years old and he didn't see how in the world I ever got the mail put up at the P.O., much less read it all, and he said if Uncle Rondo could only fathom the lengths he had gone to to get me that job! And he said on the other hand he thought Stella-Rondo had a brilliant mind and deserved credit for getting out of town. All the time he was just lying there swinging as pretty as you please and looping out his beard, and poor Uncle Rondo was *pleading* with him to slow down the hammock, it was making him as dizzy as a witch to watch it. But that's what Papa-Daddy likes about a hammock. So Uncle Rondo was too dizzy to get turned against me for the time being. He's Mama's only brother and is a good case of a one-track mind. Ask anybody. A certified pharmacist.

Just then I heard Stella-Rondo raising the upstairs window. While she was married she got this peculiar idea that it's cooler with the windows shut and locked. So she has to raise the window before she can make a soul hear her outdoors.

35   So she raises the window and says, "*Oh!*" You would have thought she was mortally wounded.

Uncle Rondo and Papa-Daddy didn't even look up, but kept right on with what they were doing. I had to laugh.

I flew up the stairs and threw the door open! I says, "What in the wide world's the matter, Stella-Rondo? You mortally wounded?"

"No," she says, "I am not mortally wounded but I wish you would do me the favor of looking out that window there and telling me what you see."

So I shade my eyes and look out the window.

40   "I see the front yard," I says.

"Don't you see any human beings?" she says.

"I see Uncle Rondo trying to run Papa-Daddy out of the hammock," I says. "Nothing more. Naturally, it's so suffocating-hot in the house, with all the windows shut and locked, everybody who cares to stay in their right mind will have to go out and get in the hammock before the Fourth of July is over."

"Don't you notice anything different about Uncle Rondo?" asks Stella-Rondo.

"Why, no, except he's got on some terrible-looking flesh-colored contraption I wouldn't be found dead in, is all I can see," I says.

"Never mind, you won't be found dead in it, because it happens to be part of my trousseau, and Mr. Whitaker took several dozen photographs of me in it," says Stella-Rondo. "What on earth could Uncle Rondo *mean* by wearing part of my trousseau out in the broad open daylight without saying so much as 'Kiss my foot,' *knowing* I only got home this morning after my separation and hung my negligee up on the bathroom door, just as nervous as I could be?"

"I'm sure I don't know, and what do you expect me to do about it?" I says. "Jump out the window?"

"No, I expect nothing of the kind. I simply declare that Uncle Rondo looks like a fool in it, that's all," she says. "It makes me sick to my stomach."

"Well, he looks as good as he can," I says. "As good as anybody in reason could." I stood up for Uncle Rondo, please remember. And I said to Stella-Rondo, "I think I would do well not to criticize so freely if I were you and came home with a two-year-old child I had never said a word about, and no explanation whatever about my separation."

"I asked you the instant I entered this house not to refer one more time to my adopted child, and you gave me your word of honor you would not," was all Stella-Rondo would say, and started pulling out every one of her eyebrows with some cheap Kress tweezers.

So I merely slammed the door behind me and went down and made some green-tomato pickle. Somebody had to do it. Of course Mama had turned both the niggers loose; she always said no earthly power could hold one anyway on the Fourth of July, so she wouldn't even try. It turned out that Jaypan fell in the lake and came within a very narrow limit of drowning.

So Mama trots in. Lifts up the lid and says, "H'm! Not very good for your Uncle Rondo in his precarious condition, I must say. Or poor little adopted Shirley-T. Shame on you!"

That made me tired. I says, "Well, Stella-Rondo had better thank her lucky stars it was her instead of me came trotting in with that very peculiar-looking child. Now if it had been me that trotted in from Illinois and brought a peculiar-looking child of two, I shudder to think of the reception I'd of got, much less controlled the diet of an entire family."

"But you must remember, Sister, that you were never married to Mr. Whitaker in the first place and didn't go up to Illinois to live," says Mama, shaking a spoon in my face. "If you had I would of been just as overjoyed to see you and your little adopted girl as I was to see Stella-Rondo, when you wound up with your separation and came on back home."

"You would not," I says.

"Don't contradict me, I would," says Mama.

But I said she couldn't convince me though she talked till she was blue in the face. Then I said, "Besides, you know as well as I do that that child is not adopted."

"She most certainly is adopted," says Mama, stiff as a poker.

I says, "Why, Mama, Stella-Rondo had her just as sure as anything in this world, and just too stuck up to admit it."

"Why, Sister," said Mama. "Here I thought we were going to have a pleasant Fourth of July, and you start right out not believing a word your own baby sister tells you!"

60   "Just like Cousin Annie Flo. Went to her grave denying the facts of life," I remind Mama.

"I told you if you ever mentioned Annie Flo's name I'd slap your face," says Mama, and slaps my face.

"All right, you wait and see," I says.

"I," says Mama, "I prefer to take my children's word for anything when it's humanly possible." You ought to see Mama, she weighs two hundred pounds and has real tiny feet.

Just then something perfectly horrible occurred to me.

65   "Mama," I says, "can that child talk?" I simply had to whisper! "Mama, I wonder if that child can be—you know—in any way? Do you realize," I says, "that she hasn't spoken one single, solitary word to a human being up to this minute? This is the way she looks," I says, and I looked like this.

Well, Mama and I just stood there and stared at each other. It was horrible!

"I remember well that Joe Whitaker frequently drank like a fish," says Mama. "I believed to my soul he drank *chemicals*." And without another word she marches to the foot of the stairs and calls Stella-Rondo.

"Stella-Rondo? O-o-o-o-o! Stella-Rondo!"

"What?" says Stella-Rondo from upstairs. Not even the grace to get up off the bed.

70   "Can that child of yours talk?" asks Mama.

Stella-Rondo says, "Can she what?"

"Talk! Talk!" says Mama. "Burdyburdyburdyburdy!"

So Stella-Rondo yells back, "Who says she can't talk?"

"Sister says so," says Mama.

75   "You didn't have to tell me, I know whose word of honor don't mean a thing in this house," says Stella-Rondo.

And in a minute the loudest Yankee voice I ever heard in my life yells out, "OE'm Pop-OE the Sailor-r-r-r Ma-a-an!" and then somebody jumps up and down in the upstairs hall. In another second the house would of fallen down.

"Not only talks, she can tap-dance!" calls Stella-Rondo. "Which is more than some people I won't name can do."

"Why, the little precious darling thing!" Mama says, so surprised. "Just as smart as she can be!" Starts talking baby talk right there. Then she turns on me. "Sister, you ought to be thoroughly ashamed! Run upstairs this instant and apologize to Stella-Rondo and Shirley-T."

"Apologize for what?" I says. "I merely wondered if the child was normal, that's all. Now that she's proved she is, why, I have nothing further to say."

80   But Mama just turned on her heel and flew out, furious. She ran right upstairs and hugged the baby. She believed it was adopted. Stella-Rondo hadn't done a thing but turn her against me from upstairs while I stood there helpless over the hot stove. So that made Mama, Papa-Daddy and the baby all on Stella-Rondo's side.

Next, Uncle Rondo.

I must say that Uncle Rondo has been marvelous to me at various times in the past and I was completely unprepared to be made to jump out of my skin, the way it turned out. Once Stella-Rondo did something perfectly horrible to him—broke a chain letter from Flanders Field[4]—and he took the radio back he had given her and gave it to me. Stella-Rondo was furious! For six months we all had to call her Stella instead of Stella-Rondo, or she wouldn't answer. I always thought Uncle Rondo had all the brains of the entire family. Another time he sent me to Mammoth Cave,[5] with all expenses paid.

But this would be the day he was drinking that prescription, the Fourth of July.

So at supper Stella-Rondo speaks up and says she thinks Uncle Rondo ought to try to eat a little something. So finally Uncle Rondo said he would try a little cold biscuits and ketchup, but that was all. So *she* brought it to him.

85   "Do you think it wise to disport with ketchup in Stella-Rondo's flesh-colored kimono?" I says. Trying to be considerate! If Stella-Rondo couldn't watch out for her trousseau, somebody had to.

"Any objections?" asks Uncle Rondo, just about to pour out all the ketchup.

"Don't mind what she says, Uncle Rondo," says Stella-Rondo. "Sister has been devoting this solid afternoon to sneering out my bedroom window at the way you look."

"What's that?" says Uncle Rondo. Uncle Rondo has got the most terrible temper in the world. Anything is liable to make him tear the house down if it comes at the wrong time.

So Stella-Rondo says, "Sister says, 'Uncle Rondo certainly does look like a fool in that pink kimono!'"

90   Do you remember who it was really said that?

Uncle Rondo spills out all the ketchup and jumps out of his chair and tears off the kimono and throws it down on the dirty floor and puts his foot on it. It had to be sent all the way to Jackson to the cleaners and re-pleated.

"So that's your opinion of your Uncle Rondo, is it?" he says. "I look like a fool, do I? Well, that's the last straw. A whole day in this house with nothing to do, and then to hear you come out with a remark like that behind my back!"

"I didn't say any such of a thing, Uncle Rondo," I says, "and I'm not saying who did, either. Why, I think you look all right. Just try to take care of yourself and not talk and eat at the same time," I says. "I think you better go lie down."

"Lie down my foot," says Uncle Rondo. I ought to of known by that he was fixing to do something perfectly horrible.

[4]in Belgium, site of graves of World War I soldiers. [5]popular tourist attraction in Kentucky.

95   So he didn't do anything that night in the precarious state he was in—just played Casino with Mama and Stella-Rondo and Shirley-T. and gave Shirley-T. a nickel with a head on both sides. It tickled her nearly to death, and she called him "Papa." But at 6:30 A.M. the next morning, he threw a whole five-cent package of some unsold one-inch firecrackers from the store as hard as he could into my bedroom and they every one went off. Not one bad one in the string. Anybody else, there'd be one that wouldn't go off.

Well, I'm just terribly susceptible to noise of any kind, the doctor has always told me I was the most sensitive person he had ever seen in his whole life, and I was simply prostrated. I couldn't eat! People tell me they heard it as far as the cemetery, and old Aunt Jep Patterson, that had been holding her own so good, thought it was Judgment Day and she was going to meet her whole family. It's usually so quiet here.

And I'll tell you it didn't take me any longer than a minute to make up my mind what to do. There I was with the whole entire house on Stella-Rondo's side and turned against me. If I have anything at all I have pride.

So I just decided I'd go straight down to the P.O. There's plenty of room there in the back, I says to myself.

Well! I made no bones about letting the family catch on to what I was up to. I didn't try to conceal it.

100   The first thing they knew, I marched in where they were all playing Old Maid and pulled the electric oscillating fan out by the plug, and everything got real hot. Next I snatched the pillow I'd done the needlepoint on right off the davenport from behind Papa-Daddy. He went "Ugh!" I beat Stella-Rondo up the stairs and finally found my charm bracelet in her bureau drawer under a picture of Nelson Eddy.[6]

"So that's the way the land lies," says Uncle Rondo. There he was, piecing on the ham. "Well, Sister, I'll be glad to donate my army cot if you got any place to set it up, providing you'll leave right this minute and let me get some peace." Uncle Rondo was in France.

"Thank you kindly for the cot and 'peace' is hardly the word I would select if I had to resort to firecrackers at 6:30 A.M. in a young girl's bedroom," I says back to him. "And as to where I intend to go, you seem to forget my position as postmistress of China Grove, Mississippi," I says. "I've always got the P.O."

Well, that made them all sit up and take notice.

I went out front and started digging up some four-o'clocks to plant around the P.O.

105   "Ah-ah-ah!" says Mama, raising the window. "Those happen to be my four-o'clocks. Everything planted in that star is mine. I've never known you to make anything grow in your life."

"Very well," I says. "But I take the fern. Even you, Mama, can't stand there and deny that I'm the one watered that fern. And I happen to know where I can send in a box top and get a packet of one thousand mixed seeds, no two the same kind, free."

"Oh, where?" Mama wants to know.

---

[6]popular American singer on radio programs of the 1930s.

But I says, "Too late. You 'tend to your house, and I'll 'tend to mine. You hear things like that all the time if you know how to listen to the radio. Perfectly marvelous offers. Get anything you want free."

So I hope to tell you I marched in and got that radio, and they could of all bit a nail in two, especially Stella-Rondo, that it used to belong to, and she well knew she couldn't get it back, I'd sue for it like a shot. And I very politely took the sewing-machine motor I helped pay the most on to give Mama for Christmas back in 1929, and a good big calendar, with the first-aid remedies on it. The thermometer and the Hawaiian ukulele certainly were rightfully mine, and I stood on the step-ladder and got all my watermelon-rind preserves and every fruit and vegetable I'd put up, every jar. Then I began to pull the tacks out of the bluebird wall vases on the archway to the dining room.

110 "Who told you you could have those, Miss Priss?" says Mama, fanning as hard as she could.

"I bought 'em and I'll keep track of 'em," I says. "I'll tack 'em up one on each side the post-office window, and you can see 'em when you come to ask me for your mail, if you're so dead to see 'em."

"Not I! I'll never darken the door to that post office again if I live to be a hundred," Mama says. "Ungrateful child! After all the money we spent on you at the Normal."[7]

"Me either," says Stella-Rondo. "You can just let my mail lie there and *rot*, for all I care. I'll never come and relieve you of a single, solitary piece."

"I should worry," I says. "And who you think's going to sit down and write you all those big fat letters and postcards, by the way? Mr. Whitaker? Just because he was the only man ever dropped down in China Grove and you got him—unfairly—is he going to sit down and write you a lengthy correspondence after you come home giving no rhyme nor reason whatsoever for your separation and no explanation for the presence of that child? I may not have your brilliant mind, but I fail to see it."

115 So Mama says, "Sister, I've told you a thousand times that Stella-Rondo simply got homesick, and this child is far too big to be hers," and she says, "Now, why don't you all just sit down and play Casino?"

Then Shirley-T. sticks out her tongue at me in this perfectly horrible way. She has no more manners than the man in the moon. I told her she was going to cross her eyes like that some day and they'd stick.

"It's too late to stop me now," I says. "You should have tried that yesterday. I'm going to the P.O. and the only way you can possibly see me is to visit me there."

So Papa-Daddy says, "You'll never catch me setting foot in that post office, even if I should take a notion into my head to write a letter some place." He says, "I won't have you reachin' out of that little old window with a pair of shears and cuttin' off any beard of mine. I'm too smart for you!"

"We all are," says Stella-Rondo.

120 But I said, "If you're so smart, where's Mr. Whitaker?"

---

[7]teachers' college.

So then Uncle Rondo says, "I'll thank you from now on to stop reading all the orders I get on postcards and telling everybody in China Grove what you think is the matter with them," but I says, "I draw my own conclusions and will continue in the future to draw them." I says, "If people want to write their inmost secrets on penny postcards, there's nothing in the wide world you can do about it, Uncle Rondo."

"And if you think we'll ever *write* another postcard you're sadly mistaken," says Mama.

"Cutting off your nose to spite your face then," I says. "But if you're all determined to have no more to do with the U.S. mail, think of this: What will Stella-Rondo do now, if she wants to tell Mr. Whitaker to come after her?"

"Wah!" says Stella-Rondo. I knew she'd cry. She had a conniption fit right there in the kitchen.

125 "It will be interesting to see how long she holds out," I says. "And now—I am leaving."

"Good-bye," says Uncle Rondo.

"Oh, I declare," says Mama, "to think that a family of mine should quarrel on the Fourth of July, or the day after, over Stella-Rondo leaving old Mr. Whitaker and having the sweetest little adopted child! It looks like we'd all be glad!"

"Wah!" says Stella-Rondo, and has a fresh conniption fit.

"*He* left *her*—you mark my words," I says. "That's Mr. Whitaker. I know Mr. Whitaker. After all, I knew him first. I said from the beginning he'd up and leave her. I foretold every single thing that's happened."

130 "Where did he go?" asks Mama.

"Probably to the North Pole, if he knows what's good for him," I says.

But Stella-Rondo just bawled and wouldn't say another word. She flew to her room and slammed the door.

"Now look what you've gone and done, Sister," says Mama. "You go apologize."

"I haven't got time, I'm leaving," I says.

135 "Well, what are you waiting around for?" asks Uncle Rondo.

So I just picked up the kitchen clock and marched off, without saying "Kiss my foot" or anything, and never did tell Stella-Rondo goodbye.

There was a nigger girl going along on a little wagon right in front.

"Nigger girl," I says, "come help me haul these things down the hill, I'm going to live in the post office."

Took her nine trips in her express wagon. Uncle Rondo came out on the porch and threw her a nickel.

140 And that's the last I've laid eyes on any of my family or my family laid eyes on me for five solid days and nights. Stella-Rondo may be telling the most horrible tales in the world about Mr. Whitaker, but I haven't heard them. As I tell everybody, I draw my own conclusions.

But oh, I like it here. It's ideal, as I've been saying. You see, I've got everything cater-cornered, the way I like it. Hear the radio? All the war news. Radio, sewing machine, book ends, ironing board and that great big piano lamp—peace, that's what I like. Butter-bean vines planted all along the front where the strings are.

Of course, there's not much mail. My family are naturally the main people in China Grove, and if they prefer to vanish from the face of the earth, for all the mail they get or the mail they write, why, I'm not going to open my mouth. Some of the folks here in town are taking up for me and some turned against me. I know which is which. There are always people who will quit buying stamps just to get on the right side of Papa-Daddy.

But here I am, and here I'll stay. I want the world to know I'm happy.

And if Stella-Rondo should come to me this minute, on bended knees, and *attempt* to explain the incidents of her life with Mr. Whitaker, I'd simply put my fingers in both my ears and refuse to listen.

(1941)

Margaret Laurence (1926–1987)

Margaret Laurence's best-known novels and short stories are set in Manawaka, a fictionalized version of her home town of Neepawa, Manitoba. However, her first novel, *This Side Jordan* (1960), grew out of her experiences living in Africa during the 1950s and reflects her lifelong concern with the repression of Native peoples. Later, in such novels as *The Stone Angel* (1964) and *A Jest of God* (1966), she depicted the social conflicts of the largely Scots-Presbyterian Manitoba community and the struggles of the women who grew up in it. "The Loons" is from *A Bird in the House* (1970), a collection of stories in which the portrayal of the maturation of Vanessa MacLeod is what Laurence called "fictionalized biography." In this story, the narrator examines the nature of her relationship to a Métis friend after the young woman's death.

THE LOONS

Just below Manawaka, where the Wachakwa River ran brown and noisy over the pebbles, the scrub oak and grey-green willow and chokecherry bushes grew in a dense thicket. In a clearing at the centre of the thicket stood the Tonnerre family's shack. The basis of this dwelling was a small square cabin made of poplar poles and chinked with mud, which had been built by Jules Tonnerre some fifty years before, when he came back from Batoche[1] with a bullet in his thigh, the year that Riel was hung and the voices of the Metis entered their long silence.[2] Jules had only intended to stay the winter in the Wachakwa Valley, but the family was still there in the thirties, when I was a child. As the Tonnerres had increased, their settlement had been added to, until the clearing at the foot of the town hill was a chaos of lean-tos, wooden packing cases, warped lumber, discarded car tyres, ramshackle chicken coops, tangled strands of barbed wire and rusty tin cans.

The Tonnerres were French half-breeds, and among themselves they spoke a *patois* that was neither Cree nor French. Their English was broken and full of obscenities. They did not belong among the Cree of the Galloping Mountain reservation, further north, and they did not belong among the Scots-Irish and Ukrainians of Manawaka, either. They were, as my Grandmother MacLeod would have put it, neither flesh, fowl, or good salt herring. When their men were not working at odd jobs or as section hands on the C.P.R., they lived on relief. In the summers, one of the Tonnerre youngsters, with a face that seemed totally unfamiliar with laughter, would knock at the doors of the town's brick houses and offer for sale a lard-pail full of bruised wild strawberries, and if he got as much as a quarter he would grab the coin and run before the customer had time to change her mind. Sometimes old Jules, or his son Lazarus, would get mixed

---

[1] near Prince Albert, Saskatchewan; in 1885, the site of a major battle in the Northwest Rebellion. [2] Louis Riel was the leader of the Métis people, who were of mixed white and Native blood.

up in a Saturday-night brawl, and would hit out at whoever was nearest, or howl drunkenly among the offended shoppers on Main Street, and then the Mountie would put them for the night in the barred cell underneath the Court House, and the next morning they would be quiet again.

Piquette Tonnerre, the daughter of Lazarus, was in my class at school. She was older than I, but she had failed several grades, perhaps because her attendance had always been sporadic and her interest in schoolwork negligible. Part of the reason she had missed a lot of school was that she had had tuberculosis of the bone, and had once spent many months in hospital. I knew this because my father was the doctor who had looked after her. Her sickness was almost the only thing I knew about her, however. Otherwise, she existed for me only as a vaguely embarrassing presence, with her hoarse voice and her clumsy limping walk and her grimy cotton dresses that were always miles too long. I was neither friendly nor unfriendly towards her. She dwelt and moved somewhere within my scope of vision, but I did not actually notice her very much until that peculiar summer when I was eleven.

"I don't know what to do about that kid," my father said at dinner one evening. "Piquette Tonnerre, I mean. The damn bone's flared up again. I've had her in hospital for quite a while now, and it's under control all right, but I hate like the dickens to send her home again."

5 "Couldn't you explain to her mother that she has to rest a lot?" my mother said.

"The mother's not there," my father replied. "She took off a few years back. Can't say I blame her. Piquette cooks for them, and she says Lazarus would never do anything for himself as long as she's there. Anyway, I don't think she'd take much care of herself, once she got back. She's only thirteen, after all. Beth, I was thinking—what about taking her up to Diamond Lake with us this summer? A couple of months rest would give that bone a much better chance."

My mother looked stunned.

"But Ewen—what about Roddie and Vanessa?"

"She's not contagious," my father said. "And it would be company for Vanessa."

10 "Oh dear," my mother said in distress, "I'll bet anything she has nits in her hair."

"For Pete's sake," my father said crossly, "do you think Matron would let her stay in the hospital for all this time like that? Don't be silly, Beth."

Grandmother MacLeod, her delicately featured face as rigid as a cameo, now brought her mauve-veined hands together as though she were about to begin a prayer.

"Ewen, if that half-breed youngster comes along to Diamond Lake, I'm not going," she announced. "I'll go to Morag's for the summer."

I had trouble in stifling my urge to laugh, for my mother brightened visibly and quickly tried to hide it. If it came to a choice between Grandmother MacLeod and Piquette, Piquette would win hands down, nits or not.

15 "It might be quite nice for you, at that," she mused. "You haven't seen Morag for over a year, and you might enjoy being in the city for a while. Well, Ewen dear, you do what you think best. If you think it would do

Piquette some good, then we'll be glad to have her, as long as she behaves herself."

So it happened that several weeks later, when we all piled into my father's old Nash, surrounded by suitcases and boxes of provisions and toys for my ten-month-old brother, Piquette was with us and Grandmother MacLeod, miraculously, was not. My father would only be staying at the cottage for a couple of weeks, for he had to get back to his practice, but the rest of us would stay at Diamond Lake until the end of August.

Our cottage was not named, as many were, "Dew Drop Inn" or "Bide-a-Wee," or "Bonnie Doon." The sign on the roadway bore in austere letters only our name, MacLeod. It was not a large cottage, but it was on the lakefront. You could look out the windows and see, through the filigree of the spruce trees, the water glistening greenly as the sun caught it. All around the cottage were ferns, and sharp-branched raspberry bushes, and moss that had grown over fallen tree trunks. If you looked carefully among the weeds and grass, you could find wild strawberry plants which were in white flower now and in another month would bear fruit, the fragrant globes hanging like miniature scarlet lanterns on the thin hairy stems. The two grey squirrels were still there, gossiping at us from the tall spruce beside the cottage, and by the end of the summer they would again be tame enough to take pieces of crust from my hands. The broad moose antlers that hung above the back door were a little more bleached and fissured after the winter, but otherwise everything was the same. I raced joyfully around my kingdom, greeting all the places I had not seen for a year. My brother, Roderick, who had not been born when we were here last summer, sat on the car rug in the sunshine and examined a brown spruce cone, meticulously turning it round and round in his small and curious hands. My mother and father toted the luggage from car to cottage, exclaiming over how well the place had wintered, no broken windows, thank goodness, no apparent damage from storm-felled branches or snow.

Only after I had finished looking around did I notice Piquette. She was sitting on the swing, her lame leg held stiffly out, and her other foot scuffing the ground as she swung slowly back and forth. Her long hair hung black and straight around her shoulders, and her broad coarse-featured face bore no expression—it was blank, as though she no longer dwelt within her own skull, as though she had gone elsewhere. I approached her very hesitantly.

"Want to come and play?"

Piquette looked at me with a sudden flash of scorn.

"I ain't a kid," she said.

Wounded, I stamped angrily away, swearing I would not speak to her for the rest of the summer. In the days that followed, however, Piquette began to interest me, and I began to want to interest her. My reasons did not appear bizarre to me. Unlikely as it may seem, I had only just realised that the Tonnerre family, whom I had always heard called half-breeds, were actually Indians, or as near as made no difference. My acquaintance with Indians was not extensive. I did not remember ever having seen a real

Indian, and my new awareness that Piquette sprang from the people of Big Bear and Poundmaker,[3] of Tecumseh,[4] of the Iroquois who had eaten Father Brebeuf's heart[5]—all this gave her an instant attraction in my eyes. I was a devoted reader of Pauline Johnson[6] at this age, and sometimes would orate aloud and in an exalted voice, *West Wind, blow from your prairie nest; Blow from the mountains, blow from the west*—and so on. It seemed to me that Piquette must be in some way a daughter of the forest, a kind of junior prophetess of the wilds, who might impart to me, if I took the right approach, some of the secrets which she undoubtedly knew—where the whippoorwill made her nest, how the coyote reared her young, or whatever it was that it said in Hiawatha.

I set about gaining Piquette's trust. She was not allowed to go swimming, with her bad leg, but I managed to lure her down to the beach—or rather, she came because there was nothing else to do. The water was always icy, for the lake was fed by springs, but I swam like a dog, thrashing my arms and legs around at such speed and with such an output of energy that I never grew cold. Finally, when I had had enough, I came out and sat beside Piquette on the sand. When she saw me approaching, her hand squashed flat the sand castle she had been building, and she looked at me sullenly, without speaking.

"Do you like this place?" I asked, after a while, intending to lead on from there into the question of forest lore.

Piquette shrugged. "It's okay. Good as anywhere."

"I love it," I said. "We come here every summer."

"So what?" Her voice was distant, and I glanced at her uncertainly, wondering what I could have said wrong.

"Do you want to come for a walk?" I asked her. "We wouldn't need to go far. If you walk just around the point there, you come to a bay where great big reeds grow in the water, and all kinds of fish hang around there. Want to? Come on."

She shook her head.

"Your dad said I ain't supposed to do no more walking than I got to."

I tried another line.

"I bet you know a lot about the woods and all that, eh?" I began respectfully.

Piquette looked at me from her large dark unsmiling eyes.

"I don't know what in hell you're talkin' about," she replied. "You nuts or somethin'? If you mean where my old man, and me, and all them live, you better shut up, by Jesus, you hear?"

I was startled and my feelings were hurt, but I had a kind of dogged perseverance. I ignored her rebuff.

"You know something, Piquette? There's loons here, on this lake. You can see their nests just up the shore there, behind those logs. At night, you can hear them even from the cottage, but it's better to listen from the beach.

---

[3]nineteenth-Century Cree chiefs who supported Louis Riel. [4]Shawnee chief, allied with the British in the War of 1812. [5]Jesuit missionary killed by Iroquois in 1649.
[6]early-twentieth-century Native writer.

My dad says we should listen and try to remember how they sound, because in a few years when more cottages are built at Diamond Lake and more people come in, the loons will go away."

Piquette was picking up stones and snail shells and then dropping them again.

"Who gives a good goddamn?" she said.

It became increasingly obvious that, as an Indian, Piquette was a dead loss. That evening I went out by myself, scrambling through the bushes that overhung the steep path, my feet slipping on the fallen spruce needles that covered the ground. When I reached the shore, I walked along the firm damp sand to the small pier that my father had built, and sat down there. I heard someone else crashing through the undergrowth and the bracken, and for a moment I thought Piquette had changed her mind, but it turned out to be my father. He sat beside me on the pier and we waited, without speaking.

40 At night the lake was like black glass with a streak of amber which was the path of the moon. All around, the spruce trees grew tall and close-set, branches blackly sharp against the sky, which was lightened by a cold flickering of stars. Then the loons began their calling. They rose like phantom birds from the nests on the shore, and flew out onto the dark still surface of the water.

No one can ever describe that ululating sound, the crying of the loons, and no one who has heard it can ever forget it. Plaintive, and yet with a quality of chilling mockery, those voices belonged to a world separated by aeons from our neat world of summer cottages and the lighted lamps of home.

"They must have sounded just like that," my father remarked, "before any person ever set foot here."

Then he laughed. "You could say the same, of course, about sparrows, or chipmunks, but somehow it only strikes you that way with the loons."

"I know," I said.

45 Neither of us suspected that this would be the last time we would ever sit here together on the shore, listening. We stayed for perhaps half an hour, and then we went back to the cottage. My mother was reading beside the fireplace. Piquette was looking at the burning birch log, and not doing anything.

"You should have come along," I said, although in fact I was glad she had not.

"Not me," Piquette said. "You wouldn' catch me walkin' way down there jus' for a bunch of squawkin' birds."

Piquette and I remained ill at ease with one another. I felt I had somehow failed my father, but I did not know what was the matter, nor why she would not or could not respond when I suggested exploring the woods or playing house. I thought it was probably her slow and difficult walking that held her back. She stayed most of the time in the cottage with my mother, helping her with the dishes or with Roddie, but hardly ever talking. Then the Duncans arrived at their cottage, and I spent my days with Mavis, who was my best friend. I could not reach Piquette at all, and I soon lost interest in trying. But all that summer she remained as both a reproach and a mystery to me.

That winter my father died of pneumonia, after less than a week's illness. For some time I saw nothing around me, being completely immersed in my own pain and my mother's. When I looked outward once more, I scarcely noticed that Piquette Tonnerre was no longer at school. I do not remember seeing her at all until four years later, one Saturday night when Mavis and I were having Cokes in the Regal Café. The jukebox was booming like tuneful thunder, and beside it, leaning lightly on its chrome and its rainbow glass, was a girl.

50 Piquette must have been seventeen then, although she looked about twenty. I stared at her, astounded that anyone could have changed so much. Her face, so stolid and expressionless before, was animated now with a gaiety that was almost violent. She laughed and talked very loudly with the boys around her. Her lipstick was bright carmine, and her hair was cut short and frizzily permed. She had not been pretty as a child, and she was not pretty now, for her features were still heavy and blunt. But her dark and slightly slanted eyes were beautiful, and her skin-tight skirt and orange sweater displayed to enviable advantage a soft and slender body.

She saw me, and walked over. She teetered a little, but it was not due to her once-tubercular leg, for her limp was almost gone.

"Hi, Vanessa." Her voice still had the same hoarseness. "Long time no see, eh?"

"Hi," I said. "Where've you been keeping yourself, Piquette?"

"Oh, I been around," she said. "I been away almost two years now. Been all over the place—Winnipeg, Regina, Saskatoon. Jesus, what I could tell you! I come back this summer, but I ain't stayin'. You kids goin' to the dance?"

55 "No," I said abruptly, for this was a sore point with me. I was fifteen, and thought I was old enough to go to the Saturday-night dances at the Flamingo. My mother, however, thought otherwise.

"Y'oughta come," Piquette said. "I never miss one. It's just about the on'y thing in this jerkwater town that's any fun. Boy, you couldn' catch me stayin' here. I don' give a shit about this place. It stinks."

She sat down beside me, and I caught the harsh over-sweetness of her perfume.

"Listen, you wanna know something, Vanessa?" she confided, her voice only slightly blurred. "Your dad was the only person in Manawaka that ever done anything good to me."

I nodded speechlessly. I was certain she was speaking the truth. I knew a little more than I had that summer at Diamond Lake, but I could not reach her now any more than I had then. I was ashamed, ashamed of my own timidity, the frightened tendency to look the other way. Yet I felt no real warmth towards her—I only felt that I ought to, because of that distant summer and because my father had hoped she would be company for me, or perhaps that I would be for her, but it had not happened that way. At this moment, meeting her again, I had to admit that she repelled and embarrassed me, and I could not help despising the self-pity in her voice. I wished she would go away. I did not want to see her. I did not know what to say to her. It seemed that we had nothing to say to one another.

60   "I'll tell you something else," Piquette went on. "All the old bitches an' biddies in this town will sure be surprised. I'm gettin' married this fall—my boyfriend, he's an English fella, works in the stockyards in the city there, a very tall guy, got blond wavy hair. Gee, is he ever handsome. Got this real classy name. Alvin Gerald Cummings—some handle, eh? They call him Al."

    For the merest instant, then, I saw her. I really did see her, for the first and only time in all the years we had both lived in the same town. Her defiant face, momentarily, became unguarded and unmasked, and in her eyes there was a terrifying hope.

    "Gee, Piquette—" I burst out awkwardly, "that's swell. That's really wonderful. Congratulations—good luck—I hope you'll be happy—"

    As I mouthed the conventional phrases, I could only guess how great her need must have been, that she had been forced to seek the very things she so bitterly rejected.

    When I was eighteen, I left Manawaka and went away to college. At the end of my first year, I came back home for the summer. I spent the first few days in talking non-stop with my mother, as we exchanged all the news that somehow had not found its way into letters—what had happened in my life and what had happened here in Manawaka while I was away. My mother searched her memory for events that concerned people I knew.

65   "Did I ever write you about Piquette Tonnerre, Vanessa?" she asked one morning.

    "No, I don't think so," I replied. "Last I heard of her, she was going to marry some guy in the city. Is she still there?"

    My mother looked perturbed, and it was a moment before she spoke, as though she did not know how to express what she had to tell and wished she did not need to try.

    "She's dead," she said at last. Then, as I stared at her, "Oh, Vanessa, when it happened, I couldn't help thinking of her as she was that summer— so sullen and gauche and badly dressed. I couldn't help wondering if we could have done something more at that time—but what could we do? She used to be around in the cottage there with me all day, and honestly, it was all I could do to get a word out of her. She didn't even talk to your father very much, although I think she liked him, in her way."

    "What happened?" I asked.

70   "Either her husband left her, or she left him," my mother said. "I don't know which. Anyway, she came back here with two youngsters, both only babies— they must have been born very close together. She kept house, I guess, for Lazarus and her brothers, down in the valley there, in the old Tonnerre place. I used to see her on the street sometimes, but she never spoke to me. She'd put on an awful lot of weight, and she looked a mess, to tell you the truth, a real slattern, dressed any old how. She was up in court a couple of times—drunk and disorderly, of course. One Saturday night last winter, during the coldest weather, Piquette was alone in the shack with the children. The Tonnerres made home brew all the time, so I've heard, and Lazarus said later she'd been drinking most of the day when he and the boys went out that evening. They had an old woodstove there—you know the kind, with exposed pipes. The shack caught fire. Piquette didn't get out, and neither did the children."

I did not say anything. As so often with Piquette, there did not seem to be anything to say. There was a kind of silence around the image in my mind of the fire and the snow, and I wished I could put from my memory the look that I had seen once in Piquette's eyes.

I went up to Diamond Lake for a few days that summer, with Mavis and her family. The MacLeod cottage had been sold after my father's death, and I did not even go to look at it, not wanting to witness my long-ago kingdom possessed now by strangers. But one evening I went down to the shore by myself.

The small pier which my father had built was gone, and in its place there was a large and solid pier built by the government, for Galloping Mountain was now a national park, and Diamond Lake had been re-named Lake Wapakata, for it was felt that an Indian name would have a greater appeal to tourists. The one store had become several dozen, and the settlement had all the attributes of a flourishing resort—hotels, a dance-hall, cafés with neon signs, the penetrating odours of potato chips and hot dogs.

I sat on the government pier and looked out across the water. At night the lake at least was the same as it had always been, darkly shining and bearing within its black glass the streak of amber that was the path of the moon. There was no wind that evening, and everything was quiet all around me. It seemed too quiet, and then I realized that the loons were no longer here. I listened for some time, to make sure, but never once did I hear that long-drawn call, half mocking and half plaintive, spearing through the stillness across the lake.

I did not know what had happened to the birds. Perhaps they had gone away to some far place of belonging. Perhaps they had been unable to find such a place, and had simply died out, having ceased to care any longer whether they lived or not.

I remembered how Piquette had scorned to come along, when my father and I sat there and listened to the lake birds. It seemed to me now that in some unconscious and totally unrecognised way, Piquette might have been the only one, after all, who had heard the crying of the loons.

(1966)

Timothy Findley   (1930–2002)

Toronto-born Timothy Findley began his artistic career as an actor and later became a dramatist. Both professions are evident is his short stories, which present events that take place in clearly defined settings. In his novels, he deals with the complex psychological motivations and actions of his characters. In two of them, *The Wars* and *Famous Last Words*, discoveries of objects from earlier times lead characters on quests to understand the significance of past events. In the short story "War," a twelve-year-old boy examining a photograph of himself, his brother, and his father recounts the events that preceded the taking of the picture two years earlier. Although he refers to the time he discusses as "when we were children," his narrative raises questions as to how much understanding he has gained about his emotions and actions on learning that his father has enrolled in the army. The title refers not only to World War II, but also to the conflicts Neil felt, and perhaps still feels, within himself.

WAR

That's my dad in the middle. We were just kids then, Bud on the right and me on the left. That was taken just before my dad went into the army.

Some day that was.

It was a Saturday, two years ago. August, 1940. I can remember I had to blow my nose just before that and I had to use my dad's hankie because mine had a worm in it that I was saving. I can't remember why; I mean, why I was saving that worm, but I can remember why I had to blow my nose, all right. That was because I'd had a long time crying. Not exactly because my dad was going away or anything—it was mostly because I'd done something.

I'll tell you what in a minute, but I just want to say this first. I was ten years old then and it was sort of the end of summer. When we went back to school I was going into the fifth grade and that was pretty important, especially for me because I'd skipped grade four. Right now I can't even remember grade five except that I didn't like it. I should have gone to grade four. In grade five everyone was a genius and there was a boy called Allan McKenzie.

5 Anyway, now that you know how old I was and what grade I was into, I can tell you the rest.

It was the summer the war broke out and I went to stay with my friend, Arthur Robertson. Looking back on it, Arthur seems a pretty silly name for Arthur Robertson because he was so small. But he was a nice kid and his dad had the most enormous summer cottage you've ever seen. In Muskoka,[1] too.

It was like those houses they have in the movies in Beverly Hills. Windows a mile long—pine trees outside and then a lake and then a red canoe tied up with a yellow rope. There was an Indian, too, who sold little

[1] a popular summer cabin area 100 km north of Toronto.

boxes made of birch-bark and porcupine quills. Arthur Robertson and I used to sit in the red canoe and this Indian would take us for a ride out to the raft and back. Then we'd go and tell Mrs Robertson or the cook or someone how nice he was and he'd stand behind us and smile as though he didn't understand English and then they'd have to buy a box from him. He certainly was smart, that Indian, because it worked about four times. Then one day they caught on and hid the canoe.

Anyway, that's the sort of thing we did. And we swam too, and I remember a book that Arthur Robertson's nurse read to us. It was about dogs.

Then I had to go away because I'd only been invited for two weeks. I went on to this farm where the family took us every summer when we were children. Bud was already there, and his friend, Teddy Hartley.

10 I didn't like Teddy Hartley. It was because he had a space between his teeth and he used to spit through it. Once I saw him spit two-and-a-half yards. Bud paced it out. And then he used to whistle through it, too, that space, and it was the kind of whistling that nearly made your ears bleed. That was what I didn't like. But it didn't really matter, because he was Bud's friend, not mine.

So I went by train and Mr and Mrs Currie met me in their truck. It was their farm.

Mrs Currie got me into the front with her while Mr Currie put my stuff in the back.

"Your mum and dad aren't here, dear, but they'll be up tomorrow. Buddy is here—and his friend."

Grownups were always calling Bud "Buddy." It was all wrong.

15 I didn't care too much about my parents not being there, except that I'd brought them each one of those birch-bark boxes. Inside my mother's there was a set of red stones I'd picked out from where we swam. I thought maybe she'd make a necklace out of them. In my dad's there was an old golf ball, because he played golf. I guess you'd have to say I stole it, because I didn't tell anyone I had it—but it was just lying there on a shelf in Mr Robertson's boathouse, and he never played golf. At least I never saw him.

I had these boxes on my lap because I'd thought my mum and dad would be there to meet me, but now that they weren't I put them into the glove compartment of the truck.

We drove to the farm.

Bud and Teddy were riding on the gate, and they waved when we drove past. I couldn't see too well because of the dust but I could hear them shouting. It was something about my dad. I didn't really hear exactly what it was they said, but Mrs Currie went white as a sheet and said: "Be quiet," to Bud.

20 Then we were there and the truck stopped. We went inside.

And now—this is where it begins.

After supper, the evening I arrived at the Curries' farm, my brother Bud and his friend Teddy Hartley and I all sat on the front porch. In a hammock.

This is the conversation we had.

BUD: (*to me*) Are you all right? Did you have a good time at Arthur Robertson's place? Did you swim?

ME: (*to Bud*) Yes.

TEDDY HARTLEY: I've got a feeling I don't like Arthur Robertson. Do I know him?

BUD: Kid at school. Neil's age. (*He said that as if it were dirty to be my age.*)

TEDDY HARTLEY: Thin kid? Very small?

BUD: Thin and small—brainy type. Hey, Neil, have you seen Ted spit?

ME: Yes—I have.

TEDDY HARTLEY: When did you see me spit? (*Indignant as hell*) I never spat for you.

ME: Yes, you did. About three months ago. We were still in school. Bud—he did too, and you walked it out, too, didn't you?

BUD: I don't know.

TEDDY HARTLEY: I never spat for you yet! Never!

ME: Two yards and a half.

TEDDY HARTLEY: Can't have been me. I spit four.

ME: Four YARDS!!

TEDDY HARTLEY: Certainly.

BUD: Go ahead and show him. Over the rail.

TEDDY HARTLEY: (*Standing up*) Okay. Look, Neil . . . Now watch . . . Come on, WATCH!!

ME: All right—I'm watching. (*Teddy Hartley spat. It was three yards-and-a-half by Bud's feet. I saw Bud mark it myself.*)

BUD: Three yards and a half a foot.

TEDDY HARTLEY: Four yards. (*Maybe his feet were smaller or something.*)

BUD: Three-and-foot. Three and *one* foot. No, no. A *half*-a-one. Of a foot.

TEDDY HARTLEY: Four.

BUD: Three!

TEDDY HARTLEY: Four! Four! Four!

BUD: Three! One-two-three-and-a-half-a-foot!!

TEDDY HARTLEY: My dad showed me. It's four! He showed me, and he knows. My dad knows. He's a mathematical teacher—yes, yes, yes, he showed me how to count a yard. I saw him do it. And he knows, my dad!!

BUD: Your dad's a crazy man. It's three yards and a half a foot.

TEDDY HARTLEY: (*All red in the face and screaming*) You called my dad a nut! You called my dad a crazy-man-nut-meg! Take it back, you. Bud Cable, you take that back.

BUD: Your dad is a matha-nut-ical nutmeg tree.

TEDDY HARTLEY: Then your dad's a . . . your dad's a . . . your dad's an Insane!

BUD: Our dad's joined the army.

That was how I found out.

They went on talking like that for a long time. I got up and left. I started talking to myself, which is a habit I have.

"Joined the army? Joined the army? Joined the ARMY! Our dad?"

Our dad was a salesman. I used to go to his office and watch him selling things over the phone sometimes. I always used to look for what it was, but I guess they didn't keep it around the office. Maybe they hid it somewhere. Maybe it was too expensive to just leave lying around. But whatever it was, I knew it was important, and so that was one thing that bothered me when Bud said about the army—because I knew that in the army they wouldn't let my dad sit and sell things over any old phone—because in the army you always went in a trench and got hurt or killed. I knew that because my dad had told me himself when my uncle died. My uncle was his brother in the first war, who got hit in his stomach and he died from it a long time afterwards. Long enough, anyway, for me to have known him. He was always in a big white bed, and he gave us candies from a glass jar. That was all I knew—except that it was because of being in the army that he died. His name was Uncle Frank.

So those were the first two things I thought of: my dad not being able to sell anything any more—and then Uncle Frank.

But then it really got bad, because I suddenly remembered that my dad had promised to teach me how to skate that year. He was going to make a rink too; in the back yard. But if he had to go off to some old trench in France, then he'd be too far away. Soldiers always went in trenches—and trenches were always in France. I remember that.

Well, I don't know. Maybe I just couldn't forgive him. He hadn't even told me. He didn't even write it in his letter that he'd sent me at Arthur Robertson's. But he'd told Bud—he'd told Bud, but I was the one he'd promised to show how to skate. And I'd had it all planned how I'd really surprise my dad and turn out to be a skating champion and everything, and now he wouldn't even be there to see.

All because he had to go and sit in some trench.

I don't know how I got there, but I ended up in the barn. I was in the hayloft and I didn't even hear them, I guess. They were looking all over the place for me, because it started to get dark.

I don't know whether you're afraid of the dark, but I'll tell you right now, I am. At least, I am if I have to move around in it. If I can just sit still, then I'm all right. At least, if you sit still you know where you are—but if you move around, then you don't know where you are. And that's awful. You never know what you're going to step on next and I always thought it would be a duck. I don't like ducks—especially in the dark or if you stepped on them.

Anyway, I was in that hayloft in the barn and I heard them calling out—"Neil, Neil"—and "Where are you?" But I made up my mind right then I wasn't going to answer. For one thing, if I did, then I'd have to go down to them in the dark—and maybe I'd step on something. And for another, I didn't really want to see anyone anyway.

It was then that I got this idea about my father. I thought that maybe if I stayed hidden for long enough, then he wouldn't join the army. Don't ask me why—right now I couldn't tell you that—but in those days it made sense. If I hid then he wouldn't go away. Maybe it would be because he'd stay looking for me or something.

The trouble was that my dad wasn't even there that night, and that meant that I either had to wait in the hayloft till he came the next day—or else that I had to go down now, and then hide again tomorrow. I decided to stay where I was because there were some ducks at the bottom of the ladder. I couldn't see them but I could tell they were there.

I stayed there all night. I slept most of the time. Every once in a while they'd wake me up by calling out "Neil! Neil!"—but I never answered.

I never knew a night that was so long, except maybe once when I was in the hospital. When I slept I seemed to sleep for a long time, but it never came to morning. They kept waking me up but it was never time.

Then it was.

70   I saw that morning through a hole in the roof of the hayloft. The sunlight came in through cracks between the boards and it was all dusty; the sunlight, I mean.

They were up pretty early that morning, even for farmers. There seemed to be a lot more people than I remembered—and there were two or three cars and a truck I'd never seen before, too. And I saw Mrs Currie holding onto Bud with one hand and Teddy Hartley with the other. I remember thinking, "If I was down there, how could she hold onto me if she's only got two hands and Bud and Teddy Hartley to look after?" And I thought that right then she must be pretty glad I wasn't around.

I wondered what they were all doing. Mr Currie was standing in the middle of a lot of men and he kept pointing out the scenery around the farm. I imagined what he was saying. There was a big woods behind the house and a cherry and plum-tree orchard that would be good to point out to his friends. I could tell they were his friends from the way they were listening. What I couldn't figure out was why they were all up so early—and why they had Bud and Teddy Hartley up, too.

Then there was a police car. I suppose it came from Orillia[2] or somewhere. That was the biggest town near where the farm was. Orillia.

When the policemen got out of their car, they went up to Mr Currie. There were four of them. They all talked for quite a long time and then everyone started going out in all directions. It looked to me as though Bud and Teddy Hartley wanted to go, too, but Mrs Currie made them go in the house. She practically had to drag Bud. It looked as if he was crying and I wondered why he should do that.

75   Then one of the policemen came into the barn. He was all alone. I stayed very quiet, because I wasn't going to let anything keep me from going through with my plan about my dad. Not even a policeman.

He urinated against the wall inside the door. It was sort of funny, because he kept turning around to make sure no one saw him, and he didn't know I was there. Then he did up his pants and stood in the middle of the floor under the haylofts.

---

[2] a city just over 65 km north of Toronto.

"Hey! Neil!"

That was the policeman.

He said it so suddenly that it scared me. I nearly fell off from where I was, it scared me so much. And I guess maybe he saw me, because he started right up the ladder at me.

"How did you know my name?"

I said that in a whisper.

"They told me."

"Oh."

"Have you been here all night?"

"Yes."

"Don't you realize that *everyone* has been looking for you all over the place? Nobody's even been to sleep."

That sort of frightened me—but it was all right, because he smiled when he said it.

Then he stuck his head out of this window that was there to let the air in (so that the barn wouldn't catch on fire)—and he yelled down, "He's all right—I've found him! He's up here."

And I said: "What did you go and do that for? Now you've ruined everything."

He smiled again and said, "I had to stop them all going off to look for you. Now,"—as he sat down beside me—"do you want to tell me what it is you're doing up here?"

"No."

I think that sort of set him back a couple of years, because he didn't say anything for a minute—except "Oh."

Then I thought maybe I had to have something to tell the others anyway, so I might as well make it up for him right now.

"I fell asleep," I said.

"When—last night?"

"Yes."

I looked at him. I wondered if I could trust a guy who did that against walls, when all you had to do was go in the house.

"Why did you come up here in the first place?" he said.

I decided I could trust him because I remembered once when I did the same thing. Against the wall.

So I told him.

"I want to hide on my dad," I said.

"Why do you want to do that? And besides, Mrs Currie said your parents weren't even here."

"Yes, but he's coming today."

"But why hide on him? Don't you like him, or something?"

"Sure I do," I said.

I thought about it.

"But he's . . . he's . . . Do you know if it's true, my dad's joined the army?"

"I dunno. Maybe. There's a war on, you know."

"Well, that's why I hid."

But he laughed.

"Is that why you hid? Because of the war?"

"Because of my dad."

"You don't need to hide because of the war—the Germans aren't coming over here, you know."

"But it's not that. It's my dad." I could have told you he wouldn't understand.

115   I was trying to think of what to say next when Mrs Currie came into the barn. She stood down below.

"Is he up there, officer? Is he all right?"

"Yes, ma'am, I've got him. He's fine."

"Neil dear, what happened? Why don't you come down and tell us what happened to you?"

Then I decided that I'd really go all out. I had to, because I could tell they weren't going to—it was just *obvious* that these people weren't going to understand me and take my story about my dad and the army and everything.

120   "Somebody chased me."

The policeman looked sort of shocked and I could hear Mrs Currie take in her breath.

"Somebody chased you, eh?"

"Yes."

"Who?"

125   I had to think fast.

"Some man. But he's gone now."

I thought I'd better say he was gone, so that they wouldn't start worrying.

"Officer, why don't you bring him down here? Then we can talk."

"All right, ma'am. Come on, Neil, we'll go down and have some breakfast."

130   They didn't seem to believe me about that man I made up.

We went over to the ladder.

I looked down. A lot of hay stuck out so that I couldn't see the floor.

"Are there any ducks down there?"

"No, dear, you can come down—it's all right."

135   She was lying, though. There was a great big duck right next to her. I think it's awfully silly to tell a lie like that. I mean, if the duck is standing right there it doesn't even make sense, does it?

But I went down anyway and she made the duck go away.

When we went out, the policeman held my hand. His hand had some sweat on it but it was a nice hand, with hair on the back. I liked that. My dad didn't have that on his hand.

Then we ate breakfast with all those people who'd come to look for me. At least, *they* ate. I just sat.

After breakfast, Mr and Mrs Currie took me upstairs to the sitting room. It was upstairs because the kitchen was in the cellar.

140   All I remember about that was a vase that had a potted plant in it. This vase was made of putty and into the putty Mrs Currie had stuck all kinds of stones and pennies and old bits of glass and things. You could look at this for hours and never see the same kind of stone or glass twice. I don't remember the plant.

All I remember about what they said was that they told me I should never do it again. That routine.

Then they told me my mother and my dad would be up that day around lunch time.

What they were really sore about was losing their sleep, and then all those people coming. I was sorry about that—but you can't very well go down and make an announcement about it, so I didn't.

*****

At twelve o'clock I went and sat in Mr Currie's truck. It was in the barn. I took out those two boxes I'd put in the glove compartment and looked at them. I tried to figure out what my dad would do with an old box like that in the army. And he'd probably never play another game of golf as long as he lived. Not in the army, anyway. Maybe he'd use the box for his bullets or something.

145 Then I counted the red stones I was going to give my mother. I kept seeing them around her neck and how pretty they'd be. She had a dress they'd be just perfect with. Blue. The only thing I was worried about was how to get a hole in them so you could put them on a string. There wasn't much sense in having beads without a string—not if you were going to wear them, anyway—or your mother was.

And it was then that they came.

I heard their car drive up outside and I went and looked from behind the barn door. My father wasn't wearing a uniform yet like I'd thought he would be. I began to think maybe he really didn't want me to know about it. I mean, he hadn't written or anything, and now he was just wearing an old blazer and some gray pants. It made me remember.

I went back and sat down in the truck again. I didn't know what to do. I just sat there with those stones in my hand.

Then I heard someone shout, "Neil!"

150 I went and looked. Mr and Mrs Currie were standing with my parents by the car—and I saw Bud come running out of the house, and then Teddy Hartley. Teddy Hartley sort of hung back, though. He was the kind of person who's only polite if there are grownups around him. He sure knew how to pull the wool over their eyes, because he'd even combed his hair. Wildroot-cream-oil-Charlie.[3]

Then I noticed that they were talking very seriously and my mother put her hand above her eyes and looked around. I guess she was looking for me. Then my dad started toward the barn.

I went and hid behind the truck. I wasn't quite sure yet what I was going to do, but I certainly wasn't going to go up and throw my arms around his neck or anything.

"Neil. Are you in there, son?"

My dad spoke that very quietly. Then I heard the door being pushed open, and some chicken had to get out of the way, because I heard it making

[3]a fictional character used in advertisements for a popular hair gel of the 1940s.

that awful noise chickens make when you surprise them doing something. They sure can get excited over nothing—chickens.

155   I took a quick look behind me. There was a door there that led into the part of the barn where the haylofts were and where I'd been all night. I decided to make a dash for it. But I had to ward off my father first—and so I threw that stone.

I suppose I'll have to admit that I meant to hit him. It wouldn't be much sense if I tried to fool you about that. I wanted to hit him because when I stood up behind the truck and saw him then I suddenly got mad. I thought about how he hadn't written me, or anything.

It hit him on the hand.

He turned right around because he wasn't sure what it was or where it came from. And before I ran, I just caught a glimpse of his face. He'd seen me and he sure looked peculiar. I guess that now I'll never forget his face and how he looked at me right then. I think it was that he looked as though he might cry or something. But I knew he wouldn't do that, because he never did.

Then I ran.

160   From the loft I watched them in the yard. My dad was rubbing his hands together and I guess maybe where I'd hit him it was pretty sore. My mother took off her handkerchief that she had round her neck and put it on his hand. Then I guess he'd told them what I'd done, because this time they all started toward the barn.

I didn't know what to do then. I counted out the stones I had left and there were about fifteen of them. There was the golf ball, too.

I didn't want to throw stones at all of them. I certainly didn't want to hit my mother—and I hoped that they wouldn't send her in first. I thought then how I'd be all right if they sent in Teddy Hartley first. I didn't mind the thought of throwing at him, I'll tell you that much.

But my dad came first.

I had a good view of where he came from. He came in through the part where the truck was parked, because I guess he thought I was still there. And then he came on into the part where I was now—in the hayloft.

165   He stood by the door.

"Neil."

I wasn't saying anything. I sat very still.

"Neil."

I could only just see his head and shoulders—the rest of him was hidden by the edge of the loft.

170   "Neil, aren't you even going to explain what you're angry about?"

I thought for a minute and then I didn't answer him after all. I looked at him, though. He looked worried.

"What do you want us to do?"

I sat still.

"Neil?"

175   Since I didn't answer, he started back out the door—I guess to talk to my mother or someone.

I hit his back with another stone. I had to make sure he knew I was there.

He turned around at me.

"Neil, what's the matter? I want to know what's the matter."

He almost fooled me, but not quite. I thought that perhaps he really didn't know for a minute—but after taking a look at him I decided that he did know, all right. I mean, there he was in that blue blazer and everything—just as if he hadn't joined the army at all.

180   So I threw again and this time it really hit him in the face.

He didn't do anything—he just stood there. It really scared me. Then my mother came in, but he made her go back.

I thought about my rink, and how I wouldn't have it. I thought about being in the fifth grade that year and how I'd skipped from grade three. And I thought about the Indian who'd sold those boxes that I had down in the truck.

"Neil—I'm going to come up."

You could tell he really would, too, from his voice.

185   I got the golf ball ready.

To get to me he had to disappear for a minute while he crossed under the loft and then when he climbed the ladder. I decided to change my place while he was out of sight. I began to think that was pretty clever and that maybe I'd be pretty good at that war stuff myself. Field Marshal[4] Cable.

I put myself into a little trench of hay and piled some up in front of me. When my dad came up over the top of the ladder, he wouldn't even see me and then I'd have a good chance to aim at him.

The funny thing was that at that moment I'd forgotten why I was against him. I got so mixed up in all that Field Marshal stuff that I really forgot all about my dad and the army and everything. I was just trying to figure out how I could get him before he saw me—and that was all.

I got further down in the hay and then he was there.

190   He was out of breath and his face was all sweaty, and where I'd hit him there was blood. And then he put his hand with my mother's hankie up to his face to wipe it. And he sort of bit it (the handkerchief). It was as if he was confused or something. I remember thinking he looked then just like I'd felt my face go when Bud had said our dad had joined the army. You know how you look around with your eyes from side to side as though maybe you'll find the answer to it somewhere near you? You never do find it, but you always look anyway, just in case.

Anyway, that's how he was just then, and it sort of threw me. I had that feeling again that maybe he didn't know what this was all about. But then, he had to know, didn't he? Because he'd done it.

I had the golf ball ready in my right hand and one of those stones in the other. He walked toward me.

I missed with the golf ball and got him with the stone.

And he fell down. He really fell down. He didn't say anything—he didn't even say "ouch," like I would have—he just fell down.

195   In the hay.

[4]in many countries, the top ranking army officer.

I didn't go out just yet. I sat and looked at him. And I listened. Nothing.

Do you know, there wasn't a sound in that whole place? It was as if everything had stopped because they knew what had happened.

My dad just lay there and we waited for what would happen next.

It was me.

I mean, I made the first noise.

I said: "Dad?"

But nobody answered—not even my mother.

So I said it louder. *"Dad?"*

It was just as if they'd all gone away and left me with him, all alone.

He sure looked strange lying there—so quiet and everything. I didn't know what to do.

"Dad?"

I went over on my hands and knees.

Then suddenly they all came in. I just did what I thought of first. I guess it was because they scared me—coming like that when it was so quiet.

I got all the stones out of my pockets and threw them, one by one, as they came through the door. I stood up to do it. I saw them all running through the door, and I threw every stone, even at my mother.

And then I fell down. I fell down beside my dad and pushed him over on his back because he'd fallen on his stomach. It was like he was asleep.

They came up then and I don't remember much of that. Somebody picked me up, and there was the smell of perfume and my eyes hurt and I got something in my throat and nearly choked to death and I could hear a lot of talking. And somebody was whispering, too. And then I felt myself being carried down and there was the smell of oil and gasoline and some chickens had to be got out of the way again and then there was sunlight.

Then my mother just sat with me, and I guess I cried for a long time. In the cherry and plum-tree orchard—and she seemed to understand because she said that he would tell me all about it and that he hadn't written me because he didn't want to scare me when I was all alone at Arthur Robertson's.

And then Bud came.

My mother said that he should go away for a while. But he said: "I brought something" and she said: "What is it, then?" and now I remember where I got that worm in my handkerchief that I told you about.

It was from Bud.

He said to me that if I wanted to, he'd take me fishing on the lake just before the sun went down. He said that was a good time. And he gave me that worm because he'd found it.

So my mother took it and put it in my hankie and Bud looked at me for a minute and then went away.

The worst part was when I saw my dad again.

My mother took me to the place where he was sitting in the sun and we just watched each other for a long time.

Then he said: "Neil, your mother wants to take our picture because I'm going away tomorrow to Ottawa for a couple of weeks, and she thought I'd like a picture to take with me."

He lit a cigarette and then he said: "I would, too, you know, like that picture."

And I sort of said: "All right."

So they called to Bud, and my mother went to get her camera.

But before Bud came and before my mother got back, we were alone for about ten hours. It was awful.

I couldn't think of anything and I guess he couldn't, either. I had a good look at him, though.

He looked just like he does right there in that picture. You can see where the stone hit him on his right cheek—and the one that knocked him out is the one over the eye.

Right then the thing never got settled. Not in words, anyway. I was still thinking about that rink and everything—and my dad hadn't said anything about the army yet.

I wish I hadn't done it. Thrown those stones and everything. It wasn't his fault he had to go.

For another thing, I was sorry about the stones because I knew I wouldn't find any more like them—but I did throw them, and that's that.

They both got those little boxes, though—I made sure of that. And in one there was a string of red beads from Orillia and in the other there was a photograph.

There still is.

(1984)

Alice Munro   (b. 1931)

Born in Wingham, Ontario, Alice Munro began writing short stories in high school but did not publish her first collection, *Dance of the Happy Shades,* winner of the Governor General's Award for fiction, until 1968. Like the American writer Eudora Welty, whose work she admires, Munro is essentially a regional writer, portraying girls and women from small-town western Ontario confronting the various stages of their lives and the nature of their relationships with other people. She has been praised for her precise depiction of the events and settings that are used to reveal aspects of the personalities of her characters. In "Wild Swans," from *Who Do You Think You Are?,* another winner of the Governor General's Award, a girl's first trip alone from her small southwestern Ontario town to the metropolis of Toronto is presented as a transition period in her coming of age.

WILD SWANS

Flo said to watch out for White Slavers. She said this was how they operated: an old woman, a motherly or grandmotherly sort, made friends while riding beside you on a bus or train. She offered you candy, which was drugged. Pretty soon you began to droop and mumble, were in no condition to speak for yourself. Oh, Help, the woman said, my daughter (granddaughter) is sick, please somebody help me get her off so that she can recover in the fresh air. Up stepped a polite gentleman, pretending to be a stranger, offering assistance. Together, at the next stop, they hustled you off the train or bus, and that was the last the ordinary world ever saw of you. They kept you a prisoner in the White Slave place (to which you had been transported drugged and bound so you wouldn't even know where you were), until such time as you were thoroughly degraded and in despair, your insides torn up by drunken men and invested with vile disease, your mind destroyed by drugs, your hair and teeth fallen out. It took about three years, for you to get to this state. You wouldn't want to go home, then, maybe couldn't remember home, or find your way if you did. So they let you out on the streets.

Flo took ten dollars and put it in a little cloth bag which she sewed to the strap of Rose's slip. Another thing likely to happen was that Rose would get her purse stolen.

Watch out, Flo said as well, for people dressed up as ministers. These were the worst. That disguise was commonly adopted by White Slavers, as well as those after your money.

Rose said she didn't see how she could tell which ones were disguised.

Flo had worked in Toronto once. She had worked as a waitress in a coffee shop in Union Station. That was how she knew all she knew. She never saw sunlight, in those days, except on her days off. But she saw plenty else. She saw a man cut another man's stomach with a knife, just pull out his shirt and do a tidy cut, as if it was a watermelon not a stomach. The stomach's owner just sat looking down surprised, with no time to protest. Flo implied that that was nothing, in Toronto. She saw two bad women (that was what Flo called whores, running the two words together, like badminton) get into a fight, and a man laughed at them, other men stopped and laughed and egged them on, and they had their fists full of each other's hair. At last the police came and took them away, still howling and yelping.

She saw a child die of a fit, too. Its face was black as ink.

"Well I'm not scared," said Rose provokingly. "There's the police, any-way."

"Oh, them! They'd be the first ones to diddle you!"

She did not believe anything Flo said on the subject of sex. Consider the undertaker.

10   A little bald man, very neatly dressed, would come into the store sometimes and speak to Flo with a placating expression.

"I only wanted a bag of candy. And maybe a few packages of gum. And one or two chocolate bars. Could you go to the trouble of wrapping them?"

Flo in her mock-deferential tone would assure him that she could. She wrapped them in heavy-duty white paper, so they were something like presents. He took his time with the selection, humming and chatting, then dawdling for a while. He might ask how Flo was feeling. And how Rose was, if she was there.

"You look pale. Young girls need fresh air." To Flo he would say, "You work too hard. You've worked hard all your life."

"No rest for the wicked," Flo would say agreeably.

15   When he went out she hurried to the window. There it was—the old black hearse with its purple curtains.

"He'll be after them today!" Flo would say as the hearse rolled away at a gentle pace, almost a funeral pace. The little man had been an undertaker, but he was retired now. The hearse was retired too. His sons had taken over the undertaking and bought a new one. He drove the old hearse all over the country, looking for women. So Flo said. Rose could not believe it. Flo said he gave them the gum and the candy. Rose said he probably ate them himself. Flo said he had been seen, he had been heard. In mild weather he drove with the windows down, singing, to himself or to somebody out of sight in the back.

> Her brow is like the snowdrift
> Her throat is like the swan

Flo imitated him singing. Gently overtaking some woman walking on a back road, or resting at a country crossroads. All compliments and courtesy and chocolate bars, offering a ride. Of course every women who reported being asked said she had turned him down. He never pestered anybody, drove politely on. He called in at houses, and if the husband was home he seemed to like just as well as anything to sit and chat. Wives said that was all he ever did anyway but Flo did not believe it.

"Some women are taken in," she said. "A number." She liked to speculate on what the hearse was like inside. Plush. Plush on the walls and the roof and the floor. Soft purple, the color of the curtains, the color of dark lilacs.

20   All nonsense, Rose thought. Who could believe it, of a man that age?

Rose was going to Toronto on the train for the first time by herself. She had been once before, but that was with Flo, long before her father died. They took along their own sandwiches and bought milk from the vendor on the train. It was sour. Sour chocolate milk. Rose kept taking tiny sips, unwilling to admit that something so much desired could fail her. Flo sniffed it, then hunted up and down the train until she found the old man in his red jacket, with no teeth and the tray hanging around his neck. She invited him to sample chocolate milk. She invited people nearby to smell it. He let her have some ginger ale for nothing. It was slightly warm.

"I let him know," Flo said looking around after he had left. "You have to let them know."

A woman agreed with her but most people looked out the window. Rose drank the warm ginger ale. Either that, or the scene with the vendor, or the conversation Flo and the agreeing woman now got into about where they came from, why they were going to Toronto, and Rose's morning constipation which was why she was lacking color, or the small amount of chocolate milk she had got inside her, caused her to throw up in the train toilet. All day long she was afraid people in Toronto could smell vomit on her coat.

This time Flo started the trip off by saying, "Keep an eye on her, she's never been away from home before!" to the conductor, then looking around and laughing, to show that was jokingly meant. Then she had to get off. It seemed the conductor had no more need for jokes than Rose had, and no intention of keeping an eye on anybody. He never spoke to Rose except to ask for her ticket. She had a window seat, and was soon extraordinarily happy. She felt Flo receding, West Hanratty flying away from her, her own wearying self discarded as easily as everything else. She loved the towns less and less known. A woman was standing at her back door in her nightgown, not caring if everybody on the train saw her. They were traveling south, out of the snow belt, into an earlier spring, a tenderer sort of landscape. People could grow peach trees in their backyards.

Rose collected in her mind the things she had to look for in Toronto. First, things for Flo. Special stockings for her varicose veins. A special kind of cement for sticking handles on pots. And a full set of dominoes.

For herself Rose wanted to buy hair-remover to put on her arms and legs, and if possible an arrangement of inflatable cushions, supposed to reduce your hips and thighs. She thought they probably had hair-remover in the drugstore in Hanratty, but the woman in there was a friend of Flo's and told everything. She told Flo who bought hair dye and slimming medicine and French safes.[1] As for the cushion business, you could send away for it but there was sure to be a comment at the Post Office, and Flo knew people there as well. She also hoped to buy some bangles, and an angora sweater. She had great hopes of silver bangles and powder-blue angora. She thought they could transform her, make her calm and slender and take the frizz out of her hair, dry her underarms and turn her complexion to pearl.

[1]condoms.

The money for these things, as well as the money for the trip, came from a prize Rose had won, for writing an essay called "Art and Science in the World of Tomorrow." To her surprise, Flo asked if she could read it, and while she was reading it, she remarked that they must have thought they had to give Rose the prize for swallowing the dictionary. Then she said shyly, "It's very interesting."

She would have to spend the night at Cela McKinney's. Cela McKinney was her father's cousin. She had married a hotel manager and thought she had gone up in the world. But the hotel manager came home one day and sat down on the dining room floor between two chairs and said, "I am never going to leave this house again." Nothing unusual had happened, he had just decided not to go out of the house again, and he didn't, until he died. That had made Cela McKinney odd and nervous. She locked her doors at eight o'clock. She was also very stingy. Supper was usually oatmeal porridge, with raisins. Her house was dark and narrow and smelled like a bank.

The train was filling up. At Brantford a man asked if she would mind if he sat down beside her.

30 "It's cooler out than you'd think," he said. He offered her part of his newspaper. She said no thanks.

Then lest he think her rude she said it really was cooler. She went on looking out the window at the spring morning. There was no snow left, down here. The trees and bushes seemed to have a paler bark than they did at home. Even the sunlight looked different. It was as different from home, here, as the coast of the Mediterranean would be, or the valleys of California.

"Filthy windows, you'd think they'd take more care," the man said. "Do you travel much by train?"

She said no.

Water was lying in the fields. He nodded at it and said there was a lot this year.

35 "Heavy snows."

She noticed his saying *snows*, a poetic-sounding word. Anyone at home would have said *snow*.

"I had an unusual experience the other day. I was driving out in the country. In fact I was on my way to see one of my parishioners, a lady with a heart condition—"

She looked quickly at his collar. He was wearing an ordinary shirt and tie and a dark blue suit.

"Oh, yes," he said. "I'm a United Church minister. But I don't always wear my uniform. I wear it for preaching in. I'm off duty today."

40 "Well as I said I was driving through the country and I saw some Canada geese down on a pond, and I took another look, and there were some swans down with them. A whole great flock of swans. What a lovely sight they were. They would be on their spring migration, I expect, heading up north. What a spectacle. I never saw anything like it."

Rose was unable to think appreciatively of the wild swans because she was afraid he was going to lead the conversation from them to Nature in general and then to God, the way a minister would feel obliged to do. But he did not, he stopped with the swans.

"A very fine sight. You would have enjoyed them."

He was between fifty and sixty years old, Rose thought. He was short, and energetic-looking, with a square ruddy face and bright waves of gray hair combed straight up from his forehead. When she realized he was not going to mention God she felt she ought to show her gratitude.

She said they must have been lovely.

45

"It wasn't even a regular pond, it was just some water lying in a field. It was just by luck the water was lying there and I had to drive by there. And they came down and I came driving by at the right time. Just by luck. They come in at the east end of Lake Erie, I think. But I never was lucky enough to see them before."

She turned by degrees to the window, and he returned to his paper. She remained slightly smiling, so as not to seem rude, not to seem to be rejecting conversation altogether. The morning really was cool, and she had taken down her coat off the hook where she put it when she first got on the train, she had spread it over herself, like a lap robe. She had set her purse on the floor when the minister sat down, to give him room. He took the sections of the paper apart, shaking and rustling them in a leisurely, rather showy, way. He seemed to her the sort of person who does everything in a showy way. A ministerial way. He brushed aside the sections he didn't want at the moment. A corner of newspaper touched her leg, just at the edge of her coat.

She thought for some time that it was the paper. Then she said to herself, what if it is a hand? That was the kind of thing she could imagine. She would sometimes look at men's hands, at the fuzz on their forearms, their concentrating profiles. She would think about everything they could do. Even the stupid ones. For instance the driver-salesman who brought the bread to Flo's store. The ripeness and confidence of manner, the settled mixture of ease and alertness, with which he handled the bread truck. A fold of mature belly over the belt did not displease her. Another time she had her eye on the French teacher at school. Not a Frenchman at all, really, his name was McLaren, but Rose thought teaching French had rubbed off on him, made him look like one. Quick and sallow; sharp shoulders; hooked nose and sad eyes. She saw him lapping and coiling his way through slow pleasures, a perfect autocrat of indulgences. She had a considerable longing to be somebody's object. Pounded, pleasured, reduced, exhausted.

But what if it was a hand? What if it really was a hand? She shifted slightly, moved as much as she could towards the window. Her imagination seemed to have created this reality, a reality she was not prepared for at all. She found it alarming. She was concentrating on that leg, that bit of skin with the stocking over it. She could not bring herself to look. Was there a pressure, or was there not? She shifted again. Her legs had been, and remained, tightly closed. It was. It was a hand. It was a hand's pressure.

Please don't. That was what she tried to say. She shaped the words in her mind, tried them out, then couldn't get them past her lips. Why was that? The embarrassment, was it, the fear that people might hear? People were all around them, the seats were full.

50   It was not only that.

She did manage to look at him, not raising her head but turning it cautiously. He had tilted his seat back and closed his eyes. There was his dark blue suit sleeve, disappearing under the newspaper. He had arranged the paper so that it overlapped Rose's coat. His hand was underneath, simply resting, as if flung out in sleep.

Now, Rose could have shifted the newspaper and removed her coat. If he was not asleep, he would have been obliged to draw back his hand. If he was asleep, if he did not draw it back, she could have whispered, *Excuse me*, and set his hand firmly on his own knee. This solution, so obvious and foolproof, did not occur to her. And she would have to wonder, why not? The minister's hand was not, or not yet, at all welcome to her. It made her feel uncomfortable, resentful, slightly disgusted, trapped and wary. But she could not take charge of it, to reject it. She could not insist that it was there, when he seemed to be insisting that it was not. How could she declare him responsible, when he lay there so harmless and trusting, resting himself before his busy day, with such a pleased and healthy face? A man older than her father would be, if he were living, a man used to deference, an appreciator of Nature, delighter in wild swans. If she did say *Please don't* she was sure he would ignore her, as if overlooking some silliness or impoliteness on her part. She knew that as soon as she said it she would hope he had not heard.

But there was more to it than that. Curiosity. More constant, more imperious, than any lust. A lust in itself, that will make you draw back and wait, wait too long, risk almost anything, just to see what will happen. *To see what will happen.*

The hand began, over the next several miles, the most delicate, the most timid, pressures and investigations. Not asleep. Or if he was, his hand wasn't. She did feel disgust. She felt a faint, wandering nausea. She thought of flesh: lumps of flesh, pink snouts, fat tongues, blunt fingers, all on their way trotting and creeping and lolling and rubbing, looking for their comfort. She thought of cats in heat rubbing themselves along the top of board fences, yowling with their miserable complaint. It was pitiful, infantile, this itching and shoving and squeezing. Spongy tissues, inflamed membranes, tormented nerve-ends, shameful smells; humiliation.

55   All that was starting. His hand, that she wouldn't ever have wanted to hold, that she wouldn't have squeezed back, his stubborn patient hand was able, after all, to get the ferns to rustle and the streams to flow, to waken a sly luxuriance.

Nevertheless, she would rather not. She would still rather not. Please remove this, she said out the window. Stop it, please, she said to the stumps and barns. The hand moved up her leg past the top of her stocking to her bare skin, had moved higher, under her suspender, reached her underpants and the lower part of her belly. Her legs were still crossed, pinched together. While her legs stayed crossed she could lay claim to innocence, she had not admitted anything. She could still believe that she would stop this in a minute. Nothing was going to happen, nothing more. Her legs were never going to open.

But they were. They were. As the train crossed the Niagara Escarpment above Dundas, as they looked down at the preglacial valley, the silver-wooded rubble of little hills, as they came sliding down to the shores of Lake Ontario, she would make this slow, and silent, and definite, declaration, perhaps disappointing as much as satisfying the hand's owner. He would not lift his eyelids, his face would not alter, his fingers would not hesitate, but would go powerfully and discreetly to work. Invasion, and welcome, and sunlight flashing far and wide on the lake water; miles of bare orchards stirring round Burlington.

This was disgrace, this was beggary. But what harm in that, we say to ourselves at such moments, what harm in anything, the worse the better, as we ride the cold wave of greed, of greedy assent. A stranger's hand, or root vegetables or humble kitchen tools that people tell jokes about; the world is tumbling with innocent-seeming objects ready to declare themselves, slippery and obliging. She was careful of her breathing. She could not believe this. Victim and accomplice she was borne past Glassco's Jams and Marmalades, past the big pulsating pipes of oil refineries. They glided into suburbs where bedsheets, and towels used to wipe up intimate stains flapped leeringly on the clotheslines, where even the children seemed to be frolicking lewdly in the schoolyards, and the very truckdrivers stopped at the railway crossings must be thrusting their thumbs gleefully into curled hands. Such cunning antics now, such popular visions. The gates and towers of the Exhibition Grounds came into view, the painted domes and pillars floated marvellously against her eyelids' rosy sky. Then flew apart in celebration. You could have had such a flock of birds, wild swans, even, wakened under one big dome together, exploding from it, taking to the sky.

She bit the edge of her tongue. Very soon the conductor passed through the train, to stir the travelers, warn them back to life.

60   In the darkness under the station the United Church minister, refreshed, opened his eyes and got his paper folded together, then asked if she would like some help with her coat. His gallantry was self-satisfied, dismissive. No, said Rose, with a sore tongue. He hurried out of the train ahead of her. She did not see him in the station. She never saw him again in her life. But he remained on call, so to speak, for years and years, ready to slip into place at a critical moment, without even any regard, later on, for husband or lovers. What recommended him? She could never understand it. His simplicity, his arrogance, his perversely appealing lack of handsomeness, even of ordinary grown-up masculinity? When he stood up she saw that he was shorter even than she had thought, that his face was pink and shiny, that there was something crude and pushy and childish about him.

Was he a minister, really, or was that only what he said? Flo had mentioned people who were not ministers, dressed up as if they were. Not real ministers dressed as if they were not. Or, stranger still, men who were not real ministers pretending to be real but dressed as if they were not. But that she had come as close as she had, to what could happen, was an unwelcome thing. Rose walked through Union Station feeling the little bag with the ten dollars rubbing at her, knew she would feel it all day long, rubbing its reminder against her skin.

She couldn't stop getting Flo's messages, even with that. She remembered, because she was in Union Station, that there was a girl named Mavis working here, in the Gift Shop, when Flo was working in the coffee shop. Mavis had warts on her eyelids that looked like they were going to turn into sties but they didn't, they went away. Maybe she had them removed, Flo didn't ask. She was very good looking, without them. There was a movie star in those days she looked a lot like. The movie star's name was Frances Farmer.[2]

Frances Farmer. Rose had never heard of her.

That was the name. And Mavis went and bought herself a big hat that dipped over one eye and a dress entirely made of lace. She went off for the weekend to Georgian Bay, to a resort up there. She booked herself in under the name of Florence Farmer. To give everybody the idea she was really the other one, Frances Farmer, but calling herself Florence because she was on holidays and didn't want to be recognized. She had a little cigarette holder that was black and mother-of-pearl. She could have been arrested, Flo said. For the *nerve*.

Rose almost went over to the Gift Shop, to see if Mavis was still there and if she could recognize her. She thought it would be an especially fine thing, to manage a transformation like that. To dare it; to get away with it, to enter on preposterous adventures in your own, but newly named, skin.

(1978)

2an American actress popular in the 1930s and early 1940s.

Austin C. Clarke   (b. 1934)

Barbadian-born novelist and short story writer Austin Clarke, who moved to Toronto in 1955, has chronicled the lives of his compatriots both in the Caribbean and in Canada, the latter often referred to as "that cold, ungodly place" by his characters. His acclaimed Toronto trilogy, *The Meeting Point, Storm of Fortune,* and *The Bigger Light,* portrays the tensions that exist among poor men and women who travelled to Toronto in search of better lives and found low-paying jobs and racial prejudice. "The Motor Car" uses the familiar initiation journey structure, tracing the move of a young man from a small town to a big city. The result of Calvin's search for happiness symbolizes the lot of the immigrant in modern Canadian society. The story exemplifies the author's sensitive understanding of his characters, the gentle humour with which he depicts their situations, and his accurate reproduction of the dialect and rhythms of Barbadian speech.

THE MOTOR CAR

That Canadian thing you see lying down there in that bed is Calvin woman, I mean *was* Calvin woman. Calvin wash motor cars back in Barbados till his back hurt and his belly burn, and when the pain stop in the body it start up fresh in his mind. Good thing Calvin was a God-faring man, cause if not he would have let go some real bad curse words that would have blow way the garage itself. But instead o' talking to the customers bout the hard work, instead o' talking to the boss bout the slave work he was making Calvin do in 1968 in these modern days, Calvin talk to God. Calvin didn' know if God did really hear him, cause the more he talk to God every morning before he went to work on his old Raleigh green three-speed bicycle, and after work when his head hit that pillow, the more the work did get harder. One day Calvin take in with a bout o' bad-feels, and the moment he come outta the fit or the trance, or the *hellucinations* as his boss call it, right that very second Calvin swear blind to God that he leffing Barbados. One time. For good. First chance. Is only the governorship or the governor-generalship that could get Calvin to stay in Barbados. That is the kind o' swearing he put pon God. And it ain't really clear, even at this time, if God really understand the kind o' message that Calvin put to him. But Calvin didn't care. Calvin decide already. Calvin start to work hard, more harder than he ever work in his life, from the very day after he decide that he pulling outta Barbados. And is to Canada he coming. Now the problems start falling pon top o' Calvin head like rainwater. First problem: he can't get a Canadian visa. He seeing Canadian tourisses morning noon and night all bout his island, walking bout like if they own the blasted place, and if you don't look out they getting on as if they want to own Calvin too. Calvin hit a low point o' studyation. The work done now and he pack already, two big big imitation leather valises; and he manage to buy the ticket too, although there is a regulation down there in the island that say a black man can't buy a ticket pon

Air Canada saving he have a job and a roof to come to in Canada, or he have family here, or some kind o' support, cause Trudeau[1] get vex vex as hell bout supporting the boys when they come up here and can't find proper ploy- ment. Calvin walking bout Bridgetown the capital all day telling people he pulling out next week for Canada. Next week come and he still walking bout Bridgetown. He ain't pull out in trute, yuh: he ain't like he pulling out at all, man; that is what the boys was beginning to think. They start laughing at Calvin behind his back, and Calvin grinning and telling them, "Gorblummuh, you laugh! *laugh*! he who laugh last, laugh . . ." And for purpose, he won't finish the saying at all, he only ordering a next round o' steam for his friends, and his mind focus-on pon a new shining motto-car that he going buy up in Canada before he even living there a year. He done make up his mind that he going work at two carwash places, and if the Lord hear his prayers, and treat he nice, he going hustle a next job on top o' them two, too. Well, the more the boys laugh, the more Calvin decide with a piece o' real bad-mind that he going buy a brand-new Chevvy, perhaps even a custom-build *Galaxie*. And then, all of a sudden, one night when the fellas drink three free-round o' rum offa Calvin, Calvin really start to laugh. He push he hand inside his pocket, and he pull out a thing that look real important and official, and all he say is, "I taking off at nine in the morning." Calvin then throw a new-brand twenty dollar bill pon Marcus rum shop counter, and the fellas gone wild, be-Christ, cause is now real drinking going begin. Calvin stand up like a man. Every one that his best friend Willy fire, Calvin fire one, too. Willy, who didn' lick he mouth too much gainst Calvin going way, when he reach the fifth straight *Mount Gay*, Calvin was right there with him. Is rum for rum. Drink for drink. They start eating raw salt fish, and Calvin iamming the cod fish as if he catch it himself off the banks o' Newfoundland in the same Canada that he heading out to. The fellas eat off all o' Marcus bad half-rotten salt fish, and then start-on pon a tin o' corn beef and raw onions and you would have think that Calvin was pon a real religious fast during the time he was worrying bout the Canadian visa. "I going tell you fellas something," Willy say, for no conceivable reason at all, cause they just then telling Calvin that he ain' going see no good cricket when he get up in that cold ungodly place call Canada. "I going tell you fellas something now," Willy say, after he clear his throat for effect, and to make the fellas stop drinking and eating and listen to him. "Godblummuh! Calvin is the most luckiest one o' we, yuh! Calvin lucky-lucky-lucky as shite!" He say the last two "lucky" like if they was one word. Anyhow, he went on, "Calvin is a king to we!" Now, nobody ain' know what the arse Willy trying to say, cause Willy is a man who does try to talk big and talk a lot o' shite in the bargain. But this time, solemn occasion as it be, the fellas decide to give Willy a listen. "We lis'ning, man, so talk yuh talk. We lis'ning." Willy take a long pull pon the rum bottle, and he stuff bout a half pound o' corn beef inside his mouth, with the biscuits flying bout the place like big drops o' spit. "You see that salt fish that we just put way? Well, it

---

[1] Pierre Elliott Trudeau, prime minister of Canada from 1968 to 1979 and 1980 to 1984.

make up in Canada. Tha's where Calvin here going. Now understand this when I say it. I only say that to say this. Comprehend? The salt fish that we does get down here, send-down by Canada, is the same quality o' salt fish that they uses to send down here to feed we when we was slaves. It smell stink. You could tell when a woman cooking salt fish. We even invent a term to go long with this kind o' salt fish and this kind o' stinkingness. We does say to a person who uses *profine* words, 'Yuh mouth smell like a fucking salt-fish barrel,' Unnerstand? I going to lay a bet pon any one o' you bitches in here now, drinking this rum. I going wager five dollars gainst a quarter that the brand o' salt fish Calvin going get to buy and eat up in that place call Canada is a better quality o' salt fish. It rass-hole bound to be, cause that is where it produce. And if you ever study Marx, you would understand the kind o' socialism I talking bout." Nobody ain' answer Willy for a time, all they do is laugh. "Laugh! laugh!" Willy say with scorn, "cause godblindme! . . ." And then Calvin say, like if he didn' really want to say the words at-all, "Be-Jesus Christ, when you see me leff this blasted backwards place, call Barbados, that is the last time I eating salt fish. I eating steaks!"

Well, they poured Calvin on pon the *Air Canada*, next morning, nine sharp, drunk as a flying-fish. Good thing Calvin mother did pack the fry dolphin steak, a bottle o' Cod Liver Oil, in case the bowels do a thing and give trouble in that cold ungodly climate, as she call Canada; and she pack some Phensic for headache, just in case; she pack some miraculous bush, for medicine, "cause they ain' have doctor no place under the sun who know the goodness in this mirac'lous bush-tea as we does, so you tek it along with you, son; you going up in that strange savage place, and you far from me, and I ain' near enough no more to run to you and rub your face with a lime and some Limacol, and tie it up with oil-leaves and candle-grease . . ."; and she put in half dozen limes and two bottle o' Limacol; man, is a good-good thing that Calvin mother had the presence o' mind to pack these things for Calvin whilst Calvin was walking bout Broadstreet in Bridgetown like if he was one o' them Canadian tourisses. Calvin mother do a real good job, and when she done pack the things, and she inspect the clothes that Calvin carrying way, she tie-up the two valises with a strong piece o' string, although they had brand-new locks pon them. "Good!" is the last thing she say to Calvin, as she was holding over the kitchen door, whilst Willy was revving up the hired car and blowing the horn—which, of course, Calvin pay for, the hired car I mean—plus dropping a ten dollar bill inside Willy hand for old times sake. "Go long in the name o' the Lord, and make yuh fortune, son." A tear or two drop outta she eye, too; but she was glad-glad in she heart that she boy-child was leffing Barbados. "Too much foreigners and tourisses and crooks living here with we, now, son. Canada more brighter than here." Calvin get vex-vex when he see the water in his mother eye, and he was embarrass as hell, cause he always use to brag how nothing he do, or don't do, could make his mother belly burn she. Good thing Willy had the car motor revving, cause Calvin get in such a state over the tears and heart-break on the part of his mother that he almost forget that deep-down he is a christian-minded man and say a bad word, whiching as he did know full-well, God would be vex as hell with him for. The motto-car was making good time moving like hell going up the airport road, and everybody Calvin know, and everybody that he barely know in the twenty-nine years he born and living in Barbados, he hold half of his body out through the car window, and yell out, "Boy, I going this morning! Canada, in your arse!" All the people who see and hear, wave back and grin their teet', if they could hear from the distance and through the speed; and some o' them say, "Bless." If everybody in Barbados, down Broadstreet, at the airport didn' know that Calvin pulling out for Canada at quarter-to-nine that morning, by nine o'clock the whole world did know. Friend or no friend, every time he see a face, or a hand, he saying, "Well, I won't be see you for a while, man, I going up." And they did all know what he meant, cause it was a time when all the young boys and young girls was pulling outta the island and going to Amer'ca, Britain, although Britain begin to tighten up things for the fellas because o' Powell; and some o' them start running up in Canada. And they was more *Air Canada* planes all bout Seawell Airport in Barbados in them days that you would have think that Barbados did own *Air Canada*. But is the other way round. Anyhow, drunk as Calvin was when he step pon that plane, and the white lady smile at him and say, "Good morning, sir"—first time in Calvin life white woman ever call him that, that way—well, Calvin know long time that he make the right move. Canada nice, he say in his heart; and he end it up with "Praise God." Canada now gone straight to Calvin head, long time and with a kind o' power, that when the airplane start up Calvin imagine that he own the whole blasted plane along with the white ladies who tell him, "Good morning, sir"; he feel that the plane is the big motto-car he intend to own one year after he land pon Canadian soil. The plane making time fast fast, and Calvin drink rum after rum till he went fast asleep and didn' even know he was in Toronto. The white lady come close to him, and tap him soft soft pon his new tropical suit and say, "Sir?", like if she asking some important question, when all she want is to wake up Calvin outta the white man plane. Well, Calvin wake up. He stretch like how he uses to stretch when he wake up in his mother bed. He yawn so hard that the white lady move back a step or two, after she see the pink inside his mouth and the black and blue gums running round them white pearly teets. Calvin eyes red red as a cheery from lack o' sleep and too much rum drinking, and the body tired like how it uses to get tired and wrap-up like a old motto-car fender. But is Canada, old man, and in a jiffy, before the white lady get to the front o' the plane to put down the last glass, Calvin looking out through the window. "Toronto in your arse!" he went to say to himself, but it come out too loud, as if he was saying it to Willy and the boys who didn' think he was really going to come through. "Toronto in your arse, man!" The plane touch down, and the first man outta the plane is, well, no need to tell you who it was. Calfuckingvin! And he pass through the customs like if he was born in Toronto. The white man didn' even ask him a question. Something like it was wrong, cause Calvin did know as far away as in Barbados that the Immigration and Customs men in Toronto is the roughest in the world, when they see a black face in front o' them. But this white gentleman must have been down in the islands recently, cause all he tell Calvin was, "Don't tell me! Don't tell me! You're a Bajun!" For years after, Calvin wondering how the hell this white man know so much bout black people. Before the first week come and gone, Calvin take up pen and paper and send off a little thing to Willy and the boys: . . . *and I am going to tell you something, this place is the greatest place for a working man to live. I hear some things about this place, but I isn't a man to complain, because while I know I am a man, and I won't take no shit from no Canadian, white, black or red, I still have another piece of knowledge which says that I didn't born here. So I controls myself to suit, and make the white man money. The car only a couple of months off. I see one already that I got my eyes on. And if God willing, by the next two months, DV, I sitting down in the drivers seat. The car I got my eyes on is a red one, with white tires. The steering wheel as you know is on the left hand side, and we drives on the right hand side of the road up here, not like back in Barbados where you drive on the left hand. Next week, I taking out my licents. I not found a church I like yet, mainly because I see some strange things happening up here in churches. You don't know, man, Willy, but black people can't or don't go in the same church as white people. God must be have two colours then. One for black people and one for white people. And a next thing. There is some fellas up here from the islands who talking a lot of shite about Black Power, and I hear that one of them is a Barbadian. But I am one man who don't want to hear no shit about Black Power. I am here working for a living and a motor car and if my mother herself come in my way and be an obstacle against me getting them two things, a living and a motor car, I would kill her by Christ* . . . Calvin was going to write more: about the room he was renting for twenty dollars a week, which a white fellow tell him was pure robbery, because he was paying ten dollars for a more larger room on the ground floor in the same house; and he didn' write Willy bout the car-wash job he got the next day down Spadina Avenue, working for a dollar a hour, and when the first three hours pass he felt he been working for three days, the work was so hard; he didn' tell Willy that a certain kind of white people in Canada didn' sit too close to him on the street car, that they didn' speak to him on the street . . . lots o' things he didn' worry to tell Willy, cause he did want Willy to think that he was really a king to the boys back home, a champion for emigrading to Canada. Willy send back a post card with a mauby[2] woman on the colour side selling mauby, and on the writing side, in his scribbly handwriting, "As man!" But be-Christ, Calvin didn' care what they do, he was here for two purpose; one, living, and number two, motto-car. If they touch my motto-car, now, well, that would be something else . . . and Calvin work hard, man, Calvin work more harder than when he was washing-off cars back in Barbados. The money was good too. Sal'ry and tips. From the two car-wash jobs he uses to clear a hundred dollars a week, and that is two hundred back home, and not even Dipper does make that kind o' money, and he is the fucking prime minister! The third job, Calvin land like a dream; nightwatchman with a big big important company which put him in big big important uniform and thing, big leather belt like what he uses to envy the officers in the Volunteer Force back home wearing pon a Queen Birthday parade on the Garrison

[2]West Indian herbal beverage.

Savannah,[3] shoes the company people even provide, and the only thing that was missing, according to what Calvin figure out some months afterwards, was that the holster at his side, join-on to the leather belt, didn' have in no blasted gun. He tell it to a next Barbadian he make friends with, and the Bajan just laugh and say, "They think you going rass-hole shoot yourself, boy!" But Calvin did already become Canadified enough to know that the only people he see in them uniforms with guns in the leather holster was certain white people, and he know he wasn' Canadified so much that he did turn white overnight. "Once it don't stop me from getting that *Galaxie!*" Work work work, a occasional postcard to Willy, cause envelopes was costing too much all of a sudden, and postage stamps was going up too, no pleasure for Calvin: he went down by the *Tropics Club* where they play calypsoes and dance, one time, and he never went back cause the ugly Grenadian fellow at the door ask him for "Three dollars to come in!", and he curse the fellow and leff. But the bank account was mounting and climbing like a woman belly when she in the family-way. Quick-quick so, Calvin have a thousand dollars pon the bank. Fellas who get to know Calvin and who Calvin won't sociate with because "sociating does cost money, boy!", them fellas so who here donkey years, still borrowing money to help pay their rent, fellas gambling like hell, throwing dice every Fridee night right into Mondee morning early, missing work and getting fired from work, fellas playing poker and betting, "Forty dollars more for these two fours, in your rass, sah! I *raise!*", them brand o' Trinidadian, Bajan, Jamaician, Grenadian and thing, them so can't understand at-all how Calvin just land and he get rich so fast. "I bet all-yuh Calvin selling pussy!" one fella say. A next bad-minded fella say, "He peddling his arse to white boys down Yonge Street," and a third fella who did just bet fifty dollars 'pon a pair o' deuces, and get broke at the poker game, say quick-quick before the words fall-out o' the other fella mouth, "I going peddle mine too, then! Bread is bread." Calvin start slacking up on the first car wash work, and he humming as he shine the white people car, he skinning his teet in the shine and he smiling, and the white people thinking he smiling because he like the work and them, cause his hands never tarried whilst he was car-dreaming, they drop a little dollar bill pon Calvin as a tip, and a regular twenty-five cent piece, and Calvin pinching pon the groceries, eating a lotta pigs feet and chicken necks and salt fish . . . "I gotta write Willy and tell him bout the brand o' salt fish in this place. Willy was right!" . . . Calvin won't spend thirty cents pon a beer with a sinner, only time he even reading is when he clean out a car in the car wash and it happen to have a used paper inside it, or a throw-away paperback book. But Calvin decide long time that he didn' come here for eddication. He come for a living and a motto-car. A new one, too! And he intend to get both. And by the look o' things, be-Christ, both almost in his hand. Only now waiting to see the right model o' motor car, with the right colour inside it, and the right mileage and thing. The motto-car must have the right colour o' tires, right colour o' gear shift and in the handle too. And it have to have-in radio; and he see a fella in the car wash with a thing inside

---

[3]race track in Barbados.

his Cadillac, and Calvin gone crazy over Cadillacs until he walk down by Bay Street and price the price of a old one. He bawl for murder. "Better stick to the *Galaxie*, boy!" he tell himself; and he do that. But he really like the thing inside the white man Cadillac and he ask the man one morning what it was, and the man tell Calvin. Now Calvin *must* have red *Galaxie*, with not more than 20,000 miles on the register, black upholstery, red gear shift, radio, *AM and FM and a tellyfone* . . . Them last three things is what the man had inside his Cadillac. Calvin working even on a Sundee, bank holidays ain' touching Calvin, and the Old Queen back home who send a occasional letter asking Calvin to remember the house rent and the Poor Box in the Nazarene Church where he was a testifying brother, preaching and thing, and also to remember "who birthed him", well, Calvin tell the Old Queen, his own-own mother; *Things hard up here, mother. Don't let nobody fool you that because a man emigrade it mean that he elevate. That isn't true. But I am sending this Canadian money order for five dollars, which is ten dollars back home, and I hope that next week I would find myself a nice job, and then I am going to send you a little something more. Your loving son, Calvin. P.S. Pray for me.* Calvin start thinking that maybe the Old Queen had a bad mind for him; he start one long stewpsing, and the fellas at work even had to ask him if he sick or something, he even stop laughing and chumming around with the Canadians at work; he refuse to play Frisbee and throw the ball in the other fellas mittens, he even stop begging the German fella for a lift home after work. Calvin start getting ingrown like a toenail: pressure in Calvin arse. The studyation take a hold o' him and one weekend it capsize him in bed, Fridee night, Sardah morning and Sardah night, Sundee and right into Mondee morning half hour before he is to leff for work. Landlady couldn' even come in and change the filthy linens and bed sheets. But Calvin make sure he went to work that Mondee. "Can't lose that money now, boy!" Willy was the next joker at this time o' hardship and studyation. Willy send a letter registered and thing, in a real pretty envelope with the colours o' the Union Jack, to Calvin: . . . *and if it isn't asking too much, Calvin, I wonder if you can see your way in sending me down a piece of change. I am thinking about emigrading too, because Barbados is at a standstill for people like me, people who don't have no high school education, no big kind of skills and no kiss-me-arse god-father in big jobs in the civil service. My kind of man in Barbados is loss. I hope I am not imposing when I ask you if you could see your way in lending me the passage money, one way, and I am going to open a new bank account with it and take a picture of it and show it to the Canadian immigration people down here, because another fellow promise to do the same thing for me with the return part of the passage money. The Canadian high commission place in Trinidad giving the fellows a hard time. But we smarter than any number of Canadian immigration people they send down here. So I asking this favour for old times sake, because not that I hard on you, but I don't want to remind you of the time when you had the accident with the motor car that didn't belongst to you, and you was in hospital, and you know who help you out, so* . . . Calvin get in a bad bad mood straightaway, thinking that everybody back home think he is a millionaire, everybody back there getting on like crabs, willing to pull him down the moment he come up for breath. "Be-Christ, not me!" and in that frame o' mind Calvin take up a

piece o' stationery he borrow from a Jamaican fellow who had a job in the
General Hospital, and a envelope to match, with the hospital name on both,
and he ask a next fellow who had a typewriter to write this letter back to
Willy: *Dear Willy, I have been laid up in this hospital for two months now. I am
getting a friend who is in the hospital too, but who is not confine to bed and who
can barely walk around, to post this letter to you for me. Things really bad, man
. . .* because all my friends back home think I is a arse or something, they see
me emigrade to this place and they think that I get rich overnight, or that I
don't work hard as hell for my money, but that ain't true. Willy didn' answer
back immediately, but a month and a half later, two days before Calvin
decide he see the right automobile, a card drop through the door where
Calvin living, address to Calvin: *What are you doing up there, then? Canadians
buying out all the island. You standing for that? Send down a couple of dollars and
let me invest it in a piece of beach land for you, Brother. Power to the people!
Salaam and love. Willy X.* Calvin get so blasted vex, so damn vex, cause he
sure now that Willy gone mad too, like everybody else he been reading bout
in the States and in England; black people gone mad, Calvin say; and he get
more vex when he think that it was the landlady, Mistress Silvermann who
take up the post card from the linoleum and hand it to him, and he swear
blind that she hand it to him after she done read the thing: and now she
must be frighten like hell for Calvin, cause Calvin getting letters from these
political extremists, and birds of a feather does flock together, she thinking
now that Calvin perhaps is some kind o' political maniac, crying Black
Power! all this damn foolishness bout Power to the People, and signing his
name Willy X, when everybody in Barbados know that that damn fool's
name is really William Fortesque: Calvin get shame-shame-shame that the
landlady thinking different bout him, because sometimes she does be in the
house alone all night with Calvin, and she must be even thinking bout
giving him notice, which would be a damn bad thing to happen right now,
cause the motto-car just two days off, the room he renting now is a nice one,
the rent come down like the temperature in May when he talk plain to
Mistress Silvermann bout how he paying twice as much as other tenants, but
what really get Calvin really vex-vex-vex as hell is that a little Canadian
thing in the room over his head come downstairs one night in a mini-dress
and thing, bubbies jumping bout inside her bosom, free and thing and
looking juicy, and giggling all the time and calling sheself a women libera-
tion, all her skin at the door, and the legs nice and fat just as Calvin like his
meats, and Calvin already gone thinking that this thing is the right woman
to drive-bout in his new automobile with, this Canadian thing coming
downstairs every night for the past month, and out of the blue asking him,
"You'll like a coffee?" When she say so the first time, coffee was as far from
Calvin mind as lending Willy twenty-five cents for the downpayment for
the house spot pon the beach back home. Now, be-Christ, Willy X, or whatever the hell that bastard calling himself nowadays, is going to stay right
there down in Barbados and mash up Calvin life so! Just so? Simple so? Oh
God, no, man! But the landlady couldn' read English, she did only uses to
pretend she is a genius; the Canadian girl is who tell Calvin not to worry;
one night when they was drinking the regular coffee in the communal

kitchen, the Canadian girl say, "Missis Silvermann is only a D.P.[4] She can't read English." Calvin take courage. The bank book walking bout with him, inside his trousers all the time, he counting the digits going to work, coming from work, in the back seat alone, pon the street car, while waiting for the subway early on a morning at the Ossington Station, and then he make a plan. He plan it down to a T. Every penny organize for the proper thing, every nickel with its own work to do: the bottle of wine that the Canadian girl gave him the name to; the new suit from Eaton's that he see in the display window one night when he get hold of the girl and he get bold bold as hell and decide to take she for a lover's walk down Yonge Street; the new shoes, brown-brown till they look red to match the car; and the shirt and tie—every-blasted-thing matching-up like if he is a new bride stepping down the aisle to the wedding march. And he even have a surprise up his sleeve for the thing, too. He isn' no longer a stingy man, cause he see his goal; and his goal is like gold. The car delivery arrange for three o'clock, Sardah; no work; the ice box in his room have in a beer or two, plus the wine; and he have a extra piece o' change in his pocket . . . "I going have to remember to change the money from this pocket," he tell himself, as if he was talking to somebody else in the room with him, "to the next pocket in the new suit" . . . and he have Chinese food now on his mind because the Canadian thing mention a nice Chinese restaurant down in Chinatown near Elizabeth Street. Calvin nervous as arse all Fridee night; all Fridee night the thing in Calvin room (here of late she behaving as if she live in Calvin room!), and Calvin is a man with ambitions: one night she tantalize Calvin head so much that he start talking bout high-rise apartment; perhaps, if she behave sheself he might even put a little gold thing pon her pretty little pink finger . . .the girl start asking Calvin if he want *some*; not in them exact words, but that is what she did mean; and Calvin turn shame-shame and nearly blush, only thing, as you know black people can't show really if they blushing or if they mad as shite with a white person, and Calvin turn like a virgin on the night before she getting hang in church and in marriage, and he saying all the time because his mind pon the mileage in the motto-car, "Want some o' what?" And the girl laugh, and she throw back she head and show she gold fillings and she pink tongue and the little speck o' dirt under she neck; and she laugh and say to sheself, "This one is a real gentleman, not like what my girlfriend say to expect from West Indian men, at all . . . " And you know something? She start one big confessing: " . . . and do you know what, Calvin? Would you like to hear something that I been thinking . . ." Calvin thinking bout motto-car and this blasted white woman humbugging him bout sex! Calvin get vex, he play he get vex bout something different from the woman and she sex, and he send she flying back upstairs to she own room. He get in bed too, but he ain' sleeping, he wide awake in the dark like a thief, and he eyes open wide-wide-wide like a owl eyes, and in that darkness in that little little room that only have one small window way up by the ceiling and facing the clothes-lines and the dingy sheets that the landlady does spend all week washing, Calvin see the

[4]displaced person; derogatory term for a post–World War II European refugee or immigrant.

whole o' Toronto standing up and watching him drive by in his new motto-car-with the Canadian thing beside o' him in the front seat!—dream turn into different dream that Fridee night, because he was free to dream as much as he like since Sardah wasn' no work. Sardah is car day. He have everything plan. Go for the motto-car, pick it up, drive it home, pick up the Canadian thing, go for a spin down Bloor as far as Yonge, swing back up by Harbord, turn left at Spadina, take in College Street, and every West Indian in Toronto bound to see him in new car, before he get back home. Park she in front o' the house, *let everybody see me getting outta she, come in, have a little bite, change, change into the new suit, give the Canadian thing the surprise, and whilst she dressing, I sit down in the car . . .* " And I hope she take a long time dressing so I would have to press the car-horn, press the horn just a little, a soft little thing, and call she outside, to see me in the . . . " Morning break nice. It was a nice morning round the middle o' September, fall time in the air, everybody stretching and holding up their head cause the weather nice. Even the cops have a smile on their fissiogomy.[5] Calvin get up at five, take a quick look at the alarm clock, curse the clock for being so damn slow, went back to sleep, had a dream in which he see Willy as the garage mechanic at the car-place taking too long over the *Galaxie*; he curse Willy in the dream and nearly didn' get up in time, then turn round and curse Willy for coming into his dream; he left without tea, travelling with the Canadian thing half-sleep beside him, and gone fast pon the subway at Ossington down Danforth for the machine. The salesman-man smile and shake Calvin hand strong, and give Calvin the history of the bird although Calvin did already hear the bird history before. The salesman-man come outta the office still smiling, holding the motto-car keys between the index finger and the big thumb, and he drop them in Calvin hand. Calvin make a shiver. A shiver o' pride and ownership. "*Galaxie* in *your arse!*" He say that in his mind, and he thinking o' Willy and the boys back in Marcus rum shop. He get in the car. He shuffle bout a bit in the leather seat. He straighten he trouser seams. He touch the leather. He start up the motor. Listen to the motor. It ticking over like a fucking charm. He put the thing in gear. And he make a little thing through the car park, and he would have gone straight back up Danforth if the Canadian thing didn' wave she handbag to remind Calvin that she come with he, cause Calvin did forget she standing up there looking at a white convertible Cadillac, which she say is the car for Calvin, that there is lots o' "Negro-men driving cars, even in Nova Scotia where I come from," that Calvin should have buy one o' them. "You start spending my blasted money already, woman! This is *mine!*" He didn' tell she out loud in words what he was really thinking bout she, but he was thinking so, though. The Canadian gash get in the motto-car, cause driving in a *Galaxie* more better than walking behind a Cadillac, and she sit down so comfortable that it look like if she own the car and she was giving Calvin a chance to try she out, and that it wasn' Calvin own-own money that pay-down pon the car. Calvin didn't like that at all: he want she to sit down in the front seat like if *he* own the motto-car. But Calvin gone up Danforth with new motto-car and white

[5]physiognomy, or face.

woman beside o' him, like if he going to a funeral: "got to break she in gently, man"; and the Canadian thing not too please that Calvin didn' listen to her advice as a woman should advise a man, and buy the Cadillac, but she still please and proud that Calvin get the *Galaxie*. She sitting in it like if she belong there by birth. And Calvin don't really mind, cause he have the car, and it driving like oil pon a tar road back home. He make a thing along Danforth as far as Bloor, turn pon Yonge and gone as far as Harbord . . .the itinerry ain' exactly as he first think it out, but it would do . . .make a thing along Harbord and meet up with Spadina, and continue according to plan. And in all this time so, not one blasted West Indian or black person in sight to look at Calvin new car and make a thing with his head, or laugh, or wave. When he make a right pon College at the corner o' Spadina, a woman with a bag mark HONEST ED'S start walking through the green light, drop a tomato, and she bend down to pick it up, and Calvin now, whether he looking for the woman tomato or he looking the wrong way, nearly run-over she. Blam! Brakes on, and the Canadian thing nearly break she blasted neck 'gainst the windshield. Calvin rattle bad like a snake. Police come. Police look inside the car, see Calvin, turn he eyes pon the Canadian thing who get frighten as hell, and he say, "Okay, move along now, buster!" Calvin shaking till he get the *Galaxie* in front o' the landlady rooming house, and he ain' remember nothing bout what he plan to do when he bring home the prize of a motto-car; the police upset him and he trembling bad. "Give me a drink o' water," he say to the Canadian thing. She rubbing she neck all the time like if it really break in truth, and she get out, and she didn' even look back at the new car, whiching as you would understand is what Calvin expect any man who just have a new motto-car, to do: yuh have to walk out of the door, close the door soft-soft because it ain' the same thing as getting out of a taxi, make sure the door close, and when you know it close, open it again to show yuh-self that it close proper, and then really close it a next time; then walk off, look at the car, turn yuh head right and left like if you escaping from a light jab to the head, rub yuh hand over the chrome, walk round to the door where the passenger does sit down, open that door too, close it, and open it, and then, lock it. Then yuh does have to forget something inside the car, so yuh could have a chance to open the doors a next time and play with the car, hoping in the meantime that somebody who never see you before with a car, see you now with this new one and would say something like, "My! How much horsepower?", because according to Calvin, a "Car in some ways is like a woman, yuh does have to care she!" Calvin do all these things, and he didn't forget to walk to the back o' the *Galaxie*, stoop down and play he looking at the tires, give them a little kick with his shoes to see if they got in enough air, look under the car to see what the muffler look like, and things like that, although he know full-well that he don't know one blasted thing bout motto-cars except to wash them off, or that yuh does drive them. He do the same thing when he walk round to the front o' the car. The Canadian thing gone inside the house long time; and Calvin remember the glass o' water and he walking up the front steps. Not one blasted person on the whole street look out at Calvin new motto-car. Then the landlady, Mistress Silvermann walk out, "Don't forget

Mr. Kingston, today your rent is due." Calvin tell her in his mind something bad, and she look at the car as she reach the sidewalk, without looking back, she say, "Do you know the owner of this car, Mr. Kingston? Tell him to move it please . . . I don't want cars blocking my driveway . . ." Well, Calvin gone mad now. He walk in the house, and he catch the Canadian thing sitting down in his room, with the glass o' water in she hand, as if she dreaming, just sitting and looking at the air. He drink the water, but it was like drinking miraculous bush-tea the Old Queen uses to make when the bowels was giving trouble back in Barbados. Calvin think bout the Old Queen, put the Old Queen outta his head, and start dressing. He noticed that something was wrong with his dresser: perhaps the landlady was looking for she rent; perhaps the Canadian thing was . . ."That's why she didn' come back outside with the water! Anyhow . . ." He put on his clothes, the new suit, shoes and tie and shirt new and matching the *Galaxie* outside shining in the sun, and meantime the Canadian thing gone upstairs. Calvin finish dress, take up a old kerchief . . ."Gotta have a shammy-cloth, gotta buy one Mondee!" . . .and he gone outside polishing the motto-car. Back inside, he gone up to the Canadian thing room, knock soft, the door open, and out from behind his back he take a thing, and say in a sweet loving voice, "I buy this for you." Ohhhhhhhh! Myyyyyyyyyyyyyyyyy! "You shouldn't real-lllllllyyyyyyy!" But all the time she did know it was dress Calvin buy for she for the occasion, cause when she went inside for the water, she start searching all the man things, and she had a nice peep at the dress. She even know it cost twenty-nine dollars without tax: and she wonder if Calvin really love she so much. Well, they dress-off and they coming out like husband and wife going to church. The *Galaxie* smiling so, like if the *Galaxie* itself in love with the two o' them, too. The dress nearly red like the car, everybody in red, and looking nice. Calvin steal a peep at the Canadian thing and she look good-good-good, like something to eat! He inspect the tires a next time, though he just done looking at them, but what the hell it is his motto-car; and then he check the gas tank and the tank say, "Let's go for a long one, man!", and Calvin get in, fix the seams in the new trousers, adjust the tie, look at the knot in the mirror, fix the mirror two times, and then ask the Canadian thing if she comfortable. "I'm fine, thank you!" Calvin rev-up the thing, she turn over nice, and he ready to go. "You not nervous?" She smile. A dimple and a gold filling show when she smile. Nice. She ain' nervous. "Don't mind what happen just now by Spadina, eh?" She smile nice again. She ain' mind what happen by Spadina. Darling come to she lips with the smile. Calvin happy as hell now. He think he might treat this Canadian thing nice, and do the right thing with a gold ring even. "I take those things in my stride usually, but now it seems like an omen," she say, just as they turn into Bloor. Calvin ain' thinking bout omen, cause the only omen he know bout is that he pray for a *Galaxie* and he get a *Galaxie*! And the horses under the bonnet roaring like hell. Well, they drive and drive like if they was two explorers exploring Toronto: through Rosedale where the Canadian thing say she would *just love* to own a house; and in his mind, Calvin promise she she going get one in Rosedale; through the Bridle Path where she say the cheapest house cost a million dollars; through

Don Mills where they see the big tall Foresters' Building, all up there by IBM; "You should get a job at IBM, dear" ("Doing wha'? Cleaning out the closets?" . . . this Canadian thing like she is the wrong kind o' woman for me, Calvin thinking: I hads better get a black woman!); all this she talk as they driving back on the Don Valley Parkway. The highway nice. The motto-car open a new whole life to Calvin, and he love Canada even better. Damn good thing he left Barbados! The *Galaxie* like a horse, prancing pon the white man road. Night fall long time as they travelling, and Calvin experimenting with the dip-lights and the high beam. It nice to play with. The FM radio thing ain' working good, cause Calvin never play one o' them radios before, and he forget to practise pon it when he was visiting the car in the lot after he pay-down something pon it, so that the salesman would keep it for him. So he working the AM thing overtime. A nice tune come on. Before the tune come on, he thinking again that the Canadian thing maybe the right woman for him: she nice, she tidy and she quiet. And he raise-up liking quiet women; his mother tell him never married a woman who ain' quiet, and like church. The tune is a calypso, man. "It's a nice calypso," Calvin say. "Sparrow, in you arse!" he shout, and he beg the Canadian pardon, he excited because it is the first time he hear a calypso on the radio. He start liking Canada bad bad again. "Look at me, though! New car! A *Galaxie*, and you beside me . . ." The Canadian thing start working up she behind beside o' Calvin; she start saying she been going down in the islands for years now, that she have more calypso records than any white woman in Toronto, and she wish she had the money to take them outta storage and play one or two for Calvin. She start singing the tune, and Calvin vex as hell, cause he don't like no woman who does sing calypso, his Old Queen didn' even let him sing calypso when he was a boy in Barbados. And he was a *man*! Besides, the calypso that the Canadian thing singing now is a thing bout " . . . *three white women travelling through Africa!*", and something bout "*Uh never had a white meat, yet!*", and this nice woman, the simple-looking Canadian girl know all the words, and she enjoying sheself too, and Calvin thinking that Sparrow watching him from through the AM radio thing, and laughing at him, and he vex as shite, cause the calypso mean that certain white women like black men to lash them, and . . . "Don't sing that!" he order the thing, as if he talking to his wife; and the Canadian thing tell him, in a sharp voice, that she isn' his damn wife, so "Don't you be uppity with me, buster!" Well, who tell she she could talk-back to a Bajan man like Calvin? Calvin slam on the brakes. The motto-car cry out, *screeennnnchhhhh*! The Canadian thing head hit the windshield, bram! and she neck like it break this time, in truth. The motto-car half-way in the middle o' the highway. Traffics whizzing by, and the wind from them like it want to smash-up Calvin new *Galaxie*. Calvin vex as shite but he can't do nothing cause he trembling like hell: the woman in the front seat turning white-white-white like a piece o' paper, and the blood gone outta she face; Calvin ain' see no dimples in she face; and she ain' moving, she ain' talking, not a muscle ain' shiver. Traffics whizzing by and one come so damn close that Calvin close he eyes, and pray. "Look my blasted crosses! And my *Galaxie* ain' a fucking day old yet!" He try to start-up the motor and the motor only coughing like it have consumption. The woman like she sleeping or dead or something. The calypso still blaring over the AM radio, and Calvin so jittery he can't find the right button to turn the blasted thing off. And sudden so, one of the traffics flying by is a police. Calvin hear, *weeeeeeeeeeeeeeeeeennnnnnnnnnnnnnnnnnnnnnn!* Sirens! A police car in the rear-view mirror. Calvin stop shaking sudden-sudden. He start thinking. White woman deading in his new motto-car, the car new, and he is a stranger in Canada. He jump out, and lift-up the hood, and he back his new jacket, and he touching this and touching that, playing he is a mechanic. The police stop. He face red as a beet. "What's holding you up, boy!" Calvin hear the "boy," and he get vex, but he can't say nothing, cause they is two against his one, and he remember that he black. But he ain' no damn fool. He talk fast and sweet, and soft, and he impress the police: ". . . and officer I *just-now-now-now* give this lady a lift as I pass she on the highway, she say she feeling bad, and I was taking she to the hospital, cause as a West Indian I learn how to be a good samaritan, and . . ." The police ask for the licents, and when he see that the ownership papers say that Calvin only had the car this morning, he smile, and say, "Help me with her in the cruiser. You *are* a good samaritan, fellow. Wish our coloured people were more like you West Indians . . . " They lift the Canadian thing with she neck half-popped outta the *Galaxie* and into the cruiser, and Calvin even had a tear in his eye too. But the police take she way, and the sireen start-up again, weeeeeeeennnnnnn . . . Calvin manage to get the *Galaxie* outta the middle o' the road, the traffics still flying by, but now the new motto-car safe at the side o' the road. He put back on his jacket, and he shrug the jacket in shape and in fit pon his shoulders, he turn off the AM radio thing with the calypso, another calypso it was playing now, and fix the seams in his trousers, look back on the highway in the rear view mirror, start-up the *Galaxie*. He driving slow slow on the highway and the traffics blowing their horn to tell him get the fuck outta the road, nigger, but all the time he smiling and holding his hand outta the window and waving them on. He hold over outta habit to say something to the Canadian thing beside him, forgetting that she ain' there no more, and he still say, "This *Galaxie* is car for so! And godblummuh, look what a close shave I had!" He see the Canadian thing handbag open on the seat beside o' him, and he run his hand through it, searching. It had in five single dollar bills. He snap the handbag shut, leaving the money, touch the automatic window-winder, and throw the blasted handbag out on the Don Valley Parkway road.

(1971)

Carol Shields   (1935–2003)

Born in Oak Park, Illinois, Carol Shields came to Canada as a young woman and taught in English Departments at the Universities of Ottawa, British Columbia, and Manitoba. She published two books of poetry while in her thirties and later wrote dramas, short stories, novels, criticism, and biography. Her novel *The Stone Diaries* (1993) won both Canada's Governor General's Award and the American Pulitzer Prize. Writing about relatively ordinary men and women, Shields said that her stories were about "the arc of a human life. " In *The Stone Diaries,* this subject takes the form of a diary in which the central character tries to give shape and meaning to her life. "Hazel," which was published four years before *The Stone Diaries,* is also about an individual examining her life. After the death of her husband, a fifty-year-old woman must, for the first time, enter the outside world to take a job. In the few months covered by the story, Hazel examines her life in relation to the death of her husband, the extreme old age of her incapacitated mother-in-law, and the dismissal of the young man who had been her supervisor.

HAZEL

After a man has mistreated a woman he feels a need to do something nice which she must accept.

In line with this way of thinking, Hazel has accepted from her husband, Brian, sprays of flowers, trips to Hawaii, extravagant compliments on her rather ordinary cooking, bracelets of dull-colored silver and copper, a dressing gown in green tartan wool, a second dressing gown with maribou trim[1] around the hem and sleeves, dinners in expensive revolving restaurants and, once, a tender kiss, tenderly delivered, on the instep of her right foot.

But there will be no more such compensatory gifts, for Brian died last December of heart failure.

The heart failure, as Hazel, even after all these years, continues to think of it. In her family, the family of her girlhood that is, a time of gulped confusion in a place called Porcupine Falls, all familiar diseases were preceded by the horrific article: *the* measles, *the* polio, *the* rheumatism, *the* cancer, and—to come down to her husband Brian and his final thrashing with life—*the* heart failure.

5   He was only fifty-five. He combed his uncolored hair smooth and wore clothes made of gabardinelike materials, a silky exterior covering a complex core. It took him ten days to die after the initial attack, and during the time he lay there, all his minor wounds healed. He was a careless man who bumped into things, shrubbery, table legs, lighted cigarettes, simple curbstones. Even the making of love seemed to him a labor and a recovery, attended by scratches, bites, effort, exhaustion and, once or twice, a mild but

---

[1]artificially colored stork feathers frequently used to trim lingerie and dressing gowns.

humiliating infection. Nevertheless, women found him attractive. He had an unhurried, good-humored persistence about him and could be kind when he chose to be.

The night he died Hazel came home from the hospital and sat propped up in bed till four in the morning, reading a trashy, fast-moving New York novel about wives who lived in spacious duplexes overlooking Central Park, too alienated to carry on properly with their lives. They made salads with rare kinds of lettuce and sent their apparel to the dry cleaners, but they were bitter and helpless. Frequently they used the expression "fucked up" to describe their malaise. Their mothers or their fathers had fucked them up, or jealous sisters or bad-hearted nuns, but mainly they had been fucked up by men who no longer cared about them. These women were immobilized by the lack of love and kept alive only by a reflexive bounce between new ways of arranging salad greens and fantasies of suicide. Hazel wondered as she read how long it took for the remembered past to sink from view. A few miserable tears crept into her eyes, her first tears since Brian's initial attack, that shrill telephone call, that unearthly hour. Impetuously she wrote on the book's flyleaf the melodramatic words "I am alone and suffering unbearably." Not her best handwriting, not her usual floating morning-glory tendrils. Her fingers cramped at this hour. The cheap ball-point pen held back its ink, and the result was a barely legible scrawl that she nevertheless underlined twice.

By mid-January she had taken a job demonstrating kitchenware in department stores. The ad in the newspaper promised on-the-job training, opportunities for advancement and contact with the public. Hazel submitted to a short, vague, surprisingly painless interview, and was rewarded the following morning by a telephone call telling her she was to start immediately. She suspected she was the sole applicant, but nevertheless went numb with shock. Shock and also pleasure. She hugged the elbows of her dressing gown and smoothed the sleeves flat. She was fifty years old and without skills, a woman who had managed to avoid most of the arguments and issues of the world. Asked a direct question, her voice wavered. She understood nothing of the national debt or the situation in Nicaragua, nothing. At ten-thirty most mornings she was still in her dressing gown and had the sense to know this was shameful. She possessed a softened, tired body and rubbed-looking eyes. Her posture was only moderately good. She often touched her mouth with the back of her hand. Yet someone, some person with a downtown commercial address and an official letterhead and a firm telephone manner had seen fit to offer her a job.

Only Hazel, however, thought the job a good idea.

Brian's mother, a woman in her eighties living in a suburban retirement center called Silver Oaks, said, "Really, there is no need, Hazel. There's plenty of money if you live reasonably. You have your condo paid for, your car, a good fur coat that'll last for years. Then there's the insurance and Brian's pension, and when you're sixty-five—now don't laugh, sixty-five will come, it's not that far off—you'll have your social security. You have a first-rate lawyer to look after your investments. There's no need."

Hazel's closest friend, Maxine Forestadt, a woman of her own age, a demon bridge player, a divorcée, a woman with a pinkish powdery face loosened by too many evenings of soft drinks and potato chips and too much cigarette smoke flowing up toward her eyes, said, "Look. You're not the type, Hazel. Period. I know the type and you're not it. Believe me. All right, so you feel this urge to assert yourself, to try to prove something. I know, I went through it myself, wanting to show the world I wasn't just this dipsy pushover and hanger-oner. But this isn't for you, Haze, this eight-to-five purgatory, standing on your feet, and especially *your* feet, your arches, your arches act up just shopping. I know what you're trying to do, but in the long run, what's the point?"

Hazel's older daughter, Marilyn, a pathologist, and possibly a lesbian, living in a women's co-op in the east end of the city, phoned and, drawing on the sort of recollection that Hazel already had sutured, said, "Dad would not have approved. I know it, you know it. I mean, Christ, flogging pots and pans, it's so public. People crowding around. Idle curiosity and greed, a free show, just hanging in for a teaspoon of bloody quiche lorraine or whatever's going. Freebies. People off the street, bums, anybody. Christ. Another thing, you'll have to get a whole new wardrobe for a job like that. Eye shadow so thick it's like someone's given you a punch. Just ask yourself what Dad would have said. I know what he would have said, he would have said thumbs down, nix on it."

Hazel's other daughter, Rosie, living in British Columbia, married to a journalist, wrote: "Dear Mom, I absolutely respect what you're doing and admire your courage. But Robin and I can't help wondering if you've given this decision enough thought. You remember how after the funeral, back at your place with Grandma and Auntie Maxine and Marilyn, we had that long talk about the need to lie fallow for a bit and not rush headlong into things and making major decisions, just letting the grieving process take its natural course. Now here it is, a mere six weeks later, and you've got yourself involved with these cookware people. I just hope you haven't signed anything. Robin says he never heard of Kitchen Kult and it certainly isn't listed on the boards. We're just anxious about you, that's all. And this business of working on commission is exploitative to say the least. Ask Marilyn. You've still got your shorthand and typing and, with a refresher course, you probably could find something, maybe Office Overload would give you a sense of your own independence and some spending money besides. We just don't want to see you hurt, that's all."

At first, Hazel's working day went more or less like this: at seven-thirty her alarm went off; the first five minutes were the worst; such a steamroller of sorrow passed over her that she was left as flat and lifeless as the queen-size mattress that supported her. Her squashed limbs felt emptied of blood, her breath came out thin and cool and quiet as ether. What was she to do? How was she to live her life? She mouthed these questions to the silky blanket binding, rubbing her lips frantically back and forth across the stitching. Then she got up, showered, did her hair, made coffee and toast, took a vitamin pill, brushed her teeth, made up her face (going easy on the eye shadow), and put on her coat. By eight-thirty she was in her car and checking her city map.

Reading maps, the tiny print, the confusion, caused her headaches. And she had trouble with orientation, turning the map first this way, then that, never willing to believe that north must lie at the top. North's natural place should be toward the bottom, past the Armoury and stockyards where a large cold lake bathed the city edges. Once on a car trip to the Indian River country early in their married life, Brian had joked about her lack of map sense. He spoke happily of this failing, proudly, giving her arm a squeeze, and then had thumped the cushioned steering wheel. Hazel, thinking about the plushy thump, wished she hadn't. To recall something once was to remember it forever; this was something she had only recently discovered, and she felt that the discovery might be turned to use.

15 The Kitchen Kult demonstrations took her on a revolving cycle of twelve stores, some of them in corners of the city where she'd seldom ventured. The Italian district. The Portuguese area. Chinatown. A young Kitchen Kult salesman named Peter Lemmon broke her in, *familiarizing* her as he put it with the Kitchen Kult product. He taught her the spiel, the patter, the importance of keeping eye contact with customers at all times, how to draw on the mood and size of the crowd and play, if possible, to its ethnic character, how to make Kitchen Kult products seem like large beautiful toys, easily mastered and guaranteed to win the love and admiration of friends and family.

"That's what people out there really want," Peter Lemmon told Hazel, who was surprised to hear this view put forward so undisguisedly. "Lots of love and truckloads of admiration. Keep that in mind. People can't get enough."

He had an aggressive pointed chin and ferocious red sideburns, and when he talked he held his lips together so that the words came out with a soft zitherlike slur. Hazel noticed his teeth were discolored and badly crowded, and she guessed that this accounted for his guarded way of talking. Either that or a nervous disposition. Early on, to put him at his ease, she told him of her small-town upbringing in Porcupine Falls, how her elderly parents had never quite recovered from the surprise of having a child. How at eighteen she came to Toronto to study stenography. That she was now a widow with two daughters, one of whom she suspected of being unhappily married and one who was undergoing a gender crisis. She told Peter Lemmon that this was her first real job, that at the age of fifty she was out working for the first time. She talked too much, babbled in fact—why? She didn't know. Later she was sorry.

In return he confided, opening his mouth a little wider, that he was planning to have extensive dental work in the future if he could scrape the money together. More than nine thousand dollars had been quoted. A quality job cost quality cash, that was the long and short of it, so why not take the plunge. He hoped to go right to the top with Kitchen Kult. Not just sales, but the real top, and that meant management. It was a company, he told her, with a forward-looking sales policy and sound product.

It disconcerted Hazel at first to hear Peter Lemmon speak of the Kitchen Kult product without its grammatical article, and she was jolted into the remembrance of how she had had to learn to suppress the article that attached to bodily ailments. When demonstrating product, Peter counseled, keep it well in view, repeating product's name frequently and withholding product's retail price until the actual demo and tasting has been concluded.

20   After two weeks Hazel was on her own, although Peter Lemmon continued to meet her at the appointed "sales venue" each morning, bringing with him in a company van the equipment to be demonstrated and helping her "set up" for the day. She slipped into her white smock, the same one every day, a smooth permapress blend with grommets down the front and Kitchen Kult in red script across the pocket, and stowed her pumps in a plastic bag, putting on the white crepe-soled shoes Peter Lemmon had recommended. "Your feet, Hazel, are your capital." He also produced, of his own volition, a tall collapsible stool on which she could perch in such a way that she appeared from across the counter to be standing unsupported.

She started each morning with a demonstration of the Jiffy-Sure-Slicer, Kitchen Kult's top seller, accounting for some sixty per cent of total sales. For an hour or more, talking to herself, or rather to the empty air, she shaved hillocks of carrots, beets, parsnips and rutabagas into baroque curls or else she transformed them into little star-shaped discs or elegant matchsticks. The use of cheap root vegetables kept the demo costs down, Peter Lemmon said, and presented a less threatening challenge to the average shopper, Mrs. Peas and Carrots, Mrs. Corn Niblets.

As Hazel warmed up, one or two shoppers drifted toward her, keeping her company—she learned she could count on these one or two who were elderly women for the most part, puffy of face and bulgy of eye. Widows, Hazel decided. The draggy-hemmed coats and beige tote bags gave them away. Like herself, though perhaps a few years older, these women had taken their toast and coffee early and had been driven out into the cold in search of diversion. "Just set the dial, ladies and gentlemen," Hazel told the discomfited two or three voyeurs, "and press gently on the Jiffy lever. Never requires sharpening, never rusts."

By mid-morning she generally had fifteen people gathered about her, by noon as many as forty. No one interrupted her, and why should they? She was free entertainment. They listened, they exchanged looks, they paid attention, they formed a miniature, temporary colony of good will and consumer seriousness waiting to be instructed, initiated into Hazel's rituals and promises.

At the beginning of her third week, going solo for the first time, she looked up to see Maxine in her long beaver coat, gawking. "Now this is just what you need, madam," Hazel sang out, not missing a beat, an uncontrollable smile on her face. "In no time you'll be making more nutritious, appealing salads for your family and friends and for those bridge club get-togethers."

25   Maxine had been offended. She complained afterward to Hazel that she found it embarrassing being picked out in a crowd like that. It was insulting, especially to mention the bridge club as if she did nothing all day long but shuffle cards. "It's a bit thick, Hazel, especially when you used to enjoy a good rubber yourself. And you know I only play cards as a form of social relaxation. You used to enjoy it, and don't try to tell me otherwise

because I won't buy it. We miss you, we really do. I know perfectly well it's not easy for you facing Francine. She was always a bit of a you-know-what, and Brian was, God knows, susceptible, though I have to say you've put a dignified face on the whole thing. I don't think I could have done it, I don't have your knack for looking the other way, never have had, which is why I'm where I'm at, I suppose. But who are you really cheating, dropping out of the bridge club like this? I think, just between the two of us, that Francine's a bit hurt, she thinks you hold her responsible for Brian's attack, even though we all know that when our time's up, it's up. And besides, it takes two."

In the afternoon, after a quick pick-up lunch (leftover grated raw vegetables usually or a hard-boiled egg), Hazel demonstrated Kitchen Kult's all-purpose non-stick fry pan. The same crowds that admired her julienne carrots seemed ready to be mesmerized by the absolute roundness of her crepes and omelets, their uniform gold edges and the ease with which they came pulling away at a touch of her spatula. During the early months, January, February, Hazel learned just how easily people could be hypnotized, how easily, in fact, they could be put to sleep. Their mouths sagged. They grew dull-eyed and immobile. Their hands went hard into their pockets. They hugged their purses tight.

Then one afternoon a small fortuitous accident occurred: a crepe, zealously flipped, landed on the floor. Because of the accident, Hazel discovered how a rupture in routine could be turned to her advantage. "Whoops-a-daisy," she said that first day, stooping to recover the crepe. People laughed out loud. It was as though Hazel's mild exclamation had a forgotten period fragrance to it. "I guess I don't know my own strength," she said, shaking her curls and earning a second ripple of laughter.

After that she began, at least once or twice a day, to misdirect a crepe. Or overcook an omelet. Or bring herself to a state of comic tears over her plate of chopped onions. "Not my day," she would croon. Or "good grief" or "sacred rattlesnakes" or a shrugging, cheerful, "who ever promised perfection on the first try." Some of the phrases that came out of her mouth reminded her of the way people talked in Porcupine Falls back in a time she could not possibly have remembered. Gentle, unalarming expletives calling up wells of good nature and neighborliness. She wouldn't have guessed she had this quality of rubbery humor inside her.

After a while she felt she could get away with anything as long as she kept up her line of chatter. That was the secret, she saw—never to stop talking. That was why these crowds gave her their attention: she could perform miracles (with occasional calculated human lapses) and keep right on talking at the same time. Words, a river of words. She had never before talked at such length, as though she were driving a wedge of air ahead of her. It was easy, *easy*. She dealt out repetitions, little punchy pushes of emphasis, and an ever growing inventory of affectionate declarations directed toward her vegetable friends. "What a devil!" she said, holding aloft a head of bulky cauliflower. "You darling radish, you!" She felt foolish at times, but often exuberant, like a semi-retired, slightly eccentric actress. And she felt, oddly, that she was exactly as strong and clever as she need be.

30   But the work was exhausting. She admitted it. Every day the crowds had
to be wooed afresh. By five-thirty she was too tired to do anything more than
drive home, make a sandwich, read the paper, rinse out her Kitchen Kult
smock and hang it over the shower rail, then get into bed with a thick
paperback. Propped up in bed reading, her book like a wimple at her chin,
she seemed to have flames on her feet and on the tips of her fingers, as
though she'd burned her way through a long blur of a day and now would
burn the night behind her too. January, February, the first three weeks of
March. So this was what work was: a two-way bargain people made with the
world, a way to reduce time to rubble.

The books she read worked braids of panic into her consciousness.
She'd drifted toward historical fiction, away from Central Park and into
the Regency courts[2] of England. But were the queens and courtesans any
happier than the frustrated New York wives? Were they less lonely, less
adrift? So far she had found no evidence of it. They wanted the same
things more or less: abiding affection, attention paid to their moods and
passing thoughts, their backs rubbed and, now and then, the tender
grateful application of hands and lips. She remembered Brian's back
turned toward her in sleep, well covered with flesh in his middle years. He
had never been one for pajamas, and she had often been moved to reach
out and stroke the smooth mound of flesh. She had not found his extra
weight disagreeable, far from it.

In Brian's place there remained now only the rectangular softness of his
allergy-free pillow. Its smooth casing, faintly puckered at the corners, had
the feel of mysterious absence.

"But why does it always have to be one of my *friends*!" she had cried out
at him once at the end of a long quarrel. "Don't you see how humiliating it
is for me?"

He had seemed genuinely taken aback, and she saw in a flash it was only
laziness on his part, not express cruelty. She recalled his solemn promises,
his wet eyes, new beginnings. She fondly recalled, too, the resonant
pulmonary sounds of his night breathing, the steep climb to the top of each
inhalation and the tottery stillness before the descent. How he used to lull
her to sleep with this nightly music! Compensations. But she had not asked
for enough, hadn't known what to ask for, what was owed her.

35   It was because of the books she read, their dense complications and
sharp surprises, that she had applied for a job in the first place. She had a
sense of her own life turning over page by page, first a girl, then a young
woman, then married with two young daughters, then a member of a bridge
club and a quilting club, and now, too soon for symmetry, a widow. All of
it fell into small childish paragraphs, the print over-large and blocky like a
school reader. She had tried to imagine various new endings or turnings for
herself—she might take a trip around the world or sign up for a course in
ceramics—but could think of nothing big enough to fill the vacant time left
to her—except perhaps an actual job. This was what other people did,

[2] many novels about the English regency period (1811–1820) trace the romantic adventures of
young women.

tucking in around the edges those little routines—laundry, meals, errands—that had made up her whole existence.

"You're wearing yourself out," Brian's mother said when Hazel arrived for an Easter Sunday visit, bringing with her a double-layered box of chocolate almond bark and a bouquet of tulips. "Tearing all over town every day, on your feet, no proper lunch arrangements. You'd think they'd give you a good hour off and maybe a lunch voucher, give you a chance to catch your breath. It's hard on the back, standing. I always feel my tension in my back. These are delicious, Hazel, not that I'll eat half of them, not with my appetite, but it'll be something to pass round to the other ladies. Everyone shares here, that's one thing. And the flowers, tulips! One or the other would have more than sufficed, Hazel, you've been extravagant. I suppose now that you're actually earning, it makes a difference. You feel differently, I suppose, when it's your own money. Brian's father always saw that I had everything I needed, wanted for nothing, but I wouldn't have minded a little money of my own, though I never said so, not in so many words."

One morning Peter Lemmon surprised Hazel, and frightened her too, by saying, "Mr. Cortland wants to see you. The big boss himself. Tomorrow at ten-thirty. Downtown office. Headquarters. I'll cover the venue for you."

Mr. Cortland was the age of Hazel's son-in-law, Robin. She couldn't have said why, but she had expected someone theatrical and rude, not this handsome curly-haired man unwinding himself from behind a desk that was not really a desk but a gate-legged table, shaking her hand respectfully and leading her toward a soft brown easy chair. There was genuine solemnity to his jutting chin and a thick brush of hair across his quizzing brow. He offered her a cup of coffee. "Or perhaps you would prefer tea," he said, very politely, with a shock of inspiration.

She looked up from her shoes, her good polished pumps, not her nurse shoes, and saw a pink conch shell on Mr. Cortland's desk. It occurred to her it must be one of the things that made him happy. Other people were made happy by music or flowers or bowls of ice cream—enchanted, familiar things. Some people collected china, and when they found a long-sought piece, *that* made them happy. What made *her* happy was the obliteration of time, burning it away so cleanly she hardly noticed it. Not that she said so to Mr. Cortland. She said, in fact, very little, though some dragging filament of intuition urged her to accept tea rather than coffee, to forgo milk, to shake her head sadly over the proffered sugar.

40   "We are more delighted than I can say with your sales performance," Mr. Cortland said. "We are a small but growing firm and, as you know"—Hazel did not know, how could she?—"we are a family concern. My maternal grandfather studied commerce at McGill and started this business as a kind of hobby. Our aim, the family's aim, is a reliable product, but not a hard sell. I can't stress this enough to our sales people. We are anxious to avoid a crude hectoring approach or tactics that are in any way manipulative, and we are in the process of developing a quality sales force that matches the quality of our product line. This may surprise you, but it is difficult to find people like yourself who possess, if I may say so, your gentleness of manner. People like yourself transmit a sense of trust to the consumer. We've heard very fine

things about you, and we have decided, Hazel—I do hope I may call you Hazel—to put you on regular salary, in addition of course to an adjusted commission. And I would like also to present you with this small brooch, a glazed ceramic K for Kitchen Kult, which we give each quarter to our top sales person."

"Do you realize what this means?" Peter Lemmon asked later that afternoon over a celebratory drink at Mr. Duck's Happy Hour. "Salary means you're on the team, you're a Kitchen Kult player. Salary equals professional, Hazel. You've arrived, and I don't think you even realize it."

Hazel thought she saw flickering across Peter's guarded, eager face, like a blade of sunlight through a thick curtain, the suggestion that some privilege had been carelessly allocated. She pinned the brooch on the lapel of her good spring coat with an air of bafflement. Beyond the simple smoothness of her pay check, she perceived dark squadrons of planners and decision makers who had brought this teasing irony forward. She was being rewarded—a bewildering turn of events—for her timidity, her self-effacement, for what Maxine called her knack for looking the other way. She was a shy, ineffectual, untrained, neutral looking woman, and for this she was being kicked upstairs, or at least this was how Peter translated her move from commission to salary. He scratched his neck, took a long drink of his beer, and said it a third time, with a touch of belligerence it seemed to Hazel, "a kick upstairs." He insisted on paying for the drinks, even though Hazel pressed a ten-dollar bill into his hand. He shook it off.

"This place is bargain city," he assured her, opening the orange cave of his mouth, then closing it quickly. He came here often after work, he said, taking advantage of the two-for-one happy hour policy. Not that he was tight with his money, just the opposite, but he was setting aside a few dollars a week for his dental work in the summer. The work was mostly cosmetic, caps and spacers, and therefore not covered by Kitchen Kult's insurance scheme. The way he saw it, though, was as an investment in the future. If you were going to go to the top, you had to be able to open your mouth and project. "Like this brooch, Hazel, it's a way of projecting. Wearing the company logo means you're one of the family and that you don't mind shouting it out."

That night, when she whitened her shoes, she felt a sort of love for them. And she loved, too, suddenly, her other small tasks, rinsing out her smock, setting her alarm, settling into bed with her book, resting her head against Brian's little fiber-filled pillow with its stitched remnant of erotic privilege and reading herself out of her own life, leaving behind her cut-out shape, so bulky, rounded and unimaginably mute, a woman who swallowed her tongue, got it jammed down her throat and couldn't make a sound.

45

Marilyn gave a shout of derision on seeing the company brooch pinned to her mother's raincoat. "The old butter-up trick. A stroke here, a stroke there, just enough to keep you going and keep you grateful. But at least they had the decency to get you off straight commission, for that I have to give them some credit."

"Dear Mother," Rosie wrote from British Columbia. "Many thanks for the waterless veg cooker which is surprisingly well made and really very attractive too, and Robin feels that it fulfills a real need, nutritionally speaking, and also aesthetically."

"You're looking better," Maxine said. "You look as though you've dropped a few pounds, have you? All those grated carrots. But do you ever get a minute to yourself? Eight hours on the job plus commuting. I don't suppose they even pay for your gas, which adds up, and your parking. You want to think about a holiday, people can't be buying pots and pans three hundred and sixty-five days a year. JoAnn and Francine and I are thinking seriously of getting a cottage in Nova Scotia for two weeks. Let me know if you're interested, just tell those Kitchen Kult moguls you owe yourself a little peace and quiet by the seaside, ha! Though you do look more relaxed than the last time I saw you, you looked wrung out, completely."

In early May Hazel had an accident. She and Peter were setting up one morning, arranging a new demonstration, employing the usual cabbage, beets and onions, but adding a few spears of spring asparagus and a scatter of chopped chives. In the interest of economy she'd decided to split the asparagus lengthwise, bringing her knife first through the tender tapered head and down the woody stem. Peter was talking away about a new suit he was thinking of buying, asking Hazel's advice—should he go all out for a fine summer wool or compromise on wool and viscose? The knife slipped and entered the web of flesh between Hazel's thumb and forefinger. It sliced further into the flesh than she would have believed possible, so quickly, so lightly that she could only gaze at the spreading blood and grieve about the way it stained and spoiled her perfect circle of cucumber slices.

She required twelve stitches and, at Peter's urging, took the rest of the day off. Mr. Cortland's secretary telephoned and told her to take the whole week off if necessary. There were insurance forms to sign, but those could wait. The important thing was—but Hazel couldn't remember what the important thing was; she had been given some painkillers at the hospital and was having difficulty staying awake. She slept the afternoon away, dreaming of green fields and a yellow sun, and would have slept all evening too if she hadn't been wakened around eight o'clock by the faint buzz of her doorbell. She pulled on a dressing gown, a new one in flowered seersucker, and went to the door. It was Peter Lemmon with a clutch of flowers in his hand. "Why Peter," she said, and could think of nothing else.

50   The pain had left her hand and moved to the thin skin of her scalp. Its remoteness as much as its taut bright shine left her confused. She managed to take Peter's light jacket—though he protested, saying he had only come for a moment—and steered him toward a comfortable chair by the window. She listened as the cushions subsided under him, and hurried to put the flowers, already a little limp, into water, and to offer a drink—but what did she have on hand? No beer, no gin. and she knew better than to suggest sherry. Then the thought came: what about a glass of red wine?

He accepted twitchily. He said, "You don't have to twist my arm."

"You'll have to uncork it," Hazel said, gesturing at her bandaged hand. She felt she could see straight into his brain where there was nothing but rags and old plastic. But where had *this* come from, this sly, unpardonable superiority of hers?

He lurched forward, nearly falling. "Always happy to do the honors." He seemed afraid of her, of her apartment with its settled furniture, lamps and end tables and china cabinet, regarding these things first with a strict, dry, inquiring look. After a few minutes, he resettled in the soft chair with exaggerated respect.

"To your career," Peter said, raising his glass, appearing not to notice how the word career entered Hazel's consciousness, waking her up from her haze of painkillers and making her want to laugh.

"To the glory of Kitchen Kult," she said, suddenly reckless. She watched him, or part of herself watched him, as he twirled the glass and sniffed its contents. She braced herself for what would surely come.

"An excellent vin—" he started to say, but was interrupted by the door-bell.

It was only Marilyn, dropping in as she sometimes did after her self-defense course. "Already I can break a collarbone," she told Peter after a flustered introduction, "and next week we're going to learn how to go for the groin."

She looked surprisingly pretty with her pensive, wet, youthful eyes and dusty lashes. She accepted some wine and listened intently to the story of Hazel's accident, then said, "Now listen, Mother, don't sign a release with Kitchen Kult until I have Edna look at it. You remember Edna, she's the lawyer. She's sharp as a knife; she's the one who did our lease for us, and it's airtight. You could develop blood poisoning or an infection, you can't tell at this point. You can't trust these corporate entities when it comes to—"

"Kitchen Kult," Peter said, twirling his glass in a manner Hazel found silly, "is more like a family."

"Balls."

"We've decided," Maxine told Hazel a few weeks later, "against the cottage in Nova Scotia. It's too risky, and the weather's only so-so according to Francine. And the cost of air fare and then renting a car, we just figured it's too expensive. My rent's going up starting in July and, well, I took a look at my bank balance and said, Maxine kid, you've got to tighten the old belt. As a matter of fact, I thought—now this may surprise you—I'm thinking of looking for a job."

Hazel set up an interview for Maxine through Personnel, and in a week's time Maxine did her first demonstration. Hazel helped break her in. As a result of a dimly perceived office shuffle, she had been promoted to Assistant Area Manager, freeing Peter Lemmon for what was described as "Creative Sales Outreach." The promotion worried her slightly and she wondered if she were being compensated for the nerve damage in her hand, which was beginning to look more or less permanent. "Thank God you didn't sign the release," was all Marilyn said.

"Congrats," Rosie wired from British Columbia after hearing about the promotion. Hazel had not received a telegram for some years. She was surprised that this austere printed sheet went by the name of telegram. Where was the rough gray paper and the little pasted together words? She wondered who had composed the message, Robin or Rosie, and whose idea it had been to abbreviate the single word and if thrift were involved. *Congrats*. What a hard little hurting pellet to find in the middle of a smooth sheet of paper.

"Gorgeous," Brian's mother said of Hazel's opal-toned silk suit with its scarf of muted pink, pearl and lemon. Her lips moved appreciatively. "Ah, gorgeous."

65 "A helluva improvement over a bloody smock," Maxine sniffed, looking sideways.

"Most elegant!" said Mr. Cortland, who had called Hazel into his office to discuss her future with Kitchen Kult. "The sort of image we hope and try to project. Elegance and understatement." He presented her with a small box in which rested, on a square of textured cotton, a pair of enameled earrings with the flying letter K for Kitchen Kult.

"Beautiful," said Hazel, who never wore earrings. The clip-on sort hurt her, and she had never got around to piercing her ears. "For my sake," Brian had begged her when he was twenty-five and she was twenty and about to become his wife, "don't ever do it. I can't bear to lose a single bit of you."

Remembering this, the tone of Brian's voice, its rushing, foolish sincerity, Hazel felt her eyes tingle. "My handbag," she said, groping blindly.

Mr. Cortland misunderstood. He leaped up, touched by his own generosity, a Kleenex in hand. "We simply wanted to show our appreciation," he said, or rather sang.

70 Hazel sniffed, more loudly than she intended, and Mr. Cortland pretended not to hear. "We especially appreciate your filling in for Peter Lemmon during his leave of absence."

At this Hazel nodded. Poor Peter. She must phone tonight. He was finding the aftermath of his dental surgery painful and prolonged, and she had been looking, every chance she had, for a suitable convalescent card, something not too effusive and not too mocking—Peter took his teeth far too seriously. Perhaps she would just send one of her blurry impressionistic hasty notes, or better yet, a jaunty postcard saying she hoped he'd be back soon.

Mr. Cortland fingered the pink conch shell on his desk. He picked it up between his two hands and rocked it gently to and fro, then said, "Mr. Lemmon will not be returning. We have already sent him a letter of termination and, of course, a generous severance settlement. It was decided that his particular kind of personality, though admirable, was not quite in line with the Kitchen Kult approach, and we feel that you yourself have already demonstrated your ability to take over his work and perhaps even extend the scope of it."

"I don't believe you're doing this," Marilyn shouted over the phone to Hazel. "And Peter doesn't believe it either."

"How do you know what Peter thinks?"

75 "I saw him this afternoon. I saw him yesterday afternoon. I see him rather often if you want to know the truth."

Hazel offered the Kitchen Kult earrings to Maxine who snorted and said, "Come off it, Hazel."

Rosie in Vancouver sent a short note saying, "Marilyn phoned about your new position, which is really marvelous, though Robin and I are wondering if you aren't getting in deeper than you really want to at this time."

Brian's mother said nothing. A series of small strokes had taken her speech away and also her ability to leave her bed. Nothing Hazel brought her aroused her interest, not chocolates, not flowers, not even the fashion magazines she used to love.

Hazel phoned and made an appointment to see Mr. Cortland. She invented a pretext, one or two ideas she and Maxine had worked out to tighten up the demonstrations. Mr. Cortland listened to her and nodded approvingly. Then she sprang. She had been thinking about Peter Lemmon, she said, how much the sales force missed him, missed his resourcefulness and his attention to details. He had a certain imaginative flair, a peculiar usefulness. Some people had a way of giving energy to others, it was uncanny, it was a rare gift. She didn't mention Peter's dental work; she had some sense.

80   Mr. Cortland sent her a shrewd look, a look she would not have believed he had in his repertoire. "Well, Hazel," he said at last, "in business we deal in hard bargains. Maybe you and I can come to some sort of bargain."

"Bargain?"

"That insurance form, the release. The one you haven't got round to signing yet. How would it be if you signed it right now on the promise that I find some slot or other for Peter Lemmon by the end of the week? You are quite right about his positive attributes, quite astute of you, really, to point them out. I can't promise anything in sales though. The absolute bottom end of management might be the best we can do."

Hazel considered. She stared at the conch shell for a full ten seconds. The office lighting coated it with a pink, even light, making it look like a piece of unglazed pottery. She liked the idea of bargains. She felt she understood them. "I'll sign," she said. She had her pen in her hand, poised.

On Sunday, a Sunday at the height of summer in early July, Hazel drives out to Silver Oaks to visit her ailing mother-in-law. All she can do for her now is sit by her side for an hour and hold her hand, and sometimes she wonders what the point is of these visits. Her mother-in-law's face is impassive and silken, and occasionally driblets of spittle, thin and clear as tears, run from the corners of her mouth. It used to be such a strong, organized face with its firm mouth and steady eyes. But now she doesn't recognize anyone, with the possible exception of Hazel.

85   Some benefit appears to derive from these handholding sessions, or so the nurses tell Hazel. "She's calmer after your visits," they say. "She struggles less."

Hazel is calm too. She likes sitting here and feeling the hour unwind like thread from a spindle. She wishes it would go on and on. A week ago she had come away from Mr. Cortland's office irradiated with the conviction that her life was going to be possible after all. All she had to do was bear in mind the bargains she made. This was an obscene revelation, but Hazel was excited by it. Everything could be made accountable, added up and balanced and fairly, evenly, shared. You only had to pay attention and ask for what was yours by right. You could be clever, dealing in sly acts of surrender, but holding fast at the same time, negotiating and measuring and tying up your life in useful bundles.

But she was wrong. It wasn't true. Her pride had misled her. No one has that kind of power, no one.

She looks around the little hospital room and marvels at the accident of its contents, its bureau and tumbler and toothbrush and folded towel. The open window looks out on to a parking lot filled with rows of cars, all their shining roofs baking in the light. Next year there will be different cars, differently ordered. The shrubs and trees, weighed down with their millions of new leaves, will form a new dark backdrop.

It is an accident that she should be sitting in this room, holding the hand of an old, unblinking, unresisting woman who had once been sternly disapproving of her, thinking her countrified and clumsy. "Hazel!" she had sometimes whispered in the early days. "Your slip strap! Your salad fork!" Now she lacks even the power to wet her lips with her tongue; it is Hazel who touches the lips with a damp towel from time to time, or applies a bit of Vaseline to keep them from cracking. But she can feel the old woman's dim pulse, and imagines that it forms a code of acknowledgment or faintly telegraphs certain perplexing final questions—how did all this happen? How did we get here?

90   Everything is an accident, Hazel would be willing to say if asked. Her whole life is an accident, and by accident she has blundered into the heart of it.

(1989)

Alistair MacLeod (b. 1936)

A professor of English and creative writing at the University of Windsor, MacLeod was born in North Battleford, Saskatchewan, but spent his later childhood and teenage years on Nova Scotia's Cape Breton Island, home of his coal miner father. He has published two collections of short stories, *The Lost Salt Gift of Blood* (1976), and *As Birds Bring Forth the Sun* (1986), and a novel, *No Great Mischief* (1999). Most of his stories are set on Cape Breton Island and examine the harsh landscape and the hard lives of coal miners and fishermen as they are remembered by the narrators, who frequently have moved away from their childhood homes. "The Boat," MacLeod's first published story, is such a recollection, as a professor in a midwestern American University recalls his childhood. The story incorporates a series of opposites, including the attitudes of the mother and father and the father's life as a fisherman and his unfulfilled desire of attending university.

THE BOAT

There are times even now, when I awake at four o'clock in the morning with the terrible fear that I have overslept; when I imagine that my father is waiting for me in the room below the darkened stairs or that the shorebound men are tossing pebbles against my window while blowing their hands and stomping their feet impatiently on the frozen steadfast earth. There are times when I am half out of bed and fumbling for socks and mumbling for words before I realize that I am foolishly alone, that no one waits at the base of the stairs and no boat rides restlessly in the waters by the pier.

At such times only the grey corpses on the overflowing ashtray beside my bed bear witness to the extinction of the latest spark and silently await the crushing out of the most recent of their fellows. And then because I am afraid to be alone with death, I dress rapidly, make a great to-do about clearing my throat, turn on both faucets in the sink and proceed to make loud splashing ineffectual noises. Later I go out and walk the mile to the all-night restaurant.

In the winter it is a very cold walk and there are often tears in my eyes when I arrive. The waitress usually gives a sympathetic little shiver and says, "Boy, it must be really cold out there; you got tears in your eyes."

"Yes," I say, "it sure is; it really is."

And then the three or four of us who are always in such places at such times make uninteresting little protective chit-chat until the dawn reluctantly arrives. Then I swallow the coffee which is always bitter and leave with a great busy rush because by that time I have to worry about being late and whether I have a clean shirt and whether my car will start and about all the other countless things one must worry about when he teaches at a great Midwestern university. And I know then that that day will go by as have all the days of the past ten years, for the call and the voices and the shapes and the boat were not really there in the early morning's darkness and I have all kinds of comforting reality to prove it. They are only shadows and echoes, the animals a child's hands make on the wall by lamplight, and the voices from the rain barrel; the cuttings from an old movie made in the black and white of long ago.

I first became conscious of the boat in the same way and at almost the same time that I became aware of the people it supported. My earliest recollection of my father is a view from the floor of gigantic rubber boots and then of being suddenly elevated and having my face pressed against the stubble of his cheek, and of how it tasted of salt and of how he smelled of salt from his red-soled rubber boots to the shaggy whiteness of his hair.

When I was very small, he took me for my first ride in the boat. I rode the half-mile from our house to the wharf on his shoulders and I remember the sound of his rubber boots galumphing along the gravel beach, the tune of the indecent little song he used to sing, and the odour of the salt.

The floor of the boat was permeated with the same odour and in its constancy I was not aware of change. In the harbour we made our little circle and returned. He tied the boat by its painter, fastened the stern to its permanent anchor and lifted me high over his head to the solidity of the wharf. Then he climbed up the little iron ladder that led to the wharf's cap, placed me once more upon his shoulders and galumphed off again.

When we returned to the house everyone made a great fuss over my precocious excursion and asked, "How did you like the boat?" "Were you afraid in the boat?" "Did you cry in the boat?" They repeated "the boat" at the end of all their questions and I knew it must be very important to everyone.

10   My earliest recollection of my mother is of being alone with her in the mornings while my father was away in the boat. She seemed to be always repairing clothes that were "torn in the boat," preparing food "to be eaten in the boat" or looking for "the boat" through our kitchen window which faced upon the sea. When my father returned about noon, she would ask, "Well, how did things go in the boat today?" It was the first question I remember asking: "Well, how did things go in the boat today?" "Well, how did things go in the boat today?"

The boat in our lives was registered at Port Hawkesbury. She was what Nova Scotians called a Cape Island boat and was designed for the small inshore fishermen who sought the lobsters of the spring and mackerel of summer and later the cod and haddock and hake. She was thirty-two feet long and nine wide, and was powered by an engine from a Chevrolet truck. She had a marine clutch and a high speed reverse gear and was painted light green with the name *Jenny Lynn* stencilled in black letters on her bow and painted on an oblong plate across her stern. Jenny Lynn had been my mother's maiden name and the boat was called after her as another link in the chain of tradition. Most of the boats that berthed at the wharf bore the names of some female member of their owner's household.

I say this now as if I knew it all then. All at once, all about the boat dimensions and engines, and as if on the day of my first childish voyage I noticed the difference between a stencilled name and a painted name. But of course it was not that way at all, for I learned it all very slowly and there was not time enough.

I learned first about our house which was one of about fifty which marched around the horseshoe of our harbour and the wharf which was its heart. Some of them were so close to the water that during a storm the sea spray splashed against their windows while others were built farther along the beach as was the case with ours. The houses and their people, like those of the neighbouring towns and villages, were the result of Ireland's discontent and Scotland's Highland Clearances and America's War of Independence. Impulsive emotional Catholic Celts who could not bear to live with England and shrewd determined Protestant Puritans who, in the years after 1776,[1] could not bear to live without.

The most important room in our house was one of those oblong old-fashioned kitchens heated by a wood- and coal-burning stove. Behind the stove was a box of kindlings and beside it a coal scuttle. A heavy wooden table with leaves that expanded or reduced its dimensions stood in the middle of the floor. There were five wooden home-made chairs which had been chipped and hacked by a variety of knives. Against the east wall, opposite the stove, there was a couch which sagged in the middle and had a cushion for a pillow, and above it a shelf which contained matches, tobacco, pencils, odd fish-hooks, bits of twine, and a tin can filled with bills and receipts. The south wall was dominated by a window which faced the sea and on the north there was a five-foot board which bore a variety of clothes hooks and the burdens of each. Beneath the board there was a jumble of odd footwear, mostly of rubber. There was also, on this wall, a barometer, a map of the marine area and a shelf which held a tiny radio. The kitchen was shared by all of us and was a buffer zone between the immaculate order of ten other rooms and the disruptive chaos of the single room that was my father's.

15   My mother ran her house as her brothers ran their boats. Everything was clean and spotless and in order. She was tall and dark and powerfully energetic. In later years she reminded me of the women of Thomas Hardy, particularly Eustacia Vye,[2] in a physical way. She fed and clothed a family of seven children, making all of the meals and most of the clothes. She grew miraculous gardens and magnificent flowers and raised broods of hens and ducks. She would walk miles on berry-picking expeditions and hoist her skirts to dig for clams when the tide was low. She was fourteen years younger than my father, whom she had married when she was twenty-six and had been a local beauty for a period of ten years. My mother was of the sea as were all of her people, and her horizons were the very literal ones she scanned with her dark and fearless eyes.

Between the kitchen clothes rack and barometer, a door opened into my father's bedroom. It was a room of disorder and disarray. It was as if this wind which so often clamoured about the house succeeded in entering this single room and after whipping it into turmoil stole quietly away to renew its knowing laughter from without.

My father's bed was against the south wall. It always looked rumpled and unmade because he lay on top of it more than he slept within any folds it might have had. Beside it, there was a little brown table. An archaic

---

[1] after the American Declaration of Independence many British colonists moved to Nova Scotia.
[2] the passionate and unhappy heroine of British novelist Thomas Hardy's *The Return of the Native* (1878) drowns.

goose-necked reading light, a battered table radio, a mound of wooden matches, one or two packages of tobacco, a deck of cigarette papers and an overflowing ashtray cluttered its surface. The brown larvae of tobacco shreds and the grey flecks of ash covered both the table and the floor beneath it. The once-varnished surface of the table was disfigured by numerous black scars and gashes inflicted by the neglected burning cigarettes of many years. They had tumbled from the ashtray unnoticed and branded their statements permanently and quietly into the wood until the odour of their burning caused the snuffing out of their lives. At the bed's foot there was a single window which looked upon the sea.

Against the adjacent wall there was a battered bureau and beside it there was a closet which held his single ill-fitting serge suit, the two or three white shirts that strangled him and the square black shoes that pinched. When he took off his more friendly clothes, the heavy woollen sweaters, mitts and socks which my mother knitted for him and the woollen and doeskin shirts, he dumped them unceremoniously on a single chair. If a visitor entered the room while he was lying on the bed, he would be told to throw the clothes on the floor and take their place upon the chair.

Magazines and books covered the battered bureau and competed with the clothes for domination of the chair. They further overburdened the heroic little table and lay on top of the radio. They filled a baffling and unknowable cave beneath the bed, and in the corner by the bureau they spilled from the walls and grew up from the floor.

20   The magazines were the most conventional: *Time, Newsweek, Life, Maclean's, Family Herald, Reader's Digest.* They were the result of various cut-rate subscriptions or the gift subscriptions associated with Christmas, "the two whole years for only $3.50."

The books were more varied. There were a few hard-cover magnificents and bygone Book-of-the-Month wonders and some were Christmas or birthday gifts. The majority of them, however, were used paperbacks which came from those second-hand bookstores which advertise in the backs of magazines: "Miscellaneous Used Paperbacks 10¢ Each." At first he sent for them himself, although my mother resented the expense, but in later years they came more and more often from my sisters who had moved to the cities. Especially at first they were very weird and varied. Mickey Spillane and Ernest Haycox vied with Dostoyevsky and Faulkner, and the Penguin Poets edition of Gerard Manley Hopkins[3] arrived in the same box as a little book on sex technique called *Getting the Most Out of Love.* The former had been assiduously annotated by a very fine hand using a very blue-inked fountain pen while the latter had been studied by someone with very large thumbs, the prints of which were still visible in the margins. At the slightest provocation it would open almost automatically to particularly graphic and well-smudged pages.

[3]Spillane and Haycox were writers of popular detective novels and westerns respectively; nineteenth-century Russian novelist Fyodor Dostoyevsky wrote *Crime and Punishment* and *The Brothers Karamazov*; William Faulkner, twentieth-century American author, wrote novels about the American South (see page 145); Hopkins was a nineteenth-century English poet.

When he was not in the boat, my father spent most of his time lying on the bed in his socks, the top two buttons of his trousers undone, his discarded shirt on the ever-ready chair and the sleeves of the woollen Stanfield underwear, which he wore both summer and winter, drawn half way up to his elbows. The pillows propped up the whiteness of his head and the goose-necked lamp illuminated the pages in his hands. The cigarettes smoked and smouldered on the ashtray and on the table and the radio played constantly, sometimes low and sometimes loud. At midnight and at one, two, three and four, one could sometimes hear the radio, his occasional cough, the rustling thud of a completed book being tossed to the corner heap, or the movement necessitated by his sitting on the edge of the bed to roll the thousandth cigarette. He seemed never to sleep, only to doze, and the light shone constantly from his window to the sea.

My mother despised the room and all it stood for and she had stopped sleeping in it after I was born. She despised disorder in rooms and in houses and in hours and in lives, and she had not read a book since high school. There she had read Ivanhoe[4] and considered it a colossal waste of time. Still the room remained, like a solid rock of opposition in the sparkling waters of a clear deep harbour, opening off the kitchen where we really lived our lives, with its door always open and its contents visible to all.

The daughters of the room and of the house were very beautiful. They were tall and willowy like my mother and had her fine facial features set off by the reddish copper-coloured hair that had apparently once been my father's before it turned to white. All of them were very clever in school and helped my mother a great deal about the house. When they were young they sang and were very happy and very nice to me because I was the youngest and the family's only boy.

25

My father never approved of their playing about the wharf like the other children, and they went there only when my mother sent them on an errand. At such times they almost always overstayed, playing screaming games of tag or hide-and-seek in and about the fishing shanties, the piled traps and tubs of trawl, shouting down to the perch that swam languidly about the wharf's algae-covered piles, or jumping in and out of the boats that tugged gently at their lines. My mother was never uneasy about them at such times, and when her husband criticized her she would say, "Nothing will happen to them there," or "They could be doing worse things in worse places."

By about the ninth or tenth grade my sisters one by one discovered my father's bedroom and then the change would begin. Each would go into the room one morning when he was out. She would go with the ideal hope of imposing order or with the more practical objective of emptying the ashtray, and later she would be found spellbound by the volume in her hand. My mother's reaction was always abrupt, bordering on the angry. "Take your nose out of that trash and come and do your work," she would say, and once I saw her slap my youngest sister so hard that the print of her hand was

---

[4]Sir Walter Scott's 1819 novel of adventure is set in the early Middle Ages and was a standard English high-school text in the first half of the twentieth century.

scarletly emblazoned upon her daughter's cheek while the broken-spined paperback fluttered uselessly to the floor.

Thereafter my mother would launch a campaign against what she had discovered but could not understand. At times although she was not overly religious she would bring in God to bolster her arguments, saying, "In the next world God will see to those who waste their lives reading useless books when they should be about their work." Or without theological aid, "I would like to know how books help anyone to live a life." If my father were in, she would repeat the remarks louder than necessary, and her voice would carry into his room where he lay upon his bed. His usual reaction was to turn up the volume of the radio, although that action in itself betrayed the success of the initial thrust.

Shortly after my sisters began to read the books, they grew restless and lost interest in darning socks and baking bread, and all of them eventually went to work as summer waitresses in the Sea Food Restaurant. The restaurant was run by a big American concern from Boston and catered to the tourists that flooded the area during July and August. My mother despised the whole operation. She said the restaurant was not run by "our people," and "our people" did not eat there, and that it was run by outsiders for outsiders.

"Who are these people anyway?" she would ask, tossing back her dark hair, "and what do they, though they go about with their cameras for a hundred years, know about the way it is here, and what do they care about me and mine, and why should I care about them?"

30   She was angry that my sisters should even conceive of working in such a place and more angry when my father made no move to prevent it, and she was worried about herself and about her family and about her life. Sometimes she would say softly to her sisters, "I don't know what's the matter with my girls. It seems none of them are interested in any of the right things." And sometimes there would be bitter savage arguments. One afternoon I was coming in with three mackerel I'd been given at the wharf when I heard her say, "Well I hope you'll be satisfied when they come home knocked up and you'll have had your way."

It was the most savage thing I'd ever heard my mother say. Not just the words but the way she said them, and I stood there in the porch afraid to breathe for what seemed like the years from ten to fifteen, feeling the damp moist mackerel with their silver glassy eyes growing clammy against my leg.

Through the angle in the screen door I saw my father who had been walking into his room wheel around on one of his rubber-booted heels and look at her with his blue eyes flashing like clearest ice beneath the snow that was his hair. His usually ruddy face was drawn and grey, reflecting the exhaustion of a man of sixty-five who had been working in those rubber boots for eleven hours on an August day, and for a fleeting moment I wondered what I would do if he killed my mother while I stood there in the porch with those three foolish mackerel in my hand. Then he turned and went into his room and the radio blared forth the next day's weather forecast and I retreated under the noise and returned again, stamping my feet and slamming the door too loudly to signal my approach. My mother was busy at the stove when I came in, and did not raise her head when I threw the mackerel in a pan. As

I looked into my father's room, I said, "Well, how did things go in the boat today?" and he replied, "Oh not too badly, all things considered." He was lying on his back and lighting the first cigarette and the radio was talking about the Virginia coast.

All of my sisters made good money on tips. They bought my father an electric razor which he tried to use for a while and they took out even more magazine subscriptions. They bought my mother a great many clothes of the type she was very fond of, the wide-brimmed hats and the brocaded dresses, but she locked them all in trunks and refused to wear any of them.

On one August day my sisters prevailed upon my father to take some of their restaurant customers for an afternoon ride in the boat. The tourists with their expensive clothes and cameras and sun glasses awkwardly backed down the iron ladder at the wharf's side to where my father waited below, holding the rocking *Jenny Lynn* in snug against the wharf with one hand on the iron ladder and steadying his descending passengers with the other. They tried to look both prim and wind-blown like the girls in the Pepsi-Cola ads and did the best they could, sitting on the thwarts where the newspapers were spread to cover the splattered blood and fish entrails, crowding to one side so that they were in danger of capsizing the boat, taking the inevitable pictures or merely trailing their fingers through the water of their dreams.

35   All of them liked my father very much and, after he'd brought them back from their circles in the harbour, they invited him to their rented cabins which were located high on a hill overlooking the village to which they were so alien. He proceeded to get very drunk up there with the beautiful view and the strange company and the abundant liquor, and late in the afternoon he began to sing.

I was just approaching the wharf to deliver my mother's summons when he began, and the familiar yet unfamiliar voice that rolled down from the cabins made me feel as I had never felt before in my young life or perhaps as I had always felt without really knowing it, and I was ashamed yet proud, young yet old and saved yet forever lost, and there was nothing I could do to control my legs which trembled nor my eyes which wept for what they could not tell.

The tourists were equipped with tape recorders and my father sang for more than three hours. His voice boomed down the hill and bounced off the surface of the harbour, which was an unearthly blue on that hot August day, and was then reflected to the wharf and the fishing shanties where it was absorbed amidst the men who were baiting their lines for the next day's haul.

He sang all the old sea chanties which had come across from the old world and by which men like him had pulled ropes for generations, and he sang the East Coast sea songs which celebrated the sealing vessels of Northumberland Strait and the long liners of the Grand Banks, and of Anticosti, Sable Island, Grand Manan, Boston Harbor, Nantucket and Block Island. Gradually he shifted to the seemingly unending Gaelic drinking songs with their twenty or more verses and inevitable refrains, and the men in the shanties smiled at the coarseness of some of the verses and at the thought that the singer's immediate audience did not know what they were applauding nor recording to take back to staid old Boston. Later as the sun was setting he switched to the laments and the wild and haunting Gaelic war songs of those spattered Highland ancestors he had never seen, and when his voice ceased, the savage melancholy of three hundred years seemed to hang over the peaceful harbour and the quiet boats and the men leaning in the doorways of their shanties with their cigarettes glowing in the dusk and the women looking to the sea from their open windows with their children in their arms.

When he came home he threw the money he had earned on the kitchen table as he did with all his earnings but my mother refused to touch it and the next day he went with the rest of the men to bait his trawl in the shanties. The tourists came to the door that evening and my mother met them there and told them that her husband was not in although he was lying on the bed only a few feet away with the radio playing and the cigarette upon his lips. She stood in the doorway until they reluctantly went away.

In the winter they sent him a picture which had been taken on the day of the singing. On the back it said, "To Our Ernest Hemingway" and the "Our" was underlined. There was also an accompanying letter telling how much they had enjoyed themselves, how popular the tape was proving and explaining who Ernest Hemingway was. In a way it almost did look like one of those unshaven, taken-in-Cuba pictures of Hemingway. He looked both massive and incongruous in the setting. His bulky fisherman's clothes were too big for the green and white lawn chair in which he sat, and his rubber boots seemed to take up all of the well-clipped grass square. The beach umbrella jarred with his sunburned face and because he had already been singing for some time, his lips which chapped in the winds of spring and burned in the water glare of summer had already cracked in several places, producing tiny flecks of blood at their corners and on the whiteness of his teeth. The bracelets of brass chain which he wore to protect his wrists from chafing seemed abnormally large and his broad leather belt had been slackened and his heavy shirt and underwear were open at the throat revealing an uncultivated wilderness of white chest hair bordering on the semicontrolled stubble of his neck and chin. His blue eyes had looked directly into the camera and his hair was whiter than the two tiny clouds which hung over his left shoulder. The sea was behind him and its immense blue flatness stretched out to touch the arching blueness of the sky. It seemed very far away from him or else he was so much in the foreground that he seemed too big for it.

Each year another of my sisters would read the books and work in the restaurant. Sometimes they would stay out quite late on the hot summer nights and when they came up the stairs my mother would ask them many long and involved questions which they resented and tried to avoid. Before ascending the stairs they would go into my father's room and those of us who waited above could hear them throwing his clothes off the chair before sitting on it or the squeak of the bed as they sat on its edge. Sometimes they would talk to him a long time, the murmur of their voices blending with the music of the radio into a mysterious vapour-like sound which floated softly up the stairs.

I say this again as if it all happened at once and as if all my sisters were of identical ages and like so many lemmings going into another sea and, again, it was of course not that way at all. Yet go they did, to Boston, to Montreal, to New York with the young men they met during the summers and later married in those far-away cities. The young men were very articulate and handsome and wore fine clothes and drove expensive cars and my sisters, as I said, were very tall and beautiful with their copper-coloured hair and were tired of darning socks and baking bread.

One by one they went. My mother had each of her daughters for fifteen years, then lost them for two and finally forever. None married a fisherman. My mother never accepted any of the young men, for in her eyes they seemed always a combination of the lazy, the effeminate, the dishonest and the unknown. They never seemed to do any physical work and she could not comprehend their luxurious vacations and she did not know whence they came nor who they were. And in the end she did not really care, for they were not of her people and they were not of her sea.

I say this now with a sense of wonder at my own stupidity in thinking I was somehow free and would go on doing well in school and playing and helping in the boat and passing into my early teens while streaks of grey began to appear in my mother's dark hair and my father's rubber boots dragged sometimes on the pebbles of the beach as he trudged home from the wharf. And there were but three of us in the house that had at one time been so loud.

45   Then during the winter that I was fifteen he seemed to grow old and ill all at once. Most of January he lay upon the bed, smoking and reading and listening to the radio while the wind howled about the house and the needle-like snow blistered off the ice-covered harbour and the doors flew out of people's hands if they did not cling to them like death.

In February when the men began overhauling their lobster traps he still did not move, and my mother and I began to knit lobster trap headings in the evenings. The twine was as always very sharp and harsh, and blisters formed upon our thumbs and little paths of blood snaked quietly down between our fingers while the seals that had drifted down from distant Labrador wept and moaned like human children on the ice-floes of the Gulf.

In the daytime my mother's brother who had been my father's partner as long as I could remember also came to work upon the gear. He was a year older than my mother and was tall and dark and the father of twelve children.

By March we were very far behind and although I began to work very hard in the evenings I knew it was not hard enough and that there were but eight weeks left before the opening of the season on May first. And I knew that my mother worried and that my uncle was uneasy and that all of our very lives depended on the boat being ready with her gear and two men, by the date of May the first. And I knew then that *David Copperfield* and *The Tempest*[5] and all those friends I had dearly come to love must really go forever. So I bade them all good-bye.

The night after my first full day at home and after my mother had gone upstairs he called me into his room where I sat upon the chair beside his bed. "You will go back tomorrow," he said simply.

50   I refused then, saying I had made my decision and was satisfied.

[5]published in 1849–50, Charles Dickens's semi-autobiographical novel *David Copperfield* traces the hero's life from his poor and unhappy childhood to his success as an author. Shakespeare's play *The Tempest* was first produced in 1611.

"That is no way to make a decision," he said, "and if you are satisfied I am not. It is best that you go back." I was almost angry then and told him as all children do that I wished he would leave me alone and stop telling me what to do.

He looked at me a long time then, lying there on the same bed on which he had fathered me those sixteen years before, fathered me his only son, out of who knew what emotions when he was already fifty-six and his hair had turned to snow. Then he swung his legs over the edge of the squeaking bed and sat facing me and looked into my own dark eyes with his crystal blue and placed his hand upon my knee. "I am not telling you to do anything," he said softly, "only asking you."

The next morning I returned to school. As I left, my mother followed me to the porch and said, "I never thought a son of mine would choose useless books over the parents that gave him life."

In the weeks that followed he got up rather miraculously and the gear was ready and the *Jenny Lynn* was freshly painted by the last two weeks of April when the ice began to break up and the lonely screaming gulls returned to haunt the silver herring as they flashed within the sea.

On the first day of May the boats raced out as they had always done, laden down almost to the gunwales with their heavy cargoes of traps. They were almost like living things as they plunged through the waters of the spring and manoeuvred between the still floating icebergs of crystal white emerald green on their way to the traditional grounds that they sought out every May. And those of us who sat that day in the high school on the hill, discussing the water imagery of Tennyson, watched them as they passed back and forth beneath us until by afternoon the piles of traps which had been stacked upon the wharf were no longer visible but were spread about the bottom of the sea. And the *Jenny Lynn* went too, all day, with my uncle tall and dark, like a latter-day Tashtego[6] standing at the tiller with his legs wide apart and guiding her deftly between the floating pans of ice and my father in the stern standing in the same way with his hands upon the ropes that lashed the cargo to the deck. And at night my mother asked, "Well, how did things go in the boat today?"

And the spring wore on and the summer came and school ended in the third week of June and the lobster season on July first and I wished that the two things I loved so dearly did not exclude each other in a manner that was so blunt and too clear.

At the conclusion of the lobster season my uncle said he had been offered a berth on a deep sea dragger and had decided to accept. We all knew that he was leaving the *Jenny Lynn* forever and that before the next lobster season he would buy a boat of his own. He was expecting another child and would be supporting fifteen people by the next spring and could not chance my father against the family that he loved.

I joined my father then for the trawling season, and he made no protest and my mother was quite happy. Through the summer we baited the tubs of

---

[6] a Native American harpooner in American novelist Herman Melville's 1851 novel *Moby-Dick*.

trawl in the afternoon and set them at sunset and revisited them in the darkness of the early morning. The men would come tramping by our house at four A.M. and we would join them and walk with them to the wharf and be on our way before the sun rose out of the ocean where it seemed to spend the night. If I was not up they would toss pebbles to my window and I would be very embarrassed and tumble downstairs to where my father lay fully clothed atop his bed, reading his book and listening to his radio and smoking his cigarette. When I appeared he would swing off his bed and put on his boots and be instantly ready and then we would take the lunches my mother had prepared the night before and walk off toward the sea. He would make no attempt to wake me himself.

It was in many ways a good summer. There were few storms and we were out almost every day and we lost a minimum of gear and seemed to land a maximum of fish and I tanned dark and brown after the manner of my uncles.

60 My father did not tan—he never tanned—because of his reddish complexion, and the salt water irritated his skin as it had for sixty years. He burned and reburned over and over again and his lips still cracked so that they bled when he smiled, and his arms, especially the left, still broke out into the oozing saltwater boils as they had ever since as a child I had first watched him soaking and bathing them in a variety of ineffectual solutions. The chafe-preventing bracelets of brass linked chain that all the men wore about their wrists in early spring were his the full season and he shaved but painfully and only once a week.

And I saw then, that summer, many things that I had seen all my life as if for the first time and I thought that perhaps my father had never been intended for a fisherman either physically or mentally. At least not in the manner of my uncles; he had never really loved it. And I remembered that, one evening in his room when we were talking about *David Copperfield*, he had said that he had always wanted to go to the university and I had dismissed it then in the way one dismisses his father's saying he would like to be a tight-rope walker, and we had gone on to talk about the Peggottys and how they loved the sea.[7]

And I thought then to myself that there were many things wrong with all of us and all our lives and I wondered why my father, who was himself an only son, had not married before he was forty and then I wondered why he had. I even thought that perhaps he had had to marry my mother and checked the dates on the flyleaf of the Bible where I learned that my oldest sister had been born a prosaic eleven months after the marriage, and I felt myself then very dirty and debased for my lack of faith and for what I had thought and done.

And then there came into my heart a very great love for my father and I thought it was very much braver to spend a life doing what you really do not want rather than selfishly following forever your own dreams and inclinations. And I knew then that I could never leave him alone to suffer the iron-tipped harpoons which my mother would forever hurl into his soul because he was a failure as a husband and a father who had retained none of his own. And I felt that I had been very small in a little secret place within me and that even the completion of high school was for me a silly shallow selfish dream.

[7]characters in *David Copperfield*.

So I told him one night very resolutely and very powerfully that I would remain with him as long as he lived and we would fish the sea together. And he made no protest but only smiled through the cigarette smoke that wreathed his bed and replied, "I hope you will remember what you've said."

65

The room was now so filled with books as to be almost Dickensian, but he would not allow my mother to move or change them and he continued to read them, sometimes two or three a night. They came with great regularity now, and there were more hard covers, sent by my sisters who had gone so long ago and now seemed so distant and so prosperous, and sent also pictures of small red-haired grandchildren with baseball bats and dolls which he placed upon his bureau and which my mother gazed at wistfully when she thought no one would see. Red-haired grandchildren with baseball bats and dolls who would never know the sea in hatred or in love.

And so we fished through the heat of August and into the cooler days of September when the water was so clear we could almost see the bottom and the white mists rose like delicate ghosts in the early morning dawn. And one day my mother said to me, "You have given added years to his life."

And we fished on into October when it began to roughen and we could no longer risk night sets but took our gear out each morning and returned at the first sign of the squalls; and on into November when we lost three tubs of trawl and the clear blue water turned to a sullen grey and the trochoidal[8] waves rolled rough and high and washed across our bows and decks as we ran within their troughs. We wore heavy sweaters now and the awkward rubber slickers and the heavy woollen mitts which soaked and froze into masses of ice that hung from our wrists like the limbs of gigantic monsters until we thawed them against the exhaust pipe's heat. And almost every day we would leave for home before noon, driven by the blasts of the northwest wind, coating our eyebrows with ice and freezing our eyelids closed as we leaned into a visibility that was hardly there, charting our course from the compass and the sea, running with the waves and between them but never confronting their towering might.

And I stood at the tiller now, on these homeward lunges, stood in the place and in the manner of my uncle, turning to look at my father and to shout over the roar of the engine and the slop of the sea to where he stood in the stern, drenched and dripping with the snow and the salt and the spray and his bushy eyebrows caked in ice. But on November twenty-first, when it seemed we might be making the final run of the season, I turned and he was not there and I knew even in that instant that he would never be again.

On November twenty-first the waves of the grey Atlantic are very very high and the waters are very cold and there are no signposts on the surface of the sea. You cannot tell where you have been five minutes before and in the squalls of snow you cannot see. And it takes longer than you would believe to check a boat that has been running before a gale and turn her ever so carefully in a wide and stupid circle, with timbers creaking and straining, back into the face of the storm. And you know it is useless and that your voice does not carry the length of the boat and that even if you knew the original spot, the relentless waves would carry such a burden perhaps a mile or so by the

[8]rolling in circles.

time you could return. And you know also, the final irony, that your father like your uncles and all the men that form your past, cannot swim a stroke.

70   The lobster beds off the Cape Breton coast are still very rich and now, from May to July, their offerings are packed in crates of ice, and thundered by the gigantic transport trucks, day and night, through New Glasgow, Amherst, Saint John and Bangor and Portland and into Boston where they are tossed still living into boiling pots of water, their final home.

And though the prices are higher and the competition tighter, the grounds to which the *Jenny Lynn* once went remain untouched and unfished as they have for the last ten years. For if there are no signposts on the sea in storm there are certain ones in calm and the lobster bottoms were distributed in calm before any of us can remember and the grounds my father fished were those his father fished before him and there were others before and before and before. Twice the big boats have come from forty and fifty miles, lured by the promise of the grounds, and strewn the bottom with their traps and twice they have returned to find their buoys cut adrift and their gear lost and destroyed. Twice the Fisheries Officer and the Mounted Police have come and asked many long and involved questions and twice they have received no answers from the men leaning in the doors of their shanties and the women standing at their windows with their children in their arms. Twice they have gone away saying: "There are no legal boundaries in the Marine area"; "No one can own the sea"; "Those grounds don't wait for anyone."

But the men and the women, with my mother dark among them, do not care for what they say, for to them the grounds are sacred and they think they wait for me.

It is not an easy thing to know that your mother lives alone on an inadequate insurance policy and that she is too proud to accept any other aid. And that she looks through her lonely window onto the ice of winter and the hot flat calm of summer and the rolling waves of fall. And that she lies awake in the early morning's darkness when the rubber boots of the men scrunch upon the gravel as they pass beside her house on their way down to the wharf. And she knows that the footsteps never stop, because no man goes from her house, and she alone of all the Lynns has neither son nor son-in-law that walks toward the boat that will take him to the sea. And it is not an easy thing to know that your mother looks upon the sea with love and on you with bitterness because the one has been so constant and the other so untrue.

But neither is it easy to know that your father was found on November twenty-eighth, ten miles to the north and wedged between two boulders at the base of the rock-strewn cliffs where he had been hurled and slammed so many many times. His hands were shredded ribbons as were his feet which had lost their boots to the suction of the sea, and his shoulders came apart in our hands when we tried to move him from the rocks. And the fish had eaten his testicles and the gulls had pecked out his eyes and the white-green stubble of his whiskers had continued to grow in death, like the grass on graves, upon the purple, bloated mass that was his face. There was not much left of my father, physically, as he lay there with the brass chains on his wrists and the seaweed in his hair.

(1968)

Margaret Atwood   (b. 1939)

Ottawa-born poet, novelist, short story writer, and critic Margaret Atwood is one of Canada's best-known authors, both at home and abroad. Such novels as *Surfacing* (1972) and *Cat's Eye* (1988) have been praised for their portrayal of introspective, contemporary women examining their pasts and their relationships as they search for new directions in their lives. In "The Resplendent Quetzal," the growing alienation between a childless husband and wife is revealed during a vacation tour of Mexico.

THE RESPLENDENT QUETZAL

Sarah was sitting near the edge of the sacrificial well. She had imagined something smaller, more like a wishing well, but this was huge, and the water at the bottom wasn't clear at all. It was mud-brown; a few clumps of reeds were growing over to one side, and the trees at the top dangled their roots, or were they vines, down the limestone walls into the water. Sarah thought there might be some point to being a sacrificial victim if the well were nicer, but you would never get her to jump into a muddy hole like that. They were probably pushed, or knocked on the head and thrown in. According to the guidebook the water was deep but it looked more like a swamp to her.

Beside her a group of tourists were being rounded up by the guide, who obviously wanted to get the whole thing over with so he could cram them back onto their pink-and-purple-striped *turismo* bus and relax. These were Mexican tourists, and Sarah found it reassuring that other people besides Canadians and Americans wore big hats and sunglasses and took pictures of everything. She wished she and Edward could make these excursions at a less crowded time of year, if they had to make them at all, but because of Edward's teaching job they were limited to school holidays. Christmas was the worst. It would be the same even if he had a different job and they had children, though; but they didn't have any.

The guide shooed his charges back along the gravel path as if they were chickens, which was what they sounded like. He himself lingered beside Sarah, finishing his cigarette, one foot on a stone block, like a conquistador.[1] He was a small dark man with several gold teeth, which glinted when he smiled. He was smiling at Sarah now, sideways, and she smiled back serenely. She liked it when these men smiled at her or even when they made those juicy sucking noises with their mouths as they walked behind her on the street; so long as they didn't touch. Edward pretended not to hear them. Perhaps they did it so much because she was blonde: blondes were rare here. She didn't think of herself as beautiful, exactly; the word she had chosen for herself some time ago was "comely." Comely to look upon. You would never use that word for a thin woman.

---

[1]Spanish invader of Mexico and Peru.

The guide tossed his cigarette butt into the sacrificial well and turned to follow his flock. Sarah forgot about him immediately. She'd felt something crawling up her leg, but when she looked nothing was there. She tucked the full skirt of her cotton dress in under her thighs and clamped it between her knees. This was the kind of place you could get flea bites, places with dirt on the ground, where people sat. Parks and bus terminals. But she didn't care, her feet were tired and the sun was hot. She would rather sit in the shade and get bitten than rush around trying to see everything, which was what Edward wanted to do. Luckily the bites didn't swell up on her the way they did on Edward.

5   Edward was back along the path, out of sight among the bushes, peering around with his new Leitz binoculars. He didn't like sitting down, it made him restless. On these trips it was difficult for Sarah to sit by herself and just think. Her own binoculars, which were Edward's old ones, dangled around her neck; they weighed a ton. She took them off and put them into her purse.

His passion for birds had been one of the first things Edward had confided to her. Shyly, as if it had been some precious gift, he'd shown her the lined notebook he'd started keeping when he was nine, with its awkward, boyish printing—robin, blue jay, kingfisher—and the day and the year recorded beside each name. She'd pretended to be touched and interested, and in fact she had been. She herself didn't have compulsions of this kind; whereas Edward plunged totally into things, as if they were oceans. For a while it was stamps; then he took up playing the flute and nearly drove her crazy with the practising. Now it was pre-Columbian[2] ruins, and he was determined to climb up every heap of old stones he could get his hands on. A capacity for dedication, she guessed you would call it. At first Edward's obsessions had fascinated her, since she didn't understand them, but now they merely made her tired. Sooner or later he'd dropped them all anyway, just as he began to get really good or really knowledgeable; all but the birds. That had remained constant. She herself, she thought, had once been one of his obsessions.

It wouldn't be so bad if he didn't insist on dragging her into everything. Or rather, he had once insisted; he no longer did. And she had encouraged him, she'd let him think she shared or at least indulged his interests. She was becoming less indulgent as she grew older. The waste of energy bothered her, because it was a waste, he never stuck with anything, and what use was his encyclopaedic knowledge of birds? It would be different if they had enough money, but they were always running short. If only he would take all that energy and do something productive with it, in his job, for instance. He could be a principal if he wanted to, she kept telling him that. But he wasn't interested, he was content to poke along doing the same thing year after year. His Grade Six children adored him, the boys especially. Perhaps it was because they sensed he was a lot like them.

He'd started asking her to go birding, as he called it, shortly after they'd met, and of course she had gone. It would have been an error to refuse. She hadn't complained, then, about her sore feet or standing in the rain under the dripping bushes trying to keep track of some nondescript sparrow, while

[2]before Columbus arrived in the New World in 1492.

Edward thumbed through his Peterson's *Field Guide* as if it were the Bible or the bird were the Holy Grail.[3] She'd even become quite good at it. Edward was nearsighted, and she was quicker at spotting movement than he was. With his usual generosity he acknowledged this, and she'd fallen into the habit of using it when she wanted to get rid of him for a while. Just now, for instance.

"There's something over there." She'd pointed across the well to the tangle of greenery on the other side.

"Where?" Edward had squinted eagerly and raised his binoculars. He looked a little like a bird himself, she thought, with his long nose and stilt legs.

"That thing there, sitting in that thing, the one with the tufts. The sort of bean tree. It's got orange on it."

Edward focused. "An oriole?"

"I can't tell from here. Oh, it just flew." She pointed over their heads while Edward swept the sky in vain.

"I think it lit back there, behind us."

That was enough to send him off. She had to do this with enough real birds to keep him believing, however.

Edward sat down on the root of a tree and lit a cigarette. He had gone down the first side-path he'd come to; it smelled of piss, and he could see by the decomposing Kleenexes further along that this was one of the places people went when they couldn't make it back to the washroom behind the ticket counter.

He took off his glasses, then his hat, and wiped the sweat off his forehead. His face was red, he could feel it. Blushing, Sarah called it. She persisted in attributing it to shyness and boyish embarrassment; she hadn't yet deduced that it was simple rage. For someone so devious she was often incredibly stupid.

She didn't know, for instance, that he'd found out about her little trick with the birds at least three years ago. She'd pointed to a dead tree and said she saw a bird in it, but he himself had inspected that same tree only seconds earlier and there was nothing in it at all. And she was very careless: she described oriole-coloured birds behaving like kingbirds, woodpeckers where there would never be any woodpeckers, mute jays, neckless herons. She must have decided he was a total idiot and any slipshod invention would do.

But why not, since he appeared to fall for it every time? And why did he do it, why did he chase off after her imaginary birds, pretending he believed her? It was partly that although he knew what she was doing to him, he had no idea why. It couldn't be simple malice, she had enough outlets for that. He didn't want to know the real reason, which loomed in his mind as something formless, threatening and final. Her lie about the birds was one of the many lies that propped things up. He was afraid to confront her, that would be the end, all the pretences would come crashing down and they would be left standing in the rubble, staring at each other. There would be nothing left to say and Edward wasn't ready for that.

She would deny everything anyway. "What do you mean? Of course I saw it. It flew right over there. Why would I make up such a thing?" With her level gaze, blonde and stolid and immoveable as a rock.

---

[3]sacred cup used by Christ at the Last Supper.

Edward had a sudden image of himself, crashing out of the undergrowth like King Kong, picking Sarah up and hurling her over the edge, down into the sacrificial well. Anything to shatter that imperturbable expression, bland and pale and plump and smug, like a Flemish Madonna's.[4] Self-righteous, that's what it was. Nothing was ever her fault. She hadn't been like that when he'd met her. But it wouldn't work: as she fell she would glance at him, not with fear but with maternal irritation, as if he'd spilled chocolate milk on a white tablecloth. And she'd pull her skirt down. She was concerned for appearances, always.

Though there would be something inappropriate about throwing Sarah into the sacrificial well, just as she was, with all her clothes on. He remembered snatches from the several books he'd read before they came down. (And that was another thing: Sarah didn't believe in reading up on places beforehand. "Don't you want to understand what you're looking at?" he'd asked her. "I'll see the same thing in any case, won't I?" she said. "I mean, knowing all those facts doesn't change the actual statue or whatever." Edward found this attitude infuriating; and now that they were here, she resisted his attempts to explain things to her by her usual passive method of pretending not to hear.

("That's a Chac-Mool,[5] see that? That round thing on the stomach held the bowl where they put the hearts, and the butterfly on the head means the soul flying up to the sun."

("Could you get out the suntan lotion, Edward? I think it's in the tote bag, in the left-hand pocket."

And he would hand her the suntan lotion, defeated once again.)

No, she wouldn't be a fit sacrifice, with or without lotion. They only threw people in—or perhaps they jumped in, of their own free will—for the water god, to make it rain and ensure fertility. The drowned were messengers, sent to carry requests to the god. Sarah would have to be purified first, in the stone sweat-house beside the well. Then, naked, she would kneel before him, one arm across her breast in the attitude of submission. He added some ornaments: a gold necklace with a jade medallion, a gold circlet adorned with feathers. Her hair, which she usually wore in a braid coiled at the back of her head, would be hanging down. He thought of her body, which he made slimmer and more taut, with an abstract desire which was as unrelated as he could make it to Sarah herself. This was the only kind of desire he could feel for her any more: he had to dress her up before he could make love to her at all. He thought about their earlier days, before they'd married. It was almost as if he'd had an affair with another woman, she had been so different. He'd treated her body then as something holy, a white-and-gold chalice, to be touched with care and tenderness. And she had liked this; even though she was two years older than he was and much more experienced she hadn't minded his awkwardness and reverence, she hadn't laughed at him. Why had she changed?

Sometimes he thought it was the baby, which had died at birth. At the time he'd urged her to have another right away, and she'd said yes, but

25

[4]painting of the Virgin Mary in the style of sixteenth-century artists from Flanders, in Belgium.
[5]Mayan and Toltec statues of the rain god.

nothing had happened. It wasn't something they talked about. "Well, that's that," she said in the hospital afterwards. A perfect child, the doctor said; a freak accident, one of those things that happen. She'd never gone back to university either and she wouldn't get a job. She sat at home, tidying the apartment, looking over his shoulder, towards the door, out the window, as if she was waiting for something.

Sarah bowed her head before him. He, in the feathered costume and long-nosed, toothed mask of the high priest, sprinkled her with blood drawn with thorns from his own tongue and penis. Now he was supposed to give her the message to take to the god. But he couldn't think of anything he wanted to ask for.

And at the same time he thought: what a terrific idea for a Grade Six special project! He'd have them build scale models of the temples, he'd show the slides he'd taken, he'd bring in canned tortillas and tamales for a Mexican lunch, he'd have them make little Chac-Mools out of papier-mâché . . . and the ball game where the captain of the losing team had his head cut off, that would appeal to them, they were bloodthirsty at that age. He could see himself up there in front of them, pouring out his own enthusiasm, gesturing, posturing, acting it out for them, and their response. Yet afterwards he knew he would be depressed. What were his special projects anyway but a substitute for television, something to keep them entertained? They liked him because he danced for them, a funny puppet, inexhaustible and a little absurd. No wonder Sarah despised him.

Edward stepped on the remains of his cigarette. He put his hat back on, a wide-brimmed white hat Sarah had bought for him at the market. He had wanted one with a narrower brim, so he could look up through his binoculars without the hat getting in his way; but she'd told him he would look like an American golfer. It was always there, that gentle, patronizing mockery.

He would wait long enough to be plausible; then he would go back.

*****

Sarah was speculating about how she would be doing this whole trip if Edward had conveniently died. It wasn't that she wished him dead, but she couldn't imagine any other way for him to disappear. He was omnipresent, he pervaded her life like a kind of smell; it was hard for her to think or act except in reference to him. So she found it harmless and pleasant to walk herself through the same itinerary they were following now, but with Edward removed, cut neatly out of the picture. Not that she would be here at all if it wasn't for him. She would prefer to lie in a deck chair in, say, Acapulco, and drink cooling drinks. She threw in a few dark young men in bathing suits, but took them out: that would be too complicated and not relaxing. She had often thought about cheating on Edward—somehow it would serve him right, though she wasn't sure what for—but she had never actually done it. She didn't know anyone suitable, any more.

Suppose she was here, then, with no Edward. She would stay at a better hotel, for one thing. One that had a plug in the sink; they had not yet stayed in a hotel with a plug. Of course that would cost more money, but she thought of herself as having more money if Edward were dead: she would have all of his salary instead of just part of it. She knew there wouldn't be any salary if he really were dead, but it spoiled the fantasy to remember this. And she would travel on planes, if possible, or first-class buses, instead of the noisy, crowded second-class ones he insisted on taking. He said you saw more of the local colour that way and there was no point going to another country if you spent all your time with other tourists. In theory she agreed with this, but the buses gave her headaches and she could do without the closeup tour of squalor, the miserable thatched or tin-roofed huts, the turkeys and tethered pigs.

He applied the same logic to restaurants. There was a perfectly nice one in the village where they were staying, she'd seen it from the bus and it didn't look that expensive; but no, they had to eat in a seedy linoleum-tiled hutch, with plastic-covered tablecloths. They were the only customers in the place. Behind them four adolescent boys were playing dominoes and drinking beer, with a lot of annoying laughter, and some smaller children watched television, a program that Sarah realized was a re-run of *The Cisco Kid*, with dubbed voices.

On the bar beside the television set there was a crèche, with three painted plaster Wise Men, one on an elephant, the others on camels. The first Wise Man was missing his head. Inside the stable a stunted Joseph and Mary adored an enormous Christ Child which was more than half as big as the elephant. Sarah wondered how the Mary could possibly have squeezed out this colossus; it made her uncomfortable to think about it. Beside the crèche was a Santa Claus haloed with flashing lights, and beside that a radio in the shape of Fred Flintstone, which was playing American popular songs, all of them ancient.

"Oh someone help me, help me, plee-ee-ee-eeze . . ."

"Isn't that Paul Anka?"[6] Sarah asked.

But this wasn't the sort of thing Edward could be expected to know. He launched into a defence of the food, the best he'd had in Mexico, he said. Sarah refused to give him the consolation of her agreement. She found the restaurant even more depressing than it should have been, especially the crèche. It was painful, like a cripple trying to walk, one of the last spastic gestures of a religion no one, surely, could believe in much longer.

Another group of tourists was coming up the path behind her, Americans by the sound of them. The guide was Mexican, though. He scrambled up onto the altar, preparing to give his spiel.

"Don't go too near the edge, now."

"Who me, I'm afraid of heights. What d'you see down there?"

"Water, what am I supposed to see?"

The guide clapped his hands for attention. Sarah only half-listened: she didn't really want to know anything more about it.

"Before, people said they threw nothing but virgins in here," the guide began. "How they could tell that, I do not know. It is always hard to tell." He waited for the expected laughter, which came. "But this is not true. Soon, I will tell you how we have found this out. Here we have the altar to the rain god Tlaloc . . ."

---

[6]popular Ottawa-born singer of the 1950s.

45   Two women sat down near Sarah. They were both wearing cotton slacks, high-heeled sandals and wide-brimmed straw hats.

"You go up the big one?"

"Not on your life. I made Alf go up, I took a picture of him at the top."

"What beats me is why they built all those things in the first place."

"It was their religion, that's what he said."

50   "Well, at least it would keep people busy."

"Solve the unemployment problem." They both laughed.

"How many more of these ruins is he gonna make us walk around?"

"Beats me. I'm about ruined out. I'd rather go back and sit on the bus."

"I'd rather go shopping. Not that there's much to buy."

55   Sarah, listening, suddenly felt indignant. Did they have no respect? The sentiments weren't that far from her own of a moment ago, but to hear them from these women, one of whom had a handbag decorated with tasteless straw flowers, made her want to defend the well.

"Nature is very definitely calling," said the woman with the handbag. "I couldn't get in before, there was such a lineup."

"Take a Kleenex," the other woman said. "There's no paper. Not only that, you just about have to wade in. There's water all over the floor."

"Maybe I'll just duck into the bushes," the first woman said.

Edward stood up and massaged his left leg, which had gone to sleep. It was time to go back. If he stayed away too long, Sarah would be querulous, despite the fact that it was she herself who had sent him off on this fool's expedition.

60   He started to walk back along the path. But then there was a flash of orange, at the corner of his eye. Edward swivelled and raised his binoculars. They were there when you least expected it. It was an oriole, partly hidden behind the leaves; he could see the breast, bright orange, and the dark barred wing. He wanted it to be a hooded oriole, he had not yet seen one. He talked to it silently, begging it to come out into the open. It was strange the way birds were completely magic for him the first time only, when he had never seen them before. But there were hundreds of kinds he would never see; no matter how many he saw there would always be one more. Perhaps this was why he kept looking. The bird was hopping further away from him, into the foliage. *Come back*, he called to it wordlessly, but it was gone.

Edward was suddenly happy. Maybe Sarah hadn't been lying to him after all, maybe she had really seen this bird. Even if she hadn't, it had come anyway, in answer to his need for it. Edward felt he was allowed to see birds only when they wanted him to, as if they had something to tell him, a secret, a message. The Aztecs thought hummingbirds were the souls of dead warriors, but why not all birds, why just warriors? Or perhaps they were the souls of the unborn, as some believed. "A jewel, a precious feather," they called an unborn baby, according to *The Daily Life of the Aztecs. Quetzal*, that was *feather*.

"This is the bird I want to see," Sarah said when they were looking through *The Birds of Mexico* before coming down.

"The Resplendent Quetzal," Edward said. It was a green-and-red bird with spectacular iridescent-blue tail plumes. He explained to her that Quetzal Bird meant Feather Bird. "I don't think we're likely to see it," he said. He looked up the habitat. "*Cloud forests.* I don't think we'll be in any cloud forests."

"Well, that's the one I want," Sarah said. "That's the only one I want."

Sarah was always very determined about what she wanted and what she didn't want. If there wasn't anything on a restaurant menu that appealed to her, she would refuse to order anything; or she would permit him to order for her and then pick around the edges, as she had last night. It was no use telling her that this was the best meal they'd had since coming. She never lost her temper or her self-possession, but she was stubborn. Who but Sarah, for instance, would have insisted on bringing a collapsible umbrella to Mexico in the dry season? He'd argued and argued, pointing out its uselessness and the extra weight, but she'd brought it anyway. And then yesterday afternoon it had rained, a real cloudburst. Everyone else had run for shelter, huddling against walls and inside the temple doorways, but Sarah had put up her umbrella and stood under it, smugly. This had infuriated him. Even when she was wrong, she always managed, somehow, to be right. If only just once she would admit . . . what? That she could make mistakes. This was what really disturbed him: her assumption of infallibility.

And he knew that when the baby had died she had blamed it on him. He still didn't know why. Perhaps it was because he'd gone out for cigarettes, not expecting it to be born so soon. He wasn't there when she was told; she'd had to take the news alone.

"It was nobody's fault," he told her repeatedly. "Not the doctor's, not yours. The cord was twisted."

"I know," she said, and she had never accused him; nevertheless he could feel the reproach, hanging around her like a fog. As if there was anything he could have done.

"I wanted it as much as you did," he told her. And this was true. He hadn't thought of marrying Sarah at all, he'd never mentioned it because it had never occurred to him she would agree, until she told him she was pregnant. Up until that time, she had been the one in control; he was sure he was just an amusement for her. But the marriage hadn't been her suggestion, it had been his. He'd dropped out of Theology, he'd taken his public-school teaching certificate that summer in order to support them. Every evening he had massaged her belly, feeling the child move, touching it through her skin. To him it was a sacred thing, and he included her in his worship. In the sixth month, when she had taken to lying on her back, she had begun to snore, and he would lie awake at night listening to these gentle snores, white and silver they seemed to him, almost songs, mysterious talismans. Unfortunately Sarah had retained this habit, but he no longer felt the same way about it.

When the child had died, he was the one who had cried, not Sarah. She had never cried. She got up and walked around almost immediately, she wanted to get out of the hospital as quickly as possible. The baby clothes she'd been buying disappeared from the apartment; he never found out what she'd done with them, he'd been afraid to ask.

Since that time he'd come to wonder why they were still married. It was illogical. If they'd married because of the child and there was no child, and there continued to be no child, why didn't they separate? But he wasn't sure he wanted this. Maybe he was still hoping something would happen, there would be another child. But there was no use demanding it. They came when they wanted to, not when you wanted them to. They came when you least expected it. A jewel, a precious feather.

"Now I will tell you," said the guide. "The archaeologists have dived down into the well. They have dredged up more than fifty skeletons, and they have found that some of them were not virgins at all but men. Also, most of them were children. So as you can see, that is the end of the popular legend." He made an odd little movement from the top of the altar, almost like a bow, hut there was no applause. "They do not do these things to be cruel," he continued. "They believe these people will take a message to the rain god, and live forever in his paradise at the bottom of the well."

The woman with the handbag got up. "Some paradise," she said to her friend. "I'm starting back. You coming?"

In fact the whole group was moving off now, in the scattered way they had. Sarah waited until they had gone. Then she opened her purse and took out the plaster Christ Child she had stolen from the crèche the night before. It was inconceivable to her that she had done such a thing, but there it was, she really had.

75   She hadn't planned it beforehand. She'd been standing beside the crèche while Edward was paying the bill, he'd had to go into the kitchen to do it as they were very slow about bringing it to the table. No one was watching her: the domino-playing boys were absorbed in their game and the children were riveted to the television. She'd just suddenly reached out her hand, past the Wise Men and through the door of the stable, picked the child up and put it into her purse.

She turned it over in her hands. Separated from the dwarfish Virgin and Joseph, it didn't look quite so absurd. Its diaper was cast as part of it, more like a tunic, it had glass eyes and a sort of pageboy haircut, quite long for a newborn. A perfect child, except for the chip out of the back, luckily where it would not be noticed. Someone must have dropped it on the floor.

You could never be too careful. All the time she was pregnant, she'd taken meticulous care of herself, counting out the vitamin pills prescribed by the doctor and eating only what the books recommended. She had drunk four glasses of milk a day, even though she hated milk. She had done the exercises and gone to the classes. No one would be able to say she had not done the right things. Yet she had been disturbed by the thought that the child would be born with something wrong, it would be a mongoloid or a cripple, or a hydrocephalic with a huge liquid head like the ones she'd seen taking the sun in their wheelchairs on the lawn of the hospital one day. But the child had been perfect.

She would never take that risk, go through all that work again. Let Edward strain his pelvis till he was blue in the face; "trying again," he called it. She took the pill every day, without telling him. She wasn't going to try again. It was too much for anyone to expect of her.

What had she done wrong? She hadn't done anything wrong, that was the trouble. There was nothing and no one to blame, except, obscurely,

Edward; and he couldn't be blamed for the child's death, just for not being there. Increasingly since that time he had simply absented himself. When she no longer had the child inside her he had lost interest, he had deserted her. This, she realized, was what she resented most about him. He had left her alone with the corpse, a corpse for which there was no explanation.

80 "*Lost*," people called it. They spoke of her as having lost the child, as though it was wandering around looking for her, crying plaintively, as though she had neglected it or misplaced it somewhere. But where? What limbo had it gone to, what watery paradise? Sometimes she felt as if there had been some mistake, the child had not been born yet. She could still feel it moving, ever so slightly, holding on to her from the inside.

Sarah placed the baby on the rock beside her. She stood up, smoothing out the wrinkles in her skirt. She was sure there would be more flea bites when she got back to the hotel. She picked up the child and walked slowly towards the well, until she was standing at the very brink.

Edward, coming back up the path, saw Sarah at the well's edge, her arms raised above her head. My God, he thought, she's going to jump. He wanted to shout to her, tell her to stop, but he was afraid to startle her. He could run up behind her, grab her . . . but she would hear him. So he waited, paralyzed, while Sarah stood immobile. He expected her to hurtle downwards, and then what would he do? But she merely drew back her right arm and threw something into the well. Then she turned, half stumbling, towards the rock where he had left her and crouched down.

"Sarah," he said. She had her hands over her face; she didn't lift them. He kneeled so he was level with her. "What is it? Are you sick?"

She shook her head. She seemed to be crying, behind her hands, soundlessly and without moving. Edward was dismayed. The ordinary Sarah, with all her perversity, was something he could cope with, he'd invented ways of coping. But he was unprepared for this. She had always been the one in control.

85 "Come on," he said, trying to disguise his desperation, "you need some lunch, you'll feel better." He realized as he said this how fatuous it must sound, but for once there was no patronizing smile, no indulgent answer.

"This isn't like you," Edward said, pleading, as if that was a final argument which would snap her out of it, bring back the old calm Sarah.

Sarah took her hands away from her face, and as she did so Edward felt cold fear. Surely what he would see would be the face of someone else, someone entirely different, a woman he had never seen before in his life. Or there would be no face at all. But (and this was almost worse) it was only Sarah, looking much as she always did.

She took a Kleenex out of her purse and wiped her nose. It is like me, she thought. She stood up and smoothed her skirt once more, then collected her purse and her collapsible umbrella.

"I'd like an orange," she said. "They have them, across from the ticket office. I saw them when we came in. Did you find your bird?"

(1977)

Maria Campbell (b. 1939)

Born in rural northern Saskatchewan, where she lived until her late teens, Maria Campbell first attracted literary notice when her autobiography, *Halfbreed,* was published in 1973. A frank account of her life as a Métis caught between the worlds of whites and full-blooded Natives, it drew attention to a group of people who had been largely ignored. Since then, she has published children's books, a drama, and *Tales of the Road Allowance People,* what she has called "translations" of stories told to her in their own languages by old Native men. In 2004, she was awarded the Molson Prize for her lifelong contributions to Canadian culture. "Joseph's Justice," in which she captures in written English the speech rhythms, of Native storytellers, is set in 1885, shortly after the defeat of the Métis army at the Battle of Batoche. The narrator, who has heard about the incidents from an uncle who witnessed some of them, makes subtle, wry comments about an event that revealed the callousness of the Canadian government toward the people they had defeated. Behind the almost humorously absurd incidents in which Joseph accidentally finds himself trapped are forces that influenced the course of Métis life for several decades.

JOSEPH'S JUSTICE

You know dah big fight at Batoche?[1]
Dah one where we fight dah Anglais?[2]
Well dat one.
Dis story he happen den
an dah name of dah man is Joseph.
He was a Halfbreed guy
An he don take part in dat war.

Dere was lots of mans like dat in dem days.
Dey wasen't scare of dah Anglais
or dah government.
Oh No!
Dey jus wasen interest in fighting for land
or edjication
cause dey don believe dat Anglais government
hees gonna give dem anyting.
So
dey just mine dere own business.

Deres lots of peoples like dat
even today.

---

[1]On May 12, 1885, Batoche, located north of Saskatoon, was the site of the battle in which Canadian government troops defeated the Métis. [2]English.

Dey jus like to stick to demselves dats all.
Well shore
some of dem dey was cowards
an udder ones dey was jus plain lazy.
But most of dem
dey just got no believing dats all.
Dis Joseph
he was one of dem dat don believe.
He was jus minding hees own business
trapping an working for hees ownself
while dah udder mans dey was fighting dah war.

An den dah war he was over
an our peoples dey lose.

Dah Anglais General he take Louis[3]
an dah udder mans to Regina
where hees gonna put dem in dah jail so dey can go to
dah court.
Of course he never got all of dem
jus Louis
cause Louis him
he give hees self up.
Dah udder ones
dey was capture but not Gabriel[4] dough.
Oh no!
Him an Michel Dumas[5]
dey run away to dah States an hide.
Ooh Gabe him
he die before he give hisself up.
Dats dah kine of man he was.

Louis him
he was differen.
Differen from Gabe an all dah udders.
I guess you can say he was a spirit man.
He give hisself to dah peoples
an he do dat when he was a small boy.
Hees Daddy you know
he was dat kine of man too.
He put dah peoples before hees family even.
Dere's not many mans you know
dere born like dat.
Yeah dat Louis

[3]Métis leader Louis Riel (1844–1885) was executed for treason after surrendering after
the Battle of Batoche. [4]Gabriel Dumont (1837–1906) was the military leader of the Métis.
[5]Michel Dumas fled with Dumont to the United States after the capture of Riel.

he give us anudder kine of membering.
But not Gabe.
Hoo
he was a wile tough man him.
He was dah kine of man he can make you believe you
can do anyting on dis eart
long as you was tough enough to stay on your feet.

But you know dis Joseph
dah one I'm telling dah story about?
He was jus ordinary.
Ordinary Halfbreed like us.
Not dah kine of mans anyone he tell stories about.

Well dere he was him
minding hees own business
when dah General he win dah war an he comes riding by
wit hees Halfbreed prisoners.

10   Joseph he say he was walking home wit hees gun an
hees beaver pelts
when dah soldiers dey see him.
He say dey was making a hell of a racket.
Celebrating I guess
cause dey win dah war.
Dey damn near scare him to det he say.

Well dem soldiers
soon as dey see him
dey grab him an dey haul him to dah General

Well my ole uncle
hees name he was Alcid
hees dah one who tell me dis story.
He say dat Anglais General
he was riding a big white horse dat dance all dah time.
An dat horse
he was dancing all over when dah soldiers dey bring
Joseph to him.
An dem soldiers
dey trowed Joseph right in front of dat dancing
horse.
Well Joseph he tell my Uncle
he jump up as fas as he can.
He don wan to get step on.
An den
dat horse he start bucking an he buck dat General

right off.
I guess dat Anglais horse
he never smell a Halfbreed trapper before.

When dat General he finely get dat horse to settle
down
he tell Joseph
"Batoche he fall an your leader
Louis Riel he surrender.
Him an all dese mans dere under arres. An you my good
man, your under arres too."

"If I'm a good man" Joseph he say to him
"den what for you arres me?"

15   Dah General he don like dat very much an he say
"Dah charge hees high treason."

Joseph him
he don know what dat word treason he mean
But he say
it sound awful dangerous
so he talk real careful
jus in case hees got something to do wit shooting.
Dem soldiers you know
dey got guns an he say
dey look like dey wan to use dem.
Joseph you know
him he don trus dah Anglais.
He never trus dem in hees whole life.

Well dah General he yell at dah soldiers to put
Joseph in dah wagon wit dah udders mans.

So dah soldiers dey put chains on him
an dey trowed him in dah wagon.
Joseph he say
dah Halfbreeds an dah Indians dey was all chained togedder.
Some of dem
dey was on dah wagons an some of dem dey was walking.
He say he look for Louis
but he can see him no wheres.

Maybe he was in a cover wagon
cause he was dah leader
an dey don wan nobody to see him or talk to him.
But Joseph
he say he knowed dah udder mans.

Dere was ole Parenteau[6]
he was wearing chains like an outlaw.
Dat ole man he can hurt nobody hees over eighty
years ole.
An dere was dah Vandal boys
an one of dah Arcands.
Even hees brudder-ing-law Moise Touronde he was
dere.

20   Boy he say
dey look rough.
He was raining and real cole an all dey was wearing
was raggy ole clothes.
Some of dem dey don even got no shoes.
An lots of dem dey was wounded
an all of dem
dey was real hungry.

Well Joseph him
he tink he better try an say someting
cause dis whole damn ting
hees starting to look pretty damn scary.
An him
he wan dem to know he wasen mix up in it.

Well he try talking to dem soldiers but dey don even
listen to him.
So he start hollering an yelling
but hees brudder-ing-law Moise
he tell him to shut up
cause nobody he gives a damn if hees guilty or not
anyways.

Well
it took dem a long time to get to Regina
an when dey get dere
dey was trowed in dah jail.
Joseph him
he was dere for six monts before he come up for trial.
An when he do
he tell dah Judge what he happen to him
an dat Judge he believe on him an he let him go.
But Joseph him
he want hees gun and hees furs back
so he ask for dem.

---

[6]Pierre Parenteau was named president of the provisional Métis government of 1885.

He say dah Judge an all dah government peoples
dey jus laugh at him
an dey tell him
he should be grateful he don get hanged or go to
Stony Mountain Jail.[7]
Well he leave dere
an he go to dah policemans.
Dey tell him he should jus forget about it an get
dah hell home as fas as he can
But dat Joseph you know
he was a real hard headed mans
not dah kine dat give up jus like dat.
He tell dem policemans
dat if it was him dat steal from dah General
he would of got charge.

25   An him
he never even done nutting
an hees dah one dat gets treated like a crimnal.

Finely
my ole Uncle he say
one of dah policemans he gets tired of him
an he say
"Okey Joseph. You can press charges. But me I
shore hope you know what your doing cause dis is
gonna be one hell of a mess before hees over."

Well
it took a long time before dey go to dah court.
An when he gets dere
Joseph he meet dis lawyer
an dis lawyer
he ask him what hees doing dere.

When Joseph he tell him
dat lawyer he laugh like hell an he tell Joseph
he'll help him.
Dat lawyer he was an Irishman
an dem Irish you know
dey don like dah Anglais eeder.
My ole Uncle Alcid
he say
dem Irish
dey was dah only ones dat really try to help us in dem days.
I guess dats because dah Anglais dey take all dere lan to.

[7]Located north of Winnipeg.

Well
Joseph he lose in dah court in Regina but he knowed
he wouldn win dere
cause Regina
he was an Anglais town.

25   So him an dat lawyer
dey take it to dah high court.
Again he took a long time
but finely he heered.
Dat General
he was foun guilty for stealing.

You know dey say everybody he steal in dah war time.
But hees agains dah law you know.
Dats true.
Dah soldiers dere suppose to honor cause dey belongs
to dah Queen.
Well at Batoche
dem soldiers
dey eeder don know dat or dey gots no respec for dere Queen
cause all of dem dey steal.
Not jus from Joseph eeder
dey steal from all dah peoples.

Dah Halfbreeds
dey wasen rich you know
dey jus gots a few little nice tings.
When dem soldiers come
dey chase dah peoples away
an dey go into dah howses
an dey clean dem out.
Dey even burn some of dah howses to dah groun.
Dey do dat to Gabe hees house you know.
Burn it to dah groun.
To damn bad nobody else he press charges agains dem.

Well Joseph him
he won hees case an dah General he don look so good.
But Joseph
he don get no compansation from no one.
He never even get hees gun back.
Well he really get mad den.
Whats dah damn use of winning if you don get your
stuff back?
He don care if dah General he look good or bad
all he want
is hees gun an hees furs back.

Well he don know what hees gonna do now
cause dat General he leave our country not long after
dah court.
He go back to hees own country in Angleterre.[8]
Dere dah Queen he make him a gentlemans
You know dah kine dat wear dah armor.
An dah Queen he even put him in charge of all hees
jools.

Dat General
he become a hell of a hero for putting down dah
Breeds at Batoche.
Fars I'm concern
he don have much to brag about.
Five tousan of dem an less den a hundred of us.

30   Oh I know dah history books dey say we was two
hundred an fifty.
But you gotta member
dey write dah history books.
My ole Uncle Alcid
he was dere
an he say dere was less den a hundred at Batoche.
An mos of dem
dey was ole mans.

Well never mine about dat
cause Joseph him
he don care anyways.
All he want is hees gun an hees furs.
He go to dah court again
Dis time hees dah high court in Angleterre
an over dere he gets in dah newspaper an dem Anglais
dey write all about it
Dat really help him you know.

But dats shore funny how he is.
Dey like dah Breeds over dere
but dey hate dem here.
Me I jus never can figure out dem Anglais.
Well dat Irish lawyer he win dah case for Joseph.
An in dah court
he make a hell of a fool out of dah General
at lees
dats what all dah ole mans dey say.

[8]England.

Jimmy Isbister
he use to say dat too
cause he read dah newspapers dat come from over
dere.
Dat Jimmy you know
he was well edjicated.
He was one of dah mans dat go wit Gabe to Montana to
get Louis.

He was a smart man dat Jimmy
he understan dah Anglais.
He was a Scotch Halfbreed
an hees Daddy
he sen him to Angleterre to get hees edjication.

35   Me I always like dah story about Joseph.
Cause you know
maybe we lose dah war
but one man he win
Cause him he believe on hisself
an he don give up.
Dat kine of man hees real important.
Jus as important as Louis an Gabe
cause hees story
he tell you a little bit about how our peoples dey
was like in dem days.

Tanks for listening to me.

(1995)

Thomas King   (b. 1943)

Thomas King, who is of Greek, German, and Cherokee ancestry, has taught at the University of Lethbridge and the University of Minnesota, where he was director of the Native Studies program. His fiction, in which, he says, comedy is used to present often tragic themes, is set in southern Alberta. "I am," he comments, "this Native writer who's out there in the middle, not of nowhere." This quality is found in many of his characters. *Medicine River*, a novel created out of the related stories of several people, focuses on a half-Blackfoot photographer who returns to his home town for his mother's funeral and discovers his own identity. In *Green Grass, Running Water*, five Native people engage in a similar quest. "Borders," from King's collection *One Good Story, That One*, presents the theme of Native people's situation in the modern world in the comic encounter between the narrator's proud mother and Canadian and American immigration officials.

BORDERS

When I was twelve, maybe thirteen, my mother announced that we were going to go to Salt Lake City to visit my sister who had left the reserve, moved across the line, and found a job. Laetitia had not left home with my mother's blessing, but over time my mother had come to be proud of the fact that Laetitia had done all of this on her own.

"She did real good," my mother would say.

Then there were the fine points to Laetitia's going. She had not, as my mother liked to tell Mrs. Manyfingers, gone floating after some man like a balloon on a string. She hadn't snuck out of the house, either, and gone to Vancouver or Edmonton or Toronto to chase rainbows down alleys. And she hadn't been pregnant.

"She did real good."

"I was seven or eight when Laetitia left home. She was seventeen. Our father was from Rocky Boy on the American side.

5   "Dad's American," Laetitia told my mother, "so I can go and come as I please."

"Send us a postcard."

Laetitia packed her things, and we headed for the border. Just outside of Milk River,[1] Laetitia told us to watch for the water tower.

"Over the next rise. It's the first thing you see."

"We got a water tower on the reserve," my mother said. "There's a big one in Lethbridge, too."

10   "You'll be able to see the tops of the flagpoles, too. That's where the border is."

---

[1] river originating in northern Montana that flows north into Alberta before flowing south to the Missouri River.

When we got to Coutts, my mother stopped at the convenience store and bought her and Laetitia a cup of coffee. I got an Orange Crush.

"This is real lousy coffee."

"You're just angry because I want to see the world."

"It's the water. From here on down, they got lousy water."

15 "I can catch the bus from Sweetgrass. You don't have to lift a finger."

"You're going to have to buy your water in bottles if you want good coffee."

There was an old wooden building about a block away, with a tall sign in the yard that said "Museum." Most of the roof had been blown away. Mom told me to go and see when the place was open. There were boards over the windows and doors. You could tell that the place was closed, and I told Mom so, but she said to go and check anyway. Mom and Laetitia stayed by the car. Neither one of them moved. I sat down on the steps of the museum and watched them, and I don't know that they ever said anything to each other. Finally, Laetitia got her bag out of the trunk and gave Mom a hug.

I wandered back to the car. The wind had come up, and it blew Laetitia's hair across her face. Mom reached out and pulled the strands out of Laetitia's eyes, and Laetitia let her.

"You can still see the mountain from here," my mother told Laetitia in Blackfoot.

20 "Lots of mountains in Salt Lake," Laetitia told her in English.

"The place is closed," I said. "Just like I told you."

Laetitia tucked her hair into her jacket and dragged her bag down the road to the brick building with the American flag flapping on a pole. When she got to where the guards were waiting, she turned, put the bag down, and waved to us. We waved back. Then my mother turned the car around, and we came home.

We got postcards from Laetitia regular, and, if she wasn't spreading jelly on the truth, she was happy. She found a good job and rented an apartment with a pool.

"And she can't even swim," my mother told Mrs. Manyfingers.

25 Most of the postcards said we should come down and see the city, but whenever I mentioned this, my mother would stiffen up.

So I was surprised when she bought two new tires for the car and put on her blue dress with the green and yellow flowers. I had to dress up, too, for my mother did not want us crossing the border looking like Americans. We made sandwiches and put them in a big box with pop and potato chips and some apples and bananas and a big jar of water.

"But we can stop at one of those restaurants, too, right?"

"We maybe should take some blankets in case you get sleepy."

"But we can stop at one of those restaurants, too, right?"

30 The border was actually two towns, though neither one was big enough to amount to anything. Coutts was on the Canadian side and consisted of the convenience store and gas station, the museum that was closed and boarded up, and a motel. Sweetgrass was on the American side, but all you could see was an overpass that arched across the highway and disappeared

into the prairies. Just hearing the names of these towns, you would expect that Sweetgrass, which is a nice name and sounds like it is related to other places such as Medicine Hat and Moose Jaw and Kicking Horse Pass, would be on the Canadian side, and that Coutts, which sounds abrupt and rude, would be on the American side. But this was not the case.

Between the two borders was a duty-free shop where you could buy cigarettes and liquor and flags. Stuff like that.

We left the reserve in the morning and drove until we got to Coutts.

"Last time we stopped here," my mother said, "you had an Orange Crush. You remember that?"

"Sure," I said. "That was when Laetitia took off."

35 "You want another Orange Crush?"

"That means we're not going to stop at a restaurant, right?"

My mother got a coffee at the convenience store, and we stood around and watched the prairies move in the sunlight. Then we climbed back in the car. My mother straightened the dress across her thighs, leaned against the wheel, and drove all the way to the border in first gear, slowly, as if she were trying to see through a bad storm or riding high on black ice.

The border guard was an old guy. As he walked to the car, he swayed from side to side, his feet set wide apart, the holster on his hip pitching up and down. He leaned into the window, looked into the back seat, and looked at my mother and me.

"Morning, ma'am."

40 "Good morning."

"Where you heading?"

"Salt Lake City."

"Purpose of your visit?"

"Visit my daughter."

45 "Citizenship?"

"Blackfoot,"[2] my mother told him.

"Ma'am?"

"Blackfoot," my mother repeated.

"Canadian?"

50 "Blackfoot."

It would have been easier if my mother had just said "Canadian" and had been done with it, but I could see she wasn't going to do that. The guard wasn't angry or anything. He smiled and looked towards the building. Then he turned back and nodded.

"Morning, ma'am."

"Good morning."

"Any firearms or tobacco?"

55 "No."

"Citizenship?"

"Blackfoot."

He told us to sit in the car and wait, and we did. In about five minutes, another guard came out with the first man. They were talking as they came,

[2]the Blackfoot Nation has reserves in both Alberta and Montana.

both men swaying back and forth like two cowboys headed for a bar or a gun-fight.

"Morning, ma'am."

"Good morning."

"Cecil tells me you and the boy are Blackfoot."

"That's right."

"Now, I know that we got Blackfeet on the American side and the Canadians got Blackfeet on their side. Just so we can keep our records straight, what side do you come from?"

I knew exactly what my mother was going to say, and I could have told them if they had asked me.

"Canadian side or American side?" asked the guard.

"Blackfoot side," she said.

It didn't take them long to lose their sense of humor, I can tell you that. The one guard stopped smiling altogether and told us to park our car at the side of the building and come in.

We sat on a wood bench for about an hour before anyone came over to talk to us. This time it was a woman. She had a gun, too.

"Hi," she said. "I'm Inspector Pratt. I understand there is a little misunderstanding."

"I'm going to visit my daughter in Salt Lake City," my mother told her. "We don't have any guns or beer."

"It's a legal technicality, that's all."

"My daughter's Blackfoot, too."

The woman opened a briefcase and took out a couple of forms and began to write on one of them. "Everyone who crosses our border has to declare their citizenship. Even Americans. It helps us keep track of the visitors we get from the various countries."

She went on like that for maybe fifteen minutes, and a lot of the stuff she told us was interesting.

"I can understand how you feel about having to tell us your citizenship, and here's what I'll do. You tell me, and I won't put it down on the form. No-one will know but you and me."

Her gun was silver. There were several chips in the wood handle and the name "Stella" was scratched into the metal butt.

We were in the border office for about four hours, and we talked to almost everyone there. One of the men bought me a Coke. My mother brought a couple of sandwiches in from the car. I offered part of mine to Stella, but she said she wasn't hungry.

I told Stella that we were Blackfoot and Canadian, but she said that that didn't count because I was a minor. In the end, she told us that if my mother didn't declare her citizenship, we would have to go back to where we came from. Then we got back in the car and drove to the Canadian border, which was only about a hundred yards away.

I was disappointed. I hadn't seen Laetitia for a long time, and I had never been to Salt Lake City. When she was still at home, Laetitia would go on and on about Salt Lake City. She had never been there, but her boyfriend Lester Tallbull had spent a year in Salt Lake at a technical school.

85   "It's a great place," Lester would say. "Nothing but blondes in the whole state."

Whenever he said that, Laetitia would slug him on his shoulder hard enough to make him flinch. He had some brochures on Salt Lake and some maps, and every so often the two of them would spread them out on the table.

"That's the temple. It's right downtown. You got to have a pass to get in."

"Charlotte says anyone can go in and look around."

"When was Charlotte in Salt Lake? Just when the hell was Charlotte in Salt Lake?"

90   "Last year."

"This is Liberty Park. It's got a zoo. There's good skiing in the mountains."

"Got all the skiing we can use," my mother would say. "People come from all over the world to ski at Banff. Cardston's got a temple, if you like those kinds of things."

"Oh, this one is real big," Lester would say. "They got armed guards and everything."

"Not what Charlotte says."

95   "What does she know?"

Lester and Laetitia broke up, but I guess the idea of Salt Lake stuck in her mind.

The Canadian border guard was a young woman, and she seemed happy to see us. "Hi," she said. "You folks sure have a great day for a trip. Where are you coming from?"

"Standoff."

"Is that in Montana?"

100   "No."

"Where are you going?"

"Standoff."

The woman's name was Carol and I don't guess she was any older than Laetitia. "Wow, you both Canadians?"

"Blackfoot."

105   "Really? I have a friend I went to school with who is Blackfoot. Do you know Mike Harley?"

"No."

"He went to school in Lethbridge, but he's really from Browning."[3]

It was a nice conversation and there were no cars behind us, so there was no rush.

"You're not bringing any liquor back, are you?"

110   "No."

"Any cigarettes or plants or stuff like that?"

"No."

"Citizenship?"

"Blackfoot."

[3] town in northern Montana that is the American headquarters of the Blackfoot Nation.

110   "I know," said the woman, "and I'd be proud of being Blackfoot if I were Blackfoot. But you have to be American or Canadian."

When Laetitia and Lester broke up, Lester took his brochures and maps with him, so Laetitia wrote to someone in Salt Lake City, and, about a month later, she got a big envelope of stuff. We sat at the table and opened up all the brochures, and Laetitia read each one out loud.

"Salt Lake City is the gateway to some of the world's most magnificent skiing.

"Salt Lake City is the home of one of the newest professional basketball franchises, the Utah Jazz.

"The Great Salt Lake is one of the natural wonders of the world."

115   It was kind of exciting seeing all those color brochures on the table and listening to Laetitia read all about how Salt Lake City was one of the best places in the entire world.

"That Salt Lake City place sounds too good to be true," my mother told her.

"It has everything."

"We got everything right here."

"It's boring here."

120   "People in Salt Lake City are probably sending away for brochures of Calgary and Lethbridge and Pincher Creek right now."

In the end, my mother would say that maybe Laetitia should go to Salt Lake City, and Laetitia would say that maybe she would.

We parked the car to the side of the building and Carol led us into a small room on the second floor. I found a comfortable spot on the couch and flipped through some back issues of *Saturday Night* and *Alberta Report*.

When I woke up, my mother was just coming out of another office. She didn't say a word to me. I followed her down the stairs and out to the car. I thought we were going home, but she turned the car around and drove back towards the American border, which made me think we were going to visit Laetitia in Salt Lake City after all. Instead she pulled into the parking lot of the duty-free store and stopped.

"We going to see Laetitia?"

125   "No."

"We going home?"

Pride is a good thing to have, you know. Laetitia had a lot of pride, and so did my mother. I figured that someday I'd have it, too.

"So where are we going?"

Most of that day, we wandered around the duty-free store, which wasn't very large. The manager had a name tag with a tiny American flag on one side and a tiny Canadian flag on the other. His name was Mel. Towards evening, he began suggesting that we should be on our way. I told him we had nowhere to go, that neither the Americans nor the Canadians would let us in. He laughed at that and told us that we should buy something or leave.

130   The car was not very comfortable, but we did have all that food and it was April, so even if it did snow as it sometimes does on the prairies, we wouldn't freeze. The next morning my mother drove to the American border.

It was a different guard this time, but the questions were the same. We didn't spend as much time in the office as we had the day before. By noon, we were back at the Canadian border. By two we were back in the duty-free shop parking lot.

The second night in the car was not as much fun as the first, but my mother seemed in good spirits, and, all in all, it was as much an adventure as an inconvenience. There wasn't much food left and that was a problem, but we had lots of water as there was a faucet at the side of the duty-free shop.

One Sunday, Laetitia and I were watching television. Mom was over at Mrs. Manyfingers's. Right in the middle of the program, Laetitia turned off the set and said she was going to Salt Lake City, that life around here was too boring. I had wanted to see the rest of the program and really didn't care if Laetitia went to Salt Lake City or not. When Mom got home, I told her what Laetitia had said.

What surprised me was how angry Laetitia got when she found out that I had told Mom.

135   "You got a big mouth."

"That's what you said."

"What I said is none of your business."

"I didn't say anything."

"Well, I'm going for sure, now."

140   That weekend, Laetitia packed her bags, and we drove her to the border.

Mel turned out to be friendly. When he closed up for the night and found us still parked in the lot, he came over and asked us if our car was broken down or something. My mother thanked him for his concern and told him that we were fine, that things would get straightened out in the morning.

"You're kidding," said Mel. "You'd think they could handle the simple things."

"We got some apples and a banana," I said, "but we're all out of ham sandwiches."

"You know, you read about these things, but you just don't believe it. You just don't believe it."

145   "Hamburgers would be even better because they got more stuff for energy."

My mother slept in the back seat. I slept in the front because I was smaller and could lie under the steering wheel. Late that night, I heard my mother open the car door. I found her sitting on her blanket leaning against the bumper of the car.

"You see all those stars," she said. "When I was a little girl, my grandmother used to take me and my sisters out on the prairies and tell us stories about all the stars."

"Do you think Mel is going to bring us any hamburgers?"

"Every one of those stars has a story. You see that bunch of stars over there that look like a fish?"

150   "He didn't say no."

"Coyote[4] went fishing, one day. That's how it all started." We sat out under the stars that night, and my mother told me all sorts of stories. She was serious about it, too. She'd tell them slow, repeating parts as she went, as if she expected me to remember each one.

Early the next morning, the television vans began to arrive, and guys in suits and women in dresses came trotting over to us, dragging microphones and cameras and lights behind them. One of the vans had a table set up with orange juice and sandwiches and fruit. It was for the crew, but when I told them we hadn't eaten for a while, a really skinny blonde woman told us we could eat as much as we wanted.

They mostly talked to my mother. Every so often one of the reporters would come over and ask me questions about how it felt to be an Indian without a country. I told them we had a nice house on the reserve and that my cousins had a couple of horses we rode when we went fishing. Some of the television people went over to the American border, and then they went to the Canadian border.

Around noon, a good-looking guy in a dark blue suit and an orange tie with little ducks on it drove up in a fancy car. He talked to my mother for a while, and, after they were done talking, my mother called me over, and we got into our car. Just as my mother started the engine, Mel came over and gave us a bag of peanut brittle and told us that justice was a damn hard thing to get, but that we shouldn't give up.

155   I would have preferred lemon drops, but it was nice of Mel anyway.

"Where are we going now?"

"Going to visit Laetitia."

The guard who came out to our car was all smiles. The television lights were so bright they hurt my eyes, and, if you tried to look through the windshield in certain directions, you couldn't see a thing.

"Morning, ma'am."

160   "Good morning."

"Where you heading?"

"Salt Lake City."

"Purpose of your visit?"

"Visit my daughter."

165   "Any tobacco, liquor, or firearms?"

"Don't smoke."

"Any plants or fruit?"

"Not any more."

"Citizenship?"

170   "Blackfoot."

The guard rocked back on his heels and jammed his thumbs into his gun belt. "Thank you," he said, his fingers patting the butt of the revolver. "Have a pleasant trip."

My mother rolled the car forward, and the television people had to scramble out of the way. They ran alongside the car as we pulled away from the border, and, when they couldn't run any farther, they stood in the middle of the highway and waved and waved and waved.

[4]trickster figure in the mythology of several Native peoples of the northern plains.

We got to Salt Lake City the next day. Laetitia was happy to see us, and, that first night, she took us out to a restaurant that made really good soups. The list of pies took up a whole page. I had cherry. Mom had chocolate. Laetitia said that she saw us on television the night before and, during the meal, she had us tell her the story over and over again.

Laetitia took us everywhere. We went to a fancy ski resort. We went to the temple. We got to go shopping in a couple of large malls, but they weren't as large as the one in Edmonton, and Mom said so.

175   After a week or so, I got bored and wasn't at all sad when my mother said we should be heading back home. Laetitia wanted us to stay longer, but Mom said no, that she had things to do back home and that, next time, Laetitia should come up and visit. Laetitia said she was thinking about moving back, and Mom told her to do as she pleased, and Laetitia said that she would.

On the way home, we stopped at the duty-free shop, and my mother gave Mel a green hat that said "Salt Lake" across the front. Mel was a funny guy. He took the hat and blew his nose and told my mother that she was an inspiration to us all. He gave us some more peanut brittle and came out into the parking lot and waved at us all the way to the Canadian border.

It was almost evening when we left Coutts. I watched the border through the rear window until all you could see were the tops of the flagpoles and the blue water tower, and then they rolled over a hill and disappeared.

(1993)

Alice Walker   (b. 1944)

Born in Eatonton in rural Georgia, where her parents were poor sharecroppers, Alice Walker published her first book—a collection of poems entitled *Once*—in 1968, shortly after graduating from Sarah Lawrence College in New York. Active in Mississippi during the civil rights movement of the 1960s, she has published several books: poetry, short stories, essays, and six novels, of which the best known, *The Color Purple* (1982), was made into a motion picture. In all her writing, Walker celebrates the lives of African-American women and their heritage. "Everyday Use" contrasts characters' attitudes toward an old quilt to reveal the differences between the narrator and her daughters Maggie and Dee. In her essay "In Search of Our Mothers' Gardens," Walker writes of quilts, now often preserved in museums, as creations of people who possessed "powerful imagination and deep spiritual feeling."

EVERYDAY USE

For Your Grandmama

I will wait for her in the yard that Maggie and I made so clean and wavy yesterday afternoon. A yard like this is more comfortable than most people know. It is not just a yard. It is like an extended living room. When the hard clay is swept clean as a floor and the fine sand around the edges lined with tiny, irregular grooves, anyone can come and sit and look up into the elm tree and wait for the breezes that never come inside the house.

Maggie will be nervous until her sister goes: she will stand hopelessly in corners, homely and ashamed of the burn scars down her arms and legs, eying her sister with a mixture of envy and awe. She thinks her sister has held life always in the palm of one hand, that "no" is a word the world never learned to say to her.

You've no doubt seen those TV shows where the child who has "made it" is confronted, as a surprise, by her own mother and father, tottering in weakly from backstage. (A pleasant surprise, of course: What would they do if parent and child came on the show only to curse out and insult each other?) On TV mother and child embrace and smile into each other's faces. Sometimes the mother and father weep, the child wraps them in her arms and leans across the table to tell how she would not have made it without their help. I have seen these programs.

Sometimes I dream a dream in which Dee and I are suddenly brought together on a TV program of this sort. Out of a dark and soft-seated limousine I am ushered into a bright room filled with many people. There I meet a smiling, gray, sporty man like Johnny Carson who shakes my hand and tells me what a fine girl I have. Then we are on the stage and Dee is embracing me with tears in her eyes. She pins on my dress a large orchid, even though she has told me once that she thinks orchids are tacky flowers.

5   In real life I am a large, big-boned woman with rough, man-working hands. In the winter I wear flannel nightgowns to bed and overalls during the day. I can kill and clean a hog as mercilessly as a man. My fat keeps me hot in zero weather. I can work outside all day, breaking ice to get water for washing; I can eat pork liver cooked over the open fire minutes after it comes steaming from the hog. One winter I knocked a bull calf straight in the brain between the eyes with a sledge hammer and had the meat hung up to chill before nightfall. But of course all this does not show on television. I am the way my daughter would want me to be: a hundred pounds lighter, my skin like an uncooked barley pancake. My hair glistens in the hot bright lights. Johnny Carson has much to do to keep up with my quick and witty tongue.

But that is a mistake. I know even before I wake up. Who ever knew a Johnson with a quick tongue? Who can even imagine me looking a strange white man in the eye? It seems to me I have talked to them always with one foot raised in flight, with my head turned in whichever way is farthest from them. Dee, though. She would always look anyone in the eye. Hesitation was no part of her nature.

"How do I look, Mama?" Maggie says, showing just enough of her thin body enveloped in pink skirt and red blouse for me to know she's there, almost hidden by the door.

"Come out into the yard," I say.

Have you ever seen a lame animal, perhaps a dog run over by some careless person rich enough to own a car, sidle up to someone who is ignorant enough to be kind to him? That is the way my Maggie walks. She has been like this, chin on chest, eyes on ground, feet in shuffle, ever since the fire that burned the other house to the ground.

10   Dee is lighter than Maggie, with nicer hair and a fuller figure. She's a woman now, though sometimes I forget. How long ago was it that the other house burned? Ten, twelve years? Sometimes I can still hear the flames and feel Maggie's arms sticking to me, her hair smoking and her dress falling off her in little black papery flakes. Her eyes seemed stretched open, blazed open by the flames reflected in them. And Dee. I see her standing off under the sweet gum tree she used to dig gum out of; a look of concentration on her face as she watched the last dingy gray board of the house fall in toward the red-hot brick chimney. Why don't you do a dance around the ashes? I'd wanted to ask her. She had hated the house that much.

I used to think she hated Maggie, too. But that was before we raised the money, the church and me, to send her to Augusta[1] to school. She used to read to us without pity; forcing words, lies, other folks' habits, whole lives upon us two, sitting trapped and ignorant underneath her voice. She washed us in a river of make-believe, burned us with a lot of knowledge we didn't necessarily need to know. Pressed us to her with the

[1]city in Georgia southeast of Atlanta.

serious way she read, to shove us away at just the moment, like dimwits, we seemed about to understand.

Dee wanted nice things. A yellow organdy dress to wear to her graduation from high school; black pumps to match a green suit she'd made from an old suit somebody gave me. She was determined to stare down any disaster in her efforts. Her eyelids would not flicker for minutes at a time. Often I fought off the temptation to shake her. At sixteen she had a style of her own: and knew what style was.

I never had an education myself. After second grade the school was closed down. Don't ask me why: in 1927 colored asked fewer questions than they do now. Sometimes Maggie reads to me. She stumbles along good-naturedly but can't see well. She knows she is not bright. Like good looks and money, quickness passed her by. She will marry John Thomas (who has mossy teeth in an earnest face) and then I'll be free to sit here and I guess just sing church songs to myself. Although I never was a good singer. Never could carry a tune. I was always better at a man's job. I used to love to milk till I was hooked in the side in '49. Cows are soothing and slow and don't bother you, unless you try to milk them the wrong way.

15   I have deliberately turned my back on the house. It is three rooms, just like the one that burned, except the roof is tin; they don't make shingle roofs any more. There are no real windows, just some holes cut in the sides, like portholes in a ship, but not round and not square, with rawhide holding the shutters up on the outside. This house is in a pasture, too, like the other one. No doubt when Dee sees it she will want to tear it down. She wrote me once that no matter where we "choose" to live, she will manage to come see us. But she will never bring her friends. Maggie and I thought about this and Maggie asked me, "Mama, when did Dee ever *have* any friends?"

She had a few. Furtive boys in pink shirts hanging about on washday after school. Nervous girls who never laughed. Impressed with her they worshiped the well-turned phrase, the cute shape, the scalding humor that erupted like bubbles in lye. She read to them.

When she was courting Jimmy T she didn't have much time to pay to us, but turned all her faultfinding power on him. He *flew* to marry a cheap city girl from a family of ignorant flashy people. She hardly had time to recompose herself.

When she comes I will meet—but there they are!

Maggie attempts to make a dash for the house, in her shuffling way, but I stay her with my hand. "Come back here," I say. And she stops and tries to dig a well in the sand with her toe.

20   It is hard to see them clearly through the strong sun. But even the first glimpse of leg out of the car tells me it is Dee. Her feet were always neat-looking, as if God himself had shaped them with a certain style. From the other side of the car comes a short, stocky man. Hair is all over his head a foot long and hanging from his chin like a kinky mule tail. I hear Maggie suck in her breath. "Uhnnnh," is what it sounds like. Like when you see the wriggling end of a snake just in front of your foot on the road. "Uhnnnh."

Dee next. A dress down to the ground, in this hot weather. A dress so loud it hurts my eyes. There are yellows and oranges enough to throw back the light of the sun. I feel my whole face warming from the heat waves it throws out. Earrings gold, too, and hanging down to her shoulders. Bracelets dangling and making noises when she moves her arm up to shake the folds of the dress out of her armpits. The dress is loose and flows, and as she walks closer, I like it. I hear Maggie go "Uhnnnh" again. It is her sister's hair. It stands straight up like the wool on a sheep. It is black as night and around the edges are two long pigtails that rope about like small lizards disappearing behind her ears.

"Wa-su-zo-Tean-o!"[2] she says, coming on in that gliding way the dress makes her move. The short stocky fellow with the hair to his navel is all grinning and he follows up with "Asalamalakim,[3] my mother and sister!" He moves to hug Maggie but she falls back, right up against the back of my chair. I feel her trembling there and when I look up I see the perspiration falling off her chin.

"Don't get up," says Dee. Since I am stout it takes something of a push. You can see me trying to move a second or two before I make it. She turns, showing white heels through her sandals, and goes back to the car. Out she peeks next with a Polaroid. She stoops down quickly and lines up picture after picture of me sitting there in front of the house with Maggie cowering behind me. She never takes a shot without making sure the house is included. When a cow comes nibbling around the edge of the yard she snaps it and me and Maggie *and* the house. Then she puts the Polaroid in the back seat of the car, and comes up and kisses me on the forehead.

Meanwhile Asalamalakim is going through motions with Maggie's hand. Maggie's hand is as limp as a fish, and probably as cold, despite the sweat, and she keeps trying to pull it back. It looks like Asalamalakim wants to shake hands but wants to do it fancy. Or maybe he don't know how people shake hands. Anyhow, he soon gives up on Maggie.

25 "Well," I say. "Dee."

"No, Mama," she says. "Not 'Dee,' Wangero Leewanika Kemanjo!"

"What happened to 'Dee'?" I wanted to know.

"She's dead," Wangero said. "I couldn't bear it any longer, being named after the people who oppress me."

"You know as well as me you was named after your aunt Dicie," I said. Dicie is my sister. She named Dee. We called her "Big Dee" after Dee was born.

"But who was *she* named after?" asked Wangero.

"I guess after Grandma Dee," I said.

30 "And who was she named after?" asked Wangero.

"Her mother," I said, and saw Wangero was getting tired. "That's about as far back as I can trace it," I said. Though, in fact, I probably could have carried it back beyond the Civil War through the branches.

"Well," said Asalamalakim, "There you are."

"Uhnnnh," I heard Maggie say.

"There I was not," I said, "before 'Dicie' cropped up in our family, so why should I try to trace it that far back?"

[2]Islamic greeting popular among some African Americans in the 1960s. 3Islamic greeting also popular during the 1960s.

He just stood there grinning, looking down on me like somebody inspecting a Model A car. Every once in a while he and Wangero sent eye signals over my head.

"How do you pronounce this name?" I asked.

"You don't have to call me by it if you don't want to," said Wangero.

"Why shouldn't I?" I asked. "If that's what you want us to call you, we'll call you."

"I know it might sound awkward at first," said Wangero.

"I'll get used to it," I said. "Ream it out again."

Well, soon we got the name out of the way. Asalamalakim had a name twice as long and three times as hard. After I tripped over it two or three times he told me to just call him Hakim-a-barber. I wanted to ask him was he a barber, but I didn't really think he was, so I didn't ask.

"You must belong to those beef-cattle peoples down the road," I said. They said "Asalamalakim" when they met you, too, but they didn't shake hands. Always too busy: feeding the cattle, fixing the fences, putting up saltlick shelters, throwing down hay. When the white folks poisoned some of the herd the men stayed up all night with rifles in their hands. I walked a mile and a half just to see the sight.

Hakim-a-barber said, "I accept some of their doctrines, but farming and raising cattle is not my style." (They didn't tell me, and I didn't ask, whether Wangero (Dee) had really gone and married him.)

We sat down to eat and right away he said he didn't eat collards and pork was unclean. Wangero, though, went on through the chitlins and corn bread, the greens and everything else. She talked a blue streak over the sweet potatoes. Everything delighted her. Even the fact that we still used the benches her daddy made for the table when we couldn't afford to buy chairs.

"Oh, Mama!" she cried. Then turned to Hakim-a-barber. "I never knew how lovely these benches are. You can feel the rump prints," she said, running her hands underneath her and along the bench. Then she gave a sigh and her hand closed over Grandma Dee's butter dish. "That's it!" she said. "I knew there was something I wanted to ask you if I could have." She jumped up from the table and went over in the corner where the churn stood, the milk in it clabber by now. She looked at the churn and looked at it.

"This churn top is what I need," she said. "Didn't Uncle Buddy whittle it out of a tree you all used to have?"

"Yes," I said.

"Uh huh," she said happily. "And I want the dasher, too."

"Uncle Buddy whittle that, too?" asked the barber.

Dee (Wangero) looked up at me.

"Aunt Dee's first husband whittled the dash," said Maggie so low you almost couldn't hear her. "His name was Henry, but they called him Stash."

"Maggie's brain is like an elephant's," Wangero said, laughing. "I can use the churn top as a centrepiece for the alcove table," she said, sliding a plate over the churn, "and I'll think of something artistic to do with the dasher."

When she finished wrapping the dasher the handle stuck out. I took it for a moment in my hands. You didn't even have to look to see where hands pushing the dasher up and down to make butter had left a kind of sink in the wood. In fact, there were a lot of small sinks; you could see where thumbs and fingers had sunk into the wood. It was beautiful light yellow wood, from a tree that grew in the yard where Big Dee and Stash had lived.

After dinner Dee (Wangero) went to the trunk at the foot of my bed and started rifling through it. Maggie hung back in the kitchen over the dishpan. Out came Wangero with two quilts. They had been pieced by Grandma Dee and then Big Dee and me had hung them on the quilt frames on the front porch and quilted them. One was in the Lone Star pattern. The other was Walk Around the Mountain. In both of them were scraps of dresses Grandma Dee had worn fifty and more years ago. Bits and pieces of Grandpa Jarrell's Paisley shirts. And one teeny faded blue piece, about the size of a penny matchbox, that was from Great Grandpa Ezra's uniform that he wore in the Civil War.

"Mama," Wangero said sweet as a bird. "Can I have these old quilts?"

55 I heard something fall in the kitchen, and a minute later the kitchen door slammed.

"Why don't you take one or two of the others?" I asked. "These old things was just done by me and Big Dee from some tops your grandma pieced before she died."

"No," said Wangero. "I don't want those. They are stitched around the borders by machine."

"That'll make them last better," I said.

"That's not the point," said Wangero. "These are all pieces of dresses Grandma used to wear. She did all this stitching by hand. Imagine!" She held the quilts securely in her arms, stroking them.

60 "Some of the pieces, like those lavender ones, come from old clothes her mother handed down to her," I said, moving up to touch the quilts. Dee (Wangero) moved back just enough so that I couldn't reach the quilts. They already belonged to her.

"Imagine!" she breathed again, clutching them closely to her bosom.

"The truth is," I said, "I promised to give them quilts to Maggie, for when she marries John Thomas."

She gasped like a bee had stung her.

"Maggie can't appreciate these quilts!" she said. "She'd probably be backward enough to put them to everyday use."

"I reckon she would," I said. "God knows I been saving 'em for long enough with nobody using 'em. I hope she will!" I didn't want to bring up how I had offered Dee (Wangero) a quilt when she went away to college. Then she had told me they were old-fashioned, out of style.

65 "But they're *priceless*!" she was saying now, furiously; for she has a temper. "Maggie would put them on the bed and in five years they'd be in rags. Less than that!"

"She can always make some more," I said. "Maggie knows how to quilt."

Dee (Wangero) looked at me with hatred. "You just will not understand. The point is these quilts, *these* quilts!"

"Well," I said, stumped. "What would *you* do with them?"

"Hang them," she said. As if that was the only thing you *could* do with quilts.

Maggie by now was standing in the door. I could almost hear the sound her feet made as they scraped over each other.

70   "She can have them, Mama," she said, like somebody used to never winning anything, or having anything reserved for her. "I can 'member Grandma Dee without the quilts."

I looked at her hard. She had filled her bottom lip with checkerberry snuff and it gave her face a kind of dopey, hangdog look. It was Grandma Dee and Big Dee who taught her how to quilt herself. She stood there with her scarred hands hidden in the folds of her skirt. She looked at her sister with something like fear but she wasn't mad at her. This was Maggie's portion. This was the way she knew God to work.

When I looked at her like that something hit me in the top of my head and ran down to the soles of my feet. Just like when I'm in church and the spirit of God touches me and I get happy and shout. I did something I never had done before: hugged Maggie to me, then dragged her on into the room, snatched the quilts out of Miss Wangero's hands and dumped them into Maggie's lap. Maggie just sat there on my bed with her mouth open.

"Take one or two of the others," I said to Dee.

But she turned without a word and went out to Hakim-a-barber.

75   "You just don't understand," she said, as Maggie and I came out to the car.

"What don't I understand," I wanted to know.

"Your heritage," she said. And then she turned to Maggie, kissed her, and said, "You ought to try to make something of yourself, too, Maggie. It's really a new day for us. But from the way you and Mama still live you'd never know it."

She put on some sunglasses that hid everything above the tip of her nose and her chin.

Maggie smiled; maybe at the sunglasses. But a real smile, not scared. After we watched the car dust settle I asked Maggie to bring me a dip of snuff. And then the two of us sat there just enjoying, until it was time to go in the house and go to bed.

(1973)

Stuart McLean   (b. 1948)

Since 1994, Stuart McLean, a former radio journalist and Ryerson University journalism professor, has hosted "The Vinyl Cafe," a CBC radio program featuring interviews, essays, performances by Canadian musicians, and episodes in the life of Dave, owner of a fictional secondhand record store, "The Vinyl Cafe," husband of Morley, father of teenager Stephanie and her younger brother Sam, and owner of dog, Arthur. The episodes have been collected in a number of books, three of which have won the Stephen Leacock Memorial Medal for Humour. "On the Roof," taken from McLean's first Leacock award winner, *Home from the Vinyl Cafe*, is one of the radio show's annual Christmas stories, episodes in which Dave, trying his best, usually experiences some kind of comic disaster. The story presents a Canadian ritual, putting up outdoor Christmas lights, often very late in the season and usually in very cold weather. In presenting Dave's thoughts, the third person narrator, gently and good naturedly satirizes a Canadian tradition.

ON THE ROOF

Betty Schellenberger and Morley were drinking coffee.

Morley said, "They've done studies about this. Even in families where men and women do equal amounts of house-work, it's always the women who organize it."

Betty nodded, her hands cradling the mug of coffee in front of her on the kitchen table.

"It's the women," said Morley, "who plan and assign. It's the women who drive the train."

5   Dave was washing the lunch dishes. It made him feel bad, listening to them talk. It felt personal—like they were criticizing him. No one, he thought grimly, assigned me these dishes. He considered stopping. I wouldn't want to overstep my boundaries, he thought. Since Morley had gone back to work in the fall Dave had been trying to shoulder his share of the chores. But Morley was right. There was no denying it. She was management. He was labour.

It was Saturday afternoon. The sky was grey and heavy. The wind was rippling the puddles on the driveway. It looked like it could snow.

The weather suited Dave's mood. When he finished the dishes he said, "I'm going to take Arthur out."

He put on an old blue sweater and a canvas jacket, stuffed a toque and a pair of gloves in his pocket and headed outside with the dog. He thought of loading Arthur into the car and driving to a park, or maybe taking him down to the lake. He stood on the front walk—Arthur looking up at him expectantly—then instead of getting in the car he headed north through the neighbourhood.

There was hardly anyone else out. There were some kids walking through the park, but there was no one in the playground. The abandoned swings hung on their yellow metal frame like a row of mourners.

10   Up ahead there was a woman walking towards Dave on the same side of the street.

"Hello," said Dave as they passed. The woman did not acknowledge him. She walked by with her jaw firmly shut, her eyes straight ahead. As if he and Arthur didn't exist.

There are lots of things that can give you the blues. The weather can give you the blues. Sometimes it is so grey out it makes you feel blue inside. Your best friends can give you the blues. In fact your friends are often better at making you feel blue than your worst enemies. Sometimes, however, it's just an overheard conversation, a stranger on the street, empty swings.

Dave had not intended to be gone long. But he kept walking. After forty-five minutes he was on a street he had never been on before, gazing into the window of a store he had never seen: Thrift Villa—"Where smart shoppers save."

He only went in to warm up, but he ended up buying two drinking glasses—sixty-nine cents each. One was a Dave Keon[1] hockey glass with a picture of Dave on one side and a referee on the other demonstrating the signal for a holding penalty. "Holding" it said in black letters under the referee. The lady at the cash told him it was a peanut butter jar from the 1960s. She couldn't remember the brand name.

15   "I'm pretty sure it was a rodent," she said, as she rolled the glasses in newspaper. "Like a beaver. Or a squirrel."

When Dave was halfway home it started to snow. He pulled his toque out of his pocket and tugged it down so it covered his ears. It was 4:30 and it was getting dark. He had been gone two hours. The weather was whispering warnings: Just wanted to remind you, said the snow, that you'll be walking home from work in the dark from now on. Just wanted to let you know, said the wind, that it will probably be raining.

He was cheered by the texture of the light from the houses he passed. It reminded him of winter nights when he was a boy, of afternoon-long games of shinny. *Maybe*, he thought, *he should take everyone to Cape Breton for Christmas*. He hadn't been home at Christmas for too many years.

He thought of the disaster that befell him when he tried to cook the turkey last year. They could do worse than spend the holidays with his mother. She would be happy to see them. The kids could cut a tree on the McCauleys' farm.

That's what started him thinking about Christmas decorations. He had been late with them last year—so late that he had ended up more or less throwing their lights over the front hedge. He had promised himself he would do better this year.

---

[1]An all-star centre who played for the Toronto Maple Leafs' Stanley Cup winning teams during the 1960s.

20   Well, it was this year now. He would get the lights up before anyone had to ask. He would beat Morley to the punch. He would be labour and management. He was feeling better when he got home.

On Tuesday Dave came home early determined to climb onto his roof and put out the Christmas lights. He wanted to be up and down before dark. But first, he had to go to Jim Scoffield's house to borrow a ladder, and they had to have a beer. Then they had to *find* the ladder. Dave had to replace all the burned-out bulbs. Suddenly it was dusk.

It was dark by the time Dave stepped gingerly onto the roof and half-walked, half-crawled across the shingles to the chimney.

It was colder than he expected. He grabbed hold of the television antenna and carefully straightened up. He could see all over the neighbourhood. He wondered why he only got up there at the worst times of the year. I should come up here more often, he thought. He sat down with his back to the chimney and began to untangle the lights that he had already untangled before he climbed the ladder.

It took him about half an hour to attach the lights to the antenna. When he was finished, he plugged them in and his roof was bathed in light—yellows, reds, greens and blues. They didn't look half bad, and miracle of miracles, no bulbs had burned out since he had checked them half an hour ago. Dave shuffled back to the ladder to get a better look.

25   The antenna reminded him of the clothesline in his yard when he was a child—they had the kind made from one centre pole—the kind that looks like an umbrella with the fabric removed. Dave remembered the winter mornings when his mother would push him into a snowsuit and out the back door like a blimp, remembered the swishing of all that nylon material between his legs. How he inevitably needed to pee once he was stuck outside.

He looked out over the neighbourhood rooftops and suddenly, as sure as she was standing beside him, Dave could hear his sweet mother's voice fill his head. She was warning him about something. She was saying, Dave, don't lick the clothesline.

Sometimes you do things just because someone tells you not to. Sometimes you do things because you have never done them before and you want to see what would happen if you did. Sometimes it's hard to figure out why you do some things at all.

Dave had never put his tongue against a television antenna on a cold night in November, although he had a pretty fair idea what would happen if he did. But the moment his mother's voice came into his head he could feel himself drawn to the antenna.

As he slowly crab-walked back across the roof towards the chimney to which the antenna was attached, Dave was thinking to himself—this won't happen. I won't do this. Why would I do this? I'm not stupid. I'm just trying to scare myself. Yet he felt as if he were outside of his body. It didn't seem to be him moving across the roof. It seemed to be someone else. And there didn't seem to be much he could do to stop him.

30   Part of Dave was saying, I don't want to put my tongue on that television antenna, but another part of him, the part that seemed to be in control—the part his tongue seemed to be listening to—was saying, Just do it, Dave. You don't have to listen to your mother any more. You're an adult. You can do whatever you want.

He was surprised by how unequivocally his tongue grabbed onto the metal. It was not at all uncertain about what it was expected to do. Dave himself was uncertain that he had even touched the metal. He thought there was still some space between him and the pole, and then suddenly he was bonded to it. At first he was intrigued by the way his tongue stuck. Almost proud of it. It hurt a bit, but it was not an excruciating pain—more the pain of melted candle wax than molten lead.

Then it hurt a bit more and Dave thought, OK, that's enough, and he tried to pull his tongue off the antenna. It didn't come. He leaned forward because it hurt when he tried to pull and then more of his tongue was stuck to the antenna and he felt a wave of panic rush through him.

His mother's voice filled his head again. She said, I told you not to do that.

And Dave said, "Why didn't you stop me?"

35   Except it sounded different ... more like "MMMMUUUUGGGHHHH." When he said it, his top lip brushed against the antenna and then his top lip was stuck as well as his tongue and he knew he was in serious trouble.

Dave stopped moving. He was very still. Then he tried to lean back a little, but it hurt, and his tongue didn't want to let go.

He thought, Maybe it's like taking a Band-Aid off a kid. Maybe you have to be sure about it. Sure and fast.

So he counted. "One. Two."

Just as he was about to say, "Three," Dave heard his mother's voice again. She said, Have you thought that you could pull your entire tongue out of your mouth and leave it on the antenna. Have you thought of that?

40   Dave stopped counting.

That's impossible, he thought.

But it occurred to him that if he didn't actually lose his entire tongue, maybe he could lose a layer of it—the layer with his taste buds. He would never taste anything ever again. For the rest of his life he might as well eat tofu and it wouldn't make any difference. That scared him so much that he didn't move a muscle for a long time. He stood on the roof, sucking on his antenna without moving.

He could see his neighbours walking up and down the street. He saw the Schellenbergers stop and look up at him. When they stopped, he began to flap his arms up and down, being careful not to move his face. The Schellenbergers stood and watched him for a few moments and then they said something to each other, turned and walked inside their house.

Dave knew they weren't going to come to his rescue. They had been admiring him. They thought he was part of the display—hanging from the antenna in the middle of all the lights.

45   This is what happens when you do things you weren't asked to do, thought Dave.

He was filled with self-loathing. His life seemed to be a parade of similar incidents.

*****

When his daughter was very small, Dave had taken her in the car on his way to a job interview. Morley was sick and he was going to drop Stephanie at Morley's mother's house while he went to the interview.

The interview was for a job that Dave thought he wanted at the time—a buyer for a record store chain. He had borrowed a briefcase from Carl Lowbeer as a prop.

It was not an easy drive. Stephanie cried all the way across town. Dave was desperate to calm her down. He needed to be calm for the interview. He decided that a stick of licorice might do the trick.

50   He pulled up in front of a corner store. As he jumped out of the car he noticed four young thugs, wearing more than their fair share of black leather, bumping up the street. He didn't want them messing with his daughter. Better lock the door, thought Dave.

He patted his pockets loolting for his keys. Silly, he thought, they're still in the ignition. Dave had left the engine running so that when he came out of the store he could be on his way as quickly as possible. He wasn't exactly late for his interview, but he didn't have a lot of time to spare.

No worries. He could lock the car door without the key. Dave reached inside the car and depressed the lock button. Then he slammed the door, carefully holding the door handle so the door would stay locked.

As he stood beside his locked car and smiled at the four thugs, Dave was vaguely troubled by a feeling that something wasn't right. But he was too uptight and in too much of a hurry to worry about it. He dashed into the store and moments later dashed out again waving the candy. When he saw his car, he stopped dead in his tracks. The doors were locked. The motor was running. His keys were in the ignition.

When Dave saw Stephanie locked in the back of the car, something inside him snapped. He was irrevocably and undeniably certain that his daughter was in danger.

55   He knew that people who wanted to end their lives often sat in running cars. He understood that they usually did this in garages, but he reasoned that even though his car was in the open air, fumes could still seep through the floorboards, and if they didn't kill his daughter, they could surely damage her brain.

Dave looked around for something to break a window with in case Stephanie started to nod off. He spotted a brick at a construction site and placed it on the sidewalk beside the passenger door. He sprinted to a phone booth.

Morley, who had a fever of 102, got dressed and took a taxi across town with their extra set of keys.

By the time she arrived, so had the police.

Morley still says she should have denied knowing Dave. When she tells this story she says she should have pressed charges. Look at the brick, she could have said, I think he was planning to steal my daughter.

60   Dave was late for the interview. He didn't get the job. This was the life that was flashing by Dave's eyes as he hunched over his chimney—sucking on his television antenna. He could hear his family moving around the living room. He could hear their voices floating up the chimney. He heard Morley say, "Wouldn't a fire be nice?"

"No," said Dave. "No, it wouldn't."

Then he heard Sam.

"Can we put on two logs?"

Dave and Morley burn synthetic wax logs. The moment the waxy smoke hit Dave he needed to pee. He thought, The fumes are probably poisonous. I am being asphyxiated. My body is trying to clear the toxins.

65   It was like being trapped in the backyard in a snowsuit when he was a kid.

His mind began to race.

What if spring never came? What if there was never a thaw? What if he died there?

He couldn't remember the last time the chimney had been cleaned. What would happen to him if the chimney caught fire? The fumes were stinging his eyes. He needed to pee badly now.

What if he peed on the antenna?

Would that warm it up enough?

70   Enough to set him free?

And what, God help him, would happen if his penis touched the metal?

And then it came to him.

Why didn't he take one of the Christmas lights and hold it against his lip so the warmth from the light would melt his mouth free?

It took less than five minutes.

75   In five minutes he was down the ladder, in the house and peering into the bathroom mirror at his tongue. It was red but not too sore.

Sam and Stephanie were snuggled on the couch watching television, and Morley, his sweet wife Morley, was sticking cloves into an orange as she watched with them. Dave thought, They didn't even know I was in trouble.

There was a commercial and Sam said, "What were you doing up there? The picture was really fuzzy for a while. Then all of a sudden it got berter."

Dave said, "I put up the Christmas lights. Come and see."

They all trooped outside.

80   Sam looked up and down the block. "We're the first. We beat everyone."

Morley was smiling. "I was thinking about the lights yesterday," she said.

The kids ran back inside.

Morley was still looking at the lights. "They always make me feel good," she said. Then she turned and put her arms around her husband. "I ordered the Christmas turkey today," she said. "I was thinking, you did such a nice job with it last year, do you think you could do it again?"

(1998)

Guy Vanderhaeghe   (b. 1951)

Born in Esterhazy, Saskatchewan, Guy Vanderhaeghe has twice won the Governor General's Award for fiction, for *Man Descending* (1982), a collection of short stories, and for *The Englishman's Boy* (1996), a novel. Influenced by the works of Margaret Laurence and Sinclair Ross, most of the short stories in *Man Descending* are set on the Prairies. In one of them, "Cages," the young narrator expresses his anger toward and love for his brother and father and reveals their feelings for him. The central symbol, introduced in the title, acquires many meanings as the story progresses.

CAGES

Here it is, 1967, the Big Birthday. Centennial[1] Year they call it. The whole country is giving itself a pat on the back. Holy shit, boys, we made it.

I made it too for seventeen years, a spotless life, as they say, and for presents I get, in my senior year of high school, my graduating year for chrissakes, a six-month suspended sentence for obstructing a police officer, and my very own personal social worker.

The thing is I don't *need* this social worker woman. She can't tell me anything I haven't already figured out for myself. Take last Wednesday, Miss Krawchuk, who looks like the old widow chicken on the Bugs Bunny Show, the one who's hot to trot for Foghorn Leghorn, says to me: "You know, Billy, your father loves you just as much as he does Gene. He doesn't have a favourite."

Now I can get bullshit at the poolroom any time I want it—and without having to keep an appointment. Maybe Pop *loves* me as much as he does Gene, but Gene is still his favourite kid. Everybody has a favourite kid. I knew that much already when I was only eight and Gene was nine. I figured it out right after Gene almost blinded me.

Picture this. There the two of us were in the basement. It was Christmas holidays and the old man had kicked us downstairs to huck darts at this board he'd give us for a present. Somehow, I must've had horseshoes up my ass, I'd beat Gene six games straight. And was he pissed off! He never loses to me at nothing ever. And me being in such a real unique situation, I was giving him the needle-rooney.

"What's that now?" I said. "Is that six or seven what I won?"

"Luck," Gene said, and he sounded like somebody was slowly strangling him. "Luck. Luck. Luck." He could hardly get it out.

And that's when I put the capper on it. I tossed a bull's-eye. "Read 'er and weep," I told him. That's what the old man says whenever he goes out at rummy. It's his needle-rooney. "Read 'er and weep."

That did it. The straw what broke the frigging camel's back. All I saw was his arm blur when he let fly at me. I didn't even have time to *think* about ducking. Bingo. Dead centre in the forehead, right in the middle of the old

[1] the one-hundredth anniversary of Canadian Confederation.

noggin he drills me with a dart. And there it stuck. Until it loosened a bit. Then it sagged down real slow between my eyes, hung for a second, slid off of my nose, and dropped at my feet. I hollered bloody blue murder, you better believe it.

10   For once, Pop didn't show that little bastard any mercy. He took after him from room to room whaling him with this extension cord across the ass, the back of the legs, the shoulders. Really hard. Gene, naturally, was screaming and blubbering and carrying on like it was a goddamn axe murder or something. He'd try to get under a bed, or behind a dresser or something, and get stuck halfway. Then old Gene would really catch it. He didn't know whether to plough forward, back up, shit, or go blind. And all the time the old man was lacing him left and right and saying in this sad, tired voice: "You're the oldest. Don't you know no better? You could of took his eye out, you crazy little bugger."

But that was only justice. He wasn't all that mad at Gene. Me he was mad at. If that makes any sense. Although I have to admit he didn't lay a hand on me. But yell? Christ, can that man yell. Especially at me. Somehow I'm the one that drives him squirrelly.

"Don't you *never, never* tease him again!" he bellowed and his neck started to swell. When the old man gets mad you can see it swell, honest. "You know he can't keep a hold of himself. One day you'll drive him so goddamn goofy with that yap of yours he'll do something terrible! Something he'll regret for the rest of his life. And it'll all be your fault!" The old man had to stop there and slow down or a vein would've exploded in his brain, or his arsehole popped inside out, or something. "So smarten up," he said, a little quieter, finally, "or you'll be the death of me and all my loved ones."

So there you are. I never pretended the world was fair, and I never bitched because it wasn't. But I do resent the hell out of being forced to listen to some dried-up old broad who gets paid by the government to tell me it is. Fuck her. She never lived in the Simpson household with my old man waiting around for Gene to do that *terrible thing*. It spoils the atmosphere. Makes a person edgy, you know?

Of course, Gene has done a fair number of *bad things* while everybody was waiting around for him to do the one great big *terrible thing*; and he's done them in a fair number of places. That's because the old man is a miner, and for a while there he was always telling some foreman to go piss up a rope. So we moved around a lot. That's why the Simpson household has a real history. But Gene's is the best of all. In Elliot Lake he failed grade three; in Bomber-town[2] he got picked up for shoplifting; in Flin Flon[3] he broke some snotty kid's nose and got sent home from school. And every grade he goes higher, it gets a little worse. Last year, when we were both in grade eleven, I'm sure the old man was positive Gene was finally going to pull off the *terrible thing* he's been worrying about as long as I can remember.

15   It's crazy. Lots of times when I think about it, I figure I don't get on with the old man because I treat him nice. That I try too hard to make him like

[2]mining town in northern Ontario. [3]mining town in Manitoba.

me. I'm not the way Gene is, I respect Pop. He slogs it out, shift after shift, on a shitty job he hates. Really hates. In fact, he told me once he would have liked to have been a farmer. Which only goes to show you how crazy going down that hole day after day makes you. Since we moved to Saskatchewan I've seen lots of farmers, and if you ask me, being one doesn't have much to recommend it.

But getting back to that business of being nice to Dad. Last year I started waiting up for him to come home from the afternoon shift. The one that runs from four p.m. in the afternoon until midnight. It wasn't half bad. Most nights I'd fall asleep on the chesterfield with the TV playing after Mom went to bed. Though lots of times I'd do my best to make it past the national news to wait for Earl Cameron[4] and his collection of screwballs. Those guys kill me. They're always yapping off because somebody or something rattled their chain. Most of those characters with all the answers couldn't pour piss out of a rubber boot if they read the instructions printed on the sole. They remind me of Gene; he's got all the answers too. But still, quite a few of them are what you'd call witty. Which Gene is in his own way too.

But most times, as I say, I'd doze off. Let me give you a sample evening. About twelve-thirty the lights of his half-ton would come shooting into the living-room, bouncing off the walls, scooting along the ceiling when he wheeled into the driveway like a madman. It was the lights flashing in my eyes that woke me up most nights, and if that didn't do it there was always his grand entrance. When the old man comes into the house, from the sound of it you'd think he never heard of door knobs. I swear sometimes I'm sure he's taking a battering-ram to the back door. Then he thunks his lunch bucket on the kitchen counter and bowls his hard hat into the landing. This is because he always comes home from work mad. Never once in his life has a shift ever gone right for that man. Never. They could pack his pockets with diamonds and send him home two hours early and he'd still bitch. So every night was pretty much the same. He had a mad on. Like in my sample night.

He flicked on the living-room light and tramped over to his orange recliner with the bottle of Boh. "If you want to ruin your eyes, do it on school-books, not on watching TV in the goddamn dark. It's up to somebody in this outfit to make something of themselves."

"I was sleeping."

20   "You ought to sleep in bed." *Keerash!* He weighs two hundred and forty-four pounds and he never sits down in a chair. He falls into it. "Who's that? Gary Cooper?" he asked. He figures any movie star on the late show taller than Mickey Rooney is Cooper. He doesn't half believe you when you tell him they aren't.

"Cary Grant."

"What?"

"Cary Grant. Not Gary Cooper. Cary Grant."

"Oh." There he sat in his recliner, big meaty shoulders sagging, belly propped up on his belt buckle like a pregnant pup's. Eyes red and sore, hair

---

[4]chief announcer for the Canadian Broadcasting Corporation's National News during the 1960s.

all mussed up, the top of his beer bottle peeking out of his fist like a little brown nipple. He has cuts all over those hands of his, barked knuckles and raspberries that never heal because the salt in the potash ore keeps them open, eats right down to the bone sometimes.

"How'd it go tonight?"

"Usual shit. We had a breakdown." He paused. "Where's your brother? In bed?"

"Out."

"Out? Out? *Out?* What kind of goddamn answer is that? Out where?"

I shrugged.

"Has he got his homework done?" That's the kind of question I get asked. *Has your brother got his homework done?*

"How the hell would I know?"

"I don't know why you don't help him with his school-work," the old man said, peeved as usual.

"You mean do it for him."

"Did I say that? Huh? I said help him. Didn't I say that?" he griped, getting his shit in a knot.

He thinks it's that easy. Just screw the top off old Gene and pour it in. No problem. Like an oil change.

"He's got to be around to help," I said.

That reminded him. He jumped out of the chair and gawked up and down the deserted street. "It's almost one o'clock. On a school night. I'll kick his ass." He sat down and watched the screen for a while and sucked on his barley sandwich.

Finally, he made a stab at acting civilized. "So how's baseball going?"

"What?"

"Baseball. For chrissakes clean out your ears. How's it going?"

"I quit last year. Remember?"

"Oh yeah." He didn't say nothing at first. Then he said: "You shouldn't have. You wasn't a bad catcher."

"The worst. No bat and no arm—just a flipper. They stole me blind."

"But you had the head," said the old man. And the way he said it made him sound like he was pissed at me for mean-mouthing myself. That surprised me. I felt kind of good about that. "You had the head," he repeated, shaking his own. "I never told you but Al came up to me at work and said you were smart back there behind the plate. He said he wished Gene had your head."

I can't say that surprised me. Gene is one of those cases of a million-dollar body carrying around a ten-cent head. He's a natural. Flop out his glove and, smack, the ball sticks. He's like Mickey Mantle. You know those stop-action photos where they caught Mickey with his eyes glommed onto the bat, watching the ball jump off the lumber? That's Gene. And he runs like a Negro, steals bases like Maury Wills for chrissake.

But stupid and conceited? You wouldn't believe the half of it. Give him the sign to bunt to move a runner and he acts as if you're asking him to bare his ass in public. Not him. He's a big shot. He swings for the fence. Nothing less. And old Gene is always in the game, if you know what I mean? I don't know what happens when he gets on base, maybe he starts thinking of the hair pie in the stands admiring him or something, but he always dozes off at the wheel. Once he even started to comb his hair at first base. Here it is, a 3 and 2 count with two men out, and my brother forgets to run on the pitch because he's combing his hair. I could have died. Really I could have. The guy is such an embarrassment sometimes.

"He can have my head," I said to Pop. "If I get his girls."

That made the old man wince. He's sure that Gene is going to knock up one of those seat-covers he takes out and make him a premature grandpa.

"You pay attention to school. There's plenty of time later for girls." And up he jumped again and stuck his nose against the window looking for Gene again. Mom has to wash the picture window once a week; he spots it all up with nose grease looking for Gene.

50 "I don't know why your mother lets him out of the house," he said. "Doesn't she have any control over that boy?"

That's what he does, blames everybody but himself. Oh hell, maybe nobody's to blame. Maybe Gene is just Gene, and there's nothing to be done about it.

"I don't know what she's supposed to do. You couldn't keep him in if you parked a tank in the driveway and strung barbed wire around the lot."

Of course that was the wrong thing to say. I usually say it.

"Go to bed!" he yelled at me. "You're no better than your brother. I don't see you in bed neither. What'd I do, raise alley cats or kids? Why can't you two keep hours like human beings!"

55 And then the door banged and we knew the happy wanderer was home. Gene makes almost as much noise as the old man does when he comes in. It's beneath his dignity to sneak in like me.

Dad hoisted himself out of the chair and steamed off for the kitchen. He can move pretty quick for a big guy when he wants to. Me, I was in hot pursuit. I don't like to miss much.

Old Gene was hammered, and grinning from ass-hole to ear-lobes. The boy's got a great smile. Even when he grins at old ladies my mother's age you can tell they like it.

"Come here and blow in my face," said my father.

"Go on with you," said Gene. All of a sudden the smile was gone and he was irritated. He pushed past Pop, took the milk out of the fridge and started to drink out of the container.

60 "Use a glass."

Gene burped. He's a slob.

"You stink of beer," said the old man. "Who buys beer for a kid your age?"

"I ain't drunk," said Gene.

"Not much. Your eyes look like two piss-holes in the snow."

65 "Sure, sure," said Gene. He lounged, he swivelled over to me and lifted my Players out of my shirt pocket. "I'll pay you back tomorrow," he said, taking out a smoke. I heard that one before.

"I don't want to lose my temper," said Dad, being patient with him as usual, "so don't push your luck, sunshine." The two of them eyeballed it, hard. Finally Gene backed down, looked away and fiddled with his matches. "I don't ride that son of a bitch of a cage up and down for my health. I do it for you two," Dad said. "But I swear to God, Gene, if you blow this year of school there'll be a pair of new work boots for you on the back step, come July 1. Both of you know my rules. Go to school, work, or pack up. I'm not having bums put their feet under my table."

"I ain't scared of work," said Gene. "Anyways, school's a pain in the ass."

"Well, you climb in the cage at midnight with three hours of sleep and see if *that* ain't a pain in the ass. Out there nobody says, please do this, please do that. It ain't school out there, it's life."

"Ah, I wouldn't go to the mine. The mine sucks."

70 "Just what the hell do you think you'd do?"

"He'd open up shop as a brain surgeon," I said. Of course, Gene took a slap at me and grabbed at my shirt. He's a tough guy. He wasn't really mad, but he likes to prevent uppityness.

"You go to bed!" the old man hollered. "You ain't helping matters!"

So off I went. I could hear them wrangling away even after I closed my door. You'd wonder how my mother does it, but she sleeps through it all. I think she's just so goddamn tired of the three of us she's gone permanently deaf to the sound of our voices. She just don't hear us any more.

The last thing I heard before I dropped off was Pop saying: "I've rode that cage all my life, and take it from me, there wasn't a day I didn't wish I'd gone to school and could sit in an office in a clean white shirt." Sometimes he can't remember what he wants to be, a farmer or a pencil-pusher.

75 The cage. He's always going on about the cage. It's what the men at the mine call the elevator car they ride down the shaft. They call it that because it's all heavy reinforced-steel mesh. The old man has this cage on the brain. Ever since we were little kids he's been threatening us with it. *Make something of yourself,* he'd warn us, *or you'll end up like your old man, a monkey in the cage!* Or: *What's this, Gene? Failed arithmetic? Just remember, dunces don't end up in the corner. Hell no, they end up in the cage! Look at me!* My old man really hates that cage and the mine. He figures it's the worst thing you can threaten anybody with.

I was in the cage, once. A few years ago, when I was fourteen, the company decided they'd open the mine up for tours. It was likely the brainstorm of some public relations tit sitting in head office in Chicago. In my book it was kind of like taking people into the slaughterhouse to prove you're kind to the cows. Anyway, Pop offered to take us on one of his days off. As usual, he was about four years behind schedule. When we were maybe eleven we might have been nuts about the idea, but just then it didn't thrill us too badly. Gene, who is about as subtle as a bag of hammers, said flat out he wasn't interested. I could see right away the old man was hurt by that. It isn't often he plays the buddy to his boys, and he probably had the idea he could whiz us about the machines and stuff. Impress the hell out of us. So it was up to me to slobber and grin like some kind of half-wit over the idea, to perk him up, see? Everybody suffers when the old man gets into one of his moods.

Of course, like always when I get sucked into this good-turn business, I shaft myself. I'd sort of forgotten how much I don't like tight places and being closed in. When we were younger, Gene used to make me go berserk by holding me under the covers, or stuffing a pillow in my face, or locking me in the garage whenever he got the chance. The jerk.

To start with, they packed us in the cage with twelve other people, which didn't help matters any. Right away my chest got tight and I felt like I couldn't breathe. Then the old cables started groaning and grinding and this fine red dust like chili powder sprinkled down through the mesh and dusted our hard hats with the word GUEST stencilled on them. It was rust. Kind of makes you think.

"Here we go," said Pop.

80 We went. It was like all of a sudden the floor fell away from under my boots. That cage just dropped in the shaft like a stone down a well. It rattled and creaked and banged. The bare light bulb in the roof started to flicker, and all the faces around me started to dance and shake up and down in the dark. A wind twisted up my pant-legs and I could hear the cables squeak and squeal. It made me think of big fat fucking rats.

"She needs new brake shoes," said this guy beside me and he laughed. He couldn't fool me. He was scared shitless too, in his own way.

"It's not the fall that kills you," his neighbour replied. "It's the sudden stop." There's a couple of horses' patoots in every crowd.

We seemed to drop forever. Everybody got quieter and quieter. They even stopped shuffling and coughing. Down. Down. Down. Then the cage started to slow, I felt a pressure build in my knees and my crotch and my ears. The wire box started to shiver and clatter and shake. *Bang!* We stopped. The cage bobbed a little up and down like a yo-yo on the end of a string. Not much though, just enough to make you queasy.

"Last stop, Hooterville!" said the guide, who thought he was funny, and threw back the door. Straight ahead I could see a low-roofed big open space with tunnels running from it into the ore. Every once in a while I could see the light from a miner's helmet jump around in the blackness of one of those tunnels like a firefly flitting in the night.

85 First thing I thought was: *What if I get lost? What if I lose the group? There's miles and miles and miles of tunnel under here.* I caught a whiff of the air. It didn't smell like air up top. It smelled used. You could taste the salt. *I'm suffocating,* I thought. *I can't breathe this shit.*

I hadn't much liked the cage but this was worse. When I was in the shaft I knew there was a patch of sky over my head with a few stars in it and clouds and stuff. But all of a sudden I realized how deep we were. How we were sort of like worms crawling in the guts of some dead animal. Over us were billions, no, trillions, of tons of rock and dirt and mud pressing down. I could imagine it caving in and falling on me, crushing my chest, squeezing the air out slowly, dust fine as flour trickling into my eyes and nostrils, or mud plugging my mouth so I couldn't even scream. And then just lying there in the dark, my legs and arms pinned so I couldn't even twitch them. For a long time maybe. Crazy, lunatic stuff was what I started to think right on the spot.

My old man gave me a nudge to get out. We were the last.

"No," I said quickly and hooked my fingers in the mesh.

"We get out here," said the old man. He hadn't caught on yet.

90   "No, I can't," I whispered. He must have read the look on my face then. I think he knew he couldn't have pried me off that mesh with a gooseneck and winch.

Fred, the cage operator, lifted his eyebrows at Pop. "What's up, Jack?"

"The kid's sick," said Pop. "We'll take her up. He don't feel right." My old man was awful embarrassed.

Fred said, "I wondered when it'd happen. Taking kids and women down the hole."

"Shut your own goddamn hole," said the old man. "He's got the flu. He was up all last night."

95   Fred looked what you'd call sceptical.

"Last time I take you any place nice," the old man said under his breath.

The last day of school has always got to be some big deal. By nine o'clock all the dipsticks are roaring their cars up and down main street with their goofy broads hanging out their windows yelling, and trying to impress on one another how drunk they are.

Dad sent me to look for Gene because he didn't come home for supper at six. I found him in the poolroom playing dollar-a-hand poker pool.

"Hey, little brother," he waved to me from across the smoky poolroom, "come on here and I'll let you hold my cards!" I went over. He grinned to the goofs he was playing with. "You watch out now, boys," he said, "my little brother always brings me luck. Not that I need it," he explained to me, winking.

100   Yeah, I always brought him luck. *I* kept track of the game. *I* figured out what order to take the balls down. *I* reminded him not to put somebody else out and to play the next guy safe instead of slamming off some cornball shot. When *I* did all that Gene won—because I brought him luck. Yeah.

Gene handed me his cards. "You wouldn't believe these two," he said to me out of the corner of his mouth, "genuine plough jockeys. These boys couldn't find their ass in the dark with both hands. I'm fifteen dollars to the good."

I admit they didn't look too swift. The biggest one, who was *big*, was wearing an out-of-town team jacket, a Massey-Ferguson cap, and shit-kicker wellingtons. He was maybe twenty-one, but his skin hadn't cleared up yet by no means. His pan looked like all-dressed pizza, heavy on the cheese. His friend was a dinky little guy with his hair designed into a duck's ass. The kind of guy who hates the Beatles. About two feet of a dirty comb was sticking out of his ass pocket.

Gene broke the rack and the nine went down. His shot.

"Dad's looking for you. He wants to know if you passed," I said.

105   "You could've told him."

"Well, I didn't."

"Lemme see the cards." I showed him. He had a pair of treys, a six, a seven, and a lady. Right away he stopped to pocket the three. I got a teacher who always talks about thought processes. Gene doesn't have them.

"Look at the table," I said. "Six first and you can come around up here." I pointed.

"No coaching," said Pizza Face. I could see this one was a poor loser.

Gene shifted his stance and potted the six.

"What now?" he asked.

"The queen, and don't forget to put pants on her." I paused. "Pop figured you were going to make it. He really did, Gene."

"So tough titty. I didn't. Who the hell cares? He had your suck card to slobber over, didn't he?" He drilled the lady in the side pocket. No backspin. He'd hooked himself on the three. "Fuck."

"The old man is on graveyard shift. You better go home and face the music before he goes to work. It'll be worse in the morning when he needs sleep," I warned him.

"Screw him."

I could see Gene eyeballing the four. He didn't have any four in his hand, so I called him over and showed him his cards. "You can't shoot the four. It's not in your hand."

"Just watch me." He winked. "I've been doing it all night. It's all pitch and no catch with these prizes." Gene strolled back to the table and coolly stroked down the four. He had shape for the three which slid in the top pocket like shit through a goose. He cashed in on the seven. "That's it, boys," he said. "That's all she wrote."

I was real nervous. I tried to bury the hand in the deck but the guy with the runny face stopped me. He was getting tired of losing, I guess. Gene doesn't even cheat smart. You got to let them win once in a while.

"Gimme them cards," he said. He started counting the cards off against the balls, flipping down the boards on the felt. "Three." He nodded. "Six, seven, queen. I guess you got them all," he said slowly, with a look on his face like he was pissing ground glass.

That's when Duck Ass chirped up. "Hey, Marvin," he said, "that guy shot the four. He shot the four."

"Nah," said Gene.

Marvin studied on this for a second, walked over to the table and pulled the four ball out of the pocket. Just like little Jack Horner lifting the plum out of the pie. "Yeah," he said. "You shot the four."

"Jeez," said Gene, "I guess I did. Honest mistake. Look, here's a dollar for each of you." He took two bills out of his shirt pocket. "You got to pay for your mistakes is what I was always taught."

"I bet you he's been cheating all along," said Duck Ass.

"My brother don't cheat," I said.

"I want all my money back," said Marvin. Quite loud. Loud enough that some heads turned and a couple of tables stopped playing. There was what you would call a big peanut gallery, it being the beginning of vacation and the place full of junior high kids and stags.

"You can kiss my ass, bozo," said Gene. "Like my brother here said, I never cheated nobody in my life."

"You give us our money back," threatened Marvin, "or I'll pull your head off, you skinny little prick."

Guys were starting to drift towards us, curious. The manager, Fat Bert, was easing his guts out from behind the cash register.

130   "Give them their money, Gene," I said, "and let's get out of here."

"No."

Well, that was that. You can't change his mind. I took a look at old Marvin. As I said before, Marvin was *big*. But what was worse was that he had this real determined look people who aren't too bright get when they finally dib on to the fact they've been hosed and somebody has been laughing up his sleeve at them. They don't like it too hot, believe me.

"Step outside, shit-head," said Marvin.

"Fight," somebody said encouragingly. A real clump of ringsiders was starting to gather. "Fight." Bert came hustling up, bumping his way through the kids with his bay window. "Outside, you guys. I don't want nothing broke in here. Get out or I'll call the cops."

Believe me, was I tense. Real tense. I know Gene pretty well and I was sure that he had looked at old Marvin's muscles trying to bust out everywhere. Any second I figured he was going to even the odds by pasting old Marv in the puss with his pool cue, or at least sucker-punching him.

135   But Gene is full of surprises. All of a sudden he turned peacemaker. He laid down his pool cue (which I didn't figure was too wise) and said: "You want to fight over this?" He held up the four ball. "Over this? An honest mistake?"

"Sure I do," said Marvin. "You're fucking right I do, cheater."

"Cheater, cheater," said Duck Ass. I was looking him over real good because I figured if something started in there I'd get him to tangle with.

Gene shrugged and even kind of sighed, like the hero does in the movies when he has been forced into a corner and has to do something that is against his better nature. He tossed up the four ball once, looked at it, and then reached behind him and shoved it back into the pocket. "All right," he said, slouching a little and jamming his hands into his jacket pockets. "Let's go, sport."

That started the stampede. "Fight! Fight!" The younger kids, the ones thirteen and fourteen, were really excited; the mob kind of swept Marvin and Gene out the door, across the street and into the OK Economy parking lot where most beefs get settled. There's lots of dancing-room there. A nice big ring.

140   Marvin settled in real quick. He tugged the brim of his Massey-Ferguson special a couple of times, got his dukes up and started to hop around like he'd stepped right out of the pages of *Ring* magazine. He looked pretty stupid, especially when Gene just looked at him, and kept his hands rammed in his jacket pockets. Marvin kind of clomped from foot to foot for a bit and he said: "Get 'em up."

"You get first punch," said Gene.

"What?" said Marv. He was so surprised his yap fell open.

"If I hit you first," said Gene, "you'll charge me with assault. I know your kind."

Marvin stopped clomping. I suspect it took too much co-ordination for him to clomp and think at the same time. "Oh no," he said, "I ain't falling for that. If I hit *you* first, you'll charge *me* with assault." No flies on Marvin. "*You* get the first punch."

"Fight. Come on, fight," said some ass-hole, real disgusted with all the talk and no action.

"Oh no," said Gene. "I ain't hitting *you* first."

Marvin brought his hands down. "Come on, come on, let fly."

"You're sure?" asked Gene.

"Give her your best shot," said Marvin. "You couldn't hurt a fly, you scrawny shit. Quit stalling. Get this show on the road."

Gene uncorked on him. It looked like a real pansy punch. His right arm whipped out of his jacket pocket, stiff at the elbow like a girl's when she slaps. It didn't look like it had nothing behind it, sort of like Gene had smacked him kind of contemptuous in the mouth with the flat of his hand. That's how it looked. It *sounded* like he'd hit him in the mouth with a ball-peen hammer. Honest to God, you could hear the teeth crunch when they broke.

Big Marvin dropped on his knees like he'd been shot in the back of the neck. His hands flew up to his face and the blood just ran through his fingers and into his cuffs. It looked blue under the parking-lot lights. There was an awful lot of it.

"Get up, you dick licker," said Gene.

Marvin pushed off his knees with a crazy kind of grunt that might have been a sob. I couldn't tell. He came up under Gene's arms, swept him off his feet and dangled him in the air, crushing his ribs in a bear hug.

"*Waauugh!*" said Gene. I started looking around right smartly for something to hit the galoot with before he popped my brother like a pimple.

But then Gene lifted his fist high above Marvin's head and brought it down on his skull, hard as he could. It made a sound like he was banging coconuts together. Marvin sagged a little at the knees and staggered. *Chunk! Chunk!* Gene hit him two more times and Marvin toppled over backwards. My brother landed on top of him and right away started pasting him left and right. Everybody was screaming encouragement. There was no invitation to the dick licker to get up this time. Gene was still clobbering him when I saw the cherry popping on the cop car two blocks away. I dragged him off Marvin.

"Cops," I said, yanking at his sleeve. Gene was trying to get one last kick at Marvin. "Come on, fucker," he was yelling. "Fight now!"

"Jesus," I said, looking at Gene's jacket and shirt, "you stupid bugger, you're all over blood." It was smeared all over him. Marvin tried to get up. He only made it to his hands and knees. There he stayed, drooling blood and saliva on the asphalt. The crowd started to edge away as the cop car bounced up over the curb and gave a long, low whine out of its siren.

I took off my windbreaker and gave it to Gene. He pulled off his jacket and threw it down. "Get the fuck out of here," I said. "Beat it."

"I took the wheels off his little red wagon," said Gene. "It don't pull so good now." His hands were shaking and so was his voice. He hadn't had half enough yet. "I remember that other guy," he said. "Where's his friend?"

I gave him a shove. "Get going." Gene slid into the crowd that was slipping quickly away. Then I remembered his hockey jacket. It was wet with blood. It also had flashes with his name and number on it. It wouldn't take no Sherlock Holmes cop to figure out who'd beat on Marvin. I picked it up and hugged it to my belly. Right away I felt something hard in the pocket. Hard and round. I started to walk away. I heard a car door slam. I knew what was in that pocket. The controversial four ball old Gene had palmed when he pretended to put it back. He likes to win.

I must have been walking too fast or with a guilty hunch to my shoulders, because I heard the cop call, "Hey you, the kid with the hair." Me, I'm kind of a hippy for this place, I guess. Lots of people mention my hair.

I ran. I scooted round the corner of the supermarket and let that pool ball fly as hard as I could, way down the alley. I never rifled a shot like that in my life. If coach Al had seen me trigger that baby he'd have strapped me into a belly pad himself. Of course, a jacket don't fly for shit. The bull came storming around the corner just as I give it the heave-ho. I was kind of caught with shit on my face, if you know what I mean?

Now a guy with half a brain could have talked his way out of that without too much trouble. Even a cop understands how somebody would try to help his brother. They don't hold it too much against you. And I couldn't really protect Gene. That geek Marvin would have flapped his trap if I hadn't. And it wasn't as if I hadn't done old Gene *some* good. After all, they never found out about that pool ball. The judge would have pinned Gene's ears back for him if he'd known he was going around thwacking people with a hunk of shatter-proof plastic. So Gene came out smelling like a rose, same suspended sentence as me, and a reputation for having hands of stone.

But at a time like that you get the nuttiest ideas ever. I watched them load Marvin in a squad car to drive him to the hospital while I sat in the back seat of another. And I thought to myself: *I'll play along with this. Let the old man come down to the cop shop over me for once. Me he takes for granted. Let him worry about Billy for a change. It wouldn't hurt him.*

165 So I never said one word about not being the guy who bopped Marvin. It was kind of fun in a crazy way, making like a hard case. At the station I was real rude and lippy. Particularly to a sergeant who was a grade A dink if I ever saw one. It was only when they took my shoe-laces and belt that I started to get nervous.

"Ain't you going to call my old man?" I asked.

The ass-hole sergeant gave me a real smile. "In the morning," he said. "All in good time."

"In the morning?" And then I said like a dope: "Where am I going to sleep?"

"Show young Mr. Simpson where he's going to sleep," said the sergeant. He smiled again. It looked like a ripple on a slop pail. The constable who he was ordering around like he was his own personal slave took me down into the basement of the station. Down there it smelled of stale piss and old puke. I kind of gagged. I got a weak stomach.

170 Boy, was I nervous. I saw where he was taking me. There were four cells. They weren't even made out of bars, just metal strips riveted into a cross hatch you couldn't stick your hand through. They were all empty.

"Your choice," said the corporal. He was real humorous too, like his boss.

"You don't have to put me in one of them, sir," I said. "I won't run away."

"That's what all the criminals say." He opened the door. "Entrez-vous."

I was getting my old crazy feeling really bad. Really bad. I felt kind of dizzy. "I got this thing," I said, "about being locked up. It's torture."

175 "Get in."

"No—please," I said. "I'll sit upstairs. I won't bother anybody."

"You think you've got a choice? You don't have a choice. Move your ass."

I was getting ready to cry. I could feel it. I was going to bawl in front of a cop. "I didn't do it," I said. "I never beat him up. Swear to Jesus I didn't."

"I'm counting three," he said, "and then I'm applying the boots to your backside."

180 It all came out. Just like that. "*It was my fucking ass-hole brother, Gene!*" I screamed. The only thing I could think of was, if they put me in there I'll be off my head by morning. I really will. "*I didn't do nothing! I never do nothing! You can't put me in there for him!*"

They called my old man. I guess I gave a real convincing performance. Not that I'm proud of it. I actually got sick on the spot from nerves. I just couldn't hold it down.

Pop had to sign for me and promise to bring Gene down in the morning. It was about twelve-thirty when everything got cleared up. He'd missed his shift and his ride in the cage.

When we got in the car he didn't start it. We just sat there with the windows rolled down. It was a beautiful night and there were lots of stars swimming in the sky. This town is small enough that street-lights and neon don't interfere with the stars. It's the only thing I like about this place. There's plenty of sky and lots of air to breathe.

"Your brother wasn't enough," he said. "You I trusted."

185 "I only tried to help him."

"You goddamn snitch." He needed somebody to take it out on, so he belted me. Right on the snout with the back of his hand. It started to bleed. I didn't try to stop it. I just let it drip on those goddamn furry seat-covers that he thinks are the cat's ass. "They were going to put me in this place, this cage, for him, for that useless shit!" I yelled. I'd started to cry. "No more, Pop. He failed! He failed on top of it all! So is he going to work? You got the boots ready on the back step? Huh? Is he going down in the fucking cage?"

"Neither one of you is going down in the cage. Not him, not you," he said.

"Nah, I didn't think so," I said, finally wiping at my face with the back of my hand. "I didn't think so."

"I don't have to answer to you," he said. "You just can't get inside his head. You were always the smart one. I didn't have to worry about you. You always knew what to do. But Gene . . ." He pressed his forehead against the steering-wheel, hard. "Billy, I see him doing all sorts of stuff. Stuff you can't imagine. I see it until it makes me sick." He looked at me. His face was yellow under the street-light, yellow like a lemon. "I try so hard with him. But he's got no sense. He just does things. He could have killed that other boy. He wouldn't even think of that, you know." All of a sudden the old man's face got all crumpled and creased like paper when you ball it up.

"What's going to happen to him?" he said, louder than he had to. "What's going to happen to Eugene?" It was sad. It really was.

I can never stay mad at my old man. Maybe because we're so much alike, even though he can't see it for looking the other way. Our minds work alike. I'm a chip off the old block. Don't ever doubt it.

"Nothing."

"Billy," he said, "you mean it?"

I knew what he was thinking. "Yes," I said. "I'll do my best."

(1982)

Amy Tan   (b.1952)

Born in Oakland, California, Amy Tan visited her ancestral homeland of China when she was 35. This visit, during which she met her sisters from her mother's first marriage, inspired the writing of her first book, *The Joy Luck Club*, a series of interrelated stories about Chinese mothers and their American-born daughters. "Two Kinds" depicts the conflicts, based on cultural differences and expectations, between one of these pairs when the young girl resists her mother's hopes of her achieving musical celebrity. The title, which refers explicitly to the piece the girl plays at the recital, implicitly refers to the many tensions the narrator feels within herself and between herself and her mother.

TWO KINDS

My mother believed you could be anything you wanted to be in America. You could open a restaurant. You could work for the government and get good retirement. You could buy a house with almost no money down. You could become rich. You could become instantly famous.

"Of course you can be prodigy, too," my mother told me when I was nine. "You can be best anything. What does Auntie Lindo know? Her daughter, she is only best tricky."

America was where all my mother's hopes lay. She had come here in 1949 after losing everything in China: her mother and father, her family home, her first husband, and two daughters, twin baby girls. But she never looked back with regret. There were so many ways for things to get better.

*****

We didn't immediately pick the right kind of prodigy. At first my mother thought I could be a Chinese Shirley Temple.[1] We'd watch Shirley's old movies on TV as though they were training films. My mother would poke my arm and say, "*Ni kan*,"—You watch. And I would see Shirley tapping her feet, or singing a sailor song, or pursing her lips into a very round O while saying, "Oh my goodness."

5   "*Ni kan*" said my mother as Shirley's eyes flooded with tears. "You already know how. Don't need talent for crying!"

Soon after my mother got this idea about Shirley Temple, she took me to a beauty training school in the Mission district[2] and put me in the hands of a student who could barely hold the scissors without shaking. Instead of getting big fat curls, I emerged with an uneven mass of crinkly black fuzz. My mother dragged me off to the bathroom and tried to wet down my hair.

"You look like Negro Chinese," she lamented, as if I had done this on purpose.

---

[1]popular child actor in motion pictures of the 1930s. [2]fashionable residential district of San Francisco.

The instructor of the beauty training school had to lop off these soggy clumps to make my hair even again. "Peter Pan is very popular these days," the instructor assured my mother. I now had hair the length of a boy's, with straight-across bangs that hung at a slant two inches above my eyebrows. I liked the haircut and it made me actually look forward to my future fame.

In fact, in the beginning, I was just as excited as my mother, maybe even more so. I pictured this prodigy part of me as many different images, trying each one on for size. I was a dainty ballerina girl standing by the curtains, waiting to hear the right music that would send me floating on my tiptoes. I was like the Christ child lifted out of the straw manger, crying with holy indignity. I was Cinderella stepping from her pumpkin carriage with sparkly cartoon music filling the air.

10 In all of my imaginings, I was filled with a sense that I would soon become *perfect*. My mother and father would adore me. I would be beyond reproach. I would never feel the need to sulk for anything.

But sometimes the prodigy in me became impatient. "If you don't hurry up and get me out of here, I'm disappearing for good," it warned. "And then you'll always be nothing."

Every night after dinner, my mother and I would sit at the Formica kitchen table. She would present new tests, taking her examples from stories of amazing children she had read in *Ripley's Believe It or Not*, or *Good Housekeeping, Reader's Digest*, and a dozen other magazines she kept in a pile in our bathroom. My mother got these magazines from people whose houses she cleaned. And since she cleaned many houses each week, we had a great assortment. She would look through them all, searching for stories about remarkable children.

The first night she brought out a story about a three-year-old boy who knew the capitals of all the states and even most of the European countries. A teacher was quoted as saying the little boy could also pronounce the names of the foreign cities correctly.

"What's the capital of Finland?" my mother asked me, looking at the magazine story.

15 All I knew was the capital of California, because Sacramento was the name of the street we lived on in Chinatown. "Nairobi!" I guessed, saying the most foreign word I could think of. She checked to see if that was possibly one way to pronounce "Helsinki"[3] before showing me the answer.

The tests got harder—multiplying numbers in my head, finding the queen of hearts in a deck of cards, trying to stand on my head without using my hands, predicting the daily temperatures in Los Angeles, New York, and London.

One night I had to look at a page from the Bible for three minutes and then report everything I could remember. "Now Jehoshaphat[4] had riches and honor in abundance and . . . that's all I remember, Ma," I said.

---

[3]Nairobi is the capital city of Kenya; Helsinki, the capital of Finland. [4]king of Judah in the ninth century B.C.

And after seeing my mother's disappointed face once again, something inside of me began to die. I hated the tests, the raised hopes and failed expectations. Before going to bed that night, I looked in the mirror above the bathroom sink and when I saw only my face staring back—and that it would always be this ordinary face—I began to cry. Such a sad, ugly girl! I made high-pitched noises like a crazed animal, trying to scratch out the face in the mirror.

And then I saw what seemed to be the prodigy side of me—because I had never seen that face before. I looked at my reflection, blinking so I could see more clearly. The girl staring back at me was angry, powerful. This girl and I were the same. I had new thoughts, willful thoughts, or rather thoughts filled with lots of won'ts. I won't let her change me, I promised myself. I won't be what I'm not.

20   So now on nights when my mother presented her tests, I performed listlessly, my head propped on one arm. I pretended to be bored. And I was. I got so bored I started counting the bellows of the foghorns out on the bay while my mother drilled me in other areas. The sound was comforting and reminded me of the cow jumping over the moon. And the next day, I played a game with myself, seeing if my mother would give up on me before eight bellows. After a while I usually counted only one, maybe two bellows at most. At last she was beginning to give up hope.

Two or three months had gone by without any mention of my being a prodigy again. And then one day my mother was watching *The Ed Sullivan Show*[5] on TV. The TV was old and the sound kept shorting out. Every time my mother got halfway up from the sofa to adjust the set, the sound would go back on and Ed would be talking. As soon as she sat down, Ed would go silent again. She got up, the TV broke into loud piano music. She sat down. Silence. Up and down, back and forth, quiet and loud. It was like a stiff embraceless dance between her and the TV set. Finally she stood by the set with her hand on the sound dial.

She seemed entranced by the music, a little frenzied piano piece with this mesmerizing quality, sort of quick passages and then teasing lilting ones before it returned to the quick playful parts.

"Ni kan," my mother said, calling me over with hurried hand gestures, "Look here."

I could see why my mother was fascinated by the music. It was being pounded out by a little Chinese girl, about nine years old, with a Peter Pan haircut. The girl had the sauciness of a Shirley Temple. She was proudly modest like a proper Chinese child. And she also did this fancy sweep of a curtsy, so that the fluffy skirt of her white dress cascaded slowly to the floor like the petals of a large carnation.

25   In spite of these warning signs, I wasn't worried. Our family had no piano and we couldn't afford to buy one, let alone reams of sheet music and piano lessons. So I could be generous in my comments when my mother badmouthed the little girl on TV.

"Play note right, but doesn't sound good! No singing sound," complained my mother.

[5]popular television variety show of the 1950s and 1960s.

"What are you picking on her for?" I said carelessly. "She's pretty good. Maybe she's not the best, but she's trying hard." I knew almost immediately I would be sorry I said that.

"Just like you," she said. "Not the best. Because you not trying." She gave a little huff as she let go of the sound dial and sat down on the sofa.

The little Chinese girl sat down also to play an encore of "Anitra's Dance" by Grieg.[6] I remember the song, because later on I had to learn how to play it.

30   Three days after watching *The Ed Sullivan Show*, my mother told me what my schedule would be for piano lessons and piano practice. She had talked to Mr. Chong, who lived on the first floor of our apartment building. Mr. Chong was a retired piano teacher and my mother had traded house-cleaning services for weekly lessons and a piano for me to practice on every day, two hours a day, from four until six.

When my mother told me this, I felt as though I had been sent to hell. I whined and then kicked my foot a little when I couldn't stand it anymore.

"Why don't you like me the way I am? I'm *not* a genius! I can't play the piano. And even if I could, I wouldn't go on TV if you paid me a million dollars!" I cried.

My mother slapped me. "Who ask you be genius?" she shouted. "Only ask you be your best. For you sake. You think I want you be genius? Hnnh! What for! Who ask you!"

"So ungrateful," I heard her mutter in Chinese. "If she had as much talent as she has temper, she would be famous now."

35   Mr. Chong, whom I secretly nicknamed Old Chong, was very strange, always tapping his fingers to the silent music of an invisible orchestra. He looked ancient in my eyes. He had lost most of the hair on top of his head and he wore thick glasses and had eyes that always looked tired and sleepy. But he must have been younger than I thought, since he lived with his mother and was not yet married.

I met Old Lady Chong once and that was enough. She had this peculiar smell like a baby that had done something in its pants. And her fingers felt like a dead person's, like an old peach I once found in the back of the refrigerator; the skin just slid off the meat when I picked it up.

I soon found out why Old Chong had retired from teaching piano. He was deaf. "Like Beethoven!" he shouted to me. "We're both listening only in our head!" And he would start to conduct his frantic silent sonatas.

Our lessons went like this. He would open the book and point to different things, explaining their purpose. "Key! Treble! Bass! No sharps or flats! So this is C major! Listen now and play after me!"

And then he would play the C scale a few times, a simple chord, and then, as if inspired by an old, unreachable itch, he gradually added more notes and running trills and a pounding bass until the music was really something quite grand.

40   I would play after him, the simple scale, the simple chord, and then I just played some nonsense that sounded like a cat running up and down on

[6] nineteenth-century Norwegian composer noted for his nationalistic music.

top of garbage cans. Old Chong smiled and applauded and then said, "Very good! But now you must learn to keep time!"

So that's how I discovered that Old Chong's eyes were too slow to keep up with the wrong notes I was playing. He went through the motions in halftime. To help me keep rhythm, he stood behind me, pushing down on my right shoulder for every beat. He balanced pennies on top of my wrists so I would keep them still as I slowly played scales and arpeggios.[7] He had me curve my hand around an apple and keep that shape when playing chords. He marched stiffly to show me how to make each finger dance up and down, staccato like an obedient little soldier.

He taught me all these things, and that was how I also learned I could be lazy and get away with mistakes, lots of mistakes. If I hit the wrong notes because I hadn't practiced enough, I never corrected myself. I just kept playing in rhythm. And Old Chong kept conducting his own private reverie.

So maybe I never really gave myself a fair chance. I did pick up the basics pretty quickly, and I might have become a good pianist at that young age. But I was so determined not to try, not to be anybody different that I learned to play only the most ear-splitting preludes, the most discordant hymns.

Over the next year, I practiced like this, dutifully in my own way. And then one day I heard my mother and her friend Lindo Jong both talking in a loud bragging tone of voice so others could hear. It was after church, and I was leaning against the brick wall wearing a dress with stiff white petticoats. Auntie Lindo's daughter, Waverly, who was about my age, was standing farther down the wall about five feet away. We had grown up together and shared all the closeness of two sisters squabbling over crayons and dolls. In other words, for the most part, we hated each other. I thought she was snotty. Waverly Jong had gained a certain amount of fame as "Chinatown's Littlest Chinese Chess Champion."

45   "She bring home too many trophy," lamented Auntie Lindo that Sunday. "All day she play chess. All day I have no time do nothing but dust off her winnings." She threw a scolding look at Waverly, who pretended not to see her.

"You lucky you don't have this problem," said Auntie Lindo with a sigh to my mother.

And my mother squared her shoulders and bragged: "Our problem worser than yours. If we ask Jing-mei wash dish, she hear nothing but music. It's like you can't stop this natural talent."

And right then, I was determined to put a stop to her foolish pride.

A few weeks later, Old Chong and my mother conspired to have me play in a talent show which would be held in the church hall. By then, my parents had saved up enough to buy me a secondhand piano, a black Wurlitzer spinet with a scarred bench. It was the showpiece of our living room.

50   For the talent show, I was to play a piece called "Pleading Child" from Schumann's *Scenes from Childhood*.[8] It was a simple, moody piece that

---

[7]playing the notes of a musical chord in succession instead of simultaneously; a standard exercise for piano students. [8]series of short, simple piano pieces by the nineteenth-century German composer Robert Schumann.

sounded more difficult than it was. I was supposed to memorize the whole thing, playing the repeat parts twice to make the piece sound longer. But I dawdled over it, playing a few bars and then cheating, looking up to see what notes followed. I never really listened to what I was playing. I daydreamed about being somewhere else, about being someone else.

The part I liked to practice best was the fancy curtsy: right foot out, touch the rose on the carpet with a pointed foot, sweep to the side, left leg bends, look up and smile.

My parents invited all the couples from the Joy Luck Club to witness my debut. Auntie Lindo and Uncle Tin were there. Waverly and her two older brothers had also come. The first two rows were filled with children both younger and older than I was. The littlest ones got to go first. They recited simple nursery rhymes, squawked out tunes on miniature violins, twirled Hula Hoops, pranced in pink ballet tutus, and when they bowed or curtsied, the audience would sigh in unison, "Awww," and then clap enthusiastically.

When my turn came, I was very confident. I remember my childish excitement. It was as if I knew, without a doubt, that the prodigy side of me really did exist. I had no fear whatsoever, no nervousness. I remember thinking to myself, This is it! This is it! I looked out over the audience, at my mother's blank face, my father's yawn, Auntie Lindo's stiff-lipped smile, Waverly's sulky expression. I had on a white dress layered with sheets of lace, and a pink bow in my Peter Pan haircut. As I sat down I envisioned people jumping to their feet and Ed Sullivan rushing up to introduce me to everyone on TV.

And I started to play. It was so beautiful. I was so caught up in how lovely I looked that at first I didn't worry how I would sound. So it was a surprise to me when I hit the first wrong note and I realized something didn't sound quite right. And then I hit another and another followed that. A chill started at the top of my head and began to trickle down. Yet I couldn't stop playing, as though my hands were bewitched. I kept thinking my fingers would adjust themselves back, like a train switching to the right track. I played this strange jumble through two repeats, the sour notes staying with me all the way to the end.

55

When I stood up, I discovered my legs were shaking. Maybe I had just been nervous and the audience, like Old Chong, had seen me go through the right motions and had not heard anything wrong at all. I swept my right foot out, went down on my knee, looked up and smiled. The room was quiet, except for Old Chong, who was beaming and shouting, "Bravo! Bravo! Well done!" But then I saw my mother's face, her stricken face. The audience clapped weakly, and as I walked back to my chair, with my whole face quivering as I tried not to cry, I heard a little boy whisper loudly to his mother, "That was awful," and the mother whispered back, "Well, she certainly tried."

And now I realized how many people were in the audience, the whole world it seemed. I was aware of eyes burning into my back. I felt the shame of my mother and father as they sat stiffly throughout the rest of the show.

We could have escaped during intermission. Pride and some strange sense of honor must have anchored my parents to their chairs. And so we watched it all: the eighteen-year-old boy with a fake mustache who did a magic show and juggled flaming hoops while riding a unicycle. The breasted girl with white makeup who sang from *Madama Butterfly*[9] and got honorable mention. And the eleven-year-old boy who won first prize playing a tricky violin song that sounded like a busy bee.

After the show, the Hsus, the Jongs, and the St. Clairs from the Joy Luck Club came up to my mother and father.

"Lots of talented kids," Auntie Lindo said vaguely, smiling broadly.

60 "That was somethin' else," said my father, and I wondered if he was referring to me in a humorous way, or whether he even remembered what I had done.

Waverly looked at me and shrugged her shoulders. "You aren't a genius like me," she said matter-of-factly. And if I hadn't felt so bad, I would have pulled her braids and punched her stomach.

But my mother's expression was what devastated me: a quiet, blank look that said she had lost everything. I felt the same way, and it seemed as if everybody were now coming up, like gawkers at the scene of an accident, to see what parts were actually missing. When we got on the bus to go home, my father was humming the busy-bee tune and my mother was silent. I kept thinking she wanted to wait until we got home before shouting at me. But when my father unlocked the door to our apartment, my mother walked in and then went to the back, into the bedroom. No accusations. No blame. And in a way, I felt disappointed. I had been waiting for her to start shouting, so I could shout back and cry and blame her for all my misery.

I assumed my talent-show fiasco meant I never had to play the piano again. But two days later, after school, my mother came out of the kitchen and saw me watching TV.

"Four clock," she reminded me as if it were any other day. I was stunned, as though she were asking me to go through the talent-show torture again. I wedged myself more tightly in front of the TV.

65 "Turn off TV," she called from the kitchen five minutes later.

I didn't budge. And then I decided. I didn't have to do what my mother said anymore. I wasn't her slave. This wasn't China. I had listened to her before and look what happened. She was the stupid one.

She came out from the kitchen and stood in the arched entryway of the living room. "Four clock," she said once again, louder.

"I'm not going to play anymore," I said nonchalantly. "Why should I? I'm not a genius."

She walked over and stood in front of the TV. I saw her chest was heaving up and down in an angry way.

70 "No!" I said, and I now felt stronger, as if my true self had finally emerged. So this was what had been inside me all along.

"No! I won't!" I screamed.

She yanked me by the arm, pulled me off the floor, snapped off the TV. She was frighteningly strong, half pulling, half carrying me toward the piano as I kicked the throw rugs under my feet. She lifted me up and onto the hard

---

[9]early twentieth-century opera by Giacomo Puccini about a Japanese woman abandoned by her American husband.

bench. I was sobbing by now, looking at her bitterly. Her chest was heaving even more and her mouth was open, smiling crazily as if she was pleased I was crying.

"You want me to be someone that I'm not!" I sobbed. "I'll never be the kind of daughter you want me to be!"

"Only two kinds of daughters," she shouted in Chinese. "Those who are obedient and those who follow their own mind! Only one kind of daughter can live in this house. Obedient daughter!"

75   "Then I wish I wasn't your daughter. I wish you weren't my mother," I shouted. As I said these things I got scared. It felt like worms and toads and slimy things crawling out of my chest, but it also felt good, as if this awful side of me had surfaced, at last.

"Too late change this," said my mother shrilly.

And I could sense her anger rising to its breaking point. I wanted to see it spill over. And that's when I remembered the babies she had lost in China, the ones we never talked about. "Then I wish I'd never been born!" I shouted. "I wish I were dead! Like them."

It was as if I had said the magic words. Alakazam!—and her face went blank, her mouth closed, her arms went slack, and she backed out of the room, stunned, as if she were blowing away like a small brown leaf, thin, brittle, lifeless.

It was not the only disappointment my mother felt in me. In the years that followed, I failed her so many times, each time asserting my own will, my right to fall short of expectations. I didn't get straight As. I didn't become class president. I didn't get into Stanford. I dropped out of college.

80   For unlike my mother, I did not believe I could be anything I wanted to be. I could only be me.

And for all those years, we never talked about the disaster at the recital or my terrible accusations afterward at the piano bench. All that remained unchecked, like a betrayal that was now unspeakable. So I never found a way to ask her why she had hoped for something so large that failure was inevitable.

And even worse, I never asked her what frightened me the most: Why had she given up hope?

For after our struggle at the piano, she never mentioned my playing again. The lessons stopped. The lid to the piano was closed, shutting out the dust, my misery, and her dreams.

So she surprised me. A few years ago, she offered to give me the piano, for my thirtieth birthday. I had not played in all those years. I saw the offer as a sign of forgiveness, a tremendous burden removed.

85   "Are you sure?" I asked shyly. "I mean, won't you and Dad miss it?"

"No, this your piano," she said firmly. "Always your piano. You only one can play."

"Well, I probably can't play anymore," I said. "It's been years."

"You pick up fast," said my mother, as if she knew this was certain. "You have natural talent. You could been genius if you want to."

"No I couldn't."

90   "You just not trying," said my mother. And she was neither angry nor sad. She said it as if to announce a fact that could never be disproved. "Take it," she said.

But I didn't at first. It was enough that she had offered it to me. And after that, every time I saw it in my parents' living room, standing in front of the bay windows, it made me feel proud, as if it were a shiny trophy I had won back.

Last week I sent a tuner over to my parents' apartment and had the piano reconditioned, for purely sentimental reasons. My mother had died a few months before and I had been getting things in order for my father, a little bit at a time. I put the jewelry in special silk pouches. The sweaters she had knitted in yellow, pink, bright orange—all the colors I hated—I put those in moth-proof boxes. I found some old Chinese silk dresses, the kind with the little slits up the sides. I rubbed the old silk against my skin, then wrapped them in tissue and decided to take them home with me.

After I had the piano tuned, I opened the lid and touched the keys. It sounded even richer than I remembered. Really, it was a very good piano. Inside the bench were the same exercise notes with handwritten scales, the same secondhand music books with their covers held together with yellow tape.

I opened up the Schumann book to the dark little piece I had played at the recital. It was on the left-hand side of the page, "Pleading Child." It looked more difficult than I remembered. I played a few bars, surprised at how easily the notes came back to me.

95   And for the first time, or so it seemed, I noticed the piece on the right-hand side. It was called "Perfectly Contented." I tried to play this one as well. It had a lighter melody but the same flowing rhythm and turned out to be quite easy. "Pleading Child" was shorter but slower; "Perfectly Contented" was longer, but faster. And after I played them both a few times, I realized they were two halves of the same song.

(1989)

Rohinton Mistry   (b. 1952)

Born and raised in Mumbai, India, Mistry is a Parsi, a religious minority much favoured by the British when they ruled in India. Mistry came to Canada in 1975 and began writing while attending the University of Toronto. *Tales from Firozsha Baag* (1987), his first book, is a collection of short stories about the frequently contentious interrelationships among the residents of a Bombay housing complex. His three novels, *Such a Long Journey* (1991), winner of the Governor General's Award, *A Fine Balance* (1995), and *Family Matters* (2002) are also set in India. "Squatter," the story of a Firozsha Baag resident's unfortunate immigration to Canada, plays on the pun of the title, which not only indicates his physical difficulties, but also his status as a new Canadian. The squatter's problems in an alien environment can be compared to those of Calvin in Clarke's "The Motor Car." In addition to portraying the difficulties faced by immigrants, Mistry also examines the role of the storyteller, an old man who frequently recounts tales to an admiring audience of boys gathered outside his Mumbai apartment.

SQUATTER

Whenever Nariman Hansotia returned in the evening from the Cawasji Framji Memorial Library in a good mood the signs were plainly evident.

First, he parked his 1932 Mercedes-Benz (he called it the apple of his eye) outside A Block, directly in front of his ground-floor veranda window, and beeped the horn three long times. It annoyed Rustomji who also had a ground-floor flat in A Block. Ever since he had defied Nariman in the matter of painting the exterior of the building, Rustomji was convinced that nothing the old coot did was untainted by the thought of vengeance and harassment, his retirement pastime.

But the beeping was merely Nariman's signal to let Hirabai inside know that though he was back he would not step indoors for a while. Then he raised the hood, whistling "Rose Marie,"[1] and leaned his tall frame over the engine. He checked the oil, wiped here and there with a rag, tightened the radiator cap, and lowered the hood. Finally, he polished the Mercedes star and let the whistling modulate into the march from *The Bridge on the River Kwai*.[2] The boys playing in the compound knew that Nariman was ready now to tell a story. They started to gather round.

"*Sahibji*,[3] Nariman Uncle," someone said tentatively and Nariman nodded, careful not to lose his whistle, his bulbous nose flaring slightly. The pursed lips had temporarily raised and reshaped his Clark Gable[4] moustache.

---

[1] title song from a 1954 Hollywood musical that depicted a romance between a Mountie and a French-Canadian girl. [2] 1957 movie about a British colonel who, with his men, is imprisoned by the Japanese during World War II. [3] Sir, an expression of respect. [4] American movie star of the 1940s and 1950s.

More boys walked up. One called out, "How about a story, Nariman Uncle?" at which point Nariman's eyes began to twinkle, and he imparted increased energy to the polishing. The cry was taken up by others, "Yes, yes, Nariman Uncle, a story!" He swung into a final verse of the march. Then the lips relinquished the whistle, the Clark Gable moustache descended. The rag was put away, and he began.

5   "You boys know the great cricketers: Contractor, Polly Umrigar, and recently, the young chap, Farokh Engineer. Cricket *aficionados*, that's what you all are." Nariman liked to use new words, especially big ones, in the stories he told, believing it was his duty to expose young minds to as shimmering and varied a vocabulary as possible; if they could not spend their days at the Cawasji Framji Memorial Library then he, at least, could carry bits of the library out to them.

The boys nodded; the names of the cricketers were familiar.

"But does any one know about Savukshaw, the greatest of them all?" They shook their heads in unison.

"This, then, is the story about Savukshaw, how he saved the Indian team from a humiliating defeat when they were touring in England." Nariman sat on the steps of A Block. The few diehards who had continued with their games could not resist any longer when they saw the gathering circle, and ran up to listen. They asked their neighbours in whispers what the story was about, and were told: Savukshaw the greatest cricketer. The whispering died down and Nariman began.

"The Indian team was to play the indomitable MCC as part of its tour of England. Contractor was our captain. Now the MCC being the strongest team they had to face, Contractor was almost certain of defeat. To add to Contractor's troubles, one of his star batsmen, Nadkarni, had caught influenza early in the tour, and would definitely not be well enough to play against the MCC. By the way, does anyone know what those letters stand for? You, Kersi, you wanted to be a cricketer once."

10   Kersi shook his head. None of the boys knew, even though they had heard the MCC mentioned in radio commentaries, because the full name was hardly ever used.

Then Jehangir Bulsara spoke up, or Bulsara Bookworm, as the boys called him. The name given by Pesi *paadmaroo*[5] had stuck even though it was now more than four years since Pesi had been sent away to boarding-school, and over two years since the death of Dr. Mody. Jehangir was still unliked by the boys in the Baag, though they had come to accept his aloofness and respect his knowledge and intellect. They were not surprised that he knew the answer to Nariman's question: "Marylebone Cricket Club."

"Absolutely correct," said Nariman, and continued with the story. "The MCC won the toss and elected to bat. They scored four hundred and ninety-seven runs in the first inning before our spinners could get them out. Early in the second day's play our team was dismissed for one hundred and nine runs, and the extra who had taken Nadkarni's place was injured by a vicious bumper that opened a gash on his forehead." Nariman indicated the spot

[5]lotus-boy, a mocking nickname.

and the length of the gash on his furrowed brow. "Contractor's worst fears were coming true. The MCC waived their own second inning and gave the Indian team a follow-on, wanting to inflict an inning's defeat. And this time he had to use the second extra. The second extra was a certain Savukshaw."

The younger boys listened attentively; some of them, like the two sons of the chartered accountant in B Block, had only recently been deemed old enough by their parents to come out and play in the compound, and had not received any exposure to Nariman's stories. But the others like Jehangir, Kersi, and Viraf were familiar with Nariman's technique.

Once, Jehangir had overheard them discussing Nariman's stories, and he could not help expressing his opinion: that unpredictability was the brush he used to paint his tales with, and ambiguity the palette he mixed his colours in. The others looked at him with admiration. Then Viraf asked what exactly he meant by that. Jehangir said that Nariman sometimes told a funny incident in a very serious way, or expressed a significant matter in a light and playful manner. And these were only two rough divisions, in between were lots of subtle gradations of tone and texture. Which, then, was the funny story and which the serious? Their opinions were divided, but ultimately, said Jehangir, it was up to the listener to decide.

"So," continued Nariman, "Contractor first sent out his two regular openers, convinced that it was all hopeless. But after five wickets were lost for just another thirty-eight runs, out came Savukshaw the extra. Nothing mattered any more."

The street lights outside the compound came on, illuminating the iron gate where the watchman stood. It was a load off the watchman's mind when Nariman told a story. It meant an early end to the hectic vigil during which he had to ensure that none of the children ran out on the main road, or tried to jump over the wall. For although keeping out riff-raff was his duty, keeping in the boys was as important if he wanted to retain the job.

"The first ball Savukshaw faced was wide outside the off stump. He just lifted his bat and ignored it. But with what style! What panache! As if to say, come on, you blighters, play some polished cricket. The next ball was also wide, but not as much as the first. It missed the off stump narrowly. Again Savukshaw lifted his bat, boredom written all over him. Everyone was now watching closely. The bowler was annoyed by Savukshaw's arrogance, and the third delivery was a vicious fast pitch, right down on the middle stump.

"Savukshaw was ready, quick as lightning. No one even saw the stroke of his bat, but the ball went like a bullet towards the square leg.

"Fielding at square leg was a giant of a fellow, about six feet seven, weighing two hundred and fifty pounds, a veritable Brobdingnagian,[6] with arms like branches and hands like a pair of huge *sapaat*,[7] the kind the Dr. Mody used to wear, you remember what big feet Dr. Mody had." Jehangir was the only one who did; he nodded. "Just to see him standing there was scary. Not one ball had got past him, and he had taken some great catches. Savukshaw purposely aimed his shot right at him. But he was as quick as

[6]the giant people in Book II of Jonathan Swift's *Gulliver's Travels*. [7]boots.

Savukshaw, and stuck out his huge *sapaat* of a hand to stop the ball. What do you think happened then, boys?"

20   The older boys knew what Nariman wanted to hear at this point. They asked, "What happened, Nariman Uncle, what happened?" Satisfied, Nariman continued.

"A howl is what happened. A howl from the giant fielder, a howl that rang through the entire stadium, that soared like the cry of a banshee right up to the cheapest seats in the furthest, highest corners, a howl that echoed from the scoreboard and into the pavilion, into the kitchen, startling the chap inside who was preparing tea and scones for after the match, who spilled boiling water all over himself and was severely hurt. But not nearly as bad as the giant fielder at square leg. Never at any English stadium was a howl heard like that one, not in the whole history of cricket. And why do you think he was howling, boys?"

The chorus asked, "Why, Nariman Uncle, why?"

"Because of Savukshaw's bullet-like shot, of course. The hand he had reached out to stop it, he now held up for all to see, and *dhur-dhur, dhur-dhur* the blood was gushing like a fountain in an Italian piazza, like a burst water-main from the Vihar-Powai reservoir, dripping onto his shirt and his white pants, and sprinkling the green grass, and only because he was such a giant of a fellow could he suffer so much blood loss and not faint. But even he could not last forever; eventually, he felt dizzy, and was helped off the field. And where do you think the ball was, boys, that Savukshaw had smacked so hard?"

And the chorus rang out again on the now dark steps of A Block: "Where, Nariman Uncle, where?"

25   "Past the boundary line, of course. Lying near the fence. Rent asunder. Into two perfect leather hemispheres. All the stitches had ripped, and some of the insides had spilled out. So the umpires sent for a new one, and the game resumed. Now none of the fielders dared to touch any ball that Savukshaw hit. Every shot went to the boundary, all the way for four runs. Single-handedly, Savukshaw wiped out the deficit, and had it not been for loss of time due to rain, he would have taken the Indian team to a thumping victory against the MCC. As it was, the match ended in a draw."

Nariman was pleased with the awed faces of the youngest ones around him. Kersi and Viraf were grinning away and whispering something. From one of the flats the smell of frying fish swam out to explore the night air, and tickled Nariman's nostrils. He sniffed appreciatively, aware that it was in his good wife Hirabai's pan that the frying was taking place. This morning, he had seen the pomfret[8] she had purchased at the door, waiting to be cleaned, its mouth open and eyes wide, like the eyes of some of these youngsters. It was time to wind up the story.

"The MCC will not forget the number of new balls they had to produce that day because of Savukshaw's deadly strokes. Their annual ball budget was thrown badly out of balance. Any other bat would have cracked under

---

[8]a popular fish in India.

the strain, but Savukshaw's was seasoned with a special combination of oils, a secret formula given to him by a *sadhu*[9] who had seen him one day playing cricket when he was a small boy. But Savukshaw used to say his real secret was practice, lots of practice, that was the advice he gave to any young lad who wanted to play cricket."

The story was now clearly finished, but none of the boys showed any sign of dispersing. "Tell us about more matches that Savukshaw played in," they said.

"More nothing. This was his greatest match. Anyway, he did not play cricket for long because soon after the match against the MCC he became a champion bicyclist, the fastest human on two wheels. And later, a pole-vaulter—when he glided over on his pole, so graceful, it was like watching a bird in flight. But he gave that up, too, and became a hunter, the might-iest hunter ever known, absolutely fearless, and so skilful, with a gun he could have, from the third floor of A Block, shaved the whisker of a cat in the backyard of C Block."

"Tell us about that," they said, "about Savukshaw the hunter!"

The fat ayah, Jaakaylee, arrived to take the chartered accountant's two children home. But they refused to go without hearing about Savukshaw the hunter. When she scolded them and things became a little hysterical, some other boys tried to resurrect the ghost she had once seen: "Ayah *bhoot*! Ayah *bhoot*!"[10] Nariman raised a finger in warning—that subject was still taboo in Firozsha Baag; none of the adults was in a hurry to relive the wild and ram-pageous days that Pesi *paadmaroo* had ushered in, once upon a time, with the *bhoot* games.

Jaakaylee sat down, unwilling to return without the children, and whispered to Nariman to make it short. The smell of frying fish which had tickled Nariman's nostrils ventured into and awakened his stomach. But the story of Savukshaw the hunter was one he had wanted to tell for a long time.

"Savukshaw always went hunting alone, he preferred it that way. There are many incidents in the life of Savukshaw the hunter, but the one I am telling you about involves a terrifying situation. Terrifying for us, of course; Savukshaw was never terrified of anything. What happened was, one night he set up camp, started a fire and warmed up his bowl of chicken-*dhansaak*."

The frying fish had precipitated famishment upon Nariman, and the subject of chicken-*dhansaak* suited him well. His own mouth watering, he elaborated: "Mrs. Savukshaw was as famous for her *dhansaak* as Mr. was for hunting. She used to put in tamarind and brinjal, coriander and cumin, cloves and cinnamon, and dozens of other spices no one knows about. Women used to come from miles around to stand outside her window while she cooked it, to enjoy the fragrance and try to penetrate her secret, hoping to identify the ingredients as the aroma floated out, layer by layer, growing more complex and delicious. But always, the delectable fragrance enveloped the women and they just surrendered to the ecstasy, forgetting what they had come for. Mrs. Savukshaw's secret was safe."

[9]holy man. [10]ghost.

35 Jaakaylee motioned to Nariman to hurry up, it was past the children's dinner-time. He continued: "The aroma of savoury spices soon filled the night air in the jungle, and when the *dhansaak* was piping hot he started to eat, his rifle beside him. But as soon as he lifted the first morsel to his lips, a tiger's eyes flashed in the bushes! Not twelve feet from him! He emerged licking his chops! What do you think happened then, boys?"

"What, what, Nariman Uncle?"

Before he could tell them, the door of his flat opened. Hirabai put her head out and said, "*Chaalo ni,*[11] Nariman, it's time. Then if it gets cold you won't like it."

That decided the matter. To let Hirabai's fried fish, crisp on the outside, yet tender and juicy inside, marinated in turmeric and cayenne—to let that get cold would be something that *Khoedaiji*[12] above would not easily forgive. "Sorry boys, have to go. Next time about Savukshaw and the tiger."

There were some groans of disappointment. They hoped Nariman's good spirits would extend into the morrow when he returned from the Memorial Library, or the story would get cold.

40 But a whole week elapsed before Nariman again parked the apple of his eye outside his ground-floor flat and beeped the horn three times. When he had raised the hood, checked the oil, polished the star and swung into the "Colonel Bogie March,"[13] the boys began drifting towards A Block.

Some of them recalled the incomplete story of Savukshaw and the tiger, but they knew better than to remind him. It was never wise to prompt Nariman until he had dropped the first hint himself, or things would turn out badly.

Nariman inspected the faces: the two who stood at the back, always looking superior and wise, were missing. So was the quiet Bulsara boy, the intelligent one. "Call Kersi, Viraf, and Jehangir," he said. "I want them to listen to today's story."

Jehangir was sitting alone on the stone steps of C Block. The others were chatting by the compound gate with the watchman. Someone went to fetch them.

"Sorry to disturb your conference, boys, and your meditation, Jehangir," Nariman said facetiously, "but I thought you would like to hear this story. Especially since some of you are planning to go abroad."

45 This was not strictly accurate, but Kersi and Viraf did talk a lot about America and Canada. Kersi had started writing to universities there since his final high-school year, and had also sent letters of inquiry to the Canadian High Commission in New Delhi and to the U.S. Consulate at Breach Candy.[14] But so far he had not made any progress. He and Viraf replied with as much sarcasm as their unripe years allowed, "Oh yes, next week, just have to pack our bags."

"Riiiight," drawled Nariman. Although he spoke perfect English, this was the one word with which he allowed himself to take liberties, indulging in a

---

[11]let's go. [12]God. [13]a marching tune whistled by captured British soldiers in *The Bridge on the River Kwai.* [14]an affluent, fashionable district of Mumbai.

broadness of vowel more American than anything else. "But before we go on with today's story, what did you learn about Savukshaw, from last week's story?"

"That he was a very talented man," said someone.

"What else?"

"He was also a very lucky man, to have so many talents," said Viraf.

"Yes, but what else?"

There was silence for a few moments. Then Jehangir said, timidly: "He was a man searching for happiness, by trying all kinds of different things."

"Exactly! And he never found it. He kept looking for new experiences, and though he was very successful at everything he attempted, it did not bring him happiness. Remember this, success alone does not bring happiness. Nor does failure have to bring unhappiness. Keep it in mind when you listen to today's story."

A chant started somewhere in the back: "We-want-a-story! We-want-a-story!"

"Riiiight," said Nariman. "Now, everyone remembers Vera and Dolly, daughters of Najamai from C Block." There were whistles and hoots; Viraf nudged Kersi with his elbow, who was smiling wistfully. Nariman held up his hand: "Now now, boys, behave yourselves. Those two girls went abroad for studies many years ago, and never came back. They settled there happily.

"And like them, a fellow called Sarosh also went abroad, to Toronto, but did not find happiness there. This story is about him. You probably don't know him, he does not live in Firozsha Baag, though he is related to someone who does."

"Who? Who?"

"Curiosity killed the cat," said Nariman, running a finger over each branch of his moustache, "and what's important is the tale. So let us continue. This Sarosh began calling himself Sid after living in Toronto for a few months, but in our story he will be Sarosh and nothing but Sarosh, for that is his proper Parsi name. Besides, that was his own stipulation when he entrusted me with the sad but instructive chronicle of his recent life." Nariman polished his glasses with his handkerchief, put them on again, and began.

"At the point where our story commences, Sarosh had been living in Toronto for ten years. We find him depressed and miserable, perched on top of the toilet, crouching on his haunches, feet planted firmly for balance upon the white plastic oval of the toilet seat.

"Daily for a decade had Sarosh suffered this position. Morning after morning, he had no choice but to climb up and simulate the squat of our Indian latrines. If he sat down, no amount of exertion could produce success.

"At first, this inability was not more than mildly incommodious. As time went by, however, the frustrated attempts caused him grave anxiety. And when the failure stretched unbroken over ten years, it began to torment and haunt all his waking hours."

Some of the boys struggled hard to keep straight faces. They suspected that Nariman was not telling just a funny story, because if he intended them to laugh there was always some unmistakable way to let them know. Only the thought of displeasing Nariman and prematurely terminating the story kept their paroxysms of mirth from bursting forth unchecked.

Nariman continued: "You see, ten years was the time Sarosh had set himself to achieve complete adaptation to the new country. But how could he claim adaptation with any honesty if the acceptable catharsis continually failed to favour him? Obtaining his new citizenship had not helped either. He remained dependent on the old way, and this unalterable fact, strengthened afresh every morning of his life in the new country, suffocated him.

"The ten-year time limit was more an accident than anything else. But it hung over him with the awesome presence and sharpness of a guillotine. Careless words, boys, careless words in a moment of lightheartedness, as is so often the case with us all, had led to it.

"Ten years before, Sarosh had returned triumphantly to Bombay after fulfilling the immigration requirements of the Canadian High Commission in New Delhi. News of his imminent departure spread amongst relatives and friends. A farewell party was organized. In fact, it was given by his relatives in Firozsha Baag. Most of you will be too young to remember it, but it was a very loud party, went on till late in the night. Very lengthy and heated arguments took place, which is not the thing to do at a party. It started like this: Sarosh was told by some what a smart decision he had made, that his whole life would change for the better; others said he was making a mistake, emigration was all wrong, but if he wanted to be unhappy that was his business, they wished him well.

65 "By and by, after substantial amounts of Scotch and soda and rum and Coke had disappeared, a fierce debate started between the two groups. To this day Sarosh does not know what made him raise his glass and announce: 'My dear family, my dear friends, if I do not become completely Canadian in exactly ten years from the time I land there, then I will come back. I promise. So please, no more arguments. Enjoy the party.' His words were greeted with cheers and shouts of hear! hear! They told him never to fear embarrassment; there was no shame if he decided to return to the country of his birth.

"But shortly, his poor worried mother pulled him aside. She led him to the back room and withdrew her worn and aged prayer book from her purse, saying, 'I want you to place your hand upon the *Avesta*[15] and swear that you will keep that promise.'

"He told her not to be silly, that it was just a joke. But she insisted. '*Kassum khà*[16] —on the *Avesta*. One last thing for your mother. Who knows when you will see me again?' and her voice grew tremulous as it always did when she turned deeply emotional. Sarosh complied, and the prayer book was returned to her purse.

"His mother continued: 'It is better to live in want among your family and your friends, who love you and care for you, than to be unhappy surrounded by vacuum cleaners and dishwashers and big shiny motor cars.' She hugged him. Then they joined the celebration in progress.

"And Sarosh's careless words spoken at the party gradually forged themselves into a commitment as much to himself as to his mother and the others. It stayed with him all his years in the new land, reminding him every

[15]sacred Zoroastrian (Parsi) text. [16]swear an oath.

morning of what must happen at the end of the tenth, as it reminded him now while he descended from his perch."

70 Jehangir wished the titters and chortles around him would settle down, he found them annoying. When Nariman structured his sentences so carefully and chose his words with extreme care as he was doing now, Jehangir found it most pleasurable to listen. Sometimes, he remembered certain words Nariman had used, or combinations of words, and repeated them to himself, enjoying again the beauty of their sounds when he went for his walks to the Hanging Gardens or was sitting alone on the stone steps of C Block. Mumbling to himself did nothing to mitigate the isolation which the other boys in the Baag had dropped around him like a heavy cloak, but he had grown used to all that by now.

Nariman continued: "In his own apartment Sarosh squatted barefoot. Elsewhere, if he had to go with his shoes on, he would carefully cover the seat with toilet paper before climbing up. He learnt to do this after the first time, when his shoes had left telltale footprints on the seat. He had had to clean it with a wet paper towel. Luckily, no one had seen him.

"But there was not much he could keep secret about his ways. The world of washrooms is private and at the same time very public. The absence of his feet below the stall door, the smell of faeces, the rustle of paper, glimpses caught through the narrow crack between stall door and jamb—all these added up to only one thing: a foreign presence in the stall, not doing things in the conventional way. And if the one outside could receive the fetor of Sarosh's business wafting through the door, poor unhappy Sarosh too could detect something malodorous in the air: the presence of xenophobia and hostility."

What a feast, thought Jehangir, what a feast of words! This would be the finest story Nariman had ever told, he just knew it.

"But Sarosh did not give up trying. Each morning he seated himself to push and grunt, grunt and push, squirming and writhing unavailingly on the white plastic oval. Exhausted, he then hopped up, expert at balancing now, and completed the movement quite effortlessly.

75 "The long morning hours in the washroom created new difficulties. He was late going to work on several occasions, and one such day, the supervisor called him in: 'Here's your time-sheet for this month. You've been late eleven times. What's the problem?'"

Here, Nariman stopped because his neighbour Rustomji's door creaked open. Rustomji peered out, scowling and muttered, "Saala[17] loafers, sitting all evening outside people's houses, making a nuisance, and being encouraged by grownups at that."

He stood there a moment longer, fingering the greying chest hair that was easily accessible through his sudra,[18] then went inside. The boys immediately took up a soft and low chant: "Rustomji-the-curmudgeon! Rustomji-the-curmudgeon!"

Nariman held up his hand disapprovingly. But secretly, he was pleased that the name was still popular, the name he had given Rustomji when the

[17]dirty. [18]woolen shirt.

latter had refused to pay his share for painting the building. "Quiet, quiet!" said he. "Do you want me to continue or not?"

"Yes, yes!" The chanting died away, and Nariman resumed the story.

"So Sarosh was told by his supervisor that he was coming late to work too often. What could poor Sarosh say?"

"What, Nariman Uncle?" rose the refrain.

"Nothing, of course. The supervisor, noting his silence, continued: 'If it keeps up, the consequences could be serious as far as your career is concerned.'

"Sarosh decided to speak. He said embarrassedly, 'It's a different kind of problem. I . . . I don't know how to explain . . . it's an immigration-related problem.'

"Now this supervisor must have had experience with other immigrants, because right away he told Sarosh, 'No problem. Just contact your Immigrant Aid Society. They should be able to help you. Every ethnic group has one: Vietnamese, Chinese—I'm certain that one exists for Indians. If you need time off to go there, no problem. That can be arranged, no problem. As long as you do something about your lateness, there's no problem.' That's the way they talk over there, nothing is ever a problem.

"So Sarosh thanked him and went to his desk. For the umpteenth time he bitterly rued his oversight. Could fate have plotted it, concealing the western toilet behind a shroud of anxieties which had appeared out of nowhere to beset him just before he left India? After all, he had readied himself meticulously for the new life. Even for the great, merciless Canadian cold he had heard so much about. How could he have overlooked preparation for the western toilet with its matutinal demands unless fate had conspired? In Bombay, you know that offices of foreign businesses offer both options in their bathrooms. So do all hotels with three stars or more. By practising in familiar surroundings, Sarosh was convinced he could have mastered a seated evacuation before departure.

"But perhaps there was something in what the supervisor said. Sarosh found a telephone number for the Indian Immigrant Aid Society and made an appointment. That afternoon, he met Mrs. Maha-Lepate at the Society's office."

Kersi and Viraf looked at each other and smiled. Nariman Uncle had a nerve, there was more *lepate* in his own stories than anywhere else.

"Mrs. Maha-Lepate was very understanding, and made Sarosh feel at ease despite the very personal nature of his problem. She said, 'Yes, we get many referrals. There was a man here last month who couldn't eat Wonder Bread—it made him throw up.'

"By the way, boys, Wonder Bread is a Canadian bread which all happy families eat to be happy in the same way; the unhappy families are unhappy in their own fashion by eating other brands." Jehangir was the only one who understood, and murmured, "Tolstoy,"[19] at Nariman's little joke. Nariman noticed it, pleased. He continued.

[19]nineteenth-century Russian author of *War and Peace*; the lines about happy and unhappy families parody the opening of his novel *Anna Karenina*.

"Mrs. Maha-Lepate told Sarosh about that case: 'Our immigrant specialist, Dr. No-Ilaaz, recommended that the patient eat cake instead. He explained that Wonder Bread caused vomiting because the digestive system was used to Indian bread only, made with Indian flour in the village he came from. However, since his system was unfamiliar with cake, Canadian or otherwise, it did not react but was digested as a newfound food. In this way he got used to Canadian flour first in cake form. Just yesterday we received a report from Dr. No-Ilaaz. The patient successfully ate his first slice of whole-wheat Wonder Bread with no ill effects. The ultimate goal is pure white Wonder Bread.'

"Like a polite Parsi boy, Sarosh said, 'That's very interesting.' The garrulous Mrs. Maha-Lepate was about to continue, and he tried to interject: 'But I—' but Mrs. Maha-Lepate was too quick for him: 'Oh, there are so many interesting cases I could tell you about. Like the woman from Sri Lanka—referred to us because they don't have their own Society—who could not drink the water here. Dr. No-Ilaaz said it was due to the different mineral content. So he started her on Coca-Cola and then began diluting it with water, bit by bit. Six weeks later she took her first sip of unadulterated Canadian water and managed to keep it down.'

"Sarosh could not halt Mrs. Maha-Lepate as she launched from one case history into another: 'Right now, Dr. No-Ilaaz is working on a very unusual case. Involves a whole Pakistani family. Ever since immigrating to Canada, none of them can swallow. They choke on their own saliva, and have to spit constantly. But we are confident that Dr. No-Ilaaz will find a remedy. He has never been stumped by any immigrant problems. Besides, we have an information network with other third-world Immigrant Aid Societies. We all seem to share a history of similar maladies, and regularly compare notes. Some of us thought these problems were linked to retention of original citizenship. But this was a false lead.'

"Sarosh, out of his own experience, vigorously nodded agreement. By now he was truly fascinated by Mrs. Maha-Lepate's wealth of information. Reluctantly, he interrupted: 'But will Dr. No-Ilaaz be able to solve my problem?'

"'I have every confidence that he will,' replied Mrs. Maha-Lepate in great earnest. 'And if he has no remedy for you right away, he will be delighted to start working on one. He loves to take up new projects.'"

Nariman halted to blow his nose, and a clear shrill voice travelled the night air of the Firozsha Baag compound from C Block to where the boys had collected around Nariman in A Block: "Jehangoo! O Jehangoo! Eight o'clock! Upstairs now!"

Jehangir stared at his feet in embarrassment. Nariman looked at his watch and said, "Yes, it's eight." But Jehangir did not move, so he continued.

"Mrs. Maha-Lepate was able to arrange an appointment while Sarosh waited, and he went directly to the doctor's office. What he had heard so far sounded quite promising. Then he cautioned himself not to get overly optimistic, that was the worst mistake he could make. But along the way to the doctor's, he could not help thinking what a lovely city Toronto was. It was the same way he had felt when he first saw it ten years ago, before all the joy had dissolved in the acid of his anxieties."

Once again that shrill voice travelled through the clear night: "*Arré*[20] Jehangoo! *Muà*,[21] do I have to come down and drag you upstairs!"

Jehangir's mortification was now complete. Nariman made it easy for him, though: "The first part of the story is over. Second part continues tomorrow. Same time, same place." The boys were surprised, Nariman did not make such commitments. But never before had he told such a long story. They began drifting back to their homes.

100   As Jehangir strode hurriedly to C Block, falsettos and piercing shrieks followed him in the darkness: "*Arré* Jehangoo! *Muà*, Jehangoo! Bulsara Bookworm! Eight o'clock Jehangoo!" Shaking his head, Nariman went indoors to Hirabai.

Next evening the story punctually resumed when Nariman took his place on the topmost step of A Block: "You remember that we left Sarosh on his way to see the Immigrant Aid Society's doctor. Well, Dr. No-Ilaaz listened patiently to Sarosh's concerns, then said, 'As a matter of fact, there is a remedy which is so new even the IAS does not know about it. Not even that Mrs. Maha-Lepate who knows it all,' he added drolly, twirling his stethoscope like a stunted lasso. He slipped it on around his neck before continuing: 'It involves a minor operation which was developed with financial assistance from the Multicultural Department. A small device, *Crappus Nan Interruptus*, or CNI as we call it, is implanted in the bowel. The device is controlled by an external handheld transmitter similar to the ones used for automatic garage door-openers—you may have seen them in hardware stores.'"

Nariman noticed that most of the boys wore puzzled looks and realized he had to make some things clearer. "The Multicultural Department is a Canadian invention. It is supposed to ensure that ethnic cultures are able to flourish, so that Canadian society will consist of a mosaic of cultures—that's their favourite word, mosaic—instead of one uniform mix, like the American melting pot. If you ask me, mosaic and melting pot are both non-sense, and ethnic is a polite way of saying bloody foreigner. But anyway, you understand Multicultural Department? Good. So Sarosh nodded, and Dr. No-Ilaaz went on: 'You can encode the hand-held transmitter with a personal ten-digit code. Then all you do is position yourself on the toilet seat and activate your transmitter. Just like a garage door, your bowel will open without pushing or grunting.' "

There was some snickering in the audience, and Nariman raised his eyebrows, whereupon they covered up their mouths with their hands. "The doctor asked Sarosh if he had any questions. Sarosh thought for a moment, then asked if it required any maintenance.

"Dr. No-Ilaaz replied: 'CNI is semi-permanent and operates on solar energy. Which means you would have to make it a point to get some sun periodically, or it would cease and lead to constipation. However, you don't have to strip for a tan. Exposing ten percent of your skin surface once a week during summer will let the device store sufficient energy for year-round operation.'

---

[20]oh. [21]a good-for-nothing.

"Sarosh's next question was: 'Is there any hope that someday the bowels can work on their own, without operating the device?' at which Dr. No-Ilaaz grimly shook his head: 'I'm afraid not. You must think very, very carefully before making a decision. Once CNI is implanted, you can never pass a motion in the natural way—neither sitting nor squatting.'

"He stopped to allow Sarosh time to think it over, then continued: 'And you must understand what that means. You will never be able to live a normal life again. You will be permanently different from your family and friends because of this basic internal modification. In fact, in this country or that, it will set you apart from your fellow countrymen. So you must consider the whole thing most carefully.'

"Dr. No-Ilaaz paused, toyed with his stethoscope, shuffled some papers on his desk, then resumed: 'There are other dangers you should know about. Just as a garage door can be accidentally opened by a neighbour's transmitter on the same frequency, CNI can also be activated by someone with similar apparatus.' To ease the tension he attempted to quick laugh and said, 'Very embarrassing, eh, if it happened at the wrong place and time. Mind you, the risk is not so great at present, because the chances of finding yourself within a fifty-foot radius of another transmitter on the same frequency are infinitesimal. But what about the future? What if CNI becomes very popular? Sufficient permutations may not be available for transmitter frequencies and you could be sharing the code with others. Then the risk of accidents becomes greater.'"

Something landed with a loud thud in the yard behind A Block, making Nariman startle. Immediately, a yowling and screeching and caterwauling went up from the stray cats there, and the *kuchrawalli's*[22] dog started barking. Some of the boys went around the side of A Block to peer over the fence into the backyard. But the commotion soon died down of its own accord. The boys returned and, once again, Nariman's voice was the only sound to be heard.

"By now, Sarosh was on the verge of deciding against the operation. Dr. No-Ilaaz observed this and was pleased. He took pride in being able to dissuade his patients from following the very remedies which he first so painstakingly described. True to his name, Dr. No-Ilaaz believed no remedy is the best remedy, rather than prescribing this-mycin and that-mycin for every little ailment. So he continued: 'And what about our sons and daughters? And the quality of their lives? We still don't know about the long-term effects of CNI. Some researchers speculate that it could generate a genetic deficiency, that the offspring of a CNI parent would also require CNI. On the other hand, they could be perfectly healthy toilet seat-users, without any congenital defects. We just don't know at this stage.'

"Sarosh rose from his chair: 'Thank you very much for your time, Dr. No-Ilaaz. But I don't think I want to take such a drastic step. As you suggest, I will think it over carefully.'

[22]security guard.

"'Good, good,' said Dr. No-Ilaaz, 'I was hoping you would say that. There is one more thing. The operation is extremely expensive, and is not covered by the province's Health Insurance Plan. Many immigrant groups are lobbying to obtain coverage for special immigration-related health problems. If they succeed, then good for you.'

"Sarosh left Dr. No-Ilaaz's office with his mind made up. Time was running out. There had been a time when it was perfectly natural to squat. Now it seemed a grotesquely aberrant thing to do. Wherever he went he was reminded of the ignominy of his way. If he could not be westernized in all respects, he was nothing but a failure in this land—a failure not just in the washrooms of the nation but everywhere. He knew what he must do if he was to be true to himself and to the decade-old commitment. So what do you think Sarosh did next?"

"What, Nariman Uncle?"

"He went to the travel agent specializing in tickets to India. He bought a fully refundable ticket to Bombay for the day when he would complete exactly ten immigrant years—if he succeeded even once before that day dawned, he would cancel the booking.

"The travel agent asked sympathetically, 'Trouble at home?' His name was Mr. Rawaana, and he was from Bombay too.

" 'No,' said Sarosh, 'trouble in Toronto.'

" 'That's a shame,' said Mr. Rawaana. 'I don't want to poke my nose into your business, but in my line of work I meet so many people who are going back to their homeland because of their problems here. Sometimes I forget I'm a travel agent, that my interest is to convince them to travel. Instead, I tell them: don't give up, God is great, stay and try again. It's bad for my profits but gives me a different, a spiritual kind of satisfaction when I succeed. And I succeed about half the time. Which means,' he added with a wry laugh, 'I could double my profits if I minded my own business.'

"After the lengthy sessions with Mrs. Maha-Lepate and Dr. No-Ilaaz, Sarosh felt he had listened to enough advice and kind words. Much as he disliked doing it, he had to hurt Mr. Rawaana's feelings and leave his predicament undiscussed: 'I'm sorry, but I'm in a hurry. Will you be able to look after the booking?'

" 'Well, okay,' said Mr. Rawaana, a trifle crestfallen; he did not relish the travel business as much as he did counselling immigrants. 'Hope you solve your problem. I will be happy to refund your fare, believe me.'

"Sarosh hurried home. With only four weeks to departure, every spare minute, every possible method had to be concentrated on a final attempt at adaptation.

"He tried laxatives, crunching down the tablets with a prayer that these would assist the sitting position. Changing brands did not help, and neither did various types of suppositories. He spent long stretches on the toilet seat each morning. The supervisor continued to reprimand him for tardiness. To make matters worse, Sarosh left his desk every time he felt the slightest urge, hoping: maybe this time.

"The working hours expended in the washroom were noted with unflagging vigilance by the supervisor. More counselling sessions followed. Sarosh refused to extinguish his last hope, and the supervisor punctiliously recorded 'No Improvement' in his daily log. Finally, Sarosh was fired. It would soon have been time to resign in any case, and he could not care less.

"Now whole days went by seated on the toilet, and he stubbornly refused to relieve himself the other way. The doorbell would ring only to be ignored. The telephone went unanswered. Sometimes, he would awake suddenly in the dark hours before dawn and rush to the washroom like a madman."

Without warning, Rustomji flung open his door and stormed: "Ridiculous nonsense this is becoming! Two days in a row, whole Firozsha Baag gathers here! This is not Chaupatty beach, this is not a squatters' colony, this is a building, people want to live here in peace and quiet!" Then just as suddenly, he stamped inside and slammed the door. Right on cue, Nariman continued, before the boys could say anything.

125   "Time for meals was the only time Sarosh allowed himself off the seat. Even in his desperation he remembered that if he did not eat well, he was doomed—the downward pressure on his gut was essential if there was to be any chance of success.

"But the ineluctable day of departure dawned, with grey skies and the scent of rain, while success remained out of sight. At the airport Sarosh checked in and went to the dreary lounge. Out of sheer habit he started towards the washroom. Then he realized the hopelessness of it and returned to the cold, clammy plastic of the lounge seats. Airport seats are the same almost anywhere in the world.

"The boarding announcement was made, and Sarosh was the first to step onto the plane. The skies were darker now. Out of the window he saw a flash of lightning fork through the clouds. For some reason, everything he'd learned years ago in St. Xavier's about sheet lightning and forked lightning went through his mind. He wished it would change to sheet, there was something sinister and unpropitious about forked lightning."

Kersi, absorbedly listening, began cracking his knuckles quite unconsciously. His childhood habit still persisted. Jehangir frowned at the disturbance, and Viraf nudged Kersi to stop it.

"Sarosh fastened his seat-belt and attempted to turn his thoughts towards the long journey home: to the questions he would be expected to answer, the sympathy and criticism that would be thrust upon him. But what remained uppermost in his mind was the present moment—him in the plane, dark skies lowering, lightning on the horizon—irrevocably spelling out: defeat.

130   "But wait. Something else was happening now. A tiny rumble. Inside him. Or was it his imagination? Was it really thunder outside which, in his present disoriented state, he was internalizing? No, there it was again. He had to go.

"He reached the washroom, and almost immediately the sign flashed to 'Please return to seat and fasten seat-belts.' Sarosh debated whether to squat and finish the business quickly, abandoning the perfunctory seated attempt. But the plane started to move and that decided him; it would be difficult now to balance while squatting.

"He pushed. The plane continued to move. He pushed again, trembling with the effort. The seat-belt sign flashed quicker and brighter now. The plane moved faster and faster. And Sarosh pushed hard, harder than he had ever pushed before, harder than in all his ten years of trying in the new land. And the memories of Bombay, the immigration interview in New Delhi, the farewell party, his mother's tattered prayer book, all these, of their own accord, emerged from beyond the region of the ten years to push with him and give him newfound strength."

Nariman paused and cleared his throat. Dusk was falling, and the frequency of B.E.S.T. buses plying the main road outside Firozsha Baag had dropped. Bats began to fly madly from one end of the compound to the other, silent shadows engaged in endless laps over the buildings.

"With a thunderous clap the rain started to fall. Sarosh felt a splash under him. Could it really be? He glanced down to make certain. Yes, it was. He had succeeded!

135   "But was it already too late? The plane waited at its assigned position on the runway, jet engines at full thrust. Rain was falling in torrents and takeoff could be delayed. Perhaps even now they would allow him to cancel his flight, to disembark. He lurched out of the constricting cubicle.

"A stewardess hurried towards him: 'Excuse me, sir, but you must return to your seat immediately and fasten your belt.'

" 'You don't understand!' Sarosh shouted excitedly. 'I must get off the plane! Everything is all right. I don't have to go anymore . . .'

" 'That's impossible, sir!' said the stewardess, aghast. 'No one can leave now. Takeoff procedures are in progress!' The wild look in his sleepless eyes, and the dark rings around them scared her. She beckoned for help.

"Sarosh continued to argue, and a steward and the chief stewardess hurried over: 'What seems to be the problem, sir? You *must* resume your seat. We are authorized, if necessary, to forcibly restrain you, sir.'

140   "The plane began to move again, and suddenly Sarosh felt all the urgency leaving him. His feverish mind, the product of nightmarish days and tortuous nights, was filled again with the calm which had fled a decade ago, and he spoke softly now: 'That . . .that will not be necessary . . .it's okay, I understand.' He readily returned to his seat.

"As the aircraft sped down the runway, Sarosh's first reaction was one of joy. The process of adaptation was complete. But later, he could not help wondering if success came before or after the ten-year limit had expired. And since he had already passed through the customs and security check, was he really an immigrant in every sense of the word at the moment of achievement?

"But such questions were merely academic. Or were they? He could not decide. If he returned, what would it be like? Ten years ago, the immigration officer who had stamped his passport had said, 'Welcome to Canada.' It was one of Sarosh's dearest memories, and thinking of it, he fell asleep.

"The plane was flying above the rainclouds. Sunshine streamed into the cabin. A few raindrops were still clinging miraculously to the windows, reminders of what was happening below. They sparkled as the sunlight caught them."

Some of the boys made as if to leave, thinking the story was finally over. Clearly, they had not found this one as interesting as the others Nariman had told. What dolts, thought Jehangir, they cannot recognize a masterpiece when they hear one. Nariman motioned with his hand for silence.

"But our story does not end there. There was a welcome-home party for Sarosh a few days after he arrived in Bombay. It was not in Firozsha Baag this time because his relatives in the Baag had a serious sickness in the house. But I was invited to it anyway. Sarosh's family and friends were considerate enough to wait till the jet lag had worked its way out of his system. They wanted him to really enjoy this one.

"Drinks began to flow freely again in his honour: Scotch and soda, rum and Coke, brandy. Sarosh noticed that during his absence all the brand names had changed—the labels were different and unfamiliar. Even for the mixes. Instead of Coke there was Thums-Up, and he remembered reading in the papers about Coca-Cola being kicked out by the Indian Government for refusing to reveal their secret formula.

"People slapped him on the back and shook his hand vigorously, over and over, right through the evening. They said: 'Telling the truth, you made the right decision, look how happy your mother is to live to see this day;' or they asked: 'Well, bossy, what changed your mind?' Sarosh smiled and nodded his way through it all, passing around Canadian currency at the insistence of some of the curious ones who, egged on by his mother, also pestered him to display his Canadian passport and citizenship card. She had been badgering him since his arrival to tell her the real reason: '*Saachoo kahé*, what brought you back?' and was hoping that tonight, among his friends, he might raise his glass and reveal something. But she remained disappointed.

"Weeks went by and Sarosh found himself desperately searching for his old place in the pattern of life he had vacated ten years ago. Friends who had organized the welcome-home party gradually disappeared. He went walking in the evenings along Marine Drive, by the sea-wall, where the old crowd used to congregate. But the people who sat on the parapet while waves crashed behind their backs were strangers. The tetrapods were still there, staunchly protecting the reclaimed land from the fury of the sea. He had watched as a kid when cranes had lowered these cement and concrete hulks of respectable grey into the water. They were grimy black now, and from their angularities rose the distinct stench of human excrement. The old pattern was never found by Sarosh; he searched in vain. Patterns of life are selfish and unforgiving.

"Then one day, as I was driving past Marine Drive, I saw someone sitting alone. He looked familiar, so I stopped. For a moment I did not recognize Sarosh, so forlorn and woebegone was his countenance. I parked the apple of my eye and went to him, saying, 'Hullo, Sid, what are you doing here on your lonesome?' And he said, 'No, no! No more Sid, please, that name reminds me of all my troubles.' Then, on the parapet at Marine Drive, he told me his unhappy and wretched tale, with the waves battering away at the tetrapods, and around us the hawkers screaming about coconut-water and sugar-cane juice and *paan*.

"When he finished, he said that he had related to me the whole sad saga because he knew how I told stories to boys in the Baag, and he wanted me to tell this one, especially to those who were planning to go abroad. 'Tell them,' said Sarosh, 'that the world can be a bewildering place, and dreams and ambitions are often paths to the most pernicious of traps.' As he spoke, I could see that Sarosh was somewhere far away, perhaps in New Delhi at his immigration interview, seeing himself as he was then, with what he thought was a life of hope and promise stretching endlessly before him. Poor Sarosh. Then he was back beside me on the parapet.

" 'I pray you, in your stories,' said Sarosh, his old sense of humour returning as he deepened his voice for his favourite *Othello* lines"—and here, Nariman produced a basso profundo of his own—" 'when you shall these unlucky deeds relate, speak of me as I am; nothing extenuate, nor set down aught in malice: tell them that in Toronto once there lived a Parsi boy as best as he could. Set you down this; and say, besides, that for some it was good and for some it was bad, but for me life in the land of milk and honey was just a pain in the posterior.' "[23]

And now, Nariman allowed his low-pitched rumbles to turn into chuckles. The boys broke into cheers and loud applause and cries of "Encore!" and "More!" Finally, Nariman had to silence them by pointing warningly at Rustomji-the-curmudgeon's door.

While Kersi and Viraf were joking and wondering what to make of it all, Jehangir edged forward and told Nariman this was the best story he had ever told. Nariman patted his shoulder and smiled. Jehangir left, wondering if Nariman would have been as popular if Dr. Mody was still alive. Probably, since the two were liked for different reasons: Dr. Mody used to be constantly jovial, whereas Nariman had his periodic story-telling urges.

Now the group of boys who had really enjoyed the Savukshaw story during the previous week spoke up. Capitalizing on Nariman's extraordinarily good mood, they began clamouring for more Savukshaw: "Nariman Uncle, tell the one about Savukshaw the hunter, the one you had started that day."

"What hunter? I don't know which one you mean." He refused to be reminded of it, and got up to leave. But there was a loud protest, and the boys started chanting, "We-want-Savukshaw! We-want-Savukshaw!"

Nariman looked fearfully towards Rustomji's door and held up his hands placatingly: "All right, all right! Next time it will be Savukshaw again. Savukshaw the artist. The story of Parsi Picasso."[24]

(1987)

---

[23]based on the dying words of Othello, Shakespeare's tragic hero who was an African living in Venice. [24]twentieth-century Spanish artist who introduced and popularized many abstract styles.

Shani Mootoo (b. 1958)

Born in Ireland of East Indian parents, Shani Mootoo grew up in Trinidad. She moved to Canada when she was 19 years old and studied fine arts at the University of Western Ontario, specializing in painting and film making. In addition to paintings, photographs, and videos, all of which have achieved wide acclaim, she has written short stories, poetry, and novels. "Out on Main Street," the title story from her first collection, is the first-person account of the unnamed narrator's visit to an East Indian restaurant in Vancouver. In her reactions to her lover, Janet, the non-Carribean East Indian customers, the male white customers, and the male East Indian waiters, she reveals many hostilities, all of which help to explain why, as she says, "Going for a outing with mih Janet on Main Street ain't easy!" Her anger toward the various people, even to Janet, suggests a range of insecurities of which she is, at best, dimly aware.

OUT ON MAIN STREET

1.

Janet and me? We does go Main Street to see pretty pretty sari[1] and bangle, and to eat we belly full a burfi and gulub jamoon,[2] but we doh go too often because, yuh see, is dem sweets self what does give people like we a presupposition for untameable hip and thigh.

Another reason we shy to frequent dere is dat we is watered-down Indians—we ain't good grade A Indians. We skin brown, is true, but we doh even think 'bout India unless something happen over dere and it come on de news. Mih family remain Hindu[3] ever since mih ancestors leave India behind, but nowadays dey doh believe in praying unless things real bad, because, as mih father always singing, like if is a mantra: "Do good and good will be bestowed unto you." So he is a veritable saint cause he always doing good by his women friends and dey chilren. I sure some a dem must be mih half sister and brother, oui!

Mostly, back home, we is kitchen Indians: some kind a Indian food every day, at least once a day, but we doh get cardamom and other fancy spice down dere so de food not spicy like Indian food I eat in restaurants up here. But it have one thing we doh make joke 'bout down dere: we like we meethai[4] and sweetrice too much, and it remain overly authentic, like de day Naana and Naani step off de boat in Port of Spain[5] harbour over a hundred and sixty years ago. Check out dese hips here nah, dey is pure sugar and condensed milk, pure sweetness!

---

[1] a brightly coloured length of light-weight cloth which is worn by Indian women as an outer garment. [2] sweet Indian confections that contain a great deal of sugar. [3] one who practices Hinduism, one of the major religions of India. [4] a sweet Indian dessert. [5] capital of Trinidad and Tobago.

But Janet family different. In de ole days when Canadian missionaries land in Trinidad dey used to make a bee-line straight for Indians from down South. And Janet great grandparents is one a de first South families dat exchange over from Indian to Presbyterian. Dat was a long time ago.

5   When Janet born, she father, one Mr. John Mahase, insist on asking de Reverend MacDougal from Trace Settlement Church, a leftover from de Canadian Mission, to name de baby girl. De good Reverend choose de name Constance cause dat was his mother name. But de mother a de child, Mrs. Savitri Mahase, wanted to name de child sheself. Ever since Savitri was a lil girl she like de yellow hair, fair skin and pretty pretty clothes Janet and John used to wear in de primary school reader—since she lil she want to change she name from Savitri to Janet but she own father get vex and say how Savitri was his mother name and how she will insult his mother if she gone and change it. So Savitri get she own way once by marrying this fella name John, and she do a encore, by calling she daughter Janet, even doh husband John upset for days at she for insulting de good Reverend by throwing out de name a de Reverend mother.

So dat is how my girlfriend, a darkskin Indian girl with thick black hair (pretty fuh so!) get a name like Janet.

She come from a long line a Presbyterian school teacher, headmaster and headmistress. Savitri still teaching from de same Janet and John reader in a primary school in San Fernando,[6] and John, getting more and more obtuse in his ole age, is headmaster more dan twenty years now in Princes Town[7] Boys' Presbyterian High School. Everybody back home know dat family good good. Dat is why Janet leave in two twos. Soon as A Level[8] finish she pack up and take off like a jet plane so she could live without people only shoo-shooing behind she back . . . "But AA! Yuh ain't hear de goods 'bout John Mahase daughter, gyul! How yuh mean yuh ain't hear? Is a big thing! Everybody talking 'bout she. Hear dis, nah! Yuh ever see she wear a dress? Yes! Doh look at mih so. Yuh reading mih right!"

Is only recentish I realize Mahase is a Hindu last name. In de ole days every Mahase in de country turn Presbyterian and now de name doh have no association with Hindu or Indian whatsoever. I used to think of it as a Presbyterian Church name until some days ago when we meet a Hindu fella fresh from India name Yogdesh Mahase who never even hear of Presbyterian.

De other day I ask Janet what she know 'bout Divali. She say, "It's the Hindu festival of lights,[9] isn't it?" like a line straight out a dictionary. Yuh think she know anything 'bout how lord Rama get himself exile in a forest for fourteen years, and how when it come time for him to go back home his followers light up a pathway to help him make his way out, and dat is what Divali lights is all about? All Janet know is 'bout going for drive in de country to see light, and she could remember looking forward, around Divali

---

[6]largest city in Trinidad. [7]town in Trinidad. [8]in the English educational system, major examinations taken by university-bound students. [9]the Hindu Festival of Lights, observed in late October or early November, celebrates the epic hero Rama's triumph over evil.

time, to the lil brown paper-bag packages full a burfi and parasad[10] that she father Hindu students used to bring for him.

One time in a Indian restaurant she ask for parasad for dessert. Well! Since den I never go back in dat restaurant, I embarrass fuh so!

I used to think I was a Hindu par excellence until I come up here and see real flesh and blood Indian from India. Up here, I learning 'bout all kind a custom and food and music and clothes dat we never see or hear 'bout in good ole Trinidad. Is de next best thing to going to India, in truth, oui! But Indian store clerk on Main Street doh have no patience with us, specially when we talking English to dem. Yuh ask dem a question in English and dey insist on giving de answer in Hindi or Punjabi or Urdu or Gujarati.[11] How I suppose to know de difference even! And den dey look at yuh disdainful disdainful—like yuh disloyal, like yuh is a traitor.

But yuh know, it have one other reason I real reluctant to go Main Street. Yuh see, Janet pretty fuh so! And I doh like de way men does look at she, as if because she wearing jeans and T-shirt and high-heel shoe and makeup and have long hair loose and flying about like she is a walking-talking shampoo ad, dat she easy. And de women always looking at she beady eye, like she loose and going to thief dey man. Dat kind a thing always make me want to put mih arm round she waist like, she is my woman, take yuh eyes off she! and shock de false teeth right out dey mouth. And den is a whole other story when dey see me with mih crew cut and mih blue jeans tuck inside mih jim-boots. Walking next to Janet, who so femme dat she redundant, tend to make me look like a gender dey forget to classify. Before going Main Street I does parade in front de mirror practising a jiggly-wiggly kind a walk. But if I ain't walking like a strong-man monkey I doh exactly feel right and I always revert back to mih true colours. De men dem does look at me like if dey is exactly what I need a taste of to cure me good and proper. I could see dey eyes watching Janet and me, dey face growing dark as dey imagining all kind a situation and position. And de women dem embarrass fuh so to watch me in mih eye, like dey fraid I will jump up and try to kiss dem, or make pass at dem. Yuh know, sometimes I wonder if I ain't mad enough to do it just for a little bacchanal, nah!

Going for a outing with mih Janet on Main Street ain't easy! If only it wasn't for burfi and gulub jamoon! If only I had a learned how to cook dem kind a thing before I leave home and come up here to live!

2.

In large deep-orange Sanskrit-style letters, de sign on de saffron-colour awning above de door read *Kush Valley Sweets*. Underneath in smaller red letters it had *Desserts Fit For The Gods*. It was a corner building. The front and side was one big glass wall. Inside was big. Big like a gymnasium. Yuh could see in through de brown tint windows: dark brown plastic chair, and

[10]food offering made to Rama. [11]languages spoken in India.

brown table, each one de length of a door, line up stiff and straight in row after row like if is a school room.

15   Before entering de restaurant I ask Janet to wait one minute outside with me while I rumfle up mih memory, pulling out all de sweet names I know from home, besides burfi and gulub jamoon: meethai, jilebi,[12] sweet-rice (but dey call dat kheer up here), and ladhoo. By now, of course, mih mouth watering fuh so! When I feel confident enough dat I wouldn't make a fool a mih Brown self by asking what dis one name? and what dat one name? we went in de restaurant. In two twos all de spice in de place take a flying leap in our direction and give us one big welcome hug up, tight fuh so! Since den dey take up permanent residence in de jacket I wear dat day!

Mostly it had women customers sitting at de tables, chatting and laughing, eating sweets and sipping masala tea.[13] De only men in de place was de waiters, and all six waiters was men. I figure dat dey was brothers, not too hard to conclude, because all a dem had de same full round chin, round as if de chin stretch tight over a ping-pong ball, and dey had de same big roving eyes. I know better dan to think dey was mere waiters in de employ of a owner who chook up in a office in de back. I sure dat dat was dey own family business, dey stomach proudly preceding dem and dey shoulders throw back in de confidence of dey ownership.

It ain't dat I paranoid, yuh understand, but from de moment we enter de fellas dem get over-animated, even amorously agitated. Janet again! All six pair a eyes land up on she, following she every move and body part. Dat in itself is something dat does madden me, oui! but also a kind a irrational envy have a tendency to manifest in me. It was like I didn't exist. Sometimes it could be a real problem going out with a good-looker, yes! While I ain't remotely interested in having a squeak of a flirtation with a man, it doh hurt a ego to have a man notice yuh once in a very long while. But with Janet at mih side, I doh have de chance of a penny shave-ice in de hot sun. I tuck mih elbows in as close to mih sides as I could so I wouldn't look like a strong man next to she, and over to de l-o-n-g glass case jam up with sweets I jiggle and wiggle in mih best imitation a some a dem gay fellas dat I see downtown Vancouver, de ones who more femme dan even Janet. I tell she not to pay de brothers no attention, because if any a dem flirt with she I could start a fight right dere and den. And I didn't feel to mess up mih crew cut in a fight.

De case had sweets in every nuance of colour in a rainbow. Sweets I never before see and doh know de names of. But dat was all right because I wasn't going to order dose ones anyway.

Since before we leave home Janet have she mind set on a nice thick syrupy curl a jilebi and a piece a plain burfi so I order dose for she and den I ask de waiter-fella, resplendent with thick thick bright-yellow gold chain and ID bracelet, for a stick a meethai for mihself. I stand up waiting by de glass case for it but de waiter/owner lean up on de back wall behind de counter watching me like he ain't hear me. So I say loud enough for him, and every body else in de room to hear, "I would like to have one piece a meethai

[12]a fried sugar and flour confection. [13]a spiced tea.

please," and den he smile and lift up his hands, palms open-out motioning across de vast expanse a glass case, and he say, "Your choice! Whichever you want, Miss." But he still lean up against de back wall grinning. So I stick mih head out and up like a turtle and say louder, and slowly, "One piece a meethai—dis one!" and I point sharp to de stick a flour mix with ghee, deep fry and den roll up in sugar. He say, "That is koorma, Miss. One piece only?"

20   Mih voice drop low all by itself. "Oh ho! Yes, one piece. Where I come from we does call dat meethai." And den I add, but only loud enough for Janet to hear, "And mih name ain't 'Miss.'"

He open his palms out and indicate de entire panorama a sweets and he say, "These are all meethai, Miss. Meethai is Sweets. Where are you from?"

I ignore his question and to show him I undaunted, I point to a round pink ball and say, "I'll have one a dese sugarcakes too please." He start grinning broad broad like if he half-pitying, half-laughing at dis Indian-in-skin-colour-only, and den he tell me, "That is called chum-chum,[14] Miss." I snap back at him, "Yeh, well back home we does call dat sugarcake, Mr. Chum-chum."

At de table Janet say, "You know, Pud (Pud, short for Pudding; is dat she does call me when she feeling close to me, or sorry for me), it's true that we call that 'meethai' back home. Just like how we call 'siu mai' 'tim sam.' As if 'dim sum' is just one little piece a food. What did he call that sweet again?"

"Cultural bastards, Janet, cultural bastards. Dat is what we is. Yuh know, one time a fella from India who living up here call me a bastardized Indian because I didn't know Hindi. And now look at dis, nah! De thing is: all a we in Trinidad is cultural bastards, Janet, all a we. *Toutes bagailles!*[15] Chinese people. Black people. White people. Syrian. Lebanese. I looking forward to de day I find out dat place inside me where I am nothing else but Trinidadian, whatever dat could turn out to be."

25   I take a bite a de chum-chum, de texture was like grind-up coconut but it had no coconut, not even a hint a coconut taste in it. De thing was juicy with sweet rose water oozing out a it. De rose water perfume enter mih nose and get trap in mih cranium. Ah drink two cup a masala tea and a lassi[16] and still de rose water perfume was on mih tongue like if I had a overdosed on Butchart Gardens.[17]

Suddenly de door a de restaurant spring open wide with a strong force and two big burly fellas stumble in, almost rolling over on to de ground. Dey get up, eyes red and slow and dey skin burning pink with booze. Dey straighten up so much to overcompensate for falling forward, dat dey find deyself leaning backward. Everybody stop talking and was watching dem. De guy in front put his hand up to his forehead and take a deep Walter Raleigh bow, bringing de hand down to his waist in a rolling circular movement. Out loud he greet everybody with *"Alarm o salay koom."*[18] A part a me wanted

---

[14]a flour, sugar, saffron confection that is covered with flaked coconut. [15]everything (all of us). [16]a drink made with yogurt, milk, and spices. [17]a famous ornamental flower garden on Vancouver Island. [18]this Islamic greeting, which is badly pronounced by the drunk customer, is inappropriately addressed to a Hindu.

to bust out laughing. Another part make mih jaw drop open in disbelief. De calm in de place get rumfle up. De two fellas dem, feeling chupid now because nobody reply to dey greeting, gone up to de counter to Chum-chum trying to make a little conversation with him. De same booze-pink *alarm-o-salay-koom*-fella say to Chum-chum, "Hey, howaryah?"

Chum-Chum give a lil nod and de fella carry right on, "Are you Sikh"[19]?

Chum-chum brothers converge near de counter, busying dey-selves in de vicinity. Chum-chum look at his brothers kind a quizzical, and he touch his cheek and feel his forehead with de back a his palm. He say, "No, I think I am fine, thank you. But I am sorry if I look sick, Sir."

De burly fella confuse now, so he try again.

30   "Where are you from?"

Chum-chum say, "Fiji, Sir."

"Oh! Fiji, eh! Lotsa palm trees and beautiful women, eh! Is it true that you guys can have more than one wife?"

De exchange make mih blood rise up in a boiling froth. De restaurant suddenly get a gruff quietness 'bout it except for a woman I hear whispering angrily to another woman at de table behind us, "I hate this! I just hate it! I can't stand to see our men humiliated by them, right in front of us. He should refuse to serve them, he should throw them out. Who on earth do they think they are? The awful fools!" And de friend whisper back, "If he throws them out all of us will suffer in the long run."

I could discern de hair on de back a de neck a Chum-chum brothers standing up, annoyed, and at de same time de brothers look like dey was shrinking in stature. Chum-chum get serious, and he politely say, "What can I get for you?"

35   Pinko get de message and he point to a few items in de case and say, "One of each, to go please."

Holding de white takeout box in one hand he extend de other to Chum-chum and say, "How do you say 'Excuse me, I'm sorry' in Fiji?"

Chum-chum shake his head and say, "It's okay. Have a good day."

Pinko insist, "No, tell me please. I think I just behaved badly, and I want to apologize. How do you say 'I'm sorry' in Fiji?"

Chum-chum say, "Your apology is accepted. Everything is okay." And he discreetly turn away to serve a person who had just entered de restaurant. De fellas take de hint dat was broad like daylight, and back out de restaurant like two little mouse.

40   Everybody was feeling sorry for Chum-chum and Brothers. One a dem come up to de table across from us to take a order from a woman with a giraffe-long neck who say, "Brother, we mustn't accept how these people think they can treat us. You men really put up with too many insults and abuse over here. I really felt for you."

Another woman gone up to de counter to converse with Chum-chum in she language. She reach out and touch his hand, sympathy-like. Chum-chum hold the one hand in his two and make a verbose speech to her as she

---

[19]an Indian religion, the male practisers of which wear turbans.

nod she head in agreement generously. To italicize her support, she buy a takeout box a two burfi, or rather, dat's what I think dey was.

De door a de restaurant open again, and a bevy of Indian-looking women saunter in, dress up to weaken a person's decorum. De Miss Universe pageant traipse across de room to a table. Chum-chum and Brothers start smoothing dey hair back, and pushing de front a dey shirts neatly into dey pants. One brother take out a pack a Dentyne from his shirt pocket and pop one in his mouth. One take out a comb from his back pocket and smooth down his hair. All a dem den converge on dat single table to take orders. Dey begin to behave like young pups in mating season. Only, de women dem wasn't impress by all this tra-la-la at all and ignore dem except to make dey order, straight to de point. Well, it look like Brothers' egos were having a rough day and dey start roving 'bout de room, dey egos and de crotch a dey pants leading far in front dem. One brother gone over to Giraffebai to see if she want anything more. He call she "dear" and put his hand on she back. Giraffebai straighten she back in surprise and reply in a not-too-friendly way. When he gone to write up de bill she see me looking at she and she say to me, "Whoever does he think he is! Calling me dear and touching me like that! Why do these men always think that they have permission to touch whatever and wherever they want! And you can't make a fuss about it in public, because it is exactly what those people out there want to hear about so that they can say how sexist and uncivilized our culture is."

I shake mih head in understanding and say, "Yeah. I know. Yuh right!"

De atmosphere in de room take a hairpin turn, and it was man aggressing on woman, woman warding off a herd a man who just had dey pride publicly cut up a couple a times in just a few minutes.

One brother walk over to Janet and me and he stand up facing me with his hands clasp in front a his crotch, like if he protecting it. Stiff stiff, looking at me, he say, "Will that be all?"

Mih crew cut start to tingle, so I put on mih femmest smile and say, "Yes, that's it, thank you. Just the bill please." De smartass turn to face Janet and he remove his hands from in front a his crotch and slip his thumbs inside his pants like a cowboy 'bout to do a square dance. He smile, looking down at her attentive fuh so, and he say, "Can I do anything for you?"

I didn't give Janet time fuh his intent to even register before I bulldoze in mih most un-femmest manner, "She have everything she need, man, thank you. The bill please." Yuh think he hear me? It was like I was talking to thin air. He remain smiling at Janet, but she, looking at me, not at him, say, "You heard her. The bill please."

Before he could even leave de table proper, I start mih tirade. "But AA! Yuh see dat? Yuh could believe dat! De effing so-and-so! One minute yuh feel sorry fuh dem and next minute dey harassing de heck out a you. Janet, he crazy to mess with my woman, yes!" Janet get vex with me and say I over-reacting, and is not fuh me to be vex, but fuh she to be vex. Is she he insult, and she could take good enough care a sheself.

I tell she I don't know why she don't cut off all dat long hair, and stop wearing lipstick and eyeliner. Well, who tell me to say dat! She get real vex and say dat nobody will tell she how to dress and how not to dress, not me and not any man. Well I could see de potential dat dis fight had coming, and when Janet get fighting vex, watch out! It hard to get a word in edgewise, yes! And she does bring up incidents from years back dat have no bearing on de current situation. So I draw back quick quick but she don't waste time; she was already off to a good start. It was best to leave right dere and den.

50   Just when I stand up to leave, de doors dem open up and in walk Sandy and Lise, coming for dey weekly hit a Indian sweets. Well, with Sandy and Lise is a dead giveaway dat dey not dressing fuh any man, it have no place in dey life fuh man-vibes, and dat in fact dey have a blatant penchant fuh women. Soon as dey enter de room yuh could see de brothers and de couple men customers dat had come in minutes before stare dem down from head to Birkenstocks, dey eyes bulging with disgust. And de women in de room start shoo-shooing, and putting dey hand in front dey mouth to stop dey surprise, and false teeth, too, from falling out. Sandy and Lise spot us instantly and dey call out to us, shameless, loud and affectionate. Dey leap over to us, eager to hug up and kiss like if dey hadn't seen us for years, but it was really only since two nights aback when we went out to dey favourite Indian restaurant for dinner. I figure dat de display was a genuine happiness to be seen wit us in dat place. While we stand up dere chatting, Sandy insist on rubbing she hand up and down Janet back—wit friendly intent, mind you, and same time Lise have she arm round Sandy waist. Well, all cover get blown. If it was even remotely possible dat I wasn't noticeable before, now Janet and I were over-exposed. We could a easily suffer from hypothermia, specially since it suddenly get cold cold in dere. We say goodbye, not soon enough, and as we were leaving I turn to acknowlege Giraffebai, but instead a any recognition of our buddiness against de fresh brothers, I get a face dat look like it was in de presence of a very foul smell.

De good thing, doh, is dat Janet had become so incensed 'bout how we get scorned, dat she forgot I tell she to cut she hair and to ease up on de makeup, and so I get save from hearing 'bout how I too jealous, and how much I inhibit she, and how she would prefer if I would grow my hair, and wear lipstick and put on a dress sometimes. I so glad, oui! dat I didn't have to go through hearing how I too demanding a she, like de time, she say, I prevent she from seeing a ole boyfriend when he was in town for a couple hours en route to live in Australia with his new bride (because, she say, I was jealous dat ten years ago dey sleep together). Well, look at mih crosses, nah! Like if I really so possessive and jealous!

So tell me, what yuh think 'bout dis nah, girl?

(1993)

Jhumpa Lahiri   (b. 1967)

Born in London, England, Jhumpa Lahiri grew up in Rhode Island. She earned a bachelor's degree in English from Barnard College, master's degrees in English, Fine Arts, and Comparative Literature, and a doctorate in Renaissance Studies from Boston University. An admirer of the stories of Alice Munro, she published her first book, *Interpreter of Maladies,* in 1999. Many of the stories in the collection focus on characters dealing with separation from their Indian heritage. In "When Mr. Pirzada Came to Dine," the narrator recalls her responses to a Pakistani professor who has come to New England on a semester's leave from his university. Lilia, who was 10 years old at the time he became a regular dinner-time visitor at her family's home, understands the sense of loneliness he feels for his wife and seven daughters back home, a loneliness that becomes anxiety when war erupts in East Pakistan. The theme of separation runs through the story, not only Mr. Pirzada's from his family, but the narrator's parents' from their Bengali homeland. Personal separation is paralleled by political separation, first Pakistan's from India and later the violent separation of East Pakistan from West Pakistan, a situation the family and their visitor view each evening on the television news.

WHEN MR. PIRZADA CAME TO DINE

In the autumn of 1971 a man used to come to our house, bearing confections in his pocket and hopes of ascertaining the life or death of his family. His name was Mr. Pirzada, and he came from Dacca, now the capital of Bangladesh, but then a part of Pakistan. That year Pakistan was engaged in civil war. The eastern frontier, where Dacca was located, was fighting for autonomy from the ruling regime in the west. In March, Dacca had been invaded, torched, and shelled by the Pakistani army. Teachers were dragged onto streets and shot, women dragged into barracks and raped. By the end of the summer, three hundred thousand people were said to have died. In Dacca Mr. Pirzada had a three-story home, a lectureship in botany at the university, a wife of twenty years, and seven daughters between the ages of six and sixteen whose names all began with the letter A. "Their mother's idea," he explained one day, producing from his wallet a black-and-white picture of seven girls at a picnic, their braids tied with ribbons, sitting cross-legged in a row, eating chicken curry off of banana leaves. "How am I to distinguish? Ayesha, Amira, Amina, Aziza, you see the difficulty."

Each week Mr. Pirzada wrote letters to his wife, and sent comic books to each of his seven daughters, but the postal system, along with most everything else in Dacca, had collapsed, and he had not heard word of them in over six months. Mr. Pirzada, meanwhile, was in America for the year, for he had been awarded a grant from the government of Pakistan to study the foliage of New England. In spring and summer he had gathered data in Vermont and Maine, and in autumn he moved to a university north of

Boston, where we lived, to write a short book about his discoveries. The grant was a great honor, but when converted into dollars it was not generous. As a result, Mr. Pirzada lived in a room in a graduate dormitory, and did not own a proper stove or a television set of his own. And so he came to our house to eat dinner and watch the evening news.

At first I knew nothing of the reason for his visits. I was ten years old, and was not surprised that my parents, who were from India, and had a number of Indian acquaintances at the university, should ask Mr. Pirzada to share our meals. It was a small campus, with narrow brick walkways and white pillared buildings, located on the fringes of what seemed to be an even smaller town. The supermarket did not carry mustard oil, doctors did not make house calls, neighbors never dropped by without an invitation, and of these things, every so often, my parents complained. In search of compatriots, they used to trail their fingers, at the start of each new semester, through the columns of the university directory, circling surnames familiar to their part of the world. It was in this manner that they discovered Mr. Pirzada, and phoned him, and invited him to our home.

I have no memory of his first visit, or of his second or his third, but by the end of September I had grown so accustomed to Mr. Pirzada's presence in our living room that one evening, as I was dropping ice cubes into the water pitcher, I asked my mother to hand me a fourth glass from a cupboard still out of my reach. She was busy at the stove, presiding over a skillet of fried spinach with radishes, and could not hear me because of the drone of the exhaust fan and the fierce scrapes of her spatula. I turned to my father, who was leaning against the refrigerator, eating spiced cashews from a cupped fist.

5   "What is it, Lilia?"

"A glass for the Indian man."

"Mr. Pirzada won't be coming today. More importantly, Mr. Pirzada is no longer considered Indian," my father announced, brushing salt from the cashews out of his trim black beard. "Not since Partition. Our country was divided. 1947."

When I said I thought that was the date of India's independence from Britain, my father said, "That too. One moment we were free and then we were sliced up," he explained, drawing an X with his finger on the countertop, "like a pie. Hindus here, Muslims there. Dacca no longer belongs to us." He told me that during Partition Hindus and Muslims had set fire to each other's homes. For many, the idea of eating in the other's company was still unthinkable.

It made no sense to me. Mr. Pirzada and my parents spoke the same language, laughed at the same jokes, looked more or less the same. They ate pickled mangoes with their meals, ate rice every night for supper with their hands. Like my parents, Mr. Pirzada took off his shoes before entering a room, chewed fennel seeds after meals as a digestive, drank no alcohol, for dessert dipped austere biscuits into successive cups of tea. Nevertheless my father insisted that I understand the difference, and he led me to a map of the world taped to the wall over his desk. He seemed concerned that Mr. Pirzada might take offense if I accidentally referred to him as an Indian, though I could not really imagine Mr. Pirzada being offended by much of anything. "Mr. Pirzada is Bengali, but he is a Muslim," my father informed me. "Therefore he lives in East Pakistan, not India." His finger trailed across the Atlantic, through Europe, the Mediterranean, the Middle East, and finally to the sprawling orange diamond that my mother once told me resembled a woman wearing a sari with her left arm extended. Various cities had been circled with lines drawn between them to indicate my parents' travels, and the place of their birth, Calcutta, was signified by a small silver star. I had been there only once and had no memory of the trip. "As you see, Lilia, it is a different country, a different color," my father said. Pakistan was yellow, not orange. I noticed that there were two distinct parts to it, one much larger than the other, separated by an expanse of Indian territory; it was as if California and Connecticut constituted a nation apart from the U.S.

10 My father rapped his knuckles on top of my head. "You are, of course, aware of the current situation? Aware of East Pakistan's fight for sovereignty?"

I nodded, unaware of the situation.

We returned to the kitchen, where my mother was draining a pot of boiled rice into a colander. My father opened up the can on the counter and eyed me sharply over the frames of his glasses as he ate some more cashews. "What exactly do they teach you at school? Do you study history? Geography?"

"Lilia has plenty to learn at school," my mother said. "We live here now, she was born here." She seemed genuinely proud of the fact, as if it were a reflection of my character. In her estimation, I knew, I was assured a safe life, an easy life, a fine education, every opportunity. I would never have to eat rationed food, or obey curfews, or watch riots from my rooftop, or hide neighbors in water tanks to prevent them from being shot, as she and my father had. "Imagine having to place her in a decent school. Imagine her having to read during power failures by the light of kerosene lamps. Imagine the pressures, the tutors, the constant exams." She ran a hand through her hair, bobbed to a suitable length for her part-time job as a bank teller. "How can you possibly expect her to know about Partition? Put those nuts away."

"But what does she learn about the world?" My father rattled the cashew can in his hand. "What is she learning?"

15 We learned American history, of course, and American geography. That year, and every year, it seemed, we began by studying the Revolutionary War. We were taken in school buses on field trips to visit Plymouth Rock,[1] and to walk the Freedom Trail,[2] and to climb to the top of the Bunker Hill Monument.[3] We made dioramas out of colored construction paper depicting George Washington crossing the choppy waters of the Delaware River, and we made puppets of King George wearing white tights and a black bow in his hair. During tests we were given blank maps of the thirteen colonies, and asked to fill in names, dates, capitals. I could do it with my eyes closed.

---

[1]location in Massachusetts where the Mayflower pilgrims landed in 1620. [2]a walking trail in Boston that passes by significant sites relating to the American War of Independence.
[3]a monument in Boston commemorating a 1775 battle between British and Colonial troops.

The next evening Mr. Pirzada arrived, as usual, at six o'clock. Though they were no longer strangers, upon first greeting each other, he and my father maintained the habit of shaking hands.

"Come in, sir. Lilia, Mr. Pirzada's coat, please."

He stepped into the foyer, impeccably suited and scarved, with a silk tie knotted at his collar. Each evening he appeared in ensembles of plums, olives, and chocolate browns. He was a compact man, and though his feet were perpetually splayed, and his belly slightly wide, he nevertheless maintained an efficient posture, as if balancing in either hand two suitcases of equal weight. His ears were insulated by tufts of graying hair that seemed to block out the unpleasant traffic of life. He had thickly lashed eyes shaded with a trace of camphor, a generous mustache that turned up playfully at the ends, and a mole shaped like a flattened raisin in the very center of his left cheek. On his head he wore a black fez[4] made from the wool of Persian lambs, secured by bobby pins, without which I was never to see him. Though my father always offered to fetch him in our car, Mr. Pirzada preferred to walk from his dormitory to our neighborhood, a distance of about twenty minutes on foot, studying trees and shrubs on his way, and when he entered our house his knuckles were pink with the effects of crisp autumn air.

"Another refugee, I am afraid, on Indian territory."

20   "They are estimating nine million at the last count," my father said.

Mr. Pirzada handed me his coat, for it was my job to hang it on the rack at the bottom of the stairs. It was made of finely checkered gray-and-blue wool, with a striped lining and horn buttons, and carried in its weave the faint smell of limes. There were no recognizable tags inside, only a hand-stitched label with the phrase "Z. Sayeed, Suitors" embroidered on it in cursive with glossy black thread. On certain days a birch or maple leaf was tucked into a pocket. He unlaced his shoes and lined them against the baseboard; a golden paste clung to the toes and heels, the result of walking through our damp, unraked lawn. Relieved of his trappings, he grazed my throat with his short, restless fingers, the way a person feels for solidity behind a wall before driving in a nail. Then he followed my father to the living room, where the television was tuned to the local news. As soon as they were seated my mother appeared from the kitchen with a plate of mincemeat kebabs with coriander chutney. Mr. Pirzada popped one into his mouth.

"One can only hope," he said, reaching for another, "that Dacca's refugees are as heartily fed. Which reminds me." He reached into his suit pocket and gave me a small plastic egg filled with cinnamon hearts. "For the lady of the house," he said with an almost imperceptible splay-footed bow.

"Really, Mr. Pirzada," my mother protested. "Night after night. You spoil her."

"I only spoil children who are incapable of spoiling."

25   It was an awkward moment for me, one which I awaited in part with dread, in part with delight. I was charmed by the presence of Mr. Pirzada's rotund elegance, and flattered by the faint theatricality of his attentions, yet

---

[4]a brimless felt hat often worn by Muslims.

unsettled by the superb ease of his gestures, which made me feel, for an instant, like a stranger in my own home. It had become our ritual, and for several weeks, before we grew more comfortable with one another, it was the only time he spoke to me directly. I had no response, offered no comment, betrayed no visible reaction to the steady stream of honey-filled lozenges, the raspberry truffles, the slender rolls of sour pastilles.[5] I could not even thank him, for once, when I did, for an especially spectacular peppermint lollipop wrapped in a spray of purple cellophane, he had demanded, "What is this thank-you? The lady at the bank thanks me, the cashier at the shop thanks me, the librarian thanks me when I return an overdue book, the overseas operator thanks me as she tries to connect me to Dacca and fails. If I am buried in this country I will be thanked, no doubt, at my funeral."

It was inappropriate, in my opinion, to consume the candy Mr. Pirzada gave me in a casual manner. I coveted each evening's treasure as I would a jewel, or a coin from a buried kingdom, and I would place it in a small keepsake box made of carved sandalwood beside my bed, in which, long ago in India, my father's mother used to store the ground areca nuts[6] she ate after her morning bath. It was my only memento of a grandmother I had never known, and until Mr. Pirzada came to our lives I could find nothing to put inside it. Every so often before brushing my teeth and laying out my clothes for school the next day, I opened the lid of the box and ate one of his treats.

That night, like every night, we did not eat at the dining table, because it did not provide an unobstructed view of the television set. Instead we huddled around the coffee table, without conversing, our plates perched on the edges of our knees. From the kitchen my mother brought forth the succession of dishes: lentils with fried onions, green beans with coconut, fish cooked with raisins in a yogurt sauce. I followed with the water glasses, and the plate of lemon wedges, and the chili peppers, purchased on monthly trips to Chinatown and stored by the pound in the freezer, which they liked to snap open and crush into their food.

Before eating Mr. Pirzada always did a curious thing. He took out a plain silver watch without a band, which he kept in his breast pocket, held it briefly to one of his tufted ears, and wound it with three swift flicks of his thumb and forefinger. Unlike the watch on his wrist, the pocket watch, he had explained to me, was set to the local time in Dacca, eleven hours ahead. For the duration of the meal the watch rested on his folded paper napkin on the coffee table. He never seemed to consult it.

Now that I had learned Mr. Pirzada was not an Indian, I began to study him with extra care, to try to figure out what made him different. I decided that the pocket watch was one of those things. When I saw it that night, as he wound it and arranged it on the coffee table, an uneasiness possessed me; life, I realized, was being lived in Dacca first. I imagined Mr. Pirzada's daughters rising from sleep, tying ribbons in their hair, anticipating breakfast, preparing for school. Our meals, our actions, were only a shadow of what had already happened there, a lagging ghost of where Mr. Pirzada really belonged.

---

[5]types of candies. [6]a palm nut believed to promote good health.

30   At six-thirty, which was when the national news began, my father raised
the volume and adjusted the antennas. Usually I occupied myself with a book,
but that night my father insisted that I pay attention. On the screen I saw tanks
rolling through dusty streets, and fallen buildings, and forests of unfamiliar trees
into which East Pakistani refugees had fled, seeking safety over the Indian
border. I saw boats with fan-shaped sails floating on wide coffee-colored rivers,
a barricaded university, newspaper offices burnt to the ground. I turned to look
at Mr. Pirzada; the images flashed in miniature across his eyes. As he watched
he had an immovable expression on his face, composed but alert, as if someone
were giving him directions to an unknown destination.

During the commercial my mother went to the kitchen to get more rice,
and my father and Mr. Pirzada deplored the policies of a general named
Yahyah Khan.[7] They discussed intrigues I did not know, a catastrophe
I could not comprehend. "See, children your age, what they do to survive,"
my father said as he served me another piece of fish. But I could no longer
eat. I could only steal glances at Mr. Pirzada, sitting beside me in his olive
green jacket, calmly creating a well in his rice to make room for a second
helping of lentils. He was not my notion of a man burdened by such grave
concerns. I wondered if the reason he was always so smartly dressed was in
preparation to endure with dignity whatever news assailed him, perhaps
even to attend a funeral at a moment's notice. I wondered, too, what would
happen if suddenly his seven daughters were to appear on television, smiling
and waving and blowing kisses to Mr. Pirzada from a balcony. I imagined
how relieved he would be. But this never happened.

That night when I placed the plastic egg filled with cinnamon hearts
in the box beside my bed, I did not feel the ceremonious satisfaction I normally did. I tried not to think about Mr. Pirzada, in his lime-scented overcoat, connected to the unruly, sweltering world we had viewed a few hours
ago in our bright, carpeted living room. And yet for several moments that
was all I could think about. My stomach tightened as I worried whether his
wife and seven daughters were now members of the drifting, clamoring
crowd that had flashed at intervals on the screen. In an effort to banish the
image I looked around my room, at the yellow canopied bed with matching
flounced curtains, at framed class pictures mounted on white and violet
papered walls, at the penciled inscriptions by the closet door where my
father recorded my height on each of my birthdays. But the more I tried to
distract myself, the more I began to convince myself that Mr. Pirzada's
family was in all likelihood dead. Eventually I took a square of white chocolate out of the box, and unwrapped it, and then I did something I had never
done before. I put the chocolate in my mouth, letting it soften until the last
possible moment, and then as I chewed it slowly, I prayed that Mr. Pirzada's
family was safe and sound. I had never prayed for anything before, had
never been taught or told to, but I decided, given the circumstances, that
it was something I should do. That night when I went to the bathroom I
only pretended to brush my teeth, for I feared that I would somehow rinse

[7]President of Pakistan from 1969 to 1971, noted for his ruthlessness.

the prayer out as well. I wet the brush and rearranged the tube of paste to prevent my parents from asking any questions, and fell asleep with sugar on my tongue.

No one at school talked about the war followed so faithfully in my living room. We continued to study the American Revolution, and learned about the injustices of taxation without representation, and memorized passages from the Declaration of Independence. During recess the boys would divide in two groups, chasing each other wildly around the swings and see-saws, Redcoats[8] against the colonies. In the classroom our teacher, Mrs. Kenyon, pointed frequently to a map that emerged like a movie screen from the top of the chalkboard, charting the route of the *Mayflower*,[9] or showing us the location of the Liberty Bell.[10] Each week two members of the class gave a report on a particular aspect of the Revolution, and so one day I was sent to the school library with my friend Dora to learn about the surrender at Yorktown.[11] Mrs. Kenyon handed us a slip of paper with the names of three books to look up in the card catalogue. We found them right away, and sat down at a low round table to read and take notes. But I could not concentrate. I returned to the blond-wood shelves, to a section I had noticed labeled "Asia." I saw books about China, India, Indonesia, Korea. Eventually I found a book titled *Pakistan: A Land and its People*. I sat on a footstool and opened the book. The laminated jacket crackled in my grip. I began turning the pages, filled with photos of rivers and rice fields and men in military uniforms. There was a chapter about Dacca, and I began to read about its rainfall, and its jute production. I was studying a population chart when Dora appeared in the aisle.

"What are you doing back here? Mrs. Kenyon's in the library. She came to check up on us."

I slammed the book shut, too loudly. Mrs. Kenyon emerged, the aroma of her perfume filling up the tiny aisle, and lifted the book by the tip of its spine as if it were a hair clinging to my sweater. She glanced at the cover, then at me.

"Is this book a part of your report, Lilia?"

"No, Mrs. Kenyon."

"Then I see no reason to consult it," she said, replacing it in the slim gap on the shelf. "Do you?"

As weeks passed it grew more and more rare to see any footage from Dacca on the news. The report came after the first set of commercials, sometimes the second. The press had been censored, removed, restricted, rerouted. Some days, many days, only a death toll was announced, prefaced by a reiteration of the

---

[8]British soldiers. [9]Ship that carried pilgrims from England to Massachusetts in 1620.
[10]Located in Philadelphia, it was, according to legend, rung in 1776, calling citizens to hear a reading of the Declaration of Independence. [11]A town in Virginia where, in 1780, the combined French and American forces defeated the British.

general situation. More poets were executed, more villages set ablaze. In spite of it all, night after night, my parents and Mr. Pirzada enjoyed long, leisurely meals. After the television was shut off, and the dishes washed and dried, they joked, and told stories, and dipped biscuits in their tea. When they tired of discussing political matters they discussed, instead, the progress of Mr. Pirzada's book about the deciduous trees of New England, and my father's nomination for tenure, and the peculiar eating habits of my mother's American coworkers at the bank. Eventually I was sent upstairs to do my homework, but through the carpet I heard them as they drank more tea, and listened to cassettes of Kishore Kumar,[12] and played Scrabble on the coffee table, laughing and arguing long into the night about the spellings of English words. I wanted to join them, wanted, above all, to console Mr. Pirzada somehow. But apart from eating a piece of candy for the sake of his family and praying for their safety, there was nothing I could do. They played Scrabble until the eleven o'clock news, and then, sometime around midnight, Mr. Pirzada walked back to his dormitory. For this reason I never saw him leave, but each night as I drifted off to sleep I would hear them, anticipating the birth of a nation on the other side of the world.

40   One day in October Mr. Pirzada asked upon arrival, "What are these large orange vegetables on people's doorsteps? A type of squash?"

"Pumpkins," my mother replied. "Lilia, remind me to pick one up at the supermarket."

"And the purpose? It indicates what?"

"You make a jack-o'-lantern," I said, grinning ferociously. "Like this. To scare people away."

"I see," Mr. Pirzada said, grinning back. "Very useful."

45   The next day my mother bought a ten-pound pumpkin, fat and round, and placed it on the dining table. Before supper, while my father and Mr. Pirzada were watching the local news, she told me to decorate it with markers, but I wanted to carve it properly like others I had noticed in the neighborhood.

"Yes, let's carve it," Mr. Pirzada agreed, and rose from the sofa. "Hang the news tonight." Asking no questions, he walked into the kitchen, opened a drawer, and returned, bearing a long serrated knife. He glanced at me for approval. "Shall I?"

I nodded. For the first time we all gathered around the dining table, my mother, my father, Mr. Pirzada, and I. While the television aired unattended we covered the tabletop with newspapers. Mr. Pirzada draped his jacket over the chair behind him, removed a pair of opal cuff links, and rolled up the starched sleeves of his shirt.

"First go around the top, like this," I instructed, demonstrating with my index finger.

He made an initial incision and drew the knife around. When he had come full circle he lifted the cap by the stem; it loosened effortlessly, and Mr. Pirzada leaned over the pumpkin for a moment to inspect and inhale its

[12]Popular Indian singer of the 1970s.

contents. My mother gave him a long metal spoon with which he gutted the interior until the last bits of string and seeds were gone. My father, meanwhile, separated the seeds from the pulp and set them out to dry on a cookie sheet, so that we could roast them later on. I drew two triangles against the ridged surface for the eyes, which Mr. Pirzada dutifully carved, and crescents for eyebrows, and another triangle for the nose. The mouth was all that remained, and the teeth posed a challenge. I hesitated.

50 "Smile or frown?" I asked.

"You choose," Mr. Pirzada said.

As a compromise I drew a kind of grimace, straight across, neither mournful nor friendly. Mr. Pirzada began carving, without the least bit of intimidation, as if he had been carving jack-o'-lanterns his whole life. He had nearly finished when the national news began. The reporter mentioned Dacca, and we all turned to listen: An Indian official announced that unless the world helped to relieve the burden of East Pakistani refugees, India would have to go to war against Pakistan. The reporter's face dripped with sweat as he relayed the information. He did not wear a tie or a jacket, dressed instead as if he himself were about to take part in the battle. He shielded his scorched face as he hollered things to the cameraman. The knife slipped from Mr. Pirzada's hand and made a gash dipping toward the base of the pumpkin.

"Please forgive me." He raised a hand to one side of his face, as if someone had slapped him there. "I am—it is terrible. I will buy another. We will try again."

"Not at all, not at all," my father said. He took the knife from Mr. Pirzada, and carved around the gash, evening it out, dispensing altogether with the teeth I had drawn. What resulted was a disproportionately large hole the size of a lemon, so that our jack-o'-lantern wore an expression of placid astonishment, the eyebrows no longer fierce, floating in frozen surprise above a vacant, geometric gaze.

55 For Halloween I was a witch. Dora, my trick-or-treating partner, was a witch too. We wore black capes fashioned from dyed pillowcases and conical hats with wide cardboard brims. We shaded our faces green with a broken eye shadow that belonged to Dora's mother, and my mother gave us two burlap sacks that had once contained basmati rice, for collecting candy. That year our parents decided that we were old enough to roam the neighborhood unattended. Our plan was to walk from my house to Dora's, from where I was to call to say I had arrived safely, and then Dora's mother would drive me home. My father equipped us with flashlights, and I had to wear my watch and synchronize it with his. We were to return no later than nine o'clock.

When Mr. Pirzada arrived that evening he presented me with a box of chocolate-covered mints.

"In here," I told him, and opened up the burlap sack. "Trick or treat!"

"I understand that you don't really need my contribution this evening," he said, depositing the box. He gazed at my green face, and the hat secured by a string under my chin. Gingerly he lifted the hem of the cape, under which I was wearing a sweater and a zipped fleece jacket. "Will you be warm enough?"

I nodded, causing the hat to tip to one side.

60   He set it right. "Perhaps it is best to stand still."

The bottom of our staircase was lined with baskets of miniature candy, and when Mr. Pirzada removed his shoes he did not place them there as he normally did, but inside the closet instead. He began to unbutton his coat, and I waited to take it from him, but Dora called me from the bathroom to say that she needed my help drawing a mole on her chin. When we were finally ready my mother took a picture of us in front of the fireplace, and then I opened the front door to leave. Mr. Pirzada and my father, who had not gone into the living room yet, hovered in the foyer. Outside it was already dark. The air smelled of wet leaves, and our carved jack-o'-lantern flickered impressively against the shrubbery by the door. In the distance came the sounds of scampering feet, and the howls of the older boys who wore no costume at all other than a rubber mask, and the rustling apparel of the youngest children, some so young that they were carried from door to door in the arms of their parents.

"Don't go into any of the houses you don't know," my father warned.

Mr. Pirzada knit his brows together. "Is there any danger?"

"No, no," my mother assured him. "All the children will be out. It's a tradition."

65   "Perhaps I should accompany them?" Mr. Pirzada suggested. He looked suddenly tired and small, standing there in his splayed, stockinged feet, and his eyes contained a panic I had never seen before. In spite of the cold I began to sweat inside my pillowcase.

"Really, Mr. Pirzada," my mother said, "Lilia will be perfectly safe with her friend."

"But if it rains? If they lose their way?"

"Don't worry," I said. It was the first time I had uttered those words to Mr. Pirzada, two simple words I had tried but failed to tell him for weeks, had said only in my prayers. It shamed me now that I had said them for my own sake.

He placed one of his stocky fingers on my cheek, then pressed it to the back of his own hand, leaving a faint green smear. "If the lady insists," he conceded, and offered a small bow.

70   We left, stumbling slightly in our black pointy thrift-store shoes, and when we turned at the end of the driveway to wave good-bye, Mr. Pirzada was standing in the frame of the doorway, a short figure between my parents, waving back.

"Why did that man want to come with us?" Dora asked.

"His daughters are missing." As soon as I said it, I wished I had not. I felt that my saying it made it true, that Mr. Pirzada's daughters really were missing, and that he would never see them again.

"You mean they were kidnapped?" Dora continued. "From a park or something?"

"I didn't mean they were missing. I meant, he misses them. They live in a different country, and he hasn't seen them in a while, that's all."

75   We went from house to house, walking along pathways and pressing doorbells. Some people had switched off all their lights for effect, or strung rubber bats in their windows. At the McIntyres' a coffin was placed in front of the door, and Mr. McIntyre rose from it in silence, his face covered with chalk, and deposited a fistful of candy corns into our sacks. Several people told me that they had never seen an Indian witch before. Others performed the transaction without comment. As we paved our way with the parallel beams of our flashlights we saw eggs cracked in the middle of the road, and cars covered with shaving cream, and toilet paper garlanding the branches of trees. By the time we reached Dora's house our hands were chapped from carrying our bulging burlap bags, and our feet were sore and swollen. Her mother gave us bandages for our blisters and served us warm cider and caramel popcorn. She reminded me to call my parents to tell them I had arrived safely, and when I did I could hear the television in the background. My mother did not seem particularly relieved to hear from me. When I replaced the phone on the receiver it occurred to me that the television wasn't on at Dora's house at all. Her father was lying on the couch, reading a magazine, with a glass of wine on the coffee table, and there was saxophone music playing on the stereo.

After Dora and I had sorted through our plunder, and counted and sampled and traded until we were satisfied, her mother drove me back to my house. I thanked her for the ride, and she waited in the driveway until I made it to the door. In the glare of her headlights I saw that our pumpkin had been shattered, its thick shell strewn in chunks across the grass. I felt the sting of tears in my eyes, and a sudden pain in my throat, as if it had been stuffed with the sharp tiny pebbles that crunched with each step under my aching feet. I opened the door, expecting the three of them to be standing in the foyer, waiting to receive me, and to grieve for our ruined pumpkin, but there was no one. In the living room Mr. Pirzada, my father, and mother were sitting side by side on the sofa. The television was turned off, and Mr. Pirzada had his head in his hands.

What they heard that evening, and for many evenings after that, was that India and Pakistan were drawing closer and closer to war. Troops from both sides lined the border, and Dacca was insisting on nothing short of independence. The war was to be waged on East Pakistani soil. The United States was siding with West Pakistan, the Soviet Union with India and what was soon to be Bangladesh. War was declared officially on December 4, and twelve days later, the Pakistani army, weakened by having to fight three thousand miles from their source of supplies, surrendered in Dacca. All of these facts I know only now, for they are available to me in any history book, in any library. But then it remained, for the most part, a remote mystery with haphazard clues. What I remember during those twelve days of the war was that my father no longer asked me to watch the news with them, and that Mr. Pirzada stopped bringing me candy, and that my mother refused to serve anything other than boiled eggs with rice for dinner. I remember some nights helping my mother spread a sheet and blankets on the couch so that Mr. Pirzada could sleep there, and high-pitched voices hollering in the middle of the night when my parents called our relatives in Calcutta to learn more details about the situation. Most of all I remember the three of them operating during that time as if they were a single person, sharing a single meal, a single body, a single silence, and a single fear.

In January, Mr. Pirzada flew back to his three-story home in Dacca, to discover what was left of it. We did not see much of him in those final weeks of the year; he was busy finishing his manuscript, and we went to Philadelphia to spend Christmas with friends of my parents. Just as I have no memory of his first visit, I have no memory of his last. My father drove him to the airport one afternoon while I was at school. For a long time we did not hear from him. Our evenings went on as usual, with dinners in front of the news. The only difference was that Mr. Pirzada and his extra watch were not there to accompany us. According to reports Dacca was repairing itself slowly, with a newly formed parliamentary government. The new leader, Sheikh Mujib Rahman,[13] recently released from prison, asked countries for building materials to replace more than one million houses that had been destroyed in the war. Countless refugees returned from India, greeted, we learned, by unemployment and the threat of famine. Every now and then I studied the map above my father's desk and pictured Mr. Pirzada on that small patch of yellow, perspiring heavily, I imagined, in one of his suits, searching for his family. Of course, the map was outdated by then.

Finally, several months later, we received a card from Mr. Pirzada commemorating the Muslim New Year, along with a short letter. He was reunited, he wrote, with his wife and children. All were well, having survived the events of the past year at an estate belonging to his wife's grandparents in the mountains of Shillong.[14] His seven daughters were a bit taller, he wrote, but otherwise they were the same, and he still could not keep their names in order. At the end of the letter he thanked us for our hospitality, adding that although he now understood the meaning of the words "thank you" they still were not adequate to express his gratitude. To celebrate the good news my mother prepared a special dinner that evening, and when we sat down to eat at the coffee table we toasted our water glasses, but I did not feel like celebrating. Though I had not seen him for months, it was only then that I felt Mr. Pirzada's absence. It was only then, raising my water glass in his name, that I knew what it meant to miss someone who was so many miles and hours away, just as he had missed his wife and daughters for so many months. He had no reason to return to us, and my parents predicted, correctly, that we would never see him again. Since January, each night before bed, I had continued to eat, for the sake of Mr. Pirzada's family, a piece of candy I had saved from Halloween. That night there was no need to. Eventually, I threw them away.

(1999)

---

[13]One of the founders and the first president of Bangladesh, he was assassinated in 1975.
[14]An isolated city in the mountains of northeast India.

Yasuko Thanh   (b. 1971)

Yasuko Thanh is a graduate student in the University of Victoria's creative writing program. She began writing stories and poetry during her teens and became interested in those writers who chose historical subjects. Even though she grew up in Victoria, she did not learn about D'Arcy Island, which, from 1891 to 1924, served as a leper colony where all but one of the members were Chinese. "While I was working on the story, I often walked alone on the beach in Victoria and found myself experiencing some of the loneliness these people felt," says Thanh Although the story is permeated with a general tone of sadness, it also celebrates what the author has termed "a resilience of spirit. They cared for each other and tried to make real homes for themselves on the island." The main conflicts of the story focus on separation: the Chinese immigrants from their homeland and from the places on Vancouver Island where they worked, the Chinese from the English for whom they worked, and from each other because of mutual hostilities.

FLOATING LIKE THE DEAD

Cleaning his ear with a long stalk of grass, Ah Sing filled his wood stove with kindling. Alder leaves were fluttering in the trees, displaying their yellow undersides, which meant rain. Ah Sing shivered but did not light the fire; instead, he put a rough wool jacket over his cotton shirt. His room had no hooks but all his clothing was tidily folded and stacked on the wooden stool in the corner by the door. On top of the clothes he laid a few bone-white sticks. Sun-bleached, lighter than the pine branches he had originally whittled down for his kite, the driftwood would make a good frame. He sneezed and shivered again. He had lost his upper incisor yesterday.

The nerves of Ah Sing's arms and legs had grown hard as jade; he was turning into a mountain, solidifying. Even his face was like a palace statue. Smooth. Hairless. Varnished-looking. He had lost his eyelashes and three-quarters of his eyebrows; and lately, his ulcerated feet left tracks of blood on the wood floor. But he refused to wear the government-issue overshoes. His extremities felt no heat, no cold, no pain, anyway. In the next life he would be a mountain, the mountain he was now turning into, eternal and hard.

He had wept at the official diagnosis of leprosy.[1]

"They sick but I not," Ah Sing would say in English to the doctors who accompanied the steamer *Alert* to the island and took flakes of skin from the backs of his hands. (Speaking English was masonry work, the words like bricks laid by hands; he spoke Cantonese with the other men on the colony, and the words flowed easily then, even when they had nothing to say.) His

---

[1] a communicable bacterial disease which causes severe lesions on the skin, numbness to the limbs, and stiffness to the muscles. Until effective cures were developed in the 20th century, people suffering from the disease were placed in colonies isolated from the general population.

lost fingers, he explained to the doctors, "Coal mine in Nanaimo. Frostbite." He had difficulty pronouncing the word and it came out sounding like "flossed bite." Grunting once or twice, he would pry an oyster off a stone with his remaining fingers and hold it up.

5   "You send away Ah Sing," he always said to the visiting doctors, "back to China."

Today Ah Sing had fallen asleep on the beach next to his half-eaten lunch of sea urchins.[2] Awoken by the sound of birds near his head, he had opened his eyes and was startled to see four black cormorants[3] flying away. They reminded him of something: the cormorants he had felt sorry for when he was six years old and had laughed at by the age of nine, black birds circling the ancient uplifted seabeds in Chongwu Bay, catching fish they could taste but never swallow because of the white choke collars around their necks.

Three men left on D'Arcy Island now. They lived in the main building. Four cubicles side by side, each with its own door that opened onto a verandah facing Cordova Bay.[4] Ge Shou hadn't been right in the head since a tree fell on him, and he spent his nights in the woods singing. Gold Tooth, who had never told Ah Sing his real name, cried all day and then sat at the edge of the forest, dulled and deadened, refusing to move. He had a cough that possessed him like a malevolent spirit, wracking his body until he spat blood. He was the newest resident.

Gold Tooth had arrived at the colony three years ago with his bowler hat and a Swiss pocket watch on a chain. Slipping on patches of seagrass in leather shoes, over barnacle-covered stones still wet from the tide, refusing any attempts at help from the government official from Victoria. Ah Sing had laughed at his vanity, but the watch—the watch—was as round as an eye. He stared at it until he felt like he was staring into a thousand tiny suns.

When they had the energy, Ah Sing and Ge Shou said they would murder the filthy thief while he slept. But the daily chores sapped their passion, the harvesting of clams and mussels, the chopping of firewood, the collection of rainwater from below the eaves or in the summer from the bog. Most days, when Ah Sing had finished, he would sit on the boulders that ringed the bay and watch the waves, pondering Buddha's question: *How does one stop a drop of water from ever drying out?*

10   Now, in his room, Ah Sing picked up his Buck knife[5] and eyed the driftwood. He was searching for the most evenly balanced of sticks. He would carve the exact spaces needed to neatly wedge two smaller sticks into either side. He would wrap the joints with sewing thread. He would cut a tail to look like phoenix wings, or find some cormorant feathers on the beach to stand in their place.

As curly shavings collected around his feet, he remembered how, as a child, he had believed the most ornate kites could talk to the spirits. His thoughts were interrupted by the sound of something heavy being dragged across a wooden floor. A sob. Another. He dropped his knife.

[2]small edible marine animals covered with sharp protective spines [3]a large, black, long-necked sea bird which, in China, is trained to catch fish [4]A bay just north of Victoria off the east coast of Vancouver Island [5]A folding knife often used by sportsmen.

Gold Tooth was on the verandah, dappled light sifting through the fir trees and falling in shadows across his back. It was hard to tell which were shadows and which were stains, for Ah Sing could not remember when Gold Tooth had last taken off the silk suit he wore. Gold Tooth's face was flushed with terror and his eyes darted like birds in the trees, afraid of being caught.

"Take it easy. What are you doing with your bed?"

Gold Tooth shook off Ah Sing's hand like a dog shakes off water. He heaved the cot against the doorframe, where it got stuck. "I can't breathe," he said. "I can't breathe in there. The walls. They'll try to crush me if, if I go to sleep." He yanked. He stumbled backward.

"Do you want me to hold up the walls while you pull your bed outside?"

Gold Tooth stopped.

Ah Sing squeezed over the straw mattress and into the room. Half-eaten plates of food had been scattered from one side to the other by raccoons. The air smelled like yeast.

Ah Sing, his legs shoulder-width apart, spread his arms wide against the two walls and held them with his clawed hands so they wouldn't crush Gold Tooth, who unhinged the bed from the doorway and wrestled it outside.

On the verandah, Gold Tooth nodded toward the forest. He motioned to Ah Sing. "Pick up that end," he said.

The two men carried the wooden bed with the straw mattress past roaming chickens and beyond the storage shed with the rice, sugar, flour, meal, gardening tools, and coffins. They carried the bed beyond the vegetable garden. Past three graves, each marked with a pile of stones—the resting places of the men who had arrived with Ah Sing when the provincial government had left them on this island four years ago with a load of construction supplies. They carried it past the bog and into the forest. Ge Shou followed them, chattering.

"Do you have any pigs' feet for me?" Ge Shou asked. Ah Sing shook his head.

"Can we fly your kite?"

"When it's ready, I promise."

"Washing Matilda, washing Matilda," Ge Shou sang, "who'll come a-washing Matilda with me?" He stopped and stretched his arms above his head. "Are you going swimming tonight, Sing, you going swimming in the ocean?"

"No, not tonight."

"Swimming, swimming." Ge Shou made breaststroke motions. "Swimming in the ocean. I feel happy. Washing Matilda, you'll come a-washing Matilda with me?"

Ah Sing and Gold Tooth set the bed down in a clearing among the ferns and salal, where the ground was soft with pine needles. Through the trees they could see the ditch system that ran from the bog to the garden, where they grew lettuce, potatoes, carrots, and onions; Ge Shou playing among the vegetables. Gold Tooth shuddered onto his bed and immediately rolled onto his side as if in a deep sleep.

Ah Sing shook his shoulder.

"Go away."

30   After sitting near Gold Tooth for a time, Ah Sing came to a decision. He shuffled past the crops, spoiled before men with waning appetites had been able to eat them, and the pigs rooting in the waste. He nodded to Ge Shou, who sat among the pigs. He passed the site where they would soon start an orchard.

Back in his cabin, Ah Sing filled his shoulder basket with a Hudson's Bay blanket, a cast-iron kettle, a wok, a dead grouse, a handful of onions, some mint leaves, a cupful of cooking oil in a canning jar, and some government-issue opium. Returning to Gold Tooth, he touched his shoulder again. Gold Tooth grunted.

Ah Sing opened the blanket over him; then he placed stones in a circle on the ground around some kindling and lit a fire with the wooden matches in his pocket. He emptied his shoulder basket, picked up the kettle, and went to the woodshed, filling his shoulder basket again. The load weighed him down. He trod to the bog, sinking deep into the mud. He dipped his kettle, filling it with brown water. When he came back, neither of the men spoke, but Ah Sing didn't mind. He added more branches to the fire and set the kettle upon it.

A few minutes later, Gold Tooth said, "Why do you talk to me?"

Ah Sing shrugged. Before the disease had made his threats to beat up the other men laughable, Gold Tooth had hoarded the best rations, stashing second barrels of salt pork in his cubicle while the others looked on with mask-like eyes. But Ah Sing, at fifty-two, had himself hit a woman; had fondled the flesh of his brother's wife; had ignored the unemployed after the smelters closed; had beaten a man when he was drunk while onlookers cheered. He sat cross-legged by the fire, poking the embers with a stick. He felt feverish, strange. Far away through the trees, he could hear Ge Shou singing.

35   Ah Sing poured the oil into the wok and dried the canning jar with the hem of his shirt. He put two stalks of mint inside it and some of the opium. The mint grew wild near the bog. Ah Sing usually hung it from his cabin's ceiling. He poured the boiling water into the canning jar. He wrapped a green maple leaf around it and passed the jar to Gold Tooth, but Gold Tooth pushed it away.

Ah Sing put the jar on the ground. The steam rose and scented the air with mint. He fussed over the flames, moving the kettle to make room for the wok. He busied himself with the onions and the grouse he had killed just that morning with his shotgun until the aroma rose into the air, overpowering the mint.

"I used to be a cook, you know," Ah Sing said. "I worked for Mr. and Mrs. Edward Price in Victoria."

"Shit work."

Ah Sing moved coals and added more kindling to adjust the heat. He rotated the wok and stirred its contents with a stick, testing the mixture frequently and inhaling its scent with his eyes closed.

Gold Tooth turned to him and snorted. "Look down. Your hand."

"Oh," Ah Sing said. "I've burned myself."

A patch of flesh two inches wide was stuck to the outside of the wok.

"No one will notice. Look at your face. Have you looked in a mirror lately?"

When the food was ready, Ah Sing placed the wok down between them. Gold Tooth eyed the food with a strange appetite Ah Sing had not seen in weeks. Ah Sing chewed in silence, watching Gold Tooth eat; his clawed fingers, scooping the mixture into his mouth, were like fingers made of tree bark or elephant's hooves—strange but beautiful.

"It gets easier," Ah Sing said.

"I'm not a leper."

"No one wants to believe they are. I'll tell you something. I'm going to escape. I've got to go back to China. To my son and wife."

Gold Tooth gave a disgusted grunt. "Has anyone escaped before?"

Ah Sing didn't answer. He told Gold Tooth he'd heard that two lepers had been shipped in a crate by the CPR as far west as Saskatchewan, and he thought they'd been deported. "My son," Ah Sing said, changing the subject, "my son would be eighteen years old now. He was five the last time I saw him. It would be good if he could come to Gold Mountain.[6] He would find work."

They sat looking at each other while dusk fell. Neither one said a word. Ah Sing cracked open grouse bones and sucked out the marrow. Gold Tooth lay on his back and smoked tobacco from the supply ship. The fire had turned to coals and the coals had turned ashy before Gold Tooth spoke.

"I used to get all the girls. Best one's name was Zao.[7] I called her 'Zao,' chirp, because of the sound she made when we had sex. On hot nights she ran ice cubes up and down my spine, and on cold nights she tickled me with cotton balls. When I couldn't sleep, she massaged my feet while humming Strauss.[8] She polished my shoes and every morning brought me my gambling spreadsheets. The way she pencilled in her eyebrows. I'm going to give you a' piece of advice. Only hit a woman when she needs it, and only with an open hand. You got to keep them in their place because they want it. You have to answer their questions for them, that's love."

"Did she turn you in?" Ah Sing asked.

"No!" Then after a moment he said, "They raided the Kwong Wo & Company Store; we were in the back, gambling."

It was pitch-black now. Ah Sing drew a stick through the ashes. The bark caught an ember and he blew at the small flame. He threw on more kindling until the wood crackled. The only light came from the small campfire; its shadows highlighted the heavy ridges of Gold Tooth's overgrown brow.

"When I was a kid I found this bottle with a note inside," Gold Tooth continued. "It'd washed up from Taiwan," he said. "Funny thing is, I don't remember what the letter said. It was a wide, fat bottle, like a medicine bottle.

---

[6]A 19th century term for British Columbia, used by Chinese who believed that they would find riches if they came to Canada [7]Morning, in Mandarin [8]A 19th century Austrian composer famous for his waltzes.

It was dull, scratched up by the rocks. I remember grabbing it and trying to open it while the older boys were gambling by the fishboats, and then it started to rain and I ran under an overturned dory. I tried to untwist the lid but it was rusted closed. Then I tried to get it off with a broken clam. I ended up smashing the neck off. I remember the bottle, but not the message. Strange, huh?"

Ah Sing drew his knees up to his chest. "Memory is a funny thing."

"I wonder what it said. Was it a love letter from some guy? Who knows? I don't remember."

Ah Sing didn't answer.

"I remember lots of other things. Swimming in the Zhu Jiang River. Ducks and geese. I ate lily roots. I loved water chestnuts and dates. Have you been to the hills of Guangxi? Limestone towers. I would visit my uncle and play in the fish ponds."

60   Gold Tooth turned on his side, away from Ah Sing, and curled up in the fetal position. Ah Sing's mother had turned on her side and died facing the wall. She had first lain in bed talking about her childhood, but when, the sun rose, she had turned inward and fallen silent.

"In Canton the laundry waved like flags. We threw cats into the fetid canals. I had no parents. Stole food from the seething mass living on boats along the waterfront. Ran through the alleys making cutthroat signs at people and they feared me. I grew up to be a Tong,[9] never did any grunt work. Laundry, houseboy, gardener. Never did any of that. I'm in extortion."

An hour or so later, Gold Tooth started to cry, softly, under his breath. He mumbled something inaudible.

"What?"

"Will you send my bones back to China?"

65   Ah Sing sat up.

"You know the worst thing about it?"

"What?"

"I never knew her real name."

"Who?"

70   "First it was the cotton balls, I couldn't feel them. Then I couldn't feel the suit against my skin. This is my best suit. My best suit."

"I called her Zao," he said. He started sobbing.

Ah Sing dozed in the forest to the sound of Gold Tooth's laboured breathing. The stretches between his exhalations grew longer, as if each breath was becoming too precious to release. Another and another. He clutched the life within him and refused to unleash it, greedily holding the air for ten seconds at a time, fifteen, twenty.

Ah Sing dreamed a man with a roomful of rice was trying to make him swallow it all, and awoke choking. Gold Tooth's eyes appeared fixed on an immature bald eagle circling overhead, and in the dawn light he almost looked alive. Ah Sing rubbed his clawed hands vigorously over his own

[9]A Chinese society involved in prostitution and other criminal activities.

cheeks. He closed Gold Tooth's eyelids and touched the man's chest. He felt along the body, found the Swiss pocket watch and slipped it into his own pocket. An object valuable enough to buy passage off the island, maybe even to pay the deportation costs back to China. Ah Sing couldn't see clearly and stumbled toward the ocean, moving branches away from his face through the brush.

He ran to the beach, to the emergency flag on the hill.

75 The Victoria Tug Company steamer *Alert* delivered quarterly supplies: tea, dried fish, axes, razors, handkerchiefs, and, in the last load, a looking glass. It was surprising to see the tug so soon; often they would raise the flag and no one would show up for weeks.

Ah Sing had fought to bury Gold Tooth in his silk suit, but Ge Shou had slipped away with the jacket. So when the boat came, Ah Sing was digging alone, near the bog, past the vegetable garden where the ground was soft, and far enough away from Ah Sing's cabin that even a spirit as restless as Gold Tooth's couldn't haunt him.

As the steamer cut through the chop, Ah Sing flung a last shovel of soil onto the coffin. Then, brushing his hands together, he scrambled down the gravelled slope to the shore, pebbles tumbling away from the edges of his footsteps. He watched as a dory was lowered from the boat, loaded with supplies, and rowed toward the shore.

Ah Sing grabbed hold of the wooden dory with two men aboard, helping to pull it onto the beach. A man with a red moustache that hid his upper lip got out of it with the doctor.

The doctor straightened his back.

80 "Good, sir. Still strong, see?" Ah Sing said, lifting a barrel from the bottom of the boat.

Ah Sing recounted what had happened the night before. The doctor pulled a bag from the dory and withdrew a ledger of dates, names, and other notes. He looked down his spectacles. "The one you call . . . Go Chou?"

"No, sir."

"Fong Wah Yuen."

Ah Sing nodded.

85 The doctor wrote something on his ledger and turned toward the main building. When he was halfway up the slope, Ah Sing tilted his head toward a termite-filigreed log to indicate he wished a word with the other man, whom the doctor had introduced as a reporter. The man's pants were cinched high upon his waist. He took two steps toward the log and stood, smoothing his hands over his thighs.

Ah Sing stepped over to the log and sat down. His mouth was dry. The man was smiling, but his gaze jumped from Ah Sing to a spot beyond his head, then back to Ah Sing, then to the doctor stumbling up the gravel slope. The man did not sit.

Ah Sing cleared his throat. "I favour you . . . no, me . . . no, you favour me." The disease in his larynx made his voice no more than a loud whisper.

"I, I have something." He stood up and pulled the Swiss watch from his pocket, where he had been clutching it so tightly that it was slick with sweat. He wiped it against the leg of his pants. He dangled it between them, letting it catch the sun.

"This is for you," Ah Sing said.

"Look at that." The man scratched his head and smiled.

90 "Nice, yes?"

The man nodded. "This is a nice island," he said, rubbing the back of his neck. He looked from the boulders that ringed one side of the bay to the mud flats on the other. He glanced at the doctor, who was talking to Ge Shou at the main building. "I hear you men hunt, and fish, too."

"You take."

"No." The man's moustache brushed his bottom lip when he smiled. "I don't think I should."

"No," Ah Sing nodded his head. "For you."

95 The man looked down at the watch.

"But is gift."

The man fingered his eyebrows.

"Gift," Ah Sing repeated. "A gift for you. Your wife?"

On the verandah of the cabin, Ge Shou danced, circling the doctor, his long black ponytail bouncing on his back.

100 A sudden gust of wind blew the reporter's hat off his head. It rolled a few feet, snagged on a log, then rolled again with the next gust. The man chased it but Ah Sing bounded ahead, stopping the hat with his bare foot. Ah Sing dusted off the sand and shards of clamshell. He held the hat toward the man.

"Oh. Well, then." The man inched his fingertips forward. "Thank you."

The man took his hat between his thumb and forefinger and walked to the dory. Leaning into the boat, he dropped the hat onto one of its wooden benches. He grabbed a heavy sack. Ah Sing did the same. Sack after sack, barrel after barrel, crate after crate, the two men, Ah Sing and the reporter, worked in this way until they were done unloading. When the man began rolling a barrel up the beach toward the slope, his shoes slapping on the gravel, Ah Sing rushed after him.

"Gift, you help me. Gift," he said, his throat tightening so he could not swallow. "Please, please, you take." He pushed out a laugh. It felt like choking on a ball of rice. "You remember Ah Sing to the CPR."[10]

The man stopped, his eyes focused on Ah Sing for the first time, clear blue eyes the colour of frozen ponds in the spring when the ice cracks. Ah Sing was sure he heard the man sigh. The man shifted his weight from one foot to the other and rubbed his wiry eyebrows that shot straight up. Ah Sing held the watch in his open palm.

105 He imagined slapping it into the man's hand. The man would laugh and throw it over his shoulder; it would shatter into a thousand golden pieces.

"It *is* a beautiful timepiece," the man said.

[10]Canadian Pacific Railroad. Thousands of Chinese performed dangerous jobs in the building of the railroad through British Columbia

"Yes, beautiful," Ah Sing answered. His throat was a bird's throat, filled with small stones.

"A gift, you take."

The man smiled. "Right, then. Thank you." The man dropped it almost without touching it into his jacket pocket.

110   Then he said, "Look, man, look what I have here." He undid the buttons of his tweed jacket and fished around in the breast pocket of his blue shirt, the same colour as his eyes. "Here, look at this. This is a Kruger coin.[11] It's all the way from the South African Republic."

Ah Sing raised what was left of his eyebrows.

"I've got some others at home, a pocketful, in fact. But they're rare, quite rare, in spite of that. You'd have to go all the way to the South African Republic; I came back with them after the Boer War.[12]" The man stopped and buffed the coin against his chest. "If you would take this to show my appreciation."

Ah Sing stared at it. He felt an ache in the bottom of his stomach. It grew worse. He would vomit. He knew it. His legs tensed, waiting for it. He imagined running. Running. The man would start chasing him. Would throw handfuls of Kruger coins. They would hit him on the back, handful after handful. Stinging, like golden hail. What a silly, infuriating man. Ah Sing could decorate his cabin. He could use them as sinkers when he fished.

Ah Sing held the coin between his thumb and forefinger. He spat on its tarnished surface.

115   The man widened his eyes.

"Superstition. It bring more money when spit. Bring good luck."

"Oh," the man said. He clapped his hands together. "Well, then."

Far from shore, the steamer bobbed in the chop. A crow cawed. The waves tumbled.

The man walked to the dory and Ah Sing followed. Reaching in, the man picked up his hat from where it lay. It was a green plaid cheese cutter,[13] wool, with yellow and orange stripes. Under the leather strap at the back he had tucked some heron feathers, and for an instant Ah Sing was reminded of the ladies of Victoria who had worn hats adorned with enough feathers to drive certain birds to extinction. These wealthy of Victoria who had called men like Ah Sing their "Celestials.[14]" Romanticizing their roast duck, their porcelain figurines for sale in every Chinatown store, their opium pipes.

120   The man held his hat out to Ah Sing. "Do you like this hat?"

"It's fine hat."

"Take it."

Ah Sing walked with the coin in his pocket where the watch had been and the hat on his head, counting his footsteps as he rolled the barrel up the

---

[11]Coin bearing the image of Paul Kruger, president of the South African Republic before its defeat by the British during the Boer War [12]A war from 1899 to 1902, after which South Africa became a British colony [13]Cap with a peak at the front [14]A derogatory term applied to Chinese immigrants.

slope. He fought against quick breaths, trying not to hyperventilate. He stacked the barrel in the storage shed next to the coffins and the axes.

He was walking toward the cabin, looking at the ground, when something hit his shoulder. He looked up. A heron in the fir tree. He looked at the ground. Frog bones. And he noticed a drop of red blood that had fallen onto a green alder leaf.

125   In his cabin, he packed an empty burlap bag, his driftwood pieces, his Buck knife, his cast-iron kettle, and his tin cup. He looked around the cabin, at the clothes folded on the stool by the door, the walls papered with the *Daily Colonist* and Chinese New Year's decorations, their glossy black characters jumping off the red background. Then he went back to the beach.

He sat in the loose shale by the boulders. He dug for his Buck knife in his bag. Waiting, he whittled eight sticks and two larger ones. He carved grooves into the two big sticks and then he fitted in the small ones, trying them each in turn. If he finished in time, he could leave the kite for Ge Shou.

Leaning against a boulder, watching the ocean, Ah Sing was reminded of his thirty-ninth year. With his back against the rock wall of Kwangtung[15] and the South China Sea spread out wide before him—trapped by famines in Anhui[16] across the border, and by the dirt and drought of Jing Gang[17] on the eastern border with Hunan—he had paid a CPR labour broker and hopped a freighter bound for Canada. He smiled now, remembering. As the journey progressed, his excitement had been replaced by tense muscles. He had felt trapped, with no breath, no arms to fight; the mountains of black waves spanned for miles in any direction. How he had trembled on the deck! How he had been convinced the waves would swallow him, the same way Gold Tooth had trembled on the verandah as he heaved his bed outside, convinced the walls would crush him—solid walls that Ah Sing himself had built. And how, on the freighter, another man from Fujien[18] had touched Ah Sing on the shoulder. The man had said, "There's nothing to be afraid of."

The sun shifted; the boulders cooled. In the distance, he saw the reporter and the doctor. They were taking off their shoes and wading out to the dory.

"Hallo! Hallo!" Ah Sing yelled.

130   They nodded to him and waved.

He stood up. He threw his bag around his shoulder.

They plunged their oars into the water. They were rowing back to the *Alert* that pitched offshore. Ah Sing narrowed his eyes at the doctor and reporter and could feel the hot sun falling onto his back.

He bent down and dropped his knife back into his bag. He could hear the waves, and Ge Shou singing in the background. He touched the coin in his pocket. His jaw tightened. He undressed so quickly his shirt got caught on his ears. He pulled down his pants and dropped his wool shirt onto the rock next to his bag.

[15]Province on the south coast of China [16]Province in eastern China [17]Area in southeast China [18]Area in southeast China. Most Chinese labourers came to Canada from areas in south east China.

"Hallo! Hallo!"

135   He dove. His breath froze inside his lungs, and his limbs froze, too: he was a stone, armless and legless. He began to sink, watching the bubbles rising past his face.

Fear made a body heavy; fear made a person sink and drown. Dead bodies floated because all the fear was gone. Once, a leper had swum toward the lights of Cordova Bay. His body had floated with the grace of a lotus flower back to the gravel slope. Then Ah Sing and Ge Shou had buried him, silently, beyond the goldenrods. If only he had let the water flow through him as if he were made of it, he could have floated to freedom. Another leper had once escaped D'Arcy Island by swallowing a vial of poison. He swallowed it on board the steamer, had died before even arriving at the colony.

Ah Sing thought he would never stop sinking, but then his arms and legs sprang to life. He kicked as fast as he could while whitecaps crashed around his ears. The doctor and the reporter were not stopping. He slapped the water. He cried into the wind, his eyes open against the salt and the horrifying green.

The seagulls laughed. Ah Sing sputtered, yet the two men ignored him and boarded the steamer. His breath felt scant and thread-like in his lungs. His ears rang, his head thudded.

He plunged his head under. When he surfaced, he squinted at Ge Shou standing on the rocky outcrop of beach, who had picked up his clothes and was waving them, flag-like. Then Ge Shou reached for the kite but stopped short of picking it up.

140   Ah Sing swam back to shore and clung to a rock. Ge Shou looked down in silence. Ah Sing breathed deeply, filling his nostrils with salt air and water droplets that burned. He wiped his eyes with the back of his hand. Water remained on his lashless lids and formed prisms, through which he looked at the setting sun. Oystercatchers circled and screeched.

Ge Shou lowered his hand to help Ah Sing onto the boulder. Ah Sing shook his head. He spat over his shoulder and then heaved his body out, panting as he clambered up. There he hunched forward and held himself.

After a while, he stood up and took the hat from the rock; he spun it around on his hand a few times. Holding it aloft, he pulled out the heron feathers. Then he tossed the hat into the ocean.

He reached for the coin. He put it in his mouth. It tasted like oak. His tongue moved it from one side of his mouth to the other and warmed the metal. He spat the coin back out, into his hand. He hurled it toward the ocean. It glinted in the air. When it hit the water, it skimmed like a cormorant before sinking into the grey-green waves.

A breeze dimpled the ocean. Ah Sing picked up the kite frame and offered it to Ge Shou. Ge Shou rubbed his forehead.

145   "Don't be scared, Ge Shou."

Ge Shou hopped from foot to foot, holding the kite.

"Don't cry, Ge Shou."

Ah Sing put his arm around Ge Shou's shoulder. He stroked him up and down. He could feel the warmth of his flesh through the damp cotton of his shirt. Ah Sing's arm was covered in goose pimples. Ge Shou's black braid tickled his armpit.

"There's nothing to be afraid of," he said to Ge Shou. "Do you want to help me fly the kite?"

150   When he was a boy, Ah Sing's bed had been a strong rush mat, and he had slept on it with his four brothers and sisters, his parents, and their parents, by the great mouth of the Yangtze River where it emptied into the East China Sea.

The sea touched everything with lapping hands, probing fingers, reaching across countries and exploring fjords with whales, bays of volcanic rock, and ancient crevasses. A single drop could circumnavigate the globe in five thousand years.

As a boy, he would float in the warm waters of Chongwu Bay[19] until he felt his body liquefying, his loose limbs pulled by small currents and pushed by gentle swells. He would float as if dead while the sun burned his back. He grew and fished with the older boys. He went to work in the tin mines of Malaysia. He went to the plantations of Borneo. He forgot how to turn into the sea.

The water dripping from his body had formed a puddle at his feet. Ah Sing shook the remaining drops from his limbs and stood on one leg to dry the bottom of his feet with his shirt. Then he used his shirt to towel the top of his head. He stepped into his pants. He pulled his shirt over his neck and the hair that was still wet dripped down his back. The fabric of the shirt stuck to his skin.

The warmth was returning to his body, but the back of his head still ached with cold. He looked out over the water.

155   "Hey Ge Shou, here's a riddle for you: *How does one stop a drop of water from ever drying out?*"

"A riddle." Ge Shou clapped. "I love riddles."

(2008)

---

[19]Bay along the southeast coast of China

Craig Boyko   (b. 1978)

Born in the small town of Humboldt, Saskatchewan, Craig Boyko studied Computer Science at the University of Regina and English and Psychology at the University of Calgary. Winner of the 2007 Journey Prize, awarded to a short story by a promising young Canadian writer, "OZY" makes use of elements of Boyko's background and training. Set in a convenience store of a small town, it examines the importance of an arcade game in the life of a 12-year-old boy and his friends. Boyko subtly gives symbolic implications to the old battered game, the elderly man who owns the store and who, for unstated reasons, has the game installed, and the three-letter name each boy uses to identify himself as a player. The incidents of early adolescence are given larger significance late in the story when the narrator, now middle-aged, compares his youth with his present situation in life.

OZY

1:	1500000	WWJ
2:	1200000	NEF
3:	1000000	RTP
4:	750000	BQD
5:	500000	TYO
6:	250000	GMV
7:	150000	DSA
8:	100000	HIV
9:	75000	THG
10:	50000	MKE

The scores were fake. They were too even, too rounded. Tenth place, bottom rung, was exactly 50,000 points. Ninth was exactly 75,000. Eighth exactly 100,000. Fifth was not a point more nor less than half a million. First place would cost you exactly 1,500,000.

"It's goddamn impossible," said my brother after his first game. He'd scored 17,455.

If the highest scores seemed too big, the lowest were too small. The top ten were spaced out in neat exponential increments, like currency—or prizes.

Even at twelve, I was old enough to know that progress was made not in great, smooth leaps but in clumsy, painful steps. I'd played piano for six months, taken swimming lessons for three, and been a scout for about two weekends—and if I'd ever found myself stranded on an island ten metres from the mainland with nothing but a Swiss Army knife and a Casiotone keyboard,[1] I'd have died of hunger or poison ivy in about twelve hours flat and wouldn't even have been able to perform my own funeral dirge.

---

[1] An electronic keyboard popular in the early 1980s

5   Genius was not a gift. Talent was not innate. Practise, and only practise, made perfect—which was just to say that the long road to perfection was paved with bumpy, potholed imperfection. If some kid calling himself "WWJ" had really scored one and a half million points, there should have been countless others who'd only made 1,450,000, 1,464,000, 1,485,975. For every Edmund Hillary[2] who reached the peak there should have been dozens of frozen carcasses littering the mountain-side below. The lack of evidence of any such carnage in the hygienic high-score list was proof of its artificiality.

And that offended something in me. I was insulted. And from my brother I'd learned a useful self-defence manoeuvre: Take every insult as a challenge.

I told him to give me a goddamn quarter.

"Suck a turd, midget."

I could tell by the mildness with which he said it that he was out of money. So were the others. We lingered around the machine like smitten suitors, jiggling its joysticks and tapping its buttons, already reminiscing over past exploits and sketching out the fiery mayhem we would unleash in the near future, until Mr. Kacvac, invoking his dead wife's long-suffering soul, told us to get out of the store. Our loitering was scaring away paying customers.

10   Everyone but me had great handles. Some—Donnie Werscezsky (DON), James Thomas (JIM), and my brother (LEO), to name but a few—had been blessed from birth with names exactly three letters long. Others—Gob McCaffrey and Pud Milligan, for instance—had had such names bestowed upon them by inadvertently generous peers. Even those whose names seemed at first glance to be as unabbreviatable as my own had little difficulty re-christening themselves. Hank Lowenthal, who occasionally claimed British heritage and could quote entire scenes from Monty Python and the Holy Grail[3] as proof, embraced his pedigree with ANK. Sanjeet Kastanzi, who everyone called Sanj, had a number of options: SAN was safe if rather dull, ANJ was bold if a little risky, and KAS had a nice rough-and-tumble ring to it. (SNJ was tacitly off-limits; we all wanted our names to be sayable.) In the end he went—a little overweeningly, I thought—with JET.

And Theodore Mandel, a friend of my brother's, tries on labels like they were shoes. Indeed, I sometimes suspected that the challenge of textual condensation was the only reason he played—just as I sometimes suspected that the only reason he hung around with my brother, Leo, was so he could refer to the pair of them in rhyming third-person.

Theo tried on TEO first, then DOR. But you could see the self-dissatis-faction of the artist in his eyes. When he discovered that numerals were permissible he came up with 3OH ("Three-oh"), 3A4 ("Three-a-four"), and

[2]In 1953, Edmund Hillary became the first man to reach the peak of Mount Everest [3]A humourous 1975 movie about the comic misadventures of questing knights

finally, his *chef d'oeuvre*, 0EO. The zero, he explained to everyone in the store, stood for the Greek letter theta, which, in the International Phonetic Alphabet, was the symbol for the "th" sound. We responded to this little lesson with a different sound. Marcel Kacvac (MUT), who we all looked up to in fear and awe because he was in high school and had a tattoo, a car, and acne, started calling Theo "Oreo" and then, because "Oreo" was not offensive enough to ever catch on, "Cookie." But Theo defused the danger by pretending to be delighted. For a week he insisted that everyone call him Cookie and for a week everyone refused. "Piss off, *Theo*" even became a schoolyard catchphrase. One night I used it to greet him at the door to our walk-up and was swatted for it later by my mom, who, seated upstairs in the kitchen, had neither heard him call me "Oozy" first, nor seen him ruffle my hair afterwards.

I was supposed to have been OLD. O.L.D. really were my initials. Fortuitously, they spelled a recognizable word. And old was something I wanted to be anyway. OLD was perfect.

I crept onto the high-score screen with my very first quarter. Naturally I took this to be an omen, a sign that I'd been earmarked for greatness. But my triumph was short-lived.

LEO—whose hard-won 76,450 points had been propelled into the abyss by my seemingly effortless 78,495—immediately pantsed me. This was to be expected, and wouldn't even have been humiliating if Mrs. Schrever, my brother's History teacher, hadn't been in the store at the time. Because she was, Mr. Kacvac felt obliged to loudly reprimand my brother—and me—for our deplorable behaviour. Normally he didn't give a damn how we comported ourselves so long as merchandise got paid for. He believed Mutt's generation to be so far beyond redemption that it didn't even trouble him anymore. On the contrary, he seemed to relish each fresh confirmation of our wickedness. When there were no adult customers in the store he encouraged us to deride volunteerism, team sports, and homework. Once, home from school with a feigned illness, I wandered into his store in the middle of a weekday afternoon and Kacvac rewarded my waywardness with a free handful of gummi fruits. But that day, with Mrs. Schrever in the store, he had to condemn my brother's wanton cruelty and my obscene immodesty until the grown-up finally paid and left.

The charge of wilful obscenity was, I thought, a little unfair. It's not that I wouldn't, but *couldn't* pull up my pants right away. There was a high score that needed claiming; I had to enter my initials first.

Whether in my excitement or because everyone was laughing at the threadbare state of my skivvies, I overshot the D and put an E in its place. The mistake proved irrevocable. So I pretended I hadn't made a mistake at all. When Theo demanded to know what the heck "Olé" was supposed to mean, I just shrugged enigmatically but with tight-lipped significance, as though we were really talking about some girl I'd banged, and whom I was too much of a gentleman, or depraved pervert, to slander by disclosing the garish details.

In the end it didn't matter. My low high score was wiped out, to my secret relief, a mere twenty minutes later by DON. OLE was dust.

But so was OLD. That name was now forever tainted. It was just as well, I realized. OLD was a stupid, terrible name. Mrs. Schrever was old. Mr. Kacvac was old. And did I really want it getting out that my middle name was "Leslie"?

20   OSS seemed the obvious choice but I didn't like it. It looked amputated. Standing on their own like that, the first three letters of my name gave no clue to their origin, their context, their pronunciation. Future generations would suppose that OSS rhymed with "floss" or "gloss"—words not known to strike fear into the human heart.

I could fix this problem by substituting Z's for the S's but I didn't like OZZ any better. It looked ugly and asymmetrical; the second Z was technically superfluous. Besides, I hated "Oz," with all its childish connotations: witches, wizards, flying monkeys, munchkins, a girl named Dorothy and a dog named Toto, for crying out loud. Yes, I had made a habit of kicking the shins of anyone who called me Oz and who was not my brother.

So what did that leave?

OSI? OZI? OZE?

Ossie's needs had been modest. He'd spent his meagre allowance on little more than junk food, model airplanes, and elastic bands and paper clips—which he and Philip O'Toole (POT) stopped firing at human targets after Jill Alistair's mom complained to their moms.

25   OZY, on the other hand, was always on the lookout for money.

I dismantled our sofas. I stuck my fingers inside pay-phones and pop machines. I trawled the gutters in our neighbourhood with my eyes. At night I stole quarters from my mother's purse and, in the morning, obfuscated my crime by demanding an advance on my allowance. (After all, no thief in his right mind would return to his victim the very next day as a supplicant.) I upturned my peanut butter jar and converted its former contents, my life savings, into a roll of pennies, two rolls of nickels, and a roll of dimes—nine dollars and fifty cents in all. At the bank I watched, redfaced, as the teller removed, with a long red fingernail, two quarters from a roll before cheerfully handing it over to me. It felt like a slap on the hand. But my mood improved as soon as I stepped back out on the street with thirty-eight quarters in my pocket, weighing the left side of my cords down almost past my hip.

Unfortunately, there was no one in Kacvac's but Kacvac. I felt the need to flourish my fortune at someone, so I squandered one play—three whole lives—on a dozen gummi fruits. Fussily, but with good-humoured resignation, like someone who has grown weary of the bank's empty promises to make their coins easier to get at, I peeled a coin from the top of my roll and slid it across the counter like a checkers pro.

"Mazel tov,[4]" said Mr. Kacvac gloomily, and in his perpetually damp eyes I saw not the dysfunction of lachrymal glands—a medical condition that my mother had warned me not to mention—but a keen, unadulterated—and unadult—envy.

In no hurry to shatter my adversaries' records in their absence, I sauntered up to the machine, performed a few limbering calisthenics, looked around the store, smiled companionably back at Mr. Kacvac, peeled off another quarter, and inserted it into the slot. *Ballistic Obliteration* chimed happily, like a baby robot gurgling at the sight of its mother. I exchanged a grim nod with my reflection in the store window, like two rugged highwaymen crossing paths out on some lonely mesa after midnight. Then I reached up over my head, gripped the joystick with one hand, and slapped the START button with the other.

30   It was not respect that we sought. Those who were better than you could not respect you, and those who were worse could not even like you. Those who did not play—my mother, our teachers, the President of the United States of America—did not really exist.

It was not respect that we were after but immortality. I dreamed of taking all ten high scores. I dreamed of an army of OZYs slaughtering anyone who would deny them their rightful place in eternity.

It never occurred to us that our high scores might not be immortal. They were as indelible as a Guinness World Record or the Permanent File that Principal Ballsack kept locked in the cabinet in his office—and which he promised to show no one but such colleges, potential employers, and juries as might someday need to be disabused of any notion of our goodness or worth. Our high scores were the high scores of all time and space. We assumed they would last forever.

For disabusing us of this notion, Roger Parker (ROG) was systematically ostracized: we put dead gophers in his locker, we squashed his lunches with our textbooks, we tied his gym shoes together and wrapped them around the football goalpost like a bola,[5] and then—worst of all—we left him alone.

ROG had been one of the real contenders, one of the Obliterati. He'd been with us from the beginning. He'd been the first to "get HIV," with 104,895 points. He'd also been the first to kill the underwater-level boss, a giant robotic octopus that sprayed clouds of ink that would freeze you to your spot for five seconds while it—rather implausibly, I thought—lobbed fireballs at you.

35   Leo smacked me in the side of the head and said that obviously *grease* fires could burn underwater. Phil, who was supposed to be my best friend, backed him up, saying that everybody knew that the army had

[4]Congratulations on your good luck   [5]A cord with weights tied to each end

flame-throwers on their attack subs. I asked if he meant the navy, and Leo smacked me again.

"Ow—what was *that* for?"

"For being a smartass."

"I wasn't," I said truthfully. (*Wasn't* it the navy who had subs?) I felt the first prickle of tears gathering somewhere beneath the skin of my cheeks. It was not hardship or cruelty but injustice that made me emotional.

"Oh shit. I was just teasing. Don't pull a Kacvac on us."

One afternoon Roger was in striking distance of usurping Jim Thomas (JIM) for sixth place. We were all cheering him on. Jim Thomas was almost eighteen and, like MUT, far too old, in our opinion, to be competing. Shouldn't he have girls to bang? we asked ourselves.

This was approximately one month after the machine had first appeared in Kacvac's, dumped indifferently, as though by some giant stork, at the front of the store between the rotating display of birthday cards and the three shopping carts that no one ever used because they were too wide for all but the frozen foods aisle. None of us ever really paused to wonder where the game had come from. Though battered and scuffed with age and rough use, it seemed to us to have simply material-ized out of thin air, like some sort of divine challenge—like Arthur's sword in the stone.[6] Some of us must have realized that Mr. Kacvac owned Kacvac's, but he never seemed like anything but a worn-out and mistreated employee in his own store. It was inconceivable that we had him to thank for *Ballistic Obliteration*.

A month after it appeared, the bottom five scores were history. MKE was long forgotten. THG's thing had fallen off. DSA had, of course, caught AIDS from HIV. We were unable to do much with GMV or TYO—which was suspicious. Indeed, with the exception of HIV, none of the default high scorers' names spelled anything even remotely dirty. They even seemed to have been chosen to rule out offensive acronyms. Not a single DIK or TIT or AZZ among them—another sure sign that they were fakes.

Then again, none of us ever resorted to such vulgarity either. We took the game, and our fame, too seriously. To pass up the chance to take personal credit for your score would be more than a tragic waste; it would be a gesture of disrespect, more obscene than any three-letter word could be. Donnie Werscezsky (DON)—who later became my prin-cipal rival, next to Gob McCaffrey (GOB)—did once enter POO after losing three lives in quick succession to the dragon on the lava level (who at least did not breathe water at you). But no one so much as smiled at POO. It had been a gesture of peevishness, we all knew, not rebelliousness. DON had two better scores on the list already, so maybe it didn't matter. But there were kids—my brother, for one—who'd have killed for what Donnie tossed so dismissively aside—namely, 589,140 points.

---

[6]In Arthurian legend, only the future King of Britain would be able to pull a sword out of the rock in which it was embedded

At the time of ROG's last game, the bottom five scores were 545,770, 532,225, 528,445, 500,000, and 476,610. They belonged to JIM, GOB, OZY, the imaginary TYO, and ROG himself. Watching him play were GOB, OZY, POT, and Wally Hersch, who never had a moniker because he never made it onto the high-scores list. The kid was hopeless. His hand and his eye were apparently operated by different brains altogether. And he never got any better despite all the quarters he plugged into the machine. We serious players respected neither his ineptitude nor his conspicuous wealth, so we never let him play unless we were all broke or he promised to lend us money—which he did gladly for anyone who would play doubles with him. But this we refused to do.

Two-person play was, at least among the Obliterati, tacitly prohibited. It was easier to get further when playing doubles, and while the points that piled up had to be split two ways, the extent of player one's contribution to player two's success and vice versa could never be teased apart. Doubles scores were an inaccurate and therefore invalid measure of one's skill. A *high* score that came out of a doubles game was deemed not just worthless but in fact immoral, because every illegitimate score displaced a legitimate one. It didn't matter if your partner *was* Wally—that is, if he contributed nothing, if he died off before you even got as far as the wild boar boss at the end of the forest level. It was a question of precision. Of honour.

I once walked into Kacvac's to find Donnie Werscezsky playing alone. I watched him mutely for ten minutes. Suddenly he let out a shriek and swiftly committed hari kari.

"Why the hell'd you do *that?*" I wanted to know. "You were creeping up on bottom rung with two damn lives left."

"No shit—why d'you think I killed myself?"

Evidently Mutt Kacvac had been labouring over the machine when Donnie came into the store. MUT never played if anyone was around. He didn't like being watched. He was not a real contender, and he concealed his lack of skill behind a mask of derisive indifference. When Donnie came in, he suddenly remembered he had to be somewhere and asked DON if he wanted to take over. Donnie hesitated, so Mutt casually crashed his ship into a toxic chemical vortex, then turned and strode out of the store without another word. Donnie couldn't bear to let most of a quarter go to waste. But nor could he claim a high score that was not completely, 100 per cent his own. When he backed away from the machine after his *felo de se*, he kept shaking his hands as though they were dripping wet and muttering to himself, "That was close, that was a real close call."

By the time Jim Thomas came into the store, Roger had 521,915 points. He'd secured ninth place and was sneaking up on me in eighth. He'd made it to the electricity level—a nightmare landscape of sparkling capacitators and fizzling dynamos swept with gleaming acid showers and arc lightning that only a few of us had ever seen with our own two eyes— and he'd done it without losing a single life. He had 521,915 points, his

Faradization upgrade, ten nukes, a triple forcefield, and three ships left. He was on fire.

50   Gob, Phil, Wally, and I fell silent. Even the buzzing coolers in the produce section seemed to hold their breath. JIM, our current scoring leader, pretended not to notice what was happening. He made a lazy circuit of the store like an old lady searching for discounts. He stood in front of Mr. Kacvac and deliberated out loud over which brand of cigarettes he should try today. In the end he bought nothing but a newspaper, which he folded neatly and tucked under his arm before finally strolling, lackadaisically and as though quite by chance, in our direction.

"What's this?" he asked primly.

"It's a video game," Gob said quietly. "Never seen one?"

Casually, and with the inattentive air of someone lighting a pipe, Jim asked, "And how's old Rog doing?"

"Fine," Phil said.

55   "Amazing, actually," Wally said. "He's got ninth place."

Roger muttered something under his breath.

Jim stooped forward slightly, turned his head to one side, and blinked rapidly out the window. "Hmm? What's that he said?"

"Eighth place," Gob said. "He just got eighth."

"There goes Ossie," said Phil.

60   I exhaled. Something tight in my chest loosened up.

"Suck a turd," I said.

"Holy, what kind of power-up is *that?*" asked Wally breathlessly.

"He's right on your ass, Jim," said Phil gloatingly, "and he's got three lives."

At precisely that moment, Roger's ship exploded. He swore loudly. Mr. Kacvac, perched on his stool behind the counter, looked up from his crossword puzzle and cleared his throat threateningly. (Mrs. Howard, a friend of my mother's, was palpating lettuce heads in the produce section.) Out of respect for the dead, and not because we were cowed by Kacvac, we fell silent for a minute. Jim, who'd been about to say something, let his mouth hang open like someone anticipating a delicacy. He brought his lips together at last:

65   "Two," he said. You could tell the word tasted good. "Two lives left."

Phil sent Gob a quick commiserative glance. "He's on you. He's right on you. Oh man, he's— that's it. You're toast."

"Nice one," said Gob.

"He's got seventh place now," Wally explained. "He just passed Gob."

"Seventh place," said Phil, "and he's got two lives left."

70   Roger's ship enrupted into flames. He swore. This time Kacvac cleared his throat inquisitively, as though politely inquiring which of us would most like to be kicked out first.

"You guys are goddamn jinxing me," Roger said under his breath. "Stop saying how many lives I have goddamn left."

"Why?" said Jim brightly. "What's the matter? Are we *jinxing* you?"

He was chuckling but there was an uneasiness in his voice. His eyes, like the rest of ours, were locked on the screen, where Roger's score continued bit by excruciating bit to rise.

"How many lives do you have left anyway? One? Just one?"

As though on cue, Roger's ship hurtled into a giant electrified razor-wire barrier and blew into pieces.

He did not swear. He slammed his palms down on the buttons and spun around to glower at Jim.

Jim grinned. Gob, Phil, Wally, and I gasped in horror. Roger's game wasn't over yet. He needed less than four thousand points to beat Jim and *he had turned his back on the game*.

He was back at the controls before we could scream at him, but the one- or two-second interruption proved fatal. Before he knew what was happening, his right wing had been grazed by a deadly blue will-o-the-wisp, sending a geyser of black smoke up into the poisonous atmosphere. Roger pulled away too late and too hard: overcompensating in space for what he'd failed to do in time, he rocketed from one side of the screen to the other and came too close to a giant electromagnet, a device that looked as harmless as a giant bedspring but was as deadly as a coiled cobra. The magnet pulled him in slowly, almost gently. Then it injected him with a billion volts. The screen went white.

GAME OVER.

545,385 points. Seventh place.

Roger spun around. Jim was bent double, clutching his newspaper to his chest. It looked to me like he was only pretending to laugh.

"You goddamn jinxed me."

Jim straightened, took a deep breath, and fanned himself with his paper. At length he brought his eyes to focus uncertainly, as though without recognition, on Roger.

"*Twice*," said Roger through his teeth.

"Hey Roger," said Wally. "Your name . . ."

The game gave you thirty seconds to enter your initials. Roger had twenty left.

He made no move. Jim stopped smiling. This was serious. Roger was going to throw his score away. He *was* throwing it away. We were watching him do it. He was hurtling towards the edge of a cliff and defying anyone to intervene. He just stood there, glaring at Jim.

Jim glared back. He was angry now too. But he was nervous as well. His eyes kept darting to the screen. Fifteen seconds.

I couldn't breathe. Wally looked ready to pee himself. Phil had to put an arm out to prevent him from rushing forward to enter the R, O, and G on Roger's behalf.

Ten seconds.

Jim flinched first. The spell was broken. A goofy, panic-stricken grin spread across his face. He lunged past Roger, dropping his newspaper, grabbed the joystick and began jiggling it madly. He managed to tap out the last letter—an M—with less than a second to spare. Then he stepped back to admire, and invite the rest of us to admire, his work.

Phil, Gob, and I were too upset to speak. Wally appeared to be working himself up to a Kacvac. Roger just peered wordlessly at the screen.

Jim sensed he'd committed a faux pas. He became defensive. "Hey, it's just a joke. He was going to waste it. Jeez, it's just a *game*."

Mr. Kacvac had time to say "Hey, you kids—" before Roger reached around behind the machine and pulled the plug out of the wall. Wally shrieked. Gob closed his eyes. Jim Thomas's face went white. Then he stepped forward and punched Roger neatly and expertly in the stomach, like a para-medic administering the Heimlich manoeuvre. Roger reeled back, then tipped forward, using his momentum to head-butt Jim in the chest. They collapsed together into the display of birthday cards. Mr. Kacvac sprang over the counter and, perhaps by invoking his dead wife's name, or perhaps by bran-dishing a baseball bat, persuaded all of us to come back another time.

95 I couldn't stay away long. The next day, under the pretense of having been delegated by my mother to purchase some goat's milk, I was able on my way out—empty-handed as planned—to confirm my fears.
   MKE, THG, HIV, and DSA had made miraculous recoveries.
   ROG, JIM, GOB, and OZY were no more.
   Gone. Just like that. Without a trace. in the blink of an eye. Forever.
   So what was the point?

100 That night I lay in bed, struggling to fill my mind with the idea of forever. I took a single summer day spent rambling through our neighbourhood with Phil, taking apart bugs, collecting pop cans, melting popsicles on our tongues, browsing through his dad's old CB radio catalogues, practising our ventriloquism, throwing rocks at stray cats, chalking our names on sidewalks exposed to the naked sky—I took one day like that and tried to hold it in my head all at once. Then I shrunk it down to a dot, a mere speck, and populated the vacated space with a hundred dots, a thousand specks. A sandstorm of days—as many as I'd ever see in all my life. I compressed the dust cloud too, squeezed it down into a tiny cube and pushed it to the very edge of my imagination. I began lining cubes up next to it, slowly at first, only one or two at a time, to give me a chance to grasp the enormity of the addition. Then I began adding half a dozen blocks at once, then half a dozen half-dozens, then a long undifferentiated row of blocks spanning the entire width of the space behind my eyes, then half a dozen rows, then half a dozen half-dozens.
   I sensed that I was cheating; for each time I moved to a higher level, the detail of the lower levels went out of focus, so that I was no longer really mul-tiplying the multiplied multiples of multiplied multiples but just pushing around individual blocks again, solid pieces that could only regain their plurality at the cost of their unity, parts of a whole that I could not simulta-neously see as wholes of yet smaller parts. But I continued until I realized that everything I'd imagined so far, every multiplication I'd performed, could itself be condensed to a single infinitesimal cube and put through the very same process, from start to finish. And *that* entire process could be taken as a unit and run through itself, and so on, and so on, forever and ever. There it was: no matter how long you imagined forever to be, your idea of it was to the real forever as a split second was to your idea of it. This truism remained true even

if you took it into account when formulating your idea of forever. Even if you took *that* into account. And that. And so on, forever and ever.

Forever, then. Forever was how long dead people stayed dead. It was how long my dad and my mom's dad and my aunt Sharon and Leo's hamster, Delorna, and Theo Mandel's mother and Jill Alistair's brother Geoff and Mr. Kacvac's wife, Eleanora, would stay dead. Forever was how long gone things stayed gone. It was how long my switchblade would stay at the bottom of Konomoke Lake, how long my magnifying glass would stay smashed (thanks, Leo), how long the key I'd lost to our old apartment building would stay lost, how long our cool old car would stay sold to a fat salesman from Wisconsin. It was how long the Alistairs' house would stay burned down, it was how long World War II would stay finished, and it was how long JIM and ROG and OZY would stay gone from the *Ballistic Obliteration* high-scores list. It wouldn't matter when the power went out or when the plug was pulled. It didn't matter if it happened tomorrow or a hundred years from tomorrow. Forever would wait.

Every message is a message to the future. The feverish, grandiloquent *billet doux*[7] stashed with trembling hand in the coat pocket of the girl you're in love with; the casual note to your wife jotted in haste and posted to the fridge before you leave in the morning; the drunken, desultory jeremiad left on your ex's answering machine—they will be read or listened to, if they are read or listened to at all, by people of the future. Even the thought scribbled carelessly in the margin of whatever novel you're reading is a variety of time travel. Every mark we make, every trace we leave is a broadcast sent out into forever. We think of our footsteps as receding behind us, but really they are beacons sent out before us.

So listen:

I was good at something once. Great, even. It was a long time ago. I was twelve. Now I'm forty-three and not good at much of anything.

I'm not complaining. You're only forty-three and not good at anything for a short time. But you will have once been twelve and good at something forever.

I can't prove it, of course. I have no evidence, no documentation. Three weeks after I obliterated Gob McCaffrey's top score by a margin that should have established my supremacy for—well, for a very long time, our neighbourhood experienced a brief power failure at about four-thirty in the morning. My mother's alarm did not go off; the three of us slept late—a real treat for Leo and me but a catastrophe for Mom, who crashed into our room bellowing and clutching her head as if bombs were being dropped on the neighbourhood.

We had to pass Kacvac's on our unhurried way to school.

Power failure. Blackout. 12:00, 12:00, 12:00.

[7]Love letter

110   I had to go inside. Leo swore at me and continued on to school, not because he minded being late but because the decision to be late, or to do anything else, always had to be made by him.

They were gone, of course. All of them, gone forever.

Or were they? Might there not persist, etched upon the air we breathe, though we haven't the sensitivity to detect it or the wit to decode it, the mark of some mark, the trace of some trace?

The universe is thought to be without memory, existing only for an eternally renewed split second. Like a sprung trap, the immediate past is supposed to inexorably propel the present into the immediate future. But I think what the past really does is stand nearby, at the present's elbow, and whisper in its ear, give it counsel, suggest how a future might be made. We listen but we don't always hear everything. Not the first time. Not right away. But there might be echoes.

I put a quarter on the counter. Mr. Kacvac held out the pail of gummi fruits. I counted five, showed him. He glanced at his wristwatch. It must have been well past nine.

115   "Oh, go on," he said. "Take a handful." And he slid my quarter back across the counter.

I stood before the machine, the coin resting in my loosely cupped palm. Forever would wait. So, let it wait.

I dropped the quarter into my left front pocket. "Later," I promised, and hurried to school.

JIM and ROG, LEO and 0EO, GOB and OZY—they're gone now. Only briefly did they stir from the dust. For a short time, a time that seemed long while it lasted, they made marks that were read and left traces that were followed by others who made marks and left traces of their own. Among the marks they left were the following.

BALLISTIC OBLITERATION

** HALL OF FAME **

TOP TEN HIGH SCORES

10:	98505	MUT
9:	212005	JET
8:	299385	0EO
7:	398510	LEO
6:	545385	ROG
5:	545770	JIM
4:	784605	POT
3:	1246325	DON
2:	1597425	GOB
1:	2069100	OZY

(2007)

Deborah Willis (b. 1982)

Calgary-born Deborah Willis studied writing at the University of Victoria. She has expressed her admiration of Alice Munro and Jhumpa Lahiri, whose stories she admires for their ability to hint at profound mysteries hidden beneath the surface of ordinary lives. "Vanishing," is the title story of her debut collection, which, she says, is about the comings and goings in people's lives and the effects of these on others. The narrative presents events of the night before the mysterious disappearance of a young girl's father, the day of his vanishing, and the days, weeks, and years that follow it. By breaking up the linear chronology of events, the narrator suggests the disruptive effect of her father's leaving on the central character and gives a sense of her frequently remembering and puzzling about the significance of specific incidents in the past.

VANISHING

WEEKS PASS and the police give up their investigations. The newspapermen who wrote "Local Writer Vanishes" find other stories. Months go by, then a year.

Marlene and Bea drink afternoon coffee and their conversation slips back to the everyday: the price of potatoes at Loblaws, who's a good doctor and who's not, what kind of pictures are showing these days. Marlene goes to *shul*[1] more often, and stands for the Mourners' Kaddish.[2]

But Tabitha imagines that her father stepped onto a bus, then onto a boat, and soon they'll receive a postcard from India. She imagines him showing up in five years, his hair greyed or gone with stories of living in Oregon, or Alaska, or the Alps. She imagines he simply moved into an apartment downtown. Sometimes—and this really puts ants in her stomach—she imagines he is hiding somewhere in the house, behind the couch or in the closets. She checks under her bed every night before she goes to sleep.

*****

THE DAY NATHAN DISAPPEARED began like any other Saturday. Marlene put a long coat over her housedress and dragged Tabitha to Honest Ed's.[3] They bought a pie plate on sale, six pairs of nylons, some patterned dishcloths, and—after Tabitha pleaded—a life-sized ceramic bust of Elvis Presley. "Where will we put that thing, Tabby?" Marlene said as they stood in line at the till. "What will your father say?"

---

[1]synagogue [2]A prayer expressing love of God and acceptance of the death of a loved one
[3]A funky discount store in downtown Toronto

5　　　But Tabitha knew her mother loved the Elvis too—the realistic folds in his collar, the glassy brown eyes, that smile. During the streetcar ride home, he sat on Tabitha's lap and she wrapped her arms around his smooth, painted shoulders. He made it all worthwhile—Marlene's housedress, the streetcar windows that steamed up from people's breath, and even Honest Ed's itself. The crowded aisles, high ceilings, and the sign outside that announced *Honest Ed's: Only the Floors Are Crooked!*

When they arrived home, Tabitha went in ahead to find the perfect place for the Elvis, and that's when she saw the attic's open hatch. She stared at the ceiling's gape. Never in her ten years had she known her father to treat his office carelessly. She thought of calling to Marlene, but Tabitha knew how slowly her mother moved—how her hips cracked when she bent to unbuckle her shoes, and how she hung each coat on its proper hanger. And Tabitha didn't want to speak her worst fear aloud, wasn't even sure if a nightmare thought like this could be spoken.

"Dad?" she called up into the dark place where he did his writing. No answer, and before she could help it, she imagined her father hanging from the ceiling. She pictured it like the movies: his crumpled face and a sinister, creaking rope. She imagined that his swinging body looked long—not tall, long. She climbed the ladder, feeling sick and dizzy as she put her foot on the final step. Then, weak-kneed with relief—initial, foolish relief—she found the attic empty.

*****

HE SEEMED TO HAVE LEFT IN A RUSH. They know he walked out the front door and locked it behind him, bringing only his thick wool coat, his scarf and hat, his umbrella. He left his typewriter, his books.

They might have assumed he'd gone to the office for a couple of hours, or out for a walk, if he hadn't taken the time to tidy the attic before he left. The scripts of his finished plays were held together with paper clips, last-minute changes indicated in pencil in the margins. The more recent works were stacked on the floor. Marlene put these in a box and tied it closed with string, because he'd left a note that read, *Unfinished.*

*****

10　　THREE YEARS LATER, the plays Nathan completed are produced in Toronto and Halifax. Marlene gets a job as a bookkeeper and discovers that she's good at it. At Tabitha's bat mitzvah, the rabbi says he's rarely seen such a dramatic reading of the *parshah.*[4]

Life is as uplifting as a musical, except that sometimes Tabitha wakes at night to find Marlene humming Paul Anka[5] songs into her ear. "You had a bad dream," says her mother, and she touches Tabitha's forehead. "What was it? A monster? That falling feeling?"

[4]A weekly reading from the Torah, the first five books of Hebrew scripture [5]Popular Canadian singer of the late 1950s

No matter how hard she tries, Tabitha can't remember. All that lingers is sweat on her pyjamas and a bad feeling in her throat.

*****

WHEN TABITHA SHOWED HER MOTHER the open hatch, the empty attic, Marlene stared at the floor and furniture, her hands hanging at her sides. She bent to look at some of the papers, then went to the window by Nathan's desk. "He's gone," she said, more to herself than to Tabitha. Then she descended to the kitchen, where afternoon light still brightened the room. She picked up the phone and Tabitha knew it was to call her sister, to ask Bea to come over, right away, please. But Marlene just held the receiver in her hand as though it were heavy, as though she were too tired to dial.

Tabitha touched Marlene's hip, where the housedress pleated. "I'll do it," she said. "I'll call her."

Half an hour later, Bea brought *mandel*[6] bread and said things like, "Maybe he was murdered. Or kidnapped."

Marlene shook her head. "Kidnapped people don't bring umbrellas with them. Besides, everybody liked him. He was a gentle man. And a good lawyer."

Marlene didn't mention Lev, but Tabitha imagined her father leaving the house to see him, putting on a suit and brushing the lint from his hat. Nothing out of the ordinary, though maybe that day Nathan hesitated when he got halfway there. Anything could have happened. Maybe he turned into a shop and fell in love with the beautiful clerk. Maybe he stepped off the Bloor Viaduct. She imagined his body buried under snow. She imagined it would turn up in spring. But she didn't say any of this, because Bea was saying, "Maybe burglars broke in and attacked him," and Marlene was holding a cup of tea to her chest, shivering.

*****

SIX YEARS AFTER NATHAN'S DISAPPEARANCE, one of his plays is performed off-Broadway, and an academic from Montreal writes about the influence of Yiddish theatre on his sense of structure. Marlene gets some royalties and moves in with Bea. They don't need to worry about coupons anymore, but they do.

At sixteen, Tabitha drops out of school and gets a job as a secretary. She buys a record player and collects LPs. She takes swimming lessons because she wants to be Esther Williams.[7]

Nearly everybody's heard of the playwright who disappeared, and when people learn Tabitha's last name, three times out of five they ask if there's any relation. When she nods they say thing like, "He must have been such

6Hard-crusted, twice-baked bread 7American actress of the 1940s and 1950s, whose movies usually featured displays of synchronized swimming

a fascinating man." Yes, she smiles. He was very clever. Vanishing, she thinks, was the smartest thing he ever did.

*****

THE FIRST TIME Tabitha had gone into the attic she was seven years old and forbidden.

"He's very busy," Marlene would say, never allowing Nathan's work to be disturbed. "He's writing."

But Tabitha needed to know what this word *writing* meant. Of course, she knew how to write. In Mrs. Hill's grade two class she was forced to spell out words in a notebook, and was learning how to form each letter: upper case, lower, cursive. But surely this wasn't connected to what her father did in the attic. *He's writing.* Marlene said it with such reverence that it was obvious she herself didn't know what, exactly, Nathan did up there.

So while Marlene weeded the small, patchy flower beds that lined the porch, Tabitha climbed the ladder. She knew her father was up there because she could hear the floorboards creak as he took a few steps or adjusted himself in his chair. She pressed against the hatch—it felt heavy to her then—and she was almost relieved when she couldn't lift it. But then it squeaked open and she saw into the cramped room. Even in the middle of the day, it was dark. She could smell the dust and the damp.

25   "Yes?" Her father sounded far away.

Tabitha knew she should gently ease the hatch down and run to the yard. She still wore her sun hat and she should be outside, helping Marlene water the marigolds.

"What is it?" Her father's voice sounded closer now, and he opened the hatch all the way. "Yes?"

It took a moment for her eyes to adjust to the dark. Then she saw his ironed pants, tucked shirt, slim and serious face.

"Does your mother want something?"

30   She shook her head. The sun hat, which was too big because Marlene wanted it to last, slipped over her eyes. He bent to fix it and she felt his hand on top of her head.

"I wanted to see the attic," she said. "I wanted to see what you do."

"I rarely do much." He nodded for her to climb into the dim room. The ceiling was so low it nearly grazed his thin hair. There were papers everywhere—organized, or perhaps not organized, on the floor, the desk, in boxes, and along the windowsill of the turret window. "Come on," he said. "You can help me with something."

She hated to hear these words from Marlene, as they meant Tabitha would be asked to put away dishes, or help pick rocks from the flower beds. But Nathan cleared some papers off an old wooden chair and nodded for her to take a seat. The chair had arms, a high back, and looked like his own. He handed her three sheets of paper that he had typewritten. "Well." He sat across from her. "You can read, can't you?"

The ink was smudged in some places, and there were pencil scratchings in the margins. It wasn't like the picture books she was used to, and she didn't know where to begin, so she said, "I'm an excellent reader." Her teacher had told her this after Tabitha read a passage aloud in class. "If only I'd spend less time daydreaming and more time concentrating on my studies." She imitated Mrs. Hill's stiff lips and intonation, her emphasis on less and more.

35   "Is that so?" Nathan smiled at her joke. For a second he looked at her the way he looked at Lev—as though she were a good show, one that captivated him. "What do they make you read in school?"

"Some poems. And the Lord's Prayer."

"Ah. Of course." He pointed to a sentence at the top of the page. "Start here and go to the bottom. It's a monologue."

So Tabitha sat across from her father and read what he told her to read. He closed his eyes, and she thought at first that he wasn't listening. But every once in a while he took the paper from her to slash out a word or add sentences in a hand she couldn't make out. He didn't explain the plot and she couldn't understand it on her own; the person on the page seemed injured, but she didn't know how or why. Still, she read—with an even intonation, the way Mrs. Hill had taught. Occasionally her father said things like, "Can you repeat the last line?" or "Not so fast. Pay attention to the rhythm."

After this, going into the attic didn't scare her. If Nathan didn't want her help, she would sit in the chair—her chair—and watch him type. She was almost sure that he liked having her there, and once he said, "You are a good reader. Damn good." After three years, she got so she could decipher his handwriting.

40   Tabitha never told her mother of these visits, and she knew this was a betrayal. But she didn't want to share what she knew of his piles of paper and his slanted, chaotic notes. It was too precious, this secret.

*****

BY THE 1970S, some critics claim him as a visionary of a socialist utopia, and the literary journals love him. A long-running production of his most popular work plays at the Eaton Auditorium.

Tabitha lives in New York, and she often sees her father. He'll be in brown polyester, or sometimes in cowboy boots. He'll be a man on a billboard, or a friendly, blurry face when she's smoked too much hash. The guy behind the counter at her local grocer's. Or a man in a dance bar, in a purple suit and fake eyelashes. She learns to ignore these visions so she can enjoy the city, her own success.

She is invited to every party worth attending and she is the life of them, sampling all New York offers her: the dancing, the threesomes, the various chemical highs. She has her mother's strong nose and dark eyes, mixed with a haunting kind of ingenuousness. This proves to be marketable. She gets cast in roles that involve crying and shrieking. As a lark, she keeps a running tally of how many times she gets to kill herself onstage.

*****

LIKE EVERY OTHER FRIDAY, the night before he vanished, Nathan invited Lev for dinner. He liked to hear the law student's opinions, and Marlene liked to cook and fuss. Lev came over at six because he usually shared a Scotch with Nathan before dinner. They would go to the attic to avoid the noise of the radio that Marlene and Tabitha played in the kitchen. The smell of their cigarettes slipped through the attic's hatch and Tabitha imagined their hushed voices, the clink of ice cube to glass, and Lev in her chair. But that night, he didn't arrive alone. That night, Lev brought a woman.

45 Her name was Sofia, and she had brown hair that curled around her ears. She wore a pencil skirt, a wide red belt, and a small leather hat. She hadn't dressed up her outfit the way Marlene would have, with makeup and pearls. She didn't have to. Her skin had a natural blush and her navy sweater brought out her eyes. Tabitha had never seen anyone so graceful, so poised. Next to this woman, she felt ashamed of her mother, and ashamed of her own awkward body. She imitated Sofia's posture, stretched her neck and held her shoulders straight.

"This beautiful lady," said Lev as he stood in the doorway, "has agreed to be my wife."

Nathan curved the corners of his mouth into something that resembled a smile and nodded to the woman.

Marlene held out her hand. "How lovely to meet you." She took Sofia's coat and gloves. "How lovely."

Over dinner, the men spoke of books. Lev had recently published a first collection, and though Nathan never wrote a single line of verse, poetry was the only topic seriously broached at the Sabbath table. From nearly two years of these dinners, Tabitha learned that Nathan was forever grateful for Klein and Lev found him depressing. Lev deemed Pound "robust and brilliant"; Nathan thought him a fascist, and a victim of his own poetic rules. Nathan admired Elizabeth Bishop, but Lev didn't pay much attention to her. And they never agreed on Layton.[8]

50 "I love him," Lev stated that Friday night. He was extremely handsome, which was maybe what gave him so much confidence in his own opinions. "I love him the way a son loves a father."

Nathan leaned back in his chair and shook his head, his cheeks reddened from wine. Their conversations sounded like arguments, but Nathan rarely appeared happier. He listened when Lev spoke and seemed to find everything about him—his youth, his ego—engaging. If Marlene noticed, she seemed to treat it as a necessary ill, like the arthritis in her fingers, the fluid that collected in her legs. "Now," she said. "Would anyone like more beans?"

"A tough, brutish father. That's the way I love the man."

"He's a drunk," said Sofia. She seemed older than Lev. Maybe it was her rich voice, or the way she so confidently helped Marlene in the kitchen before the meal.

"So he's picked his poison." Lev turned to her. "That's his right."

[8]Irving Layton and A. M. Klein were twentieth century Jewish-Canadian poets; Ezra Pound was a twentieth century anti-Semitic American poet; Elizabeth Bishop was a twentieth century American poet

55 "Of course." Sofia placed her fork and knife on her plate with a click. "But I hardly find it charming."

"Sofia has little use for certain kinds of men." Lev smiled and showed his pleasantly crooked teeth. He picked up her hand and kissed the tips of her fingers. "Men who are wholeheartedly male."

"Then she's an astute young woman." Nathan looked Lev in the eye. He smiled the kind of smile people use to cover up anger, or simple heartache. The kind of smile that never quite succeeds. "She's a prize."

*****

IN THE 1980S, someone publishes a biography that gets it all wrong, Marlene and Bea spend half of every year in Florida, and Tabitha has become brash, too loud, a lush.

She is well liked, though fat and poor, and she wakes one morning to find that her hair has become a brazen, phony blond. There is nothing of Sofia in her now. She has lost her grace, her ingenuousness, her youth. She treats it like a joke, a big joke, the way her old self has disappeared inside this other woman. But in private, she doesn't find it funny. She has nightmares—sweaty, waking nightmares—that her father will find her like this. In this body, in this hair, tipsy and hysterical.

*****

60 TWO DAYS AFTER NATHAN VANISHED, Lev knocked on the door. He'd come from the office and said he didn't have much time, was just dropping by. He sat on the couch in a dark, pressed suit. Marlene took Nathan's leather chair and sat on the edge of it. Tabitha curled up on the couch, as far from Lev as possible.

Without Nathan in the house, he seemed less warm, less assured. He was interested in the legalities: what the police had said, how the search was proceeding. He interrogated Marlene and she repeated what had happened, exactly as it had happened. The streetcar trip, the shopping, the empty house. She answered Lev's questions but seemed worn by them. When she finished, he pointed to the corner of the room and said, "Is that Elvis Presley?"

Marlene refilled his coffee cup.

"There are only so many possibilities." He bit into a lemon cookie. "Either your husband's disappearance was planned or accidental. Either he's alive or dead." Lev seemed to find comfort in this kind of statement.

"He's probably just taking an extended day of rest," said Marlene. This was a joke, but even she didn't laugh.

65 "I'm sure this will all be cleared up," he said. "There's probably an explanation."

Marlene put her cup on the table. She hadn't touched her coffee.

"I can see him waltzing in here tomorrow like nothing happened." Lev smiled at Marlene, smiled at Tabitha, then laughed—a short, coughing laugh. "Wouldn't that be so like him?"

"Anyway, he'll be glad to know you dropped by." Marlene stood. "He cares so much about you."

Then Lev made a noise that was quieter than his laugh, and sounded even more like coughing. When he wiped his face, Tabitha realized he was crying.

70 "I'm sure there's no need for that," Marlene said, in the same voice she used to tell Tabitha to Stop dawdling or Quit picking at your food.

But when Lev turned away and choked out the word "Sorry," Marlene settled herself beside him on the couch and put her arm around him. Despite the suit, he looked like a child, helpless and shaky. He rested his head on her shoulder. "It's okay," Marlene said, and rocked him back and forth.

Tabitha heard Lev's strange sobbing and understood what her mother must have known. Marlene let him press his wet, closed eyes into her cotton shirt. "You poor thing," she said. "You poor boy."

*****

IN THE EARLY 1990S, Tabitha checks into rehab, where she meets Charlie Sheen,[9] then meets her future husband. His name is Stanley and he is shy. He admits that he wasted his life, and Tabitha finds this very honest, very brave. There is nothing like Betty Ford sex, and the first time they make love, he cries.

When they check out, he proposes. Two months later, they are married. One year after that, he is rebuilding his law practice and she is making a comeback, playing disturbed mothers and oversexed divorcees. They rent an apartment in Manhattan, and Tabitha learns him: his elaborate tea ritual, his fitful sleep, his splendid reading voice.

75 She eases away from friends and considers teaching theatre rather than acting. She takes up cooking and purchases things for their comfort—dishes and wineglasses and soft wool blankets. She feels a dedication as simple and big-hearted as Marlene's.

*****

THE YEAR BEFORE HE LEFT, Nathan had begun to say things like, "Not now, Tabitha," or "I need to concentrate, please," when he heard her steps on the ladder. For a month before he disappeared, she hadn't ventured into the attic at all.

But that Friday evening, she silently climbed the steps after dinner. What drew her there was the look on his face when he'd stood and left the table in the middle of the meal. The defeated way he'd said, "I've got work to see to."

After Lev and Sofia went home, and while Marlene changed out of the blouse and green skirt she wore for company, Tabitha opened the hatch and pulled herself up, edging along the dusty floor until she slid into the office.

Nathan hadn't heard her come in—or if he had, he didn't find her presence important. He sat at his desk, facing away from her, and she stared at the back of his neck. He didn't turn to her or clear the stack of books from

[9]An American film star whose tempestuous personal life has been widely publicized

the chair. There was a blank sheet of paper rolled into the typewriter, so white it glowed under the lamp. He stared out the window, not even attempting to punch the keys.

*****

80   BEA PASSES AWAY SUDDENLY, and Tabitha flies home to help Marlene with the details: obituary, casket, stone. Maybe it comes from age, or from living with a sister for decades, but Marlene has lost any sense of propriety. She rinses dishes instead of washing them with soap, and forgets to close the door when she pees.

After sitting shiva,[10] they give Bea's clothes and her cribbage board to the Goodwill. Then they pack Marlene's dishes and the canned goods she stockpiles—*might as well buy lots when they're on sale*—so Marlene can move to a smaller place. As Tabitha fills a box with her mother's old records, she finds the Elvis. He's at the back of Marlene's closet, looking out like a ghost. He smells of mothballs, and his slim ceramic nose has broken off. Still, there's something about him. He's as strange and charming as ever.

*****

TABITHA STRETCHED up on the tips of her toes and her head nearly touched the attic's ceiling. She wanted, like her father, to see out the window. When she did this, the light must have changed, or the floorboards shifted, because he turned around. His wooden chair squeaked as it swivelled. "What are you doing here, Tabitha?" He was the only one, then, who called her by her full name.

"Nothing."

"Have they gone?"

85   She nodded. "I'm supposed to be helping with the dishes."

"I shouldn't have left the table like that. Tell your mother I'm sorry."

When she wasn't reading the lines he gave her, she didn't know how to talk to him, so she said the only thing that came into her head. "Wasn't Lev's fiancée pretty? Like a movie star?"

"Prettier," he said quietly. "Because it's real life."

Tabitha nodded and looked toward his desk. The typewriter, the blank sheet of paper.

90   "Did you know I haven't written anything in nearly a year?" He spoke as though it were a statistic, a fact that piqued his interest.

She shook her head. She understood exactly what this meant: that he wouldn't need her anymore, that there was no reason for her to be in the attic. That the chair was no longer hers.

"'But that's a secret." He raised one eyebrow, an exaggerated expression that reminded her of when he would read bedtime stories. When he terrified her, doing all the voices. "Can you keep a secret?"

She heard Marlene in the kitchen, running water for the dishes. Tabitha had a few minutes before her mother needed her to dry. "Sometimes."

---

[10]In Judaism, a week-long period of mourning after the death of a close relative

"That's a truthful answer." He leaned back in his chair. "Of course, I've written reviews and letters and things. But I haven't really written."

95 There was the sound of Marlene opening and closing a cupboard. "I should go down soon," said Tabitha. "She wouldn't want me here."

"Your mother is a very sweet person," he said. "I think that's why I married her. Because she seemed like the only honest person on earth." He laughed then, and it sounded hollow in the low-ceilinged attic. "Isn't that incredible? I married the only honest person on earth."

Tabitha stared at his shoes. They were brown leather and polished. "If it's just that you're not really writing," she said, imitating his emphasis on *really*, "then you should tell her the truth. It would probably make her happy, because then you could come downstairs more."

"The truth? It would break her heart," he said. "I don't suppose you're old enough yet. I don't suppose you've had your heart broken."

"Yes, I have." This was a lie. But Tabitha had seen enough romances to know how to cast her eyes down and pause, breathlessly, before adding, "Once."

100 "Then I'm sorry for you," he said, and turned back to the window. His voice had a harshness that told her she hadn't fooled him. He was the only audience, she would later realize, that she hadn't been able to fool.

*****

WITHIN A YEAR OF BEA, Marlene dies. And after her mother's stroke, Tabitha can't think of a single thing to say to Stanley. He holds her, tries to give comfort, but everything about him seems foreign: his smell, his pilled sweaters. He is a stranger, a man she never knew. So Tabitha walks out of her own life.

She leaves her marriage and New York and moves to a more manageable city. One with glass-fronted buildings, and bridges that stretch over waterways. She doesn't know anyone there, though once she runs into Lev as she's buying groceries. "Tabby," he says. "Is that really you?"

He looks tired, less handsome, and he wears an expensive suit that doesn't fit his soft body. He says that Sofia left him long ago, after she too became a successful lawyer. He says he visits the kids every Hanukkah.

She wants to ask him questions. "Have you heard anything about my father?" Or, "Do you still miss him?" But it seems ridiculous to say those things under fluorescent lights, beside shelves of microwaveable popcorn and freeze-dried soups. And Lev is talking about how he'd seen her picture in a magazine years ago and couldn't believe it. "I said to myself, that can't be the same girl!"

105 Neither of them suggests staying in touch, and they never see each other again. Tabitha gets a job in a bookstore, where the owner finds it amusing that she was once well known on the stage. Eventually, she too finds it amusing. So she settles, for a while, into this role behind the counter. And cultivates—perfectly—the sad, knowledgeable smile that customers seem to like.

*****

TABITHA STOOD IN THE ATTIC surrounded by Nathan's books and the dim light, faced with her father's back. She wanted to say something—apologize for her lie, or ask why he had left the table, who had broken his heart. But he stared out the turret window as though there was something out there. So she slipped down the ladder, closed the hatch, and ran to the living room. She looked out the big window, the one Marlene washed with vinegar every week. She wanted to see whatever he'd seen. But there was nothing outside. Just the usual street lamps and lawns. Houses with drawn curtains. The everyday, falling snow.

(2009)

GLOSSARY OF LITERARY TERMS—SHORT FICTION

action What happens in a literary work; the activity, whether physical or mental, represented in the work; also the mental activity stimulated in a reader.

allusion A reference to CHARACTERS, places, events, or objects from history, religion, mythology, or literature, which the reader is supposed to recognize and connect to the subject of the work in which the allusion appears.

ambiguity The presence of multiple meanings in a word or phrase, whether intentional or accidental.

antagonist Any CHARACTER who opposes another; most often applied to one opposing the main character (the PROTAGONIST).

archetype A CHARACTER type, SYMBOL, PLOT, or THEME that appears frequently in works of literature and therefore seems to have universal meaning.

character A person in a work of literature or one of the *dramatis personae* of a play; also the moral, psychological, and intellectual traits of such a person. A round character possesses the complexities, contradictions, and subtle depths of personality associated with actual human beings. A *flat* character, in contrast, seems relatively two-dimensional: the character is presented briefly and has little depth of personality. Both kinds may be *dynamic*—a character who changes, for better or worse, during the course of a literary work—or *static*, a character who undergoes no development.

characterization The techniques used to depict the traits of a character in a literary work. See CHARACTER.

classic A work considered to be the best of its class.

climax The crucial or high point of tension, understanding, or recognition in a plot and the turning point of the ACTION.

complication The problem near the beginning of a story or drama that causes the CONFLICT.

conflict The opposition of forces within a CHARACTER, or the struggles either between characters (PROTAGONISTS) and other characters (ANTAGONISTS) or between characters and natural or supernatural forces.

connotation The implications of a word; that is, the feelings, ideas, or associations suggested by a word in addition to its denotation, or dictionary meaning.

contextual symbol See SYMBOL.

denotation The dictionary meaning of a word, which depends significantly on context, without reference to its implications and associations.

dénouement See RESOLUTION.

dialogue The direct presentation of the spoken words of characters in a story or play.

diction The choice of types of words, specific words, and levels of language. Levels may be *formal* (lofty language such as that used in epics and in the speeches of nobles in Shakespearean drama), *informal* (the speech and idiom of daily life), or *colloquial* (the speech and idioms of particular social classes or groups, such as the Cockneys in England).

dynamic character See CHARACTER.

epiphany A religious term meaning a "manifestation" or "showing forth"; western Christianity celebrates the Feast of the Epiphany on January 6 to mark Christ's manifestation of divinity to the Magi; James Joyce applied the term to short fiction to describe the moment when events show forth their meaning, bringing illumination or revelation to a character.

exposition The presentation, usually at or near the beginning of a narrative or drama, of necessary background information about characters and situations.

expressionism An early-twentieth-century artistic movement that emphasized the inner world of emotions and thought and projected this inner world through distortions of real-world objects; unlike impressionism, expressionist literature and drama distort and abstract the external world, creating works that are symbolic, anti-realistic, and often nightmarish in vision; in prose, stream-of-consciousness NARRATION is one of its major techniques.

figurative language Language that uses figures of speech (such as METAPHORS or SIMILES) so that it means more than the simple denotation of the words and, therefore, must be understood in more than a literal way.

flashback An interruption of the chronological sequence of events to present an event that occurred at an earlier time.

flat character See CHARACTER.

foil A minor CHARACTER who, through contrast, highlights and emphasizes distinct features of the main character.

foreshadowing The presentation of incidents, CHARACTERS, or objects that hint at important events that will occur later.

genre A classification of literature into separate kinds, such as drama, poetry, and prose fiction; a major literary form that sometimes contains other related forms, which are known as subgenres.

image See IMAGERY.

imagery At its most basic, the verbal creation of images, or pictures, in the imagination; also applied to verbal appeals to any of the senses.

irony A figure of speech that creates a discrepancy between appearance and reality, expectation and result, or surface meaning and implied meaning; traditionally categorized as *verbal irony* (a reversal of denotative meaning in which the thing stated is not the thing meant), *dramatic irony* (in which the discrepancy is between what a CHARACTER believes or says and the truth possessed by the reader or audience), and *situational irony* (in which the result of a situation is the reverse of what a character expects).

leitmotif A recurring word, phrase, situation, or THEME running through a literary work. Also see MOTIF.

metafiction A work of fiction that makes the nature of fiction itself a major concern; it is, therefore, considered to be a self-referential text.

metaphor A figure of speech that makes a comparison by equating things, as in "His heart is a stone."

modernism An artistic movement of the early twentieth century that deliberately broke from the reliance on established forms and insisted that individual consciousness, not something objective or external, was the source of truth. Modernist literature may be structurally fragmented; its themes tend to emphasize the philosophy of existentialism, the alienation of the individual, and the despair inherent in modern life.

mood A general emotional atmosphere created by the characters and SETTING and by the language chosen to present these.

motif An image, CHARACTER, object, setting, SITUATION, or THEME recurring in many works. Also see LEITMOTIF.

motivation The psychological reason behind a CHARACTER'S words or actions.

myth A traditional story embodying ideas or beliefs of a people; also a story setting forth the ideas or beliefs of an individual writer.

narration The recounting, in summarized form, of events and conversations.

narrator The person telling a story, either a fictional character or the implied author of the work; see POINT OF VIEW.

naturalism A literary movement based on philosophical determinism, the belief that the lives of ordinary people are determined by biological, economic, and social factors; naturalists tend to use the techniques of REALISM in order to present a tragic vision of the fate of individuals crushed by forces they cannot control.

oxymoron An ironic figure of speech containing an overt contradiction, as in the word *oxymoron* itself, which means "sharp stupidity" in Greek, or in such phrases as "fearful joy" or "paper coin"; see IRONY and PARADOX.

paradox An apparent contradiction that, upon deeper analysis, contains a degree of truth.

persona Literally, "the mask"; the speaking personality through which the author delivers the words in a poem or other literary work; the fictional "I" who acts as the actual author's mouthpiece in a literary work.

personification The attribution of human traits to inanimate objects or abstract concepts.

plot The arrangement of ACTIONS in a drama or story, often in a sequence according to cause and effect.

point of view The angle of vision or perspective from which a story is told. The point of view may be *first person* (in which the NARRATOR is a CHARACTER within the story), *third person* (a character or an implied author outside the story), or, very rarely, *second person* (in which the narrator, as in "choose your adventure" books, addresses the reader as "you"). Narrative point of view also involves questions of knowledge and reliability. Narrators may be omniscient, knowing both external events and internal thoughts and motivations, or they may be *limited* to some degree, knowing only some external details. *Reliable* narrators (a category that includes omniscient narrators) tell the truth completely. *Unreliable* narrators have personal limitations, such as youth or lack of education, that make them misunderstand what they narrate.

postcolonial criticism Explorations of the literature written within and about cultures that have experienced European colonization, such as India or Jamaica after British colonial rule; the focus of postcolonial critical approaches is often differences between the way formerly colonized peoples view their own cultural, social, and narrative practices and the way Europeans interpreted them.

postmodernism A highly contested term that can refer to both literary production in the period since about 1965 (although various critics see it beginning to develop as early as the 1950s) and the analysis of that literature and society in general; as a literary attitude, postmodernism is sometimes described as pushing modernism to extremes because, while sharing its sense of meaninglessness and despair, it rejects the elaborate textual constructions and symbolism that characterize many modernist texts and, instead, playfully manipulates conventions, using random, even absurd, organization and including alternative and discontinuous narrative lines to prevent a text from having fixed meanings and to insist that texts are not representations of reality but metafictional, or self-referential, constructions; applied to critical or theoretical approaches to literature, the term has no precise meaning, but postmodernist literary criticism often focuses on the instability or limitations of language and on the self-consciousness or self-referentiality of art. See METAFICTION, MODERNISM.

protagonist The main character of a drama or story.

realism The attempt to represent accurately the actual world; a literary movement that developed in reaction to the artificialities of romantic literature and melodramatic drama and that tended to focus on the lives of ordinary people, to use the language of daily speech, and to develop themes that offered social criticism and explored the problems of mundane life.

resolution A portion of a story or drama occurring after the CLIMAX that reveals the consequences of the PLOT and resolves CONFLICTS.

rising action The progression of events and development of the CONFLICT of a story or play up to the point of the CLIMAX.

round character See CHARACTER.

satire A literary form that uses wit and humour to ridicule persons, things, and ideas, frequently with the declared purpose of effecting a reformation of vices or follies.

setting The emotional, physical, temporal, and cultural context in which the action of the story, play, or poem takes place.

simile A figure of speech making a direct comparison between things by using *like* or *as* or similar words, as in "His heart is like a stone."

static character See CHARACTER.

stream of consciousness A narrative presenting the flow of thoughts and emotions of a CHARACTER.

structure The arrangement of elements within a work; the organization of and relationship between parts of a work; the plan, design, or form of a work.

style A writer's selection and arrangement of words.

suspense The anxiety created by a situation in which the outcome is uncertain.

symbol A figure of speech that links a person, place, object, or action to a meaning that is not necessarily inherent in it; a word so charged with implication that it means itself and also suggests additional meanings, which are the product of convention (the culture traditionally associates a particular image with a particular meaning) or of context (the placement of the image in a work and the details and emphases within that work add suggestiveness to the image, making it symbolic).

theme The central idea or meaning of a work; a generalization, or statement of underlying ideas, suggested by the concrete details of language, CHARACTER, SETTING, and ACTION in a work.

tone The speaker's attitude toward the subject matter or audience, as revealed by the choice of language and the rhythms of speech.

understatement A figure of speech, the opposite of exaggeration, that intensifies meaning ironically by deliberately minimizing, or underemphasizing, the importance of ideas, emotions, and situations.

unity The cohesiveness of a literary work in which all the parts and elements harmonize.

CREDITS

Alcott, Louisa May "A Whisper in the Dark" from *Plots and Counterplots: More Unknown Thrillers of Louisa May Alcott*, edited by Madeleine Stern (New York: William Morrow and Company, 1976).

Atwood, Margaret "The Resplendent Quetzal" from *Dancing Girls and Other Stories* by Margaret Atwood © 1977, 1982 by O.W. Toad, Ltd. Published by McClelland & Stewart Ltd. Used with permission of the publisher.

Boyko, Craig "OZY" from *Blackouts: Stories by Craig Boyko*. Copyright © 2008 by Craig Boyko. Published by McClelland & Stewart Ltd. and used with permission.

Campbell, Maria "Joseph's Justice" © 1995 Reprinted by permission of the author.

Chopin, Kate "The Story of an Hour" from *The Complete Works of Kate Chopin*, Vol. 1 (Baton Rouge: Louisiana State University Press, 1969).

Clarke, Austin C. "The Motor Car" copyright © 1971 by Austin Clarke. Published in *Choosing His Coffin: The Best Stories of Austin Clarke* in Canada by Thomas Allen in 2003. Reprinted by permission of the author.

Conrad, Joseph "An Outpost of Progress" from *The Medallion Edition of the Works of Joseph Conrad*, Vol. 1 (London: Gresham Publishing, 1925).

Faulkner, William "A Rose for Emily" by William Faulkner, copyright 1930 and renewed 1958 by William Faulkner; from *Collected Stories of William Faulkner* by William Faulkner. Used by permission of Random House, Inc.

Findley, Timothy "War". From *Dinner Along the Amazon* by Timothy Findley. Copyright © Timothy Findley, 1996. Reprinted by permission of Penguin Group (Canada).

Gilman, Charlotte Perkins "The Yellow Wallpaper" from *The Charlotte Perkins Gilman Reader*, Volume 1 (New York: Pantheon, 1980).

Hawthorne, Nathaniel "Young Goodman Brown" from *The Centenary Edition of the Works of Nathaniel Hawthorne, Volume X: Mosses from an Old Manse*, Ohio State University Press, 1974.

Hemingway, Ernest "A Clean, Well-Lighted Place". Reprinted with the permission of Scribner, a Division of Simon & Schuster, Inc., from *The Short Stories of Ernest Hemingway*. Copyright 1933 by Charles Scribner's Sons. Copyright renewed ©1961 by Mary Hemingway.

Joyce, James "Araby" from *Dubliners* by James Joyce.

King, Thomas "Borders" by Thomas King, from *One Good Story, That One*. Published by HarperCollins Publishers Ltd. Copyright © 1993 by Thomas King. All rights reserved.

Lahiri, Jhumpa "When Mr. Pirzada Came to Dine" from *Interpreter of Maladies: Stories* by Jhumpa Lahiri. Copyright © 1999 by Jhumpa Lahiri. Reprinted by permission of Houghton Mifflin Harcourt Publishing Company. All rights reserved.

INDEX OF AUTHORS AND TITLES